# *THE HISTORY OF AL-ṬABARĪ*

AN ANNOTATED TRANSLATION

---

## VOLUME V

*The Sāsānids, the Byzantines, the Lakhmids, and Yemen*

The History of al-Ṭabarī



---

Center for Iranian Studies
Columbia University

---

SUNY

SERIES IN NEAR EASTERN STUDIES

Said Amir Arjomand, Editor

*The preparation of this volume was made possible in part by a grant from the National Endowment for the Humanities, an independent federal agency.*

**Bibliotheca Persica**
Edited by Ehsan Yar-Shater

# The History of al-Ṭabarī

*(Ta'rīkh al-rusul wa'l-mulūk)*

VOLUME V

## The Sāsānids, the Byzantines, the Lakhmids, and Yemen

translated and annotated
by

*C. E. Bosworth*

University of Manchester

State University of New York Press

Published by
State University of New York Press, Albany

Printed in the United States of America

For information, address State University of New York Press, State University Plaza, Albany, N.Y., 12246

**Library of Congress Cataloging-in-Publication Data**

Ṭabarī, 838?-923.

[Tārīkh al-rusul wa-al-muluk. English. Selections]

The Sāsānids, the Byzantines, the Lakhmids, and Yemen / translated and annotated by C. E. Bosworth.

p. cm. — (SUNY series in Near Eastern studies) (The history of al-Ṭabarī = Ta'rīkh al-rusul wa'l-mulūk ; 5) (Bibliotheca Persica)

Includes bibliographical references and index.

ISBN 0-7914-4355-8 (hc : alk. paper). — ISBN 0-7914-4356-6 (pb : alk. paper)

1. Iran—History—To 640. 2. Iran—History—640-1256.
I. Bosworth, Clifford Edmund. II. Title. III. Series. IV. Series: Ṭabarī, 838?-923. Tārīkh al-rusul wa-al-muluk. English ; v. 5.
V. Series: Bibliotheca Persica (Albany, N.Y.)

DS38.2.T313 1985 vol. 5
[DS286]
909'.1 s—dc21
[955'.02] 99-38279
CIP

10 9 8 7 6 5 4 3 2 1

# Preface

The History of Prophets and Kings (*Ta'rīkh al-rusul wa'l-mulūk*) by Abū Jaʿfar Muḥammad b. Jarīr al-Ṭabarī (839–923), here rendered as *The History of al-Ṭabarī*, is by common consent the most important universal history produced in the world of Islam. It has been translated here in its entirety for the first time for the benefit of non-Arabists, with historical and philological notes for those interested in the particulars of the text.

In his monumental work al-Ṭabarī explores the history of the ancient nations, with special emphasis on biblical peoples and prophets, the legendary and factual history of ancient Iran, and, in great detail, the rise of Islam, the life of the Prophet Muḥammad, and the history of the Islamic world down to the year 915. The first volume of this translation contains a biography of al-Ṭabarī and a discussion of the method, scope, and value of his work. It also provides information on some of the technical considerations that have guided the work of the translators. The thirty-ninth volume is a compendium of biographies of early members of the Muslim community, compiled by al-Ṭabarī; although not strictly a part of his *History*, it complements it.

The *History* has been divided here into thirty-nine volumes, each of which covers about two hundred pages of the original Arabic text in the Leiden edition. An attempt has been made to draw the dividing lines between the individual volumes in such a way that each is to some degree independent and can be read as such. The page numbers of the Leiden edition appear in the margins of the translated volumes.

Al-Ṭabarī very often quotes his sources verbatim and traces the chain of transmission (*isnād*) to an original source. The chains of transmitters are, for the sake of brevity, rendered by only a dash (—) between the individual links in the chain. Thus, "According to Ibn Ḥumayd—Salamah—Ibn Isḥāq" means that al-Ṭabarī received the report from Ibn Ḥumayd, who said that he was told by Salamah, who said that he was told by Ibn Isḥāq, and so on. The numerous subtle and important differences in the original Arabic wording have been disregarded.

The table of contents at the beginning of each volume gives a brief survey of the topics dealt with in that particular volume. It also includes the headings and subheadings as they appear in al-Ṭabarī's text, as well as those occasionally introduced by the translator.

Well-known place names, such as, for instance, Mecca, Baghdad, Jerusalem, Damascus, and the Yemen, are given in their English spellings. Less common place names, which are the vast majority, are transliterated. Biblical figures appear in the accepted English spelling. Iranian names are usually transcribed according to their Arabic forms, and the presumed Iranian forms are often discussed in the footnotes.

Technical terms have been translated wherever possible, but some, such as *dirham,* and *imām,* have been retained in Arabic forms. Others that cannot be translated with sufficient precision have been retained and italicized, as well as footnoted.

The annotation is aimed chiefly at clarifying difficult passages, identifying individuals and place names, and discussing textual difficulties. Much leeway has been left to the translators to include in the footnotes whatever they consider necessary and helpful.

The bibliographies list all the sources mentioned in the annotation.

The index in each volume contains all the names of persons and places referred to in the text, as well as those mentioned in the notes as far as they refer to the medieval period. It does not include the names of modern scholars. A general index, it is hoped, will appear after all the volumes have been published.

For further details concerning the series and acknowledgments, see the preface to Volume I.

Ehsan Yar-Shater

# Contents

# Abbreviations

*AAE*: *Arabian Archaeology and Epigraphy*
*AJSLL*: *American Journal of Semitic Languages and Literatures*
*AKAW Berlin*: *Abhandlungen der Königlichen Akademie der Wissenschaften zu Berlin*
*AKGW Göttingen*: *Abhandlungen der Königlichen Gesellschaft der Wissenschaften zu Göttingen*
*AM*: *Asia Major*
*AO*: *Acta Orientalia*
*AO Hung.*: *Acta Orientalia Hungarica*
*BAR*: *British Archaeological Reports*
*BEO*: *Bulletin d'Etudes Orientales*
*BGA*: *Bibliotheca Geographorum Arabicorum*
*BIFAO*: *Bulletin de l'Institut Française d'Archéologie Orientale*
*BSOAS*: *Bulletin of the School of Oriental and African Studies*
*BZ*: *Byzantinische Zeitschrift*
*CAJ*: *Central Asiatic Journal*
*CHI III*: *The Cambridge History of Iran. III. The Seleucid, Parthian and Sasanian Periods*, ed. E. Yarshater, 2 parts. Cambridge, 1983.
*CHI IV*: *The Cambridge History of Iran. IV. The Period from the Arab Invasion to the Saljuqs*, ed. R. N. Frye. Cambridge, 1975.
*CRAIBL*: *Comptes Rendus de l'Académie des Inscriptions et Belles-Lettres*
*DOP*: *Dumbarton Oaks Papers*
*EI*[1]: *Encyclopaedia of Islam, first edition*
*EI*[2]: *Encyclopaedia of Islam, second edition*
*EIr*: *Encyclopaedia Iranica*
*GAS*: Fuat Sezgin, *Geschichte des arabischen Schrifttums*, 9 vols. Leiden, 1975– .

*GMS: Gibb Memorial Series*
*HdO: Handbuch der Orientalistik*
*IA: Iranica Antiqua*
*IC: Islamic Culture*
*Iran JBIPS: Iran, Journal of the British Institute of Persian Studies*
*IIJ: Indo-Iranian Journal*
*IJMES: International Journal of Middle East Studies*
*IS: Iranian Studies*
*Isl.: Der Islam*
*JA: Journal Asiatique*
*JAOS: Journal of the American Oriental Society*
*JESHO: Journal of the Economic and Social History of the Orient*
*JIS: Journal of Islamic Studies*
*JRAS: Journal of the Royal Asiatic Society*
*JSAI: Jerusalem Studies in Arabic and Islam*
*JSS: Journal of Semitic Studies*
*MO: Le Monde Oriental*
*MUSJ: Mélanges de l'Université Saint-Joseph*
*NC: The Numismatic Chronicle*
*OC: Oriens Christianus*
*OS: Orientalia Suecana*
*PSAS: Proceedings of the Seminar for Arabian Studies*
*PW: Paulys Real-Encyclopädie der classischen Altertumswissenschaft,* ed. G. Wissowa *et alii,* 34 vols. + 15 vols. Supplement. Stuttgart, 1893-Munich, 1972. *Der Kleine Pauly,* 5 vols. Stuttgart, 1964-Munich, 1975.
*RHR: Revue de l'Histoire des Religions*
*RMMM: Revue du Monde Musulman et la Méditerranée*
*RSO: Rivista degli Studi Orientali*
*SbWAW: Sitzungsberichte der Wiener Akademie der Wissenschaften*
*SI: Studia Islamica*
*St Ir: Studia Iranica*
*TAVO: Tübinger Atlas des Vorderen Orients*
*WbKAS: Wörterbuch des klassischen arabischen Sprache*
*WO: Die Welt des Orients*
*WZKM: Wiener Zeitschrift für die Kunde des Morgenlandes*
*ZA: Zeitschrift für Assyriologie*
*ZDMG: Zeitschrift der Deutschen Morgenländischen Gesellschaft*

In citations from the Qur'ān, where two different numbers are given for a verse, the first is that of Flügel's text and the second one that of the official Egyptian edition.

# Translator's Foreword

## *I*

The section of al-Ṭabarī's *History* on the four centuries preceding the rise of the Prophet Muḥammad continues the nonannalistic treatment of the pre-Islamic period as a whole, but it departs from the previous retailing of stories about the Children of Israel, the earlier prophets and the ancient peoples of the Near East and Arabia, which formed the first tier of Islamic salvation history, that of a pristine monotheism which had become clouded over by idolatry and a time of ignorance before God had sent His Prophet to mankind. Instead, although we do not get the year-by-year treatment of events used for post-Islamic times, we emerge instead into something that is recognizable as real history: the origins of the successors to the Parthian Arsacids of Persia, the Sāsānids, and the subsequent four centuries' history of the dynasty; the Sāsānids' sporadic episodes of warfare with the Romans/Byzantines, and, on the eastern frontiers of the Sāsānid empire, occasional wars with the peoples of Inner Asia, the Tūrān of Firdawsī's version of the Persian national epic, the *Shāh-nāmah;* the Sāsānids' attempts to maintain a buffer-state on the desert fringes of Mesopotamia in the shape of the Arab Lakhmid princes who, it was hoped, would protect Mesopotamia from depredations by the Bedouins of inner Arabia; the Sāsānids' installing of military bases on the western shores of the Persian Gulf in order to turn the gulf into a Persian lake, safe for their commerce; from the fifth century onwards, an interventionist policy across central Arabia, culminating in the Persian occupation of Yemen in 570 for some sixty years; but then, at the end, the sudden disintegration of the empire at the hands of first the Byzantines and then the Muslim Arabs.

This section of al-Ṭabarī's work is thus by no means exclusively concerned with the affairs of the Persian imperial heartland proper, the Iranian plateau and Mesopotamia, where the capital Seleucia-Ctesiphon lay, but is to a considerable extent concerned with its western and southwestern fringes; that is, the Roman/ Byzantine provinces of eastern Anatolia and the Semitic Near East, including such ruling Arab families as the Lakhmids of al-Ḥīrah and the chiefs of Kindah of the family of Ḥujr Ākil al-Murār in central Arabia. Much of the material in al-Ṭabarī on the Sāsānids' external relations can be corroborated or amplified from outside contemporary or near-contemporary sources. For the warfare with the Romans/Byzantines, there is a rich array of Byzantine chroniclers, some of them, like Procopius, closely connected with the military commanders concerned or, like Agathias, with a special channel of communication for knowledge of Persian affairs. For the Arabian peninsula, there is a fair amount of Arabic information, admittedly post-Islamic in the form we know it, about the Lakhmid kings and the chiefs of Kindah, arising out of the Arabs' passion for genealogical information and its historical background and out of the need to elucidate the background of poetic activity at the court of al-Ḥīrah or in the person of a poet-chief like Imru' al-Qays. In his translation, *Geschichte der Perser und Araber zur Zeit der Sasaniden* (see on this, below), Nöldeke omitted some sections of al-Ṭabarī's material on pre-Islamic Yemen, since he considered it as "zu fabelhafte" ($880^{17}$–$882^{4}$, but with $881^{19}$–$882^{4}$ inserted out of order in his translation at 147–48; $890^{4}$–$892^{14}$; $901^{1}$–$917^{17}$). He also omitted as irrelevant to his general topic $966^{15}$–$981^{2}$, on the miraculous birth and early upbringing of the Prophet Muḥammad, and the closing section in this *Prima series*, vol. 2, $1069^{17}$–$1072^{20}$, on the chronology of the world from Adam to the Prophet's birth. With regard to the South Arabian material, during the 1870s, with little more secondary material available on the history of the pre-Islamic Arabs than A. P. Caussin de Perceval's attempt at making historical bricks without straw, his *Essai sur l'histoire des Arabes avant l'Islamisme, pendant l'époque de Mahomet et jusqu'à la réduction de toutes les tribus sous la loi musulmane* (Paris 1847–48), this must have seemed substantially the case. Only from the early 1870s, through the pioneer efforts of scholarly travelers like Halévy in copying inscriptions on the spot, with his subsequent decipherment of the script and then further elucidation of the material by D. H. Müller and others, did knowledge begin to emerge of the rich but patchy heritage of South Arabian inscriptions (and also, around this time, of inscriptions in other languages of the peninsula like Thamudic, Lihyanitic, Safaitic, etc.). Nöldeke was of course aware of the pioneer discoveries and publications here, but the material was still meager in quantity and philologically difficult to evaluate. During the course of the present century, the study of Epigraphic South Arabian has emerged as a fully grown branch of Semitic studies, and we now have confirmation—if at times in an allusive rather than direct manner—of several apparently "fabelhafte" events in al-Ṭabarī's presentation of South Arabian history. Nor should one forget the significant quantity of material in Syriac and other languages of the Christian Orient that has now come to light and has illuminated the formation of an indigenous Christian church in Southwestern Arabia and such episodes as the struggle for political power and influence there involving such outside powers as Abyssinia, Byzantium, and Persia. Even the history of the lands beyond Persia's northeastern frontier has had a certain amount of fresh illumination thrown upon it by recent work on the Western Turk empire and on the Kushans, Kidarites, and Hephthalites, utilizing the results of such disciplines as archaeology, numismatics, and epigraphy; and the emergence in the last decade of material from a family archive in what is now northern Afghanistan will almost certainly increase our knowledge of the history and language of Bactria, the later Islamic Ṭukhāristān, in its pre-Islamic phase.

We have been talking about the peripheries of Persia, but there remains central to this section of al-Ṭabarī's *History* the Persian and Mesopotamian core of the Sāsānid empire. The populations and resources of these territories, the firm social structure, the cohesive power within society of the Zoroastrian state church and its ethos, the richness of the irrigated lands of the Sawād of Iraq and the oases of the Iranian plateau, all these provided the motive power for Sāsānid expansionism and military success. For nearly four centuries there was a perceptible trend of Sāsānid military success over the Romans/Byzantines: in the great battleground of Upper Mesopotamia, the Persian captured Nisibis in 363 and held it continuously thereafter as a bastion of Persian power threatening the Greeks, with the supreme success of final breakthrough in 614. Recently, James Howard-Johnston has perceptively weighed up the comparative positions and rôles of the two great empires of the Near and Middle East, concluding that it was above all the Persians' possession of Mesopotamia, with its populousness, its advanced, irrigated agriculture and its position at the head of the Persian Gulf with trade routes stretching thither from the East—all these advantages complementing the results of a similar exploitation of the oasis economies of the Iranian plateau—which gradually gave the Sāsānids the edge over Byzantium, enabling *inter alia* the emperors to use the threat of renewed military action to impose humiliating, tribute-paying conditions on the Greeks.[1]

Unfortunately, our knowledge of whole stretches of Sāsānid internal history and of the mechanisms driving the empire remains very imperfect. Such basic topics as the nature of the social structure and the rôles of the aristocracy, gentry, priesthood, and merchants, and the nature of the landholding and financial system on which the state apparatus rested, continue to excite discussion and controversy among scholars. Sources of information like that from the rich corpus of Sāsānid royal and priestly inscriptions and reliefs, the testimony of coins and sealings, the material concerning subordinate faiths of the empire such as that from the conciliar acts of the Nestorian Church and from the Babylonian Talmud, have all been carefully sifted, but cannot compensate for the almost total absence of contemporary records and literature in Middle Persian; and the exact dating and provenance of such exiguous material as we do have, like the *Letter of Tansar* (see on this p. 17 n. 66, below) continue to be debated. Hence the continued, central importance of al-Ṭabarī's historical information on Sāsānid history, supplemented by equally valuable if scantier information in writers like Ibn Qutaybah, al-Ya'qūbī, al-Dīnawarī, al-Mas'ūdī, and Ḥamzah al-Iṣfahānī.

1. Howard-Johnston, "The Two Great Powers in Late Antiquity: A Comparison," 180–97.

It is undeniably true, as Howard-Johnston has again observed, that the version of Sāsānid history that reached al-Ṭabarī from one or other versions of the *Khwadāy-nāmag* or *Book of Kings*, probably from that translated into Arabic by the late Umayyad writer Ibn al-Muqaffaʿ, almost certainly involved much distortion, suppression, and invention.[2] The penchant for entertaining anecdotes, memorable sayings, curiosa, moralizing tales, and the like, which seem to go back to the *Book of Kings*'s Pahlavi original, was characteristic also of early Arabic *udabā'* or littérateurs. In his endeavor to produce a plausible, straightforward historical narrative, al-Ṭabarī must have tried valiantly to cut his way through a mass of entertaining but historically irrelevant information presented to him in these royal annals, but he could not entirely break free of the *adab* tradition (cf. his inclusion of the totally unhistorical story of Shābūr II's wandering disguised in the Roman camp and capture, p. 60 below, and the tale of Kawād I's escape from imprisonment at the end of the interregnum of Jāmāsp's rule, p. 135 below). Al-Ṭabarī's efforts at pruning less relevant material can be seen in the shortened Persian translation produced by Abū ʿAlī Balʿamī (see on this, below), in which the Sāmānid vizier put back in his narrative certain items from the Sāsānid historical tradition where he thought al-Ṭabarī had pruned it overzealously. The fact that anecdotal material of the examples given above remained in al-Ṭabarī's *History* detracts only a little from confidence in his search for sober history.

There is nevertheless a certain unevenness of treatment, perhaps inevitable considering the material within al-Ṭabarī's hands. Sometimes confirmation or amplification of incidents in al-Ṭabarī's narrative can be found in, for example, the Greek, Syriac, or Armenian sources, but when the internal history of the Sāsānid empire did not impinge upon or affect the Christians of Persia, there was little reason for Eastern Christian sources to notice events there. Hence we are left with many blank or little-known periods in Sāsānid history, such as the reigns of Bahrām II in the later third century (covering seventeen years), of Bahrām IV at the end of the fourth century (eleven years) and of Yazdagird II in the

2. Ibid., 170–72.

mid fifth century (almost two decades), skated over by al-Ṭabarī (see pp. 46, 69, 106–109 below). For a crucial subject like Khusraw Anūsharwān's financial, tenurial, and military reforms, vital for our understanding of the internal dynamics of the later Sāsānid empire, we are still largely dependent on al-Ṭabarī's account; it is detailed and informative, but capable of varying interpretation, and hence has not surprisingly attracted a substantial body of comment and interpretation (see p. 258 n. 624, below). The same applies to the slightly earlier episode of Mazdak and his religioso-cial movement in the reign of Kawād I and the earlier part of Anūsharwān's reign, which has given rise to widely varying interpretations, often not unconnected with the political and social views of the scholars concerned (see p. 132 n. 342, below).

We must be grateful to al-Ṭabarī for preserving as much as he did of hard historical material, among the less valuable episodes of his *History* that were meant more for entertainment than instruction. Writing a history of the Sāsānids without the Arabic chronicles, even though these last date from two or three centuries after the empire's demise, would be a daunting task.

## *II*

The achievement of Theodor Nöldeke (1836–1930) in producing in 1878 his *Geschichte der Perser und Araber zur Zeit der Sasaniden* and its stupendous commentary, was uniformly praised on its publication (save for one petulant French reviewer, although one recalls that this was only seven years after the French loss of Alsace-Lorraine to the German empire and that Nöldeke was at that moment sitting in Alsace in a professorial chair at Strassburg/Strasbourg University). In his extended review article of the work, Alfred von Gutschmid stated that Nöldeke's utilization of al-Ṭabarī had made it possible for the first time to write a real history of the Sāsānids.[3] Succeeding generations of scholars—and not only orientalists but those from other disciplines like Byzantine studies—have continued to use Nöldeke's work and will doubtless continue to do so, when so

3. See F.-C. Muth, *Die Annalen von aṭ-Ṭabarī im Spiegel der europäischen Bearbeitungen*, 57 and nn. 323–37.

much of the material he brought to bear on the elucidation and amplification of the Arabic text, that from the Greek, Latin, Syriac, Hebrew, Georgian, and Armenian sources (the latter via his Berlin colleague von Gutschmid), remains still valid. Nöldeke himself regarded his translation as perhaps his *chef d'oeuvre.*[4] Nevertheless, a plethora of new information has emerged in the intervening 120 years, and this needs to be integrated with any new translation of the Arabic text. Today we live in an age of many specialists but not of polymaths like Nöldeke. How can any single person nowadays—not least the present *ʿabd ḥaqīr*—attempt to gather up and integrate all this new information? Thus as noted above, since Nöldeke's time, a whole new field within Semitic studies, that of Epigraphic South Arabian and South Arabian history, has emerged and matured. The obvious answer to the problem would be a team of experts collaborating on the project of a translation plus a commentary that would almost certainly exceed by many times the length of the translation itself. Such projects are easy to conceive but hard to finance and even harder to realize. The final volume of the *History of al-Ṭabarī* project cannot wait a further twenty years or so, which is what such a team of experts in different fields might well require (though Nöldeke finished his translation in one year!); and their finished product would almost inevitably be outdated in many respects before the end of the period of time involved. Hence the present work is offered now for readers' consideration as one which had to be completed within a period of two years only. The present translator and commentator is conscious of whole areas of new scholarship which should, in ideal conditions, be brought into consideration for the commentary; for instance, much exciting and relevant work is coming out of the Workshops on Late Antiquity and Early Islam, and this has been only partially tapped. But a halt must be called at some point, and I have reluctantly arrived at this; whether the achievement is worthwhile, the reader must judge for himself.

4. His view here was expressed in a letter to Goldziher, cited by F. Rosenthal, *The History of al-Ṭabarī, an Annotated Translation. I. General Introduction* and *From the Creation to the Flood,* 144 n. 469.

The generations of Arabists who have used Nöldeke's *Geschichte* cannot have failed to be impressed by the degree of accuracy which he achieved in his translation.[5] Where, as with so much of pre-Islamic poetry, replete as it is with recondite allusions, often totally unrecoverable today, doubt and uncertainty remained, he noted this. Since he actually published the translation a year before the appearance of the edited text (volume 1 of the *Prima Series*) on which it was based, a more complete understanding of the text led him on occasion to revise his translation (see, e.g., p. 65 n. 177 below). But such occasions were few and far between. What has happened since Nöldeke's time is that several Arabic texts that he had to use in manuscript, such as Ibn Qutaybah's *'Uyūn al-akhbār,* al-Ya'qūbī's *Ta'rīkh,* al-Dīnawarī's *al-Akhbār al-ṭiwāl,* and various poetical *dīwāns*, have now been critically edited, and wherever possible, I have taken advantage of improved readings in these editions.

When the project for an edition of the *History* was first mooted in the early 1870s under the stimulus of the Leiden Arabist M. J. de Goeje,[6] Nöldeke undertook to edit the section on the Sāsānids (*Prima series,* 813–1067) and, after the unexpected death of Otto Loth, the ensuing section 1067–1572; that is, up to almost the end of the events of A.H. 6. Basically, Nöldeke had at his disposal for the section on the Sāsānids the three manuscripts (1) L = Leiden 497, covering the whole period except for a lacuna at $878^{12}$–$899^{17}$; (2) C = Constantinople/Istanbul, Köprülü 1040; and (3) T and t = Tübingen Ma. VI, 2 (Wetzstein Collection), with two parts, the second copied later than the first. Other manuscripts in part supplemented these, including P = Paris, Bibliothèque Nationale, ancien fonds 627 (a manuscript cognate with L), from $899^{12}$ (i.e., soon after the beginning of the reign of Khusraw I Anūsharwān); and BM = British Library, Add. 23,263, from $915^{9}$ (i.e., in the section on the Tubba' king of Yemen As'ad Abū Karib). Nöldeke also mentioned that he had found useful Ibn Hishām's version of Ibn

5. Cf. Irfan Shahīd, "Theodor Nöldeke's 'Geschichte der Perser und Araber,' an Evaluation," 119–21.

6. See on the project and its genesis, *Introductio,* pp. XXII–XXXV; J. W. Fück, *Die arabischen Studien in Europa bis in den Anfang des 20. Jahrhunderts,* 212–14; Muth, *Die Annalen von aṭ-Ṭabarī,* 8–13; Rosenthal, *The History of al-Ṭabarī, an Annotated Translation,* I, 141–42.

Isḥāq's *Sīrat al-nabī* (available in the printed edition of 1858–60 by F. Wüstenfeld); the anonymous history contained in the manuscript Sprenger 30 (in the collection acquired in 1858 from Sprenger by the Prussian State Library in Berlin, and still unpublished; it corresponds to one of the two main versions used by al-Ṭabarī for the history of the Sāsānids; see on the work the dissertation of J. G. Rothstein, *De chronographo arabo anonymo, qui codice Berolinensi Sprengriano tricesimo continetur*); and the Gotha manuscript 24–25 of Balʿamī's abbreviated, and in places slightly amplified, Persian translation of al-Ṭabarī's *History* (H. Zotenberg's French translation was not published until 1867–74).[7] The Cairo 1960–69 text of al-Ṭabarī's *History* by the veteran Egyptian editor Muḥammad Abū al-Faḍl Ibrāhīm, which incorporates some readings from Istanbul Topkapi Saray manuscripts and certain other ones, has been compared by the present translator with the Leiden text; the additional information gleaned has, however, proved negligible.

The rendering of Arabic names and terms follows the usual system of *The History of al-Ṭabarī.* In regard to Epigraphic South Arabian, I have endeavored to follow the generally acknowledged system as exemplified in A. F. L. Beeston's *Sabaic Grammar.* It is the rendering of pre-Islamic Iranian names and terms that causes difficulties, and no watertight system seems possible here. At the suggestion of Mr F. C. de Blois, for the spelling of Middle Persian words and names I have endeavored to follow the principles laid down by D. N. MacKenzie in his *A Concise Pahlavi Dictionary* (cf. his exposition of the ambiguities and difficulties involved in handling the Pahlavi script, Introduction, pp. x–xv) and now generally accepted by specialists; namely, a strict distinction between *transliteration* of the consonantal script and *transcription* of the reconstructed Sāsānid pronunciation. For example, the name of the first Sāsānid ruler is transliterated *ʾrtḥštr* but transcribed as Ardaxšīr. His father's name is transliterated *pʾpky* but transcribed as Pābag. Ardaxšīr's son's name is spelled etymologically as *šḥpwḥly* (for *šāh* + *puhr*), and the contemporary Sāsānid pronunciation was Šābuhr, as we know from the Manichaean Middle Per-

7. See *Introductio,* pp. L–LII, and for Balʿamī's translation specifically, Muth, *Die Annalen von aṭ-Ṭabarī,* 20–27.

sian spelling *š'bwḥr*; although in the commentary to al-Ṭabarī's *History* I have used the later Middle Persian (and early New Persian) form for this last name of Shābūr, as being closer to the Arabic version of the name. A further slight anomaly is that I have used the later form Ardashīr rather than the strictly correct, earlier form Ardakhshīr, as again reflecting early New Persian usage and as being also the familiar Arabic equivalent.

Such institutions as the John Rylands University Library, Manchester; the Widener Library, Harvard University; and the Oriental Institute Library, Oxford, have aided completion of the work. Several colleagues have been helpful in making books available to me, providing xeroxes of articles difficult of access to me, sending offprints of their own articles, and giving information and guidance on various obscure or contested points. Thus I am grateful to Mr. Mohsen Ashtiany (Columbia University); Dr. S. P. Brock (Oxford University); Dr. Paul M. Cobb (Wake Forest University, N.C.); the Rev. Professor J. A. Emerton (Cambridge University); Dr. G. Greatrex (University of Wales, Cardiff); Dr. R. G. Hoyland (Oxford University); Dr. Ph. Huyse (Paris); Mr. M. C. A Macdonald (Oxford); Prof. D. N. MacKenzie (Anglesey); Dr. M. I. Mochiri (Paris); Professor Chr. Robin (CNRS, Aix-en-Provence); Professor N. Sims-Williams (SOAS, London); Professor G. Rex Smith (Manchester University); and Professor Edward Ullendorff (Oxford). My colleague in Manchester, Professor W. C. Brice, has drawn the maps in an expert fashion. In particular, Mr. F. C. de Blois (Royal Asiatic Society, London), with his special expertise in such fields as Iranian, South Arabian, and Syriac studies, has been kind enough to read through a draft of the commentary and to make a considerable number of corrections and valuable suggestions for improvement; some of these are explicitly acknowledged in the commentary, but there are many other, unacknowledged places where he has saved me from error or has enriched the documentation. Hence I am deeply grateful to him. But at the end, the usual confession must be made: responsibility for the final product remains my own.

C. Edmund Bosworth

Table 1. The Sāsānid Emperors
*(the dates of some of the early rulers are tentative)*

- Ardashīr I, son of Pābag (224 or 226–242)
  - Shābūr I, Sābūr al-Junūd (coruler 240, sole rule 242–70)
    - Hormizd Ardashīr (270–71)
    - Bahrām I (271–74)
      - Bahrām II (274–91)
        - Bahrām III (292)
    - Narseh (292–302)
      - Hormizd II (302–309)
        - Ardashīr II (379–83)
        - Shābūr II, Dhū al-Aktāf (309–79)
          - Shābūr III (383–88)
          - Bahrām IV (388–99)
            - Yazdagird I (399–420)
              - Bahrām V Gūr (420–38)
                - Yazdagird II (438–57)
                  - |

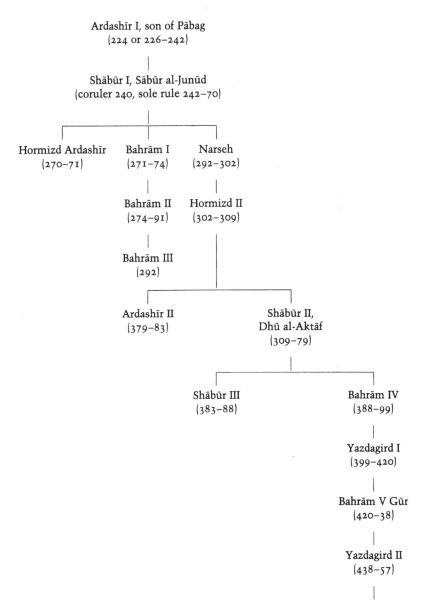

Hormizd III
(457–59)

Pērōz I
(459–84)

Walāsh
(484–88)

Kawād I
488–96, 498 or 499–531)

Jāmāsp
(496–498 or 499)

Khusraw I Anūsharwān
(531–79)

Hormizd IV
(579–90)

Bahrām VI Chōbēn,
son of Bahrām Gushnasp
(590–91)

Khusraw II Abarwēz
(591–628)

Shahriyār

Kawād II Shērōy
(628)

Būrān(dukht)
(630–31)

Āzarmīgdukht
(631–32)

Ardashīr III
(628–29)

Khusraw III Khurrah-zādh
(between 630 and 632)

Hormizd V
(between 630 and 632)

Yazdagird III
(632–51)

Pērōz (II)
(died in China after 661)

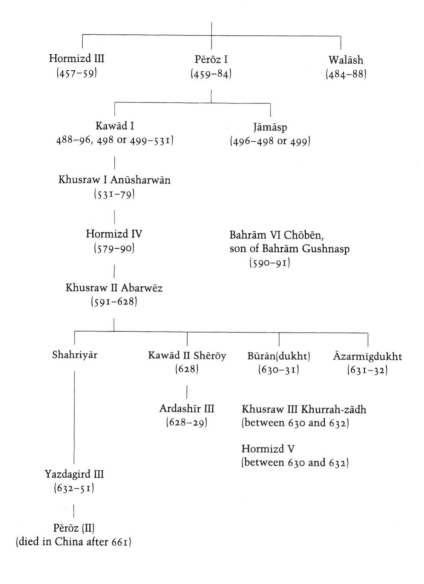

Table 2. The Roman and Byzantine Emperors, from Constantine the Great to Heraclius

| | |
|---|---|
| Constantine I | 324–37 |
| Constantius II | 337–61 |
| Julian | 351–63 |
| Jovian | 363–64 |
| Valens | 364–78 |
| Theodosius I | 379–95 |
| Arcadius | 395–408 |
| Theodosius II | 408–50 |
| Marcian | 450–57 |
| Leo I | 457–74 |
| Leo II | 474 |
| Zeno, first reign | 474–75 |
| Basiliscus | 475–76 |
| Zeno, second reign | 476–91 |
| Anastasius I | 491–518 |
| Justin I | 518–27 |
| Justinian I | 527–65 |
| Justin II | 565–78 |
| Tiberius II Constantine | 578–82 |
| Maurice | 582–602 |
| Phocas | 602–10 |
| Heraclius | 610–41 |

Table 3. The Lakhmid Rulers
(*many dates are tentative*)

ʿAdī

Imru' al-Qays I al-Bad', "King of all the Arabs"
(d. 328)

ʿAmr I

Imru' al-Qays II
(ruled for 25 years, died in the early fifth century)

al-Nuʿmān I
(ca. 400–ca. 418)

al-Mundhir I
(ca. 418–ca. 462)

al-Aswad
(ca. 462–ca. 482)

al-Mundhir II
(482–89)

al-Nu'mān II
(499–503)

al-Mundhir III m. Hind, daughter of al-Ḥārith (Arethas) of Ghassān
(ca. 504–54)

ʿAmr II (b. Hind)
(554–69)

Qābūs
(569 or 570–573 or 574)

al-Mundhir IV
(ca. 575–80)

al-Nuʿmān III
(580–602)

al-Mundhir, al-Gharūr
(d. 633 or thereafter)

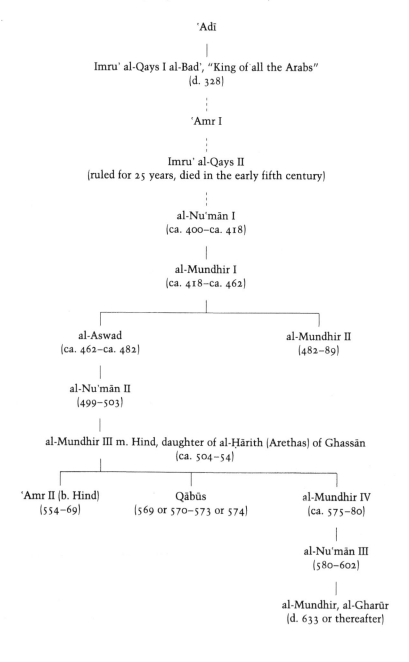

Table 4. The Chiefs of Kindah

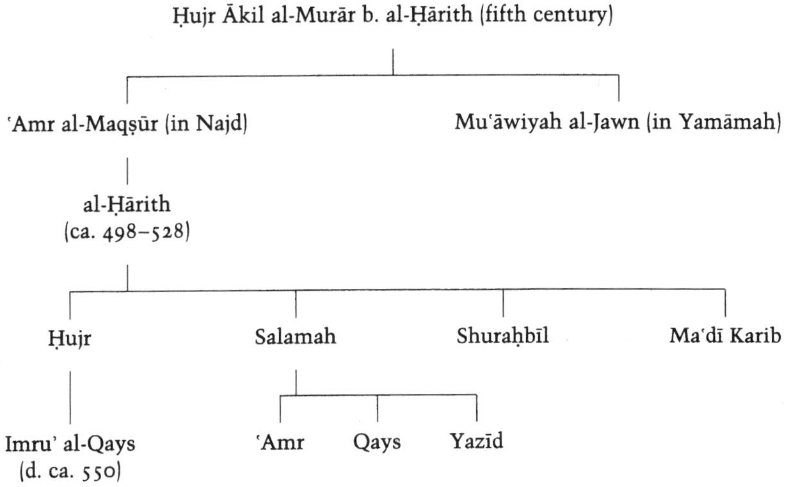

Table 5. Rulers in South Arabia during the Sixth and Early Seventh Centuries
(*many dates are tentative*)

Marthad-īlān Yanūf, to end of 518 or beginning of 519

Ma'dī Karib Ya'fur, last Tubba' king, began ruling end of 518 or beginning of 519

Yūsuf (or Yanūf ?) As'ar Yath'ar, called Dhū Nuwās, 521 or 522, died 525

Abraham, king under Abyssinian suzerainty, killed after 525

Sumu-yafa' Ašwa' (Esimiphaios), king under Abyssinian suzerainty 530 or 531

Abrahah, former slave, ruler ca. 533 till after 552 or 553, nominally on behalf of the king of Abyssinia

Yaksūm, son of Abrahah

Masrūq, son of Abrahah

Sayf b. Dhī Yazan, local Yemeni noble, rebel against Abyssinian domination 570, placed on the throne by the Persian commander Wahriz

Wahriz, governor on behalf of the king of Persia till ca. 575

Marzubān, his son

Bīnajān (?), Marzubān's son

Khurrah Khusrah, Bīnajān's son

Bādhān, till ca. 630

Shahr, his son, killed in 632 by the Yemeni local rebel and religious leader al-Aswad or Dhū al-Khimār

al-Muhājir b. Abī Umayyah al-Makhzūmī, first Muslim governor 632

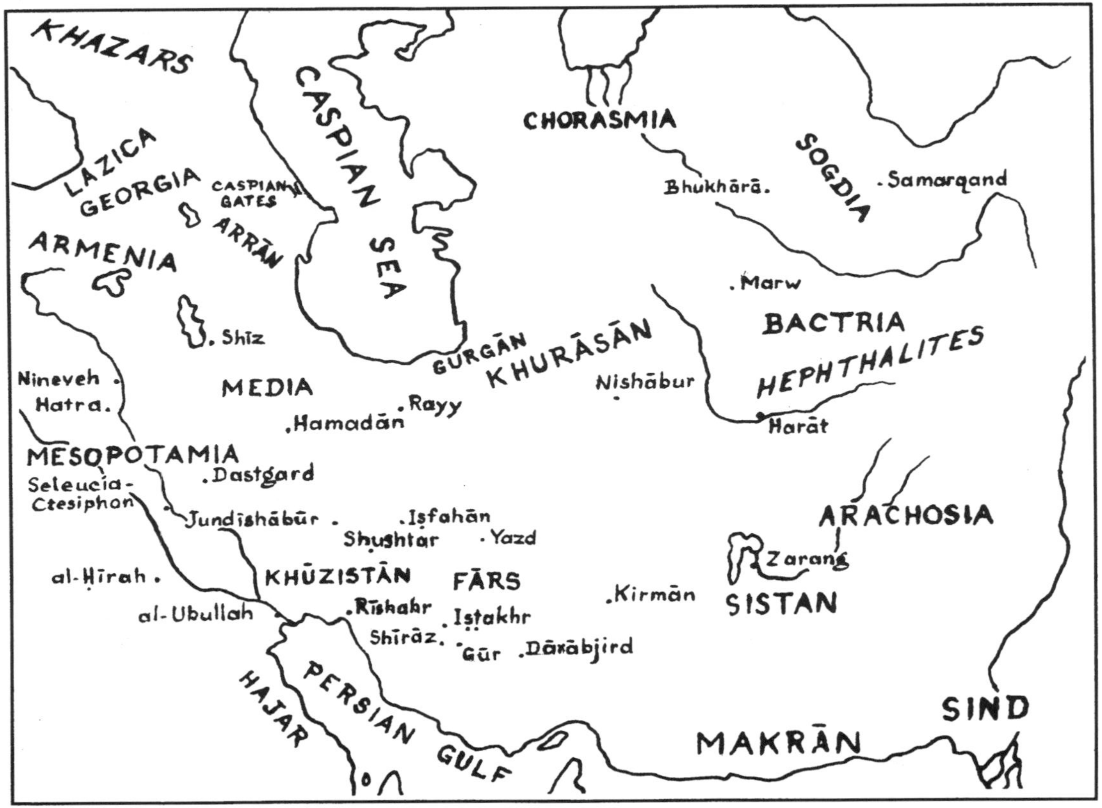


Map 1. The Sāsānid Empire

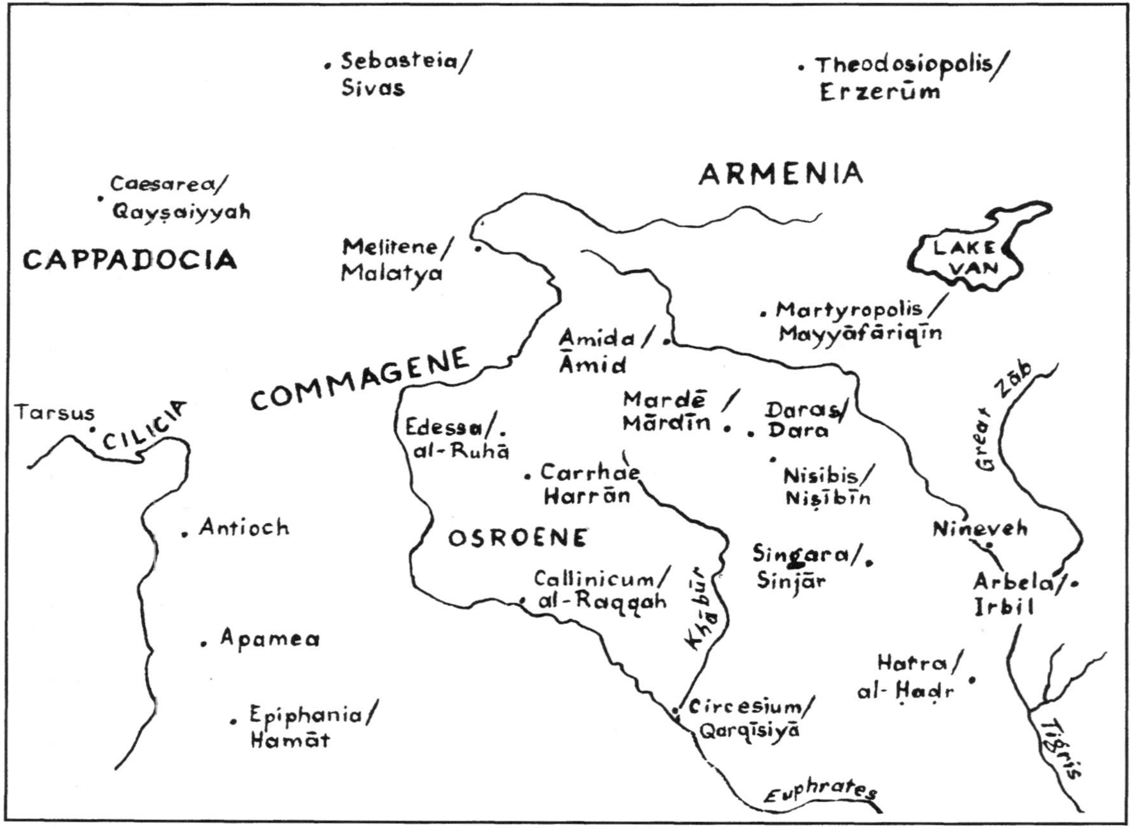


Map 2. The Roman-Byzantine and Persian Frontierlands

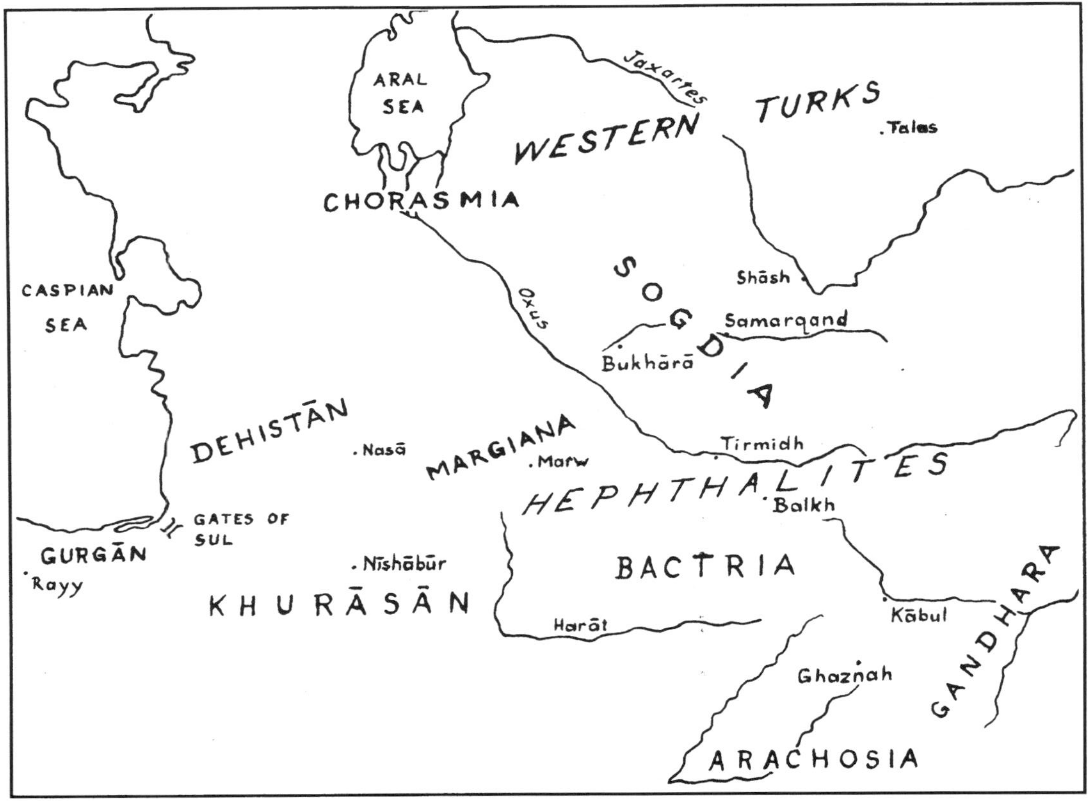


Map 3. The Northeastern Frontier of the Sāsānids

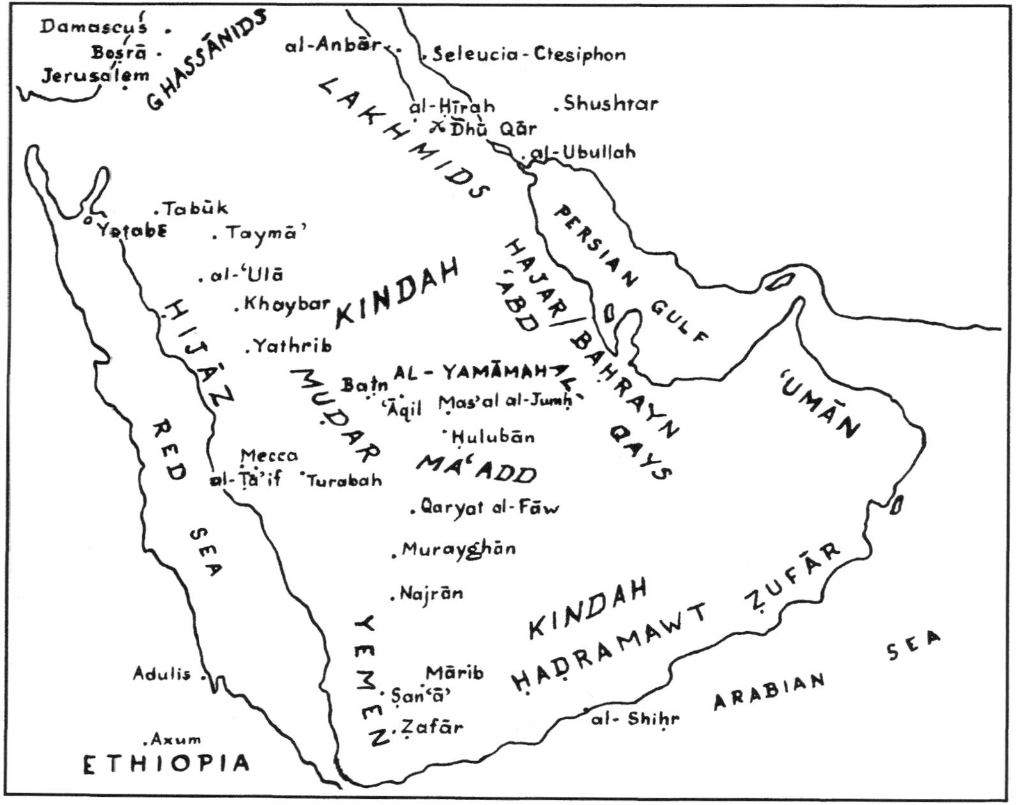


Map 4. The Arabian Peninsula: The Lands of the Lakhmids, Kindah, etc.

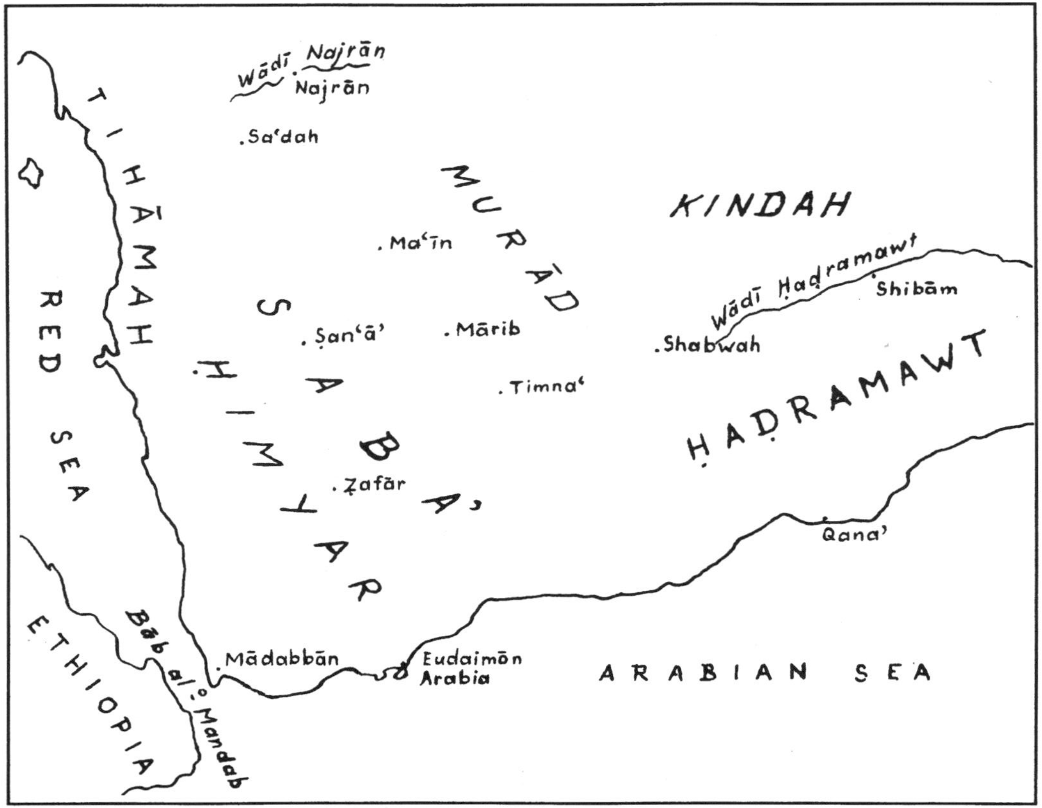


Map 5. Southwestern Arabia

# [The Kings of the Persians]

The kings of the Persians and the duration of their rule according to the entire course of [their] history, since we have already mentioned the major events that took place in the time of the Party Kings (*Mulūk al-Ṭawāʾif*)[1] among the Persians, the Children of [I, 813]

1. Al-Ṭabarī intends by this term, as he has earlier explained (I, 706), the Parthians or Arsacids, considered as regional powers in comparison with such universal monarchs as the Achaemenid emperors of Persia and Alexander the Great. The Sāsānids themselves regarded the "Party Kings," comprising the Arsacids' predecessors the Seleucids (in fact, little known in Iranian historical tradition) and the Arsacids themselves, as an interruption in the development through the ages, from legendary times onward, of the legitimate, unified Persian monarchy, even though the Arsacids ruled for the very respectable span of 474 years. But historical mention of the Achaemenids in indigenous Persian sources seems to be exiguous, beyond some knowledge of the last kings, the Dārās (Darius III being the only monarch mentioned, e.g., in Zoroastrian sources like the *Dēnkard* and the *Bundahišn,* and in Firdawsī's *Shāh-nāmah*) (M. A. Dandamayev and V. G. Lukonin, however, have suggested that, in the Sāsānid national consciousness, these two Darius were in any case attached to the Kayanids; see their *The Culture and Social Institutions of Ancient Iran,* 372–73). The problem has exercised modern scholars, who have tended to draw the conclusion that the Sāsānids had little or no knowledge of the Achaemenids, hence could not in any significant way have considered themselves as heirs of the Achaemenids. The arguments have been set forth and discussed, with a wealth of pertinent information, by Ehsan Yarshater in his "Were the Sasanians Heirs to the Achaemenids?" 517–39, and his "Iranian National History," 378; and cf. A. Christensen, *Les Kayanides,* 35–43. Subsequent Iranian historical scholarship has overwhelmingly endorsed Yarshater's view; see, e.g., G. Gnoli, *The Idea of Iran,* 136–38; J. Wiesehöfer, *Die 'dunklen Jahrhunderte' des Persis,* 19; and idem, *Ancient Persia from 550 B.C. to 650 A.D.,* 167–69. Only Touraj Daryaee has recently challenged this consensus, assembling references to the

Israel, the Romans (*al-Rūm*), and the Arabs, up to the time of Ardashīr.[2]

## [Ardashīr I]

When there had elapsed, according to what the Christians and the possessors of the early Scriptures relate, 523 years, but according to the Zoroastrians (*al-Majūs*), 266 years, since Alexander had taken control of the land of Babylon,[3] there arose Ardashīr,[4] son of Bābak Shāh, King of Khīr, son of the younger Sāsān, son of Bābak, son of Sāsān, son of Bābak, son of M.h.r.m.s, son of Sāsān, son of

---

Achaemenids from earlier Sasanid sources, citing the veneration by the Sāsānids of Persepolis as a sacred site (but they regarded it as stemming from legendary or semilegendary times!) and suggesting that non-Persian authors such as Greek, Armenian, Jewish, and Muslim ones (including, of these last, the Khwarazmian al-Bīrūnī in his *al-Āthār al-bāqiyah*) were well aware of the Achaemenids; see his "National History or Keyanid History? The Nature of Sasanid Zoroastrian Historiography," 129–41. Nevertheless, as emphasized above, the weight of opinion concurs in the view that the Sāsānids did not regard themselves as heirs to the Achaemenids, but to the Kayānids.

2. See *The History of al-Ṭabarī*, vol. III, *The Children of Israel*, and vol. IV, *The Ancient Kingdoms*.

3. The chronology attributed by al-Ṭabarī to the Christians here, and elsewhere, as the "Years of Alexander," is based on the Seleucid era, that commemorating Seleucus I's assumption of power at Babylon, commonly fixed at 1 October 312 B.C. The Byzantine historian Agathias dated the beginning of Ardashīr's reign to the year 538 of the era of Alexander, i.e., A.D. 226–27, probably with Ardashīr's coronation at Ctesiphon in mind (cf. Averil Cameron, "Agathias on the Sassanians," 117). Interpretation of the bilingual, i.e., Parthian and Middle Persian, inscription at Bīshāpūr would seem to point to the "official" beginning of the Sāsānid dynasty's rule as being in the calendar year 27 September 223 to 25 September 224; but the topic remains uncertain and controversial. Since Alexander's era was considered to have begun with his accession, the traditional figure for the length of his reign, fourteen years (e.g., in al-Ṭabarī, I, 702, citing "the Persians"), these years had to be subtracted from the known figure of 537 years to give 524 years as the interval separating Ardashīr from Alexander's death. The lesser figure of the Magians or Zoroastrians given here reflects Sāsānid ideological considerations, foreshortening the actual 474 years of Parthian rule in an attempt to depreciate the duration of their predecessors' power (in reality, this had been longer than the rule of the Sāsānids was to extend). See Th. Nöldeke, trans. 1 n. 1; *EIr* s.v. Arsacids. V. The Arsacid Era, and VI. Arsacid Chronology in Traditional History (A. Sh. Shahbazi).

4. MP *'.r.t.ḥ.š.t.r*, pronounced Ardaxšīr, from a hypocoristic form **Ṛtaxšira* of the full OP form **Ṛtaxšathra*, i.e., Artaxerxes. The name had apparently continued in use among local princes of Fārs during the Arsacid period, on numismatic evidence. See Nöldeke, trans. 1 n. 2; D. Sellwood, "Minor States in Southern Iran," 304–305; *EIr*, s.v. Ardašīr I. i. History (J. Wiesehöfer).

Rulers based on military strength
Military was well trained
religious

HIST 3180 Prof. Thabit Abdullah
Essay #3 due 29 Nov. in class.

Please write a 6-page essay (typed, double-spaced, 12 pt font, 1 inch margins all around) in which you answer the following question. Please use all of the relevant parts of the readings for this term:

Many of our sources repeat the fact that the Sasanians suffered from a low population compared to their chief rivals the Romans/Byzantines. Nevertheless, they successfully defended their realm and scored some impressive victories along the way. What, in your view accounts for Sasanian strength? Answer by referring to the interaction between the political, social, religious and military institutions.

Note: This essay is a bit longer than the previous two so you have the space to discuss the background to the topic. Be careful you don't turn this into a simple descriptive paper which repeats the lectures. Make sure you use the sources well and always remember to go beyond the obvious and try to deal with the complex ideas which will surely arise.

1. Militar+ - use Sylases resource

vert well organized

able to adapt ~~the~~ - new tech [seiges]

rulers often chosen through militart histort

2. religion

- Ardashir came from Preist family

- religion with king as state ruler and religious leader easier to control tons of peeps

1. Political

- Strong administration could continue without king

- centralized economy - cities with rulers ~~names~~ names

3. Social

very religious peoples

religion was every thing

- maybe combine with religion

King Bahman, son of Isfandiyār, son of Bishtāsb, son of Luhrāsb, son of Kaywajī (?), son of Kaymanush. According to another genealogy, [he was] Ardashīr, son of Bābak, son of Sāsān, son of Bābak, son of Zarār, son of Bihā-Afrīdh, son of the elder Sāsān, son of Bahman, son of Isfandiyār, son of Bishtāsb, son of Luhrāsb.[5] [He arose] in Fārs seeking, as he alleged, to avenge the blood of his paternal cousin Dārā, son of Bahman, son of Isfandiyār, on whom Alexander had made war and had killed two of the latter's chief commanders. As he said, he wished to recover the royal power (or: the kingdom) for its rightful holders and for those who had held it continuously in the previous time of his predecessors and forefathers, before the "Party Kings," and [wished] to gather it together again under one head and one monarch.[6] [814]

It is mentioned that he was born in a village (*qaryah*) of the Iṣṭakhr region called Ṭīrūdih, situated in the rural district (*rustāq*)

---

5. On the problems in the Sāsānid genealogies, see G. Morrison, "The Sassanian Genealogy in Mas'ūdī," 42–44; R. N. Frye, *The Heritage of Persia,* 207–208; idem, "The Political History of Iran under the Sasanians." 116–17. The genealogies go back to personages like Zarār and Bihā-Āfrīdh who were attached (nonhistorically) to the Arsacids, and then back to the legendary Kayānids, the Achaemenids having by Sāsānid times (apart from the Dariuses) receded into a legendary haze. See Nöldeke, trans. 2, nn. 1–3, 3 n. 1.

The question of the nearer descent of Ardashīr, whether Sāsān was actually his grandfather or a more remote ancestor (the *jadd* of al-Ṭabarī's text could imply either of these), or directly connected with the line of Pābag at all, has aroused considerable discussion, since the sources, literary and epigraphic, offer differing interpretations. Thus, noting the description of Sāsān as a lord but with no explicit filiation of Pābag as the son of Sāsān in the Ka'ba-yi Zardusht inscription at Naqsh-i Rustam, R. N. Frye is inclined to believe that Sāsān was a remote ancestor whose name was used for the dynasty as a whole, just as the Achaemenids took their name from the totally obscure Haxāmaniš/Achaemenēs, while noting the epic tradition that, since Sāsān died just after his son Ardashīr's birth, the boy was adopted, following current Zoroastrian practice, as Pābag's own son. The popular Persian tradition, exemplified in the Middle Persian romance, the *Kār-nāmag-ī Ardašīr-ī Pābagān, pace* the view expressed here by al-Ṭabarī, makes Ardashīr the son of Sāsān, the local ruler Pābag having given his daughter in marriage to Sāsān after hearing of the latter's noble descent from Dārā, i.e., the last Achaemenid Darius III (considered by the Sāsānids as the last Kāyanid king). See the discussions in R. N. Frye, "History and Sasanian Inscriptions," 215–16; idem, "The Political History of Iran under the Sasanians," 116–17; *EIr,* s.v. Ardašīr I. i. History (Wiesehöfer).

6. Again reflecting Sāsānid imperial propaganda that Ardashīr restored the unity of the state as the heir of earlier, pre-Arsacid rulers whom he now avenged on Artabanus V.

good stuff

of Khīr[7] in the administrative division (*kūrah*) of Iṣṭakhr.[8] His grandfather Sāsān was a courageous and mighty warrior whose courage and military might were such that he fought single-handed eighty of the strong and valiant men of Iṣṭakhr and put them all to flight. His wife stemmed from one of the royal families in Fārs called the Bāzranjīn.[9] She was named Rāmbihisht, and possessed beauty and perfection. Sāsān was the custodian of the fire temple of Iṣṭakhr called that of Anāhīdh.[10] He was also a devotee of the chase and of equestrian pursuits (*al-furūsiyyah*).

---

7. This town of Fārs (other forms such as Khayr and Khiyār are found in the geographers) lay near the southeastern tip of Lake Bakhtigān in the district of Nīrīz, and marked a stage on the Shīrāz-Kirmān road. See G. Le Strange, *The Lands of the Eastern Caliphate*, 289–90; P. Schwarz, *Iran im Mittelalter*, 104–105. The location of Ṭīrūdih, and the exact form of its name, remain unclear.

8. In Sāsānid times, Stakhr (thus written in Pahlavi script, *stxr*) was regarded as both the religious and political center for the dynasty, given the origins of the Sāsānids themselves from the district. It lay on the Pulvar river north of Persepolis, and may have come into prominence after Alexander the Great's destructions at Persepolis. In Islamic times, it remained moderately significant as the center of the *kūrah* or administrative district (see on this term n. 119 below) of the same name but was gradually overshadowed by the foundation in early Umayyad times of Shīrāz, which became the capital for the whole of Fārs. See Nöldeke, trans. 3 n. 2; Le Strange, *Lands*, 275–76; Schwarz, *Iran*, 13–16; W. Barthold, *An Historical Geography of Iran*, 151–53; *EI²*, s.v. Iṣṭakhr (M. Streck-G. C. Miles); *EIr*, s.v. Eṣṭakr (A. D. H. Bivar and Mary Boyce), This tradition identifying Ṭīrūdih as Ardashīr's birthplace may well deserve credence; before the Sāsānids, the Arsacids had continued to venerate their original home in northeastern Persia, on the evidence of Isidore of Charax.

9. The correct form of this name is unclear. Nöldeke, trans. 4 n. 1, compared it with a mountainous district of western Fārs, Bāzrang, mentioned by the Islamic geographers al-Iṣṭakhrī and Ibn Ḥawqal (see Le Strange, *Lands*, 171–72; Schwarz, *Iran*, 118–19), so that we might possibly have a family name derived from a place. The Bāzrangīs were apparently a family of local potentates in Fārs, acknowledging the Arsacids as their suzerains but in practice largely autonomous; after the time of Ardashīr, however, they disappear from historical record. See *EIr*, s.v. Bāzrangī (R. N. Frye). Whether Ardashīr really was related to one of these families cannot now be ascertained, but such a link is by no means improbable; A. von Gutschmid, "Bemerkungen zu Tabari's Sasanidengeschichte, übersetzt von Th. Nöldeke," 734, was less skeptical than Nöldeke about such a possibility.

10. The Avestan Arədvī Sūrā Anāhita "mighty, immaculate one of the waters," a goddess of fertility, nurturer of crops and herds, and also of success in battle, MP Ardwīsūr Anāhīd, had also become identified with the Western Iranian Anāhiti, apparently the goddess of the planet Venus. Venerated by the Achaemenids from the time of Artaxerxes II onward, the cult was popular among the early Sāsānids, and Shāpūr I called his daughter and queen Ādur Anāhīd, "Fire (and) Anāhīd," i.e., this was a dvandva name, from the names of two deities. According to al-Ṭabarī's source, presumably the *Khwadāy-nāmag* or "Book of Kings," Ardashīr was now laying claim to custodianship of the fire temple that had grown out of a shrine to

Rāmbihisht provided Sāsān with a son, Bābak, whose hair, at the moment he was born, was already over a span long.[11] When he reached the age of sound judgment, he assumed rule over the people after his father. Then his son Ardashīr was born to him. The ruler of Iṣṭakhr at that time was a man from the Bāzranjīn family called, according to what I have been told from information going back to Hishām b. Muḥammad (i.e., Ibn al-Kalbī),[12] Jūzhir,[13]

---

Anāhīd, the beginning of a tradition among the Sāsānids that their founder had been at once warrior hero, prince, and priest. See Nöldeke, trans. 4 n. 2; *EIr*, s.v. Anāhīd. i. Ardwīsūr Anāhīd (M. Boyce).

11. A legendary touch, like being born with a full set of teeth, presaging future strength and greatness. See Nöldeke, trans. 4, n. 3.

12. The major early Islamic historian of pre-Islamic Arabia, including Yemen and the fringes of the northern and central Arabian Desert facing the empires of the Byzantines and the Sāsānids, and also a prime authority, as his *magnum opus* the *Jamharat al-nasab* shows, on Arab tribal genealogy and history, born in Kūfah ca. 120/737 and died there in 204/819 or 205/821. His interest in pre-Islamic Arabian history seems to have arisen partly from a desire to elucidate the background of the Qur'ān, and partly from his Kalbī family origins, for the Kalb had played a glorious role in South Arabian tribal history as the mainstay of the Quḍā'ah, and then in early Islamic times had been the principal military backing for the Umayyad caliphs in Syria. Moreover, his home town of al-Kūfah lay close to al-Ḥīrah, in pre-Islamic times the capital of the Lakhmid kings, whose history Hishām was especially concerned to elucidate (see, e.g., al-Ṭabarī, I, 821–22, pp. 20–22 below). His interest here was such that he called one of his sons al-Mundhir, the name so typical of Lakhmid kings that they are often referred to as al-Manādhirah, and thus himself acquired the *kunyah* or patronymic of Abū al-Mundhir.

This interest in the Lakhmids further gave him a desire to make available to his contemporaries in early 'Abbāsid Iraq the history of the Lakhmids' suzerains, the rulers of Persia. This explains why Hishām provided so much material for al-Ṭabarī on the Persian monarchs (which al-Ṭabarī, being himself of Iranian stock, was probably not averse from using); he wrote a special monograph, no longer extant, on the Parthian Arsacids, the *Kitāb Mulūk al-ṭawā'if*. This material on the Lakhmids and Sāsānids is much greater in quantity and richer in caliber than the exiguous material al-Ṭabarī could find on the Ghassānids of Syria and their suzerains the Byzantines. Apart from his careful use of written sources, including historical traditions and narratives, *akhbār*, derived from his father Muḥammad, a noted Qur'ānic scholar and exegete, Hishām apparently had access to some written documents on the Lakhmids still available in al-Ḥīrah during his own lifetime. He combed local churches and monasteries for their inscriptions and for documents preserved there. He was especially familiar with the verses of the poet of the last Lakhmids at al-Ḥīrah, 'Adī b. Zayd (see n. 116 below), but must have had the whole corpus of pre-Islamic poetry and that of the interval between the Jāhiliyyah and the new Islamic dispensation, the *mukhaḍram*, at his fingertips.

See on Hishām and his father Ibn al-Kalbī, trans. W. Caskel and G. Strenziok, *Jamharat al-nasab*, introduction; Fuat Sezgin, *GAS*, I, 268–71; A. A. Duri, *The Rise of Historical Writing among the Arabs*, 51–52, 146–47; Irfan Shahîd, *Byzantium*

[815] and, according to others, Juzhir. This last had a eunuch called Tīrā,[14] whom he had appointed castellan (*arjabadh*)[15] of Dārābjird.[16] When Ardashīr reached the age of seven years, his father took him to Juzhir, whose seat was at al-Bayḍā',[17] made his son stand before Juzhir, and asked the latter if he would attach the boy to Tīrā as a foster child of his and as the future castellan in Tīrā's stead. Juzhir agreed to his request and had the terms of the request written out for him in a formal sealed document (*sijill*).[18] Bābak

---

*and the Arabs in the Fourth Century*, 349–66; *EI*², s.v. al-Kalbī (W. Ataullah).

13. Older forms Gōchithr, Gōchihr, rendered in Greek sources as Gōsithrēs "a former king of the Persians." It means "whose seed is cattle," i.e., parent of the cattle, *gaočithra* being used in the Avesta as an epithet of the moon. See Nöldeke, trans. 4 n. 4; F. Justi, *Iranisches Namenbuch*, 110. No coins from Gōchihr (or from any other Bāzranjīs) are extant, but his historical existence seems likely.

14. This name stems from such a compound name as Tīr- dād "given, created by Tīr or Mercury." In Greek sources a king of Characene is named as Tiraios (from whom coins are known), and it may have been this ruler who gave his name to the Nahr Tīrā or Tīrīn river or canal of early Islamic al-Ahwāz (Yāqūt, *Mu'jam al-buldān*, V, 319; Le Strange, *Lands*, 241; Schwarz, *Iran*, 308, 313–15). See Nöldeke, trans. 4 n. 5; Justi, *Namenbuch*, 325, 326–27; P. Gignoux, *Noms propres sassanides en moyen-perse épigraphique*, no. 899.

15. Nöldeke, trans. 5 n. 1, took *(h)argabadh* to mean "castellan," but the coexistence of the specific Middle Persian term *dizbed*, meaning "commander of a fortress," led some scholars subsequently to doubt this interpretation and suggest a meaning like "tax collector" for an MP **hargbed*. However, Christensen, *L'Iran sous les Sassanides*, 107, noted that, at the outset of the Sāsānid state, it was an office held by the prince Ardashīr (I) (see al-Ṭabarī, I, 815, p. 7 below), and in *EIr*, s.v. Argbed, M.-L. Chaumont opts for the former meaning, "commander of an *arg*," to use the NP term corresponding to MP **argbed*. Both readings of the word are possible. It clearly became a very prestigious office, and later, al-Ṭabarī, I, 869, p. 104 below, states that it was close in status to that of the commander-in-chief of the army.

16. A town and *kūrah* of eastern Fārs, in modern times having the curtailed form Dārāb, corresponding to what in Seljuq and Il-Khānid times was known as the lands of the Shabānkāra'ī Kurds. See Yāqūt, *Buldān*, ii, 446; Le Strange, *Lands*, 288–89; Schwarz, *Iran*, 92–97; *EI*², s.v. Dārābdjird (D.N. Wilber).

17. Literally, "the white [fortress, town, etc.]," a town of Fārs lying to the north of Shīrāz and in the Kāmfīrūz district. This region flourished as far back as Elamite times as that of Anshan (see *EIr*, s.v. Anshan [J. Hansman]), but al-Bayḍā' is today little more than a village. See Yāqūt, *Buldān*, I, 529; Le Strange, *Lands*, 280; Schwarz, *Iran*, 16–17, 54; Barthold, *Historical Geography*, 153, 161; *EI*², s.v. al-Bayḍā' (O. Löfgren); *EIr*, s.v. Bayżā (C. E. Bosworth).

18. Derived from Latin *sigillum* "seal" and then in Late Latin and Byzantine Greek usage applied to the document or scroll to which a seal had been affixed, this term came into Arabic certainly by Qur'ānic times (cf. Sūrah XXI, 104). It later acquired various technical legal and administrative senses. See *EI*² s.v. Sidjill. 1. Ḳur'ānic and early Arabic usage (F. C. de Blois).

took him along to Tīrā, who received him handsomely and adopted him as his own son. When Tīrā died, Ardashīr took over his office, and performed the function admirably. A group of astrologers and diviners informed him that he had been born under an auspicious star and that he would rule the lands (sc., the whole of Iran). It is related that, after this, Ardashīr behaved in a modest and unpretentious manner in pursuance of this forecast, and continued each day to grow in good deeds and conduct, and that he saw in a dream an angel sitting by his head who told him that God was going to give him rulership over the lands, so he was to prepare for this. When he awoke, he rejoiced at this and felt within himself power and great strength such as he had never before known.

The first thing he did was to proceed to a place in the Dārābjird district called Jūbānān,[19] and killed a ruler there named Fāsīn.[20] Then he went along to a place called Kūn.s (?) and killed a ruler there called Manūshihr,[21] and after that to a place called L.r.wīr (?),[22] where he killed a ruler there named Dārā.[23] In all these places he appointed persons [as governors] responsible to him. He then wrote to his father (sc., to Bābak) telling him what he had accomplished, and called upon him to rise up against Juzhir, who [816]

19. Literally, "cowherds," MP *gōbānān, in this form or the singular Jūbān, is the name of several villages in Persia, cf. Yāqūt, *Buldān*, II, 176 (Jūbānān), IV, 487 (Kūbān(ān)); but most probably here is meant what was in early Islamic times the town of Jūbānān on the northern shore of Lake Bakhtigān (now, it seems, vanished from the map) and on the Iṣṭakhr-Sīrajān-Kirmān road. See Nöldeke, trans. 6 n. 3; Le Strange, *Lands*, 278–79; Schwarz, *Iran*, 109.

20. Thus the reading of the ms. Sprenger 30, an anonymous chronographical work (see *Introductio*, p. LII), i.e., Pisīn, Pasīn, a name familiar in the Iranian national legend, see Justi, *Namenbuch*, 252–53; but other mss. have readings that could be *Wās.f.r* (see text, n. g), cf. Wāsbuhr, etc.

21. This name of a hero in the Iranian national legend (literally, "from the race of Manu," in Indian legend, the first man; see Yarshater, "Iranian National History," 433–35, and Gignoux, *Noms propres sassanides*, no. 559) is attested on pre-Sāsānid coins, or on coins roughly contemporary with the advent of Ardashīr to power, issued by kings of Persis. See Nöldeke, trans. p. 6 n. 6.

22. Both Kūn.s and Lurwīr are unidentified.

23. This ancient name of Achaemenid kings had survived among local rulers during the Arsacid period, and one of these may have been the eponymous founder of Dārābjird (according to the Middle Persian geography used by J. Markwart, ed. G. Messina, in his *A Catalogue of the Provincial Capitals of Ērānshahr*, 19, by a Dārā, son of Dārā), since names of towns composed of a personal name and the ending *-gird* do not occur before the time of Alexander the Great. See Nöldeke, trans. 6 n. 7.

was at al-Bayḍā'; this Bābak did, killing him and seizing his crown,[24] and then he wrote to Ardawān the Pahlawī, king of the mountain regions (al-Jibāl, i.e., Media) and the adjoining lands,[25] humbly entreating and requesting from him permission to place upon his son Sābūr's head the crown of Juzhir. Ardawān, however, wrote back to him in harsh terms informing him that he and his son Ardashīr were to be regarded as rebels, since the two of them had killed people; but Bābak took no notice of this.

Bābak died around that time, and Sābūr, son of Bābak, was invested with the crown and reigned in his father's place as king.[26] He wrote to Ardashīr instructing him to proceed to his court, but Ardashīr held back. Accordingly, Sābūr grew angry at Ardashīr's recalcitrance; he gathered together troops and set off at the head of them to make war on Ardashīr. He left Iṣṭakhr [and encamped in the building (*binā'*) of Khumāy[27] on the road to Dārābjird, but part of the building fell on top of him and killed him. When news of this reached Ardashīr, he proceeded to Iṣṭakhr].[28] He found there a number of his brothers, some of them older than himself. They

24. The account transmitted by al-Ṭabarī seems to magnify Ardashīr's role in the fighting against Artabanus; it may well have been Bābak and not his son who took the initiative here. See Nöldeke, trans. 7 n. 1.

25. That is, the last Arsacid king, Artabanus IV (in the older reckoning, Artabanus V), r. ca. 213–ca. 224. The Greek form Artabanus, Parthian and MP Ardawān, represents OP *Arta-bānu "the glory of Arta" (i.e., the divine order of the Avesta, cf. *EIr* s.v. Ardwahišt [M. Boyce]). See Nöldeke, trans. 7 n. 2; A. D. H. Bivar, "The Political History of Iran under the Arsacids," 94–96, 99; *EIr,* s.v. Artabanus (M.R. Dandamaev, K. Schippmann). The form Ardawān was taken over by the Arab historians; see the citations detailed in al-Mas'ūdī, *Murūj al-dhahab,* ed. Ch. Pellat, VI, *Index généraux,* 137.

26. The name Shābūr, MP Shāhpuhr, "son of the king," ultimately going back to OP **Xšāyathiya.pūthra,* was not apparently used before the Sāsānids (see Justi, *Namenbuch,* 284–87; Gignoux, *Les noms propres sassanides,* no. 858). Whether Shābūr was thus named by his father to buttress his right to succeed to the throne is uncertain. His reign was long enough for him to mint coins. In any case, Ardashīr's theoretical role as a usurper was subsequently validated by his succession on Shābūr's accidental death. See Nöldeke, trans. 7 n. 3; *EIr,* s.v. Ardašīr I. i. History (Wiesehöfer).

27. Humāy, Avestan Humāyā, is in the Avesta the daughter of Wīshtāspa, playing a role in later Persian epic tradition somewhat like that of the Assyrian queen Semiramis. Early Islamic authors such as al-Dīnawarī, al-Mas'ūdī, and Ḥamza al-Iṣfahānī attribute to Humāy the building of palaces in the vicinity of Iṣṭakhr, in one of which Shābūr now met his death, possibly in an earthquake. See Nöldeke, trans. 8 n. 2; Justi, *Namenbuch,* 131–32; M. Mayrhofer, *Die altiranischen Namen,* no. 177.

28. These words are supplied from the ms. Sprenger 30.

nevertheless gathered together and brought in the crown and the royal throne, and then offered them all to Ardashīr. Hence he was crowned and sat down on the throne.

He began his reign with vigorous and incisive measures. He appointed various persons to diverse offices, and nominated a man called Abarsām to the position of Chief Minister (*buzurg framadhār*), lavishing largesse on him and giving him numerous charges.[29] He appointed a man named Fāh.r (?) as Chief Mōbadh (*mūbadhān mūbadh*).[30] He got wind of a plot on the part of his brothers and some other persons in his entourage to assassinate him, hence he slew a great number of them. Then news came to him that the people of Dārābjird had risen against him, so he returned thither and conquered the town after killing a number of [817] its citizens. He proceeded to Kirmān, where there was a king called Balāsh.[31] There was a fiercely fought battle, in which Ar-

29. Abarsām is a fully historical figure, attested as a high-ranking official of Ardashīr's in Shābūr I's Naqsh-i Rustam inscription, in which the latter monarch lists those court dignitaries in whose memory Shābūr had set up a pious foundation. He could not have been the chief minister, since this official for both Ardashīr and Shābūr is named as a Bābag, and his exact rank and title are uncertain, but he was obviously exalted enough for the late Sāsānid tradition, as transmitted by al-Ṭabarī, to consider him as chief minister. See *EIr*, s.v. Abarsām (E. Yarshater). For Abarsām's supposed part in the preservation and then production at an opportune moment of the prince Shābūr, see al-Ṭabarī, I, 823–25, pp. 24–27 below.

It is, however, an anachronism of al-Ṭabarī's source that he introduces already the office of *buzurg framadhār*, which is not attested till the early fifth century (see on the office, n. 257 below). Court and administration cannot have been so neatly organized at this early time; the highest offices under the Sāsānids in their first century of power were actually those of the *(h)argbed* (see above, n. 15) and the *bidakhsh*, a kind of viceroy, cf. *EIr*, s.v. Bidaxš (W. Sundermann). See Nöldeke, trans. 9 n. 2, and on the name Abarsam, Justi, *Namenbuch*, 1, and Gignoux, *Noms propres sassanides*, no, 14.

30. This renders MP *mowbed mowbedān* "supreme priest," in Syriac the *rēš məghūšē*; see Nöldeke, trans. 451, Excursus 3. The title comes into usage comparatively late in the Sāsānid period and is not an early one. As Nöldeke remarks, trans. 9 n. 3, the new ruler, whether from personal conviction or for reasons of state, showed himself eager to establish the Zoroastrian clergy in a leading role under his dynasty.

31. This, or Walāsh, is the NP form of MP Wardākhsh, well known in the Greek forms Vologesos, etc., and it was a frequent name for the Arsacid kings, later appearing also in the Sāsānid royal line in the shape of Balāsh, son of Yazdajird II (484–88), see, p. 126 below. This Balāsh of Kirmān must have been a local ruler of the last Arsacids, and he may have been the founder of the town of Walāshgird, on the road connecting Jīruft with Hurmuz, mentioned by the Islamic geographers (Yāqūt, *Buldān*, V, 383; Le Strange, *Lands*, 317–18; Schwarz, *Iran*, 248). See

dashīr took part personally, until he captured Balāsh and seized control of the city. Ardashīr thereupon appointed as governor over Kirmān one of his sons, also called Ardashīr.

Ruling in the coastlands along the Persian Gulf was a king called 'b.t.n.b.w.d (Haftānbūkht ?),[32] who was accorded divine attributes and worship. Ardashīr marched against him, killed him by cutting him in half with his sword, put to death the members of his entourage, and brought forth from their subterranean store rooms (*maṭāmīr*)[33] extensive treasures that had been piled up there. He wrote to Mihrak, the king of Abarsās (?)[34] in the district of Ardashīr Khurrah,[35] and to a group of his fellow rulers, summoning them to his obedience. When they refused to submit, he

---

Nöldeke, trans. 10 n. 2; *EIr*, s.v. Balāš (M. L. Chaumont).

In Sāsānid times and in early Islamic times up to the fourth/tenth century, the *shahr-i Kirmān*, the provincial capital, was what became the early Islamic city of Sīrajān, in the western part of the province and near the modern Sa'īdābād. It may have been this first Sāsānid governor, Ardashīr, son of Ardashīr I, who laid out what was perhaps a military encampment, rather than a city, at Weh Ardashīr in the northeastern part of the province (Ḥamzah al-Iṣfahānī, *Ta'rīkh*, 43), the place that became in later times Guwāshīr or Bardasīr, provincial capital under the Būyids and, afterward, became the modern city of Kirmān. See Nöldeke, trans. 10 n. 3; Le Strange, *Lands*, 300–301; J. Marquart, *Ērānšahr nach der Geographie des Ps. Moses Xorenac'i*, 30; Markwart-Messina, *Catalogue of the Provincial Capitals*, 90; Barthold, *Historical Geography*, 137–38; *EI*², s.v. Kirmān (A. K. S. Lambton).

32. Thus according to text, n. *b*. Nöldeke, trans. 10 n. 1 renders the reading '.*s.w.w.d* of the Sprenger ms. as Astawadh (?). The spelling Haftānbūkht (?) is probably a misrendering of an Achaemenid term for an administrative district, denoting a component part of a province, a term that survived through Islamic times as the modern place-name Haftuwān, a village to the southwest of Khunj, in the western part of Lāristān, in southern Fārs.

33. Sing. *maṭmūrah*, meaning a subterranean chamber, either natural or man-made, used essentially for the storage of foodstuffs like grain (i.e., as a silo) or, as here, for treasure. The plural form is not infrequently a toponym in early Islamic times, as in Byzantine Asia Minor, see al-Ṭabarī, III, 1104, year 216/831–32, and in general, *EI*², s.v. Maṭmūra (Ch. Pellat).

34. Thus in Ibn al-Athīr, *Kāmil*, I, 382, but regarded by Nöldeke as dubious; the mss. have various incomprehensible readings, see text, n. *d*. For Mihrag, older form Mithrak, see Justi, *Namenbuch*, 207–208; Gignoux, *Noms propres sassanides*, no. 629.

35. One of the five *kūrah*s or administrative districts making up the province of Fārs, in which was later situated the Islamic provincial capital Shīrāz. The *kūrah*'s MP name, "Ardashīr's glory," commemorated the founder of the Sāsānid dynasty, while the original town there of Gūr, the Islamic Jūr and then Fīrūzābād, was said to have been built on the site of Ardashīr's decisive victory over the last Arsacid Ardawān or Ardabanus IV in ca. A.D. 224. See Nöldeke, trans. 11 n. 2, 446 Excursus 3; Yāqūt, *Buldān*, IV, 283; Le Strange, *Lands*, 248–49; Schwarz, *Iran*, 43ff.; Barthold, *Historical Geography*, 152–53, 158–59; *EI*², s.v. Fīrūzābād (L. Lockhart).

proceeded against them and killed Mihrak. He then went to Jūr; he founded the city [there] and began the construction of the palace called al-Ṭirbāl[36] and also of a fire temple.

While he was engaged in these activities, an envoy from Ardawān (Azdawān, Lāzdawān ?)[37] arrived bearing a letter from the latter. Hence Ardashīr assembled the leading men in the state (*al-nās*)[38] for this purpose and read out the document in their presence. The contents were as follows: "You have presumed beyond your rank in society, and have brought down on yourself destruction, O Kurd brought up amongst the tents of the Kurds![39] Who gave you leave to assume the crown on your head, and permission to seize all the territories you have assembled together and whose rulers and peoples you have subdued? Who ordered you to build the city which you have founded in the desert of . . . ?"—he meant Jūr[40]—"When we allow you to go ahead and construct it, then build a city in the desert which is ten farsakhs across and call it Rām Ardashīr!"[41] He went on to inform Ardashīr that he had dispatched the king of al-Ahwāz against him, with orders to bring back Ardashīr to him in bonds. Ardashīr replied, "It [818] is God who has bestowed on me the crown which I have assumed, who has given me authority over the lands which I have conquered, and who has aided me against the mighty potentates (*jabābirah*) and kings whom I have slain. As for the city which I am to build and which I am to name Rām Ardashīr, I very much hope to get my hands on you and then send your head and your

36. This appears in the Arabic dictionaries, defined as "high building, tower" (see E. W. Lane, *Lexicon*, 1836c), but must in reality be a loanword from MP *talwār* "audience hall," a synonym of *īwān*. There are impressive remains above ground of Ardashīr's palace at Gūr/Jūr; see *EIr*, s.v. Architecture. iii. Sasanian (D. Huff), at II, 331 (Plate V), 332. Concerning the fire temple at Jūr, see al-Ṭabarī, I, 1067, p. 410 below.

37. Nöldeke, text, n. *e*, preferred the reading of the Sprenger ms. Lāzdawān.

38. Here, as often in premodern Islamic history in all times and places, *al-nās* does not mean "people in general" but "the people who matter, *the* people"; cf. the Mamlūk *awlād al-nās*, sons of amīrs and mamlūks within the *ḥalqah* unit of the Mamlūk army; i.e., sons of the ruling military caste.

39. A looking-forward to later Islamic times when, certainly from the ʿAbbāsid period onward, *kurd*, "shepherd, nomad," is virtually a synonym for "robber, bandit, brigand."

40. See for Jūr, n. 35 above.

41. Literally, "joy of Ardashīr." Ardashīr's words here are of course ironic: you may plan a city, but you won't be able to carry out the plan! See Nöldeke, trans. 12 n. 3.

treasuries to the fire temple which I have founded at Ardashīr Khurrah."[42]

Then Ardashīr headed toward Iṣṭakhr, and left Abarsām [as governor] in Ardashīr Khurrah. Not much time had elapsed before a letter reached him from Abarsām with the news that the king of al-Ahwāz had appeared but that he had retreated after being defeated in battle.[43] Whereupon Ardashīr proceeded to Iṣbahān, took its king Shādh Sābūr prisoner and then killed him,[44] after which he returned to Fārs, and went forth to give battle to Nīrūfarr (?), ruler of al-Ahwāz, marching to Arrajān,[45] Sanbīl (?),[46] and Ṭāshān,[47] dependencies of [the district of] Rām Hurmuz, and then to Surraq.[48] When he reached these places, he rode on with a group of his retainers until he stood on the banks of the Dujayl (here, the Kārūn river),[49] took control of the city [already existing there], and founded the [new] city of Sūq al-Ahwāz;[50] then he returned to Fārs

42. Again ironically, Ardashīr asserts that he has no need of a new city, but will adorn his existing one with his enemy's head. See Nöldeke, tr. 12 n. 5.

43. This ruler would be the ruler of Elymais, a vassal of the last Arsacids, the region of southeastern Khūzistān, with its center at the modern Tang-i Sarvak; coins are extant from these petty rulers.

44. Ardashīr is now for the first time moving out of Fārs against neighboring potentates. Nothing is known of the rulers in Iṣfahān at this time; Nöldeke, trans. 13 n. 1, surmised that Shādh Sābūr, literally "joy of Shābūr," should perhaps be read as Shāh Sābūr, since the name in the text would be more fittingly that of a town.

45. The name of a city and of the westernmost *kūrah* of Fārs, adjacent to the border with the province of Ahwāz. Al-Ṭabarī's mention of it here would be anachronistic in the light of the information in many Arabic authors that it was founded by the emperor Qubādh (I) (i.e., some two-and-a-half centuries after Ardashīr's time), but clearly an older town existed on the site, which Qubādh may have rebuilt. See Yāqūt, *Buldān*, I, 142–44; Nöldeke, trans. 13 n. 2; Le Strange, *Lands*, 248, 268–69; Schwarz, *Iran*, 111ff.; Barthold, *Historical Geography*, 164–65; H. Gaube, *Die südpersische Provinz Arraǧān/Kūh-Gīlūyeh*, 28–31, 74–76; *EI²*, s.v. Arradjān (M. Streck-D. N. Wilber); *EIr*, s.v. Arrajān (H. Gaube).

46. Nöldeke's preferred reading, n.c, for the text's *s.sār*.

47. Ṭāshān or Ṭasan probably survives today as the ruined site of Tāshūn. See Schwarz, *Iran*, 344; Gaube, *Die südpersische Provinz Arraǧān/Kūh-Gīlūyeh*, 112,

48. The region of which Dawraq [al-Furs] was the chief town. See Le Strange, *Lands*, 242; Schwarz, *Iran*, 370–71; Sir Arnold T. Wilson, *The Persian Gulf. An Historical Sketch from the Earliest Times to the Beginning of the Twentieth Century*, 186–87; Gaube, *Die südpersische Provinz Arraǧān/Kūh-Gīlūyeh*, 22ff; *EI²*, s.v. Dawraḳ (L. Lockhart); *EIr*, s.v. Dawraq (C. E. Bosworth).

49. Dujayl, "Little Tigris." See Nöldeke, trans. 13 n. 3; Le Strange, *Lands*, 232–34, 245–46; Schwarz, *Iran*, 296–99; Barthold, *Historical Geography*, 189–92; *EI²*, s.v. Kārūn (M. Streck-J. Lassner).

50. A city of lower Khūzistān or Ahwāz (the latter an Arabic broken plural of Hūzī, Khūzī, the name of the Iranian tribe originally occupying the region), the

laden with plunder. He set off from Fārs once again, and went back to al-Ahwāz by the road through Jirih and Kāzarūn,[51] and then from al-Ahwāz to Maysān, where he killed a ruler there called B.n.dū (?) and built there Karkh Maysān.[52]

Yet again, he set off back to Fārs, and dispatched a message to Ardawān demanding [that he name] a place where the two of them could fight together. Ardawān replied that he would meet Ardashīr on a plain called Hurmuzjān[53] at the end of the month of Mihr. Ardashīr, however, reached the place before the appointed time in order to take up a [favorable] position on the plain. He dug out a ditch to protect himself and his army, and took possession of [819] a spring there.[54] Ardawān came up against him, and the troops deployed themselves in battle order. Sābūr, Ardashīr's son, had

---

name Ahwāz also being applied to the province's capital, further defined as the province's "market" (*sūq*), given the agricultural and commercial prosperity of the province. There was probably an Achaemenid settlement on the site of Sūq Ahwāz, which Ardashīr rebuilt and refounded as his own city, Hurmuz Ardashīr (see al-Ṭabarī, I, 820, p. 16 below), and in Sāsānid times it prospered greatly as the capital of the province of Susiana after the decay of Susa. See Yāqūt, *Buldān*, I, 284–86; Le Strange, *Lands*, 232–34; Schwarz, *Iran*, 315–24; *EI²*, s.v. al-Ahwāz (L. Lockhart); *EIr*, s.v. Ahvāz. 1. History (C. E. Bosworth).

51. These two places, often mentioned together by the geographers, lay to the southwest and west, respectively, of Shīrāz. See Yāqūt, *Buldān*, II, 131, IV, 429–30; Le Strange, *Lands*, 266–68; Schwarz, *Iran*, 33, 35; Barthold, *Historical Geography*, 162–63; *EI²*, s.v. Kāzarūn (J. Calmard).

52. The Greek Mesēnē, MP Mēshān, Arabic Maysān, was the region along the lowest reaches of the Tigris in Mesopotamia to the east of the Baṭīḥa, or Great Swamp. Its center was the Seleucid foundation of Charax Spasinou, with the province in Arsacid times being known as Characene, with the subsequent Syriac name Karkhā dhə Mēshān (*karkhā*, "fortified town"), eventually yielding the Arabic form given by al-Ṭabarī. Ardashīr conquered Characene in ca. 224, but there seems to be no confirmatory evidence that the rebuilt and refounded town of Charax acquired the name Ast(ar)ābādh Ardashīr. See Nöldeke, trans. 13 n. 5; *PW*, III/2, s.v. Charax, Mesēnē (Weissbach); Le Strange, *Lands*, 43, 80; Marquart, *Ērānšahr*, 40–42; M. J. Morony, *Iraq after the Muslim Conquest*, 155–61; W. Eilers, "Iran and Mesopotamia," 487; Bosworth, "Iran and the Arabs before Islam," 594; *EI²*, s.v. Maysān (M. Streck-M. Morony); *EIr*, s.v. Characene and Charax (J. Hansman).

53. Unattested in the Islamic geographers.. See Nöldeke, trans. 14 n. 1; the name appears in al-Dīnawarī's *al-Akhbār al-ṭiwāl* with an intrusive *d*, i.e., Hurmuzdijān

54. The exact location of the battlefield is unknown. It has been fixed as probably somewhere near the later Islamic town of Gulpāyagān to the northwest of Iṣfahān; the date of the battle was 30 Mihr of Seleucid era 535/28 April 224. See *EIr*, s.v. Artabanus (K. Schippmann), at II, 650a. There remains, nevertheless, the possibility that the encounter took place in eastern Khūzistān if the name Hurmuzdijān should have some connection with the town of Rām-Hurmuz; the terrain there would certainly be suitable for extensive cavalry maneuvering.

already gone forward in order to shield his father. Fierce fighting got under way, in the course of which Sābūr killed Dādhbundādh,[55] Ardawān's secretary (sc., the writer of the letter) with his own hand. Ardashīr rushed forward from his battle position toward Ardawān and killed him. There was great slaughter among Ardawān's troops, and the survivors fled the field. It is said that Ardashīr dismounted and trampled Ardawān's head with his feet. On that day of battle, Ardashīr received the title of "Supreme King" (*Shāhanshāh,* literally "King of Kings").[56]

Then he went from there to Hamadhān and conquered it by force of arms, as also the mountain region (al-Jabal), Azerbaijan, Armenia, and [the region of] al-Mawṣil. The he went from al-Mawṣil to Sūristān, that is, the Sawād,[57] and took possession of it for himself. On the banks of the Tigris, opposite the city of Ctesiphon (which is the city that forms the eastern part of al-

55. The rendering preferred by Nöldeke, text n. *a,* for the *dār.n.b.dādh* of the text (Sprenger ms., *dād.b.n.dār*).

56. Ardashīr commemorated his victory in a rock relief, the largest surviving Sāsānid one, on a mountainside near his town of Ardashīr Khurrah. See *EIr,* s.v. Ardašīr I. ii. Rock reliefs (H. Luschey) (with illustrations).

Ardashīr's symbolic investiture with the ancient title of "King of Kings" is depicted in a relief at Naqsh-i Rustam, in which the king receives the diadem of sovereignty from Ahura Mazdā, and in other reliefs depicting god and king at the bridge near Ardashīr-Khurrah and at Naqsh-i Rajab. See Georgina Herrmann, *The Iranian Revival,* 82–88, 90 (illustration); Luschey, loc. cit. (with illustrations). His assumption of the title is also noted in the other Arabic sources on the Sāsānids: al-Ya'qūbī, *Ta'rīkh,* I, 179; al-Dīnawarī, *al-Akhbār al-ṭiwāl,* 43; al-Mas'ūdī, *Murūj,* II, 161 = §585. It was from the date of his victory over Ardawān (see above, n. 54), i.e., the regnal year 223–24, or at his formal accession to the throne shortly afterwards (probably therefore at some point between 224 and 226, see Frye, "The Political History of Iran," 118–19, and n. 68 below) that Ardashīr dated the beginning of his reign, which extended till his death, most probably in 242 (the chronology of the early Sāsānids is in many places uncertain). See Nöldeke, trans. 15 n. 1; the genealogical table of Sāsānid rulers in Frye, *The Heritage of Persia,* 295 (in which several dates for the early Sāsānids need correction), and his list in "The Political History of Iran under the Sassanians," 178 (again with some early dates to be corrected); *EIr,* s.v. Ardašīr I. i. History (J. Wiesehöfer).

57. Nöldeke, trans. 15 n. 3, took Sūristān to be a Persian translation of Bēth Aramāyē, "land of the Syrians." It could also denote "the region of the Nahr Sūrā," this being the name the Arabs gave to what was then the eastern branch of the middle Euphrates (now the river's main channel; see Yāqūt, *Buldān,* III, 279; Le Strange, *Lands,* 70; Marquart, *Ērānšahr,* 21; Markwart-Messina, *Catalogue of the Provincial Capitals,* 103). It is equated with the Sawād, "the dark lands" (contrasted, in its vegetation and greenery, with the dazzling whiteness of the surrounding desert), the irrigated region of Mesopotamia. See *EI*[2], s.v. Sawād (C. E. Bosworth).

Madā'in), he built a city on the western side, which he called Bih Ardashīr. He formed this into a province (*kūrah*), adding to it Bihrasīr, al-Rūmaqān, Nahr Darqīṭ, Kūthā and Nahr Jawbar,[58] and appointed local governors (*'ummāl*) over them. Then he went back from the Sawād to Iṣṭakhr, and thence to Sijistān, thence to Jurjān, and thence to Abarshahr,[59] Marw, Balkh, and Khwārazm, as far as the farthest frontiers of Khurāsān, after which he returned to Marw. He killed a large number of people, and despatched their heads to the fire temple of Anāhīdh. Then he returned from Marw to Fārs and took up his quarters at Jūr. Envoys from the kings of [820] the Kūshān, of Ṭūrān, and of Makrān, came to him offering their submission.[60] From Jūr, Ardashīr went to al-Baḥrayn and laid siege to its king Sanaṭruq. The latter was reduced to the extremity of need, till finally he threw himself down from the walls of the citadel and perished. Ardashīr returned to al-Madā'in and estab-

---

58. For these places, see Nöldeke, trans. 16 nn. 3, 4; Le Strange, *Lands*, 34, 68–70; Marquart, *Ērānšahr*, 164–65; Morony, *Iraq after the Muslim Conquest*, 143ff. As Nöldeke observed, tr. 16 n. 4, these administrative arrangements reflect late Sāsānid administrative geography, not that of Ardashīr's time, shown by the inclusion of Rūmaqān, the settlement of Weh-Andiyōg-Khusraw, founded by Anūshar-wān for the people of Antioch carried off after the Persian conquest of that city in 540, and called in Arabic al-Rūmiyyah. See Fry, "The Political History of Iran under the Sasanians," 155; *EIr*, s.v. "Deportations. ii. In the Parthian and Sasanian Periods" (E. Kettenhofen), at VII, 301a; pp. 157–58 below.

59. That is, the region around Nīshāpūr, the central part of Khurāsān, the province to which Ardashīr turned his attention once he had secured western Persia. The name Abarshahr probably reflected an old **Aparn-xšathr* "country of the Aparnak," Greek Aparnoi, the leading tribe of the Dahae who founded the Parthian empire. For the city of Nīshāpūr and its foundation, see n. 163 below. See Yāqūt, *Buldān*, I, 65–66; Nöldeke, trans. 17 n. 2, 59 n. 3; Le Strange, *Lands*, 382–88; Marquart, *Ērānšahr*, 36, 74–75 (his rendering of Abarshahr as "upper country" is to be rejected); Markwart-Messina, *Catalogue of the Provincial Capitals*, 52–53; Barthold, *Historical Geography*, 94ff.; *EI*², s.v. Nīsh̲āpūr (E. Honigmann-C. E. Bosworth).

60. These potentates were neighbors of the Sāsānids in what is now northern Afghanistan and the Sijistān-Baluchistan region. The demise of the Kushan empire, which had in its heyday straddled the Hindu Kush and extended over northern India, seems to have taken place ca. 225, and is probably to be connected with Ardashīr's campaigns against the Kushan Shāh, laconically referred to here. See Nöldeke, tr. 17 n. 5; Bivar, "The History of Eastern Iran," 203. Ṭūrān was in early Islamic times a region of east-central Baluchistan associated with Quṣdār or Khuzdār, i.e., it lay to the north of the coastal region of Makrān and, as Nöldeke observed, trans. 18 n. 1, is not to be confused with Tūrān, the name the Iranians gave to the peoples beyond the Oxus. The Paikuli inscriptions of some two generations after Ardashīr's time mention the Makurān Shāh as a vassal of the Sāsānids but not the Tūrān Shāh. See *EI*¹, s.v. Ṭūrān (V. Minorsky).

lished himself there, and he had his son Shābūr crowned within his own lifetime.[61]

It is related that there was in a village called Alār, in the district of Kūjarān, which is one of the rural districts of the coastland of Ardashīr Khurrah, a queen who was accorded the respect and worship of a divinity and who possessed wealth, treasuries, and soldiers. Ardashīr made war on her priestly custodians (*sadanah*), killed her, and seized as booty immense wealth and treasures belonging to her. [It is further related] that he built eight cities: in Fārs, the city of Ardashīr Khurrah, that is, Jūr, the city of Rām Ardashīr, and the city of Rīw Ardashīr;[62] in al-Ahwāz, Hurmuz Ardashīr, that is, Sūq al-Ahwāz; in the Sawād, Bih Ardashīr, that is, the western side of al-Madā'in,[63] and Astābādh Ardashīr, that is, Karkh Maysān; in al-Baḥrayn, Fasā (?) Ardashīr, i.e the city of al-Khaṭṭ;[64] and in [the region of] al-Mawṣil, Būdh Ardashīr, that is, Ḥazzah.[65]

---

61. These movements by Ardashīr mark the beginning of Sāsānid attempts to control the western shores of the Gulf, and we now have the start of a Persian political, cultural, and religious penetration into eastern Arabia that was to continue until the advent there of Islam in the 630s. The appearance of the Parthian name Sanaṭrūq/Sinatrices, so common among the Arsacids and their dependents in Adiabene and Commagene, may mean that this local ruler in Baḥrayn was an Arsacid vassal. See Nöldeke, trans. 18 n. 3; A. Siddiqi, *Studien über die persischen Fremdwörter im klassischen Arabisch,* 77–79; Bosworth, "Iran and the Arabs before Islam," 603–604.

The coronation of Shāpūr with his father's crown and the joint rule of father and son is confirmed by Ardashīr's late coins, which, inter alia, depict Ardashīr and a youthful king symbolizing the son, and also by rock reliefs, including one at Dārābgird apparently depicting Shāpūr, victorious over the Romans, and wearing his father's crown. See *EIr,* s.v. Dārāb. iii. Rock Reliefs (Georgina Herrmann).

62. This name later became Rēshahr/Rīshahr. Its modern ruins lie at the southern end of the Bushire peninsula; the name survived at least until the sixteenth century in that of the Portuguese fort of "Reixer." See Nöldeke, trans. 19 n. 4; Schwarz, *Iran,* 120–21; Wilson, *The Persian Gulf,* 73–74; Barthold, *Historical Geography,* 164; *EI²,* s.v. Būshahr (Būshīr) (L. Lockhart).

63. That is, the newly refounded Seleucia. See J. M. Fiey, "Topographie chrétienne de Mahozé," 400, 409–10.

64. Al-Khaṭṭ was a term applied by early Islamic historians and geographers to the coastlands of eastern Arabia from the head of the Persian Gulf down to Oman, without any more precise definition. The particular settlement of al-Khaṭṭ was said to be held by the 'Abd al-Qays tribe and to be an entrepôt for a famous type of spear, the Khaṭṭī, imported from India and sold to the Bedouins, but it is impossible to locate it firmly. The name would appear to be old and to be connected with the Chatenia of the classical geographers. See Nöldeke, tr. 20 n. 3; *PW,* III/2, s.v. Chattenia (D. H. Müller); Bosworth, "Iran and the Arabs before Islam," 593–4; *EI²,* s.v. al-Khaṭṭ (A. Grohmann).

65. Ḥazzah, marked today by an entirely Muslim village Heza to the southwest

It is mentioned that, when Ardashīr first came to power, he wrote to the Party Kings eloquently phrased letters setting forth his rightful claim to authority over them and summoning them to obedience. When he came to the end of his life, he set forth his testament for his successor.[66] All through his career he was the object of praise and was victorious in war. No military force of his was ever put to flight nor was any banner of his ever hurled down. [821]

---

of Irbil, was the administrative center of a region of the same name in Adiabene, the region between the Greater and the Lesser Zāb rivers in northern Mesopotamia (see on it, *EIr*, s.v. Adiabene [D. Sellwood]). The town is frequently mentioned in Nestorian Christian literature as the seat of a bishopric in the metropolitanate of Irbil (and ca. 1200 a Jacobite bishopric is mentioned there). Ibn Ḥawqal in the fourth/tenth century still speaks of the *arḍ Ḥazzah* and its component *rustāq*s. See Nöldeke, tr. 20 n. 4; M. Canard, *Histoire des H'amdanides*, 123; Fiey, *Assyrie chrétienne*, I, 165–67; Morony, *Iraq after the Muslim Conquest*, 132–33. Ḥamzah al-Iṣfahānī devotes much of his section on Ardashīr in *Ta'rīkh*, 42–44, to the many cities the emperor founded and his many fire temples and other buildings. Although a zealous adherent of Zoroastrianism, Ardashīr seems to have been tolerant of the Christian communities within his realm, although it was only toward 250 that what might be called a catholic Christianity, with a defined dogma, evolved with a proper ecclesiastical hierarchy, at least as far as the Tigris. See J. Labourt, *Le Christianisme dans l'empire perse sous la dynastie sassanide, 224–632*; 10–17; M.-L. Chaumont, "Les Sassanides et la Christianisme de l'Empire iranien au IIIe siècle de notre ère," 167–68.

66. This is a reference to what was in Islamic times known as the *'ahd Ardashīr*, in fact a good example of the "Mirrors for Princes" genre, listed by Ibn al-Nadīm in his *Fihrist*, 377–78, trans. Bayard Dodge, *The Fihrist of al-Nadīm. A Tenth-Century Survey of Muslim Culture*, II, 740, as the *Kitāb 'Ahd Ardashīr Bābakān ilā ibnihi Sābūr* and described as a translation from Pahlavi. Whether any material from the time of Ardashīr is actually contained in it is unknown, but it is more likely that material ostensibly from Ardashīr was imputed to him later. The text and a translation of it, at that time still in manuscript, were given by Mario Grignaschi in his "Quelques spécimens de la littérature sassanide conservée dans les bibliothèques d'Istanbul," 46–90, and the work has been subsequently edited and published by Iḥsān 'Abbās, *'Ahd Ardashīr*, Beirut 1967. A related text is the *Ā'īn-i Ardashīr*, a collection of aphorisms and advice on statecraft, also edited and translated by Grignaschi in op, cit., 91–133. Also relevant here is mention of the so-called *Letter of Tansar*, known subsequently to the Islamic world through an Arabic translation, probably by Ibn al-Muqaffa' from a lost Pahlavi original, but now known substantially in a New Persian version. It purports to be the work of Ardashīr's Chief Priest, Tōsar or Tansar; it adjures a local prince of Ṭabaristān to submit to the Sāsānid ruler and, in general, justifies Sāsānid rule and political conduct. Although it is generally accepted that the *Letter* in its existing form dates substantially from the time of Khusraw Anūsharwān, i.e., the sixth century, it may well have a core going back to the third century. See *EI*[2], s.v. Tansar, Kitāb (F. C. de Blois). See also for a recent consideration of all three of these texts as part of the movement for translating works from the Pahlavi into Arabic, and their place in the subsequent development of Islamic political and social thinking, Louise Marlow, *Hierarchy and Egalitarianism in Islamic Thought*, 72–88.

He reduced to submission[67] and humiliated all the rulers of the lands around his own kingdom, and conquered the lands totally. He divided up the land into provinces, laid out cities, established the various ranks and offices in the state, and exerted himself in multiplying the fertility and flourishing of the land. His reign lasted, from the time when he killed Ardawān till he himself perished, fourteen years, but according to others, fourteen years and ten months.[68]

There was related to me a narrative going back to Hishām b. Muḥammad (i.e., Ibn al-Kalbī) that states:[69] Ardashīr moved for-

67. *wa-athkana fī al-arḍ*, echoing Qur'ān, VIII, 68/67.

68. Ardashīr I reigned from spring 224, the date his victory over Ardawān took place, or 226 (see n. 56 above) to 240 as sole ruler, and then for two more years till his death as coruler with his son Shāpūr. There has, in fact, been much discussion about the chronology of Ardashīr's last years and the exact date of his death; this latter event should probably be placed, in Wiesehöfer's estimation (see below), in early 242, most likely in February of that year. Ardashīr's name appears on his coins as 'ARTHŠTR. See, on his coins, Furdoonjee D. I. Paruck, *Sāsānian Coins*, 51–52, 305–16, 413–16, Plates I-III, Table I; R. Göbl, *Sasanian Numismatics*, 42, Tables I-Ia, Plates 1–2; D. Sellwood, P. Whitting, and R. Williams, *An Introduction to Sasanian Coins*, 21, 73–78; Hodge Mehdi Malek, "A Survey of Research on Sasanian Numismatics," 232–33.

The Arabic sources on the rise of the Sāsānids and Ardashīr's reign include Ibn Qutaybah, *Ma'ārif*, 653–54; al-Ya'qūbī, *Ta'rīkh*, I, 179 (very brief); al-Dīnawarī, *al-Akhbār al-ṭiwāl*, 42–45 (Ardashīr's rise to power and defeat of Ardawān's son Farrukhān, the extension of his authority over outlying provinces and the story of the clandestine birth and upbringing of his son Sābūr (I), see below, al-Ṭabarī, I, 823–25); Ḥamzah al-Iṣfahānī, *Ta'rīkh*, 42–44 (Ardashīr's rise and consolidation of power, his new cities and his building operations); al-Mas'ūdī, *Murūj*, II, 148, 151–63 = §§ 573, 576–88 (his defining of the various ranks in the Persian social, military, and religious structures, his emphasis on court ceremonial, his urban foundations and building works, and his aphorisms on statecraft and monarchical power, as set forth in the *Kār-nāmag* [-*ī Ardašīr-ī Pābagān*], on which see n. 5 above); idem, *Tanbīh*, 98–100, trans. B. Carra de Vaux, *Le livre de l'avertissement et de la revision*, 141–44; and Ibn al-Athīr, *Kāmil*, I, 380–84. Among Persian sources, see al-Ṭabarī, Persian abridged trans. Bal'amī, trans. H. Zotenberg, *Chronique de Abou-Djafar-Mo'hammed-ben-Djarîr-ben-Yezid Tabari*, I, 527–28, II, 66–75.

For studies on the reign of Ardashīr in general, see e.g., Christensen, *Sassanides*, 86–96; Frye, *The Heritage of Persia*, 207–21; idem, "The Political History of Iran under the Sasanians," 118–25, 178; *EIr*, s.v. Ardašīr I. i. History (J. Wiesehöfer). Nöldeke, trans. 21 n. 4, thought that the picture of the first Sāsānid emperor as an exemplary ruler, while not without some basis, was exaggerated. Ardashīr can nevertheless be accounted a firm and successful ruler who brought unity to the Persian lands after the chaotic conditions of the late Arsacid period. It is probably true that he extirpated the Arsacid royal family within Persia (though not in Armenia, see n. 84 below), but he conciliated and took into his service many of the great Parthian military and administrative families, thus providing some element of continuity within the state.

69. The change to Ibn al-Kalbī's narrative, with material emanating from the

ward at the head of an army of the men of Fārs seeking to gain military and political ascendancy over Iraq. He encountered there Bābā, the king of the Aramaeans, and he also encountered Ardawān, the king of the Ardawānīs.[70] Hishām explains: The Aramaeans are the Nabataeans (*al-Anbāṭ*) of the Sawād, and the Ardawānīs are the Nabataeans of Syria.[71] He goes on to relate: Each one of these two groups used to fight with each other over the possession of power, but then they came together and agreed to fight Ardashīr. So the two of them fought against Ardashīr, each assisting the other (or: going forth in separate groups, alternately, *mutasānidayn*)[72] one of them would fight one day, and the other would fight on another day. When it was Bābā's day for combat, Ardashīr was unable to withstand him, but when it was Ardawān's day for combat, the latter was unable to withstand Ardashīr. So when Ardashīr realized that, he made a peace agreement with Bābā, on the basis that Bābā would let Ardashīr alone and leave the latter to fight it out with Ardawān, while Ardashīr, for his part, would leave Bābā in control of his own territories and all

---

Arab milieu of al-Ḥīrah, brings with it more poetic and anecdotal elements into the story (seen here immediately in the story of the warfare between Ardashīr and his two opponents Ardawān and Bābā) as compared with the more sober, straightforward material of the Persian national historical tradition going back to the *Xwadāy-nāmag*. See Nöldeke, trans. 22 n. 2.

70. The "Aramaeans" (*al-Aramāniyyūn*) can hardly refer to the whole nation of Aramaic-speaking peoples of the Syro-Mesopotamian region, those in Islamic times called al-Nabaṭ/al-Anbāṭ (see n. 71 below). Nöldeke, loc. cit., thought that in this context the term appears to refer to the people of Bēth Aramāyē or Lower Iraq, with the king Bābā being the unidentified Bābā, son of Bandīnā, described by al-Mas'ūdī, *Murūj*, II, 161 = § 585, as ruler of (the forerunner of) Qaṣr Ibn Hubayrah (which in early Islamic times lay between Baghdad and al-Kūfah, see *EI*², s.v. Ḳaṣr Ibn Hubayra [J. Lassner]). As for the Ardawānīs, these were not of course an ethnic or national group at all, but the partisans and troops of king Ardawān.

71. The term *Nabaṭ*, pl. *Anbāṭ*, was especially applied in early Islamic times, often with a contemptuous tinge, to the indigenous, Aramaic-speaking cultivators of the Sawād of Iraq as compared with the Bedouin Arab pastoralists. By then, little was remembered or known of the proto-Arab Nabataeans of northwestern Arabia, modern Jordan, and southern Syria, the Nabaṭ al-Shām of the Muslims. There was much confusion in the Arab historians concerning the ancient peoples who had inhabited Mesopotamia, with all of these—Sumerians, Akkadians, Assyrians, etc.—tending to be lumped together as Chaldaeans, *al-Kaldāniyyūn*. See *EI*², s.v. Nabaṭ. 2. The Nabaṭ al-'Irāḳ (T. Fahd). The false distinction between the Ardawānīs = the Nabataeans of Syria, and the Aramāniyyūn = the Nabataeans of Iraq, appears also in Ḥamzah al-Iṣfahānī, *Ta'rīkh*, 85.

72. See for this term, Lane, *Lexicon*, 1443b, 1444b, and Dozy, *Supplément*, I, 691–92.

within them. In this way, Ardashīr was free to combat Ardawān alone; he speedily killed him and conquered all his possessions and dependencies. He also compelled Bābā to give obedience [to him]. Thus Ardashīr took firm control of the realm of Iraq; its rulers became subject to him; and he finally brought into submission all the people there who had resisted him, thereby compelling them to to do what he wished and what was in accordance with his plans, however distasteful though it was to them.

## [The History of al-Ḥīrah]

[Hishām b. Muḥammad continues:] When Ardashīr conquered Iraq and seized power there, a large part of the Tanūkh (group of tribes)[73] disliked the prospect of remaining in his kingdom and becoming his subjects. Hence those of them belonging to the tribes of Quḍāʿah who had come with Mālik and ʿAmr, the two sons of Fahm, together with Mālik b. Zuhayr and others, went forth and eventually joined with those of Quḍāʿah already in Syria.[74] Now
[822] there was a group of the Arabs who were guilty of committing

73. This important tribal confederation, accounted as South Arabian in genealogy when they were in Iraq, and said to have spread out from the southern part of the Arabian peninsula toward the fringes of Iraq and Syria, was certainly an ancient one, apparently referred to by Ptolemy as the *Thanouitai.* Their history in the peninsula is very shadowy, but they are attested on the fringes of the Fertile Crescent by the third century A.D. and, as al-Ṭabarī relates, they became a significant population element in al-Ḥīrah and Mesopotamia as "Arabs of the Marches" (i.e., of the Sāsānid empire, *ʿArab al-Ḍāḥiyah*), and seem to have had some kinship connection with the ruling Lakhmids of al-Ḥīrah. It was in these places that some at least of the Tanūkh acquired Christianity, which they retained well into the Islamic period. See G. Rothstein, *Die Dynastie der Laḫmiden in al-Ḥîra,* 18–40, 134–38; I. Shahîd, *Byzantium and the Arabs in the Fourth Century,* 360–62, 366ff., 418ff.; *EI*[1], s.v. Tanūkh (H. Kindermann); *EI*[2], s.v. Tanūkh (I. Shahîd); and see the next note.

74. Quḍāʿah were an old group of tribes, whose components included Balī, Juhaynah, Kalb, Khawlān, Salīḥ, Tanūkh, ʿUdhrah, etc. The genealogists were uncertain whether they belonged to the North or South Arabs; there are indications that, in the Umayyad period, the Quḍāʿah of central Syria may have changed their affiliation, for military and political reasons, from Maʿadd, the North Arabs, to Qaḥṭān, the South Arabs (see W. Robertson Smith, *Kinship and Marriage in Early Arabia,* 246–53; M. J. Kister and M. Plessner, "Notes on Caskel's Ǧamharat an-nasab," 56–58; G. R. Hawting, *The First Dynasty of Islam, The Umayyad Caliphate A D 661–750,* 36). The Tanūkh of Quḍāʿah were certainly installed in northern Syria and northern Jazīrah during the eighth and ninth centuries, still Christian in faith and considering themselves Qaḥṭānīs. See Ibn al-Kalbī-Caskel-Strenziok, *Jamharat al-nasab,* I, tables 274, 279, II, 73–76, 470; *EI*[2], s.v. Ḳuḍāʿa (M. J.Kister).

various misdeeds among their own people,[75] or who were becoming reduced by hardship in their daily life to extremities, so that they were moving into the agricultural lands (*rīf*) of Iraq and settling at al-Ḥīrah.[76] [The population of al-Ḥīrah] thus comprised three elements. The first element was that of the Tanūkh, who dwelled in shelters and tents of hair and skins on the western banks of the Euphrates, between al-Ḥīrah and al-Anbār and beyond.[77] The second element were the ʿIbād ("devotees"), that is, those who had [originally] settled in al-Ḥīrah and built themselves permanent houses there.[78] The third element were the Aḥlāf

---

75. That is, had brought down upon their heads blood feuds. See Nöldeke, trans. 24 n. 1.

76. This was the great city, strategically situated on the borderland between the cultivated lands of the Sawād of Mesopotamia and the northeastern fringes of the Arabian Desert; its ruins (first noted by B. Meissner, *Von Babylon nach den Ruinen von Ḥîra und Ḫuarnaq*, Deutsche Orientgesellschaft Sendschriften 2, 1899, Leipzig 1901) can be seen today to the southeast of al-Najaf. It owed its rise, as the most important city of the Arabs for three centuries, to the Lakhmids and was always closely associated with that dynasty, with a peak of splendor under al-Mundhir III b. al-Nuʿmān II (r. 504–54), the appointee of Qubādh and Khusraw Anūsharwān (see al-Ṭabarī, I, 899–900, pp. 159, 161 below). The decline of the city came with the end of the Lakhmids, when in 602 Khusraw Abarwēz deposed and killed al-Nuʿmān III b. al-Mundhir IV (see text, I, 1026–28, below) and entrusted the city to Persian nominee governors, and then with the city's surrender in 12/633 to the Muslim general Khālid b. al-Walīd (see al-Ṭabarī, I, 2019). It continued to exist, however, for at least four more centuries, but was gradually eclipsed by the nearby, newly founded *miṣr* or armed camp of al-Kūfah. See Yāqūt, *Buldān*, II, 328–31; Nöldeke, trans. 25 n. 1; Rothstein, *Laḫmiden*, 12–40; Le Strange, *Lands*, 75–76; Siddiqi, *Studien über die persischen Fremdwörter*, 76–77; Eilers, "Iran and Mesopotamia," 487–88; Bosworth, "Iran and the Arabs before Islam," 597; *EI²*, s.v. al-Ḥīra (I. Shahîd).

The etymology of the name al-Ḥīrah has traditionally been connected with Syriac *ḥērtā*, "enclosure," but Shahîd has argued that an etymology from the languages of the Arabian peninsula, with the sense of "military encampment," is more likely, especially since we have in Sabaic *ḥyrt, ḥrt*= "encampment," and a verb *ḥyr*, "to encamp" (see for these, A. F. L. Beeston et al., *Sabaic Dictionary*, 74; Joan C. Biella, *Dictionary of Old South Arabic, Sabaean Dialect*, 175). Shahîd propones that we should accordingly consider Syriac *ḥērtā* as a loanword from the Arabian peninsula, not vice versa. See his *Byzantium and the Arabs in the Fourth Century*, 490–98.

77. These dwellers in shelters and (permanent?) tents must have represented a transitional way of life between those of the pure nomadic Bedouins and the house-dwelling ʿIbād. See Nöldeke, trans. 24 n. 3.

Anbār (Persian, "storehouse," "granary") was an ancient town of central Iraq, at a crossing-point of the Euphrates and further strategically important as the approach from the west to Ctesiphon-al-Madāʾin and, later, to Baghdad. Its value had led Shābūr I to rebuild it in early Sāsānid times and to rename it Fīrūz-Shāpūr. See Yāqūt, *Buldān*, I, 257–58; *PW*, I/2, s.v. Ambara (F. C. Andreas); Le Strange, *Lands*, 65–66; A. Musil, *The Middle Euphrates*, 353–57; *EI²*, s.v. al-Anbār (M. Streck and A. A. Duri); *EIr*, s.v. Anbār (M. Morony).

("confederates"), who had joined with the people of al-Ḥīrah and settled among them but who belonged neither to the tent-dwelling Tanūkh nor the ʿIbād, who had both submitted to Ardashīr.[79]

Al-Ḥīrah and al-Anbār were both built in the time of Bukht Naṣṣar (Nebuchadnezzar), but al-Ḥīrah fell into ruins when its population migrated to al-Anbār at the time of Bukht Naṣṣar's death. In this way, al-Anbār flourished for 550 years, until al-Ḥīrah revived in the time of ʿAmr b. ʿAdī, when the latter took up his residence there. Al-Ḥīrah accordingly flourished for 530-odd years, until al-Kūfah was founded and [the people of] Islam took up residence there. The complete extent of ʿAmr b. ʿAdī's tenure of power was 118 years, of which ninety-five fell within the time of Ardawān and the "Party Kings" and twenty-three years within the time of the Persian kings, comprising fourteen years and ten months of Ardashīr son of Bābak's reign and eight years and two months in his son Sābūr's reign.[80]

---

78. The Arab Christian ʿIbād, "devotees," of al-Ḥīrah represented the culturally most advanced Arabs of their time, even though their Lakhmid rulers remained generally pagan, at times fiercely so. The last Lakhmid king, al-Nuʿmān III, may have been the first Christian ruler since the time of Imruʾ al-Qays I al-Badʾ (see al-Ṭabarī, I, 834, p. 44 below). Modern archaeological investigations, from an Oxford expedition in 1931 to the work of the Japanese Archaeological Expedition to Iraq in the 1970s and 1980s, have uncovered the sites of many Christian churches both at the site of al-Ḥīrah itself and in the surrounding district; see the details given in Erica C. D. Hunter, "Syriac Inscriptions from al Hira," 66–67, and nn. 2, 4–5; and also J. S. Trimingham, *Christianity among the Arabs in Pre-Islamic Times*, 197 and n. 114. Early Arab traditions state that the Arabic alphabet, having evolved among the literate scribes of al-Ḥīrah, was carried thence to the Arabian interior and Mecca (but note the doubts of G. Endress, "Die arabische Schrift," 169). Certainly, the Lakhmid kings were great patrons of the Bedouin poets who flocked to their court, but the city itself also produced several noted poets, headed by the celebrated ʿAdī b. Zayd (see al-Ṭabarī, I, 1016–24, pp. 339–51, below, and n. 116, below). See Rothstein, *Laḫmiden*, 18–28; Bosworth, Iran and the Arabs before Islam, 597–99; and for al-Ḥīrah as a literary center, R. Blachère's section "La poésie à la cour des Laḫmides de Ḥîra," in his *Histoire de la littérature arabe*, II, 293–301.

79. These must have been Bedouins sedentarized within the city; see Rothstein, *Laḫmiden*, 18ff., and Bosworth. "Iran and the Arabs before Islam," 599. The Lakhmid kings' policy of balancing rival tribal groups within Arabia against each other, one of divide and rule, is discussed in F. McG. Donner, *The Early Islamic Conquests*, 45–48.

80. ʿAmr b. ʿAdī, the father of the Imruʾ al-Qays I al-Badʾ, "king of the Arabs," of the Namārah inscription (as this has customarily been read), lived toward the end of the third century and in the early part of the fourth century; he was regarded as the father of the dynasty, but cannot have ruled for such a span of years. See al-Ṭabarī, I, 834–35, p. 44 below; Nöldeke, trans. 25 n. 1; Rothstein, *Laḫmiden*, 50ff.

# Mention of the Holders of Power in the Kingdom of Persia after Ardashīr b. Bābak

## *[Sābūr I, called Sābūr al-Junūd]*[81]

When Ardashīr b. Bābak died, there succeeded to power in Persia[82] his son Sābūr. When Ardashīr b. Bābak had attained the royal power, he wrought great slaughter among the Arsacids (al-Ashakāniyyah),[83] to whom belonged the "Party Kings," until he had exterminated them, in accordance with an oath which Sāsān the elder, son of Ardashīr, son of Bahman, son of Isfandiyār, the ancestor of Ardashīr b. Bābak, had sworn: that, if at some point, he should attain the royal power, he would not spare a single one of the progeny of Ashak, son of Khurrah. He had further laid this charge on his descendants, and had instructed them in his testament not to leave alive a single one of the Arsacids if they should succeed to power [immediately after him] or if one of them should [eventually] attain to royal power one day. The first of his descendants and progeny to achieve this power was Ardashīr, son of [823]

81. That is, "Sābūr of the Armies."

82. Here, for the first time in the present text, *Fār(i)s* seems to mean the land of Persia in general rather than the province of Fārs, cradle of ancient Persian monarchy, in particular.

83. The Arabic name for the dynasty goes back to the eponymous founder of the line, Arshaka, Parthian *'ršk*, Greek Arsacēs, who seized power in northern Parthia ca. 247 B.C., henceforth the beginning of the Parthian era. See Nöldeke, trans. 26 n.1; Bivar, "The Political History of Iran under the Arsacids," 28, 98.

Bābak. Hence Ardashīr massacred the Arsacids en bloc, women and menfolk alike, not sparing a single one of them, in accordance with the intention of his forefather Sāsān.[84]

It is mentioned that he left no one alive except a maiden whom he had found in the royal palace. He was struck by her beauty, and asked her—she was really the slaughtered king's daughter—about her origins. She stated that she was the handmaiden of one of the king's wives. He then asked her whether she was a virgin or had previously been married. She told him that she was a virgin. So he had sexual intercourse with her and took her as one of his concubines, and in due course she became pregnant by him. Now when she became assured of her own safety in regard to him, because of her firm position in his affections through her pregnancy, she informed him that she was really from the progeny of Ashak. However, he recoiled from her, and summoned Harjand, son of Sām,[85] a man of great seniority and advanced years, and told him that she was from Ashak's progeny. Ardashīr went on to say, "It is incumbent upon us to keep faith with our forefather Sāsān's vow, even though she has become dear to my own heart, as you
[824] well know. So take her away and kill her!" The old man went off to kill her. She told him that she was pregnant. He took her along to the midwives, who confirmed that she was indeed pregnant. He consigned her to an underground cellar. Then he cut off his own

84. Whether the Arsacid royal family, the line of Ardawān, was so thoroughly exterminated is hard to determine, but the Arsacid dynasty in Armenia, which had come to power when Tiridates I was crowned king of Armenia by the Roman emperor Nero in A.D. 66, continued to rule there till the early fifth century; the Armenian Arsacids considered themselves the holders of legitimate Iranian rule and, not surprisingly, their relations with the upstart Sāsānid supplanters of their kinsmen in Persia always remained strongly hostile. See D. M. Lang, "Iran, Armenia and Georgia," 517–18. Whatever the fate of members of the Arsacid royal house in Persia, many of the great Parthian "feudal" families seem gradually to have made their peace with the Sāsānids and to have entered their service; such was certainly the case with the Kāren, Sūrēn, and Mihrān families. See Nöldeke, trans. 26 n. 1; Frye, "The Political History of Iran under the Sasanians," 119–20.

85. Perhaps one should read here *Abarsām* (on Abarsām, see n. 29 above) for the text's *H.r.j.n.d ibn Sām*, as in al-Dīnawarī, *al-Akhbār al-ṭiwāl*, 43–45, where he is described as Ardashīr's *wazīr*. This last historian in fact gives the story of Abarsām's self-mutilation and the birth of Shāpūr I, the only one of the other Arabic sources on the Sāsānids to note it. See also Nöldeke, trans. 27 n. 2.

genitalia and placed them in a box, which he sealed. He returned to the king. The king said to him, "What have you done?" He replied, "I have consigned her to the bowels of he earth," and he handed over the box to the king, asking him to seal it with his personal seal and to place it in one of his treasuries; this Ardashīr did.

The girl remained with the old man until she gave birth to a baby boy. The old man did not want to give the king's son a name inferior to his status, nor did he wish to tell him about his real rank when he was still a child, but only when he was grown up and had completed his education and acquisition of good manners (*adab*). The old man had actually determined the astral conjunctions at the moment of the boy's birth and had worked out for him his horoscope; he realized from this that the child would eventually become a ruler, hence he gave him a name which would be both a description and also a true personal name, in that he would subsequently have a choice regarding it when he knew all about it (i.e. whether it was intended for him as a descriptive or a personal name). Hence he called him Shāh Būr, which means in Arabic "king's son" (*ibn al-malik*), and he was the first person to be thus named.[86] This was Ardashīr's son, Sābūr al-Junūd. Other authorities say, on the other hand, that he called him Ashah Būr, meaning in Arabic "the son of Ashak," from whose progeny the boy's mother stemmed.

Ardashīr passed several years in a childless state. Then the faithful old man, who had the child in his care, went into the king's presence and found him deep in sorrow. He asked him, "What is making you so sad, O King?" Ardashīr replied, "Why should I not be sad? Although by means of my sword I have seized everything between the East and the West, although I have conquered everything I wanted and although I have complete control over the kingdom, the kingdom of my forefathers, yet I shall die in the end, leaving no offspring behind to succeed to my authority, and there will be no enduring trace of me within the royal power during the

86. Conveniently forgetting here Ardashīr's prematurely deceased brother Shābūr, see al-Ṭabarī, I, 816, p. 8, above, and taking no account of the fact that the future Shābūr (I) must have been born well before the defeat of Ardawān and the overthrow of the Arsacids. See Nöldeke, trans. 28 n. 1.

future." But the old man said to him, "May God grant you joy, O King, and give you long life! I have in my care a fine, noble son of yours. Call for the box which I entrusted to you, and which you personally sealed, to be brought in, and I will show you the decisive proof of that." Ardashīr sent for the box. He examined the
[825] impression of his seal, and then he broke it and opened the box. In it he found the old man's genitalia and a document on which it was written: "When we ascertained that the daughter of Ashak had indeed conceived by the King of Kings Ardashīr, at the same time when the latter ordered us to kill her, she being pregnant, we did not consider it lawful to destroy the noble seed of the king. So we consigned her to the bowels of the earth, as our monarch had commanded us, and we exonerated ourselves in his sight from any guilt (i.e., by the self-mutilation), lest any calumniator find any means to forge lies against her. We made it our concern to protect the rightfully sown seed until it should be united once again with its own kindred. This took place at so-and-so time in so-and-so year."

On hearing all this, Ardashīr ordered the old man to place the boy among a group of a hundred youths—according to others, among a thousand youths—all of exactly the same appearance and height as the boy, and then to parade them before him in a body, avoiding any distinguishing features of clothing, height, and demeanor. The old man did this. When Ardashīr looked at this group of youths, his instinct immediately recognized his own son out of all the throng, and he found him pleasing, without there having been made any indication of him or muttered hint concerning him to the king. Then he gave commands for them all to be brought into the antechamber of the royal palace (*ḥujrat al-aywān*). They were provided with polo sticks, and they set to playing with a ball, the king meanwhile being seated on his throne inside the palace proper (*al-aywān*).[87] The ball flew into the palace chamber where the king was. All the youths held back from entering the place chamber, but Sābūr pushed his way forward from their midst and went in. Ardashīr now deduced from Sābūr's entry into his pres-

87. Historical romance and legend does in fact describe Ardashīr as the first prominent enthusiast for polo, as, e.g., in the *Kārnāmag-ī Ardašīr-ī Pābagān*. See *EI*², s.v. Čawgān (H. Massé).

ence, his thrusting forward and his temerity—all this being in addition to the feeling in his heart for acceptance of Sābūr, which he had felt on the first occasion when he saw him, and his tender sentiments toward him, quite lacking in regard to all his comrades—that he was indeed his own son. Ardashīr said to him in Persian, "What is your name?" The youth answered, "Shāh Būr." Ardashīr exclaimed, "The king's son (*shāh būr*)!" When he was completely certain that the youth really was his son, he publicly acknowledged him and hailed him as heir after himself.[88]

The Persian people had already experienced, before the royal [826]
power passed to Sābūr and during his father's lifetime, Sābūr's intelligence, virtue, and knowledge, combined with ardor in battle, eloquence, and wit, tenderness toward the subjects, and mildness. When the crown was [eventually] placed on his head (i.e., after his father's death), he gathered together before him all the great men of state. They then sent up prayers for his long life and went on at length in mentioning his father and the latter's excellent characteristics. Sābūr informed them that they could not have invoked his benevolence by any means more acceptable to him than by what they had said about his father, and he gave them promises of beneficence. Then he gave orders that the riches in the treasuries were to be lavished on the people (*al-nās*, i.e., the landed and military classes who were the supports of the state), sharing them out among those whom he deemed worthy of receiving them—the prominent persons, the troops, and those [of them] who had fallen into indigence (*ahl al-ḥājah*). He wrote to his governors in the provinces and outlying districts that they were to do likewise with the wealth under their control.[89] In this way, he distributed his bounty and beneficence to those near and far, noble and humble, the aristocracy and the generality of people, so that all shared in this benevolence and their standard of daily life was thereby raised. Then he chose governors over the populace, and

88. As Nöldeke notes, trans. 30 n. 2, this tale of Ardashīr's recognition of Shābūr as his son and his appointing him his heir, is pure fantasy.

89. Nöldeke, trans. 31 n. 1, regarded it as highly unlikely that a powerful monarch like Shābūr, who intended vigorously to prosecute the wars with the Romans, would thus dissipate the wealth in his treasuries, especially as Persian rulers seem, even at the best of times, always to have been short of money for their military ventures.

kept a keen watch over them and over the subjects in general. Thus the meritoriousness of his good conduct became clear, his fame spread widely and he stood out above all other monarchs.

It is said that, in the eleventh year of his reign, he marched against the city of Niṣībīn,[90] where there was a garrison of Roman troops, and besieged them for a considerable period of time.[91] But then he received news of happenings in one of the regions of Khurāsān that required his personal attention, so he headed for there, restored order and returned to Niṣībīn. They allege that the city's wall split asunder of its own accord, and a breach was opened up for Sābūr, by means of which he was able to gain entry. He then killed the [defending] soldiers, enslaved the women and children, and seized an immense sum of wealth stored up there for Qayṣar (i.e., the Roman emperor). Then he traversed the territory to Syria and Roman Anatolia (*bilād al-Rūm*), and conquered a

90. Niṣībīn or Naṣībīn, Greek Nasibis, was one of the most important towns and fortresses of Upper Mesopotamia, situated on the Hirnas river, an affluent of the Khābūr, in the plain to the south of the mountainous region of Ṭūr ʿAbdīn. In Roman and Byzantine times it came within the district of Bēth ʿArabhāyē, and in early Islamic times, in that of Diyār Rabīʿah within the province of al-Jazīrah. Known as a settlement in Assyrian times, possession of it oscillated between the Parthians and the Romans, until in A.D. 195 Septimius Severus came to Niṣībīn and made it the capital of the new province of *Septimia Nesibi Colonia.* Control of the region was disputed by the Romans and Persians more or less continuously in the third and fourth centuries, with this campaign of Shābūr I's falling in the 250s (see n. 91 below); but after the peace agreement of 363 between Jovian and Shābūr II, Niṣībīn and Sinjār or Singara passed under Persian control more or less permanently. This period of Persian domination enabled Niṣībīn to become an especially flourishing center of the (to the Byzantines, heretical) Nestorian Church; under this last, it functioned as the metropolitan seat for the region of Bēth ʿArabhāyē. See Yāqūt, *Buldān,* V, 288–89; *PW,* XVII/1, s.v. Nisibis (J. Sturm); Le Strange, *Lands,* 94–95; Labourt, *Le Christianisme dans l'empire perse,* 83; Christensen, *Sassanides,* 218–24; Canard, *Histoire de la dynastie des H'amdanides,* 100–101; Frye, "The Political History of Iran under the Sasanians," 125, 137–38; *EI*², s.v. Naṣībīn (E. Honigmann-C. E. Bosworth).

91. No clear picture emerges from the scattered details in the sources about Shābūr's wars against Rome, with a resultant uncertainty about chronology. The eleventh year of Shābūr's reign would be 251, and it is possible that Niṣībīn was attacked (and for at least the second time) in 251 or 252; but Shābūr's expeditions into Asia Minor and Syria must have extended beyond that date, and the emperor Valerian did not in any case begin his reign until 253. See Nöldeke, trans. 31 n. 3; E. Stein, *Histoire du Bas-Empire. I. De l'état romain à l'état byzantin (284–476),* 6; and the discussion of the dating of the Persian capture of Niṣībīn at this time in E. Kettenhofen, *Die römisch-persischen Kriege des 3. Jahrhunderts nach Chr. nach der Inschrift Šāpuhrs I. an der Kaʿbe-ye Zartošt (ŠKZ),* 44–46.

large number of the cities there. Among these, he is said to have conquered Qālūqiyyah (Cilicia) and Qadhūqiyyah (Cappadocia) and to have besieged one of the [Roman] kings who happened to be in Anatolia called al-Riyānūs (Valerian[us])[92] in the city of Antioch. He took him prisoner, and transported him, and a large num- [827]
ber of the troops who were with him, and settled them at Junday Sābūr (Jundīshāpūr).[93] It is mentioned that he compelled al-

---

92. That is, the emperor Valerian, Publius Licinius Valerianus (r. 253–60). See on him *Der kleine Pauly*, V, s.v. Valerianus (G. Winckler). W. B. Henning observed that it was strange that the tradition that came down to al-Ṭabarī from the *Xwadāy-nāmag*, with the name as al-Riyānūs, rendered the Roman emperor's name more correctly than did Shābūr's victory inscription (see next note), with its *wry'rnswy*. See his "The Great Inscription of Shāpūr I," 834.

93. According to the trilingual (in Parthian, Middle Persian, and Greek) inscription erected by Shābūr on the Ka'bah-yi Zardusht at Naqsh-i Rustam in 260 or shortly afterward, the Persian emperor captured Valerian with his own hands. The question of the exact dating of the capture of the Roman emperor—for which August or September 260 would seem to be *termini post quem*—is discussed by Kettenhofen, *Die römisch-persischen Kriege des 3. Jahrhunderts nach Chr.*, 97–99.

The discovery of the Ka'ba-yi Zardusht trilinguis (ŠKZ) by the Chicago University Persepolis Expedition of 1936–39 marked a great step forward in our knowledge of the campaigns of Shābūr against the Romans and of the history of the early Sāsānid rulers in general. Wiesehöfer has emphasized that inscriptions like this one at Naqsh-i Rustam, the inscription of Narseh at Paikuli (see n. 141 below) and that of the High Priest Kerdēr at Naqsh-i Rajab, are important inter alia for their information on the early Sāsānid court and its officials, and on the contemporary conception of royal power and its relationship to the divinity Ahura Mazdā, and, in part, as *res gestae*, the exploits of the Sāsānids, thus supplying a corrective to non-Persian sources such as the Byzantine ones; see his *Ancient Persia*, pp. 154–55.

The information of the three texts making up the complete Ka'ba-yi Zardusht inscription, as edited by Martin Sprengling (the two Middle Iranian texts) and André Maricq (the Greek text) has been compared and integrated with the information of the Greek and Latin historical texts, of coin legends, etc., by Kettenhofen in his monograph mentioned in the previous paragraph, meant to accompany his TAVO map (BV 11) *Vorderer Orient. Römer und Sāsāniden in der Zeit der Reichskrise (224–284 n. Chr.)* and its *Sonderkarte, Die Kriege Šāpuhrs I. mit Rom nach ŠKZ;* the monograph itself includes three maps illustrating Roman and Sāsānid campaigns in Asia Minor, Syria, and Mesopotamia. A new *Gesamtedition* of the three ŠKZ texts is being prepared by Dr. Philip Huyse and will appear as part of the *Corpus Inscriptionum Iranicarum* under the title *Die dreisprachige Inschrift Šābuhr's I. an der Ka'ba-i Zardušt (ŠKZ).*

Shābūr's victories over the Romans were also immortalised for him in such rock reliefs as at Naqsh-i Rustam and in those of the Bīshāpūr gorge. See Henning, "The Great Inscription of Shāpūr I," 833–35; Christensen, *Sassanides*, 221–24; Herrmann, *The Iranian Revival*, 92–94, 96–98; Gignoux, "Middle Persian Inscrip-

Riyānūs to set to work building a dam (*shādurwān*) at Tustar, whose breadth was to be one thousand cubits.[94] The Roman [emperor] constructed this with the aid of a group of men whom he had caused to be brought from Anatolia, and he held Sābūr to a promise to free him once the dam was completed. It is said that

---

tions," 1207–1209.

The Sāsānid foundation, or rather re-foundation, in al-Ahwāz or Khūzistān of Gondēshabūr is given by al-Ṭabarī, I, 830–31, pp. 38–39 below, the original name in New Persian of Bih-az-Andiyū Sābūr "Better than Antioch (has) Sābūr (built this)," repeated thus in Ḥamzah al-Iṣfahānī, 45 (the MP equivalent would be *Weh az Andiyōg Shāhbuhr [kird]). Nöldeke, trans. 42 n. 2, was skeptical, and thought that Wandēw-Sābūr "Acquired by Shābūr" was the true form, eventually yielding Gondēshābūr and the Arabised form Jundaysābūr; but Mr F. C. de Blois tells me that he is in turn skeptical of Nöldeke's theory, since "Acquired by Sābūr" would be *Windād Shāhbuhr. D. T. Potts has recently discussed the etymology of the place's name in the light of two Greek inscriptions found at Susa which mention a local river Gondeisos, and has suggested that the name of this river derives from a military center and fortress there of the Parthian period, *Gond-dēz, subsequently called *Gond-dēz-i Shābūr when the Sāsānid ruler restored and refounded it. The alternative name *Weh az Andiyōg Shāhbuhr would have been applied to it when the people from Antioch were planted there. See his "Gundešapur and the *Gondeisos*," 323–35. Al-Dīnawarī, *al-Akhbār al-ṭiwāl*, 46, has the cryptic information that, in *al-khūziyyah* (i.e., the local language of Khūzistān), the town was called N.y.lāṭ, now rendered by the people there as N.y.lāb. Under the Sāsānids, Gondēshabūr flourished as the main urban center of Khūzistān. In early Islamic times it was famed as a center of medical knowledge and practice, skills that must have been brought thither in Sāsānid times by Nestorian Christians. See Nöldeke, trans. 41 n. 2; Yāqūt, *Buldān*, II, 170–71; Le Strange, *Lands*, 238; Schwarz, *Iran im Mittelalter*, 346–50; Barthold, *Historical Geography*, 187–88; Frye, "The Political History of Iran under the Sasanians," 126; *EI*[2] s.v. Gondēshāpūr (Cl. Huart and Aydin Sayılı). On the improbability of Indian influence there, cf. n. 180 below.

Al-Ṭabarī does not actually mention the building of what was Shābūr's most favored urban foundation, that of Bīshāpūr to the west of Iṣṭakhr, probably completed by him ca. 266. As at Gondēshabūr and at Shushtar (see on this last n. 94 below), Roman prisoners of war are said to have been settled there. Many buildings of the Sāsānid and Islamic period remain on the site, although by the tenth century the town was in ruins, eclipsed by the rising town of Kāzarūn. Also notable are the nearby reliefs carved at Shābūr's behest on the bank of the Tang-i Chawgān river. See Herrmann, *The Iranian Revival*, 101–104; *EIr*, s.v. Bīšāpūr (E. J. Keall).

94. This dam, popularly known as the Band-i Qayṣar "Emperor's dam" from the alleged, but probably legendary, role of the captured Roman ruler in building it (although Roman prisoners of war were very probably involved in this work, as also at the monuments of Bīshābūr; cf. Christensen, *Sassanides*, 220–21, and Nina Garsoïan, "Byzantium and the Sasanians," 581), came to be regarded as one of the wonders of the world by the mediaeval Muslims. It was in reality only one of many *shādurwān*s on the Dujayl or Kārūn, barriers that divided up the river's waters into irrigation channels running off from the main flow and that at the same time relieved the pressure of waters in winter and spring from the snows that fell in the

Sābūr took from al-Riyānūs a great financial indemnity, and set him free after cutting off his nose; others, however, say that Sābūr killed him.[95]

Now there was, facing Takrīt[96] and between the Tigris and Euphrates, a city called al-Ḥaḍr (Hatra),[97] and there was there a man

---

Zagros Mountains, where the Kārūn and its affluents rise.

Tustar (Persian, Shus(h)tar) was in early Islamic times the next most important town of Khūzistān after the provincial capital al-Ahwāz, and was situated on the Kārūn; but its pre-Islamic history goes back at least to the time of Pliny (first century A.D.), who mentions it. See Yāqūt, *Buldān*, II, 29–31; Le Strange, *Lands*; Markwart-Messina, *Catalogue of the Provincial Capitals*, 97; *EI*², s.v. Shushtar (J. H. Kramers-C. E. Bosworth).

The term *shādurwān* has many meanings in early Islamic usage, often in connection with irrigation devices, but the basic meaning seems to be that of a raised platform or dais, this being then extended to masonry walls and revetments for storing and controling waters and their flow. E. Benveniste thought that this obviously Iranian word was probably Parthian in origin. See his "Le sens du mot persan shâdurvân," 31–37; Bosworth, "Some Remarks on the Terminology of Irrigation Practices and Hydraulic Constructions in the Eastern Arab and Iranian Worlds in the Third–Fifth Centuries A.H.," 83–84.

95. Nothing definite is known of Valerian's death. The Byzantine historian Agathias (who derived much of his information on the Sāsānids from the interpreter Sergius, who had been given access to the Persian royal annals while in the Persian capital on diplomatic work) says that Shābūr, a notoriously bloodthirsty monarch, had Valerian flayed alive, but this is unconfirmed elsewhere. See Averil Cameron, "Agathias on the Sassanians," 120–21, 138.

96. Reading *bi-ḥiyāl* as in Nöldeke's text, whereas he had in his translation, 33, followed a defective reading, *bi-jibāl*. There are, of course, no hills, let alone mountains, near Takrīt, lying as this town does on the Tigris; see *EI*², s.v.Takrīt (J. H. Kramers and C. E. Bosworth).

97. The city of Hatra, Greek Atrai, lay to the southwest of Mawṣil on the Nahr Tharthar, an affluent of the Tigris, but even by early Islamic times the exact site was not known to the Arabs. In the Parthian period, Hatra was the center of one of a chain of Arab principalities along the fringes of the Syrian Desert through Commagene and Edessa to Emesa and Palmyra, but was clearly under considerable Iranian political and cultural influence. Various of its princes bore Iranian names, such as the typically Parthian one of Sanatrūk (which may be behind the Arabic name of the ruler given here, al-Sāṭirūn; for suggestions on the etymology of the name Sanatrūk itself, see Eilers, "Iran and Mesopotamia," 491 n. 3) and that of Vologases, and Hatra was usually an ally of the Arsacids against Roman pressure. With the fall of its Parthian protectors, Hatra declined in power. It passed temporarily under Roman control, bringing down on it the wrath of Shāpūr I in the middle years of the third century, as related here (other, less likely, dates for this are given in Arabic sources other than al-Ṭabarī).

Hatra became famed in early Islamic lore as a symbol of the transience of earthly power, since it seemed by then to have disappeared from the face of the earth, and the story of the city's betrayal by al-Ḍayzan's daughter al-Naḍīrah struck the popular imagination. It must have entered into Arabic literature either through Ibn

from the Jarāmiqah[98] called al-Sāṭirūn. He is the person about whom Abu Du'ād al-Iyādī speaks:[99]

I see how death has come down from al-Ḥaḍr upon the leader of its people, al-Sāṭirūn.

The Arabs, however, called him al-Ḍayzan.[100] It is said that he was a man from the people of Bā Jarmā, but according to Hishām b. [Muḥammad] al-Kalbī, he was an Arab from Quḍā'ah, his genealogy being al-Ḍayzan b. Mu'āwiyah b. al-'Abīd b. al-Ajrām b. 'Amr b. al-Nakha' b. Salīḥ b. Ḥulwān b. 'Imrān b. al-Ḥāfi b. Quḍā'ah, that his mother Jayhalah was from the tribe of Tazīd b. Ḥulwān

al-Muqaffa''s Arabic version of the *Khwadāy-nāmag* or through the traditions transmitted by Ibn al-Kalbī, and here utilized by al-Ṭabarī, based inter alia on references in the verses of the poets of al-Ḥīrah, Abū Du'ād al-Iyādī, and 'Adī b. Zayd. As Yarshater has noted, "Iranian National History," 400–401, intriguing anecdotes and touches like this may have evolved to provide an element of entertainment within the narratives of dynastic and political history. See Nöldeke, trans. 33 n. 4; *PW*, VII/2, s.v. Hatra (M. Streck); Christensen, *Sassanides*, 218–19; F. Altheim and R. Stiehl, *Die Araber in der alten Welt*, II, 191ff., IV, 263ff.; Eilers, "Iran and Mesopotamia," 490–91; Bosworth, "Iran and the Arabs before Islam," 594–96; *EI*², s.v. al-Ḥaḍr (Ch. Pellat).

98. That is, from the inhabitants of Bā Jarmā, Syriac Bē(th) Garmē, the region to the east of the middle Tigris and of Takrīt, lying south of the Lesser Zāb and the region of Adiabene; it extended to Shahrazūr and the fringes of the Zagros range. As an important Christian region in Sāsānid times, it was the seat of a metropolitan bishopric. Arabic Jarāmiqah, sing. Jarmaqī, derives from Syriac Garmaqāyē. See Nöldeke, trans. 35 n. 1; Marquart, *Ērānšahr*, 21–22; Fiey, *Assyrie chrétienne*, III, 11–145; Morony, *Iraq after the Muslim Conquest*, 335–36.

99. Pre-Islamic poet of al-Ḥīrah, *floruit* in the middle years of the sixth century under the Lakhmid al-Mundhir III; he was classed among the *muqillūn*, those poets who only composed a small amount of verse. This verse is given in G. E. von Grunebaum, "Abū Du'ād al-Iyādī. Collection of Fragments," as one of a fragment of thirteen verses. See on the poet, Abū al-Faraj al-Iṣfahānī, *Kitāb al-Aghānī*³, XVI, 373–81; Rothstein, *Laḫmiden*, 28, 133; Blachère, *Histoire de la littérature arabe*, II, 294–95; *EI*², s.v. Abū Du'ād al-Iyādī (Ch. Pellat).

100. Nöldeke, trans. 35 n. 1, nevertheless thought that al-Sāṭirūn and Ḍayzan were two separate persons: the first name a non-Arabic one (see n. 97 above), and the second one Arabic, and averred that the only sure name of a king of Hatra that we know is the Barsēmias/Barsēmios, a clearly Aramiac name, in Herodian, which he interpreted as Barsamyā but which von Gutschmid, "Bemerkungen zu Tabari's Sasanidengeschichte," 735, preferred to read as Barsēnios = Barsīn. Nöldeke surmised that the Ḍayzan mentioned here might possibly have been the founder of the Ḍayzanābādh/Ṭayzanābādh of al-Balādhurī, *Futūḥ*, 284, and likewise connected with the Marj al-Ḍayāzin on the middle Euphrates near al-Raqqah of Yāqūt, *Buldān*, V, 101.

and that he was exclusively known by his mother's name.[101] Ibn al-Kalbī goes on to assert that he was the ruler over the land of al-Jazīrah and that he had with him [as his supporters] innumerable numbers of the Banū 'Abīd b. al-Ajrām and [other] tribes of Quḍā'ah. [It is said that] his kingdom stretched as far as Syria.

When Sābūr, son of Ardashīr, was away in the region of Khurāsān, al-Ḍayzan made an incursion into the Sawād. When [828] Sābūr got back from his period of absence, he was told what al-Ḍayzan had been up to. 'Amr b. Ilah (?) b. al-Judayy b. al-Dahā' b. Jusham b. Ḥulwān b. 'Imrān b. al-Ḥāfi b. Quḍā'ah composed these verses in connection with al-Ḍayzan's actions:[102]

We encountered them [in battle] with a host of the [Banū] 'Ilāf
and with [a troop of] strong-hoofed stallions.
The Persians received at our hands exemplary punishment, and
we massacred the Hērbadhs of Shahrazūr.[103]
We advanced toward the Persians (*al-A'ājim*) from afar with a
host from al-Jazīrah as in a blaze of fire.[104]

When Sābūr was informed about what al-Ḍayzan had done, he headed towards him until he halted before al-Ḍayzan's fortress, while al-Ḍayzan entrenched himself within it. Ibn al-Kalbī asserts that Sābūr was involved in the siege of the fortress for four years, completely unable to destroy it or to get his hands on al-Ḍayzan.

---

101. That is, as Ibn Jayhalah; cf. al-Balādhurī, *Futūḥ*, 284.

102. Nöldeke, trans. 39 n. 1, was skeptical about the contemporaneity of this poet with the events alluded to and thought that the (later) author must have had al-A'shā's verses in mind. In Abū al-Faraj al-Iṣfahānī, *Aghānī*[3], II, 142–43, giving the story of Sābūr's destruction of al-Ḥaḍr, the poet's name appears as 'Amr b. Alah.

103. The place-name Shahrazūr in western Kurdistān, though admittedly a place with a pre-Islamic history (see *EI*[2], s.v. Shahrazūr (V. Minorsky-C. E. Bosworth), gives little sense in this context. Nöldeke, trans. 36 n. 3, endeavoring to improve the reading of these verses from parallel sources, opined that the reading *Bahrasīr* = Bih Ardashīr (cf. al-Ṭabarī, I, 820, p. 16 above) of Abū al-Faraj al-Iṣfahānī, *Aghānī*[1], II, 37 (wrongly corrected to *Shahrazūr* in *Aghānī*[3] ?) was certainly the right one. It undoubtedly makes more sense that Zoroastrian priests, hērbeds, should be encountered in the central Mesopotamian plain than in the mountains of Kurdistān.

104. Following Nöldeke's suggestion, loc. cit., that one should follow the reading of Abū al-Faraj al-Iṣfahānī, *Aghānī*[1], *mil-jazīrati*, for the text's *ka-al-jazīrati*.

However, al-Aʿshā Maymūn b. Qays[105] has mentioned in his poem that Sābūr was engaged in the siege of the fortress for only two years, saying:

Have you not seen al-Ḥaḍr, whose people always enjoyed ease of life? But does anyone favored with ease of life enjoy it for ever?
Shāhabūr of the Hosts (al-Junūd) remained before it for two years, wielding his battle axes there.
But his (i.e., the ruler of al-Ḥīrah's) Lord vouchsafed him no access of strength, and pivots such as his could not remain firm (i.e., the ease of life he had enjoyed could not endure forever).
When his Lord saw what he was doing, He swept down on him
[829] with a violent blow, without him being able to retaliate.
He had called upon his partisans, "Come forward to your affair, which has been already severed,
And die noble deaths through your own swords; I see that the real warrior takes on for himself the burden of death with equanimity."[106]

One of al-Ḍayzan's daughters, called al-Naḍīrah,[107] was menstruous, hence was segregated in the outer suburb of the city, as was the custom of the time with women during their menstrual periods. According to what was generally acknowledged, she was one of the most beautiful women of her time, just as Sābūr was one of the most handsome men of his age. The two of them saw each other, and fell madly in love with each other. She sent a

105. Here giving the full name of the poet (on whom see n. 106, below) in order to distinguish him from several Arabic poets with the cognomen *al-Aʿshā* "the night-blind one."

106. R. Geyer, *Gedichte von Abú Baṣír Maimún ibn Qais al-'Aʿshà*, Arabic text 33–34, poem no. 4, vv. 60–65. For this *mukhaḍram* poet (d. after 3/625) who frequented the Lakhmid court at al-Ḥīrah in the early part of his life, see Rothstein, *Laḫmiden*, 21; Siddiqi, *Studien über die persische Fremdwörter*, 77; Blachère, *Histoire de la littérature arabe*, II, 321–25; *EI²*, s.v. al-Aʿshā, Maymūn b. Ḳays (W. Caskel). Nöldeke, trans. 37 n. 4, pointed out that there is no mention—at least, in this fragment of what was probably a longer poem—of Ḍayzan and his daughter al-Naḍīrah's treachery; the verses merely stress the well-worn theme of the fragility and perishability of human endeavor.

107. In al-Dīnawarī, *al-Akhbār al-ṭiwāl*, 48, she is called Mulaykah.

message to him with the words, "What would you give me if I were to indicate to you how you could bring about the destruction of the wall of this city and how you could kill my father?" He replied, "Whatever you might choose; and I would elevate you above all my other wives and would make you my closest spouse to their exclusion." She instructed him, "Take a silver-colored collar dove, and write on its leg with the menstrual blood of a blue-eyed virgin girl. Then release it, and it will alight on the city wall, and the latter will crumble away."[108] That was in fact the talisman of the city, and only this could destroy the city. So Sābūr did that and got ready to attack them (sc., the city's defenders). The king of al-Ḥaḍr's daughter went on to say, "I will give the guards wine, and when they are laid out on the ground [by its stupefying effects], kill them and enter the city."[109] He did all this; the city's defenses collapsed totally, and he took it by storm and killed al-Ḍayzan on that very day. The splinter groups from Quḍā'ah, who were with al-Ḍayzan, were annihilated, so that no part of them known as such remains to this present day. Some clans of the Banū Ḥulwān[110] were likewise completely destroyed. 'Amr b. Ilah, who was with al-Ḍayzan, has said:

Have you not been filled with grief as the reports come in about
  what has happened to the leading men of the Banū 'Abīd,
And of the slaying of [al-] Ḍayzan and his brothers, and of the

108. In many premodern societies, menstrual blood has been regarded as possessing special power, in certain cases for healing but more often for wreaking violent and harmful effects; whence the taboos that usually surround menstruous women and the menstrual flow and which often cause them to be separated from the rest of the community at times of menstruation (as was the case here with al-Naḍīrah, see above). Pliny the Elder wrote in his *Natural History,* Book XXVIII. XXIII. 77, "Over and above all this there is no limit to women's power . . . Wild indeed are the stories told of mysterious and awful power of the menstruous discharge itself . . ." (tr. Rackham, VII, 55).

Here, the violent effect, the shock to the order of nature that spontaneously brings about the destruction of the walls of Hatra, arises from the passage of unclean menstrual blood from the pure virgin to the pure dove and its consequent supernatural effect.

109. Nöldeke, trans. 38 n. 4, notes that this additional explanation for the fall of the city is superfluous, given the magical effect of the dove smeared with menstrual blood, and must be an attempt at a rationalizing explanation of events.

110. Ḥulwān was the great-grandson of Quḍā'ah; see Ibn al-Kalbī-Caskel-Strenziok, *Jamharat al-nasab,* I, Table 279, II, 331.

men of Tazīd, who were wont to ride forth in the cavalry squadrons?
Sābūr of the Hosts attacked them with war elephants, richly caparisoned, and with his heroic warriors,
And he destroyed the stone blocks of the fortress's columns, whose foundation stones were like iron blocks.[111]

Sābūr then reduced the city to ruins and carried off al-Ḍayzan's daughter al-Naḍīrah, marrying her at ʿAyn al-Tamr.[112] It is mentioned that she complained volubly the whole night through about the hardness of her bed, even though this was of finely woven silk cloth stuffed with raw silk. A search was made for what was distressing her, and behold, it turned out to be a myrtle
[830] leaf stuck in one of the folds of the skin of her abdomen which was irritating her.[113] [Ibn al-Kalbī] goes on to relate: Because her skin was so fine, one could see right to her marrow. Sābūr thereupon said to her, "Tell me then, what did your father give you to eat?" She replied, "Cream, marrow from bones and honey from virgin bees, together with the choicest wine!" He exclaimed, "By your father! I have known you more recently than your father, and am dearer to you than him, who gave you such food as you mention!" (i.e., you should not therefore start complaining). So he commanded a man to mount a wild, unbroken horse; he tied her locks of hair to its tail, and then made the horse gallop off[114] until it tore her into pieces.

---

111. These verses are also given in Abū al-Faraj al-Iṣfahānī, *Aghānī*[3], II, 142–43; al-Masʿūdī, *Murūj*, IV, 85 = § 1411 (three verses); Yāqūt, *Buldān*, II, 268–69. Nöldeke, trans. 39 n. 1, doubted very much the authenticity of Arabic poetry from so early a period.

112. This was a *ṭassūj* or administrative subdistrict to the west of the Euphrates and south of Hīt on the Syrian Desert fringes; the settlement of ʿAyn al-Tamr "the spring of the date palm" still had a small fortress in al-Maqdisī's time (fourth/tenth century), but the site has now disappeared. See Yāqūt, *Buldān*, IV, 176–77; Le Strange, *Lands*, 65, 81; Musil, *The Middle Euphrates*, 41–42, 285, 289–90, 295–311. For the term *ṭassūj*, see *EI*[2], s.v. Ṭassūdj (M. J. Morony), and the remarks on Sāsānid administrative geography in n. 117 below.

113. This folkloric motif turns up in Hans Christian Andersen's story of "The Princess and the Pea." Cf. Christensen, "La princess sur la feuille de myrte et la princesse sur la poie," 241–57.

114. For this verb *istarkaḍa*, see *Glossarium*, p. CCLXIX. Nöldeke, trans. 39 n. 4, compared al-Naḍīrah's fate with the (apparently authentic) account of the death of the Merovingian queen Brunhilda, dragged to her death at a horse's tail in 613, as narrated by the chronicler Fredegar.

A poet has said in connection with this:

The fortress has become desolate on account of [al-] Naḍīrah,
likewise al-Mirbāʿ because of her and the banks of the Tharthār.[115]

The poets have written extensively about this [al-] Ḍayzan in their verse. ʿAdī b. Zayd alludes to him in his words:[116]

And [where is now] the ruler (*akhū*) of al-Ḥaḍr, who once built it and for whom the taxation of the Tigris and the Khābūr was collected?
He raised it up firmly with marble and covered it over with plaster, yet the birds have found nesting places in its pinnacles.
The blows of ill fortune did not frighten him, yet kingly power ebbed away from him and his portals are now forsaken.

It is also said that Sābūr built in Maysān [the town of] Shādh Sābūr, which is called in Aramaic (*al-nabaṭiyyah*) Dīmā.[117]

---

115. This verse is in fact by ʿAdī b. Zayd (see n. 116 below) and is included in the collected *Dīwān ʿAdī b. Zayd al-ʿIbādī*, ed. al-Muʿaybidī, 135, fragment no. 67. The Tharthār river flowed past al-Ḥaḍr, and al-Mirbāʿ ("place with vegetation from spring rains") must have been a local site.

116. ʿAdī b. Zayd, of Tamīmī origin, flourished in the second half of the sixth century as the most notable exponent of the Ḥīran school of poets, in whom the indigenous Arabic, the Christian culture of the ʿIbād and, probably, Persian culture, all combined. Hence ʿAdī's poetry mingles Christian and Biblical themes with the ascetic and fatalist strains of desert life. His administrative career was spent in the Persian capital Ctesiphon as a translator and advisor on Arab affairs for Khusraw Abarwēz and, after 580, at al-Ḥīrah with al-Nuʿmān III, till the jealousies and intrigues of his enemies brought about his death ca. 600, as detailed by al-Ṭabarī, I, 1016–24, pp. 339–51 below. His complete *Dīwān* has not survived and only scattered verses are known. See Rothstein, *Laẖmiden*, 109–11; Siddiqi, *Studien über die persische Fremdwörter*, 76–77; Blachère, *Histoire de la littérature arabe*, II, 300–301; *EI²*, s.v. ʿAdī b. Zayd (F. Gabrieli).

These famous verses by ʿAdī on the lost glories of al-Ḥaḍr are from the long poem in the *Dīwān*, ed. al-Muʿaybidī, 88, fragment no. 16.

117. Shādh Sābūr was both a town and a *kūrah* or administrative district in Maysān, the later Islamic administrative division of Arḍ Kaskar; see Morony, *Iraq after the Muslim Conquest*, 155. Marquart suggested that the place's full name might have been Ērān-shād Shābuhr "the joy of the Iranians [is] Shābūr"; see Markwart-Messina, *Catalogue of the Provincial Capitals*, 102. The local *nabaṭī* name of Dīmā (in the Cairo text, the equally incomprehensible Rīmā) remains obscure.

In the time of Sābūr, there arose Mānī the Zindīq.[118]

It is said that, when Sābūr proceeded to the site of Junday Sābūr in order to lay down the city's foundations, he came across an aged man there called Bīl. So he asked him, "Is it permissible for a city to be constructed on this spot?" Bīl replied, "If I am vouchsafed the ability to write, despite my having reached an advanced age, then it is allowable for you to build a city in this place." Sābūr said
[831] to him, "Now indeed, the two things whose possibility you deny shall come to pass," and he thereupon sketched out the plan of the city and handed Bīl over to an instructor, with instructions to teach him to write and to be able to do arithmetical calculations within one year. The instructor shut himself up with Bīl, and began by shaving off Bīl's hair and his beard, lest these two things distract him, and then taught him thoroughly. After this, he brought Bīl to the king, Bīl having bcome effective and skillful in his studies. So Sābūr entrusted to him the job of calculating expenditure on the city and of setting up a proper accounting procedure for these payments. The king established the region (i.e., of the city and its surrounding rural areas) as a separate administrative division (*kūrah*)[119] and called it Bih-az-Andīw-i Sābūr, which

118. On the rise of Mani, son of Pātik, and his movement at this time, see G. Widengren, "Manichaeism and Its Iranian Background," 965–90. The founder of the new faith actually stemmed, according to the much later Islamic historian al-Bīrūnī, from Kūthā to the south of Ctesiphon, on the canal connecting the Tigris and the Euphrates. In later Arabic lore, he appears as Mānī b. Fātik or Fāttik; see *EI*², s.v. Mānī b. Fāttik (C. E. Bosworth).

The term *zindīq* came to be applied in Sāsānid times not only to the Manichaeans but also, subsequently, to the Mazdakites, while in early Islamic times its use was generalized to cover adherents of many heretical movements, especially within ʿAbbāsid Iraq, and as a general term of abuse for any religious deviants. See G. Vajda, "Les zindîqs en pays d'Islam au début de la periode abbaside," 173–229; F. Gabrieli, "La «zandaqa» au Ier siècle abbaside," 23–38; *EI*¹, s.v. Zindīḳ (L. Massignon). Some older authorities sought an etymology for *zindīq* in Aramaic *zaddīqā* "righteous (one)" or even Greek, but more recently the view has been put forward that it is an indigenous Iranian term, from MP *zandīk*, a person who has a deviant interpretation (*zand*) of the sacred text of the Avesta; hence early Armenian writers contrast the *zandīk*s with the orthodox Zoroastrian Magians. The question remains open. See Sir Harold Bailey's *Note* appended to Widengren's chapter, in *CHI*, III/2, 907; *EI*², s.v. Zindīḳ (F. C. de Blois), opting for an Aramaic origin.

119. For this term, probably stemming from Greek *chōra*, see *EI*², s.v. Kūra (D. Sourdel). It denoted something like an administrative division within a province (Fārs, for instance, having within it five *kūrah*s in Sāsānid and early Islamic times), the equivalent, according to Yāqūt, quoting Ḥamzah al-Iṣfahānī, of the Persian

means "the city of Sābūr's which is better than Antioch."[120] This is the city that is [now] called Junday Sābūr, which the people of al-Ahwāz, however, call Bīl, from the name of the man who was overseer of the city's construction.[121]

When Sābūr was near to death, he appointed as ruler his son Hurmuz and laid upon him testamentary instructions, ordering him to base his conduct upon them. There are differing views on the length of Sābūr's reign. Some authorities put it at thirty years and fifteen days, others at thirty-one years, six months, and nineteen days.[122]

---

*istān/ustān*, and was itself divided up into component *ṭassūj*s and *rustāq*s. F. Løkkegaard, *Islamic Taxation in the Classic Period, with Special Reference to Circumstances in Iraq*, 164–67, assumed a descending order of *istān/kūrah—ṭassūj—rustāq—dih/qaryah* for the hierarchy of administrative subdivisions in Sāsānid Mesopotamia and Persia and these same lands during early Islamic times, but the texts are, however, inconsistent and at times contradictory. The *Sīrat Anūsharwān* (see on this n. 624 below) posits, in the context of Khusraw Anūsharwān's administrative and fiscal reforms (see al-Ṭabarī, I, 960–63, pp. 255–62 below) a hierarchy of province or region (*balad*), administrative division (*kūrah*), rural district (*rustāq*), village (*qaryah*), down to individual taxpayer, and this corresponds largely to how al-Ṭabarī, I, 814, pp. 3–5 above, describes Ardashīr I's origins. See Nöldeke, trans. 446–47 Excursus 3; Wadie Juwaideh, *The Introductory Chapters of Yāqūt's Mu'jam al-Buldān*, 56, 57–58; Valeria F. Piacentini, "*Madīna/shahr, qarya/dih, nāḥiya/rustāq*. The city as political-administrative institution: the continuity of a Sasanian model," 96–99; and above all, the detailed discussion of G. Widengren, "Recherches sur le feudalisme iranien," 122–48.

120. See nn. 58, 93 above.

121. This tale of Bīl's educational achievement revolves round learning the notoriously difficult and ambiguous Pahlavi script.

122. Shābūr I's reign was 240–70, since he was crowned as coruler with his father Ardashīr I in 240, probably in April of that year, almost two years before the latter's death; see the discussion on the regnal dates of Shābūr by Kettenhofen in his *Die römisch-persischen Kriege des 3. Jahrhunderts nach Chr.*, 46–49. Shābūr's name appears on his coins as ŠHPWHRY = Shābuhr. See on his coins Paruck, *Sāsānian Coins*, 52–53, 316–22, 416–19, Plates IV-V, Table II; Göbl, *Sasanian Numismatics*, 43, Table II, Plate 2; Sellwood, Whitting, and Williams, *An Introduction to Sasanian Coins*, 21, 79–83; Malek, "A Survey of Research on Sasanian Numismatics," 233.

The other Arabic sources on his reign include Ibn Qutaybah, *Ma'ārif*, 654 (brief entry); al-Ya'qūbī, *Ta'rīkh*, I, 180–81 (brief note of Sābūr's Roman campaign, but mainly concerned with the appearance of Mani, the polemical works he composed, and Sābūr's own attraction to Manichaeism before he was brought back to *al-majūsiyyah* by the Chief Mōbadh); al-Dīnawarī, *al-Akhbār al-ṭiwāl*, 46 (only a short notice, on Sābūr's Roman campaign and capture of the Roman emperor, and his construction works in Khūzistān and at Jundaysābūr); al-Mas'ūdī, *Murūj*, II, 163–66 = §§589–93 (Mani's rise to prominence and Sābūr's part in it, together with

## [Hurmuz I]

Then after Sābūr (I), son of Ardashīr (I), son of Bābak, the royal power was assumed by his son Hurmuz (I).[123]

He was called "the Bold" (*al-jārī'*),[124] and resembled Ardashīr in bodily constitution and appearance, but did not come up to him in judgment and skillful management.[125] Nevertheless, he was outstanding for his fortitude in battle, boldness, and massive build. His mother, according to what is said, was one of the daughters of King Mihrak, whom Ardashīr killed at Ardashīr Khurrah.[126] This arose from the fact that Ardashīr's astrologers had told him that a person would arise from Mihrak's stock who would attain the royal power. So Ardashīr hunted down all of his stock and killed them. However, Hurmuz's mother, who was an intelligent, beautiful, perfectly formed, and physically strong person, slipped

---

the latter's counsels on good rule and the maintenance of an efficient army); idem, *Tanbīh*, 100, trans. 144; Ḥamzah al-Iṣfahānī, *Ta'rīkh*, 44–45 (enumerates in fair detail all the cities Sābūr built, with their names and comments on their plans); Ibn al-Athīr, *Kāmil*, I, 385–88. Of Persian sources, see Ṭabarī-Bal'amī, trans. II, 75–85.

Shābūr seems to have been a less zealous adherent of Zoroastrianism than his father, and is even said by some sources to have been favorable toward Manichaeism, although Zoroastrianism was at this time being consolidated as the state religion of Persia through the untiring efforts of men like the Chief Hērbed Kerdēr. During his time, the influence in the state of Kerdēr and the prophet Mani seems to have been evenly balanced. Shābūr's deportations from Antioch and elsewhere in Syria and in Upper Mesopotamia actually brought increased numbers of Christians into the Persian Empire, so that Christian communities were now implanted in the towns of the heartland Fārs and in places like Ardashīr Khurrah, the preferred residence of Ardashīr I. See Labourt, *Le Christianisme dans l'empire perse*, 19–20; Chaumont, "Les Sassanides et la Christianisme de l'Empire iranien," 168–80; S. Brock, "Christians in the Sasanian Empire: A Case of Divided Loyalties," 1ff.

For recent studies on Shābūr's reign in general, see, e.g., Christensen, *Sassanides*, 179ff, 218–26; Frye, *The Heritage of Persia*, 208–17; idem, "The Political History of Iran under the Sasanians," 124–27, 178; *EI*², svv. Sāsānids (M. Morony), Shāpūr (C. E. Bosworth).

123. In Pahlavi, Ohrmazd, Greek Hōrmisdēs, from Ahura Mazdā, the name in the Avesta of the great divinity of ancient Iranian religion. See Justi, *Namenbuch*, 7–9; Gignoux, *Noms propres sassanides*, no. 702; *EIr*, s.v. Ahura Mazdā (M. Boyce).

124. In al-Mas'ūdī, *Murūj*, II, 166 = §593, and al-Khwārazmī, *Mafātīḥ al-'ulūm*, 102, we have for this *al-baṭal* "the warrior, hero." Cf. Nöldeke, trans. 43 n.2.

125. Nöldeke, trans., 43 n. 3, observes that the forty years or so from Shāpūr I's death to the accession of Shāpūr II were ones of comparative weakness and decline for the Sāsānids.

126. See al-Ṭabarī, I, 817, pp. 10–11 above.

away surreptitiously into the desert and took refuge with some shepherds.

Now Sābūr set out one day hunting. He pursued his quarry enthusiastically, and became very thirsty. At that point, the tents where Hurmuz's mother had sought refuge came into his view. He made for them, but found the shepherds away. He asked for water, and the woman there gave him some. He perceived that she was outstandingly beautiful and had a remarkable carriage and a noble face. Shortly afterward, the shepherds returned. Sābūr asked them about her, and since one of the shepherds gave out that she was a member of his family, Sābūr asked him to give her to him in marriage. The shepherd conceded this to him, so Sābūr went off with her to his own encampment, commanded her to be washed clean, suitably clothed, and adorned. He wanted to have conjugal relations with her. But when he was alone wih her, and sought from her what men usually seek from women, she held back and fended him off when he tried to get near her, with a degree of force he found unpleasing, and he marveled at her physical strength. When she behaved like this for some time, it aroused his anger, and he enquired after the cause. So she told him that she was the daughter of Mihrak, and that she had only done what she had done in order to spare him from Ardashīr. He made an agreement with her to conceal her real position, and had sexual congress with her. She then gave birth to Hurmuz, but Sābūr subsequently concealed the whole matter. [832]

When Hurmuz was several years old, Ardashīr rode out one day, and turned aside to Sābūr's dwelling because he wanted to tell Sābūr something. He went into the house unexpectedly. When Ardashīr had stretched himself out comfortably, Hurmuz came forth, having by this time grown into a sturdy youth. He had in his hand a polo stick that he was playing with, and was crying out in pursuit of the ball. When Ardashīr's eye fell on him, this perturbed him, and he became aware of the resemblance in the youth to his own family, because the qualities of Persian kingship (*al-kayiyyah*)[127] characteristic of Ardashīr's house could not be con-

127. An Arabic abstract noun coined from the name of the ancient, at best semilegendary, ruling dynasty of the Kayānids, Kay (Avestan Kawi) being the princely title used by these, passing into MP and NP with the generalized sense of

cealed and could not be disregarded by anyone, because of certain specific traits visible in members of that house: a handsome face, a stout physique, and other bodily features by which Ardashīr's house was distinguished. So Ardashīr made him come near, and asked Sābūr about him. The latter fell down [before him] in obeisance, acknowledging his fault over all that he had done, and told
[833] his father the truth about the whole affair. Ardashīr, nevertheless, expressed joy over him, and told him that he had now [for the first time] realized the truth of what the astrologers had said regarding Mihrak's offspring and regarding the one from them who would reign as king; the astrologers had simply been envisaging Hurmuz in this connection, since he was from the stock of Mihrak; and this had now provided consolation for the perturbation in his mind and had dispelled it.

When Ardashīr died, and the royal power passed to Sābūr, he appointed Hurmuz governor of Khurāsān and dispatched him thither. Hurmuz adopted an independent policy, subdued the rulers of the nations in adjacent lands, and behaved as a highly proud and effective ruler. Hence various calumniators delated him to Sābūr and implanted the delusion in the latter's mind that, if Sābūr were to summon Hurmuz [to his court], the latter would not respond, and that he was planning to seize the royal power from him. News of this reached Hurmuz. It is said that he went aside into a private place, and cut into his hand and severed it, placed on the hand some preservative, wrapped it up in a piece of costly clothing, put it in a casket and sent it off to Sābūr. He wrote a letter to him about what he had heard (sc., the calumnies concerning him), and [explained] that he had only done what he had done (i.e., cut off and dispatched the hand) in order to dispel all suspicions about him, for among their customs was the practice of not raising anyone to kingly power who had a physical defect.[128] When the letter and the accompanying casket reached Sābūr, he

---

"king." See Christensen, *Les Kayanides*, 9–10, 17ff., 43; Yarshater, "Iranian National History," 436ff.; *EI*², s.v. Kayānids (ed.).

128. Nöldeke, trans. 45 n. 1, noted the information of the Byzantine historian Procopius that "a one-eyed person or someone afflicted by any other serious defect, could not become king of Persia"; but this was probably a near-universal principle in the Ancient Near East and the classical Eastern Mediterranean world, and was one of continued validity in later times, since physical wholeness was certainly required for the Byzantine emperors and the Islamic caliphs.

became cut up through grief, and wrote back to Hurmuz telling him how filled with affliction he had become at Hurmuz's action, excused himself and informed him that, if Hurmuz were to cut up his body limb by limb, he would not choose anyone else for the royal power. He then proclaimed him [his successor as] king.

It is said that, when Sābūr placed the crown on Hurmuz's head, the great men of state came into his presence and invoked blessings on him. He returned a kindly answer to them, and they then realized from him the [real] truth of the affair. He behaved benevolently toward them, meted out justice to the subjects, and followed the [praiseworthy] ways of his forefathers, and he laid out the district (*kūrah*) of Rām Hurmuz.[129] Hurmuz's reign lasted one year and ten days.[130]

## *[Bahrām I]*

After him, there succeeded to the royal power his son Bahrām (I). He was Bahrām, son of Hurmuz (I), son of Sābūr (I), son of Ardashīr (I), son of Bābak.[131]

---

129. A town of southeastern Khūzistān, in early Islamic times a flourishing market town and in the modern period a center for the oil industry. It was clearly an old town, though little mentioned by the historians. The Pahlavi town list confirms al-Ṭabarī's information here that it was founded by Hormizd I, son of Shābūr I (Markwart-Messina, *Catalogue of the Provincial Capitals*, 19, 95–96), but some sources, e.g., Ḥamzah al-Iṣfahānī, 43, attribute it to Ardashīr I. See Marquart, *Ērānšahr*, 145; Le Strange, *Lands*, 243–44; Schwarz, *Iran*, 332–35; Barthold, *Historical Geography*, 194; *EI²*, sv. Rām-Hurmuz (V. Minorsky and C. E. Bosworth).

130. Hormizd I Ardashīr's reign was 270–71. Hormizd's name appears on his coins as 'WHRMZDY. See on his coins Paruck, *Sāsānian coins*, 53, 322–23, 419, Plate V, Table III; Göbl, *Sasanian Numismatics*, 43, Table II, Plate 3; Sellwood, Whitting, and Williams, *An Introduction to Sasanian Coins*, 21, 84–85; Malek, "A Survey of Research on Sasanian Numismatics," 233.

The other Arabic sources on his reign include Ibn Qutaybah, *Ma'ārif*, 654; al-Ya'qūbī, *Ta'rīkh*, I, 187 (extremely brief); al-Dīnawarī, *al-Akhbār al-ṭiwāl*, 47 (mainly on his execution of Mani, thus attributed to Hurmuz); al-Mas'ūdī, *Murūj*, II, 166–67 = §593 (his counsels to his commanders); idem, *Tanbīh*, 100, trans. 144; Ḥamzah al-Iṣfahānī, 45 (notes his considerable gifts, but that he fell short of his father); Ibn al-Athīr, *Kāmil*, I, 388–89. Of Persian sources, see Ṭabarī-Bal'amī, trans. II, 85–89.

For recent studies on Hormizd's reign in general, see Christensen, *Sassanides*, 102, 226–28; Frye, "The Political History of Iran under the Sasanians," 127–28, 178; Morony, *EI²*, s.v. Sāsānids.

131. MP Warahrān, Wahrām, Greek Ouararanēs, Baramas, etc., Syriac Warathrān, from the name of the Avestan god of victory Vərəthraghna. See Nöldeke,

## [The History of al-Ḥīrah]

After the demise of ʿAmr b. ʿAdī b. Naṣr b. Rabīʿah, the governor for Sābūr b. Ardashīr, and for Hurmuz b. Sābūr, and for Bahrām [b. [834] Hurmuz] b. Sābūr, over the frontier region of [the land of] the Arabs of Rabīʿah, Muḍar, and the rest of the tribes in the deserts of Iraq, Ḥijāz, and Jazīrah,[132] was at that time a son of ʿAmr b. ʿAdī called Imruʾ al-Qays al-Badʾ. He was the first of the kings from the house of Naṣr b. Rabīʿah and the governors for the kings of the Persians who became a Christian.[133] According to what Hishām b. Muḥammad (sc., Ibn al-Kalbī) has mentioned, he ruled over his charge as a vassal prince for 114 years, comprising twenty-three years and one month under Sābūr, son of Ardashīr, one year and

---

trans. 46 n. 3; Justi, *Namenbuch*, 361–65; Gignoux, *Noms propres sassanides*, no. 926; *EIr*, s.v. Bahrām, heading.

132. This enormous sphere of control and influence attributed to the early Lakhmid governors is vastly exaggerated, since their authority as representatives of imperial Persia was mainly exercised along the Syrian Desert fringes of Mesopotamia and in northeastern Arabia, and only sporadically within the Arabian interior. The two great tribal groups of Rabīʿah and Muḍar dominated northern Arabia, with members of their component tribes pushing northward through Iraq into Jazīrah, where the names of their dwelling places and pasture grounds, the Diyār of Rabīʿah, Muḍar, and Bakr, reflect their presence in early Islamic times. See *EI*², s.v. Rabīʿa and Muḍar (H. Kindermann). It was, however, true that elements of the South Arabian Lakhm had spread from their original home quite early in the pre-Islamic period not only into Iraq but also into Syria. See Ibn al-Kalbī-Caskel-Strenziok, *Jamharat al-nasab*, I, Tables 176, 246, II, 54–56, 375–76; *EI*², s.v. Lakhm (H. Lammens-Irfan Shahîd).

133. *al-Badʾ*, "the first, the originator." This is Imruʾ al-Qays (I), the famous "Imruʾ al-Qays, King of all the Arabs" of the proto-Arabic al-Namārah tomb inscription of 328, al-Namārah being situated in the district of al-Ṣafāʾ between Damascus and Boṣrā in what was then the Roman province of Arabia. In explanation of the apparent paradox why this Lakhmid king in al-Ḥīrah should have been buried far from his homeland of the desert fringes of Iraq, Irfan Shahîd has plausibly suggested that Imruʾ al-Qays was the first of his line to become a Christian and therefore deserted his allegiance to the Zoroastrian Sāsānids and went over to the Romans in Syria, becoming one of their client rulers; also, he may have been affronted by Shābūr II's campaign against the Arabs of eastern Arabia (see al-Ṭabarī, I, 838–39, pp. 54–56 below), which challenged his own claim to the headship of all the Arabs, however inflated this might have been (see n. 132 above). Nöldeke, tr. 47 n. 2, denied that Imruʾ al-Qays al-Badʾ could have been a Christian, in the light of the vigorous paganism of later Lakhmid kings, and thought that al-Ṭabarī's source Ibn al-Kalbī had here confused this Imruʾ al-Qays (I) with a later one of the same name. But Nöldeke was writing before the discovery of the Namārah inscription in Syria at the end of the nineteenth century. See Shahîd's detailed discussion of the king and his inscription, in *Byzantium and the Arabs in the Fourth Century*, 31–47, and also Rothstein, *Laḫmiden*, 52, 55ff., 61, 63–64, 139.

ten days under Hurmuz, son of Sābūr, and three years, three months, and three days under Bahrām, son of Hurmuz, son of Sābūr, and eighteen years under Bahrām, son of Bahrām, son of Hurmuz, son of Sābūr, son of Ardashīr.[134]

According to what has been mentioned, Bahrām b. Hurmuz was a forebearing and mild person, so that the people rejoiced when he came to power. He behaved in a praiseworthy manner toward them, and in his policy of rule over the people followed the practices of his forefathers.

According to what has been mentioned, Mānī the Zindīq summoned him to his religion. So Bahrām enquired exhaustively into Mānī's beliefs, and found that he was a propagandist for Satan. So he ordered him to be executed and his body to be skinned and stuffed with straw, and then for it to be hung from one of the city gates of Junday Sābūr, which is [because of this] called Mānī's Gate. He also killed his followers and those who had joined his faith.[135] Bahrām's reign lasted, according to what is said, for three years, three months, and three days.[136]

---

134. A total, in reality, of forty-five years, four-and-a-half months (but Shābūr I's reign is usually taken as thirty or thirty-one years, as in al-Ṭabarī, I, 831, p. 39 above). Also, Bahrām I was the son of Shābūr I, not of Hormizd I, and Bahrām II was the son of Bahrām I, hence Hormizd I's nephew and not his son.

135. The date of Mani's execution is controversial, and its exact placing is bound up with uncertainty over the chronology of the early Sāsānid rulers. see n. 56 above, and, specifically, with the dates for Bahrām I's brief reign, during which it appears Mani was killed. Hence the chronology for the dating of Shābūr I's death, Hormizd I's reign, Bahrām I's reign, and Bahrām II's accession proposed by Henning is followed here (see nn. 122, 130 and 134 above, and nn. 136–37 below). Basing himself on the dating of 271–74 for Bahrām I's reign and on evidence from a wide range of sources, including Manichaean ones, Henning suggested that Mani may have been executed on Monday, the 4th of the Babylonian month of Addaru in the year 584 of the Seleucid era = 2 March A.D. 274; but he allowed the possibility of divergent dates, such as a date in A.D. 277 proposed by S. H. Taqizadeh. See Taqizadeh and Henning, "The dates of Mani's Life," 505–20 and especially 515–20. See also for further suggestions regarding the date, such as that of 276, W. Hinz, "Mani and Kardēr," 490–92; Widengren, "Manichaeism and Its Iranian Background," 971–72.

136. Bahrām I's reign was 271–74, but very little is known about his reign. His name appears on his coins as WRḤR'N. See on his coins Paruck, *Sāsānian Coins*, 53–54, 324–25, 419–22, Plates V-VI, Table III; Göbl, *Sasanian Numismatics*, 43, Table II, Plate 3; Sellwood, Whitting, and Williams, *An Introduction to Sasanian Coins*, 21, 86–87; Malek, "A Survey of Research on Sasanian Numismatics," 233.

The other Arabic sources on his reign include Ibn Qutaybah, *Maʿārif*, 655; al-Yaʿqūbī, *Taʾrīkh*, I, 182 (on his relations with Mani, and his execution of him); al-Dīnawarī, *al-Akhbār al-ṭiwāl*, 47 (lists his name only); al-Masʿūdī, *Murūj*, II, 147–

## *[Bahrām II]*

Then there succeeded him in the royal power his son Bahrām (II). [He was] the son of Bahrām [I], son of Hurmuz (I), son of Sābūr (I), son of Ardashīr (I). He is said to have been knowledgeable about the affairs [of government]. When he was crowned, the great men of state called down blessings on his head, just as they had done for
[835] his forefathers, and he returned to them greetings in a handsome manner and behaved in a praiseworthy fashion toward them. He was wont to say: "If fortune furthers our designs, we receive this with thankfulness; if the reverse, we are content with our share." There are varying reports about the duration of his reign. Some say that he ruled for eighteen years, others for seventeen years.[137]

---

48 = §594 (Mani's rise, Bahrām's feigned sympathy for his, and an explanation of the term *zindīq* = one who makes (heretical) interpretations, *zands*, of the Avesta; cf. n. 118 above); idem, *Tanbīh*, 100, trans. 144; Ḥamzah al-Iṣfahānī, *Ta'rīkh*, 47 (his interrogation and execution of Mani); Ibn al-Athīr, *Kāmil*, I, 390. Of Persian sources, see Ṭabarī-Bal'amī, trans. II, 89–90. Of modern studies, see Christensen, *Sassanides*, 226–27; Frye, "The Political History of Iran under the Sasanians," 127–28, 178; *EI²*, s.v. Sāsānids (M. Morony); *EIr*, s.v. Bahrām I (A. Sh. Shahbazi).

137. Bahrām II's reign was 274–91. His reign was a troubled one, although few details of its events are known. There was the lengthy rebellion of his brother Hormizd centered on Sijistān, so that the Romans were able to take advantage of Bahrām's preoccupation with the east of his realm and invade Mesopotamia, an attack on Ctesiphon only being averted by the death in 283 of the Roman emperor Carus. Bahrām II's name appears on his coins as WRḤR'N. See on his coins Paruck, *Sāsānian Coins*, 54–55, 326–34, 422–25, Plates VI-VIII, Table IV; Göbl, *Sasanian Numismatics*, 43–45, Tables III-IV, Plates IV-V; Sellwood, Whitting, and Williams, *An Introduction to Sasanian Coins*, 21, 88–92; Malek, "A Survey of Research on Sasanian Numismatics," 233.

The other Arabic sources on his reign include Ibn Qutaybah, *Ma'ārif*, 655; al-Ya'qūbī, *Ta'rīkh*, I, 182 (name and length of reign only); al-Dīnawarī, al-*Akhbār al-ṭiwāl*, 47 (name only); al-Mas'ūdī, *Murūj*, II, 168–74 = §§595–99 (lengthy entry: stresses Bahrām's life of pleasure and neglect of state affairs); idem, *Tanbīh*, 100, trans. 144; Ḥamzah al-Iṣfahānī, *Ta'rīkh*, 46; Ibn al-Athīr, *Kāmil*, I, 390. Of Persian sources, see Ṭabarī-Bal'amī, trans. II, 90.

Bahrām was a fervent Zoroastrian and was strongly under the influence of Kerdēr, whom he regarded as his mentor and on whom he bestowed the title of "Saviour of Bahrām's soul"; also, Kerdēr appears on all but one of Bahrām's numerous rock reliefs with the sovereign himself (see Herrmann, *The Iranian Revival*, 98–99, 106). In the previous reigns of Shābūr I and Bahrām I, Kerdēr had had to share royal patronage and favor with the prophet Mani. Now, with the advent of Bahrām II, as Hinz has pointed out, the balance tipped definitely in Kerdēr's favor, and some two years into the new reign, Mani was arrested and died in imprisonment (see n. 135 above). With Kerdēr's ascendancy now complete, non-Zoroastrian faiths within Persia came under attack, as is seen in his Ka'ba-yi Zardusht inscription, where it is stated that Kerdēr humbled, among others like the Manichaeans

## [*Bahrām III*]

Then there reigned Bahrām (III), who had the honorific title of Sakānshāh.[138] [He was] the son of Bahrām [II], son of Bahrām [I], son of Hurmuz (I), son of Sābūr (I), son of Ardashīr (I). When he was crowned, the great men of state gathered together around him, and called down on his head blessings for the auspiciousness of his rule and for his long life, and he returned to them greetings in a handsome manner. Before he had succeeded to the royal power, he had been appointed ruler of Sijistān. He reigned for four years.[139]

---

and Jews, the "Nazarenes" (Jewish Christians?), and the *Krīstīyān* (mainstream, Catholic, Nicene Christians?) (the exact defintion of the latter two terms is disputed; thus Wiesehöfer, *Ancient Persia*, 203, following Brock, "Christians in the Sasanian Empire," 3, 6, and n. 21, assumes a distinction based on territorial-cultural origins, so that "Nazarenes = the indigenous Persian Christians, and *Krīstīyān* = the Christian deportees from lands further west and their descendants); the *Chronicle of Arbela* has some mention of persecutions during Bahrām's reign. It seems to have been the Jews who, in practice, suffered the least molestation. See; Chaumont, "Les Sassanides et la Christianisme de l'Empire iranien," 187–97; J. Neusner, "Jews in Iran," 914–15.

Of modern studies, see Christensen, *Sassanides*, 227–31; Frye, "The Political History of Iran under the Sasanians," 128–29, 178; *EI²*, s.v. Sāsānids (M. Morony); *EIr*, s.v. Bahrām II (A. Sh. Shahbazi).

138. al-Ṭabarī's text has *Shāhanshāh* "Supreme king," but as is apparent from the words at the end of this section on him, this is an old misreading; the correct reading appears in Ḥamzah al-Iṣfahānī, *Ta'rīkh*, 46, and al-Khwārazmī, *Mafātīh al-ʿulūm*, 102. Sakān Shāh means literally "king of the Sakas," i.e., of the people controling or inhabiting Sakastān/Sagastān, Islamic Sijistān, Sīstān; see *EI²*, s.v. Sīstān (C. E. Bosworth). Bahrām III had acquired his post during his predecessor's reign, following the early Sāsānid practice of granting out provincial appanages to royal princes; in this case, he was appointed to Sagastān because of its importance as a bastion against powerful peoples of the eastern fringes, such as the Sakas and Kushans, or because it had recently been conquered by Bahrām II after the revolt there of his brother Hormizd (n. 137 above). Agathias says that it was the custom of the Persian kings, when they had subdued a land or people, to give their sons titles expressing dominion over that people. See Nöldeke, trans. 49 n. 2; Christensen, *Sassanides*, 228–29; Cameron, "Agathias on the Sassanians," 122–23, 143; Frye, "The Political History of Iran under the Sasanians," 128–29.

139. Bahrām III's reign was for four months only in the early part of the year 292 until he was deposed after a revolt by his great-uncle Narseh (see below). Coins attributed to Bahrām's name are exiguous in number, and the readings of their legends are ambiguous, with coins variously assigned to him and to his successor Narseh. See on these Paruck, *Sāsānian Coins*, 56, 334–35, 425–26, Plate VIII, Table V; Sellwood, Whitting, and Williams, *An Introduction to Sasanian Coins*, 21, 93–94; Malek, "A Survey of Research on Sasanian Numismatics," 234.

The other Arabic sources on his reign, all very laconic (with al-Dīnawarī omitting him altogether), are Ibn Qutaybah, *Maʿārif*, 655; al-Yaʿqūbī, *Ta'rīkh*, I, 182; al-Masʿūdī, *Murūj*, II, 174 = § 600; idem, *Tanbīh*, 100, trans. 144; Ibn al-Athīr, *Kāmil*,

## [Narsī]

Then there took charge of the royal power after him Narsī, son of Bahrām (I) and also the brother of Bahrām (II).[140] When he was crowned, the nobles and great men of state came into his presence and called down blessings on him. He gave them promises of benevolence and adjured them to aid him in the business of ruling. He behaved toward them in a highly just manner. On the day he became king he said, "We must never lose an opportunity in giving thanks to God for His bountifulness to us." He reigned for nine years.[141]

---

I, 391. Of modern studies, see Christensen, *Sassanides,* 231; Frye, "The Political History of Iran under the Sasanians," 129, 178; *EI*², s.v. Sāsānids (M. Morony); *EIr,* s.v. Bahrām III (O. Klíma).

140. The name Narseh, Greek Narsēs, Narsaios, goes back to Nairyōsaṇha, the name in the Avesta of the messenger of Ahura Mazdā. See Justi, *Namenbuch,* 221–25; Gignoux, *Noms propres sassanides,* no. 678. Narseh was actually yet another son of Shābūr I, hence brother of Bahrām I, uncle of Bahrām II and great-uncle of Bahrām III. Cf. Nöldeke, tr. 50 n. 2; Christensen, *Sassanides,* 231; Frye, "The Political History of Iran under the Sasanians," 129, 178; *EI*², s.v. Sāsānids (M. Morony). Only in al-Mas'ūdī, *Murūj,* II, 238 = § 660, quoting from Abū 'Ubaydah's history of Persia, taken from 'Umar called Kisrā (?), is the correct filiation "Narsī, son of Sābūr (I)" given in the other Arabic sources, for which see n. 141 below.

141. Narseh's reign was 292–302. His name appears on his coins as NRSḤY. See on his coins Paruck, *Sāsānian Coins,* 56, 335–36, 426–28, Plate VIII, Table V; Göbl, *Sasanian Numismatics,* 45, Table V, Plate 5; Sellwood, Whitting, and Williams, *An Introduction to Sasanian Coins,* 21, 95–96; Malek, "A Survey of Research on Sasanian Numismatics," 234.

The other Arabic sources on his reign include Ibn Qutaybah, *Ma'ārif,* loc. cit.; al-Ya'qūbī, *Ta'rīkh,* loc. cit. (name and length of reign only); al-Dīnawarī, *al-Akhbār al-ṭiwāl,* 47 (name and length of reign); al-Mas'ūdī, loc. cit.; idem, *Tanbīh,* loc. cit.; Ḥamzah al-Iṣfahānī, *Ta'rīkh,* 46–47; Ibn al-Athīr, *Kāmil,* loc. cit. Of Persian sources, see Ṭabarī-Bal'amī, trans. II, 90. Of modern studies, see Christensen, *Sassanides,* 102, 231–32; Frye, *The Heritage of Persia,* 218, 220–21; idem, "The Political History of Iran under the Sasanians," 129–31, 178.

Narseh had become "High King of Armenia" on his father Shābūr I's death. The story of his eventual achievement of the throne and the setting aside of Bahrām III; the enumeration of local kings or princes on the fringes of the Sāsānid empire who were presumably tribute to him; and the exposition of his concept of his own royal power, are set forth in the inscription (NPi) which he had carved on the commemorative tower built by him at Paikuli in Kurdistan. He also made known his feeling that his legitimate right to the throne after Hormizd Ardashīr's death had been usurped by the succession of the three Bahrāms, by altering Bahrām II's investiture relief at Bīshāpūr and substituting his own name for that of his elder brother; and he added to the relief the prostrate figure of a vanquished foe under the monarch's horse (this enemy being probably the noble Wahnām who had organized the putsch in Fārs raising Bahrām III to the throne). See E. Herzfeld, *Paikuli. Monument and Inscriptions of the Early History of the Sasanian Empire,* I, 94–

## [Hurmuz II]

Then there ruled Hurmuz (II), son of Narsī, son of Bahrām (II),[142] son of Bahrām (I), son of Hurmuz (I), son of Sābūr (I), son of Ardashīr (I). The people had been in awe of him, and had experienced harshness and severity [from him]. But he told them that he had been fully aware of their fears over his severity and strong rule, and informed them that he had exchanged the roughness and harshness in his nature for mildness and clemency. He then ruled them in the most considerate fashion and behaved in the most equitable manner possible. He was eager to succor and revive the [836]
weak, to render the land prosperous and flourishing, and to spread justice among the subjects. Then he died without leaving any son. The people were distressed at that and, because of their favorable feeling for him, they asked about his wives and were told that a certain one of them was pregnant. Others have said, moreover, that Hurmuz had entrusted the royal power to that unborn child in his mother's womb, and that the woman in question gave birth to [the future] Sābūr (II) Dhū al-Aktāf ("The Man with the Shoulders").[143] Hurmuz's tenure of royal power, according to

119, and now H. Humbach and P. O. Skjaervø, *The Sassanian Inscription of Paikuli*, III/1–2; Herrmann, *The Iranian Revival*, 99, 106–107; Wiesehöfer, *Ancient Persia*, 184–85.

Narseh's warfare against the Romans was not very successful, though we have little information on the actual course of events. The Romans were able to restore their protégé, the Armenian Arsacid Tiridates I, to the throne of Armenia, and the Persian had to cede part of Little Armenia to Rome. However, the peace of 298 between Narseh and Diocletian was to endure for forty years. Narseh is also said to have been tolerant toward the Christians and Manichaeans, possibly in the hope of securing the support of their coreligionists within the boundaries of the Roman territories. See Nöldeke, trans. 50 n. 3; Christensen, *Sassanides*, 233; Stein, *Histoire du Bas-Empire*, I, 79–80; Chaumont, "Les Sassanides et la Christianisme de l'Empire iranien," 200; Frye, "The Political History of Iran under the Sasanians," loc. cit.; *EIr*, s.v. Armenia and Iran. ii. The Pre-Islamic Period (M. -L. Chaumont), at II, 426.

142. For the correct filiation here, see p. 45 n. 134 above.

143. Nöldeke, trans. 52 n. 1, surmised that this sobriquet was initially one of honor, "the man with broad shoulders." i.e., suitable for bearing the burdens of royal power and leadership in war. The folkloric explanation of the Arabic sources, given by al-Ṭabarī, I, 843–44, p. 63 below, that Shābūr acquired the title from piercing the shoulders of Arab captives from eastern Arabia, would accordingly be a later, fanciful explanation. Al-Ṭabarī's younger contemporary, Ḥamzah al-Iṣfahānī, *Ta'rīkh*, 47, followed by al-Khwārazmī, *Mafātīḥ al-ʿulūm*, 102–103, give the alleged Persian original of "shoulder borer" as *hūyah sunbā* (thus vocalized by al-Khwārazmī's editor Van Vloten: NP *hūyah/hūbah* "shoulder" + *sunbā*, "auger,

what some authorities say, was six years and five months, but according to others, seven years and five months.[144]

## [Sābūr II Dhū al-Aktāf]

Then there was born Sābūr Dhū al-Aktāf, son of Hurmuz (II), son of Narsī, son of Bahrām (II), son of Bahrām (I),[145] son of Sābūr (I), son of Ardashīr (I), who succeeded to the royal power by virtue of the testament of his father Hurmuz's appointment of him as his successor.[146] The people rejoiced at his birth; they spread the news about it to the farthest lands, they wrote letters and the couriers of the postal and intelligence system (*al-burud*) conveyed news of it to the most distant regions and frontiers.[147] The viziers

---

instrument for boring"). Whether this goes back to a Pahlavi original or is a later, back formation from the Arabic, is, as Nöldeke observed, impossible to determine.

144. Hormizd II's reign was 302–309. His name appears on his coins as 'WHRMZDY. See on his coins Paruck, *Sāsānian Coins,* 57–58, 337–41, 428–30, Plates VIII-IX, Table VI; Göbl, *Sasanian Numismatics,* 45–46, Table V, Plate 5; Sellwood, Whitting, and Williams, *An Introduction to Sasanian Coins,* 21, 97–98; Malek, "A Survey of Research on Sasanian Coins," 234.

The other Arabic sources on his reign include Ibn Qutaybah, *Ma'ārif,* 655; al-Ya'qūbī, *Ta'rīkh,* I, 182 (name and length of reign, death while Sābūr (II) was still a baby) al-Dīnawarī, *al-Akhbār al-ṭiwāl,* 47 (information that he died when his wife was several months pregnant; the succession of his putative son was confirmed by placing the crown on his wife's abdomen, a tale known also to Western historians such as Agathias, see Cameron, "Agathias on the Sassanians," 122–25, 144); al-Mas'ūdī, *Murūj,* II, 174 = § 600; idem, *Tanbīh,* 100, trans. 144 (name and reign only); Ḥamzah al-Iṣfahānī, *Ta'rīkh,* 47 (he founded a *rustāq* in the Rām-Hurmuz district); Ibn al-Athir, *Kāmil,* I, 391–92. Of Persian sources, See Ṭabarī-Bal'amī, trans. II, 90–91. Of modern studies, see Nöldeke, trans. 51 nn. 1, 2; Christensen, *Sassanides,* 233–34; Frye, "The Political History of Iran under the Sasanians," 131–32, 178; *EI*², s.v. Sāsānids (M. J. Morony).

145. For the correct filiation here, see p. 45 n. 134 above.

146. Concerning the folkloric touch of Hormizd's entrusting the royal power to his infant Shābūr while he was still in his mother's womb, aside from the fact that he could not have known the sex of the child at that point, the ascertainable historical facts are that Hormizd left several sons by various wives, all older than Shābūr. The great men of state and the Zoroastrian priesthood saw their chance of securing a dominant influence in affairs, hence killed the natural successor to power, Hormizd's eldest son Ādhar Narseh, blinded another, forced a third to flee to Roman territory, and then raised to nominal headship of the realm the infant Shābūr, born forty days after his father's death. See the references in n. 144 above, and *EIr,* s.v. Ardašīr II (A. Sh. Shahbazi)

147. The institution of a state-organized postal and intelligence network was an ancient Near Eastern one, known in Persia from as far back as Achaemenid times and in such neighbors of the Sāsānids as the Romans and Byzantines. While there is

and secretaries retained the official functions they had held during his father's reign. They continued in these positions until news about them (sc., about these officials) spread, and there was disseminated on the distant frontiers of the land of the Persians [the news] that the people there had no king and that the Persians were merely waiting for a child, [at that time] in the cradle, not knowing how he would turn out. Hence the Turks[148] and the Romans cast envious eyes on the lands of the Persians.

Now the lands of the Arabs were the nearest ones to Fārs,[149] and these Arabs were among the most needy of all the nations for something to provide them with daily sustenance and with lands, because of their wretched condition and the harshness of their way of life. So a great horde of them crossed the sea from the region of the lands of 'Abd al-Qays, al-Baḥrayn, and al-Kāẓimah, until they set up military encampments against (*anākhū 'alā*) [the town of] Abruwān, on the shores that had Ardashīr Khurrah as their hinterland (*sawāḥil Ardashīr Khurrah*) and in the coastlands (*asyāf*) of Fārs.[150] They seized the local people's herds of cattle,

---

little direct information on the postal and intelligence network of the Sāsānids, a certain amount of information can be inferred from both Pahlavi sources and from Firdawsī's *Shāh-nāmah*; see B. Geiger, "Zum Postwesen der Perser," 309–14. As well as the rapid conveyance of information and intelligence, such a system of riding-beasts and post-houses provided one of the few possible means for rulers to exercise control over the remoter parts of their kingdoms. Popular early Islamic etymology derived the term *barīd* (sing. of *burud*) from Persian *burīdah-dunb* "having a docked tail," but the true derivation is from Late Latin *veredus* "post-horse" (whence *veredarius* "courier"), as was recognized by Quatremère over a century and a half ago. See Bosworth, "Abū 'Abdallāh al-Khwārazmī on the Technical Terms of the Secretary's Art," 141–42; *EI*², s.v. Barīd (D. Sourdel); *EIr*, s.v. Barīd (C. E. Bosworth).

148. Nöldeke, trans. 53 n. 2, held that mention here of "Turks" was anachronistic and pointed to al-Ṭabarī's source having been composed in the later sixth century at the earliest, because only in that century did Khusraw Anūsharwān come into contact with the Turks, those of the Western Türk empire, which had established its influence over both sides of the Tien Shan and over Transoxania (see al-Ṭabarī, I, 895–96, pp. 152–53 below). This is probably true, but it is not totally impossible that the "Turks" whom Bahrām V Gūr repelled from the eastern borders of his kingdom in the second quarter of the fifth century included elements of genuine Turks, but perhaps as members of the following of the hordes like those of the Kidarites or Chionites. See the discussion in n. 244 below.

149. Altheim and Stiehl have pointed out (*Die Araber*, II, 346) that Nöldeke, trans. 53, was mistaken in rendering *Fārs* here as "Persien" when the geographical context makes it clear that the province of Fārs is meant. When, as in I, 839, p. 55 below, al-Ṭabarī specifically means "the land of Persia," he has *mamlakat Fārs*.

150. 'Abd al-Qays were an ancient Arab tribe, originally from the inland regions

their cultivated lands, and their means of subsistence, and did a
[837] great deal of damage in those regions.

They (sc., the Arab invaders) remained engaged in these activities for a considerable time, with none of the Persians able to launch a counterattack because they had set the royal crown on the head of a mere child and because of people's [consequent] lack of awe and respect for him. [This continued] until Sābūr grew up and became stirred to action. When he was grown up, the first thing that was manifested of his good management of affairs and his acute understanding, so it has been mentioned, was that he was awakened from sleep one night, toward early morning, in the royal palace at Ctesiphon, by the anguished clamor of the people. He enquired what that was, and was told that it was the clamor of the people crowded together on the bridge over the Tigris, coming and going. So he gave orders for another bridge to be built, so that one of the bridges could be used for people crossing in one direction and the other bridge for people crossing from the opposite direction; thus people using the two bridges would no longer be crowded together. When the people perceived the acuteness of his mind in

---

of eastern Najd, and accounted genealogically as part of Rabī'ah. They early migrated toward the western shores of the Persian Gulf, to Qaṭīf and Baḥrayn, which, as al-Ṭabarī shortly relates (I, 838–39, pp. 54–56 below) were from Shābūr II's time directly under Persian rule, with garrisons and governors, and then made over to the Persians' representatives, the Lakhmids. The 'Abd al-Qays were thus well placed, under the stimulus of inadequate resources for supporting them in the oases of the eastern Arabian coastlands, to make incursions across the gulf to the coast (*sīf*, pl. *asyāf*) of Fārs. See Ibn al-Kalbī-Caskel-Strenziok, *Jamharat al-nasab*, I, Tables 141, 168, II, 28–29, 127; *EI*[2], s.v. 'Abd al-Qays (W. Caskel); *EIr*, s.v. 'Abd-al-Qays (P. Oberling). Al-Kāẓimah was a place on the Baḥrayn coast south of the mouth of the Shaṭṭ al-'Arab but not further specified. See al-Bakrī, *Mu'jam mā ista'jam*, III, 1109–10; Yāqūt, *Buldān*, IV, 431.

The reading of the name rendered here as Abruwān (tentatively translated by Nöldeke, trans. 53, as Rīshahr, on which see al-Ṭabarī, I, 820, p. 16 and n. 62 above) varies greatly in the mss. Altheim and Stiehl, *Die Araber in der Alten Welt*, II, 347–48, have suggested that this is the town of *Abruwān mentioned by al-Ṭabarī, I, 870, p. 105 below, as being in the province of Ardashīr Khurrah and as a place where Mihr Narsī erected lofty buildings (see p. 105 n. 267 below, for varying suggestions about this place-name). Also, Altheim and Stiehl have suggested, as certainly seems appropriate in the context, that one should follow ms. C's reading *anākhū 'alā*, "they set up encampments against . . ." (thus likewise in the Cairo edition, II, 55, apparently following here the Constantinople/Istanbul ms.), instead of the text's weaker *anākhū bi-*, "they halted at . . ." (cf. Dozy, *Supplément*, II, 734, on *anākha 'alā*: "se présenter hostilement devant [une place ou un homme]").

working out a solution for this problem, despite his tender years, they rejoiced at this, and hastened to fulfil what had been commanded regarding this [construction of the new bridge]. It is mentioned that the [second] bridge was constructed in the vicinity of the existing bridge before sunset of that day. In this way, the people were relieved of the necessity of endangering their lives when crossing the bridge. The child [Sābūr] grew in stature and prestige in that single day, what for others would have taken a long period.

The secretaries and viziers began successively to lay before Sābūr various state matters. Among the matters they brought to his notice was the position of the troops along the frontiers and those directly facing enemies there, for news had arrived that the greater part of them had been reduced to a sorry state. The secretaries and viziers stressed to him the seriousness of the situation, but Sābūr told them, "Don't worry about this excessively, since the remedy for it is simple." Then he ordered a letter to be sent to the whole of these troops, stating that he had learned about how long they had been stationed in those regions of the provinces where they were, and about the intensity of their deprivation of [838] their dependents and brothers.[151] Hence whosoever wished to return to his family was free to do so, with full permission for that; and whosoever wished to complete the rest of his service by remaining standfast in his post, that would be reckoned to him favorably. He further ordered that those who chose to return could remain with their families on their own lands until the time when they were needed again. When the viziers heard all these words of his, they approved of them highly and said, "Even if this youth had had long experience of state affairs and the management of troops, his judgment and the soundness of his eloquent speech could not be greater than what we have just heard!"

---

151. Complaints about the long periods of service along distant frontiers, entailing separation from homes and families, were among the accusations hurled two centuries or so later at Khusraw II Abarwēz by his own son and supplanter Shērōy, see al-Ṭabarī, I, 1047, p. 383 below. Also, in early Islamic times complaints about this process, called in Arabic *tajmīr* (literally, "bringing together, collecting," i.e., of troops in garrisons, with the Arab warriors or *muqātilah* being stationed on the inhospitable fringes of what is now Afghanistan, were a powerful factor in the revolt of ʿAbd al-Raḥmān Ibn al-Ashʿath and the "Peacock Army" in 81–82/700–701 which nearly toppled the Umayyad government. See *EI*², s.vv. Ibn al-As̲h̲ʿat̲h̲ (L. Veccia Vaglieri) and Tad̲j̲mīr (C. E. Bosworth).

Then there were issued successively his instructions to the provinces and the frontier lands, which gave heart to his own troops and humbled his enemies. At last he reached sixteen years of age and was able to bear weapons and ride cavalry horses, and his physical strength became great. He summoned together the commanders of his guards and troops and made an oration to them. He mentioned how bountiful God had been to him and to them through his forefathers, what these last had accomplished through their good conduct and how they had crushed their enemies, and how all these achievements of theirs had, however, fallen into confusion in the period that had elapsed during his youth. He then told them that he was going to make a start on the work [of restoring the position] by securely defending the heartland; and that [after that] he was making plans to move against one of his enemies and make war on him, and that he was going to take with him a force of one thousand warriors only. The assembled people rose up, calling down blessings [on him] and expressing their thanks, but asking that he should remain in his place and send forward in his stead the commanders and troops on this expedition he had planned.

He rejected their request, however, that he should stay in his capital. Then they requested him to increase the number [of troops] he had mentioned, but again he refused. [On the contrary,] he selected one thousand cavalrymen from among the stoutest and most heroic of the troops. He commanded them to go forward and accomplish his design and forbade them to spare any of the Arabs they encountered or to turn aside in order to seize booty. Then he led them forth, and fell upon those Arabs who had treated Fārs as their pasture ground while they were unaware, wrought great slaughter among them, reduced [others of] them to the harshest form of captivity, and put the remainder to flight.[152]
[839] Then he crossed the sea at the head of his troops and reached al-Khaṭṭ. He marched through the land of al-Baḥrayn, killing its people, not letting himself be bought off by any kind of payment and not turning aside to take plunder. He went back on his tracks and reached Hajar,[153] where there were Bedouins from the tribes of

152. Reading here *wa-harraba.*
153. That is, the western Persian Gulf coastland, of what is now Kuwait, Qatar, and eastern Saudi Arabia, the term appearing in Syriac sources as Hagar; it was also

Tamīm, Bakr b. Wā'il, and 'Abd al-Qays. He spread general slaughter among them, and shed so much of their blood that it flowed like a torrent swollen by a rainstorm. Those who were able to flee realized that no cave in a mountain nor any island in the sea was going to save them.

After this he turned aside to the lands of the 'Abd al-Qays and destroyed all the people there except for those who fled into the desert sands. He passed on to al-Yamāmah,[154] where he made general slaughter like that of the previous occasion. He did not pass by any of the local Arabs' springs of water without blocking them up, nor any of their cisterns without filling them in. He approached the neighborhood of Medina and killed the Arabs whom he found there and took captives. Then he turned aside to the lands of the Bakr and Taghlib, which lie between the land of Persia (*mamlakat Fārs*) and the frontier fortresses (*manāẓir*)[155] of the Romans in the land of Syria. He killed the Arabs he found there, took captives, and filled in their water sources. He settled members of the tribe of Taghlib, who were in al-Baḥrayn, at Dārīn and al-Samāhīj, and at al-Khaṭṭ;[156] members of the 'Abd al-Qays

---

called al-Baḥrayn (in this sense comprehending both the island and the adjacent mainland) in early Islamic times and, right up to modern times, al-Aḥsā' or al-Ḥasā. See Nöldeke, trans. 56 n. 1; *EI*², s.v. al-Ḥasā (F. S. Vidal). For al-Khaṭṭ, see n. 64 above.

154. An extensive region of eastern Arabia, with several important oases, running westward to the scarp of the Jabal Ṭuwayq and eastward to the Dahnā', i.e., comprising much of the modern Saudi provinces of al-Riyāḍ, al-Kharj, and al-'Āriḍ. At the beginning of the Islamic period, Yamāmah was the home of the semi-Christianized Banū Ḥanīfah and the epicenter of activity by the rival prophet to Muḥammad, Musaylimah. See *EI*¹, s.v. al-Yamāma (A. Grohmann).

155. Sing. *manẓarah,* literally "look-out posts," largely synonymous with the more common term for these frontier guard stations, *maslaḥa,* pl. *masāliḥ.*

156. Taghlib b. Wā'il were an important tribe of the Rabī'ah group who lived in Najd till their defeat in the famous "War of Basūs" (early sixth century), and already within the sphere of the Sāsānids and their Lakhmid allies, as Shābūr I's policy here shows. When the Lakhmids regained control of al-Ḥīrah after the interlude of Kindah control there in the 520s, the considerably Christianized Taghlib became one of the firm supports of Lakhmid power there. See Ibn al-Kalbī-Caskel-Strenziok, *Jamharat al-nasab,* I, Tables 141, 163, II, 27–28, 541–42; *EI*², s.v. Taghlib b. Wā'il (M. Lecker).

The mediaeval geographers were confused and vague about these places in al-Baḥrayn. According to Yāqūt, *Buldān,* II, 432, Dārīn was either on Baḥrayn island or on the nearby Persian Gulf coast. Concerning Samāhīj, see al-Bakrī, *Mu'jam,* III, 754, IV, 1382: "a place in al-Baḥrayn belonging to the 'Abd al-Qays" (but in Yāqūt, op. cit., III, 432, an island in the gulf). Al-Ṭabarī's text here, *Dārīn wa-ismuhā*

and some groups of the Banū Tamīm in Hajar; and those members of the Bakr b. Wā'il who were in Kirmān (the so-called Bakr Abān)[157] and those of them from the Banū Ḥanẓalah at al-Ramaliyyah in the province of al-Ahwāz.[158]

He gave orders for the building of a city in the Sawād, which he called Buzurj Sābūr, [that is, Ukbarā, and another city which he

---

*Hayj*, is disturbed, and should should be corrected to *Dārīn wa-Samāhīj* in the light of the parallel passage in Ibn al-'Adīm's *Bughyat al-ṭalab*. It is not surprising that Nöldeke, trans. 57 n. 2, was unable to find anything about a putative place called Hayj. In fact, we have here reference to two distinct places. Dārīn was the main town of the island of Tarut, still known today as such and lying in the bay off the eastern Arabian coast near the modern towns of al-Qaṭīf and al-Dammām. Samāhij was a village on the island of al-Muḥarraq lying just off the northern edge of the main al-Baḥrayn island (and now linked to it by a causeway); it is mentioned around this time as the seat of a Nestorian Christian bishopric. See the detailed discussion of these place-names by Joëlle Beaucamp and Chr. Robin, "L'évêché nestorien des Mâšmâhîg dans l'archipel d'al-Baḥrayn (V$^{e}$–IX$^{e}$ siècle)," 171–96; D. T. Potts, *The Arabian Gulf in Antiquity*, II, 151–52.

157. Bakr b. Wā'il were also a tribe of Rabī'ah, originally nomadizing in the Yamāmah region, but, also like the Taghlib, migrating northward to the desert fringes of the lower and middle Euphrates. Hence they came into contact with the Lakhmids, especially after Taghlib moved on again into Upper Mesopotamia, and began to clash with the rival pastoralists of Tamīm, a discord subsequently reflected in the events leading up to the skirmish of Dhū Qār (see al-Ṭabarī, I, 1030, pp. 359–60 below). Several leading poets of Bakr, including Ṭarafah b.'Abd, al-Ḥārith b. Ḥillizah, and al-A'shā Maymūn, came within the cultural ambit of the Lakhmid court. See Ibn al-Kalbī-Caskel-Strenziok, *Jamharat al-nasab*, I, Tables 141, 162–66, II, 22–23, 223; *EI*$^{2}$, s.v. Bakr b. Wā'il (W. Caskel).

Abān was a place in eastern Fārs, lying to the southeast of Yazd in the district of Rūdhān, and is now the modern town of Anār. See Nöldeke, trans., 57 n. 3; Le Strange, *Lands*, 286; Schwarz, *Iran*, 21, 191–92.

158. Ḥanẓalah b. Mālik were a subdivision of the great tribe of Tamīm b. Murrah or Ma'add, forming the main group within its branch of Zayd Manāt. Tamīm's center was in Yamāmah, where they were rivals and opponents of the Rabī'ah tribes of Taghlib and Bakr. Tamīm in general had close connections with the Sāsānids and Lakhmids, cooperating with the Persian authorities in Hajar and policing trade routes across central Arabia to Yemen for the above two powers. See Ibn al-Kalbī-Caskel-Strenziok, *Jamharat al-nasab*, I, Tables 59, 68, 72–73, II, 7–10, 298; *EI*$^{2}$, s.vv. Ḥanẓala b. Mālik (W. Montgomery Watt) and Tamīm b. Murra (M. Lecker).

Al-Ramaliyyah may well be the Qaryat al-Ramal of subsequent Islamic times situated in western Khūzistān, between Qurqūb and the Nahr Tīrā on or near the Karkhā affluent of the Kārūn. In the later third/eighth century, it was the scene of amphibious operations led by the Regent al-Muwaffaq against the Zanj rebels, according to al-Ṭabarī, III, 1952–53, tr. P. M. Fields, *The History of al-Ṭabarī, an Annotated Translation*, XXXVII, *The 'Abbāsid Recovery. The War against the Zanj Ends*, 17–18. See Nöldeke, trans. 57 n. 4; Schwarz, *Iran*, 368.

called Fayrūz Sābūr, that is] al-Anbār.[159] He further founded in the province of al-Ahwāz two cities, one called Īrān-Khurrah-Sābūr, [840] which means "Sābūr and his land," and which is called in Syriac al-Karkh, and the other al-Sūs, a city he built at the side of the fortress that has within it a sarcophagus containing the corpse of the prophet Dāniyāl (Daniel), may God pray over him and grant him peace.[160] He led an expedition into the land of the Romans, took a great number of prisoners there, and then planted [them] in the city of Īrān-Khurrah-Sābūr, which the Arabs called al-Sūs after

159. The interpolated words were supplied by Nöldeke; see text, n. *e*, and trans. 57 n. 5. 'Ukbarā, Syriac 'Okbarā, was a town on the east bank of the Tigris above Ctesiphon, famed for its gardens and vineyards. Arabic authorities like Ibn Khurradādhbih, Ḥamzah al-Iṣfahānī and Yāqūt confirm that its Persian name was indeed Buzurg Shāpūr. See Yāqūt, *Buldān*, IV, 142; Le Strange, *Lands*, 50–51. Anbār (for which, see n. 77 above) was doubtless meant as one of the fortified points in the belt of strongholds and garrisons (*masāliḥ*) protecting the Sawād, and would have had Arab auxiliaries planted along this line as frontier guards, the equivalent of the *limitanei* of the Romans and Byzantines on the opposite, western side of the Syrian Desert. Not mentioned by al-Ṭabarī but known from other Arabic sources, e.g., al-Balādhurī, *Futūḥ*, 298, is the defensive trench and rampart, the *khandaq Sābūr*, which the Sāsānid ruler had dug out from Hīt in the north to al-Kāẓimah, south of where the Islamic *miṣr* of al-Baṣrah was later to be laid out. See Altheim and Stiehl, *Die Araber in der Alten Welt*, II, 349–50; Frye, "The Political History of Iran under the Sasanians," 138.

160. The text is somewhat disturbed here, as pointed out by Altheim and Stehl, *Die Araber*, II, 352. The definition "Sābūr and his land" must in reality go with Īrān-Shahr-Sābūr, this being the first of Shābūr's two foundations; the second, Īrān-Khurrah-Sābūr, must be Sūs, especially as Ḥamzah al-Iṣfahānī, 47, specifically equates Khurrah Sābūr with al-Sūs. We thus have Īrān-Shahr-Sābūr = Karkh, and Irān-Khurrah-Sābūr = Sūs.

Both towns lay in the ancient region of Susiana. Al-Karkh(ah) (Syriac *karkh* = "fortified town") appears in the Eastern Christian sources as Karkhā dhə Lēdhān or Rēdhān, and was the seat of a Nestorian bishop; it was situated near Susa/al-Sūs, with its present site marked by the ruins called locally Aywān-i Karkh. See Yāqūt, *Buldān*, IV, 449, Marquart, *Ērānšahr*, 145; Le Strange, *Lands*, 240; Barthold, *Historical Geography*, 185; Markwart-Messina, *Catalogue of the Provincial Capitals*, 97; Altheim and Stiehl, op. cit., II, 353–55; *EI*[2], s.v. Karkha (P. Schwarz-A. Miquel); *EIr*, s.v. Ērān-Xwarrah-Šābuhr (Rika Gyselen).

(Al-)Sūs was the early Islamic form for the ancient city of Susa (also the seat of a bishopric in later Sāsānid and early Islamic times), which lay on the plain between the Kārūn and Kharkhā rivers. One of its greatest attractions for religious devotees was that it claimed to have the tomb of Daniel, the Islamic prophet Dāniyāl, although another town of Khūzistān, Rustar or Shushtar, also claimed to have it. See Yāqūt, *Buldān*, III, 280–81; Nöldeke, trans. 58 n. 1; Marquart, *Ērānšahr*, 144–45; Le Strange, *Lands*, 240–41; Schwarz, *Iran*, 358–64; Markwart-Messina, *Catalogue of the Provincial Capitals*, 96–90; Barthold, *Historical Geography*, 185–86; *EI*[2], s.vv. Dāniyāl (G. Vajda), al-Sūs (M. Streck-C. E. Bosworth).

shortening the name.[161] He gave orders also for the building of a city in Bā Jarmā, which he called Khunī[162] Sābūr (?), which he laid out as an administrative region (*kūrah*) and for the building of a city in the land of Khurāsān, which he named Naysābūr and likewise laid it out as an administrative region.[163]

Sābūr had made a truce with Qusṭanṭīn (Constantine), the King of the Romans, the one who built Constantinople and who was the first king of the Romans who became a Christian.[164] Qusṭanṭīn died, and his kingdom was divided between three of his sons, who also died, so that the Romans appointed as their king a man from Qusṭanṭīn's house named Lulyānūs (Julian[us]), who was an adherent of the religion of the Romans that had prevailed before Christianity.[165] He used to conceal this, and ostensibly follow Christianity before he became king, but when he actually came to power he openly proclaimed his adhesion to the religion of the [ancient] Romans, restored it in its former state, and gave orders for its revival. He commanded that the churches should be pulled

---

161. On Shābūr's deportations and plantations of prisoners of war, see Nöldeke, trans. 59 n. 1; *EIr*, s.v. Deportations. ii. In the Parthian and Sasanian Periods (E. Ketterhofen), at VII, 299.

162. Text, *J.nī*, thought Nöldeke though that the whole name was dubious. For Bā Jarmā, see al-Ṭabarī, I, 827, p. 32 and n. 98 above.

163. Naysābūr, the Arabised form of MP Nēw-Shāhbuhr, NP Nīkū Shābūr Nīshābūr, less correctly Nīshāpūr, "fair [city] of Shābūr." Some sources attribute its foundation to Shābūr I, e.g., Ḥamzah al-Iṣfahānī, *Ta'rīkh*, 44, presumably to be considered as part of his consolidation of power in the realm described in al-Ṭabarī, I, 819–20, pp. 14–15 above. Others attribute its foundation to Shābūr II, and if he was its founder, this action may have been part of his activities in the East against the "Kushans," *Cuseni*, which are poorly documented but which apparently fell within the 350s or 360s while Shāpūr was also disputing control of Armenia with the Romans. What may have happened was a rebuilding by Shābūr II of his great-grandfather's original foundation. See in addition to the references in n. 59 above, Yāqūt, V, 331–33; Nöldeke, trans. 59 n. 3; Marquart, *Ērānšahr*, 50; R. Ghirsham and T. Ghirshman, *Les Chionites-Hephtalites*, 70–74.

164. Constantine the Great (r. 324–37). See on him *PW*, IV/1, s.v. Constantinus (der Grosse) (Benjamin).

165. Julian the Apostate (r. 361–63), successor to Constantine I's second son Constantine II, was actually the son of a half-brother of Constantine the Great. See on him *PW*, XI/1, s.v. Iulianus (Apostata) (E. von Borries). The rendering here with initial *l-* stems from a Syriac form of the name, see Nöldeke, trans. 60 n. 1, who also in 59 n. 4 points out that the following information is of no historical value, but must stem from the Syriac romance of the Emperor Julian, see his "Ueber den syrischen Roman von Kaiser Julian," 291–92 (see on this romance p. 63 n. 173 below).

down and that the bishops and learned scholars of the Christians should be killed. He assembled contingents of the Romans and Khazars,[166] and of the Arabs who were within his kingdom, in order to use them for making war on Sābūr and the armies of Persia.

The Arabs seized that opportunity as an occasion for revenge on Sābūr for his killing the Arabs. One hundred and seventy thousand Arab warriors were gathered together in Lulyānūs's army.[167] The latter sent them forward under the command of one of the Patricians of the Romans called Yūsānūs (Jovian[us]),[168] whom he placed in charge of his vanguard. Lulyānūs marched on until he [841]

---

166. Nöldeke, trans. 60 n. 2, thought that this anachronistic mention of the Turkish Khazars was an interpolation in the text of al-Ṭabarī's source, since the Khazars do not firmly appear in Middle Eastern history till the early seventh century, when they were allies of Byzantium against the Persians in Transcaucasia; see *EI²*, s.v. Khazar (W. Barthold and P. B. Golden). Shahîd has suggested, in his *Byzantium and the Arabs in the Fourth Century*, 116 n. 38, that al-Ṭabarī's "Khazars" were probably Goths (an important auxiliary element in the Roman forces at this time, the same nation whom Ammianus Marcellinus (see below, n. 167) calls "Scythians"), but this seems unlikely. It is admittedly true that the Scythians, the original Goths, and the Khazars all inhabited the South Russia-lower Volga basin region.

167. The undeniable, if in many ways obscure, Arab dimension to Julian's short, eighteen-months' reign, has been considered in close and perspicuous detail by Shahîd in his *Byzantium and the Arabs in the Fourth Century*, especially at 82–86, 110ff. and 132–37, depending, on the classical side, on such sources as the Latin historian Ammianus Marcellinus's *Res gestae*, the Greek Libanius's *Orations* and some church historians. Julian's own attitude toward the Arabs was somewhat ambiguous, but became generally hostile: he himself describes them as *lēstas* "robbers," echoing Ammianus's stigmatizing of them as a *natio perniciosa*. But here it is very probably the *Sarakenoi*, the nomadic Arabs of the desert interiors of Syria, Palestine, Sinai, and Egypt who are envisaged; whereas, the Romans' prime contact with the Arabs was with the sedentary or semisedentary ones of the borderlands between the desert and the town, the *foederati* or confederates, many of them Christianized, those who at the time of the Arab conquests are described in the sources as *musta'ribah*. Shahîd argues that Julian failed to make the best use of the Arab auxiliary element in his forces when he thrust through the northern part of the Syrian Desert via his concentration point at Callinicum (the later Islamic al-Raqqah) across the Euphrates at Ctesiphon. For the Arabs were familiar with the terrain, as well as with the Middle Eastern climate, whereas the Roman troops were more used to fighting in the temperate climes of Europe and the Mediterranean basin. Also, whereas many elements back in Rome were lukewarm about the Persian campaign, arguing that the threat from the Goths was a more imminent one than that from the Persians, the Arabs were, as al-Ṭabarī notes, eager to take vengeance for Shābūr's savage treatment of their compatriots in eastern Arabia.

168. The Syriac form of Jovian's name, according to Nöldeke, trans. 60 n. 4.

reached the land of Persia. When Sābūr got news of the magnitude of Lulyānūs's army—Romans, Arabs, and Khazars—he became alarmed, and sent out spies to bring back to him information about the size of their forces and their state of fighting spirit and effectiveness for wreaking damage. But the reports these spies brought back to him concerning Lulyānūs and his troops were at variance with each other. Hence Sābūr disguised himself and went along with a group of some men from his trusty entourage to see for themselves the opposing army. When he drew near to the army of Yūsānūs, the commander of Lulyānūs's vanguard, he sent forward a small group from those accompanying him to Yūsānūs's army, in order that they might ferret out information and bring back to him authentic reports. However, the Romans became aware of them, seized them, and brought them back to Yūsānūs. Not one of them confessed the purpose for which they had gone out to Yūsānūs's army except for one man, who told Yūsānūs about the whole affair, exactly as it was, and where Sābūr was, and who asked Yūsānūs to send back with him a detachment of troops so that he might bring Sābūr back to them. But when Yūsānūs heard this story, he sent to Sābūr one of his own close intimates who would tell him what Yūsānūs had learned about Sābūr's position and warn him. Sābūr accordingly rode away rapidly, back to his own army. The Arab troops in Lulyānūs's army asked him for
[842] permission to launch an attack on Sābūr and he acceded to their request. So they advanced toward Sābūr, fought with him, routed his force and wrought great slaughter among them. Sābūr fled, together with what remained of his army, and Lulyānūs took possession of Sābūr's seat of power, the city of Ctesiphon, and seized Sābūr's stores of wealth and treasuries there.[169]

169. Julian's army advanced into Persian Mesopotamia in spring 363 and won a great victory over Shābūr outside Ctesiphon. Al-Ṭabarī emphasizes the outstanding role of the Arab auxiliary troops here, presumably as mounted lancers within the cavalry division of the army, whereas Ammianus Marcellinus does not mention it. Shahîd, *Byzantium and the Arabs in the Fourth Century,* 117, notes the Latin historian's dislike of the Arabs, and thinks that the truth may be somewhere in between the two partisan viewpoints; for Nöldeke, however, trans. 61 n. 1, the emphasis on the Arab role was a later addition to the story by an Arab hand concerned to vaunt the exploits of his nation. Despite the victory in the field over the Persian army, Ctesiphon resisted a siege by the Romans (*pace* al-Ṭabarī's information here that it was captured), and in June 363 Julian and his forces turned

Sābūr at that point sent letters to those elements of his army in distant regions, telling them what he had suffered at the hands of Lulyānūs and his Arab contingents, and he ordered all the commanders there to hasten back to him with the troops of his army under their command. Very soon, armies from all quarters of the land had gathered round him. He then marched back again, attacked Lulyānūs, and recovered from him the city of Ctesiphon. Luliyānūs encamped with his army at the city of Bih-Ardashīr[170] and in the region nearby. Envoys were at this point going backward and forward between him and Sābūr. One day, however, Lulyānūs was seated in his chamber when a stray arrow, from an invisible hand, struck him in the heart and killed him.[171]

The hearts of his troops were thrown into perturbation, and they became fearful because of what had happened to him. They fell into despair about extracting themselves from the land of Persia. They coalesced into an advisory council, with no king or leader, and asked Yūsānūs if he would take over the business of ruling, and they would accordingly raise him to the throne. He refused this, however, and when they pressed him, he told them that he was a Christian and that he would not rule over a people who were opposed to him in religion; but the Romans told him that they were really Christians too, and that they had only concealed this in fear of Lulyānūs. So he agreed to their request, and they made him their king and publicly displayed their Christian faith.[172]

---

back toward Antioch. Al-Dīnawarī, *al-Akhbār al-ṭiwāl,* 50, states that Julian's army occupied the city of Ctesiphon but were held up outside its citadel (*qaṣr*), with Julian killed by a stray arrow in the course of the siege.

170. That is, Seleucia, the Bihrasīr of al-Ṭabarī, I, 819, p. 15 above.

171. The circumstances of Julian's sudden death in June 363 were mysterious. Contemporaries were unsure whether he was killed, as al-Ṭabarī says, by a stray arrow or lance thrust, or whether he was struck down by an assassin; and if the latter, was the murderer in the pay of the Persians or one from Julian's own troops? The possibility that the assassin was an Arab and that it was the result of a grudge against the emperor (since according to Ammianus, Julian had withheld the Arab troops' pay) is discussed by Shahîd, *Byzantium and the Arabs in the Fourth Century,* 124–31.

172. On Julian's death, the Roman troops offered the imperial crown first to the Praetorian Prefect Salutius Secundus, who refused it, and then to the commander Jovian. See E. Stein, *Histoire du Bas-Empire,* I, 169–71.

Sābūr came to know about Lulyānūs's death, and sent a message to the commanders of the Roman army in which he said, "God has brought you into our power and has made us to prevail over you, in return for your violence towards us and your trampling over our
[843] land. We hope that you will perish there from hunger without our having to wield a sword against you in battle or to point a spear at you; but dispatch to us a leader [to treat with us], if you have appointed a leader over yourselves." Yūsānūs resolved to go to Sābūr, even though none of his army commanders agreed with his judgment in this. Nevertheless, he insisted on following his own view here and went to Sābūr with a guard of eighty of the noble warriors from his camp and from his army, and wearing his crown. Sābūr received news of his coming; he went out to meet him, and each of them prostrated themselves before the other [in obeisance], and then Sābūr embraced Yūsānūs out of thankfulness for what he had previously done for him (i.e., letting him escape back to his camp). He feasted with Sābūr that day and felt at ease. Sābūr sent a message to the commanders of the Roman army and their leaders informing them that, if they had raised to power anyone except Yūsānūs, their destruction in the land of Persia would have ensued, and that their appointing Yūsānūs as their king had [alone] preserved them from his violence. Yūsānūs's prestige became strong through his action [on this occasion].

Sābūr continued: "The Romans have launched attacks into our land and have killed a great number of people. They have chopped down date palms and other trees in the Sawād, and have ruined its agricultural prosperity. So either you must pay us the full value of what you have destroyed and ruined, or else you must hand over to us, in recompense for all that damage, the town of Niṣībīn and its surrounding region." Niṣībīn had previously been part of the kingdom of Persia, but the Romans had then conquered it. Yūsānūs and the leading commanders of his army agreed to Sābūr's demand for reparations, and handed over Niṣībīn to him. The people of Niṣībīn heard about this, and emigrated from there to various cities in the Roman empire, fearful of their safety under the power of a king opposed to their own religion (sc., to Christianity). When news of this reached Sābūr, he transferred twelve thousand persons of good lineage from among the people of Iṣṭakhr, Iṣbahān, and other regions of his country and his provinces, to Niṣībīn, and settled them there. Yūsānūs returned with his troops to Roman territory, where he reigned for only a short time and then died.[173]

Right up to his death, Sābūr became occupied with great eagerness in killing the Arabs and tearing out the shoulder-blades of [844] their leaders; this was why they called him Dhū al-Aktāf "The Man of the Shoulders." Certain of the historians (*ahl al-akhbār*) mention that after Sābūr had wrought great slaughter among the Arabs and had expelled them from the regions they had entered, namely the lands adjoining Fārs, al-Baḥrayn and al-Yamāmah,[174] he went down into Syria and proceeded to the frontiers of the Roman empire.[175] He explained to his companions that he intended to enter the territory of the Romans in order to find out

173. Jovian died at Dadastana in central Anatolia en route from Antioch to Constantinople, thus terminating his brief reign of slightly more than six months (363–64). See on him *PW*, IX/2, s.v. Iovianus (Seeck). It seems quite likely that may Christians did flee from Niṣībīn before the Persians and that Shāpūr did resettle Persians from the interior of his kingdom in this strategically placed city of Niṣībin. The infusion of a Persian ethnic element there helps perhaps to explain the city's preference thereafter for the Persian connection. Jovian's action in making peace with Shāpūr enabled the Roman army to withdraw intact, but at the price of the cession of Niṣībīn, Singara (Sinjār), and the territories in Upper Mesopotamia conquered by Diocletian more than sixty years before. The peace treaty was, however, regarded by contemporaries in the Roman empire as a dishonorable one. Agathias expressed this view when he called it "a shameful and disgraceful truce, so bad that it is even now (i.e., ca. 570) harmful to the Roman state"; see Cameron, "Agathias on the Sassanians," 124–25, 146. From this time onward, Niṣībīn was to be the great bastion of Persian arms against Roman and Byzantine attacks and pressure from the west, and was never to return to Christian control.

The preceeding story of the Roman-Persian warfare during Shabūr's reign is paralleled in the account of these events in the Syriac romance of the Emperor Julian, an original Syriac work and not a translation from Greek, probably written in Roman-held Edessa. Nöldeke thought that it was directly or indirectly known to the Arabs, since al-Ṭabarī's account, derived from Ibn al-Kalbī, accords in general with the romance, especially in such episodes as Julian's being killed by a stray arrow, Shābūr's secret visit to the enemy encampment and his personal understanding with Jovian. See his "Ueber den syrischen Roman von Kaiser Julian," 263–92.

174. This is a sketchy and not very accurate résumé of Shabūr's campaigns in eastern Arabia in the year 326 already described by al-Ṭabarī, I, 836–37, pp. 51–52 above.

175. The following story apparently contradicts the previous narrative of the warfare of Julian and Jovian with Shābūr, but is in Nöldeke's view, trans. 64 n. 2, really a genuine Persian recounting, not of events in the time of Shābūr II but of those in the time of Shābūr I (see al-Ṭabarī, I, 826–27, pp. 28–31 above), the captured Qayṣar being, of course, Valerian.

their secrets and to acquire information about their cities and the numbers of their troops. Accordingly, he entered Roman territory and wandered about there for a considerable period of time. News reached him that Qayṣar had given a great feast and had ordered all the people to be gathered together to attend his feast. Sābūr set out, therefore, disguised as a beggar, with the aim of attending that gathering, so that he might thereby see Qayṣar, familiarize himself with his appearance, and discern how he behaved at his feast. But his identity was discovered; he was arrested and Qayṣar gave orders for him to be wrapped in a bull's hide.

Qayṣar now traveled with his troops toward the land of Persia, bearing with him Sābūr in that condition. He made extensive slaughter and destroyed many cities and villages, and cut down date palms and other trees until finally he came to the city of Junday Sābūr. The local people had fortified themselves in it, but Qayṣar set up ballistas (*majānīq*) and demolished part of the city. While matters stood thus, the Roman guards entrusted with watching over Sābūr were negligent one night. There were some prisoners from al-Ahwāz in his vicinity, so he instructed them to pour oil from nearby skins on to his bonds. They did this; the ox hide became soft, and he wriggled out of the bonds. He then slipped quietly away until he drew near to the city gate. He told the city guards who he was. When he came out among its people,
[845] they were overjoyed at seeing him. Their voices were raised in praise and invocations to God, to such an extent that Qayṣar's troops woke up at the sound of the voices.[176]

Sābūr gathered together all those who were in the city, provided them with weapons and equipment, and marched out against the Romans that very same night toward the morning. He killed the Romans, took Qayṣar captive and seized as booty his treasuries

176. The whole story of Sābūr's foray into the Roman camp, his capture, and escape, is part of a well-known topos, that of the prince slipping behind enemy lines in disguise for spying purposes. Nöldeke, trans. 65 n. 1, cites such a role being ascribed to Alexander the Great in the *Alexander Romance*, the legendary biography of the emperor by Pseudo-Callisthenes (whence taken over by Firdawsī into the Persian epic) (see Nöldeke, "Beiträge zur Geschichte des Alexanderromans," 1–56); to a Roman emperor, probably Galerius (r. 305–11) by Synesius; and here to Shābūr, being taken, as already noted, from the Syriac Julian Romance.

and his womenfolk. Then he loaded Qayṣar with iron fetters and required him to restore to prosperity all that he had ruined. It is said that Sābūr required him to bring earth from the Roman lands to al-Madā'in and Junday Sābūr, so that he might thereby restore what he had destroyed, and to plant olive trees in place of the date palms and other trees he had chopped down. Then he cut off Qayṣar's heels, sewed them up, and sent him back to the Romans on an ass with the words, "This is your punishment for your crimes against us." Because of that, the Romans abandoned the use of straps over the heels (i.e., for shoes and sandals) and sewed up the parts of the shoes hanging down over the feet.[177]

Sābūr remained in his kingdom for a considerable time, and then he led an expedition against the Romans. He killed many of them and took many captives. He settled these last in a city he built in the vicinity of al-Sūs and called it Īrānshahr-Sābūr. Then he sought peace with the Arabs, and settled some tribes of Taghlib, 'Abd al-Qays, and Bakr b. Wā'il in Kirmān, Tawwaj,[178] and al-Ahwāz. He built the city of Naysābūr and other cities in Sind and Sijistān.[179] He had a physician brought from India and established him at al-Karkh by al-Sūs; when this man died, the people of Sūs

177. Nöldeke observed in his text, n. *b*, that he had not correctly understood this last sentence when he made his translation, 66. Other Arabic sources, including Ibn Qutaybah, *Ma'ārif*, 657–58, and al-Mas'ūdī, *Murūj*, II, 181–83 = §§ 605–606, 608, give the story of Sābūr's spying mission, his capture, his being sewn up in a bull's hide, and his escape. This last historian, ibid., II, 184 = § 607, gives the story of Sābūr's mutilation of the captured Qayṣar in a slightly different form: that he shod with iron the Roman's feet after cutting his Achilles tendons and cauterizing his heels, which is why the Rūm subsequently did not shoe their horses with iron or themselves wear boots with heels (*al-khifāf al-mu'aqqabah*).

178. Tawwaj or Tawwaz was an ancient town, the Taokē mentioned in the itinerary of Alexander's Indian campaign and in the classical geographers. It lay in western Fārs on the Shābūr river about midway between Kāzarūn and the Persian Gulf shore. In early Islamic times it was an important center of the textile trade, but in later mediaeval times it fell into ruins, and its exact site is now unknown. See Yāqūt, *Buldān*, II, 56–57; Le Strange, *Lands*, 259–60; Schwarz, *Iran*, 66–68; Wilson, *The Persian Gulf*, 74–75; Markwart-Messina, *A Catalogue of the Provincial Capitals*, 94–95; Barthold, *Historical Geography*, 163; *EI*, s.v. Tawwadj (C. E. Bosworth).

179. It is unlikely that Shābūr could have built cities in a frontier province like Sijistān, disputed with the Sakas and their epigoni, and almost impossible that he could have constructed any in the Indian province of Sind, at this time under local Brahman rulers.

inherited his medical skill, and for this reason the people of that region are the most expert of medical practitioners among the Persians.[180] Shābūr bequeathed the royal power to his brother Ardashīr (II). Sābūr's reign lasted seventy-two years.[181]

---

180. Although the Arabic sources mention an Indian connection for the foundation of medical studies as Sūs and Jundayshābūr, it is difficult to discern any factual basis for this beyond a general belief in early Islamic society that Indian physicians were especially skillful, a belief that was perpetuated because of the infinitesimal number of Indian physicians known against which the belief could be tested (but cf. the story given by al-Ṭabarī, III, 747–48, of Hārūn al-Rashīd's summoning from India the physician Mankah to treat an obstinate illness). Much clearer than Indian influences are the undoubted Hellenistic ones brought by persons resettled in Khūzistān from the Byzantine lands and by Nestorian Christian immigrants, who brought the traditions and techniques of the medical schools of Antioch and Alexandria. See *EI²*, s.v. Gondēshāpūr (Aydın Sayılı).

181. Shābūr II's reign was 309–79. Shabūr's name appears on his coins as ŠḤPW-ḤRY. See on his coins Paruck, *Sāsānian Coins*, 58–59, 341–52, 430–35, Plates IX–XI, Tables VI–VIII; Göbl, *Sasanian Numismatics*, 46–47, Table VI, Plates 6–7; Sellwood, Whitting, and Williams, *An Introduction to Sasanian Coins*, 21, 99–103; Malek, "A Survey of Research on Sasanian Numismatics," 234–35.

The other Arabic sources on his reign include Ibn Qutaybah, *Ma'ārif*, 656–59; al-Ya'qūbī, *Ta'rīkh*, I, 182–83 (his raids on and violence against the Arabs, and his wars with the Romans); al-Dīnawarī, *al-Akhbār al-ṭiwāl*, 47–51 (a very detailed section: the raids into Jazīrah and the Sawād by a Ghassānid king [cf. Shahîd, *Byzantium and the Arabs in the Fourth Century*, 117], Shabūr's attacks on al-Ḥaḍr, his war with Julian [here called Mānūs!] and acquisition of Niṣībīn, and his urban foundations); al-Mas'ūdī, *Murūj*, II, 175–89 = §§ 601–11 (much detail on the attacks of the Arabs on Iraq and Shābūr's revenge, his adventures in Rūm and his plantation of Byzantine captives in Khūzistān); idem, *Tanbīh*, 100, trans. 144; Ḥamzah al-Iṣfahānī, *Ta'rīkh*, 47–48 (his raids on the Arabs, his being captured while spying in Rūm, his captivity, his gaining of Niṣībīn, and his building works); Ibn al-Athīr, *Kāmil*, I, 392–97. Of Persian sources, see Ṭabarī-Bal'amī, trans. II, 91–102. Of modern studies on Shābūr II's reign in general, see Christensen, *Sassanides*, 234–53; Frye, *The Heritage of Persia*, 224; idem, "The Political History of Iran under the Sasanians," 132–41, 178; *EI¹*, s.v. Shāpūr (V. F. Büchner); *EI²*, s.vv. Sāsānids (M. J. Morony), Shāpūr (C. E. Bosworth).

Nöldeke, trans. 68 n. 1, noted that the Arabic and Persian sources used by al-Ṭabarī and other Islamic writers mention nothing of Shābūr's persecutions of the Christian community in Persia and, to a lesser extent, of the Jews and Manichaeans. The great sufferings of the Christians are, however, known to us from the Syriac *Acts of the Martyrs* and from such works as Sozomenus's *Ecclesiastical History*. Thus in 341 the Catholicos in the see of Seleucia-Ctesiphon (whose primacy had only become established with difficulty in the mid-fourth century), Simon Bar Ṣabba'ē, was martyred after he had protested his inability to burden his indigent community with the capitation tax at double rate in order to finance Shābūr's wars with the Romans/Byzantines; and two years later, Narsēs, the metropolitan of Bēth Garmāyē, was arrested and executed. Given that Shābūr was

## *[The History of al-Ḥīrah]*

During the reign of Sābūr, his governor over the desert fringes of Muḍar and Rabī'ah was Imru' al-Qays al-Bad' b. 'Amr b. 'Adī b. Rabī'ah b. Naṣr, and then Sābūr appointed over the latter's governorship his son, 'Amr b. Imri' al-Qays, according to what has been mentioned. He remained in the office for the remainder of Sābūr's reign, the whole of his brother Ardashīr (II), son of Hurmuz (II) b. Narsī's reign and part of that of Sābūr (III), son of Sābūr (II). The [846] total length of his governorship over the Arabs, as I have just mentioned, and his exercise of authority over them, amounted to thirty years, according to Ibn al-Kalbī.[182]

## *[Ardashīr II]*

Then there took charge of the royal power, after Sābūr (II) Dhū al-Aktāf, his brother Ardashīr.

[He was] the son of Hurmuz (II), son of Narsī, son of Bahrām (II), son of Bahrām (I), son of Hurmuz (I), son of Sābūr (I), son of Ardashīr (I), son of Bābak. After he was crowned, he sat there [to receive] the great men of state. When they came into his presence, they prayed for his victoriousness and conveyed thanks to him for his brother Sābūr. Ardashīr replied to them enthusiastically and told them about the warm place in his heart for their thanks to him regarding his brother. When he was securely on the throne, he turned his attention to the great men and the holders of authority,

---

indeed much involved with warfare against the Christian Romans/Byzantines, a political element was doubtless at work here, but the king is known to have hated the Christians and to have been a keen enforcer of Zoroastrian orthodoxy within his dominions. Christians could not accept elements like the sun, earth, and fire as objects of cultic reverence, and found such Zoroastrian practices as marriage within close degrees of relationship as equally abhorrent. Shābūr's reign was the worst thirty or forty years or so that the Christians of Persia had to endure, and the total ruin of Christianity within Persia was only averted by his death and the succession of kings who either did not wish to continue his policy or did not have the means to do so. See Labourt, *Le Christianisme dans l'empire perse,* 20–25, 43–82; J. P. Asmussen, "Christians in Iran," 936–39. Shabūr's reign concomitantly saw a rise in power and prestige of the Zoroastrian priesthood, whom a strong monarch like Shābūr could afford to cultivate and shower with favors.

182. The middle and later decades of the fourth century are an obscure period in the history of the Lakhmids. See Rothstein, *Laḫmiden,* 41ff.

and killed a great number of them, The people then deposed him from power after a reign of four years.[183]

## *[Sābūr III]*

Then there assumed the royal power Sābūr.

He was the son of Sābūr (II) Dhū al-Aktāf, son of Hurmuz (II), son of Narsī. The subjects rejoiced at his accession and at the return of his father's royal authority to him. He met with them in the most handsome way possible, and wrote letters to the provincial governors enjoining them to good conduct and to kindness with the subjects, and he ordered the same thing to his viziers, secretaries, and court entourage, and addressed them in eloquent terms. He continued to behave justly to his subjects, showing compassion to them because of the love, affection, and obedience they clearly bore him. His paternal uncle, the deposed Ardashīr (II), behaved submissively toward him and vouchsafed obedience to him. But the great men of state (*al-ʿuẓamāʾ*) and the members of noble houses (*ahl al-buyūtāt*) cut the ropes of a large tent Sābūr had had erected in one of his palace courts, and the tent fell down on top of him [and killed him]. He had reigned for five years.[184]

---

183. Ardashīr II's reign was 379–83. As Nöldeke, trans. 69 n. 2, remarked, Ardashīr must have been an old man when he came to the throne, since he was only slightly younger than his half-brother Shabūr II, and he lived on into the next reign of Shābūr III (see below). Ardashīr had been a governor at Ḥajab in Adiabene for Shābūr II, and his depiction of himself in the Tāq-i Bustān rock reliefs, together with his brother, as subduers of a slain Roman emperor (possibly Julian; see R. Sellheim, "Ṭāq-i Bustān und Kaiser Julian (361–363)," 354–66), implies that he participated in Shābūr's wars with the Romans. Al-Ṭabarī's information that Ardashīr slaughtered many of the nobility points to his being a strong personality who continued Shābūr's policy of firm rule. Ardashīr's name appears on his coins as 'RTḤŠTR. See on his coins Paruck, *Sāsānian Coins,* 59, 352–53, 435–36, XII, Table VIII; Göbl, *Sasanian Numismatics,* 47, Table VII, Plate 7; Sellwood, Whitting, and Williams, *An Introduction to Sasanian Coins,* 21, 104–105; Malek, "A Survey of Research on Sasanian Numismatics," 235.

The other Arabic sources on his reign include Ibn Qutaybah, *Maʿārif,* 659; al-Yaʿqūbī, *Taʾrīkh,* I, 183; al-Masʿūdī, *Murūj,* II, 189 = § 611; idem, *Tanbīh,* 100, trans. 144; Ḥamzah al-Iṣfahānī, 48; Ibn al-Athīr, *Kāmil,* I, 397. Of Persian sources, see Ṭabarī-Balʿamī, trans. II, 102. Of modern studies, see Christensen, *Sassanides,* 254–55; Frye, "The Political History of Iran under the Sasanians," 141, 178; *EIr,* s.v. Ardašīr II (A. Sh. Shahbazi).

184. Shābūr III's reign was 383–88. As Nöldeke, trans., 70 n. 2, observed, the

[847]

## [Bahrām IV]

Then there assumed the royal power after him his brother Bahrām (IV).

[He was] the son of Sābūr (II) Dhū al-Aktāf, and had the title of Kirmān-Shāh, since his father Sābūr had made him governor of Kirmān during his own lifetime.[185] He wrote a letter to his army commanders urging them to obedience and adjuring them to fear God and to furnish sound advice to the king. At Kirmān he built a city. He governed his subjects in a commendable fashion and was praised for his rule. His reign lasted eleven years. A group of murderous evildoers rose up against him, and one of them killed him by shooting an arrow at him.[186]

---

briefness of the reigns of Shābūr III and his two successors, as well as their violent ends, show that this was a "time of troubles" for the Sāsānid state, with enfeeblement of the crown and aggrandizement of the nobility. It was fortunate for the Persians that Rome was largely preoccupied with the Goths; the readjustments to the frontiers between Persian-protected Armenia and the smaller, Roman-protected part were achieved peacefully in the reigns of Shabūr III and Bahrām IV. Shābūr' s name appears on his coins as ŠḤPWḤRY. See on his coins Paruck, *Sāsānian Coins,* 59–60, 3534–56, 437–40, Plate XII, Table IX; Göbl, *Sasanian Numismatics,* 47–48, Table VII, Plate 8; Sellwood, Whitting, and Williams, *An Introduction to Sasanian Coins,* 21, 106–107; Malek, "A Survey of Research on Sasanian Numismatics," 235.

The other Arabic sources on Shābūr's reign include Ibn Qutaybah, *Ma'ārif,* 659; al-Ya'qūbī, *Ta'rīkh,* I, 183 (his death under the collapsing tent); al-Mas'ūdī, *Murūj,* II, 189 = § 611 (his wars against the Arabs of Iyād and other tribes; a confusion with the activities of Shābūr II?); idem, *Tanbīh,* 100, trans. 144; Ḥamzah al-Iṣfahānī, 48; Ibn al-Athīr, *Kāmil,* I, 397–98. Of Persian sources, see Ṭabarī-Bal'amī, trans. II, 89. For recent studies on his reign, see Christensen, *Sassanides,* 256–57, 259; Frye, "The Political History of Iran under the Sasanians," 141, 178.

185. It nevertheless seems more probable, as already noted by Nöldeke, trans. 71 n. 2, that Bahrām was a son of Shābūr III.

186. Bahrām IV's reign was 388–99. His name appears on his coins as WRḤR'N. See on his coins Paruck, *Sāsānian Coins,* 60–61, 356–60, 440–43, Plates XII–XIII, Table X; Göbl, *Sasanian Numismatics,* 48, Table VIII, Plate 8; Sellwood, Whitting, and Williams, *An Introduction to Sasanian Coins,* 21, 108–11; Malek, "A Survey of Research on Sasanian Numismatics," 235.

The other Arabic sources on his reign include Ibn Qutaybah, *Ma'ārif,* 659; al-Ya'qūbī, *Ta'rīkh,* I, 183 (his pursuit of justice and good rule); al-Dīnawarī, *al-Akhbār al-ṭiwāl,* 51 (makes him the direct successor of his father Shabūr II) (*recte* III?); al-Mas'ūdī, *Murūj,* II, 190 = § 612; idem, *Tanbīh,* 101, trans. 144; Ḥamzah al-Iṣfahānī, *Ta'rīkh,* 48 (a proud, harsh ruler, negligent of his subjects' welfare); Ibn al-Athīr, *Kāmil,* I, 398. Of Persian sources, see Ṭabarī-Bal'amī, trans. II, 90–91. Of modern studies on his reign, see Christensen, *Sassanides,* 253–54, 269; Frye, "The Political History of Iran under the Sasanians," 142–43, 178; *EIr,* sv. Bahrām IV (O.

## [Yazdajird I]

Then there assumed the royal power after him Yazdajird (I).[187] He had the epithet of "The Sinful One" (*al-Athīm*),[188] and was the son of Bahrām (IV), who was called Kirmān-Shāh, son of Sābūr (II) Dhū al-Aktāf. Some of the scholars knowledgeable about the genealogies of the Persians say [on the other hand] that this Yazdajird the Sinful One was the brother of Bahrām, who had the title Kirmān-Shāh, and not his son, and they state that he was Yazdajird, son of Sābūr Dhū al-Aktāf. Among those who attribute this filiation to him and assert this, is Hishām b. Muḥammad (sc., Ibn al-Kalbī).[189]

According to what has been mentioned, he was rough and harsh and possessed many defects. One of the worst and most serious of these last, it is said, was that he did not use his keenness of intellect, his good education, and the wide-ranging varieties of knowledge he had thoroughly mastered in their proper place, and also his extensive delving into harmful things and his use of all the powers he possessed for deceiving people, using his sharpness, wiles, and
[848] trickery —all this together with his keen mind, which had a propensity toward evil-doing, and his intense enjoyment in employing these faculties of his. Also, he scoffed at and poured scorn upon other people's knowledge and cultural attainments, counting them as of no account, and he paraded at length before people his own achievements. In addition to all that, he was ill-natured, of

---

Klíma). The name of the town Bahrām built (when he was governor?) survives today as the small town of Kirmānshāh to the south-southeast of Yazd (and perhaps survives also in the name of the better-known Kirmānshāh of western Persia, cf. Nöldeke, trans., 71 n. 3).

187. Literally, "made by a god," Yazdgird being a MP formation from *yazad* (< Avestan *yazata-*) and *kird* (< Old Persian *kṛta-*) (*yazata-* denotes the lesser deities of Zoroastrianism, below the supreme position of Ahura Mazdā), Greek Isdigerdēs. See Nöldeke, trans. 72 n. 3; Justi, *Namenbuch*, 148–49; Chr. Bartholomae, *Altiranisches Wörterbuch*, cols. 443–48, 1279–80; Gignoux, *Noms propres sassanides*, no. 1047.

188. Ḥamzah al-Iṣfahānī, *Ta'rīkh*, 49, and al-Khwārazmī, *Mafātīḥ al-ʿulūm*, 103, give a Persian equivalent for *al-athīm al-mujrim*, which Nöldeke, trans. 72 n. 4, interpreted as *dabz* ("rough, harsh" = Arabic *ghalīẓ*) + *bazah* ("sin," whence *bazagar* "sinner").

189. The filiation is obviously confused here. Yazdagird I was the son of Shābūr III and thus the brother of Bahrām IV. See Nöldeke, trans. 73 n. I; Frye, *The Heritage of Persia*, genealogical table at p. 295.

bad morals, and of depraved propensities, to the point that his bad nature and violent temper made him consider minor lapses as great sins and and petty slips as enormities. As a result, no one, whatever close relationship he might have with him, ever dared to intercede on behalf of a person who had offended him in the slightest way. He was suspicious of people for the whole period of his life, and trusted no one in any thing whatever. He would never recompense anyone who had done a good service, but if he conferred the most exiguous benefit on a person, he made that out to be a great favor. If anyone was bold enough to speak to him over some matter which another person had already spoken to him about, he would say to him, "The person on whose behalf you have spoken to me, how much did he give you, or how much have you already received from him?"[190] Only delegations of envoys coming to him from the rulers of the various nations could speak with him on these things and similar topics. His subjects could only preserve themselves from his harshness and the affliction of his tyranny, and from the tout ensemble of his evil defects, by holding fast to the good customs of the rulers before his period of power and to their noble characters. They could only band together and help each other in the face of his reprehensible conduct and fear of his harshness. It was part of his policy that he should punish anyone guilty of an error in regard to him, or who had committed an offense against him, with such a severe penalty that the sum stipulated could never be gathered together by the offender in the space of three hundred years; and for the same reason, such a person would never be beaten with a number of lashes without expecting further punishment later on, which would be even more unpleasant. Whenever he received a report that one of his entourage had shown especial favor toward one of those dependent on him, or whom he had encouraged and patronized (*min ahl ṣināʿatihi*), or one of those of equal social standing (*[min ahl] ṭabaqatihi*), he sent him away from his service.[191]

---

190. A recognition, if evidence were necessary, of the antiquity in Persian life of the tradition of offering presents, *pīshkash,* in return for expected favors from a superior. See *EI*², s.vv. Hiba. iv. Persia (H. Busse), Pīshkash (A. K. S. Lambton).

191. The universally black picture of Yazdagird in the Islamic sources depending on the Persian historical tradition has been seen by modern scholars as the

When Yazdajird had achieved power, he had appointed as his [849] vizier Narsī, the outstandingly wise man of his age; Narsī was perfect in manners and education, excellent in all his conduct, and the preeminent figure among the men of his time. They used to call him Mihr Narsī or Mihr Narsih, and he had the by-name of al-Hazārbandah.[192] The subjects hoped that his policies and his abilities would take away some of Yazdajird's [bad] characteristics and that Narsī would have a beneficial effect on him. But when Yazdajird became firmly established on his throne, his contempt for the

---

reflection of a struggle between the king and such powerful and ambitious classes in the state as the nobility and the Zoroastrian priesthood. Nöldeke, trans. 74 n. 3, adduced as a counterbalance to this image, promulgated by aristocratic and clerical circles, the very favorable image of the king in contemporary Christian sources, and other faiths such as Judaism seem to have enjoyed more freedom during his time. According to one story (not, however, very probable), he married Shōshendukht, daughter of the Rēsh Gālūthā, the Jewish Exilarch; see Neusner, "Jews in Iran," 915. While Frye, "The Political History of Iran under the Sasanians," 143–44, states that not all Christian sources are eulogistic, and there was some persecution toward the end of his reign, he does agree that Yazdagird was, in comparison with earlier emperors, tolerant toward minority faiths in Persia, even if this may have involved an element of *Realpolitik,* in that he sought the maintenance of peace and good relations with the Romans. One source optimistically states that Yazdagird was on the verge of becoming a Christian himself. Agathias calls Yazdagird "friendly and peaceable," a ruler who never once made war on the Romans; see Cameron, "Agathias on the Sassanians," 126–27. Procopius likewise praises Yazdagird's peace policy and retails the colorful story that the Roman emperor Arcadius (r. 383–408) entrusted his young son, the future Theodosius II, to Yazdagird's guardianship. See *The Persian Wars,* I.ii.1–10; Garsoïan, "Byzantium and the Sasanians," 578–79; Cameron, *Procopius and the Sixth Century,* 153–54. Also, it was during Yazdagird's reign, in 410, that the first synod of the Nestorian Church on Sāsānid territory was held, under the headship of the Catholicos Mār Isḥāq of Seleucia-Ctesiphon, and a hierarchy of metropolitan bishoprics, headed by Seleucia-Ctesiphon, set up. See Labourt, *Le Christianisme dans l'empire perse,* 87–109; Asmussen, "Christians in Iran," 939–40; *EI*², s.v. Sāsānids (M. J. Morony); *EIr,* s.v. Christianity. I. In Pre-Islamic Persia (J. R. Russell), at V, 525.

192. Literally, "having or commanding a thousand slaves," see Justi, *Namenbuch,* 128. Mihr Narsēh was from one of the noblest families in Persia, the Spendiyārs; for his genealogy, see al-Ṭabarī, I, 868–69, pp. 103–104 below. See on him Nöldeke, trans., 439, and Lukonin, "Political, Social and Adminstrative Institutions: Taxes and Trade," 704. That the emperor made him his chief minister immediately on his accession is improbable, as Nöldeke, trans. 76 n. 1, noted, seeing that Mihr Narsēh was active as a minister and field commander until forty years later in the reigns of Bahrām V and Yazdagird II; see al-Ṭabarī, I, 866, 868, 871, 872, pp. 99–100, 103, 106, 108 below.

nobles and great men of state grew intense, he bore down hard on the weak, shed copious amounts of blood, and exercised power in so tyrannical a manner as the subjects had never experienced in his time. When the prominent personages and the nobles perceived that Yazdajird was only rushing further into the paths of tyranny, they came together and complained [to God] about the oppression by Yazdajird from which they were suffering. They made humble supplications to their Lord and implored Him to send them a speedy deliverance from Yazdajird.

They assert that Yazdajird was in Jurjān.[193] One day, he looked out from his palace at a horse coming toward him, the like of whose fine appearance and perfection of form had never before been seen in a horse. It stopped at his gate. The people marveled at it because the beast was of an extraordinary nature. Yazdajird was told about it, and he then gave orders for it to be saddled and bridled. His grooms and the master of his stables all tried to do this but failed. Yazdajird was informed of the horse's refractoriness with them, so he went out personally to the spot where that horse was, placed a bridle on it with his own hand, threw a saddle blanket over its back and a saddle on top of it, secured the girth strap, and put a halter round its neck, without the horse moving an inch at any of this. Finally, he lifted its tail to fix the crupper, when the horse wheeled round behind him and struck him such a blow on the heart that he died from it. Subsequently, that horse [850]
was never seen again. It is said that the horse galloped off at a great pace, without anyone being able to catch up with it, nor could anyone ascertain the reason for its behavior. The subjects were thus freed from him and exclaimed, "This is God's work and a manifestation of His beneficence to us."[194]

193. That is, the region at the southeastern end of the Caspian Sea, Gurgān, OP Vṛkāna, classical Hyrcania. See Yāqūt, *Buldān*, II, 119–22; Marquart, *Ērānšahr*, 72–74; Le Strange, *Lands*, 376–78; Barthold, *Historical Geography*, 88; *EI*², s.v. Gurgān (R. Hartmann-J. A. Boyle).

194. Following the reading of the Sprenger ms. given in Nöldeke's text, n. *a*, *khalaṣat al-raʿiyyah minhu*. The remarkable mode of Yazdagird's death is closely linked with the story in the Perso-Islamic sources concerning his evil ways, as being a fittingly mysterious end for such an impious tyrant. See Nöldeke, trans. 77 n. 1.

Some state that Yazdajird reigned for twenty-two years, five months, and sixteen days, others that he reigned for twenty-one years, five months, and eighteen days.[195]

## *[The History of al-Ḥīrah]*

When ʿAmr b. Imriʾ al-Qays al-Badʾ b. ʿAmr b. ʿAdī died during the time of Sābūr, son of Sābūr,[196] the latter appointed to his office Aws b. Qal(l)ām, according to Hishām [Ibn al-Kalbī]; Aws was one of the Amalekites, from the tribe of ʿAmr b. ʿAmalīq (or ʿImlīq). But Jaḥjabā b. ʿAtīk b. Lakhm rose up against him and killed him, Aws having reigned for five years.[197] His death fell in the time of Bahrām, son of Sābūr Dhū al-Aktāf. There was appointed to succeed him in the office Imruʾ al-Qays al-Badʾ,[198] the son of ʿAmr b.

---

195. Yazdagird I's reign was 399–420. His name appears on his coins as (L'MŠ-TRY) YZDKRTY, i.e., (Rāmshahr) Yazdagird. See on his coins Paruck, *Sāsānian Coins,* 61–62, 360–62, 443–47, Plates XIII–XIV, Table XIII; Göbl, *Sasanian Numismatics,* 48, Table VIII, Plate 9; Sellwood, Whitting, and Williams, *An Introduction to Sasanian Coins,* 21, 112–15; Malek, "A Survey of Research on Sasanian Numismatics," 235.

The other Arabic sources on his reign include Ibn Qutaybah, *Maʿārif,* 659–60; al-Yaʿqūbī, *Taʾrīkh,* I, 183 (both sources on his evil ways and tyrannical rule); al-Dīnawarī, *al-Akhbār al-ṭiwāl,* 51–52 (his harsh rule and his sending his son Bahrām [V] to al-Ḥīrah for his education); al-Masʿūdī, *Murūj,* II, 190 = § 612; idem, *Tanbīh,* 101, trans. 144; Ḥamzah al-Iṣfahānī, *Taʾrīkh,* 49; Ibn al-Athīr, *Kāmil,* I, 398–401. Of Persian sources, see Ṭabarī-Balʿamī, trans. II, 127–28. For recent studies of his reign, see Christensen, *Sassanides,* 269–73; Frye, "The Political History of Iran under the Sasanians," 143–44, 178; *EI²,* s.v. Sāsānids (M. J. Morony).

196. Correctly, "during the time of Sābūr (II), great-grandson of Sābūr (I)." The father of ʿAmr, Imruʾ al-Qays al-Badʾ, was the "King of the Arabs" of the Namārah inscription; see al-Ṭabarī, I, 834, p. 44 and n. 133 above.

197. The five years' rule of Aws b. Qal(l)am (fuller genealogy in Ḥamzah al-Iṣfahānī, 87: . . . b. Buṭayn(ah) . . . b. Liḥyān al-ʿAmalīqī) forms the first interregnum of Lakhmid domination in al-Ḥīrah. Very little is known of Aws, whose reign must have fallen within the 380s or 390s if he died during Bahrām IV's reign, but he must have been a member of one of the leading Arab families of al-Ḥīrah. It was a descendant of his, the Christian bishop of the town, Jābir b. Shamʿūn, who lent the impoverished last Lakhmid king al-Nuʿmān III b. al-Mundhir IV (see al-Ṭabarī, I, 1016ff., pp. 339ff. below) eighty thousand dirhams so that he could live in a royal style (see Abū al-Faraj al-Iṣfahānī, *Aghānī¹,* II, 26 = *Aghānī³,* II, 115). If al-ʿAmalīqī did occur as a tribal *nisbah* among the ancient Arabs, it cannot of course have had any direct connection with the Old Testament Amalekites; cf. Nöldeke, trans. 78 n. 1.

198. That is, Imruʾ al-Qays (II), see Rothstein, *Laḫmiden,* 52, 55, 58, 65. As Nöldeke, 79 n. 1, observed, it is highly improbable that two Lakhmid rulers could both have had the cognomen *al-Badʾ* "the first"; accordingly, we find in the text of

Imri' al-Qays [al-Bad'] (?) b. 'Amr, [who ruled for] twenty-five years; he died in the time of Yazdajird the Sinful one. The latter appointed in his stead his son al-Nu'mān b. Imri' al-Qays al-Bad' b. 'Amr b. Imri' al-Qays b. 'Amr b. 'Adī,[199] whose mother was Shaqīqah, daughter of Rabī'ah b. Dhuhl b. Shaybān, [al-Nu'mān being], the rider of [the celebrated horse] Ḥalīmah and the builder of al-Khawarnaq.

The reason for his building al-Khawarnaq,[200] according to what has been mentioned, was that Yazdajird the Sinful One, the son of Bahrām the Kirmān-Shāh, son of Sābūr Dhū al-Aktāf, had [at that [851] time] no surviving son. Hence he made enquiries concerning a spot that was healthy and free from diseases and maladies. As a result, he was directed to the elevated region of al-Ḥīrah, and he sent his [subsequently born] son Bahrām Jūr to this al-Nu'mān, ordering the latter to build al-Khawarnaq as a residence for him. He made him reside there, and instructed him to send out Bahrām Jūr into the deserts of the Arabs. The actual builder of al-Khawarnaq was a man called Sinnimār.[201] When Sinnimār had completed its construction, people were amazed at its beauty and the perfection of its workmanship. Sinnimār, however, commented, "If I had believed that you (sc., al-Nu'mān) would pay me

Ḥamzah al-Iṣfahānī, 87, the second occurrence of al-Bad' changed to (the meaningless in the context) al-Badan.

199. That is, al-Nu'mān (I), called al-A'war "the one-eyed" and al-Sā'iḥ "the wanderer, ascetic" (cf. regarding this last cognomen, p. 81 n. 217 below). See Rothstein, *Laḫmiden,* 52, 55, 56, 58, 65–68; *EI*², s.v. Lakhmids (Irfan Shahîd).

200. This famous palace of the Lakhmids would accordingly date from the first two decades of the fifth century. It lay just to the east of al-Ḥīrah, hence of the Islamic al-Najaf also, and was regarded by the early Arabs as one of the wonders of the world. The name is most probably of Iranian origin. F. C. Andreas suggested an etymology from **huwarna,* "having a fine roof," but Mr F. C. de Blois has pointed out to the present writer the great unlikelihood of this, given that there is no trace of a word **warna-* "roof" in Middle Persian. Al-Khawarnaq was used as a palace in early 'Abbāsid times, but later fell into ruins. Its site is visible today. See Yāqūt, *Buldān,* II, 401–403; Rothstein, *Laḫmiden,* 15–16; Le Strange, *Lands,* 75–76; Musil, *The Middle Euphrates,* 35, 103–106; *EI*², s.v. al-Khawarnaḳ (L. Massignon). The story that it was built specially for the prince Bahrām Gūr would be, according to Noldeke, 79 n. 3, a later suggestion.

201. Ḥamzah al-Iṣfahānī, 90, gives him the *nisbah* of *al-Rūmī,* "the Greek," and makes him the builder of a palace called Ṣinnīn (?). Sinnimār's being described as a *Rūmī* is a reflection of the Romans' reputation as architects and fine builders. Nothing is known of the historicity of Sinnimār; see Nöldeke, 80 n. 1.

the whole of my due and would have treated me as I deserve, I would have constructed a building which would have gone round with the sun, wherever it went in its course." The king then exclaimed, "So you could have built something more splendid than this, yet you didn't do it?" and he ordered him to be thrown down from the top of al-Khawarnaq.[202] It is in connection with this that Abū al-Ṭamaḥān al-Qaynī has recited:[203]

He paid a recompense to her and her lord, just as Sinnimār was paid a recompense—by Allāt and al-ʿUzzā![204]—the recompense which must be paid by someone seeking release from an oath.

Salīṭ b. Saʿd has likewise said,[205]

Abū Ghaylān's sons recompensed him for his advanced age and his handsome behaviour just as Sinnimār was recompensed.

Also, Yazīd b. Iyās al-Naḥshalī has said,[206]

May God recompense Kammāl for his most evil action with the recompense of Sinnimār, one which is paid out in full!

ʿAbd al-ʿUzzā b. Imriʾ al-Qays al-Kalbī also related poetry [with this reference].[207] It happened that he gave a present of some

---

202. Hence "the reward of Sinnimār" became proverbial; see Rothstein, loc. cit.

203. Abū al-Ṭamaḥān Ḥanẓalah b. al-Sharqī was a *ṣuʿlūk* or bandit poet of the *mukhaḍram.* See Abū al-Faraj al-Iṣfahānī, *Aghānī*[3], XIII, 3–14, with this verse quoted at II, 145; Blachère, *Histoire de la littérature arabe,* II, 318; *EI*[2] Suppl., s.v. Abu 'l-Ṭamaḥān al-Ḳaynī (ed.).

204. That is, the two goddesses of the pre-Islamic Arabs of Ḥijāz, who with Manāt made up the so-called Daughters of Allāh, mentioned specifically in Qurʾān, LIII, 19–20. The shrine of Allāt was at al-Ṭāʾif and that of al-ʿUzzā at al-Nakhlah near Mecca. See Ibn al-Kalbī, *Kitāb al-aṣnām,* text in F. Klinke-Rosenberger, *Das Götzenbuch. Kitâb al-Aṣnâm des Ibn al-Kalbî,* 10–17, Ger. trans. 37–44, Eng. trans. N. A. Faris, *The Book of Idols,* 14–23; J. Wellhausen, *Reste arabischen Heidentums*[2], 24, 29–45; T. Fahd, *Le panthéon de l'Arabie centrale à la veille de l'hégire,* 111–20, 163–82; *EI*[1], s.v. al-ʿUzzā (F. Buhl); *EI*[2], s.v. al-Lāt (Fahd).

205. The poet himself is obscure, but the verse is quoted in Abū al-Faraj al-Iṣfahāhī, *Aghānī*[3], II, 145.

206. This poet is not traceable, but the Naḥshal were a subtribe of Dārim of Tamīm. See Ibn al-Kalbī-Caskel-Strenziok, *Jamharat al-nasab,* I, Tables 60, 62, II, 8, 433.

207. The story of ʿAbd al-ʿUzzā and the Ghassānid king is given in Abū al-Faraj al-Iṣfahānī, *Aghānī*[3], loc. cit., with the first two verses of the following poem.

horses to al-Ḥārith b. Māriyah al-Ghassānī and went to him.[208] The horses delighted al-Ḥārith, as did ʿAbd al-ʿUzzā's own presence and conversation. The king had a son who had been put out for suckling among the Banū al-Ḥamīm b. ʿAwf of the Banū ʿAbd Wudd of Kalb.[209] A snake bit the son [and killed him], but the king imagined that they had fallen upon and murdered him. He said to ʿAbd al-ʿUzzā, "Bring these fellows to me!" ʿAbd al-ʿUzzā replied, "These are a free people, I have no superiority over them in lineage [852] or achievements [that I might compel them to come back with me]." The king threatened, "Either you bring them to me or else I shall do such-and-such [to you]!" He replied, "We expected something as a gift from you, but we are getting punishment from you instead!" He summoned his two sons Sharāḥīl and ʿAbd al-Ḥārith, and sent the following verses with them to his people:

---

208. The Ghassān were a section of the great tribal group of Asd or Azd. The tribe apparently migrated to west-central Arabia during the course of the fourth century, and the *Gs'n* are mentioned in a South Arabian inscription dated 470 of the Ḥimyarite era/A.D. 360–61 (on the correspondence of these eras, see n. 409 below) as located in western Najd at Sijah/Siyyan (roughly midway between Mecca and the modern al-Riyāḍ). Some of the Ghassān, though not necessarily all of them, migrated to the fringes of the Byzantine province of Arabia in the later fifth century, where they then assumed the role of frontier auxiliaries for the Byzantine emperors—a role corresponding to that of the Lakhmids for the Sāsānids on the other side of the Syrian Desert—under chiefs from the family of Jafnah. See Chr. Robin, "Le royaume ḥujride, dit «royaume de Kinda» entre Ḥimyar et Byzance," 693 and n. 101, 697 n. 118, who, because of the fact that not all members of the Banū Ghassān necessarily established themselves in Syria, would prefer to style the chiefs in Syria who were allies of Byzantium "Jafnids" (see n. 211 below), a point already made implicitly by Nöldeke in the title of his pioneer monograph on the family. See in general on the Jafnid/Ghassānid chiefs at this time, Ibn al-Kalbī-Caskel-Strenziok, *Jamharat al-nasab,* I, Table 176,II, 31–33, 273; Nöldeke, *Die Ghassânischen Fürsten aus dem Hause Gafna's,* 5ff.; Shahîd, *Byzantium and the Arabs in the Fourth Century,* 89–91; idem, *Byzantium and the Arabs in the Fifth Century,* 32–49, 61–72; *EI*², s.v. Ghassānids (Shahîd).

The greatest of the Jafnid/Ghassānid princes, Abū Shamir al-Ḥārith b. Jabalah al-Aṣfar (r. 529–69) is here attributed to his mother, the famous Kindī princess Māriyah. According to al-Masʿūdī, *Murūj,* II, 217 = § 1079, al-Ḥārith, the son of Māriyah Dhāt al-Qurtayn bt. Arqam, was the third of the Jafnid/Ghassānid governors of Syria for the Byzantines. See *EI*², s.v. al-Ḥārith b. Djabala (Irfan Shahîd).

209. This ancient custom of placing babies with foster mothers in the healthy environment of the desert is later seen in the infant Muḥammad the Prophet's being entrusted for suckling (*riḍāʿ*) to a woman of the Saʿd b. Bakr tribe of the Hawāzin groups outside Mecca. See F. Buhl, *Das Leben Muhammeds,* 117, noting that such a custom goes back well before Muḥammad's time; W. M. Watt, *Muhammad at Mecca,* 33.

He has recompensed me—may God recompense him with the
  worst of His recompenses—just as Sinnimār, who was
  entirely innocent, was recompensed.
[It was] simply that he raised up the building over a period of
  twenty years long, lavishing on it repeatedly fired bricks
  and molten lead.
When [the king] saw that the building had reached a great
  height and had become like a lofty mountain with steep
  and difficult slopes,
It rendered him suspicious (or: he became suspicious of him)
  after a long period of time and after the people of East and
  West had shown abhorrence of him.
Sinnimār imagined that he would gain from him all sorts of joys
  of life and achieve a position of affection and close
  friendship with him.
But the king exclaimed, "Throw the barbarian (*al-ʿilj*)[210] from
  the top of his own tower!" By God, this is one of the most
  remarkable affairs!
And, as you well know, I am guilty of no offense against Ibn
  Jafnah[211] that could make him swear an oath [to act]
  against Kalb (sc., the poet's own tribe).
He will certainly seek out the heart of their lands with his
  cavalrymen, but—may you avoid all curses![212]—become
  free of it by your far-traveling words!

---

210. In its original meaning, *ʿilj* means "coarse, strong, burly," but it was applied—obviously with a deprecatory meaning—by the Arabs to non-Arabs, and especially to the Aramaic-speakers of Iraq and to the Persians. The implicit contrast is with the spare, lean Arabs, devoid of any superfluous flesh through their harsh and frugal desert way of life; cf. n. 813 below, where ʿAdī b. Zayd counsels the Lakhmid al-Nuʿmān III to impress the emperor Hormizd IV by appearing before him as a lean, half-starved, battle-hardened desert warrior.

211. That is, the Jafnid/Ghassānid prince referred to in the poem, the name "Ibn Jafnah" going back to the eponymous founder of the line in its original Yemen home, Jafnah b. ʿAmr Muzayqiyā b. ʿAmīr. See al-Masʿūdī, *Murūj*, II, 182, 217, III, 391 = §§ 1037, 1079, 1276; Ḥamzah al-Iṣfahānī, *Taʾrīkh*, 99; Nöldeke, *Die Ghassânischen Fürsten*, 6.

212. *abayta ʾl-laʿna*, a common formula in addressing Arab chiefs and princes of the Jāhiliyyah, with the implication "may you not do anything which will merit your being cursed!" Used here, as Nöldeke notes, trans. 82 n. 5, with a contemptuous tinge to the wish. Numerous examples from early Arabic literature of its use are collected in M. Ullmann, *WbKAS*, II/2, 859–60.

Opposing what Ibn Jafnah has willed for himself are men who repel the perpetrator of evil from the tribe! [853]
Already the man Ḥārith sent before you[213] has launched an attack on us, but he has been left mortally wounded in the lungs (literally, "afflicted by consumption") on the reddish-colored hills.

Hishām has related: This al-Nuʿmān had raided Syria many times and had brought down numerous calamities on its people, taking captives and plunder.[214] He was one of the most violent of kings in inflicting hurt on his enemies and one of the most effective in penetrating deeply into their lands. The king of Persia had given him two corps of troops, one called Dawsar—these being from Tanūkh—and the other one called al-Shahbāʾ ("the Brightly Gleaming Ones"), these being Persians.[215] These are the two

213. One could also vocalize here *min qibalika* "on your authority."

214. Nöldeke, trans. 83 n. 3, thought that such attacks were not impossible, even within the period of general peace between Byzantium and Persia negotiated by Theodosius II and Shābūr III, but that it was more likely that a confusion has been made with the Lakhmid al-Nuʿmān II (r. ca. 499–503), who was certainly active in the Byzantine-Persian warfare in Upper Mesopotamia toward the end of the fifth century. See Shahîd, *Byzantium and the Arabs in the Fifth Century*, 121–22.

215. The Arabic sources mention various groups on whom the Lakhmids relied for military backing. Since they were a family in al-Ḥīrah ruling over a population which was in large part an urban, sedentary one, with the ʿIbād different also from their rulers in their Christian faith, the Lakhmids had generally to rely on foreign or mercenary troops except when they could take advantage of tribal conflicts within Arabia and thus utilize as allies one of the tribal groups involved. As well as these two groups of the Dawsar and the Shahbāʾ, supplied, according to al-Ṭabarī, by the Persian emperors, the sources mention other groups in Lakhmid service. These include the Waḍāʾiʿ (sing *waḍīʿah*, "those set down, planted, *mawḍūʿ*," perhaps "garrison troops set down on the desert frontiers." or else "levied, stipulated according to an agreement," *waḍīʿah*); the Ṣanāʾiʿ (sing. *ṣanīʿah*, "creatures [of the king], those attached to his service through royal favor and patronage"); the Rahāʾin (sing. *rahīnah*, "pledges, hostages," taken from the nearby Arabian tribes); and others.

Rothstein, *Laḫmiden*, 134–38, discussed these various bodies of troops at length, and the discussion has been taken up more recently by M. J. Kister in his "Al-Ḥīra. Some Notes on Its Relations with Arabia," 165–68, who was able to use important additional information on the Lakhmids in the British Library ms. of Abū al-Baqāʾ Hibat Allāh al-Ḥillī's *al-Manāqib al-mazyadiyyah fī akhbār al-mulūk al-asadiyyah* (since Kister wrote, available in the printed edition of Ṣāliḥ Mūsā Danādikah and Muḥammad ʿAbd al-Qādir Khuraysāt).

The Dawsar(ah), says Abū al-Baqāʾ, were an élite force of valiant and courageous

groups known as "the two tribes." He used to raid the land of Syria and the Arabs who did not recognize his authority, by means of these troops.

Hishām related: It has been mentioned to us—but God knows best [the truth of it]—that al-Nuʿmān sat one spring day in his audience chamber at al-Khawarnaq and looked down at al-Najaf, with the gardens, date-palms, orchards, and canals adjoining it, on his western side, and down at the Euphrates on his eastern side, he being on the ridge of al-Najaf.[216] He was pleased with all the greenness, the flowers, and the water courses he could see, and exclaimed to his vizier and companion, "Have you ever seen the like of this view?" The vizier replied, "No; if only it were to last!" The king said, "What then endures?" He replied, "That which is with God in the next world." The king asked, "How can that be attained?" He replied, "By your abandoning this present world, by devoting yourself to God and by seeking that which is laid up with Him." So the king renounced his kingdom that very night; he put on coarse garments and left secretly in flight, without anybody knowing. The people came next morning, knowing nothing about

---

cavalrymen. The Shahbā' were called al-Ashāhib (pl. of *ash'hab*, fem. *shahbā'*, literally, "white mingled with grey," often applied to armies because of the glint of their weapons and breastplates) because of their handsomeness and splendid appearance ("the shining ones") (but according to an alternative tradition, these were a detachment of Persians, the Waḍā'iʿ). A third group, according to this author, were the Malḥā' (fem. of *amlaḥ*, "greyish, ashen colored," thus called from their grey, iron cuirasses). See *al-Manāqib al-mazyadiyyah*, 110, and cf. Kister, op. cit., 167, and Bosworth, "Iran and the Arabs before Islam," 599–600. No source offers an etymology for the name Dawsar, but Nöldeke, trans. 83 n. 4, influenced by al-Ṭabarī's information that these were troops sent by the Persian monarch, saw clearly in it Persian *du sar* "having two heads," without being able to suggest any reason for this designation. One might speculate that the contingent had two component detachments, each with its own commander. Shahîd, in his *Byzantium and the Arabs in the Fifth Century*, 29 n. 26, cf. 30, has recently suggested a possible link with the Arabian tribe Dawsar, the modern Dawāsir, whose name is enshrined in that of the Wādī al-Dawāsir in southern Najd, see *EI²*, s.v. al-Dawāsir (G. Rentz). The question remains unresolved.

216. Al-Najaf, in Islamic times known also as Mash'had ʿAlī from its being the last resting place of the fourth caliph, lay on the edge of the desert some six miles to the west of where the early Islamic *miṣr* or military encampment of al-Kūfah was to arise; nothing, however, appears to be known of the pre-Islamic history of the place or whether this history was in any way separate from al-Ḥīrah. See Yāqūt, *Buldān*, V, 271–22; Le Strange, *Lands*, 76–78; Musil, *The Middle Euphrates*, 34–35; *EI²*, s.v. al-Nadjaf (E. Honigmann-C. E. Bosworth).

what had happened to him; they came to his door, but received no permission to enter into his presence, as he normally gave. When they had waited for a considerable time without this permission to enter, they made enquiries about him, but could find no trace of him.[217]

Concerning this, ʿAdī b. Zayd al-ʿIbādī says:

Consider the example of the lord of al-Khawarnaq, when he
looked out one day, and he had an [inward] vision of divine
guidance. [854]
His position made him rejoice, and the great extent over which
he ruled, the river [Euphrates] stretched out before him, and
al-Sadīr.[218]
But his heart became troubled and he said, "What happiness can
a king enjoy, when he is heading toward death?"
Then after prosperity, royal power, and ease of life, the graves
have closed over them there.
Then they have become like shriveled leaves, which the east
and west winds snatch away.[219]

Al-Nuʿmān's reign, up to the point when he renounced the world and wandered the earth, was twenty-nine years and four months. Ibn al-Kalbī says that fifteen years of that fell within Yazdajird's time and fourteen years within that of Bahrām Jūr,[220]

---

217. The theme of the ruler experiencing a revulsion from the world and suddenly renouncing it is a topos, but the Arabic sources do attribute ascetic tendencies to al-Nuʿmān (whether ex post facto is unknown), whence his by-name of al-Sāʾiḥ, "the wanderer," and he is said to have visited the Syrian pillar saint, Simeon Stylites, between 413 and 420. See Nöldeke, trans. 85 n. 1; Shahîd, *Byzantium and the Arabs in the Fifth Century,* 162–64; *EI*², s.v. Lakhmids (Shahîd).

218. Another famed palace of the Lakhmids, often mentioned in Arabic lore and linked with al-Khawarnaq. Some of the Arabic philologists sought a forced etymology for its name in *si dihlī(z)* "having three compartments, porticoes." See Yāqūt, *Buldān,* III, 201–202; Rothstein, *Laḫmiden,* 15–16, 96; Le Strange, *Lands,* 75.

219. The complete poem is in ʿAdī's *Dīwān,* 84–92, no. 16. Its atmosphere of world-weariness would lead one to place it among ʿAdī's *ḥabsiyyāt,* poems composed when he was in the prison to which a credulous and ungrateful al-Nuʿmān had consigned him.

220. Jūr, the Arabized form of Persian *gōr,* "wild ass," famed for its endurance and hardiness. The epithet would thus be parallel to that of al-Ḥimār given to the last Umayyad caliph Marwān II b. Muḥammad, and would be applied here to Bahrām for his heroic qualities. One could also take Bahrām-i Gōr as meaning "Bahrām of the wild asses," i.e., a hunter of those beasts. Popular romance con-

son of Yazdajird; but as for the Persian scholars knowledgeable about their historical accounts and affairs, they relate concerning this what I am [now] about to relate.

## *[Bahrām V Jūr]*

[He was] the son of Yazdajird the Harsh One (*al-Khashin*), son of Bahrām (IV) Kirmān-Shāh, son of Sābūr Dhū al-Aktāf.

It is mentioned that his birth took place on Hurmuzd day in the month of Farwardīn at the seventh hour of the day.[221] At the instant of Bahrām's birth, his father Yazdajird summoned all the astrologers who were at his court and ordered them to cast his horoscope and to explain it in such a clear way that what was going to happen to him in the whole of his life would be indicated. They measured the height of the sun and observed the ascension of the stars. Then they informed Yazdajird that God would make Bahrām the heir to his father's royal power, that he would be suckled in a land not inhabited by the Persians, and that it was advisable that he should be brought up outside his own land. Yazdajird had it in mind that he should commit the child for suckling and rearing to one of the Romans or Arabs or other non-
[855] Persians who were at his court. It now seemed best to Yazdajird to choose the Arabs for rearing and bringing him up. Hence he sum-

---

nects Bahrām's acquisition of the name with a hunting feat when he killed both a lion and a wild ass with a single arrow, see the story as given by al-Ṭabarī, I, 857, pp. 85–86 below, and n. 226 below; thus the etymology from *gōr* "wild ass" became hallowed in romance and story. Various other bases for the name have been proposed, including one from a supposed Sogdian royal title, *gula*, which the Indo-Europeanist Olaf Hansen thought occurred, e.g., in the name of the Hephthalite or "White Hun" ruler over northern India Mihrakula/Mihragula, r. ca. 515–44 (but of which there is actually no trace in Sogdian), and an Indian one (cf. Ghirshman, *Les Chionites-Hephtalites*, 109 n. 4). In our present state of knowledge, the traditional explanation seems most feasible.

221. That is, toward midday on the Persian New Year's Day; it is emphasised in the popular romantic legends surrounding Bahrām that he was born at this most auspicious and fortunate hour and date. Firdawsī's information that he was born in the eighth year of Yazdagird I's reign would make Bahrām fourteen or fifteen years old at his accession, but the statement in al-Ṭabarī, I, 863, p. 93 below, that Bahrām was twenty years old when he became king seems more historically correct.

moned al-Mundhir b. al-Nuʿmān[222] and he committed to his charge the upbringing of Bahrām. He lavished on al-Mundhir signs of nobility and honour and gave him rule over the Arabs, and he bestowed on him two high ranks, one of them called Rām-abzūd-Yazdajird, meaning "Yazdajird's joy has increased,"[223] and the other called Mihisht, meaning "chiefest servant." He also singled him out for presents and robes of honor befitting his high rank, and he ordered al-Mundhir to take Bahrām to the land of the Arabs.

So al-Mundhir went with Bahrām to his dwelling place in the land of the Arabs. He selected for suckling him three women, daughters of the nobles, with healthy bodies, keen intelligence, and acceptable education: two of them from the Arab ladies and one Persian lady. He gave orders for them to be provided with all the clothing, carpets, food, drink, and other items they needed, and they then took turns in suckling him over a period of three years.

In the fourth year, he was weaned. When he was five, he said to al-Mundhir, "Bring me knowledgeable teachers, well trained in methods of instruction, who can teach me writing, archery, and knowledge of law (*fiqh*; or perhaps just "intellectual skills"). Al-Mundhir replied, "You are still young in years, and the time is not yet ripe for you to embark on education. Occupy yourself with the things young children concern themselves with until you reach an age ready for being educated and for being taught good behavior; then I will appoint teachers for everything in which you have sought instruction." But Bahrām told al-Mundhir, "By God, I am indeed young in years, but my intelligence is that of a man of adult judgment; whereas, you are old in years, yet your mind is that of a weak child. Do you not know, O man, that everything which is

---

222. This is al-Mundhir I (r. ca. 418–62), son of al-Nuʿmān I (r. ca. 400–18), on whom see Rothstein, *Laḫmiden*, 52, 55, 58, 69–70; for al-Mundhir's role in Lakhmid-Persian relations and his share in the war of 421–22 between Bahrām and Byzantium, see Shahîd, *Byzantium and the Arabs in the Fifth Century*, 28–32.

223. This title was restored, with difficulty, by Nöldeke from the mss., see text, n. *b*. In his trans., 86 n. 1, he noted that one would expect *Rām-abzūd* (for *aβzūd*, *afzūd*) *ba-Yazdagird* and that this seems to be an isolated attestation of the epithet in the sources for Sāsānid history, leading him to wonder whether its form has arisen from a misunderstanding by the older Arab transmitters/authors.

[856] sought after prematurely is reached in its right time, that which is sought in its own time is reached at some other time, and that which is not sought at the right time (i.e., too late) is lost and not attained at all? I am the offspring of kings, and with God's permission, royal power will come to me. Now the most appropriate obligation for kings and the most important thing they should see is beneficial knowledge, for this last is an adornment for them and a pillar of their royal power; by means of it they become powerful. So busy yourself and procure quickly for me the teachers for whom I have asked you!"

The very moment that al-Mundhir heard these words of Bahrām's, he sent envoys to the king [of Persia's] court who would bring back to him a group of scholars of the Persians versed in law, instructors in archery and the equestrian arts, and teachers in writing and in all the share of attainments of those possessing a good education.[224] He furthermore assembled for Bahrām wise men from among those of the Persians and Romans and retellers of the stories of the Arabs. Bahrām thereupon gave them binding instructions, and he appointed specific times for the specialists in each sector of those skills in which they were to come to him, and he laid down a fixed period of time within which they had to communicate to him all their appropriate knowledge. Bahrām devoted his skills exclusively to learning everything that he had asked to be taught and to listening to the wise men and the transmitters of stories. He firmly comprehended everything he heard and quickly grasped everything he was taught with the minimum of tuition. It was found that after he had reached twelve years of age he had derived benefit from everything that had been taught him, had stored it all in his mind, and had surpassed his teachers and all the highly educated persons round him to such an extent that they acknowledged to him his superiority over themselves.[225]

Bahrām now expressed his gratitude to al-Mundhir and his

224. The Cairo text has *khāṣṣatan*, "and especially those knowledgeable about polite education," for Leiden's *ḥiṣṣati.*

225. Bahrām's education in both the Persian and the Arabic sciences and knightly virues is also described, in much less detail, in al-Ya'qūbī, *Ta'rīkh*, I, 183; al-Dīnawarī, *al-Akhbār al-ṭiwāl*, 51–52; Ṭabarī-Bal'amī, trans. II, 110–12.

teachers, and commanded the latter to return home. He now ordered the instructors in archery and the equestrian arts to be present with him, in order that he might acquire from them everything requisite for him to be trained in and to achieve mastery over. Then, [after having acquired these skills,] Bahrām sent for al-Nuʿmān b. al-Mundhir and instructed him to make the Arabs come forward and bring their horses, both stallions and mares, with information on their pedigrees. Hence al-Nuʿmān instructed the Arabs to do that. When al-Mundhir was informed about Bahrām's intention of selecting a horse as his mount, he said to [857]
Bahrām, "Don't require the Arabs to let their horses run forth [in competition with each other], but order each of them to pass in review his horse before you, and then take your pick, just as it pleases you, and tether the horse for your own use." Bahrām replied, "You have spoken well; but I am the most outstanding of men in rulership and nobility, and its is necessary that my mount should only be the very best of horses. The superiority of one horse over another can only be known by trial, and there can be no trial without a competitive race." Al-Mundhir approved of his words, and al-Nuʿmān ordered the Arabs to bring forward their horses. Bahrām and al-Mundhir rode out to the horses assembled for the race. The horses went off from [a place which was] two farsakhs [from the winning post]. A sorrel horse of al-Mundhir's outstripped all these horses and came in first, and then the rest of them came along in successive groups, of two or three horses following each other or coming in separately or coming right at the end. Al-Mundhir led that sorrel horse over to Bahrām with his own hand, saying, "May God bring you blessing by means of it!" Bahrām ordered the steed to be secured for him; his joy was great, and he gave thanks to al-Mundhir.

One day, Bahrām rode the sorrel horse, which al-Mundhir had given him as a mount, out hunting. He spotted a herd of wild asses, loosed an arrow at them, and rode towards them, but lo and behold, there was a lion that had seized one of the asses in the herd, and had gripped its back with its jaws in order to smash it and kill it! Bahrām shot an arrow into the lion's back; the arrow pierced through its body to its belly, and then to the wild ass's back and its navel, until it ended up in the ground, penetrating into it to about a third of its length, and was fluttering there for a considerable time. All this took place in the presence of a group of Arabs and of Bahrām's guards and other persons. Bahrām gave orders for the episode of him, the lion, and the wild ass to be set down in picture form in one of his court chambers.[226]

Then Bahrām informed al-Mundhir that he was going to return to his father, so he set out to see the latter. But his father Yazdajird, because of his evil character, paid no attention to any of his children and merely took Bahrām as one of his servants, so that Bahrām suffered great hardship in this.[227] At that point, an em-
[858] bassy came to Yazdajird under a brother of the Roman Emperor, called Thiyādhūs (Theodosius), seeking a peace agreement and a truce in fighting for the emperor and the Romans.[228] Hence Bahrām asked Thiyādūs to speak with Yazdajird and to secure for Bahrām permission to return to al-Mundhir. So he returned to the land of the Arabs, where he devoted himself to a life of ease and enjoyment.

Bahrām's father Yazdajird died while Bahrām was away. A group of the great men of state and nobles came together and made an agreement among themselves not to raise to the throne any of Yazdajird's offspring because of his evil conduct. They said, "Yazdajird has not left any son capable of assuming the royal power except for Bahrām; but he has not yet governed any province [of the realm] by means of which his abilities may be tested and his capabilities thereby known. Nor has he had an education

---

226. The tale of Bahrām's prowess in the chase—thus explaining his sobriquet "the Wild Ass," see n. 220 above—figures in or is echoed by various other sources. See, e.g., Ibn Qutaybah, *'Uyūn al-akhbār*, I, 178; al-Dīnawarī, *al-Akhbār al-ṭiwāl*, 52; Ṭabarī-Bal'amī, trans. II, 117–18; al-Mas'ūdī, *Murūj*, II, 191 = § 613, referring for further details to his *Akhbār al-zamān* and his *Kitāb al-Awsaṭ* (both now lost, despite the existence of apocryphal works bearing these titles, see Ahmad M. H. Shboul, *Al-Mas'ūdī and His World. A Muslim Humanist and His Interest in Non-Muslims*, 72–73 and nn. 126–27; *EI²*, s.v. al-Mas'ūdī [Ch. Pellat]). Hunting scenes depicting Bahrām, such as this adventure with the lion and wild ass, became favorite subjects for later Persian miniature painting. See *EIr*, s.v. Bahrām. vi. Bahrām V Gūr in Persian Legend and Literature (W. L. Hanaway).

227. Although this piece of information would seem to be just one more item with which to blacken Yazdagird's reputation, Nöldeke, trans. 90 n. 2, thought that there might conceivably have been some bad blood between father and son, with Bahrām's being sent to al-Ḥīrah as a sort of exile. This is, however, pure conjecture.

228. The name of the "brother of the Roman Emperor" is in fact that of the then emperor himself, Theodosius II (r. 408–50).

in Persian ways, but his education has been solely in Arab ways, so that his nature is like the Arabs' nature, seeing that he has grown up among them." The view of the great men of state and the nobles agreed with that of the mass of people (*'āmmah*) (i.e., of the military and landed classes below the topmost ranks of society): that the royal power should be diverted from Bahrām to a man from the family of Ardashīr, son of Bābak (i.e., a man from a collateral line of descent from the first Sāsānid emperor) called Kisrā, and without delay they raised this last to the royal power.[229]

The news of Yazdajird's death, and the leading men's raising of Kisrā to the throne, reached Bahrām at a time when he was out in the Arabian Desert. He sent for al-Mundhir and his son al-Nu'mān, plus a group of the chiefs of the Arabs, and said to them, "I feel sure that you will not deny my father's special favor (*khiṣṣīsā*) which you have enjoyed, O Arabs, and the beneficence and largesse he has showered upon you, while at the same time he has been harsh and savage against the Persians." He then passed on to them the information that had reached him announcing his father's death and the Persians' appointment of a king as a result of deliberations among themselves. Al-Mundhir replied, "Don't let that make you apprehensive; I will find some stratagem for dealing with the situation." Al-Mundhir therefore fitted out a force of ten thousand cavalrymen from the Arabs and sent them, under his son's command, against Ctesiphon and Bih-Ardashīr, the two royal cities.[230] He further ordered him to encamp near to them and to keep sending forward reconnaissance units against them. If [859]
anyone were to make a move toward giving battle to him, he should fight him, and he should raid into the territory adjacent to

229. Before this happened, Shābūr, the eldest of Yazdagird's three sons, in fact hastened from Persian Armenia, where he had acted as king since the death of its Arsacid ruler in 414, to Ctesiphon in order to enforce his claim by seniority to the crown, but was killed at the capital by the nobles and priests, according to the Armenian writer Moses Khorenac'i. See Nöldeke, trans. 91 n. 4; Christensen, *Sassanides*, 274–75; Frye, "The Political History of Iran under the Sasanians," 144; *EIr*, s.v. Bahrām V (O. Klíma).

230. Presumably from the Dawsar, the Shahbā' and other units of the Lakhmid forces. The forces sent to the Sawād and to Bih Ardashīr near Ctesiphon in order to support Bahrām's bid for the throne may well have been numerous, but ten thousand looks like a suspiciously round number.

the two cities, take captives, adults and children; but he forbade him to shed blood. Al-Nuʿmān advanced until he encamped near to the two cities, sent out advanced reconnaisance units toward them, and made fighting with the Persians his chief task.

Then the great men of state and the nobles at the [Persian] court dispatched Juwānī,[231] the head of Yazdajird's chancery, to al-Mundhir, and they wrote letters to the latter informing him of what al-Nuʿmān was doing. When Juwānī reached al-Mundhir and read out the letter that had been written to him, al-Mundhir said, "Go and meet King Bahrām," and he provided him with someone who would conduct him to Bahrām. Juwānī went into Bahrām's presence, but the sight of Bahrām's handsomeness and splendid appearance reduced him to a state of alarm and, out of confusion, he forgot to prostrate himself before Bahrām. Bahrām realized at that moment that Juwānī had only omitted the prostration because he had been awe-stricken by his own outstandingly beautiful form.[232] Bahrām spoke to him and personally assured him of promises of favor. He sent him back to al-Mundhir, whom he told that he would give an answer to what he had written. Al-Mundhir said to Juwānī, "I have been thinking about the letter which you have brought to me. It was only King Bahrām who sent al-Nuʿmān to your region, since God has given him the royal power after his father and conferred [power] on him over you." When Juwānī heard al-Mundhir's words, and recalled to mind Bahrām's outstandingly beautiful form, which he had seen face to face, and the awe for Bahrām he had felt in his spirit, [he realized] that all those who

231. Thus in Nöldeke's text, but interpreted by him in his trans., 92 n. 1, as Juwānūyah, with the Persian hypocoristic ending *-ōy/ ūyah,* which the Arab philologists turned into *-wayhi,* and as probably being a contracted form of some compound name like Juwānmard or Juwānshīr. Cf. Justi, *Namenbuch,* 123.

232. This is the royal *xvarənah* of the Avesta, MP *xwarrah* or *farr(ah),* NP *farr,* the divine aura of the ruler, one of the most enduring concepts in Persian national history, the "royal glory" that legitimized the authority of theocratic rulers and brought them success. See Marquart, "Beiträge zur Geschichte und Sage von Erān," 667–69; Yarshater, "Iranian Common Beliefs and World View," 345–46, and the references at 345 n. 2; Almut Hintze, *Der Zamyād-Yašt. Edition, Übersetzung, Kommentar,* 15–33, with further literature (the most up-to-date discussion of the term's etymology and meaning; she believes that it means "Glücksglanz").

had advised depriving Bahrām of his royal power were revealed as persons to be discounted and rejected in argument. He said to al-Mundhir, "I am not going to take back any reply.[233] But you yourself, if you see fit, go to the royal residence, so that the great men of state and the nobles who are there may gather round you and take counsel together about the matter. Bring forward good arguments, for they will oppose you in nothing which you advise."

Al-Mundhir then sent back Juwānī to those who had sent him in the first place. He made his preparations and went forth, just one day after Juwānī's departure, in company with Bahrām and at the head of thirty thousand cavalrymen, courageous and mighty [860]
warriors, from amongst the Arabs, against the two cities of the [Persian] king. When they reached the two cities, he gave orders, and the people gathered together, with Bahrām seated on a golden throne (*minbar*) encrusted with jewels and al-Mundhir at his right hand. The great men of state and the nobles of the Persians spoke, and in their speech set out before al-Mundhir how harsh Bahrām's father had been and his evil conduct; how, through his perverted judgment, the land had been ruined; and how he had killed large numbers of people unjustly and had even slaughtered the people of his own land; and [they recounted] many other enormities. They mentioned that it was only because of these facts that they had taken counsel together and made an agreement to divert the royal power away from Yazdajird's offspring. They asked al-Mundhir not to force them to accept anything in regard to the royal power that they would dislike. Al-Mundhir fully comprehended all that they had pointed out regarding this matter, but he said to Bahrām, "It is more fitting that you, rather than me should answer the people."

Bahrām replied, "I cannot deny as false, O group of spokesmen, any part of the deeds for which you have accused Yazdajird of responsibility, because I am myself convinced of its truth. I have personally denounced him for his evil example and have avoided him, on account of his way of behavior and belief; hence I have unceasingly asked God graciously to bestow upon me the royal

233. Reading, with the Cairo text, *muḥīr^an* for the Leiden text's *mukhbir^an*.

power so that I might put right all that he has done wrong and repair what he has split asunder.[234] If I reign for just one year and have not fulfilled all the things I have enumerated to you, then I will freely and willingly renounce all claim to the throne. I call upon God, His angels, and the Chief Mōbadh to bear witness that I do this, and let the last named be the arbiter and judge between us. Moreover, despite what I have explained to you, I am ready to tell you that I am content to accept your appointing as king the person who can snatch the crown and the regalia from between two ravening lions with their cubs;[235] let such a person be king!"

When the people heard these words of Bahrām's and what he had, personally and from the heart, promised, they rejoiced at that,
[861] their hopes were raised, and they said among themselves, "We cannot reject Bahrām's words. Seeing that, if we carry to its conclusion the decision to exclude Bahrām from the throne, we will thereby be thrown into fear of bringing about our own destruction, given the large numbers of Arabs he has brought to his aid and has summoned up. We shall, on the other hand, be able to test him in regard to what he has laid before us, promises which only confidence in his own strength, bravery, and boldness would have led him to make. If he is really as he has described himself, our decision can only be to hand over the royal power to him and to show him obedience and submsission. But if he perishes through weakness and impotence, we shall be guiltless of any part in his death and secure from any malevolence and trouble from him."

With this resolution, they dispersed. Bahrām came back again [on the next day] after he had originally spoken to them and sat down just has he had sat down the previous day. The persons who had previously opposed him were also there. He told them: "Either you agree to what I proposed to you yesterday or else you keep silent, humbling yourselves and giving obedience." The people answered: "We ourselves have made the choice of Kisrā to direct the affairs of state, and have only experienced good actions from

234. According to Nöldeke, trans. 94 n. 2, the Sprenger manuscript elaborates on this prayer: that Bahrām promises to lower the land tax, to increase the army's pay, and to give the nobles and great men still higher offices. Nöldeke thought that these express promises certainly belonged to the original source used here.

235. That is, alluding to the contest, described below, between himself and the rival contender for the throne, Khusraw.

him. Nevertheless, we are willing that the crown and regalia should be set down, as you have suggested, before two lions and that you and Kisrā should contend together for them; to whichever of you manages to snatch them from among the lions we will transfer the royal power."

Bahrām was agreeable to what they proposed, so the Chief Mōbadh, who was responsible for placing the crown on the head of every king who was invested with royal power,[236] brought in the crown and regalia, and he placed them at one side. Bisṭām the Iṣbahbadh[237] brought in two fierce, hungry lions with their cubs, and stationed one of them at the side of the place where the crown and regalia had been set down and the other opposite it, and released their chains. Bahrām said to Kisrā, "You have first go at the crown and regalia!" Kisrā responded, "It is more fitting that you should have the first attempt at getting them for yourself, because you are seeking the royal power by right of inheritance while I am an usurper in regard to it." Bahrām had nothing against his words [862]
because of his confidence in his own bravery and strength. He took up a mace[238] and made toward the crown and regalia. The

236. Nöldeke, trans. 96 n. 1, noted that, among the Persian Arsacids and in Armenia, it was one of the leading nobles who had the hereditary right to crown the ruler.

237. The *Spāhbed* or "Army chief," Arabized as *Iṣbabadh,* whose title goes back to Achaemenid times, was the supreme military commander and war minister in the Sāsānid empire. In the first three centuries or so of the dynasty's rule, there was a single, supreme *Spāhbed,* but in the sixth century Khusraw Anūsharwān, fearing such a concentration of power in the hands of a single person, divided the office and appointed four *Spāhbed*s for each of the quarters of the realm. See Justi, *Namenbuch,* 306; Marquart, "Beiträge zur Geschichte und Sage von Erān," 635–39; Christensen, *Sassanides,* 99, 104, 130–31, 370–71, 519–21; Eilers, "Iranisches Lehngut im arabischen Lexikon," 215; Wiesehöfer, *Ancient Persia,* 198; $EI^2$, s.v. Ispahbadh (C. E. Bosworth).

Bisṭām is the Arabized form of NP Bistahm, from the unattested OP *Vistaxma, with the parallel form Gustahm, literally, "wielding far-extending power." See Justi, *Namenbuch,* 371–72; *EIr,* s.v. Besṭām (W. Eilers). The *Spāhpat* named here as Bistahm or Bisṭām is apparently the Bisṭām, "*Iṣbahbadh* of the Sawād, who held the rank of Hazār-raft" (on which latter title, see Nöldeke, trans. 76 n. 2, and Justi, op. cit., 88, 128), who, according to al-Dīnawarī, *al-Akhbār al-ṭiwāl,* 55, was one of the great men of state who had met together on Yazdagird's death to exclude any descendant of the deceased ruler from the succession in favor of the remote kinsman Khusraw (al-Ṭabarī, I, 858, p. 86 above, cf. also I, 993, p. 303 and n. 711 below).

238. The mace or club (Pers. *gurz,* here Arabized to *jurz*) appears in Persian lore

Chief Mōbadh said to him "What you have embarked upon puts you in mortal danger; this is all done freely and of your own accord, and none of the Persians has put the idea into your head. We are blameless before God of your [possible] self-destruction." Bahrām replied, "[Yes], you are absolved of all responsibility and have no burden of blame regarding it." Then he darted quickly toward the lions. When the Chief Mōbadh perceived Bahrām's vigor in confronting the lions, he cried out to him [again], saying, "Confess openly your sins and show repentance for them, then step forward, if you are completely determined on doing so." Bahrām confessed the sins he had committed[239] and advanced towards the two lions. One of them sprang towards him, but when it got near, Bahrām leapt with a single bound onto its back, squeezed the lion's flanks with his thighs so firmly that he threw the lion into distress, and he set about beating its head with the mace he had brought.

At that point, the other lion hurled itself at him, but he seized it by its two ears, rubbed them violently with both his hands, and kept on dashing its head against the head of the other lion on which he was riding until he had battered out their brains; then he killed them both by raining blows on their heads with the mace he had with him. This action he did before the eyes of Kisrā and all the persons assembled for the occasion.[240] After that, Bahrām took up for himself the crown and regalia. Kisrā was the first to call out to him, saying, "May God grant you long life, Bahrām, to whom all around are giving their ear and their obedience, and may He give you rule over the seven climes of the earth!"[241] At that, all

and epic as the weapon par excellence of heroes. Ḥamzah al-Iṣfahānī, *Ta'rīkh*, 49, describes Bahrām Gūr, after representations which he had seen, as seated on his throne with a mace in his hand.

239. A touch noted by Nöldeke, trans. 97 n. 1, as very characteristic of the Perso-Islamic transmission of this story.

240. The story of Bahrām's contest with the lions appears in al-Ya'qūbī, *Ta'rīkh*, I, 183–84; al-Mas'ūdī, *Murūj*, II, 191 = § 613; Ṭabarī-Bal'amī, trans. II, 117–18. It became a favorite tale in the Islamic *adab* works; see, e.g., Ps.-al-Jāḥiẓ, *Kitāb al-tāj fī akhlāq al-mulūk*, tr. Ch. Pellat, *Le livre de la couronne*, 182–84.

241. Here, *aqālīm*, sing. *iqlīm*, refers to the ancient Iranian idea of the seven *kishwars* or "regions of the earth" grouped round the central *kishwar*, the inhabited world, the region most favored by nature for human life and human development, the Avestan *xʷaniratha-*, MP *khwanirah*; see C. Brunner, "Geographical

those present cried out, saying, "We submit to King Bahrām, we humble ourselves before him and are content to have him as king," and they sent up profuse prayers for him. The great men of state, the nobles, the provincial governors and the viziers came to al-Mundhir after that day, and besought him to speak with [863] Bahrām, asking forgiveness for their injurious conduct toward him, pardon, and overlooking of their faults. Al-Mundhir spoke to Bahrām regarding their request, and asked him to bestow now as benevolence all the personal animus he had [previously] borne against them. Bahrām satisfied al-Mundhir in what he had asked, and gave them hopes of future beneficence.[242]

Bahrām assumed the royal power when he was twenty years old. On the very same day, he ordered his subjects to celebrate a general holiday and festivities. After that, he sat in public audience for all the people for seven days continuously, giving them promises of his benevolent rule and enjoining upon them fear of God and obedience to Him. But when he had become king, Bahrām continuously devoted himself to pleasure, to the exclusion of everything else, until his subjects reproached him profusely for this conduct and the neighboring monarchs became desirous of conquering his land and seizing his kingdom.[243]

---

and Administrative Divisions: Settlements and Economy," 747. The idea later took shape that the six lands surrounding Persia were those of India, China, the Turks, the Rūm, Africa, and the Arabs; see *EI*², s.v. Iḳlīm (A. Miquel).

242. Nöldeke, trans. 98 n. 1, held that Bahrām had succeeded to power against the desires of the nobility and priesthood, and was now in a position of strength vis-à-vis those two classes. In fact, this inital lack of support from the nobility probably placed Bahrām in a somewhat weak position, and explains his cooperation with the commanding figure in the state of Mihr Narsēh. The latter was known as an implacable foe of the Christians, and almost immediately on Bahrām's accession, the emperor ordered, or at least condoned, a savage persecution of the Persian Christians; several members of the Persian nobility suffered. It was reaction to the plight of refugees from the western frontier regions of Persia fleeing to Byzantine territory which led to the Perso-Byzantine war of 421–22, mentioned by al-Ṭabarī, I, 868, p. 103, and see n. 261 below. See Labourt, *Le Christianisme dans l'empire perse,* 109; Christensen, *Sassanides,* 280–81; Frye, "The Political History of Iran under the Sasanians," 148; Asmussen, "Christians in Iran," 940–41.

243. Other sources, such as al-Ya'qūbī, *Ta'rīkh,* I, 184, and al-Dīnawarī, *al-Akhbār al-ṭiwāl,* 56, describe Bahrām's excessive love of sport and diversion (*lahw*) and of hunting, until he was reproached for this by the great men of the kingdom, and ambitious neighboring rulers, like the king of the Turks, were emboldened to

The first ruler to set himself up as a rival to Bahrām in power was Khāqān, the king of the Turks, who attacked Bahrām with an army of 250,000 Turks.[244] News of Khāqān's approaching their land with a powerful force reached the Persians. It appeared to them a catastrophe and terrified them. A group of the Persian great men of state, known for their firm judgment and their solicitude

---

attack Persia. Ḥamzah al-Iṣfahānī, 49, has a story about Bahrām's passion that people should enjoy themselves and busy themselves with music making, to the extent that he sent to the king of India a request for musicians (*mulhīn*). The king sent twelve thousand of these, whom Bahrām spread throughout his realm; this was the origin of the Zuṭṭ, i.e., gypsies. Al-Mas'ūdī, *Murūj*, II, 157–58 = § 582, states that Bahrām promoted musicians to a higher rank in society than previously.

244. The mention here of the Turks, with their grossly inflated army, is, as noted in n. 148 above, probably an anachronism, although there seem to have been Turks in the Eurasian steppelands by the fifth century, as was certainly the case in the sixth century when the first Turk empire, with its western and eastern wings, was constituted. See D. Sinor and S. G. Klyashtorny, "The Turk Empire," 332–35; Sinor, "The Establishment and Dissolution of the Türk Empire," 285, 287; *EI*², s.v. Turks. I. History. 1. The Pre-Islamic Period (L. Bazin). The "Turks" mentioned here by al-Ṭabarī were, in Bahrām's time, quite likely the Kidarites or Chionites, successors to the Kushans in Bactria, i.e., the upper Oxus lands and what is now northern Afghanistan; the Sprenger manuscript speaks of a *marzbān-i Kūshān* who guarded the eastern frontiers of the Sāsānid kingdom, but "the land of the Kushans" was by now a generic term for all the lands in the east. See Nöldeke, trans. 99 n. 1, 102 n. 2; Ghirshman, *Les Chionites-Hephtalites*, 83–84; Frye, "The Political History of Iran under the Sasanians," 142; A. D. H. Bivar, "The History of Eastern Iran," 211–14.

The rendering in Arabic, Khāqān, of the Turkish ruler's title corresponds to the oldest attestation of the title in Turkish, the Qaghan of the Tonyuquq inscription in Mongolia (ca. 720), and in the Orkhon inscriptions it has the meaning of "an independent ruler over a people or tribe," hence not only applicable to the Qaghans of the two empires of the Eastern and Western Turks but also, e.g., to the Chinese emperor, referred to as Tabghach Qaghan in both the Tonyuquq and the Kül Tigin inscriptions. In Byzantine Greek sources of this time it appears as *Chaganos* (Gy. Moravcsik, *Byzantinoturcica. II. Sprachreste der Türkvölker in den byzantinischen Quellen*, 332–34). The title is undoubtedly an ancient one, clearly recognizable as a royal title of such Inner Asian peoples as the Juan-juan and the T'u-yü-hu (ca. A.D. 400) but possibly recognisable from Chinese transcriptions as a title of the much earlier Hsiung-nu, according to E. G., Pulleyblank, "The Consonantal System of Old Chinese. Part II," 260–62, and Doerfer, confirming the earlier opinion of Marquart, *Ērānšahr*, 54. Its etymology must accordingly be lost in the obscurity surrounding these Inner Asian peoples known to us only as names from the Chinese sources. See the discussions in C. E. Bosworth and Sir Gerard Clauson, "Al-Xwarazmī on the Peoples of Central Asia," 9; G. Doerfer, *Türkische und mongolische Elemente im Neupersischen. Türkische Elemente*, II, 141–79 no. 1160; Clauson, *An Etymological Dictionary of Pre-Thirteenth-Century Turkish*, 611.

for the masses of the people, went into Bahrām's presence and told him, "O king, there has suddenly come upon you the calamitous appearance of the enemy, and this should be enough to rouse you from the pleasure and merrymaking in which you are sunk. So get ready to tackle it, lest we become afflicted by something which will entail revilement and shame for you." Bahrām merely replied, "God, our Lord, is powerful, and we are under His protection," and he only increased in his exclusive pursuit of pleasure and merry-making. But then he fitted out an expedition and proceeded to Azerbaijan, in order to worship at the fire temple there,[245] then to Armenia to seek game for hunting in its thickets and to enjoy himself on the way. He was accompanied by a group [864]
of seven of the great men of state and the nobles plus three hundred mighty and courageous men from his personal guard. He left one of his brothers, called Narsī, to act as his governor over the kingdom.

When the people heard about Bahrām's expedition and his appointment of his brother as his deputy to govern the kingdom, they felt sure that this was an act of flight from his enemy and an act of abandonment of his kingdom. They took counsel together and resolved to send an embassy to Khāqān and to undertake that they would pay him tribute, out of fear that he would invade their land and would annihilate their own troops unless they showed themselves submissive to him by handing the money over. Khāqān heard about what the Persians had agreed upon, that they would submit and show themselves submissive to him, so he gave a guarantee of security for their land and ordered his army to hold back. Bahrām, however, had sent forward a spy to bring back to him information about Khāqān; the spy now returned and told him about Khāqān's doings and intentions. So Bahrām marched against him with the force accompanying him and fell on him by

245. This is the ancient, celebrated fire temple of Ādur-Gushnasp at Shīz, by or near Ganzak or Ganjak, the Greek Ganzaka, to the southeast of Lake Urmiya (to be distinguished from the Ganjah in Arrān, in Transcaucasia), in more recent times known as Takht-i Sulaymān. In the next century after this, Khusraw Anūsharwān transferred the fire to a site in the mountains of southern Azerbaijan less open to Byzantine attack. See on its location, V. Minorsky, "Roman and Byzantine Campaigns in Atropatene," 97–101; also Nöldeke, trans. 100 n. 1; Herrmann, *The Iranian Revival,* 113–18, 128–31; *EI*², s.v. Shīz (J. Ruska and C. E. Bosworth).

night, killing Khāqān with his own hand and spreading slaughter among Khāqān's troops. Those who escaped being killed were put to flight and showed their backs. They left behind their encampment, their wives and children and their baggage. Bahrām exerted himself assiduously in hunting them down, killing them, gathering up the plunder he had seized from them and enslaving their women and children, and returned with his own army intact.[246]

Bahrām had seized Khāqān's crown and diadem and had conquered his country in the land of the Turks. He appointed a Warden of the Marches (*Marzbān*)[247] over these conquered territories, providing him with a silver throne. A group of people from the regions bordering on the land of the Turks that he had conquered came to Bahrām, submissive and offering him obedience, and they asked him to demarcate for them the boundary between his and their territories, which they would not then cross. So he duly delimited the frontier for them, and ordered the construction of a tall and slender tower (*manārah*); this is the tower which Fayrūz, son of Yazdajird (II) [later] gave orders for its [re]building, and it was erected in a forward position on [the frontier of] the land of the Turks. Bahrām also sent one of his military commanders to
[865] Transoxania in the land of the Turks and instructed him to fight the people there. So he made war on them and wrought great slaughter among them, until they promised submission to Bahrām and the payment of tribute.

Bahrām now went back to Azerbaijan and then to his residence

---

246. Al-Dīnawarī, *al-Akhbār al-ṭiwāl*, 56–57, gives details of Bahrām's itinerary as he marched to engage the "Turkish" army through Ṭabaristān and the Caspian coastlands to Gurgān, then across northern Khurāsān via Nasā to Marw. The battle then took place at Kushmayhan, a village in the Marw oasis (see on this village, Le Strange, *Lands*, 400; *Ḥudūd al-ʿālam*, trans. 105). As Nöldeke commented, trans. 101 n. 2, there seems no reason to doubt the authenticity of this location for the battle, and Marquart equated this more or less exactly with the site of the battle between Wishtāsp and the Chionites in the *Ayādgār ī Zarērān* "Memorial of Zarēr," see his *Ērānšahr*, 51–52.

247. *Marzbān* "protector of the frontier," Arabized as *marz(u)bān*, is used in Sāsānid administrative and military terminology from the fourth century onward for the military governor of such frontier provinces as Upper Mesopotamia (the commander here being based on Niṣībīn), Bēth Aramāyē, and, as here, Khurāsān. See Nöldeke, trans. 102 n. 2; Justi, *Namenbuch*, 197–98; Eilers, "Iranisches Lehngut im arabischen Lexikon," 219; *EI*², s.v. Marzpān (J. H. Kramers-M. J. Morony).

in the Sawād [of Iraq]. He ordered that the rubies and other jewels in Khāqān's diadem should be hung up in the fire temple of Azerbaijan, and then he set off and came to the city of Ctesiphon. He took up his quarters in the administrative headquarters (*dār al-mamlakah*) there. He sent letters to his troops and provincial governors announcing how he had killed Khāqān and what he and the Persian army had accomplished. Then he appointed his brother Narsī governor of Khurāsān, instructed him to make his way thither and to establish his residence at Balkh, and ordered for him whatever he required.[248]

Toward the end of his life, Bahrām went to Māh for hunting there.[249] One day he rode out to the chase, fastened tenaciously onto a wild ass and pursued it closely. But he fell into a pit and sank into the mud at the bottom. When his mother heard of that accident, she hurried along to that pit, taking with her a large sum of money. She remained near the pit, and ordered that the money should be paid out to whoever might rescue Bahrām from the hole. They excavated a vast amount of earth and mud from the pit, until they had made a number of large mounds from this; but they were never able to find Bahrām's corpse.[230]

---

248. Balkh lay in the heart of Bactria, the early Islamic Ṭukhāristān, and must at this time have been in the hands of a power like the Kushans or their epigoni; subsequently, it was a principal residence of the king of the northern Hephthalites. It is highly unlikely that any Sāsānid control could have been exerted at this time as far east as Balkh; Marw was probably the northeasternmost bastion of Persian power. See Nöldeke, trans. 103 n. 1.

249. The OP Māda-, i.e., Media or northwestern Persia, a name that survived into Islamic times as Māh, included in the toponyms Māh al-Baṣrah = Nihāwand, and Māh al-Kūfah = Dīnawar. See Le Strange, *Lands*, 190 and n. 2; *EI*², s.v. Māh al-Baṣra (M. J. Morony).

250. This story of Bahrām's end also appears, very cursorily in al-Ya'qūbī, *Ta'rīkh*, I, 184, and al-Mas'ūdī, *Murūj*, II, 190 = § 612, but in detail in al-Dīnawarī, *al-Akhbār al-ṭiwāl*, 58, who says that the story of Bahrām's death was still current in the area of Dāy-marj, the place where the king was swallowed up (this lay near Hamadhān and was later famous as the site of a battle in 584/1188 when the last Seljuq sultan of the East, Ṭoghrïl III, defeated the 'Abbāsid caliph al-Nāṣir's forces; see Schwarz, *Iran*, 553). This whole region of Māh or Media was a favorite one of Bahrām's, and he is said to have had a splendid palace at Mādharūstān near Ḥulwān and a fortress near Hamadhān (Le Strange, *Lands*, 191, 195). Nöldeke, trans. 103 n. 3, thought that this tale of the manner of Bahrām's death originated in an attempt to provide an alternative explanation to his by-name Gūr/Jūr in the sense of "wild ass," i.e., one from *gōr* in the sense of "pit, grave."

It is mentioned that, when Bahrām returned to his realm from his expedition against the Turks, he addressed the people of his kingdom for several days continuously, urging them in his speech to maintain their obedience and informing them that his intention was to render circumstances easy for them and to bring them a good way of life; but if they should stray from the straight way of righteousness, they would suffer treatment from him more severe than what they had experienced under his father. The latter had begun his reign over them with lenience and equity; but then they, or at least some of them, had rejected that policy and not shown themselves submissive, as servants and slaves should in fact show themselves toward kings. This had impelled him into harsh policies: he had beaten people and had shed blood.

Bahrām's return journey from that expedition [against the
[866] Turks] was via the road to Azerbaijan; he presented to the fire temple at al-Shīz the rubies and jewels that were in Khāqān's diadem, a sword belonging to Khāqān encrusted with pearls and jewels, and many other precious adornments. He gave Khātūn, Khāqān's wife,[251] to the temple as a servant there.[252] He remitted to the people three years' land tax as a thank offering for the victory he had achieved in his expedition, and he divided up among the poor and destitute a great sum of money, and among the nobles and persons of meritorious behavior twenty million dirhams. He sent letters to the distant lands with news about his

251. In Orkhon Turkish, *qatun/khatun* denoted the wife of the Qaghan, borrowed into Mongolian as *qadun,* but later it tended to mean "noble woman" and, eventually, by Ottoman times, little more than "married lady, woman" in the form *kadïn* (a relationship noted by Nöldeke, trans. 104 n. 2). It has traditionally been considered as a loan word from Sogdian *xwt'yn,* "wife of the lord or ruler," but from Paul Pelliot onward, doubts have been raised over this. Pulleyblank, "The Consonantal System of Old Chinese. Part II," 262–64, states that related forms are to be found among the Inner Asian Altaic people of the T'o-pa, successors of the Hsiung-nu in the early centuries A.D. G. Doerfer has pointed out the phonological difficulties in the transition Sogdian *khwatēn* > Old Turkish **khaghatun/ qaghatun.* Instead, he posits an ultimate origin in the Inner Asian peoples of Turco-Mongolian stock known to us from Chinese sources, perhaps from as far back as the eastern Hsiung-nu. See *Türkische und mongolische Elemente im Neupersischen. Türkische Elemente,* II, 132–41 no. 1149; Clauson, *Etymological Dictionary,* 602–63.

252. That is, as a manifestation of contempt for the paganism of the captured queen; cf. Nöldeke, trans. 104 n. 3.

dealings with Khāqān, in which he mentioned how reports had reached him that Khāqān had invaded his lands, and how he had extolled and magnified God and had depended completely on Him, how he had marched against Khāqān with a guard of [only] seven men from the nobility and three hundred cavalrymen from the choicest warriors of his personal guard, via the Azerbaijan and Caucasus Mountains road until he had reached the deserts and wastes of Khwārazm, and how God had then tested him [in battle] with a most successful outcome. He further mentioned to them how much land tax he had remitted to them. His letter containing this information was an eloquent and penetrating one.

When Bahrām had first achieved the royal power, he had given orders that the arrears of the land tax from previous years (*al-baqāyā*) and for which the taxpayers were still liable, should be cancelled.[253] He had been informed that these arrears amounted to seventy million dirhams, but had nevertheless given orders that they were to be remitted. He also remitted one-third of the land tax for the year in which he had acceded to power.[254]

It is said that, when Bahrām Jūr returned to Ctesiphon from his expedition against Khāqān the Turk, he appointed his brother Narsī as governor of Khurāsān and assigned him Balkh as his capital [there].[255] He appointed as his vizier Mihr Narsī, son of Burāzah,[256] made him one of his intimates and nominated him as Buzurjfarmadhār.[257] He then announced to him that he was going

---

253. In Arabic administrative literature of the fourth/tenth century, *al-baqāyā* "arrears of taxation from previous years" seems to be distinguished from *al-bāqī* "taxation of the current year still uncollected." See Bosworth, "Abū 'Abdallāh al-Khwārazmī on the Technical Terms of the Secretary's Art," 135.

254. If the report is authentic, this concession was presumably possible because of the great amount of plunder taken from the Turks; cf. Nöldeke, trans., 105 n. 5.

255. See al-Ṭabarī, I, 865, p. 97 and n. 248 above.

256. This paternal name is somewhat problematical. Nöldeke, trans. 106 n. 2, unconvincingly connected it with place names in Fārs. Justi, *Namenbuch,* 70, noted the Greek form Bōrazē for Hebrew Bigtā, the name of one of the seven eunuchs who served King Ahasuerus as chamberlains in Esther, i.10.

257. The *framadār* was originally, it appears, the steward of the royal household and then administrator of the royal estates, and finally, by Sāsānid times, the first civilian minister in the state. The extended title of *wuzurg* "great" *framadār* is characteristic of the later Sāsānid period, and this Mihr Narsēh (whose genealogy al-Ṭabarī subsequently traces back to pre-Sāsānid times (see I, 868–69, p. 104 below) appears as one of the first persons mentioned as holding the office. See

to the land of India in order to get information about conditions there and to find out by subtle means whether he could add part of the Indian lands to his own territory, in order that he might [867] thereby lighten some of the tax burden on his own subjects. He gave him (sc., Mihr Narsī) the necessary orders concerning all the matters relative to his apppointment as regent up to the time of his own return, and set off on the journey from his kingdom until he reached Indian territory, traveling in disguise. He remained there a considerable time, without any of the local people asking at all about him and his situation, except that they were favorably impressed by what they saw regarding him: his equestrian skill, his killing of wild beasts, his handsomeness, and the perfection of his form.

He continued thus until he heard that there was in one region of their land an elephant, which had made the roads unsafe for travelers and had killed a great number of people. He accordingly asked one of the local people to direct him toward the beast so that he might kill it. This intention came to the ears of the king; he summoned Bahrām and sent an envoy to accompany him, who was to go back to him with an account of Bahrām's actions. When Bahrām and the envoy came to the patch of dense jungle where the elephant was, the accompanying envoy shinned up a tree in order to see what Bahrām would do. Bahrām went forward to try and lure out the elephant, and shouted to it. The elephant came forth toward him, foaming with rage, trumpeting loudly and with a fearsome appearance. When it got near, Bahrām shot an arrow at it right between the eyes, in such a way that the arrow almost disappeared in the beast's head, and he showered arrows on it until he

---

Christensen, *Sassanides*, 114–16, 136, 265–66, 519–26; V. J. Lukonin, "Political, Social and Administrative Institutions: Taxes and Trade," 737–38.

The *wuzurg framadār* has been seen by some scholars as a forerunner of the early Islamic vizier, the chief minister of the caliphs from ʿAbbāsid times onward (for whose name, *wazīr*, some have sought a Persian etymology, see below, although more recent opinon favors an indigenous Arabic one—not that this philological question is particularly relevant anyway to the question of continuity in function and practice). See the discussion in D. Sourdel, *Le vizirat ʿabbāside de 749 à 936 (132 à 324 de l'Hégire)*, I, 41–61; and for a reassertion of a Persian origin for the word, in MP *wizīr* (apparently attested, however, in the opinion of Mr F. C. de Blois, only as an abstract noun "decision, judgment"), see Eilers, "Iranisches Lehngut im arabischen Lexikon," 207.

reduced it to a sorry state. He then leaped upon it, seized it by the trunk and dragged it downward, which made the elephant sink down on its knees. He kept on stabbing it until he got the upper hand over it and was then able to cut off its head. He rolled it over on to its back and brought it forth to the roadside. The king's envoy was meanwhile watching all this.

When the envoy returned, he related the whole story of Bahrām's doings to the king. The king was full of wonder at Bahrām's strength and boldness, gave him rich presents and questioned him about himself and his background. Bahrām told him that he was one of the great men of the Persians, but had incurred the wrath of the king of Persia for a certain reason, hence had fled from him to the king of India's protection. Now that latter monarch had an enemy who had tried to deprive him of his kingdom and had marched against him with a large army. The king, Bahrām's patron, had become fearful of the enemy because of what he knew of this enemy's might and the fact that the latter demanded of him submission and payment of tribute. Bahrām's patron was on the point of acceeding to the enemy's demands, but [868]
Bahrām dissuaded him from that, and guaranteed to him that the affair would be brought to a satisfactory conclusion. The king's mind became tranquil and confident in Bahram's words, and Bahrām set out, prepared for war.

When the two armies encountered each other, Bahrām said to the Indian cavalrymen (*asāwirah*),[258] "Protect my rear," and then

258. This is the Arabic broken pl. formed from the sing. *aswār/uswār*, from MP *aswār*, "cavalryman," used specifically in Sāsānid times for the heavy, mailed cavalrymen who formed the backbone of the army. It seems originally to have denoted a high military rank, the chief of a military unit, but in Sāsānid times came to be applied to the cavalrymen in general. These *aswārān* were certainly ranked among what might be called the aristocracy and landed gentry of Persia, and in the fiscal reforms of Khusraw Anūsharwān they were one of the classes exempted from paying the poll tax on account of their great services to the state (thus enumerated by al-Ṭabarī, I, 962, p. 259 below, where *al-muqātilah* = *aswārān*; in his equivalent passge, al-Dīnawarī specifically has *asāwirah*, see n. 625 below). In the accounts of the battles of the Muslim Arabs with the armies of the last Sāsānids, e.g., in al-Balādhurī's *Futūḥ al-buldān*, the *asāwirah* emerge as an élite of mounted archers. See Løkkegaard, *Islamic Taxation in the Classic Period*, 171, and the detailed discussion in Widengren, "Recherches sur le feudalisme iranien," 170–76; and for later usage of the term *aswārī*, extending up to Mughal and British Indian times as *suwār*, Anglicised as sowar, see *EIr*, s.v. Asāwera (C. E. Bosworth).

he led an assault on the enemy. He began to strike their heads with blows that split the head down to the mouth; to strike another in midbody so that he cut him in half; to go up to an elephant and sever its trunk with his sword; and to sweep a rider off his saddle. The Indians are a people who are not very skillful in archery, and most of them fought on foot, not having horses; when, on the other hand, Bahrām shot an arrow at one of the enemy, the shaft penetrated right through him. When the enemy saw what was happening, they wheeled round and fled, without turning aside to do anything. Bahrām's patron seized as plunder everything in the enemy's camp, and returned home rejoicing and glad, in company with Bahrām. As a reward for Bahrām's efforts, the king bestowed on him his daughter in marriage and granted to him al-Daybul, Makrān, and the adjacent parts of Sind.[259] He wrote out for him an investiture patent for all this, had the grant to him confirmed before witnesses, and gave orders for those territories to

---

259. Daybul, the Arabized form of a possible original something like Dēwal, was the great port of Sind in pre-Islamic and early Islamic times, and the first city of the province to be captured by the Arab commander Muḥammad b. al-Qāsim al-Thaqafī in 92/711–12. Moses Khorenac'i (later sixth century to early eighth century ?) mentions the district of *Dēpuhl, linking it, as here, with Makrān and Sind in general (see Marquart, *Ērānšahr*, 45). It lay in the Indus delta region to the west of the river's then main channel, but its location is still a matter for conjecture since an identification with the archaeological site Bhanbore is by no means certain. See S. Qudratullah Fatimi, "The Twin Ports of Daybul. A Study in the Early Maritime History of Sind," 97–105; *EI*², s.v. Daybul (A. S. Bazmee Ansari).

Makrān is the coastal region of what is now Pakistani and Persian Baluchistan. Whether it embraced the region known from Sumerian and old Akkadian texts as Magan, in the OP inscriptions Maka (where it is described as a satrapy of Darius the Great), and also from Akkadian texts as Melukhkha, has called forth varying opinions. Recently, de Blois, on the evidence of the texts of two Elamite tablets from the so-called Persepolis fortification tablets, has argued that Maka denotes the region called in Middle Iranian, Syriac, Armenian, and Arabic sources, from the third century A.D. onward, Mazūn = 'Umān; see his "Maka and Mazūn." 160–67. Whatever the truth, Greek historians of the time of Alexander call Makrān Gedrosia; and the region appears in the Naqsh-i Rustam inscription of Kerdēr as *Mkwl'n*. Despite the reported pretensions of early Persian monarchs to control it, as here with Bahrām Gūr, Makrān probably remained always within the Indian rather than the Persian political and cultural sphere, in Bahrām's time under the influence of the Brahman kings of Sind. See *Ḥudūd al-'ālam*, trans. 123, comm. 373; Marquart, op. cit., 33–34; Le Strange, *Lands*, 329–30; *EI*², s.v. Makrān (C. E. Bosworth).

be added to the Persian lands, with their land tax to be paid to Bahrām. Bahrām then returned [to his homeland] rejoicing.[260]

After this, Bahrām sent Mihr Narsī, son of Burāzah, on an expedition against the Roman lands, at the head of a force of forty thousand warriors. He ordered him to make for their supreme ruler (*'aẓīm*) and discuss with him the question of the tribute and other things, tasks that only a man of Mihr Narsī's caliber could undertake. Mihr Narsī then marched off with this army and matériel, and entered Constantinople. He played a notable role there, and the supreme ruler of the Romans made a truce with him. He returned homeward having achieved all that Bahrām had desired, and the latter heaped honors unceasingly on Mihr Narsī.[261]

His name was sometimes rendered in a "lightened" (*mukhaffaf*) form as just Narsī, and sometimes people would say Mihr Narsih.

---

260. Naturally, there is no question of the historicity of these fabulous Indian adventures of Bahrām, which appear, however, in other Arabic sources such as Ibn Qutaybah, *Ma'ārif,* 660–61 (detailed account, clearly based on the same source as al-Ṭabarī); al-Mas'ūdī, *Murūj,* II, 191 = § 612 (describes Bahrām's secret mission to the court of King Shubrumah, probably to be identified with the Gupta monarch Chandragupta II, r. 376–415); Ḥamzah al-Iṣfahānī, *Ta'rīkh,* 49 (very brief mention); and Ṭabarī-Bal'amī, trans. II, 122–25.

261. This is a cursory mention of the war with Byzantium that broke out in 421 shortly after Bahrām's accession. It ran counter to the general trend in Byzantine-Persian relations of the period, which had been one of peace since the treaty of 384 between Theodosius II and Shābūr III. It seems to have been provoked, on the one hand, by the violent persecution of Christians within the Persian lands that broke out at the beginning of the new reign (see n. 242 above), and, on the other hand, by Byzantine attempts to use Christian missionary activities in order to secure the allegiance of Arab tribes of the Syrian Desert fringes and by the Byzantines' sheltering of Christian converts from those fringes under Persian control.

The war was ended by a peace treaty in the following year. It promised religious freedom for Christians of Persia and for Zoroastrians in the Byzantine lands; each side was prohibited from accepting and sheltering Arab allies of the other side if these Arabs should rebel; and the Greeks were to pay an annual tribute, ostensibly for the defense of the pass at Darband against the barbarians beyond the Caucasus, but which contained no territorial changes to the boundary between the two powers. See J. B. Bury, *A History of the Later Roman Empire from Arcadius to Irene (395 A.D. to 800 A.D.),* I, 304–305; idem, *History of the Later Roman Empire from the Death of Theodosius to the Death of Justinian (A.D. 395 to A.D. 565),* I, 4–5; Labourt, *Le Christianisme dans l'empire perse,* 118; Christensen, *Sassanides,* 281; Frye, "The Political History of Iran under the Sasanians," 145; Z. Rubin, "Diplomacy and War in the Relations between Byzantium and the Sassanids in the Fifth Century A.D.," 679–81; G. Greatrex, "The Two Fifth-Century Wars between Rome and Persia," 1–14.

[869] He was Mihr Narsī, son of Burāzah, son of Farrukhzādh, son of Khūrahbādh, son of Sīsfādh, son of Sīsanābrūh, son of Kay Ashak, son of Dāra, son of Dāra, son of Bahman, son of Isfandiyār, son of Bishtāsb.[262] Mihr Narsī was held in high honor by all the kings of Persia because of his fine education and manners, the excellence of his judgment, and the contentedness and tractability of the masses of the people with him. He had, moreover, several sons, who approached him in worth and who fulfilled various offices for the monarchs that almost reached his own office [in rank and importance]. There were three of them who had reached an outstanding position. One was Zurwāndādh,[263] whom Mihr Narsī had intended for religion and the religious law. In this sphere he attained such a leading position that Bahrām Jūr appointed him Chief Hērbadh (Hirbadhān Hirbadh), a rank near to that of Chief Mōbadh. The second was called Mājusnas, who remained in charge of the department of the land tax all through the reign of Bahrām Jūr, the name of his rank in Persian being Wastrā'i'ūshān Sālār.[264] The third was called Kārd[ār], supreme commander of the army, the name of his rank in Persian being Rathāshtārān Sālār;[265] this is a rank higher than that of al-Iṣbahbadh and is near to that of al-Arjabadh.[266]

262. Mihr Narseh's Arsacid descent, in fact linking the first Arsacids with a Darius of the Achaemenids and then with the legendary kings of early Persia (only detailed here and in the Sprenger ms.), shows that scions of the previous, fallen dynasty could nevertheless rise to high office under the Sāsānids; cf. n. 84 above.

263. Following here the version of this name preferred by Nöldeke from the Sprenger ms., set forth in his n. *e*, instead of the text's Zarāwandadh; the name Zurvandād is, in fact, attested, see Gignoux, *Noms propres sassanides*, no. 1091. The name would then mean "given by Zurvān," i.e., by the deification of time put forward by some heretical (?) Zoroastrian circles, erecting it into a guiding principle for the universe as the father of both Ahura Mazdā and Ahriman, hence above all gods and men. See R. C. Zaehner, *The Dawn and Twilight of Zoroastrianism*, 236–47 (his chapter here being more manageable than his exhaustive work, *Zurvan, a Zoroastrian Dilemma*, Oxford, 1955).

264. Following the form reconstructed by Nöldeke, in n. *g* for the text's *Rās.t.r.āī w.shān.s.lān*, i.e., *Wāstaryōshān-sālār*. The title would then be that of "head of [the class of] cultivators."

265. Following the form reconstructed by Nöldeke in n. *i* for the text's *As.ṭ.rān s.lān*, i.e., *Artēshtārān-sālār*. The title would then mean "head of [the class of] warrors." Cf. for this and the preceding note, Nöldeke, trans. 110 n. 4.

266. For the exalted title of *argabadh*, "commander of a fortress," see al-Ṭabarī, I, 815, p. 6 and n. 15 above.

Mihr Narsī's own title of rank was in Persian Buzurjfarmadhār, [870]
which means in Arabic "supreme vizier" (*wazīr al-wuzarā'*) or "supreme executive" (*ra'īs al-ru'asā'*). He is said to have come from a town (*qaryah*) called Abruwān[267] in the rural district of Dasht-i Bārīn[268] in the province of Ardashīr Khurrah. He had lofty buildings erected there and at Jirih, in the province of Sābūr, because of the contiguity of that and Dasht-i Bārīn, and he constructed there for himself a fire temple, which is said to be still in existence today,[269] with its fire still burning to this present moment. It is called Mihr Narsiyān. In the vicinity of Abruwān he founded four villages, with a fire temple in each one. He set up one of these for himself and called it Farāz-marā-āwar-khudāyā, meaning [in Arabic] "come to me, O my lord,"[270] with the aim of showing great veneration for the fire. The second one was meant for Zarāwandādh, and he called it Zarāwandādhān. The third was for Kārd[ār], and he called it Kārdādhān; and the last was for Mājushnas, and he called it Mājushnasfān.[271] He also laid out three gardens in this region: in one of them he planted twelve thousand date palms; in another, twelve thousand olive trees; and in [the third] garden, twelve thousand cypress trees. These villages, with [871]
the gardens and the fire temples, have remained continuously in the hands of his descendants, who are well known till today, and it has been mentioned that all these remain in the best possible condition at the present time.

It has been mentioned that, after he had finished with Khāqān and the King of the Romans, Bahrām proceeded to the land of the

---

267. The text has *'b.r.wān*, but the form of this name is uncertain. It may possibly be the Artuwān of al-Maqdisī, *Aḥsan al-taqāsīm*, 258, in the list of the towns and districts of Sāsānid Persia attributed to Qubādh (I), son of Fayrūz, or the Arduwāl/Arduwān of Yāqūt, *Buldān*, I, 149, as a small town of southwestern Persia.

268. The "plain of Bārīn" was a district of southwestern Fārs whose urban center was in Islamic times Ghundijān. See Nöldeke, trans. 111 n. 4; Le Strange, *Lands*, 260, 268, 294; Schwarz, *Iran*, 68–70.

269. When "today" and "at the present time" were, is unfortunately not known.

270. With feminine forms in the Arabic: *iqbalī ilayya sayyidatī, nār*, "fire" being a feminine noun. Cf. Nöldeke, trans. 111 n. 7.

271. These names of estates or places in *-ān* demonstrate connections with their founders or developers (the *-ān* being originally a genitive pl. ending) and were especially notable in Iraq during early Islamic times for the names of estates, canals, etc.; e.g., Go Masrūqān, Not Artashīrakān, Nahr Sūrān.

blacks, in the region of Yemen,[272] and fell upon them, wreaking great slaughter among them and taking large numbers of captives before returning to his kingdom. Then followed his death in the manner we have described. There are differing views on the length of his reign. Some say that it was eighteen years, ten months, and twenty days, others that it was twenty-three years, ten months, and twenty days.[273]

## *[Yazdajird II]*

Then there succeeded to the royal power after him Yazdajird, son of Bahrām Jūr. When the crown had been placed on his head, the great men of state and the nobles (*ashrāf*) came into his presense, invoked blessings on his head, and congratulated him on his accession to the royal power. He replied to them in pleasant terms and mentioned his father, his virtues, how he had behaved toward the subjects, and how lengthy his sessions for them (sc., for hearing complaints and receiving petitions) had been. He told them that if they did not experience from him just what they had been used to experience from his father, they should not condemn him, for his periods of withdrawal from public gaze at court were only for some aspect of public good for the kingdom and to trick enemies. [He went on to say] that he had appointed Mihr Narsī, the son of Burāzah, his father's aide, as his vizier, that he would

272. The *bilād al-sūdān* would be the regions of the Horn of Africa and East Africa adjacent to South Arabia, but the story that Bahrām penetrated to there is quite legendary, and may have been influenced by the Persian expeditions to Yemen in the later sixth century, see al-Ṭabarī, I, 948ff., pp. 239ff. below.

273. Bahrām V Gūr's reign was 420–38. His name appears on his coins as (R'MŠTRY) WRḤR'N, i.e., (Rāmshahr) Bahrām See on his coins Paruck, *Sāsānian Coins,* 62, 363–66, 447–48, Plates XIV–XV, Table XII; Göbl, *Sasanian Numismatics,* 49, Table IX, Plate 9; Sellwood, Whitting, and Williams, *An Introduction to Sasanian Coins,* 21, 116–18; Malek, "A Survey of Research on Sasanian Numismatics," 235. The other Arabic sources on his reign include Ibn Qutaybah, *Ma'ārif,* 661; al-Ya'qūbī, *Ta'rīkh,* I, 183–84; al-Dīnawarī, *al-Akhbār al-ṭiwāl,* 56–58; al-Mas'ūdī, *Murūj,* II, 190–93 = §§ 612–14; idem, *Tanbīh,* 101, trans. 144; Ḥamzah al-Iṣfahānī, *Ta'rīkh,* 49; Ibn al-Athīr, *Kāmil,* I, 401–406. Of Persian sources, see Ṭabarī-Bal'amī, trans. II, 118–26. Of modern studies of his reign in general, see Christensen, *Sassanides,* 274–82; Frye, "The Political History of Iran under the Sasanians," 144–46, 178; *EI*², s.vv. Bahrām (Huart-H. Massé) and Sāsānids (M. J. Morony); *EIr,* s.vv. Bahrām V Gōr (O. Klíma), Bahrām V Gōr in Persian Legend and Literature (W. L. Hanaway).

behave with them in the best possible manner and would lay down for them the best of ways of conduct, and that he would unceasingly humble his enemies but continuously behave with mildness and benevolence to his subjects and his troops.[274]

Yazdajird had two sons, one called Hurmuz, who was ruler over Sijistān, and the other called Fayrūz. It was Hurmuz (II) who seized the royal power after his father Yazdajird's death. Fayrūz [872] fled from him and reached the land of the Hephthalites (*al-Hayāṭilah*).[275] He told their king the story of what had happened between him and his brother and that he had a better right to the throne than Hurmuz. He asked the king to provide him with an army with which he could combat Hurmuz and gain control of his father's kingdom, but the king of the Hephthalites refused to respond to his request until he received information that Hurmuz really was a tyrannical and unjust king. He said, "God is not pleased with injustice, and He does not let the works of those

274. Christian sources nevertheless describe Yazdagird II as a savage persecutor of the Christians, both within his kingdom proper (with records of many martyrs in Mesopotamia) and also in Armenia, where his edict of 449 imposing Zoroastrianism on Armenia and Georgia provoking the revolt there, mentioned in n. 277 below. Jews also suffered when in 454–55 Yazdagird forbade the observance of their Sabbath, and later the Persian authorities are said to have closed all Jewish schools. See Nöldeke, trans. 114 n. 1; Labourt, *Le Christianisme dans l'empire perse,* 126–30; Christensen, *Sassanides,* 283–89; Lang, "Iran, Armenia and Georgia," 520–21; Neusner, "Jews in Iran," 915–16; Asmussen, "Christians in Iran," 942.

275. Hayāṭilah is the Arabic broken plural of Hayṭal, correctly *Habṭal. This last seems originally to have been a dynastic name, with forms of it appearing in, e.g., Byzantine sources (*Hephthalitai*) and Chinese ones (*Ye-tai-i li-to*), the Greek form corresponding to the Sogdian nominative pl. **Heβtalīt*; see W. B. Henning, "Neue Materialen zur Geschichte des Manichäismus," 17 n. 2. At the time of Fayrūz/Fīrūz's flight to the land beyond the eastern frontiers of the Sāsānid realm (i.e., in 457), the Kidarites were still ruling in Bactria and Gandhara, but were about to be replaced there, in the second half of the fifth century, by the Hephthalites (J. Harmatta places the Hephthalite attack on the Kidarite territories in Transoxania in 466). The Hephthalites did not apparently arrive in a sudden wave from the Inner Asian steppes, but had doubtless been infiltrating into Transoxania, Bactria, and the northern fringes of Khurāsān for some time. It was to these that the fugitive Fīrūz was able to appeal for the help that enabled him to gain his father's old throne. See Nöldeke, trans. 115 n. 2; Moravcsik, *Byzantinoturcica. I. Die byzantinischen Quellen der Geschichte der Türkvölker,* 69–70; Sinor, "The Establishment and Dissolution of the Türk Empire," 298–99; E. V. Zeimal, "The Kidarite Kingdom in Central Asia," 124–26; B. A. Litvinsky, "The Hephthalite Empire," 138–39.

committing it prosper; under the rule of an unjust king, a man cannot succeed properly in any enterprise or practice any trade successfully except by injustice and tyranny likewise." Then, after Fayrūz had made over al-Ṭālaqān to him, he provided Fayrūz with an army.[276] Fayrūz advanced with it and gave battle to his brother Hurmuz, killing him, scattering his forces, and seizing control of his kingdom.

The Romans had been dilatory in forwarding to Yazdajird, the son of Bahrām, the tribute they used to pay to his father. Hence Fayruz sent against them Mihr Narsī, the son of Burāzah, with an army and matériel such as Bahrām had originally sent against them for that purpose (sc., of exacting tribute), and Mihr Narsī secured the imposition of his master's will for him.[277]

---

276. There was more than one Ṭālaqān in the eastern Persian lands and their fringes. See Nöldeke, trans. 116 n. 1; *EI*², s.v. Ṭālaḳān (C. E. Bosworth and J. R. Lee). The Ṭālaqān intended here is most likely the one in what was the later mediaeval Islamic province of Gūzgān, at a site now unknown but somewhere in the vicinity of modern Maymanah in northwestern Afghanistan. At the time of the Arab invasions of Bactria/Ṭukhāristān, it had a local (Iranian?) ruler of its own. Less likely to be the Ṭālaqān mentioned here is the one beyond Balkh and toward Badakhshān. See Yāqūt, *Buldān*, IV, 6–8; Le Strange, *Lands*, 423; *EI*², art. cit., sections 1 and 3. The mention here of the cession of Ṭālaqān to the Hephthalites implies that the Sāsānid territories never extended as far as the Oxus.

277. This was the war launched by Yazdagird II in 439 soon after he had achieved the throne. It caught the Roman empire at a critical moment when its North African provinces had just been invaded by the Germanic Vandals and when the Huns from Inner Asia were pressing on the Balkans and eastern parts of the empire. As al-Ṭabarī implies in his mention of the arrears of tribute, there were financial reasons behind the outbreak of war, the Byzantines' refusal to contribute to the cost of defenses in the Caucasus to keep out barbarians pressing down from the north, as well as continuing disputes over the allegiance of Arab tribes in the Mesopotamian frontier region, which had caused the war with Yazdagird I twenty years previously (see n. 261 above). The war was terminated by the commander of Theodosius II's eastern army, the *Strategus Anatolicus*, coming to an agreement with Yazdagird, essentially on a basis of retaining the status quo, and with the additional proviso that neither side should erect new fortresses in the frontier zone between the two empires. See Nöldeke, trans. 116 n. 2; Stein, *Histoire du Bas Empire*, I, 291; Frye, "The Political History of Iran under the Sasanians," 146; Rubin, "Diplomacy and War in the Relations between Byzantium and the Sassanids in the Fifth Century AD," 681ff.; Greatrex, "The Two Fifth-Century Wars between Rome and Persia," 2–14.

In addition to this war against the Byzantines, Nöldeke notes, trans. 113 n. 4, that Yazdagird II was involved in several other wars during his reign, unmentioned by the Arabic sources but known from Greek, Armenian, and Syriac authors. The emperor suppressed with difficulty a revolt of the Christian princes of Armenia

According to some authorities, Yazdajird's period of royal power was eighteen years and four months, but according to others, seventeen years.[278]

## [Fayrūz I]

Then there succeeded to the royal power Fayrūz,[279] son of Yazdajird (II), son of Bahrām Jūr, after he had killed his brother and three [other] members of his family. There was related to me a report going back to Hishām b. Muḥammad [in which] he said: Fayrūz prepared for war with the resources of Khurāsān and called upon the men of Ṭukhāristān and regions neighboring on it for support,[280] and marched against his brother Hurmuz, son of Yazdajird (II), who was at al-Rayy. Both Fayrūz and Hurmuz had a common mother, called Dīnak, who was at al-Madā'in governing that part of the kingdom adjacent to it. Fayrūz captured and im-

(see n. 274 above), the battle of 451 between the Persians and Armenians leaving behind the memory of a host of slain Armenian martyrs whose deaths are commemorated by the Armenian Church to this day. Yazdagird also repelled an invasion of the Huns through the Caucasus that had penetrated to Darband and Shīrwān; and, most importantly, he engaged in strife with the Kidarites or their supplanters, defeating their king in a battle near Marw al-Rūdh. It was probably in the course of this last campaign on his eastern frontiers that Yazdagird subdued the local ruler of Ṣūl or Chöl in the vicinity of Gurgān (see on Ṣūl, al-Ṭabarī, I, 874, pp. 112–13 and n. 290 below) and founded there a town, Shahristān-i Yazdagird, whose exact location is unknown.

278. Yazdagird II's reign was 438–57. His name appears on his coins as (KDY) YZDKRTY, i.e., (Kay) Yazdagird. See on his coins Paruck, *Sāsānian Coins*, 63, 366–67, 450–52, Plate XV, Table XIII: Göbl, *Sasanian Numismatics*, 49, Table IX, Plate 10; Sellwood, Whitting, and Williams, *An Introduction to Sasanian Coins*, 21, 119–21; Malek, "A Survey of Research on Sasanian Numismatics," 236.

The other Arabic sources on his reign are Ibn Qutaybah, *Ma'ārif*, 661; al-Ya'qūbī, *Ta'rīkh*, I, 184; al-Dīnawarī, *al-Akhbār al-ṭiwāl*, 58–59; al-Mas'ūdī, *Murūj*, II, 193–94 = §§ 615–16; idem, *Tanbīh*, 101, tr. 144–45; Ḥamzah al-Iṣfahānī, *Ta'rīkh*, 49; Ibn al-Athīr, *Kāmil*, I, 407. Of Persian sources, see Ṭabarī-Bal'amī, trans. II, 127–28. Of modern studies of his reign in general, see Christensen, *Sassanides*, 282–89; Frye, "The Political History of Iran under the Sasanians," 146–47, 178; *EI*², s.v. Sāsānids (M. J. Morony).

279. In Pahlavi, Pērōz, NP Pērōz/Fīrūz, literally, "successful, victorious." See Nöldeke, trans. 117 n. 3; Justi, *Namenbuch*, 247–51; Gignoux, *Noms propres sassanides*, no. 759.

280. That is, the Kidarites or Hephthalites of Bactria.

prisoned his brother.[281] He displayed just rule and praiseworthy
[873] conduct, and showed piety.[282] During his time, there was a seven-year-long famine, but he arranged things very competently: he divided out the monies in the public treasury, refrained from levying taxation, and governed his people to such good effect that only one person died through want in all those years.

He then marched against a people called the Hephthalites, who had taken over Ṭukhāristān. At the outset of his reign, he had strengthened their power, because they had helped him against his brother (sc., Hurmuz).[283] They allegedly practiced sodomy, hence Fayrūz did not deem it permissible (or: it was not deemed permissible) to leave the land in their hands.[284] He attacked the Hephthalites, but they killed him in battle, together with four of his sons and four of his brothers, all of whom bore the title of king. The Hephthalites conquered the whole of Khurāsān, until there rose up against them a man of Fārs, from the people of Shīrāz,

---

281. The Arabic sources on the civil war include Ibn Qutaybah, *Ma'ārif*, 661; al-Ya'qūbī, *Ta'rīkh*, I, 184; al-Dīnawarī, *al-Akhbār al-ṭiwāl*, 58–59 (the most detailed account); al-Mas'ūdī, *Murūj*, II, 195 = § 617; Ibn al-Athīr, *Kāmil*, I, 408. Of Persian sources, see Ṭabarī-Bal'amī, trans. II, 127–28.

282. *kāna yatadayyanu*, reflecting the fact that, in the civil warfare between the two brothers, Fīrūz had the support of the Zoroastrian priesthood. Subsequently in his reign, he enforced harsh measures against the Christians and Jews of the empire. See Nöldeke, trans. 118 n. 4; Labourt, *Le Christianisme dans l'empire perse*, 130; Christensen, *Sassanides*, 290–92. Reflecting the state of affairs in the middle of the fifth century, i.e., at this time, al-Mas'ūdī, *Tanbīh*, 193, trans. 147–48, places the Chief Mōbadh at the head of the social hierarchy in the state, just below the king himself. See Christensen, op. cit., 265, 290.

283. At the time of his first war with the powers of the eastern lands, Fīrūz's enemies there were probably still the Kidarites, who controled Balkh, as they were likewise the Persian ruler's foes in his second war of 467, in the opinion of Zeimal, "The Kidarite Kingdom in Central Asia," 125–26, and see n. 275 above. It would thus have been natural for Fīrūz to have sought aid from the Kidarites' enemies, soon to replace them as the dominant power in Transoxania and Bactria, the Hephthalites, and equally natural that he should fall out with his erstwhile allies once the formidable power of the Hephthalites was firmly established just across his eastern frontiers.

284. This accusation laid against the Hephthalites is also in al-Balādhurī, *Futūḥ*, 403, cf. Nöldeke, trans. 120 n. 1. In the Shu'ūbiyyah controversies of the third/ninth century within the Islamic caliphate, the Arabs asserted that it was the Persians, and especially the Khurāsānians, who had brought the vice into the central lands of the caliphate.

among whom he was a chief, called Sūkhrā.[285] Sūkhrā went forth with a band of followers, like a volunteer fighter and one seeking a heavenly reward for his action, until he encountered the ruler of the Hephthalites and expelled him from the land of Khurāsān. The two sides now disengaged and made peace; all those members of Fayrūz's army who had not by then perished and had been made captive—men, women and children—were repatriated. Fayrūz had reigned for seven years.[286]

Another purveyor of historical traditions other than Hishām[287] has stated that Fayrūz was a man of limited capability, generally unsuccessful in his undertakings, who brought down evil and misfortune on his subjects, and the greater part of his sayings and the actions he undertook brought down injury and calamity upon both himself and the people of his realm. During his reign, a great famine came over the land for seven years continuously. Streams, qanāts, and springs dried up; trees and reed beds became dessicated; the major part of all tillage and thickets of vegetation were reduced to dust in the plains and the mountains of his land alike,

---

285. The form of the name is uncertain, but it appears to have been a family name rather than one of an individual; at all events, Sūkhrā clearly represented a powerful family of the Shīrāz region. In al-Ṭabarī, I, 877–78, 880, pp. 116–18, 120 below, and see n. 298, he is linked with the great family of Qārin and his genealogy given back to legendary Iranian times. See Nöldeke, trans. 120 n. 3.

286. There were actually three wars of Fīrūz with the powers of the East; in the first two he made no headway, while the third campaign ended in the supreme disaster of his death. In the first campaign, Fīrūz may have been taken prisoner and later released in exchange for a ransom, paid in part by the Byzantines, on the evidence of the history attributed to Joshua Stylites, *The Chronicle of Joshua the Stylite*, tr. W. Wright, 8. He was certainly captured at the end of the second campaign, and his son Qubādh/Kawādh, the future king, had to spend two years in the East as a hostage until sufficient ransom money could finally be raised. The third and last campaign was undoubtedly against the Hephthalites proper, who had by now overrun Transoxania and Bactria and were pressing southward over the Hindu Kush into northern India, where there were to appear in Indian chronicles as the "White Huns." See Litvinsky, "The Hephthalite Empire," 138–39. Al-Ṭabarī, or his source, was not able to distinguish these three campaigns, but conflated them into one calamitous war that destroyed the Persian king himself and left his country tributary to the Hephthalites for several years.

287. According to Nöldeke, trans 121 n. 1, this new authority for Fīrūz's reign is Ibn al-Muqaffaʿ, who is indeed cited in Ibn Qutaybah's *ʿUyūn al-akhbār* as "the author of the *Kitāb siyar al-ʿAjam*" for Fīrūz's débâcle with the Hephthalite king Akhshunwār, see al-Ṭabarī, I, 874ff., pp. 113ff. below.

bringing about the deaths there of birds and wild beasts; cattle and horses grew so hungry that they could hardly draw any loads; and the water in the Tigris became very sparse. Dearth, hunger, hardship, and various calamities became general for the people of his
[874] land. He accordingly wrote to all his subjects, informing them that the land and capitation taxes were suspended, and extraordinary levies (*nā'ibah*)[288] and corvées (*sukhrah*) were abolished, and that he had given them complete control over their own affairs, commending them to take all possible measures in finding food and sustenance to keep them going. He wrote further to them that anyone who had a subterranean food store (*maṭmūrah*), a granary, foodstuffs, or anything that could provide nourishment for the people and enable them to assist each other, should release these supplies, and that no one should appropriate such things exclusively for himself. Furthermore, rich and poor, noble and mean, should share equally and aid each other. He also told them that if he received news that a single individual had died of hunger, he would retaliate upon the people of that town, village, or place where the death from starvation had occurred, and inflict exemplary punishment on them.

In this way, Fayrūz ordered the affairs of his subjects during that period of dearth and hunger so adroitly that no one perished of starvation except for one man from the rural district of Ardashīr Khurrah, called Dīh. The great men of Persia, all the inhabitants of Ardashīr Khurrah and Fayrūz himself considered that as something terrible. Fayrūz implored his Lord to bestow His mercy on him and his subjects and to send down His rain (or, assistance, *ghayth*) upon them. So God aided him by causing it to rain. Fayrūz's land once more had a profusion of water, just as it had had previously, and the trees were restored to a flourishing state.[289]

Fayrūz now gave orders for a town to be built near al-Rayy and called it Rām Fayrūz; another town between Jurjān and the Gate of

288. See for this meaning, *Glossarium*, p. DXXXIII.

289. Fīrūz employs here what would have been called, in an Arabian context, *istisqā'*, "offering up pleas, prayers [to God] for rain," and this is in fact the very term used here by al-Dīnawarī, al-*Akhbār al-ṭiwāl*, 59, in his account of Fīrūz's measures to relieve the famine and dearth and to restore fertility. See $EI^2$, s.v. Istiṣkā' (T. Fahd and P. N. Boratav).

Ṣūl and called it Rūshan Fayrūz; and a third one in the region of Azerbaijan, which he named Shahrām Fayrūz.[290]

When Fayrūz's land had revived and his kingly rule there was firmly established, when he had inflicted condign violence on his enemies and subdued them, and when he had completed the building of these three towns, he set off with his army for Khurāsān, with the aim of making war on Akhshunwār, king of the Hephthalites.[291] When news of this reached Akhshunwār, he

---

290. Fīrūz's building activities are also recorded by al-Dīnawarī, al-*Akhbār al-ṭiwāl,* 59–60, and Ḥamzah al-Iṣfahānī, *Ta'rīkh,* 50 (in the latter source, as far as Hind!). Rām Fīrūz is mentioned by the Arabic geographers, but they are uncertain whether it was the predecessor of the mediaeval Islamic city of Rhagae/Rayy or a town near it, as al-Ṭabarī states here. See Yāqūt, *Buldān,* IV, 283; Schwarz, *Iran,* 744–45. The "Gate of Ṣūl" guarded the ancient corridor for peoples from the steppe passing via Dihistān and Gurgān on to the Persian plateau. The Ṣūl in question is possibly the Ṣūl or Chūl known as a family or tribal name; Marquart, *Ērānšahr,* 51, 73, connected it with Turkish *chöl,* "steppe, desert," regarded skeptically by Barthold, *Four Studies on the History of Central Asia. III. A History of the Turkmen People,* 87–88. Von Gutschmid, however, in his "Bemerkungen zu Tabari's Sasanidengeschichte," 736, preferred to connect Ṣūl with the Qaghan of the Western Turks known in Chinese sources as Su-lu and the Arabic ones as Abū Muzāḥim, r. 717–38. De Blois adduces the MP name for "Sogdian," *sūlīg* (*sughdī* > *sughlī* > *sūlī*). Whatever the origin of this name, the local rulers of Ṣūl are certainly described as "Turks" at the time of the first Arab probes into Gurgān and Dihistān, i.e., in the mid-first/seventh century; see al-Balādhurī, *Futūḥ,* 335–36. But the family of these rulers must gradually have bcome Islamized and integrated into Perso-Islamic life and culture. A Ṣūl [Er-] Tigin was a leading commander under the caliphs al-Mu'taṣim and al-Wāthiq in the first half of the third/ninth century (al-Ṭabarī, III, 1194, 1313), and the family produced several scholars and *adībs* in Arabic, most notably Abū Bakr Muḥammad b. Yaḥyā al-Ṣulī (d. 335/947) (see *EI*[2], s.v. al-Ṣūlī [S. Leder]).

The Sāsānids constructed walls across the coastal plain of Gurgān between the Caspian and the inland Elburz mountain chain to keep out the barbarians, including Fīrūz himself (al-Ṭabarī, I, 895, p. 152 below) and Khusraw Anūsharwān (Ibn Rustah, *Kitāb al-a'laq al-nafīsah,* 150, tr. 173). Rūshan Fīrūz seems, however, to be the wrong appellation for Fīrūz's foundation in Gurgān, since certain other sources place this in the district of Kaskar on the lower Tigris (see Nöldeke, trans., 123 n. 2). Later, at I, 894–95, pp. 150–52 below, al-Ṭabarī mentions Khusraw Anūsharwān's stone defenses in the regions of the Ṣūl and the Alan region of the Caucasus, his quelling of the Ṣūl people and his settling them at the (already existing?) Shahrām (= Shahr Rām) Fīrūz. This last is most likely the correct name for Fīrūz's foundation in Gurgān, especially as there seem to be no other mentions, apart from the one here of a Shahr Rām Fīrūz in Azerbaijan. See Nöldeke, trans. 123 nn. 1–3.

291. It is not immediately obvious whether this is a personal name or a title; the *Khushnawāz* of Firdawsī and other Persian sources looks like an attempt to mold this into an intelligible Persian name. Nöldeke, trans. 123 n. 4, connected the name Akhshunwār with the Kougchas, king of the Kidarites in ca. 485, mentioned

[875] was stricken with terror. It is mentioned that one of Akhshunwār's retainers offered up his life for him and told him, "Cut off my hands and feet and hurl me down in Fayrūz's way; but look after my children and family." He intended by this, so it has been mentioned, to trick Fayrūz. Akhshunwār did this to the man, and threw him down in Fayrūz's way. When Fayrūz passed by him, he was distressed at the man's state, and asked him what had happened to him. The man informed him that Akhshunwār had done that to him because he had told Akhshunwār that he would be unable to stand up against the Persian troops. Fayrūz accordingly felt pity and compassion for him, and ordered him to be carried with him. The man told Fayrūz, by way of advice, so it is alleged, that he would show him and his followers a short cut, which no one had ever previously used, to get to the king of the Hephthalites. Fayrūz was taken in by this trickery, and he and his troops set off along the route the mutilated man had told him about. They kept on floundering through one desert after another, and whenever they complained of thirst, the man would tell them that they were near to water and had almost crossed the desert. Finally, when the man had brought them to a place where, he knew, they could neither go forward nor back, he revealed to them what he had done. Fayrūz's retainers said to him, "We warned you about this man, O King, but you would not be warned. Now we can only go forward until we encounter the enemy, whatever the circumstances may be." So they pressed ever onward; thirst killed the greater part of them, and Fayrūz went on with the survivors against the enemy. When they contemplated the state to which they had been reduced, they appealed to Akhshunwār for a peace

---

by the Byzantine historian Priscus (see on this Greek rendering, Moravcsik, *Byzantinoturcica,* II, 165–66), and this was followed up by Ghirshman, who adduced a coin of Fīrūz's with the counterstamp of a ruler called Akūn, which he connected with Kougchas; see his *Les Chionites-Hephtalites,* 87–88. The name looks like a distinctly Iranian one, and certainly not a Turkish one, and Henning put forward the view that it was a title, which should be read as *'.kh.sh.n.dār* = Sogdian *'xš'wnd'r* "power holder"; see his "Neue Materialen zur Geschichte des Manichäismus," 17 n. 2. Widengren, however, saw no need to amend the *w* of the ending of the name, and suggested that it represents Sogdian *'xš'wnw'r* "power bearer"; see his "Xosrau Anōšurvān, les Hephtalites et les peuples turcs. Etude préliminaire des sources," 75 n. 1.

agreement, on the basis that he would allow them freely to return to their homeland, while Fayrūz would promise Akhshunwār, with an oath and an agreement sworn before God, that he would never in the future mount raids against him, covet his territories, or send against him an army to make war on them. Fayrūz further undertook to establish a boundary between the two kingdoms, which he would not cross. Akhshunwār was content with these promises. Fayrūz wrote for him a document, properly sealed and with his obligations guaranteed by professonal witnesses. Akhshunwār then allowed him to depart, and he returned home. [876]

However, once Fayrūz arrived back in his kingdom, overweening pride and uncontrollable rashness led him to renew the war with Akhshunwār. He led an attack on Akhshunwār, despite the advice of his viziers and his close advisers against this, since it involved breaking the agreement; but he rejected their words and would only persist in following his own judgment.[292] Among those who counseled against this course of action was a man called Muzdbuwadh (?) who was especially close to Fayrūz and whose opinion Fayrūz used to seek out. When Muzdbuwadh perceived Fayrūz's firm determination, he set down what had passed between him and the king in a document, which he asked Fayrūz to seal.[293]

Fayrūz now set off on his expedition toward Akhshunwār's territory. Akhshunwār had dug a great trench (*khandaq*) between his own and Fayrūz's territory. When Fayrūz came to this, he threw bridges across it and set up on them banners which would be guiding markers for him and his troops on the way back home, and then crossed over to confront the enemy. When Akhshunwār came up to their encampment, he publicly adduced before Fayrūz the document with the agreement he had written for Akhshunwār, and warned him about his oath and his undertaking; but Fayrūz rejected this and only persisted in his contentiousness and

292. The narrative emphasizes Fīrūz's personal responsibility, as the breaker of his oath, for the ensuing catastrophe; but as Nöldeke skeptically observes, if Fīrūz had been victorious, all mention of his oath-breaking would have been tossed aside!

293. That is, so that the record should be clear, that he had opposed Fīrūz's planned attack and was thus in no way responsible for the consequences.

squaring up to his opponent. Each one of them addressed his opponent in lengthy speeches, but in the end, they became enmeshed in the toils of war. Fayrūz's followers were, however, in a weakened and defeatist state because of the agreement that had existed between them and the Hephthalites. Akhshunwār brought forth the document Fayrūz had written out for him and raised it up on the tip of a lance, calling out, "O God, act according to what is in
[877] this document!"[294] Fayrūz was routed, mistook the place where the standards had been set up [as markers], fell into the trench, and perished. Akhshunwār seized Fayrūz's baggage, his womenfolk, his wealth, and his administrative bureaus (*dawāwīnuhu*). The Persian army suffered a defeat the like of which they had never before experienced.

There was in Sijistān a man of the Persians, from the people of the district of Ardashīr Khurrah, who had insight, strength in battle, and bravery, and who was called Sūkhrā.[295] He had with him a detachment of cavalrymen. When he received the news about Fayrūz, he rode off that same night, traveling as far as he could, till he came up with Akhshunwār. He sent a messenger, announcing to him his intention of making war and threatening him with destruction and ruin. Akhshunwār dispatched a mighty army against Sūkhrā. When the two sides met, Sūkhrā rode out against them, and found them eager for battle. It is said that he shot an arrow at a man who had ridden out to attack him; the arrow struck the latter's horse between the eyes and became almost totally sunk in its head. The horse fell down dead, and Sūkhrā was able to capture its rider. Sūkhrā spared his life, and instructed him to go back to his master and inform him about what he had seen. The (Hephthalite) troops went back to Akhshunwār bearing with them the horse's corpse. When Akhshunwār saw the effects of the arrow shot, he was amazed, and sent a message to Sūkhrā, saying, "Ask whatever you want!" Sūkhrā told him, "I want you to return to me the government exchequer (*al-dīwān*) and to release the captives: The king did that. When Sūkhrā had taken possession of the ex-

294. That is, bring down upon Fīrūz the stipulated curse for his breaking the agreement he had made with Akhshunwār.

295. Presumably the Sūkhrā mentioned by al-Ṭabarī, I, 873, pp. 110–11 above, as from Fārs, Ardashīr Khurrah being the district in which Shīrāz lay.

chequer and had secured the release of the captives, he extracted from the exchequer records a certified statement of the monies[296] that Fayrūz had had with him, and then wrote to Akhshunwār that he was not going to leave without this money. When Sūkhrā's determination became apparent to Akhshunwār, he purchased his freedom (i.e., from the threatenings of Sūkhrā, by handing over the missing money).

Sūkhrā was able thus to return to the Persian land after rescuing the captives and after getting hold of the exchequer, with the money and all the contents of the treasuries that had been with Fayrūz, now given back. When he arrived back to the Persians, they received him with great honor, extolled his feats, and raised him to a lofty status such as none but kings were able to attain
after him. He was Sūkhrā, son of Wīsābūr,[297] son of Z.hān, son of [878]
Narsī, son of Wīsābūr, son of Qārin, son of K.wān, son of 'b.y.d, son of 'w.b.y.d, son of Tīrūyah, son of K.r.d.n.k, son of Nāw.r, son of Ṭūs, son of Nawdhar,[298] son of M.n.shū, son of Nawdar, son of Manūshihr.

---

296. Reading, with the Sprenger ms., *thabat* (or *thubūt*), "certification, record," as in n. *b*, for the text's *buyūt*.

297. For Wihshāpūr, as in Nöldeke, trans. 127 n. 1.

298. Text, *N.w.d.kā*. The *Addenda*, p. DXCI, refer back to the name Ṭūs, son of Nawdharān, in al-Ṭabarī, I, 601, amended there by the editor from the form in the *Bundahishn* and the *Shāh-nāmah*, the name Nawdhar being in Persian legendary history the son and successor of king Manūchihr, killed by Afrāsiyāb. See Nöldeke, *Das iranische Nationalepos*, 8–9; Yarshater, "Iranian National History," 373, 404, 435. The Naōtara/Nawdhar were, in fact, one of the great princely houses of legendary history, figuring in the Avesta. From the time of Wištāspa onward—apparently through Wištāspa's marriage connection with Hutaosā, of the Naōtara—the Naōtara were reckoned as the royal house, now prominent in the national epic. See Christensen, *Les Kayanides*, 23–25; Yarshater, op. cit., 413, 460–61; and on the family name, appearing in the Avesta as the eponymous epithet *naōtairya-*, see Mayrhofer, *Die altiranischen Namen*, no. 228, regarding it as of uncertain origin.

This impressive genealogy for Sūkhrā, going back to mythological times, indicates the importance of the family and places it as one of the great Arsacid families, that of Qārēn or Qārin, which was to survive the Islamic conquest of Persia and play a role in Islamic history for some two centuries further. Qārin, son of Sūkhrā, received from the Sāsānid monarch lands in Ṭabaristān, the Wandā-Ummīd Kūh in the hinterland of Amul, and in early Islamic times the Qārinid principality may have been centered on Firrīm. The most famed representative of the line in the Islamic period was Māzyār b. Qārin, then only a recent convert to Islam, who rebelled against the Ṭāhirid governors of Khurāsān in the caliphate of al-Mu'taṣim and was executed in 225/840, with the line disappearing from history after this point. See al-Ṭabarī, III, 1268–98; Nöldeke, trans. 127 n. 2, 438 Excursus 3; *EI*[1], s.v.

Another authority knowledgeable about the historical narratives of the Persians has mentioned the story of Fayrūz and Akhshunwār in similar terms to what I have just recounted,[299] except that he has stated that when Fayrūz set out and headed toward Akhshunwār, he appointed as his deputy over the cities of Ctesiphon and Bahurasīr—the two royal residences—this person Sūkhrā.[300] He related: The latter was called, on account of his rank, Qārin,[301] and used to be governor of Sijistān as well as of the two cities. Fayrūz came to a tower (*manārah*) Bahrām Jūr had constructed in the zone between the border of the land of Khurāsān and the land of the Turks in order that the latter should not cross the frontier into Khurāsān—all this in accordance with the covenant between the Turks and the Persians providing that each side should renounce transgressing the other's frontiers. Fayrūz likewise had made an agreement with Akhshunwār not to pass beyond the tower into the land of the Hephthalites.

[After reaching the tower,] Fayrūz gave orders, and had fifty elephants plus three hundred men linked together,[302] and had it (sc., the tower) dragged forward, while he came along behind it. He intended by means of this to assert that he had ostensibly kept
[879] faith with Akhshunwār regarding his agreement with him.[303]
Akhshunwār got news of what Fayrūz was up to in connection with that tower. He sent an envoy to Fayrūz with the message, "Desist, O Fayrūz, from what your forefathers abandoned, and don't embark on what they didn't attempt to do!" Fayrūz took no notice of his words and Akhshunwār's message left him unmoved. He began to try and tempt Akhshunwār into a direct military

---

Māzyār (V. Minorsky); *EI*², sv. Ḳārinids (M. Rekaya).

299. In this version, Fīrūz's enemies in the East have become not Hephthalites but Turks, and Fīrūz's offense consists in advancing beyond the tower that Bahrām Gūr had set up as a boundary between the two powers. Cf. Nöldeke, trans. 128 n. 3.

300. Al-Dīnawarī, *al-Akhbār al-ṭiwāl*, 60, has Shūkhar for this name and also states that Fīrūz was accompanied on the expedition by, among others, the Chief Mōbadh.

301. Nöldeke, trans 128 n. 4, notes that Greek sources also tend to attach family or clan names, associated with great offices in the state, to the offices themselves.

302. The Cairo text, II, 96, has *fa-ṣuffida* "were linked together," with the same meaning as the Leiden text's *fa-ḍumida*.

303. That is, by not leading the attack on Akhshunwār directly from the front of his troops.

engagement and summoned him to this, but Akhshunwār kept on holding back and showing an aversion for this, because the Turks' method of warfare consists for the most part in trickery, deceitfulness, and stratagems. Furthermore, Akhshunwār ordered a trench to be dug behind the lines of his own army, ten cubits wide and twenty cubits deep. He had light branches of wood laid over it and then had it covered with earth. Then he retired with his troops to a spot not too far away. Fayrūz received news of Akhshunwār's departure from his encampment with his troops, and had no doubt that this meant Akhshunwār's withdrawal and flight. He ordered the drums to be beaten, and rode out at the head of his troops in pursuit of Akhshunwār and his followers. They rushed forward impetuously, heading directly toward that trench. But when they reached it, they rushed blindly on to the trench's covering.[304] Fayruz and the whole mass of his army fell into the pit and perished to the last man. Akhshunwār wheeled round to Fayrūz's encampment and took possession of everything there. He took captive the Chief Mōbadh, and among Fayrūz's womenfolk who fell into his hands was Fayrūzdukht,[305] his daughter. Akhshunwār gave orders for the corpses of Fayrūz and all those who had fallen into that trench with him to be retrieved, and they were laid out on funerary structures (*al-nawāwīs*).[306] Akhshunwār sent for Fayrūzdukht, wishing to join with her in sexual congress, but she refused.[307]

---

304. The *Addenda*, p. DXCI, suggest reading the text's *'alā ghimā'ihi* (*ghimā'* = "roof made of reeds and earth" as *'alā 'amāyat^in^*, "erroneously." Cf. *Glossarium*, p. CCCSCII.

305. Literally, "daughter of Fīrūz"; cf. Justi, *Namenbuch*, 250, and Gignoux, *Noms propres sassanides*, no. 761. As Nöldeke, trans. 130 n. 2 notes, her true name would not be known outside the royal harem and its circle of attendants.

306. In conformity thereby with the Zoroastrian practice of exposing corpses to the air rather than inhumation. The *nawāwīs* would be hastily assembled, temporary structures for dealing with large numbers of the slain, corresponding to the more permanent *dakhma*s or "towers of silence."

307. Nöldeke, trans 130 n. 3, notes that this is a distortion of the apparent truth, meant here to emphasize Persian royal pride. According to Ps.-Joshua Stylites, *Chronicle*, trans. 15–16, the victorious Akhshunwār took Fīrūz's daughter into his harem, and she gave birth to a daughter who subsequently married her own paternal uncle Kawādh, son of Fīrūz; the king's daughter was obviously not given back with any other royal womenfolk.

When the news of Fayrūz's death reached the Persian lands, the people were thrown into perturbation and terror. However, when
[880] Sūkhrā became convinced of the exact truth of Fayrūz's fate, he got ready and advanced with the greater part of the troops at his disposal against the Hephthalite lands. When Sūkhrā reached Jurjān, Akhshunwār received news of his expedition to attack him, so he prepared for war and moved toward engaging Sūkhrā in battle; and at the same time he sent to Sūkhrā asking him about his intentions and enquiring what his name and his official position were. Sūkhrā sent back the message that he was a man with the personal name of Sūkhrā and the official rank of Qārin, and that his intention in marching against Akhshunwār was to take vengeance on him for Fayrūz's death. Akhshunwār returned a message to him: "Your way of proceeding in this affair you have undertaken is exactly like Fayrūz's was, since despite the numerousness of his troops, the sole consequence of his attacking me was his own destruction and perdition." But Akhshunwār's words did not deter Sūkhrā, and he paid no heed to them. He gave orders to his troops, and they got ready for battle and girded on their weapons. He moved forward against Akhshunwār, advancing with firm determination and a keen mind (literally, "heart"). Akhshunwār sought a truce and a peace agreement with Sūkhrā, but the latter refused to contemplate any peace agreement with him unless he could recover everything Akhshunwār had appropriated from Fayrūz's encampment. So Akhshunwār returned to him everything he had seized from Fayrūz's camp, including his treasuries, the contents of his stables, and his womenfolk, including Fayrūzdukht, and he handed back to him the Chief Mōbadh and every single one of the great men of the Persians in his possession. Sūkhrā then went back to the land of the Persians with all that.[308]

---

308. The Arabic sources on Fīrūz's last campaign and Sūkhrā's putative campaign of vengeance include Ibn Qutaybah, *Ma'ārif*, 661–62; idem, *'Uyūn al-akhbār*, I, 117–21 (from the *Kitāb siyar al-'Ajam*); al-Ya'qūbī, *Ta'rīkh*, I, 184–85; al-Dīnawarī, *al-Akhbār al-ṭiwāl*, 60; al-Mas'ūdī, *Murūj*, II, 195 = § 617, placing the battle in which the Persian monarch was killed at Marw al-Rūdh, whereas Firdawsī places it in the vicinity of Marw; Ibn al-Athīr, *Kāmil*, I, 408–409. The Persian ones include Ṭabarī-Bal'amī, trans. II, 131–44. Nöldeke, trans. 131 n. 2, saw in the campaign of Sūkhrā a reminiscence of Bahrām Gūr's campaigns in the East, and in his *Das iranische Nationalepos*, 9, drew attention to the role of Sūkhrā

The authorities differ concerning [the length of] Fayrūz's reign. Some say it was twenty-six years, others twenty-one years.[309]

## *Mention of Events in the Reigns of Yazdajird (II), Son of Bahrām (V), and Fayrūz and the Relations of Their Respective Governors with the Arabs and the People of Yemen*[310]

Information was transmitted to me from Hishām b. Muḥammad, who said: The sons of the nobles of Ḥimyar and others from the Arab tribes used to serve the kings of Ḥimyar during their

---

as retriever of the military situation and restorer of Persian national honor after Fīrūz's ill-omen actions had abased it, and he mentioned the parallel role of the house of Qārin (to which al-Ṭabarī attaches Sūkhrā; see above) in Iranian legendary history, possibly an attempt to glorify the house of Qārin by giving it a splendid part in the nation's remote past. Christensen, *Sassanides,* 296, notes that the whole episode of Sūkhrā's campaign of revenge against the Hephthalite king is unmentioned in the contemporary sources (i.e., the Christian chroniclers), and may likewise have been a patriotic Persian invention by circles unwilling to accept the possibility of such a dismal defeat for Fīrūz, especially when the latter had been the darling of the Zoroastrian clergy. Of Byzantine sources on the wars with the Hepthalites, Procopius, *The Persian War,* I.iii.1–iv.35 is detailed but inclined very much to the anecdotal, with undue space devoted to, e.g., the story of a pearl earring of Fīrūz's; see Cameron, *Procopius and the Sixth Century,* 154–55. Agathias, however, has a more lively account, influenced by Syrian and Armenian traditions very hostile to Fīrūz; see Cameron, "Agathias on the Sassanians," 152–54. Of modern studies on the wars, see Ghirshman, *Les Chionites-Hephthalites,* 87–90; K. Hannestad, "Les relations de Byzance avec la Transcaucasie et l'Asie Centrale aux 5ᵉ et 6ᵉ siècles," 438–40; Litvinsky, "The Hephthalite Empire," 138–40.

309. Fīrūz I's reign was 459–84; hence more like twenty-six (lunar) years. His name appears on his coins as (KDY) PYRWCY, i.e., (Kay) Pērōz. See on his coins Paruck, *Sāsānian Coins,* 63, 367–70, 452–57, Plate XVI, Table XIV; Göbl, *Sasanian Numismatics*, 49–50, Table IX, Plate 10; Sellwood, Whitting, and Williams, *An Introduction to Sasanian Coins,* 21, 123–27; Malek, "A Survey of Research on Sasanian Numismatics," 236.

The other Arabic sources for his reign include Ibn Qutaybah, *Maʿārif,* 661–62; al-Yaʿqūbī, *Taʾrīkh,* I, 184–85; al-Dīnawarī, *al-Akhbār al-ṭiwāl,* 58–60; al-Masʿūdī, *Murūj,* II, 195 = § 617; idem, *Tanbīh,* 101, trans. 145; Ḥamzah al-Iṣfahānī, *Taʾrīkh,* 50; Ibn al-Athīr, I, 407–11. Of Persian sources, see Ṭabarī-Balʿamī, trans. II, 128–44. For modern studies of his reign in general, see Christensen, *Sassanides,* 290–96; Frye, "The Political History of Iran under the Sasanians," 147–8, 178.

310. From this point, I, 880 l. 17 to 882, l. 4, Nöldeke did not bother to translate, considering the events narrated there as too "fabelhafte" (but see regarding such omissions, Translator's Foreword, p. xvi above).

period of royal power.[311] Among those who served Ḥassān b.
[881] Tubba' was 'Amr b. Ḥujr al-Kindī, the chief of Kindah during his time.[312] When Ḥassān b. Tubba' led an expedition against the Jadīs,[313] he appointed 'Amr as his deputy over certain affairs.[314] When 'Amr b. Tubba' killed his brother Ḥassān b. Tubba' and

311. The earliest firm mention of Ḥimyar (Sabaic *ḥmyr*) and the Ḥimyarites comes from Pliny the Elder in the late first century A.D., but it is unclear whether the term originally denoted an ethnic identity or a grouping of diverse ethnic elements. It then appears, in what is probably the next century, in the *Periplus of the Erythraean Sea,* where is mentioned Charibael "king of the two nations (*ethnē*), the Homeritae and the Sabaeans." In the first centuries A.D., the Ḥimyarites seem to have been led by minor princes, *qayl*s, and chiefs, rather than kings. Only in the sixth century do we find epigraphic evidence for kings of Ḥimyar, when the Ḥiṣn al-Ghurāb inscription (CIH 621) speaks of their being killed by the Abyssinians. See Beeston, "The Himyarite Problem," 1–7.

312 Kindah (*kdt* = *kndt* in the South Arabian inscriptions, with assimilation of the intervocalic *n*) was the great Arabian tribe which, according to Arab tradition, migrated from Ḥaḍramawt to central Arabia, though this may be an inversion of what actually happened. It was accordingly accounted South Arabian in *nasab* by the overwhelming majority of genealogists (see for certain exceptions to these, Kister and Plessner, "Notes on Caskel's Ǧamharat an-nasab," 58–59). Certainly, in the third century A.D., Kindah was established in southwestern Najd with their center at Qaryat al-Fāw, an important settlement on the main caravan route from Yemen and Najrān northward to Najd (see A. R. al-Ansary, *Qaryat al-Fau. A Portrait of Pre-Islamic Civilisation in Saudi Arabia*); they appear in recorded history as nomad auxiliaries of the kings of Saba, and then, after ca. A.D. 275, of the Ḥimyarite kings. In the second half of the fifth century, Kindah are found further to the north in Najd, with what seems to have been a semipermanent camp/capital at Baṭn 'Āqil (localized by U. Thilo, *Die Ortsnamen in der altarabischen Poesie,* 29, in the wadi of that name, an affluent of the Wādī al-Rummah, to the west of modern 'Unayzah and Buraydah) under the celebrated Ḥujr b. 'Amr, called Ākil al-Murār (on this cognomen, n. 408 see below). It seems that, as part of the general policy of extending Ḥimyarite power into central Arabia at this time, this chief of Kindah was placed in power as a "king" (in fact, merely a tribal chief) over the local Arab tribes there of Ma'add. The Arab historical tradition makes the Ḥimyarite ruler involved here either the Tubba' As'ad Abū Karib or his son Ḥassān (in the South Arabian inscriptions, *ḥs³n*) Yuha'min, whose reigns should be placed, according to the inscriptions, in the second quarter of the fifth century. As well as appearing in the Arabian historical tradition, it now seems likely that Ākil al-Murār is the "Ḥujr b. 'Amr, king (*mlk*) of Kiddat" of a Sabaean rock inscription found near Kawkab, roughly half-way between Najrān and al-Fāw (see Iwona Gajda, "Ḥuǧr b. 'Amr roi de Kinda et l'établissement de la domination ḥimyarite en Arabie centrale," 65–73). The fortunes of Kindah were thus for long connected with the rulers of South Arabia, until the fall of the Ḥimyarites under Abyssinian pressure deflected many elements of the tribe in southwestern Najd into Ḥaḍramawt. See, in general, Ibn al-Kalbī-Caskel-Strenziok, *Jamharat al-nasab,* I, Tables 176, 233, II, 47–53, 371–2; G. Olinder, *The Kings of Kinda of the Family of Ākil al-Murār,* 32–50; Chr. Robin, in idem (ed.), *L'Arabie antique de Karib'īl à*

assumed the royal power in his stead, he took ʿAmr b. Ḥujr al-Kindī into his personal service. ʿAmr b. Ḥujr was a man of sound judgment and sagacity. ʿAmr b. Tubbaʿ intended to honor him and at the same time to diminish the status of his brother Ḥassān's sons, and as part of this policy he gave Ḥassān b. Tubbaʿ's daughter in marriage to ʿAmr b. Ḥujr. The Ḥimyarites grumbled at this, and among them were some young men who were concerned about her, because none of the Arabs had previously been bold enough to desire a marriage alliance with that house (sc., the Ḥimyarites).

---

*Mahomet. Nouvelles données sur l'histoire des Arabes grâce aux inscriptions,* 80–81; idem, "Le royaume ḥujride, dit «royaume de Kinda», entre Ḥimyar et Byzance," 666–68; idem, in *Supplément au Dictionnaire de la Bible,* s.v. Sheba. 2, col. 1141; *EI*2, s.v. Kinda (Irfan Shahîd).

Ḥujr's son ʿAmr, mentioned here, had the cognomen al-Maqṣūr, apparently because he was "limited, confined" to his father's sphere of power and unable to expand it (regarding his personal qualities, al-Ṭabarī, below, stresses his judgment and sagacity). He succeeded Ḥujr in the main center of Kindī authority, Najd, with another branch of the family under his brother Muʿāwiyah al-Jawn controling the eastern Najd regions of Yamāmah, Hajar and Baḥrayn. See Olinder, op. cit., 47–50, and nn. 314, 408 below.

313. This was one of the extinct tribes of the Arabs, *al-ʿArab al-bāʾidah,* according to Arabic lore and legend, which relates that Jadīs and his brother Thamūd were three generations after Sām b. Nūḥ, i.e., Noah's son Shem. The story goes that Jadīs, living in Yamāmah, rebelled against the tyranny of a sister tribe, Ṭasm, but that the sole survivors of the latter called in Ḥassān Tubbaʿ, whose army exterminated the Jadīs. See al-Ṭabarī, I, 215, 217, 219–21, 771–75; Ibn al-Kalbī-Caskel-Strenziok, *Jamharat al-nasab,* I. 40; *EI*2, s.v. Ṭasm (W. P. Heinrichs).

314. Tubbaʿ, with the Arabic broken plural Tabābiʿah, is used by writers of Islamic times as a dynastic title (comparable to Firʿawn, pl. Farāʿinah, for the Pharaohs of Egypt and Kisrā, pl. Akāsirah, for the Sāsānid kings (on this last title, see n. 374 below), etc.) for this line of Ḥimyarite rulers who controled the southwestern part of Arabia from the late third century A.D. to the early sixth century. It is probably true that Tubbaʿ was a title rather than a personal name, but its meaning and/or etymology are unknown; the explanations of the Arabic lexicographers (see Lane, *Lexicon,* 295b–c) can be disregarded. At all events, ca. 275 the Ḥimyarite Shamir Yurʿish or Yuharʿish overthrew the Sabaean rulers in Yemen, together with the independent rulers in Ḥaḍramawt, and constituted himself "king of Saba and Dhū Raydān and of Ḥaḍramawt and *Ymnt*" (see further on him, al-Ṭabarī, I, 890, p. 142 and n. 364 below). Almost all the Tubbaʿ rulers mentioned by Islamic authors, most notably by al-Ḥasan b. Aḥmad al-Hamdānī (d. 334/945) in his *Iklīl,* can be validated from South Arabian inscriptions, but there remain lacunae, and a definitive dynastic list cannot be worked out. See Beeston, "Hamdānī and the Tabābiʿah," 5–15; *EI*2, s.v. Tubbaʿ (A. F. L. Beeston).

ʿAmr b. Tubbaʿ's patronage of ʿAmr b. Ḥujr al-Kindī further illustrates the closeness of the links between Kindah and the kings of Ḥimyar, as does his giving in marriage his own niece to ʿAmr b. Ḥujr, mentioned a few lines below. Cf. Olinder, *The Kings of Kinda,* 48, who is unnecessarily skeptical about this marriage.

Ḥassān b. Tubbaʻ's daughter bore al-Ḥārith b. ʻAmr to ʻAmr b. Ḥujr.

After ʻAmr b. Tubbaʻ, ʻAbd Kulāl b. Muthawwib succeeded to the royal power. This was because the sons of Ḥassān were only small, except for Tubbaʻ b. Ḥassān, whom the jinn had rendered mentally unbalanced. Hence Abū Kulāl b. Muthawwib assumed the royal power [temporarily], fearing lest someone outside the royal house of the kingdom might covet it. He was qualified to exercise this power through his mature years, his experience, and his excellent powers of governing. According to what has been mentioned, he was an adherent of the original form of Christianity (*ʻalā dīn al-Naṣrāniyyah al-ūlā*), but used to conceal this from his people. He had been converted to that faith by a man of Ghassān who had come from Syria, but whom the Ḥimyarites had then attacked and killed.[315]

At that point, Tubbaʻ b. Ḥassān recovered his sanity and was restored to health. He was highly knowledgeable about the stars, the most intelligent among those who had learned [the sciences] in his time, and the one with the most information and lore concerning both the past and what was to come after him in the future. Hence Tubbaʻ b. Ḥassān b. Tubbaʻ b. Malikay Karib b. Tubbaʻ al-Aqran was raised to the kingship. Ḥimyar and the Arabs stood in intense awe of him. He then sent his sister's son al-Ḥārith b. ʻAmr b. Ḥujr al-Kindī at the head of a powerful army against the
[882] lands of Maʻadd,[316] al-Ḥīrah , and the districts adjacent to them both. Al-Ḥārith marched against al-Nuʻmān b. Imri' al-Qays b. al-Shaqīqah and fought with him; al-Nuʻmān and a number of his family were killed, and his companions were routed. Only al-Mundhir b. al-Nuʻmān al-Akbar,[317] whose mother was Mā' al-

315. That is, by al-Nuʻmān I b. Imri' al-Qays II (r. ca. 400–18). See Rothstein, *Lahmiden*, 52, 65–68, 70.

316. Maʻadd is a general designation for the North Arab tribes in Islamic times, as is also that of his father ʻAdnān and his son Nizār. Maʻadd was originally, in pre-Islamic times, a tribal group in central Arabia, presumably the Nizār of the Namārah inscription of A.D. 328, and then in the early sixth century the Maʻadd are mentioned in South Arabian inscriptions as the North Arab subjects of Kindah. See Ibn al-Kalbī-Caskel-Strenziok, *Jamharat al-nasab*, I, Table 1, II, 1–2, 379; *EI*², s.v. Maʻadd (W. M. Watt).

317. That is, al-Mundhir I b. al-Nuʻmān I (r. ca. 418–76). See Rothstein, *Lahmiden*, 53, 68–70.

Samā', a woman of the Banū al-Namir,[318] managed to escape from al-Ḥārith. In this way the royal power of the house of al-Nu'mān passed away, and al-Ḥārith b. 'Amr al-Kindī succeeded to their former power and possessions.[319]

Hishām related: After al-Nu'mān, his son al-Mundhir b. al-Nu'mān succeeded to the royal power, al-Mundhir's mother being Hind bt. Zayd Manāt b. Zayd Allāh b. 'Amr al-Ghassānī,[320] for forty-four years, of which eight years and nine months fell within

---

318. The Namir b. Qāsiṭ were a minor tribe of Rabī'ah. See Ibn al-Kalbī-Caskel-Strenziok, *Jamharat al-nasab,* I, Table 141, II, 444; Ibn Durayd, *Kitāb al-Ishtiqāq,* 334–35.

319. Al-Ḥārith b. 'Amr al-Maqṣūr (*fl.* in the first thirty years or so of the sixth century) was a dominating personality on the political and military scene of Arabia and the adjacent fringes of the Byzantine and Persian lands. The Lakhmids and the chiefs of Kindah had had connections, despite being rivals for the control of northern and eastern Arabia; already in the later fifth century al-Aswad b. al-Mundhir I had married a daughter, Umm al-Malik, of the Kindī 'Amr b. Ḥujr Ākil al-Murār.

The campaign against the Lakhmids mentioned here was preceded by an attack on the Byzantine frontiers in Syria led by two of al-Ḥārith's sons, Ḥujr and Ma'dī Karib, in ca. 500, forcing the Greeks to agree to a peace treaty in 502. According to the South Arabian tradition of Ibn al-Kalbī and the Bakrī tribal one set forth in Abū Muḥammad al-Qāsim b. Muḥammad al-Anbārī's commentary on the *Mufaḍḍaliyyāt* poetical anthology, al-Ḥārith and the Rabī'ah attacked al-Nu'mān al-Akbar, al-Mundhir's father, and then al-Ḥārith became head of the Arabs of Iraq. This accords *grosso modo* wiith the South Arabian tradition of Ibn al-Kalbī also given here by al-Ṭabarī, that al-Nu'mān was killed but his son al-Mundhir III b. al-Nu'mān II b. Mā' al-Samā' managed to escape. All other Arabic traditions are concerned only with al-Mundhir, variously described as the son of Imru' al-Qays, of al-Nu'mān, and of Mā' al-Samā', and not with his father. Concerning the date of the event, the Ps.-Joshua the Stylite, *Chronicle,* trans. 45–46, states that the Arab (i.e., Kindī) invasion of the Lakhmid lands took place when al-Nu'mān was away with the Persian army combatting the Greeks, which would place an attack by al-Ḥārith on al-Ḥīrah in 503. It is probable that the Kindī ruler was then able to control the greater part of the Lakhmid dominions from 503 till 506, the years when the Byzantine-Persian war was at its most intense, and Kawād was unable to afford the Lakhmids any assistance. According to the Bakrī tradition again, al-Mundhir, bereft of Persian help, had to agree to marry al-Ḥārith's daughter Hind, who, as a Christian, was subsequently held in great honor at al-Ḥīrah and was the founder of a monastery in the region of al-Ḥīrah, the Dayr Hind (al-Ṣughrā); see al-Shābushtī, *Kitāb al-diyārāt,* 244–46, and n. 914 below. See for these events, Rothstein, *Laḫmiden,* 69–71, 87ff.; Olinder, *The Kings of Kinda,* 57–63; S. Smith, "Events in Arabia in the 6th Century A.D.," 445–46; *EI*², s.v. Kinda (Irfan Shahîd). For the general background of relations between Byzantium and Kindah, Shahîd, "Byzantium and Kinda," 57–63.

320. As Rothstein pointed out, *Laḫmiden,* 68, this *nasab* does not necessarily imply that Hind was a princess of the Jafnid/Ghassānid royal house in Syria; there were members of Ghassān living in al-Ḥīrah, e.g., the Āl Buqaylah.

the time of Bahrām (V) Jūr, son of Yazdajird (I), eighteen years fell within the time of Yazdajird (II), son of Bahrām, and seventeen years within the time of Fayrūz b. Yazdajird (II). After him there reigned his son al-Aswad b. al-Mundhir, whose mother was Hirr bt. al-Nuʻmān from the descendants of al-Hayjumānah bt. ʻAmr b. Abī Rabīʼah b. Dhuhl b. Shaybān.[321] It was he whom the Persians imprisoned. [He reigned for] twenty years, of which ten years fell within the time of Fayrūz, son of Yazdajird (II), four years in the time of Balāsh, son of Yazdajird (II), and six years in the time of Qubādh, son of Fayrūz.[322]

## *[Balāsh]*

Then there succeeded to the royal power after Fayrūz, son of Yazdajird (II), his son Balāsh.[323]

(He was) the son of Fayrūz, son of Yazdajird (II), son of Bahrām (V) Jūr. His brother Qubādh had disputed the succession with him, but Balāsh had emerged victorious and Qubādh had fled to Khā-
[883] qān, king of the Turks, seeking his help and military aid.[324] When the crown was placed on Balāsh's head, the great men of state and the nobles gathered round him, hailed him with congratulations, and invoked divine blessings on him. They requested him to re-

---

321. Nöldeke, trans. 133 n. 1, thought that the unusual name al-Hayjumānah (found in ancient Arab onomastic in both masculine and femine forms) stemmed from Greek *hegoumenē* or *hegemōn*, and this seems very probable.

322. The reign of al-Aswad b. al-Mundhir I is poorly documented, but must have fallen substantially within the third quarter of the fifth century and just beyond it, apparently from 462 onward in Rothstein's computation.. The lists of the Lakhmid kings in the Arabic sources, where they mention al-Aswad (here from Ibn al-Kalbī, and also in al-Masʻūdī, *Murūj*, III, 200 = § 1060) accord in giving him a reign of twenty years, which would take his reign up to 482. See Rothstein, *Laḫmiden*, 55, 70.

323. Correctly, the brother of Fayrūz and not his son. See Frye, *The Heritage of Persia*, 295. On the name Balāsh/Walāsh, see n. 31 above.

324. Some sources, both Christian and Muslim, mention two flights of Kawād from Walāsh to the rulers of the East, others only one. He had certainly been a hostage for two years with the Hephthalite king Akhshunwār, according to al-Yaʻqūbī and other authorities. Further sources state, however, that Walāsh had to struggle for the succession of his father's death with another brother, Zarēr. See Nöldeke, trans. 133 n. 6.

ward Sūkhrā for what he had done, so Balāsh marked him out as one of his special favorites, honored him and gave him rich presents.[325] Balāsh invariably behaved in a praiseworthy manner and had an intense care for the prosperity of the land. His laudable concern for this reached the extent that, whenever he heard of the ruin of a house and the flight of its inhabitants, he would punish the owner of the village[326] because of his lack of lively concern for them and lack of relief for their need, so that they would not have been compelled to abandon their homes. He built in the Sawād a city he called Balāshāwādh, which is Sābāṭ near al-Madā'in.[327] His reign lasted four years.[328]

---

325. Sūkhrā was clearly a dominant influence during Walāsh's short reign. It may well be that Sūkhrā and his son Zārmihr, mentioned just below, are one and the same person. See Nöledke, trans. 134 n. 1.

326. *ṣāḥib al-qaryah,* i.e., the *dihqān,* a member of the lesser nobility of rural and small-town landowners.

327. This is a false equation of the two places mentioned, which extracts a fictitious name from the later port of Balāshābād; a genuine Sābāṭ, Sābāṭ al-Madā'in, in Persian, Walāshābād, existed as the port of Ctesiphon from Arsacid times, having been founded by Vologeses I (r. ca. A.D. 51–80), whose name really lies behind al-Ṭabarī's Balāshāwādh. See Nöldeke, trans. 134 n. 4; Fiey, "Topographie chrétienne de Mahozé," 398–99.

328. Walāsh's reign was 484–88. His name appears on his coins as (ḤWKDY) WLK'Š, i.e., Hu Kay Wālakhsh. See on his coins Paruck, *Sāsānian Coins,* 63–64, 370–73, 457–59, Plates XVI–XVII, Table XVI; Göbl, *Sasanian Numismatics,* 50–51, Table X, Plate 11; Sellwood, Whitting, and Williams, *An Introduction to Sasanian Coins,* 21, 128–29; Malek, "A Survey of Research on Sasanian Numismatics," 236.

Of the other Arabic sources on his reign, al-Ya'qūbī, al-Dīnawarī, and al-Mas'ūdī merely give his name and the length of his reign. Ibn Qutaybah, *Ma'ārif,* 610, mentions him in connection with a popular proverb, *ḥijām Sābāṭ,* and 662–63 in regard to his brief reign and his deposition in favor of his brother Qubādh. Ḥamzah al-Iṣfahānī, *Ta'rīkh,* 50, notes that he built Balāshābād and another town near Ḥulwān called Balāshfarr (read thus for the text's *Balāsh.'.z*). See also Ibn al-Athīr, *Kāmil,* I, 411. Of Persian sources, see Ṭabarī-Bal'amī, trans. II, 144–46. For modern studies of his reign, see Christensen, *Sassanides,* 295–96; Frye, "The Political History of Iran under the Sasanians," 149, 178.

Despite Walāsh's good rule, he was overthrown and blinded by a conspiracy of the great men of state and the Zoroastrian clergy; Ps.-Joshua the Stylite, *Chronicle,* trans. 12–13, says that the clergy hated him and condemned him for introducing public baths into Persia, presumably because it was a foreign, Roman practice and such use of water profaned one of the sacred elements of creation. His measures had perhaps clashed with the interests of the aristocracy and the *dihqāns,* while his conciliatory policy toward the Christians had aroused the ire of the priesthood of the state church. See Nöldeke, trans. 134 n. 5; Labourt, *Le Christianisme dans l'empire perse,* 154.

## *[Qubādh I]*

Then there succeeded to the royal power Qubādh, son of Fayrūz, son of Yazdajird (II), son of Bahrām (V) Jūr.[329] Before Qubādh attained the throne, he had fled to Khāqān, seeking help from him against his brother Balāsh. On his way there, he passed through the vicinity of Naysābūr, accompanied by a small band of companions fleeing with him in disguise. Among these was Zarmihr, son of Sūkhrā. Qubādh had an intense desire for sexual satisfaction, complained about this to Zarmihr, and asked the latter to seek out a wife of good family (*dhāt ḥasab*) for him.[330] Zarmihr did that, and went along to the wife of his major-domo (*ṣāḥib manzilihi*), who was one of his cavalrymen; she had a virgin daughter, of outstanding beauty. He asked her, as a sincere friend, for her daughter, and indicated to her that he would send her along to Qubādh. The wife told her husband about that, while Zarmihr kept on setting forth to the two of them how attractive a proposition it was and spelling out to them how alluring a prospect it was
[884] for them, until finally they consented. The girl, who was called Nīwāndukht,[331] came to Qubādh; he lay with her that very night, and she became pregnant with Anūsharwān.[332] He ordered for her

329. Qubādh is the Arabized form of MP Kawād, Greek form Kabatēs, on his coins KW'T and KDY KW'T, i.e., (Kay) Kawād, which goes back to Kawi Kawāta, the legendary founder of the Kayānid dynasty. Following Nöldeke, Christensen, *Les Kayanides*, 40–41, and *Sassanides*, 350–51, noted the increasing popularity from the fifth century onward of personal names from Persian legendary history and that it was from this time that the legendary, epic history assumed the form as we know it in the *Xwadāy-nāmag*. See Nöldeke, trans. 135 n. 1, 147 n. 1; Justi, *Namenbuch*, 159–60; Mayrhofer, *Die altiranischen Namen*, no. 209; Gignoux, *Noms propres sassanides*, no. 493; Yarshater, "Iranian National History," 374.

330. Necessary for her, since she was to be the mother of the great Anūsharwān. For the name Zarmihr ("golden Mithra"), see Justi, *Namenbuch*, 383; P. Gignoux, *Noms propres sassanides*, no. 1082. The historicity of this whole episode of Kawād's flight to the Khāqān of the Turks during his brother Balāsh's reign is, however, difficult to accept, and may be a confusion arising from the fact of Kawād's undoubted one, probably two, stays among the Hephthalites. The begetting of Anūsharwān at Nīshābūr must, at all events, be pure fable.

331. Following the reading of this name by Nöldeke in text, n. *a*; cf. his trans. 502. Justi, *Namenbuch*, 228–29, interpreted Nēwāndukht as "daughter of heroes."

332. Anūshrawān or Anūsharwān (the most common form of the name in later Islamic times), in its original form Anōshag-ruwān, literally "of immortal soul"; see Justi, *Namenbuch*, 17–18; Gignoux, *Noms propres sassanides*, no. 102. According to Nöldeke, 136 n. 2, we do not possess any contemporary evidence for this

a handsome present and gave her a noble reward. It has been said that the mother of that girl asked her about Qubādh's appearance and bodily form: The girl told her that she knew nothing about that except that she noticed that his trousers were embroidered with gold.[333] Her mother knew thereby that he was a royal prince, and this gave her happiness.

Qubādh traveled on to Khāqān, and when he reached him, he told him that he was the son of the king of Persia and that his brother had contested the throne with him and had gained the upper hand. Hence he was now coming to Khāqān seeking help. The latter gave him fine promises, but Qubādh remained at Khāqān's court for four years, during which Khāqān kept putting off his promise to Qubādh. Qubādh became tired of waiting and sent a message to Khāqān's wife requesting her to adopt him as her own child, and requesting her to speak with her husband regarding him and ask him to fulfill his promise. She did this, and kept on at length pressing Khāqān until he dispatched an army with Qubādh.[334]

---

cognomen of the future Khusraw I, hence we cannot say whether this original form of the by-name was used for him or whether a shorter form was current. De Blois has, moreover, pointed out that this epithet is commonly used in Middle Persian with the simple meaning of "deceased" (hence the equivalent of Arabic *al-marḥūm* "the one on whom [God] has had mercy"), thus strengthening the probability that it was not applied to Khusraw till after his death; see *Burzōy's Voyage to India and the Origin of the Book of Kalīlah wa Dimnah,* 96.

333. Trousers were regarded by classical writers as a characteristic garment for the Persians (according to Herodotus, *History,* I.71, adopted by the Persians from the Scythians, steppe people of Inner Asia). A Byzantine author like Theophylactus Simocatta speaks of the "gold-embroidered trousers" of the Persian kings. Ḥamzah al-Iṣfahānī, *Ta'rīkh,* 50, says that Kawād's trousers were red. The Arabic word for trousers, *sirwāl* is of doubtful etymology, though often assumed to be a loanword from Persian (cf. Siddiqi, *Studien über die persischen Fremdwörter,* 18, 24; the parallel Persian form *shalwār* is often derived from a word *shāl* said to mean "thigh," but an origin in a putative OP word *zārawāro,* as asserted by W. Björkman in his *EI*[2] article "Sirwāl," is impossible (personal communication from Professor N. Sims-Williams).

334. According to some Western sources, when Kawād was in exile among the Hephthalites, he married the king's daughter, the offspring of the ruler and Fīrūzdukht (see n. 307 above). This would appear to be the basis for the story here in al-Ṭabarī's text, in which he becomes the adoptive son of the Khāqān's wife and, by extension, of the Khāqān himself. He would in any case now be in a strong position to secure military help from a father-in-law/adoptive father in gaining the Persian throne.

When Qubādh departed with the military force and reached the vicinity of Naysābūr, he asked the man who had brought the girl to him about what had happened to her. The man made enquiries of the girl's mother, who told him that she had given birth to a boy. Qubādh gave orders for the child to be brought to him. She came to him, bringing Anūsharwān by her hand. When she entered his presence, he asked her about the boy's history, and she informed him that he was his own son, that the boy resembled him in his bodily form and handsomeness. It is said that the news of Balāsh's death reached him on that very spot. He regarded the child's birth as a good augury, and ordered him and his mother to be conveyed in wagons of the type customary for royal womenfolk.[335]

When Qubādh reached al-Madā'in and had gathered together firmly in his hands all the reins of royal power, he sought out Sūkhrā for special honor, delegated to him all his executive
[885] powers, and gave him thanks for the service rendered to him by his son (sc., by Zarmihr). He then sent out troops to the distant frontiers, which inflicted hurt on his enemies and brought back numerous captive women and children.[336] Between al-Ahwāz and Fārs he built the town of Arrajān, and likewise he built the town of Ḥulwān, and, in the administrative district (*kūrah*) of Ardashīr Khurrah, in the neighborhood of Kārazīn, a town called Qubādh Khurrah. All this was in addition to [other] towns and villages he founded and to [other] canals he had dug and bridges he had constructed.[337]

---

335. Carts and wagons, originally with two wheels and shafts for the animals drawing them, are known to have been used by the steppe peoples of Inner Asia from early Christian times onward, hence this form of transport would be familiar to Kawād from his residence among the Hephthalites; but they seem in any case to have been employed in Persia, on the testimony of classical authors, from Achaemenid times onward for conveying royal consorts. See also *EI*[2], s.v. 'Araba. II. (M. Rodinson).

336. According to al-Balādhurī, *Futūḥ*, 194, Kawād sent one of his commanders into the region of Arrān in Transcaucasia to secure the Caucasus passes against the Khazars (at this early period, this is probably an anachronism, and the steppe peoples to the north of the Caucasus were probably Huns, the Turkish Onughurs, and/or Avars, since it is only ca. 630 that a distinct Khazar state begins to emerge; see P. B. Golden, *Khazar Studies*, I, 28ff., 58–59). Kawād then ordered the building in Arran of various towns and defences between Shīrwān and the Alan Gates.

337. For Arrajān, see al-Ṭabarī, I, 818, p. 12 and n. 45 above. Ḥulwān, at the entrance from the Iraq plain to the pass through the Zagros mountains and thence

Now when the greater part of Qubādh's days had gone by, with Sūkhrā in charge of the government of the kingdom and the management of affairs, the people came to Sūkhrā and undertook all their dealings with him, treating Qubādh as a person of no importance and regarding his commands with contempt.[338] At last, Qubādh became desirous of resuming power and was no longer able to endure that state of affairs or remain content with it. He wrote to Sābūr of al-Rayy, [a man] from the house called Mihrān, who was Supreme Commander of the Land (*iṣbahbadh al-bilād*),[339] to come to him with the troops under his command.[340] Sābūr came to him with these, and Qubādh sketched out for him the position regarding Sūkhrā and gave him the necessary orders concerning this last. The next morning, Sābūr went into Qubādh's presence and found Sūkhrā seated there with the king. He walked toward Qubādh, passing before Sūkhrā and paying no attention to him. Sūkhrā [for his part] gave no heed to this part of Sābūr's

---

to Khurāsān, is a much older town than this, being known in Assyrian times as *Khalmanu;* at most, Kawādh can only have refounded it. Kārzīn, to the southwest of Jahrum, within the bend of the Sakkān river in southern Fārs, was still in early Islamic times a town of significance, with the surrounding region still known as "the glory of Qubādh." See Yāqūt, *Buldān,* II, 290–93, IV, 428–29; Nöldeke, trans. 138 n. 3; Le Strange, *Lands,* 191, 254; Schwarz, *Iran,* 70–71, 677–83; Barthold, *Historical Geography,* 198–99; *EI*[2], s.v. Ḥulwān (L. Lockhart).

338. Nöldeke, trans. 138 n. 4, thought that the opening words "when the greater part of Qubādh's days had gone by . . ." required emendation, since they would place the fall of Sūkhrā in the later part of his reign, well after his exile among the Hephthalites and his restoration. On this analysis, the obvious sense of the episode would be that the newly acceeded Kawād was at first under the tutelage of Sūkhrā but grew to resent this tutelage once he had acquired experience and the will to govern independently. This view is ostensibly confirmed by such Arabic sources as al-Ya'qūbī, *Ta'rīkh,* I, 185, and al-Dīnawarī, *al-Akhbār al-ṭiwāl,* 64–65, which state that Kawād was fifteen years old on his accession and remained under Sūkhrā's dominance for the first five years of his reign, i.e., till 493, until he rebelled against this control. On the other hand, further sources make Kawād eventually die as an old man (Firdawsī, at the age of eighty; the Byzantine historian John Malalas, at the age of eighty-two), who must therefore have begun a reign spanning forty-three years in his late thirties; also, the account in al-Ṭabarī, I, 886, places the fall of Zarmihr-Sūkhrā after Kawād's restoration, see nn. 342–43, 345 below.

339. An attempt to render the title *Ērān-spāhbed;* see n. 237 above.

340. The Mihrāns were one of the greatest noble families at this time, in part at least descended from the Arsacid royal house, and Bahrām Chūbīn (see al-Ṭabarī, I, 992ff., pp. 301ff. below) was to be one of their most illustrious members. See the references gathered together in Nöldeke, trans. 139 n. 3, 438–39 Excursus 3, and also Lukonin, "Political, Social and Administrative Institutions: Taxes and Trade," 704.

cunning plan, until Sābūr threw round his neck a noose he had with him and then dragged him off. He was taken away, loaded with fetters, and consigned to gaol. People commented at that time, "Sūkhrā's wind has died away, and a wind belonging to Mihrān has now started to blow," and this became proverbial. After that, Qubādh ordered Sūkhrā to be executed, and this was done.[341]

When ten years had elapsed of Qubādh's reign, the Chief Mōbadh and the great men of state agreed together on deposing Qubādh from his throne, so they did this and imprisoned him. This was because he had become a follower of a man named Mazdak and his partisans, who proclaimed, "God has established
[886] daily sustenance in the earth for His servants to divide out among themselves with equal shares, but men have oppressed each other regarding it." They further asserted that they were going to take from the rich for the poor and give to those possessing little out of the share of those possessing much; moreover, [they asserted that] those who had an excessive amount of wealth, womenfolk, and goods had no more right to them than anyone else. The lower ranks of society took advantage of this and seized the opportunity; they rallied to Mazdak and his partisans and banded together with them. The people (*al-nās*, i.e., the higher levels of society) suffered from the activities of the Mazdakites, and these last grew strong until they would burst in on a man in his own house and appropriate his dwelling, his womenfolk, and his possessions without the owner being able to stop them. They contrived to make all these doctrines attractive to Qubādh, but also threatened him with deposition (if he did not cooperate with them). Very soon it came to pass that a man among them (i.e., the Mazdakites?) no longer knew his own son, nor a child his father, nor did a man any longer possess anything with which he could enjoy ampleness of life.[342]

341. As Nöldeke observed, 140 n. 2, Kawād's seeming ingratitude here may have sprung from fear of Sūkhrā's ascendancy in the state and of his behavior as an overmighty subject; if so, it would accord with the information given in n. 338 above.

342. No episode in Sāsānid history has engendered so much discussion by modern scholars, from Nöldeke himself (in his trans., 455–67 Excursus 3 on Mazdak and the Mazdakites) through Christensen to recent scholars like F. Altheim and Ruth Stiehl, N. V. Pigulevskaya, O. Klíma, Mansour Shaki (viewing the Mazdakite revolt as an upsurge of oppressed peasantry had obvious attractions for scholars

They now consigned Qubādh to a place to which only they had access and set up in his place a brother of his called Jāmāsb.[343] They told Qubādh, "You have incurred sin by what you have done in the past, and the only thing that can purify you from it is handing over your womenfolk." They even wanted him to make

---

writing behind the Iron Curtain), H. Gaube, and Patricia Crone, as the appearance of the Mazdakite movement and Kawād's involvement in it. Two recent summations of the problem are Ehsan Yarshater's chapter "Mazdakism" and, more controversially, Patricia Crone's article "Kavad's Heresy and Mazdak's Revolt." In brief, it seems unlikely that Mazdak espoused a thoroughgoing program of communism of property and wives, entailing a total upheaval in society, or that Kawād would adopt such a program in its entirety, thereby subverting the hierarchy of classes on which Persian monarchy and society had rested from time immemorial and laying a disordered land open to attacks from the Byzantines on one side and the Hepthalites on the other.

What Yarshater and Crone bring out, despite their different emphases, is that, when Mazdakism came to prominence in the first part of Kawād's reign (488–96), at a time when the emperor was still a youth or young man, it clearly appeared as a Zoroastrian heresy. As such it stemmed from the ideas of a third century A.D. heresiarch, Zarādusht of Fasā in Fārs (the Zarādhusht, son of Khurrakān, of al-Ṭabarī, I, 893, p. 148 below), not connected in any way with Manichaeism, and in *Weltanschauung* and ethos directly opposed to Mani's asceticism and suspicion of the present world. Kawād could never have become, by definition as a Sāsānid monarch, a fervid communist, but did see the utility of some of Mazdak's ideas in his endeavors to reduce the excessive power of the nobility, to modernize the Sāsānid state, to make its social structure more flexible, and to render it more able to withstand attacks from its powerful external enemies in both east and west. His proposed reform of marriage practices did not involve communism of wives, *ibāḥat al-nisā'*, but rather a widening of such existing practices as wife lending, a redistribution of women immured within princely and noble harems, and the allowing of women to marry outside their own class. Regarding property, some redistribution, rather than confiscation, was probably envisaged. Such policies would have reduced social distinctions and destroyed the purity of noble lineages. They must have been anathema to the Persian nobility, and only Kawād's youth explains how he thought he could enforce such measures, given that the only coercive power at his disposal was that of an army staffed by the great nobility and *dihqāns* themselves, members of the classes most likely to be directly affected by the reforms. Hence the ending of what was apparently the first phase of the Mazdakite movement with Kawād's deposition in 496 by a conspiracy of the nobility, who replaced him by what was hoped would be a more pliant Jāmāsb/Zāmāsp, is wholly explicable.

343. Nöldeke, 142 n. 1, noted that all is straightforward in the narrative up to this point, but that it now becomes illogical and absurd, with Kawād dethroned by the Mazdakites but with them influential enough once more after his restoration to procure the killing of Sūkhrā/Zarmihr. Nöldeke attributed this section to Ibn al-Muqaffa'.

Jāmāspa- is in Persian legendary history a son of Kay Khusraw. Whether this is the name appearing here as Jāmāsb/Zāmāsp, Greek form Zamaspēs, on his coins

over himself to them as a sacrifice, so that they could kill him and make him an offering to the fire. When Zarmihr, son of Sūkhrā, perceived this, he went forth with an accompanying group of the nobles, ready to expend his own life, and then killed a great number of the Mazdakites, restored Qubādh to his royal power and drove out his brother Jāmāsb. After this, however, the Mazdakites kept on inciting Qubādh against Zarmihr to the point that Qubādh killed him.[344] Qubādh was always one of the best of the Persian kings until Mazdak seduced him into reprehensible ways. As a result, the bonds linking the outlying parts of the realm became loosened and the defense of the frontiers fell into neglect.[345]

---

Z'M'SP, i.e., Zāmāsp, is unclear. See on Jāmāsb's coins Paruck, *Sāsānian Coins,* 64, 375–76, 461–63, Plate XVII, Table XVIII; Göbl, *Sasanian Numismatics,* 51, Table X, Plate 11; Sellwood, Whitting, and Williams, *An Introduction to Sasanian Coins,* 21, 137–39; Malek, "A Survey of Research on Sasanian Numismatics," 236–37. See on the name, Nöldeke, trans. 142 n. 2; Justi, *Namenbuch,* 109. His brief reign, separating the two parts of Kawādh's one, was 496–98. See on it, Christensen, *Sassanides,* 349–51; Frye, "The Political History of Iran under the Sasanians," 150.

344. It is strange, as pointed out by Nöldeke, trans. 140 n. 2, that after putting Sūkhrā to death, Kawād should take into his service the son Zarmihr and that Zarmihr should then take a leading part in the release and restoration of Kawād after the Mazdakite ascendancy, only to be killed in his turn by the emperor. He suggested that we do not need to assume that Kawād killed successively father and son, but that we have to deal instead with one minister only, Sūkhrā Zarmihr, who had been with Kawād in exile among the Hephthalites but who now, after the emperor's return, had arrogated too much power in the state to himself, leading to his elimination in the usual fashion. This event would have been split into two episodes corresponding to the two elements making up Sūkhrā Zarmihr's name. The actual occasion of the execution must, on this analysis, be accordingly pushed back to the second part of Kawād's reign; but see n. 338 above.

345. That Kawād was a weakling who allowed his empire to fall apart as alleged here (and in al-Ṭabarī, I, 888–89, pp. 139–41 below, in regard to Kawād's relations with the Kindī chief al-Ḥārith b. 'Amr) could well be a slanderous report going back to the Zoroastrian priestly and Persian aristocratic tradition exemplified in the *Book of Kings* which Ibn al-Muqaffa' made available for later Arabic authors, and reflecting Kawād's involvement early in his reign with Mazdakite doctrines and attempts to curb the Zoroastrian clergy and the nobility (see n. 342 above and n. 349 below). It is further reflected, for instance in the report of al-Balādhurī, *Futūḥ,* 292, that in Kawād's reign the irrigation channels in the district of Kaskar on the Tigris in Lower Iraq were allowed to fall into disrepair.

Nöldeke, trans. 142 n. 3, endeavored at length to refute this partisan verdict, pointing out that Kawād held the throne, with just a two or three years' break, for the lengthy period of forty-three years. During this time he undertook two protracted wars against the Greeks (see al-Ṭabarī, I, 887, p. 137 and n. 351 below).

A certain person knowledgeable about the history of the Persians has [on the other hand] mentioned that it was the great men of state of the Persians who imprisoned Qubādh when he became a partisan of Mazdak and one of the followers of his doctrines, and who raised to the royal power in his stead his brother Jāmāsb, son [887] of Fayrūz. Now a sister of Qubādh's went to the prison where he was incarcerated[346] and tried to gain entry, but the offical responsible for guarding the prison and its inmates prevented her from entering. This man became roused by the desire to ravish her at that opportunity, and told her how much he desired her; she informed him that she would not resist him in anything he might desire of her, so he let her in. She entered the prison, and spent a day with Qubādh. Then at her bidding, Qubādh was rolled up in one of the carpets in the gaol, and this was borne by one of his male attendants, a strong and hardy youth, and brought out of the prison. When the lad went past the prison commander, the latter asked him what he was carrying. He was unable to answer, but Qubādh's sister came up behind the lad and told the prison commander that it was a bed roll she had slept on during her menstrual periods and that she was only going forth to purify herself and would then return. The man believed her, and did not touch the carpet or go near it, fearing lest he become polluted by it, and he allowed the lad who was bearing Qubādh to pass freely out. So he went along with Qubādh, the sister following after him.

---

Procopius regarded Kawād as exceptionally clever and energetic. He also maintained a general peace with the Hephthalites in the east; see n. 348 below. Similarly, Crone, "Kawad's Heresy and Mazdak's Revolt," 25–26, stresses that, while Kawād ruled in a mild and pacific fashion, and abstained during his pro-Mazdakite phase from meat (al-Ṭabarī, I, 889, p. 142 below), after his restoration he behaved in a bellicose enough manner and in his warfare with the Byzantines was as savage as any of his predecessors.

346. According to Greek sources, Kawād's fortress-prison lay in Susiana. Procopius, who makes the ingenious woman here Kawād's wife and not his daughter (followed in this by Agathias, see Cameron, "Agathias on the Sassanians," 128–29, 157–58), simply calls it "the fortress of oblivion" and has a lengthy digression on its past history within his already extended account of Kawād's enforced interregnum, imprisonment, and escape. See *The Persian War,* I.v.1–vi.19; Cameron, *Procopius and the Sixth Century,* 155. Theophrastes, however, calls the fortress Giligerda, which led the nineteenth-century traveler and historian Sir Henry Rawlinson to identify it with Gilgird in the mountains to the east of Shushtar. See Nöldeke, trans. 144 n. 1.

Qubādh now took to flight until he reached the land of the Hepththalites, in order to ask their king to help him and to provide him with an army, so that he might make war on those who had rebelled against him and deposed him. It has been further related that, on his outward journey to the Hepththalites, he halted at Abarshahr at the house of one of its leading citizens, who had a daughter of marriageable age, and it was on the occasion of this journey that he had sexual relations with the mother of Kisrā Anūsharwān.[347] It has been also related that Qubādh returned from that journey with his son Anūsharwān and the latter's mother.[348]

He defeated his brother Jāmāsb in the contest for royal power after the latter had reigned for six years.[349] Then after that,

---

347. Abarshahr was the district around Nīshābūr, see al-Ṭabarī, I, 819, p. 15 and n. 59 above. Al-Ya'qūbī, *Ta'rīkh*, I, 185–86, has Abatrshar here, but al-Dīnawarī, *al-Akhbār al-ṭiwāl*, 65–66, in a more detailed account than that of al-Ṭabarī, has Kawād fleeing for refuge in the house of a *dihqān*, whose ancestry went back to Farīdūn, on the borders of Khūzistān and Iṣfahān, and Firdawsī follows al-Dīnawarī substantially. The emperor's flight to a refuge in southwestern-western Persia obviously accords better with his incarceration just before this in Susiana. Cf. Nöldeke, trans. 145 nn. 2–4.

348. There is little information in the Arabic sources on Kawād's stay among the Hephthalites (with whom he already had links from his time as a hostage at the Hephthalite court during his father's reign), but useful information in Procopius and the Western sources. The fugitive Kawād was sheltered—after what must have been a lengthy journey right across Persia—by the king of the Hephthalites (whose personal name is unknown, unless Akhshunwār was still ruling). The king gave to Kawād in marriage his daughters, actually the child of the Persian princess who had been captured by the Hepththalites on the defeat of her father Fīrūz, hence Kawād's niece; such a union would not have been regarded in Zoroastrian custom as at all incestuous. Kawād regained his throne with Hephthalite assistance, but at the price of continued dependence on them. He had to finance the Hephthalite army that placed him back on the throne, to cede territory along the Oxus to them, and to pay a tribute, in Sāsānid coinage counterstamped with the Hephthalite name. This last was in fact paid for over thirty years till the opening of Khusraw Anūsharwān's reign. See Marquart, *Ērānšahr*, 63–64; Christensen, *Sassanides*, 349–50; Ghirshman, *Les Chionites-Hephtalites*, 16–17 and Pl. II (coins) 92–93; Litvinsky, "The Hephthalite Empire," 140.

349. The reign of Jāmāsb/Zāmāsp seems in reality to have been shorter than this, with Kawād resuming power—apparently without striking a blow—in 498 or 499, which would make his period of deposition, imprisonment, and exile only two or three years. The fate of Zāmāsp, now in turn deposed, is uncertain. Elias of Nisibis alone states that Kawād had him killed. More probable is the leniency toward his brother attributed to Kawād by the well-informed Agathias, that Zāmāsp renounced the throne of his own accord, preferring a life of safe obscurity, and was pardoned (confirmed in the Arabic source of al-Dīnawarī, *al-Akhbār al-*

Qubādh led an expedition against the land of the Romans, conquered one of their towns in al-Jazīrah called Āmid[350] and carried off the women and children as captives.[351] He gave orders for a town to be built in the borderland between Fārs and the land of al-Ahwāz and named it Wām Qubādh;[352] this is the town named [888]

---

ṭiwāl, 66). The Christian Arabic *Chronicle of Se'ert* does, however, record a purge of the Zoroastrian priesthood by Kawād, with executions and imprisonments. See Nöldeke, trans. 145 n. 5; Christensen, *Sassanides,* 350–51; Cameron, "Agathias on the Sassanians," 130–31; eadem, *Procopius on the Sixth Century,* 155 (Procopius in his *The Persian War* confuses Jāmāsb with Fīrūz's successor Balāsh/Blasēs); Frye, "The Political History of Iran under the Sasanians," 150.

350. Āmid, classical Amida, was a key point in the fighting between the Byzantines and Sāsānids. It lay on the west bank of the upper Tigris, in what was in early Islamic times the district of Diyār Bakr in the province of Jazīrah, and is now the modern Turkish city of Diyarbakir. See *PW,* I/2, col. 1833, s.v. Amida (Baumgartner) Le Strange, *Lands,* 108–11; Canard, *H'amdanides,* 79–81; *EIr,* s.v. Amida (D. Sellwood). Al-Dīnawarī, *al-Akhbār al-ṭiwāl,* 66, adds that Kawād also captured another town of the region, Mayyāfāriqīn (the Greek Martyropoplis).

351. These are the sole details in the oriental sources on the great four years' war launched by Kawād against the Byzantines (summer 502–autumn 506) soon after his regaining the Persian throne. Kawād's pretext for opening hostilities was the emperor Anastasius's refusal to contribute to Kawād's expenses in financing the Hephthalite army, which had backed him, and in paying the ongoing tribute to the Hephthalites. The Byzantines must have had the hope that, if Kawād were unable to pay his former allies, a rupture between these two latter powers would occur. It seems that the Byzantine frontier fortresses and fortified towns had not been kept in good repair during the fifth century and, as a result, were at this time inadequate to withstand the Persians, especially as the Persians had acquired important stretches of territory in the later fourth century, above all the important bridgehead of Niṣībīn (see al-Ṭabarī, I, 826, p. 28, and nn. 90–91 above). Hence early successes for Kawād's army, which included Hephthalite contingents, were the sack of Theodosiopolis (the later Erzerum) in western Armenia, this capture of Amida/Āmid (see n. 350 above), and that of Martyropolis or Mayyāfāriqīn (the bare information recorded in al-Dīnawarī, *al-Akhbār al-ṭiwāl,* 66, and Yāqūt, *Buldān,* I, 143). However, the war is fully documented in Greek and Syriac sources, such as Procopius's *The Persian War,* I.vii.1–I.x.19; cf. Cameron, *Procopius and the Sixth Century,* 155–56; Ps. Joshua the Stylite's *Chronicle,* trans. 37–62, 63–75. See Nöldeke, trans. 146 n. 1; Bury, A *History of the Later Roman Empire from Arcadius to Irene,* I, 307–309; idem, *History of the Later Roman Empire from the Death of Theodosius I to the Death of Justinian,* I, 10–15; Christensen, *Sassanides,* 352; Ghirshman, *Les Chionites-Hephtalites,* 92–93; Hannestad, "Les relations de Byzance avec la Transcaucasie et l'Asie Centrale aux 5e et 6e siècles," 442; Stein, *Histoire du Bas-Empire,* II, 267–72; Frye, "The Political History of Iran under the Sasanians," 150–51; M. Whitby, "Procopius and the Development of Roman Defences in Upper Mesopotamia," 725–26; Greatrex, *Rome and Persia at War, 502–532,* 73–119.

The fame of the Persian victory at Amida resonated several decades later in a verse of the Ḥīran poet 'Adī b. Zayd:

We struck to the ground Qubādh, the lord of all the Persians, even though they

Būqubādh,[353] also called Arrajān.[354] He laid out an administrative division (*kūrah*) and added to it rural districts (*rasātīq*) from the *kūrah* of Surraq and that of Rām Hurmuz.[355] He then nominated his son Kisrā as his successor in the royal power, and wrote this out in a document, which he sealed with his seal ring.[356] When

---

had stirred up with their hands the glistening swords of Āmid. (*Dīwān*, 124 no. 41)

352. Following *Addenda et emendanda*, p. DXCI, as being a crasis of *Weh-Āmid-Kawād for the text's Rām Qubādh.

353. Following *Addenda et emendanda*, loc. cit., for the text's Barqubādh.

354. These two alternative names for Arrajān are somewhat dubious; the second one should be read as *Abarqubādh, as the consonant ductus in al-Dīnawarī, *al-Akhbār al-ṭiwāl*, 66, and Yāqūt, *Buldān*, I, 143, allows. Cf. Nöldeke, trans. 146 n. 2.

355. Al-Dīnawarī, *al-Akhbār al-ṭiwāl*, 66–67, mentions a number of changes in administrative geography carried out by Kawād in the provinces of *Abarqubādh (locating this, however, in central Iraq), Bihqubādh al-Awsaṭ and al-Asfal, and Iṣfahān. These may have been connected with the cadastral survey of the Sawād of Iraq instituted by Kawād, accompanied by a new tax system, to be continued by his successor Khusraw Anūsharwān, which is mentioned in the Arabic sources. See Crone, "Kawad's Heresy and Mazdak's Revolt," 33–34.

356. According to al-Dīnawarī, *al-Akhbār al-ṭiwāl*, 67, Kawād had several sons, out of whom Khusraw was the most favored, despite the emperor's having certain grounds for suspicion (*ẓinnah*) regarding him. According to Procopius, Kawād's eldest son was Kaosēs, i.e., Kāwūs (called by Theophanes *Pthasouarsan* in an attempt to render *Padashkhwār-shāh*, this being Kāwūs's title as provincial ruler of Ṭabaristān), and there was another son Zamēs, i.e., Jam. But Kawād wished his third, younger son Khusraw to succeed him, since, according to Theophanes, Kāwūs had been brought up (in the first part of his father's reign?) as a Mazdakite.

Toward the end of his reign, Kawād was in a stronger position vis-à-vis the nobility, and was able to make these succession arrangements himself rather than leave the choice and the election of his successor to the nobles and clergy; but he cannot have wished to provoke a strong reaction by nominating Kāwūs if the latter was still indeed an adherent of the Mazdakites. Procopius, *The Persian War*, I.x.1–18, further relates that Kawād had sought from the Byzantine emperor Justin I (518–27) that the latter should adopt Khusraw (just as, at the end of the fourth century, the emperor Arcadius had made the Sāsānid Yazdagird I protector of his son and desired heir Theodosius (II) (see n. 191 above). No doubt Kawād had the intention of strengthening Khusraw's claim to the succession, which might then have been backed, if necessary, by Byzantine arms; but Justin had refused. The second son Jāmāsb (= Procopius's Zamēs/Jam) was disqualified from succeeding to the throne through the loss of an eye. Hence when Kawād fell mortally ill in 531, he wrote out this succession document (al-Ṭabarī's *kitāb*, al-Ya'qūbī's *waṣiyyah*) for Khusraw. According to the Byzantine chronicler John Malalas, he actually had him crowned. Again according to Procopius, ibid., I.xxi.20–22, Kāwūs laid claim to the throne on his father's death, and according to the later historian of Ṭabaristān Ibn Isfandiyār, raised a rebellion, which failed and caused him to lose his life. See Nöldeke, trans. 147 n. 1; Christensen, *Sassanides*, 353–55; Frye "The Political History of Iran under the Sasanians," 151; Crone, "Kawad's Heresy and Mazdak's Revolt," 31–32.

Qubādh died after having reigned for forty-three years, including the years of his brother Jāmāsb, Kisrā put into execution the measures which Qubādh had commended to him.[357]

### *Mention of What Has Been Recorded Concerning the Events Taking Place among the Arabs in Qubādh's Reign in His Kingdom and Involving His Governors*

There was related to me a narrative going back to Hishām b. Muḥammad, who said: Al-Ḥārith b. ʿAmr b. Ḥujr b. ʿAdī al-Kindī met al-Nuʿmān b. al-Mundhir b. Imriʾ al-Qays b. al-Shaqīqah in battle and killed him, with al-Mundhir b. al-Nuʿmān al-Akbar escaping from al-Ḥārith. Al-Ḥārith b. ʿAmr al-Kindī then assumed power over the lands al-Nuʿmān had ruled. At this point, Qubādh, son of Fayrūz, the ruler of Persia, sent a message to al-Ḥārith b. ʿAmr, informing him that there had been formerly an agreement between him and his predecessor as king [among the Arabs] and that he would welcome a meeting with al-Ḥārith.[358]

Qubādh was a Zindīq who did only good deeds, who abhorred shedding blood and who, in his dislike for shedding blood, treated

357. Kawād I's reign was 488–531, with the interlude of Jāmāsb/Zāmāsp's two or three years from 496 to 498 or 499. Concerning his possible age at death, see n. 338 above. Concerning his name on his coins, see n. 329 above. See on his coins, Paruck, *Sāsānian Coins*, 64–65, 373–75, 376–80, 459–61, 464–70, Plates XVII–XVIII, Tables XVII, XIX ; Göbl, *Sasanian Numismatics*, 51–52, Table X, Plate 11; Sellwood, Whitting, and Williams, *An Introduction to Sasanian Coins*, 21, 130–36; Malek, "A Survey of Research on Sasanian Numismatics," 236.

The other Arabic sources for his reign include Ibn Qutaybah, *Maʿārif*, 663; al-Yaʿqūbī, *Taʾrīkh*, I, 185–86 (mainly on Kawād's flight to the Hephthalites and the circumstance of Khusraw's birth); al-Dīnawarī, *al-Akhbār al-ṭiwāl*, 64–67 (considerable detail on Mazdak's movement); al-Masʿūdī, *Murūj*, II, 195–96 = §§ 617–18 (brief note of Mazdak); idem, *Tanbīh*, 101, trans. 145; Ḥamzah al-Iṣfahānī, *Taʾrīkh*, 50–51 (concentrates on his foundation of cities); Ibn al-Athīr, *Kāmil*, I, 412–14, 421. Of the Persian sources, see Ṭabarī-Balʿamī, trans. II, 146–55.

Of modern studies on his reign in general, see Christensen, *Le règne du roi Kawādh I et le communisme mazdakite*; idem, *Sassanides*, 336–62; Frye, "The Political History of Iran under the Sasanians," 149–51, 178; *EI²*, s.v. Sāsānids (M. J. Morony); also references on the Mazdakite movement in n. 338.

358. This is a repetition *grosso modo* of the events treated by al-Ṭabarī at I, 881–82, pp. 124–25 above, but bringing in Kawād at the end causes chronological difficulties, since Kawād only acceeded to power in 488, and the events involving al-Nuʿmān I's death and the succession of his son al-Mundhir I are probably to be placed in the second decade of the century, hence some seventy years earlier; see nn. 315, 319 above.

his enemies with leniency.[359] In his time, heretical opinions (*al-ahwā'*) became rife, and the people came to regard Qubādh as a weak ruler. Al-Ḥārith b. ʿAmr al-Kindī, however, set out with a numerous and well-equipped army, until the two forces met at the bridge of al-Fayyūm.[360] Qubādh ordered a dish of dates and extracted their stones. Then he ordered another dish and placed in it dates in which the stones had been left. These two dishes were placed before them (sc., Qubādh and al-Ḥārith). The dish of dates
[889] with stones by al-Ḥārith b. ʿAmr, and the one with no date stones in it was placed by Qubādh. Al-Ḥārith began to eat the dates and to spit out the stones. Qubādh set about eating [everything in] the dish in front of him, and said to al-Ḥārith, "What's the matter with you? Why aren't you eating exactly what I'm eating?" Al-Ḥārith replied, "Among us, only camels and sheep eat date stones," and he realized that Qubādh was deriding him. After this, the two of them made peace on the basis that al-Ḥārith b. ʿAmr and those he wished of his followers should bring their horses to drink from the Tigris up to their saddle girths but not pass any further beyond that point.[361]

But when al-Ḥārith saw Qubādh's weakness, he began to covet the Sawād, and ordered the men in his garrison posts (*masāliḥihi*) to cross the Euphrates and carry out raids into the Sawād.[362] The

359. See on the term Zindīq, n. 118 above.

360. According to Yāqūt, *Buldān*, IV, 286, this was in central Iraq, near Hīt on the Euphrates; cf. Musil, *The Middle Euphrates*, 350. As a bridge, it would be regarded as neutral ground, hence suitable for a meeting between the two opposing sides. Cf. Nöldeke, trans. 149 n. 1.

361. According to Nöldeke, trans. 149 n. 3, citing the Talmud, this occurs as a formulaic legal expression.

362. These garrison posts must in reality have been part of the Sāsānid defenses along the desert fringes against Arabs from the interior of the peninsula like those of Kindah. From this point onward, al-Ṭabarī's account slides into legend, as recognized by Nöldeke, trans. 150 nn. 1–2, and Rothstein, *Laḫmiden*, 88–89. What is, nevertheless, firmly historical is that between approximately 525 and 528 al-Ḥārith was indeed able to expel the Lakhmids from al-Ḥīrah, having taken over parts of the Iraqi borderlands some twenty years before (see al-Ṭabarī, I, 881–82, pp. 124–25 and n. 319 above). From 528 till his death in 531, Kawād was preoccupied with warfare with the Byzantines, with the emperor Justin I at the outset and then with the great Justinian I, this warfare being centered on Georgia and Transcaucasia on one front and on the Upper Mesopotamian frontier on another one (see Bury, *A History of the Later Roman Empire from Arcadius to Irene*, I, 372–80; idem, *History of the Later Roman Empire from the Death of Theodosius I to the*

cries for help [of the local people] reached Qubādh when he was at al-Madā'in, and he exclaimed: "This has occurred under the protection of their king," and he then sent a message to al-Ḥārith b. ʿAmr that some robbers of the Arabs had mounted raids and that he wanted a meeting with him. When al-Ḥārith came, Qubādh said to him, "You have done something which no one before you has ever done," but al-Ḥārith replied, "I haven't done anything, and don't know anything about it; it was some Arab robbers, and I myself cannot keep a firm hand over the Arabs except by financial subsidies and regular troops." Qubādh said to him, "What do you want, then?" and he replied, "I want you to make over to me a grant of part of the Sawād so that I can get weapons ready by means of it." So Qubādh made over to him the side of the lower Euphrates bordering on the Arabs, comprising six *ṭassūj*s. Al-Ḥārith b. ʿAmr al-Kindī at that point sent a messenger to Tubbaʿ in Yemen,

---

*Death of Justinian*, I, 79–89; Stein, *Histoire du Bas-Empire*, II, 267–71, 283–84, 287–94; Greatrex, *Rome and Persia at War, 502–532*, 139–212). It seems, however, to have been a withdrawal of support from al-Mundhir III by Kawād that allowed al-Ḥārith to take over al-Ḥīrah. Al-Mundhir had apparently been negotiating with the Persians' enemy, Byzantium. Hence credence should not be placed in the information retailed in some Arabic sources (e.g., Abū al-Faraj al-Iṣfahānī, *Aghānī*[1], VIII, 63 = *Aghānī*[3], 78–79; Ibn al-Athīr, *Kāmil*, I, 434) that Kawād tried first to impose Mazdakism on al-Mundhir but failed, whereupon al-Ḥārith b. ʿAmr agreed to accept Mazdakism, and was rewarded by a grant of the former Lakhmid lands. See Christensen, *Le règne du roi Kawādh I et le communisme mazdakite*, and (regarding the tale with skepticism), Olinder, *The Kings of Kinda*, 63–64. In any case, Kawād had broken decisively with the Mazdakites on his restoration in 498 or 499, and it seems highly unlikely that he would make adherence to the heresy an instrument of diplomacy nearly thirty years later. Abū al-Baqā', *al-Manāqib al-mazyadiyyah*, 121, simply states that Kawād was unable to answer al-Mundhir's appeal for help because his kingdom was disturbed by the Mazdakites

Al-Mundhir regained control of al-Ḥīrah in 528. The sources all state that it was Khusraw Anūsharwān who restored him, but Khusraw did not come to the throne until 531; it thus seems that al-Mundhir had somehow regained possession of his capital and that Khusraw merely confirmed this. At all events, Lakhmid power was now firmly reestablished on the Iraq fringes, backed by the might of their traditional patrons and supporters, the Sāsānids. At some unspecified point, al-Mundhir managed to get hold of al-Ḥārith b. ʿAmr, who had had to retreat into the interior of northern Arabia after clashing with the Byzantines and Ghassānids on the Syrian frontiers. Al-Mundhir seized the Kindī leader's camels, killed al-Ḥārith himself, and massacred forty-eight members of the ruling house of Kindah, an event alluded to in the *Dīwān* of al-Ḥārith's grandson Imru' al-Qays (*Dīwān*, ed. Muḥammad Abū al-Faḍl Ibrāhīm, 200, no. 37 vv. 1–2). Other traditions make al-Ḥārith's death at the hands of the Kalb. See Rothstein, *Laḫmiden*, 89–90; Olinder, *The Kings of Kinda*, 63–68.

saying, "I covet strongly the kingdom of the Persians, and have already acquired six *ṭassūj*s of it. So gather your troops together and advance, for there is nothing between you and their kingdom, since the king does not eat meat and does not consider the shedding of blood lawful, for he is a Zindīq." So Tubbaʿ assembled his troops and advanced until he encamped at al-Ḥīrah. He drew near
[890] to the Euphrates, where the midges plagued him. Al-Ḥārith b. ʿAmr ordered a canal to be dug for him as far as al-Najaf, and this was done: this is the Canal of al-Ḥīrah. He encamped against there and sent his nephew Shamir Dhū al-Janāḥ ("Shamir of the Wing") against Qubādh.[363] He fought with Qubādh and routed him, compelling him to flee as far as al-Rayy. He then caught up with Qubādh there and killed him.[364]

Tubbaʿ now sent Shamir Dhū al-Janāḥ to Khurāsān and his son Ḥassān to Sogdia (al-Ṣughd), telling them, "Whichever of you

---

363. See on Shamir Yurʿish or Yuharʿish, n. 314 above and n. 364 below, and al-Ṭabarī, I, 910, pp. 176–77 and n. 451 below.

364. All this is pure fantasy. As implied by al-Ṭabarī in I, 888, pp. 138–39 above, Kawād died a natural death, doubtless at an advanced age after such a long reign. Ibn al-Athīr, *Kāmil,* I, 411, criticizes al-Ṭabarī for his confusion here and lack of critical acumen, such defects of an absense of discrimination and discernment being common, he says, to all writers dealing with the ancient Arabs; Nöldeke in his translation omitted this passage on the legendary exploits of the Tubbaʿ kings, that from I, 890 l. 4 to 892 l. 14. The only genuine feature in al-Ṭabarī's account is that the Tubbaʿ prince Shamir Yurʿish mentioned in al-Ṭabarī, I, n. 910, pp. 176–77 below, the first recorded Tubbaʿ king (on this dynasty, see n. 314 above), really did exist.

For the king's name, *Sh.m.r,* the vocalization is of course speculative, there being no indication of vowels in the South Arabian script with the probable exception of *w* and *y* used both consonantally and vocalically (see Beeston, *Sabaic Grammar,* 6–7). But Shamir or Shimr seem to have better claims that Shammar for the vocalization of the first component of the king's full name, despite the fact that the rather late author Nashwān b. Saʿīd al-Ḥimyarī (d. 573/1178) expressly gives Shammar in his *Shams al-ʿulūm* (see ʿAẓīmuddīn Aḥmad, *Die auf Südarabien bezüglichen Angaben Našwāns im Šams al-ʿulūm,* 56–57). The choice of this latter form by such later writers as Nashwān was probably influenced by the rise of the North Arabian tribe of Shammar and their home, the Jabal Shammar, since there is no orthographic sign in the South Arabian script to indicate gemination (Beeston, ibid., 7–8). G. Ryckmans, *Les noms propres sud-sémitiques,* I, 210, has Šimr, comparing this with Classical Arabic *shimr,* "energetic, capable"; G. Lankester Harding, *An Index and Concordance of Pre-Islamic Names and Inscriptions,* 357, has Šamir; and Robin, *Supplément à la dictionnaire du Bible,* s.v. Sheba. 2., writes Shammir. In the line of verse (apocryphal, naturally) placed in Shamir's mouth in al-Ṭabarī, I, n. 910, p. 177 below, the *wāfir* metre does require *ShVmVr*$^{un}$ or *ShVmr*$^{un}$.

reaches China first shall become ruler over it." Each one headed a mighty army, said to be of 640,000 men. He further sent his nephew Ya'fur against the Romans; it was he who recited:

O my companion, you may well be full of wonder at Ḥimyar,
when they encamped at al-Jābiyah![365]
Eighty thousand is the number of their chiefs,[366] and for each
group of eight men there is a chief!

Ya'fur proceeded until he reached Constantinople (al-Qusṭanṭīniyyah), whose people then gave him their obedience and promised to pay tribute, and then went on to Rome (Rūmiyyah), a journey of four months, and besieged it. The troops accompanying him suffered great hunger, were afflicted by plague, and became weakened. The Romans perceived what had hit them, so fell upon them and killed them, with not a single man escaping. Shamir Dhū al-Janāḥ traveled on until he reached Samarqand.[367] He besieged it but was unable to capture any part of it. When he realized that, he went round to the city guard, captured one man of it, and interrogated him about the city and its ruler. The man told him that, regarding its ruler, he was the most stupid of mankind, with no interest except in drinking and eating, but that he had a daughter and it was she who decided the affairs of the populace. Hence Shamir sent the man back to her with a present, telling him, "Inform her that I have only come from the land of the Arabs because of what I have heard about her intelligence, and in order [891]
that she might marry me and I might acquire through her a boy

365. This settlement in the Jawlān or Golan region south of Damascus was a main residence of the Byzantines' allies, the chiefs of the Jafnid family of Ghassān, probably their summer encampment, and it was further important in the periods of the Arab conquest of Syria and of the early Umayyads as a military encampment and concentration point for troops. See Yāqūt, *Buldān*, II, 91–92; Le Strange, *Palestine under the Moslems*, 460–61; Nöldeke, *Die Ghassânischen Fürsten*, 47–49; H. Lammens, "L'evènement des Marwānides et le califat de Marwān Ier," 77–79; Donner, *The Early Islamic Conquests*, 44.; *EI*², s.v. Djābiya (H. Lammens-J. Sourdel-Thomine).

366. Thus interpreting *rawāyāhum*, pl. of *rāwiyah*, "a camel used for drawing water," such a camel being likened to the chief who bears the burden of blood money, to be paid in camels by his tribe. See Lane, *Lexicon*, 1196c; *Glossarium*, p. CCLXXIII: *rāwiyah* = *dux*.

367. Presumably to Transoxania via Khurāsān, Ḥassān having, as it later appears, preceded him to Sogdia and then China.

who will rule over both the Persians and the Arabs. [Tell her also] that I have not come seeking wealth but that I have here with me four thousand chests of gold and silver and that I will hand it over to her and proceed onward to China. If I succeed in gaining the land, she will become my wife; but if I perish, all that wealth will be hers."

When his message was brought to her, she said, "I have fallen in with his wishes, so let him send what he has mentioned." Hence he sent to her four thousand chests, with two men inside each chest. Now Samarqand had four gates, with four thousand men by each gate. He fixed as a sign of recognition between himself and them the striking of camel bells, and gave orders regarding that to the envoys he sent with them. When they got inside the city, he had the camel bells struck; they sprang out [from the chests] and seized control of the gates. Shamir led a frontal attack with his troops and entered the city, killing its populace and seizing as plunder everything within it.[368] He then marched onward to China. He encountered the hosts of the Turks, put them to flight, and went on to China, but found that Ḥassān b. Tubbaʿ had preceeded him by three years. According to what certain people have mentioned, the two of them remained in China until they died, their stay there extending to twenty-one years.

He related: Those who have asserted that they both remained in China until they died have said that Tubbaʿ built [a chain of] lighthouses (*al-manār*) spanning the expanse between him and them, and when any affair of moment occurred, they lit fire beacons at night, and the news was thereby conveyed in a single night. He laid down as a sign between him and them that, "If I light two fires at my end, this signifies the death of Yaʿfur, and if I light three fires, that means the death of Tubbaʿ; whereas, if a single fire is kindled at their end, it means the death of Ḥassān, and if two fires, the death of both of them." They kept to this arrangement, until he lit two fires, and that signified the death of Yaʿfur, and then he lit three fires, and that signified the death of Tubbaʿ.

---

368. A Persian popular etymology derived the city's name (presumably after its supposed rebuilding) from this legendary episode, *Shamir kand* "Shamir destroyed, uprooted (it)," according to Ḥamzah al-Iṣfahānī, 108.

He related: According to the story generally agreed upon, Shamir and Ḥassān returned via the road they had previously taken when they had originally started out, until they came into Tubba''s presence with the wealth they had obtained in China plus various kinds of jewels, perfumes, and slave captives. Then they all went back together to their own land, Tubba' traveled onward till he reached Mecca, where he lodged in the ravine of the cook shops (*al-maṭābikh*).[369] Tubba' died in Yemen. None of the kings of Yemen after him ever sallied forth from Yemen on raids to any other land. His reign lasted for one hundred and twenty-one years. [892]

He related: It is said that Tubba' had become a convert to Judaism because of the rabbis (*al-aḥbār*), a large group of whom had gone from Yathrib to Mecca with him.[370] He related: They say that Ka'b al-Aḥbār's lore came from the surviving material those rabbis had bequeathed; Ka'b al-Aḥbār came from the Ḥimyar.[371]

---

369. Tubba''s coming to Mecca and his designs against the Ka'bah are treated in more detail by al-Ṭabarī at I, 901ff., pp. 164ff. below. In giving this story, also from Ibn Isḥāq, the historian of Mecca al-Azraqī specifies that *al-shi'b min al-maṭābikh* got its name because Tubba' set up his own kitchens in the ravine of Mecca later called that of the early Umayyad governor of the city, 'Abdallāh b. 'Āmir b. Kurayz (*Kitāb akhbār Makkah*, I, 85).

370. We certainly know of the presence of Judaism in pre-Islamic Yathrib, the Islamic Medina, notably from the story of the Prophet Muḥammad's relations with the local Jewish tribes there after he had made the *hijrah* from Mecca to Medina. These Jews must have emigrated from Palestine to setlements along the Wādī al-Qurā in western Arabia, Yathrib being the farthest south of these colonies; the stimulus for this migration may well have been the fall of Jerusalem in A.D. 70 or the aftermath of Bar Kokhba's revolt. i.e., after A.D. 135. The term used for "rabbi" in early Arabic, *ḥabr/ḥibr*, given the Arabic broken plural *aḥbār*, stems directly from Hebrew *ḥaber*, and was already known in pre-Islamic Arabia. See C. C. Torrey, *The Jewish Foundation of Islam*, 34; A. Jeffery, *The Foreign Vocabulary of the Qur'ān*, 49–50. Al-Khwārazmī, *Mafātīḥ al-'ulūm*, 35, equates *al-ḥabr* with the Muslim *al-'ālim*.

How the town which became the Islamic Medina/al-Madīnah had acquired its earlier name of Yathrib (still appearing in Qur'ān, XXXIII, 13) is uncertain, but the name is undoubtedly ancient. A cuneiform inscription from Ḥarrān mentions *ya-at-ri-bu* as one of the towns in Arabia to which Nabū-nā'id or Nabonidus of Babylon (r. 556–539 B.C.) penetrated; in the Greek geographer Ptolemy we have *Iathrippa*; and in Minaean inscriptions we find *Ytrb*. See Buhl, *Das Leben Muhammeds*, 201 n. 1; F. Rosenthal, introd. to Torrey, *The Jewish Foundation of Islam*, repr. p. xi; *EI²*, s.v. al-Madīna. i. History to 1926 (W. M. Watt).

371. Abū Isḥāq Ka'b al-Aḥbār ("Ka'b of the rabbis") was a Yemeni convert from Judaism to Islam, probably in 17/638 (thus in al-Ṭabarī, I, 2514), dying in 32/652–

As for Ibn Isḥāq's account, he has mentioned that the member of the Tubbaʿ dynasty who went to the Orient was Tubbaʿ the Second (*al-ākhar*); namely, Tubbaʿ Tubān Asʿad Abū Karib b. Malkī Karib b. Zayd b. ʿAmr Dhī al-Adhʿār, who was the father of Ḥassān.[372] Ibn Ḥumayd transmitted that information to us, saying that he had it from Salamah.[373]

## *[Kisrā I Anūsharwān]*

Then there assumed the royal power Kisrā Anūsharwān, son of Qubādh, son of Fayrūz, son of Yazdajird (II), son of Bahrām (V) Jūr.[374] When he became king, he wrote letters to the four Fādhūsbāns, each of whom was governor over a region of the land of Persia, and to their subordinate officials.[375] The text of his letter to the Fādhūsbān of Azerbaijan is as follows:

---

53 or shortly afterward. He was considered the greatest authority of his time on Judaeo-Islamic traditions, the *Isrāʾīliyyāt*, and also on South Arabian lore. See *EI²*, s.vv. Isrāʾīliyyāt (G. Vajda) and Kaʿb al-Aḥbār (M. Schwitz).

372. This genealogy in Ibn Hishām, *Sīrat al-nabī*, ed. Wüstenfeld, 12 = ed. al-Saqqā *et alii*, I, 20, tr. A. Guillaume, 6. Asʿad Abū Karib is attested in the inscriptions as reigning ca. A.D. 425.

373. Abū ʿAbdallāh Muḥammad b. Ḥumayd al-Rāzī (d. 248/862) was one of al-Ṭabarī's most important transmitters, in both his *History* and his *Tafsīr*, especially as a second-generation *rāwī* for Ibn Isḥāq, and it is very often Abū ʿAbdallāh Salamah b. al-Faḍl al-Anṣārī (d. 191/806) who provides the link between the two scholars. See Sezgin, *GAS*, I, 242; Rosenthal, *The History of al-Ṭabarī, an Annotated Translation*, I, *General Introduction and From the Creation to the Flood*, 17–19, 172 n. 26, 174 n. 49.

374. . Kisrā, the Arabized form of MP Husraw (thus according to Gignoux) or Khusrōy, and NP Khusraw, Greek Chosroēs, going back to Avestan *haosrawah-*, "of good reputation," a name stemming from the Persian legendary past; in Firdawsī, Kay Khusraw is the son of Siyāwush and Farangīs (for Wasfāfrīd), daughter of Afrāsiyāb, who is the victorious leader of the host of Iran against Turan, and the vanquisher and slayer of Afrāsiyāb. See Justi, *Namenbuch*, 134–39; Bartholomae, *Altiranisches Wörterbuch*, cols. 1737–38; Mayrhofer, *Die altiranischen Namen*, no. 167; Gignoux, *Noms propres sassanides*, no. 465; Yarshater, "Iranian National History," 375–76. Because the two prolonged reigns of Khusraw I Anusharwān (531–79) and Khusraw II Abarwēz (590 and 591–628) made them especially well known to the Arabs, and because those monarchs' actions impinged very much on the history of the pre-Islamic Arabs and the beginnings of Islam, the assumption arose among the Arabs that Kisrā was a generic term for all the Persian kings, and it actually acquired a broken plural, *al-Akāsirah*. See Nöldeke, trans. 151 n. 1. For the component Anūsharwān, see n. 332 above.

375. The exalted title Pādhūspān stems from a non-Persian form corresponding to MP *pāygōs*, "land, region," + the suffix *-pān*. The Pādhūspāns of the four quarters of the Sāsānid empire seem to have been the civil administration counterparts

In the name of God, the Merciful, the Compassionate,[376] from the King Kisrā, son of Qubādh, to Wārī, [893] son of the Nakhīrjān,[377] Fādhūsbān of Azerbaijan and Armenia and their territories, and Dunbāwand and Ṭabaristān and their adjacent territories,[378] and his subordinate officials, greetings! The thing that most strikes fear into the hearts of people is the feeling of deprivation felt by those who fear the ending of their state of comfortable living, the eruption of civil disorders, and the advent of unpleasant things to the best of individuals, one after the other of such individuals, in regard to their own persons, their retainers, their personal wealth, or what is dearest to them. We know of no cause for fear or absence of a thing that brings more crushing ill-fortune for the generality of people, nor one likely to bring about universal disaster, than the absence of a righteous king.[379]

---

of the Ispahbadhs or provincial military commanders (on Khusraw Anūsharwān's division of the supreme military command into four commands corresponding to the quarters of the empire, see al-Ṭabarī, I, 894, p. 149 below), although the civil and military functions doubtless often overlapped in frontier regions. In some sources, notably al-Ya'qūbī, *Ta'rīkh,* I, 260, the Pādhūspān is placed under the control of the Ispabadh. See Nöldeke, trans. 151 n. 2, 445–46 Excursus 3; Christensen, *Sassanides,* 139, 265, 352, 519.

376. It is hardly conceivable that the Sāsānids should have used the exact form of the Islamic *basmalah;* whether they used a corresponding formula at the opening of their chancery documents, etc., is unknown, although Mr F. C. de Blois points out that extant Pahlavi texts (known, of course, in Islamic-period manuscripts) often begin with the formula *pad nām ī yazadān* "by the name of the gods," or words to the same effect. He cites Saul Shaked, "Some Iranian Themes in Islamic Literature," 152–54, who is skeptical, however, that there was any Persian influence on Islam in this regard.

377. This appears both as a family name and as a title, but was perhaps originally a patronymic. In al-Balādhurī, *Futūḥ,* 262, we have this same form, al-Nakhīrjān, as the name or title of the defender of al-Madā'in against the Arabs of 'Umar's army. See Nöldeke, trans. 152 n. 2. N. *a* of Nöldeke's text suggests the possible reading Zādhūyah for the son of the Nakhīrjān, which would make more sense than the unusual Wārī.

378. These would be the territories making up the "northern quarter" of the realm, the arrangements made by Khusraw Anūsharwān being variously defined in an Armenian source and in the later Islamic historians and geographers: see n. 385 below.

379. As Nöldeke remarks, trans. 153 n. 2, the sententious and moralizing tone of the document (this being merely its introduction) is not untypical of what we know of Sāsānid chancery documents.

When Kisrā had gained firm control of power, he took measures to extirpate the religious beliefs of a hypocritical person from the people of Fasā, called Zarādhusht, son of Khurrakān,[380] a new faith which he had brought into existence within the Mazdaean religion. A considerable number of people followed him in that heretical innovation, and his movement became prominent on account of this. Among those who carried out missionary work for him among the masses was a certain man from M.dh.riyyah (?) called Mazdaq, son of Bamdādh.[381] Among the things he ordained for people, made attractive to them, and urged them to adopt, was holding their possessions and their families in common. He proclaimed that all this was part of the piety that is pleasing to God, and that He will reward with the most handsome of recompenses, and that, if that religious faith he commanded them to observe and urged them to adopt were not to exist, the truly good way of behavior, the one which is pleasing to God, would lie in the common sharing or property. With those doctrines, he incited the lower classes against the upper classes. Through him, all sorts of vile persons became mixed up with the best elements of society, criminals seeking to despoil them of their possessions found easy ways to do this, tyrannical persons had their paths to tyranny facilitated, and fornicators were able to indulge their lusts and get their hands on high-born women to whom they would never have
[894] been able to aspire. Universal calamity overwhelmed the people to an extent they had never before experienced.[382]

---

380. Fasā was an important town and district of southeastern Fārs. See Yāqūt, *Buldān*, IV, 260–61; Le Strange, *Lands*, 290; Schwarz, 97–100; Barthold, *Historical Geography*, 152–53; *EI*², s.v. Fasā (L. Lockhart). That Zarādhusht came from Fasā is stated in the *Dēnkard*. See Nöldeke, trans. 456; Crowe, "Kavad's Heresy and Mazdak's Revolt," 24.

381. The sources variously attribute Mazdak to this mysterious M.dh.riyya (which Nöldeke, trans. 154 n. 3, compared with Manādhir in Susiana and which Christensen, *Le règne du roi Kawādh Ier*, 100, sought to interpret as Mādharayyā in Lower Iraq), to Iṣṭakhr in Fārs (al-Dīnawarī, *al-Akhbār al-ṭiwāl*, 65), and to Nasā in Khurāsān (al-Bīrūnī, *al-Āthār al-bāqiyah*, 209). See Nöldeke, trans. 457 and n. 3; Crone, "Kawad's Heresy and Mazdak's Revolt," 24.

382. The question of whether there were two Mazdakite revolts, one toward the end of Kawād's reign and another one at Khusraw's accession or shortly after it, and the exact timing of the revolt(s) anyway, has been much discussed. Most recently, Crone has suggested that it is simplest to assume that a single revolt broke out on Khusraw's acession in 531, at a time when he was combating the rival succession

Hence Kisrā forbade the people[383] to act in accordance with any of the heretical innovations of Zarādusht, son of Kharrakān, and Mazdaq, son of Bamdādh. He extirpated all their heresy, and he killed a great number of their fervid adherents and did not allow himself to be deflected from any of what he had forbidden the people. [He further killed] a group of the Manichaeans, and made firm for the Magians the religion they had always held.

Before Kisrā became king, the office of Iṣbahbadh—that is, the supreme commander of the armed forces—was held by one man, who was responsible for this supreme command over all the land.[384] Kisrā now divided this office and rank between four Iṣbahbadhs, namely, the Iṣbahbadh of the East, comprising Khurāsān and its adjoining regions; the Iṣbahbadh of the West; the Iṣbahbadh of Nīmrūz, that is, the land of Yemen; and the Iṣbahbadh of Azerbaijan and its adjoining regions, that is, the Khazar lands.[385] He

---

claims of his elder brother Kāwūs and military control over the realm was obviously relaxed. Khusraw may have bought time by offering the Makdakites some degree of toleration, and he certainly brought the protracted, but by now rather desultory war with Justinian to an end. Once firmly in command of affairs, *lammā istaḥkama lahu al-mulk*, as al-Ṭabarī, I, 893, puts it, he turned on the Mazdakites, massacred them and gradually restored order in the land. A *terminus ad quem* for this would be 540, when Khusraw resumed the war with Byzantium. See Crone, 30–33.

383. The syntax here is somewhat unusual in that we have verb-object-subject instead of the normal verb-subject-object, but one only derives sense if *Kisrā* is taken as the subject and *al-nās* as the object, as here and as in Nöldeke's translation, "Da verbot nun Chosrau . . ."

384. This is the *iṣbahbadh al-bilād/Ērān-spahbed* of al-Ṭabarī, I, 885, p. 131 above.

385. The division of the realm into four quarters (probably in MP, *kustag;* Arabic, *rub'*, *nāḥiya*), described by their geographical orientation, is attested to in the Armenian geography ascribed to Moses Khorenac'i, which considers the various places in the Persian lands according to a division of (1) *K'usti Khorbaran,* the West; (2) *K'usti Nemroy,* the midday region, thc South; (3) *K'usti Khorasan,* the East; and *K'usti Kapkoh,* the direction of the Caucasus, the North. See Marquart, *Ērānšahr,* 16–17, and for the exact delimitation in this work of the Quarter of the South, see n. 969 below. The Islamic sources have similar information about these divisions. Thus Ibn Khurradadhbih, *Kitāb al-masālik wa-al-mamālik,* 118: Jibāl and its components, Rayy, Azerbaijan, Ṭabaristān, Dunbāwand, and Qūmis; al-Ya'qūbī, *Ta'rīkh,* I, 201–202: Ṭabaristān, Rayy, Jibāl, and its components, and Azerbaijan; al-Dīnawārī, *al-Akbār al-ṭiwāl,* 67: Iṣfahān, Qum, Jibāl, Azerbaijan and Armenia. See Nöldeke, trans. 155 n. 2; and the discussion in Marquart, *Ērānšahr,* 94–95. The Khazar lands were never, of course, controled by the Sāsānids (or any other rulers of Persia), and the mention of this Turkish people in a context as early

saw in this new arrangement a way of improving the good ordering of his kingdom. He strengthened the fighting quality of the soldiers with weapons and mounts.[386] He recovered lands belonging to the kingdom of Persia, some of which had slipped out of the hand of King Qubādh and into the control of other monarchs of the nations, through various causes and reasons, including Sind, Bust, al-Rukhkhaj, Zābulistān, Ṭukhāristān, Dardistān, and Kābulistān.[387] He inflicted extensive slaughter among a people called the Bāriz, transported the remaining ones of them from their land, and resettled them in various places of his kingdom. They submitted to him as his servants, and he utilized them in his military campaigns.[388] He gave orders for another people, called the Ṣūl, to be made captives, and they were brought before him.

---

as the first part of the sixth century is an anachronism anyway; see further n. 390 below.

386. For Khusraw's military reforms, see al-Ṭabarī, I, 963–65, pp. 262–63, and n. 633 below.

387. Bust, al-Rukhkhaj (classical Arachosia), Zābulistān, Kābulistān, and Dardistān (the pre-Islamic region of Gandhara, this name properly read in Nöldeke's text, whereas in his translation, 156, he had read it, with justifiable doubt, as "Dihistān") were all in the southeastern or eastern part of what is now Afghanistan, while Ṭukhāristān (older Bactria) was in its northern part. It is possible that the success in the mid-560s of the Western Turks against the Hephthalites north of the Oxus, with the resultant fragmentation of the northern Hephthalite kingdom, enabled the Persian king to extend Sāsānid control toward the Oxus and into Bactria (cf. al-Ṭabarī, I, 899, p. 160 below). But Marquart, in his *Ērānšahr,* 32–33, was dubious that Persian armies ever penetrated south of the Hindu Kush into eastern Afghanistan at this time, where the southern Hephthalite kingdom was to persist for a considerable time further, and hardly credible that they should have reached Sind. Later, however, in his "Das Reich Zābul und der Gott Žūn vom 6.-9. Jahrhundert," 257 n. 2, he apparently accepted that Khusraw did actually conquer the Hephthalite lands south of the Hindu Kush as far as the borders of India. See Nöldeke, trans. 156 n. 1; Ghirshman, *Les Chionites-Hephtalites,* 94; Widengren, "Xosrau Anōšurvān, les Hephtalites et les peuples turcs," 69–74 (a penetrating critique of the information in the various sources and the traditions they represent); Frye, "The Political History of Iran under the Sasanians," 156. For the regions mentioned above, see *EI*², s.vv. Bust (J. Sourdel-Thomine), Dardistān (A. S. Bazmee Ansari), Kābulistān (C. E. Bosworth), al-Rukhkhadj (idem), Zābulistān (idem, forthcoming).

388. The mountain people of the Jabal Bāriz in the southeastern part of Kirmān province seem to have supplied infantry for the Achaemenid armies, and were always regarded as a bellicose and predatory race. In early Islamic times, various of the ruling dynasties of Persia launched punitive expeditions against these Kūfichīs. See Bosworth, "The Kūfichīs or Qufṣ in Persian History," 9–17; *EI*² Suppl., s.v. Bāriz, Djabal (idem).

He commanded that they should be killed, except for eighty of their boldest warriors, whom he spared and had settled at Shahrām Fayrūz, where he could call upon them for his military [895] campaigns.[389] There was also a people called the Abkhaz, and other ones of the B.n.j.r, Balanjar, and al-Lān, who came together in a coalition to raid his lands.[390] They made an incursion into Armenia in order to raid and despoil its people. Their route thither was at that moment easy and unimpeded, and Kisrā closed his eyes to their activities until, when they had firmly established themselves in his territories, he dispatched against them contingents of troops, who fought with them, and exterminated them apart for ten thousand of them, whom they took prisoner and then settled in Azerbaijan and the neighboring regions.[391]

---

389. For the Ṣūl and Shahrām Fayrūz, see al-Ṭabarī, I, 874, pp. 112–13 and n. 290 above.

390. The Abkhāz were, and still are, a people living on the eastern shores of the Black Sea to the northwest of Georgia and on the southern slopes of the northwestern prolongation of the Caucasus range; under Soviet Russian rule there was an Abkhazian ASSR within the Georgian SSR, now part of the independent Georgian Republic. The lands of the Abkhāz were invaded by the Byzantine armies of Justinian and the people converted to Christianity; subsequently, their history was closely linked with the oher Christian peoples of the Georgians and Alans. See Marquart, *Osteuropäische und ostasiatische Streifzüge*, 175–78; *EI*², s.v. Abkhāz (W. Barthold-V. Minorsky). However, Marquart read al-Ṭabarī's *Abkhaz* as *al-Khazar*, without any discussion of the questions involved. If this were correct, it would be an early mention of the appearance of this Turkish people in the steppes north of the Caucasus; cf. D. M. Dunlop, *The History of the Jewish Khazars*, 23. But whether it is possible to speak of the Khazars, in what was at this time their prehistory, as a separate Turkish people or just part of the Inner Asian Türk empire, is impossible to decide. See Moravcsik, *Byzantinoturcica*, II, 335–36; P. B. Golden, *Khazar Studies*, I, 49–50.

The Alans originally lived north of the Caucasus, but as a result of pressure from the Huns, were pushed into the central Caucasus. At the time of Khusraw Anūsharwān they must have been still pagan, and were not converted to Christianity till the early tenth century. Their modern descendants are the Ossetians. See Marquart, *Ērānšahr*, 65, 95, 105–06; idem, *Streifzüge*, 164–72; *EI*², s.v. Alān (Barthold-Minorsky), Marquart, op. cit., 16, also in *Addenda et emendanda*, p. DXCI, took *B.n.j.r* for *Bulghār*, adducing the Pahlavi form *Burgar* for this Turkish people of the middle Volga basin and South Russian steppe; see *EI*², s.v. Bulghār (I. Hrbek). The Balanjar are here a people, but subsequently they gave their name to what became a well-known city of the Turkish Khazars, in eastern Caucasia to the north of Darband or Bāb al-Abwāb. See Nöldeke, 157 n. 3; Marquart, op. cit., 16–18; *EI*², s.v. Balandjar (D. M. Dunlop).

391. On this Caucasian campaign of Khusraw, see Christensen, *Sassanides*, 369–70; Hannestad, "Les relations de Byzance avec la Transcaucasie et l'Asie

King Fayrūz had previously erected in the regions of the Ṣūl and al-Lān buildings of stone, with the intention of strengthening his lands against the encroachments there of those nations. Moreover, King Qubādh, son of Fayrūz, had begun the construction, after his father, of a great number of building works in those regions, until, when Kisrā achieved the royal power, he gave orders for the construction in the region of the Ṣūl, with stone hewn in the vicinity of Jurjān, of towns, castles, fortified mounds, and many other buildings, which would serve as a protection for the people of his lands, where they might seek refuge from the enemy in the event of a sudden attack.[392]

The Khāqān Sinjibū was the most implacable, the most courageous, the most powerful, and the most plentifully endowed with troops of all the Turks. It was he who attacked W.r.z (?) the king of the Hephthalites, showing no fear of the numerousness or the fierce fighting qualities of the Hepththalites, and then killed their king W.r.z and the greater part of his troops, seizing their possessions as plunder and occupying their lands, with the exception of the part of them that Kisrā had conquered.[393] Khāqān won

---

Centrale aux 5e et 6e siècles," 444–56; Dunlop, *The History of the Jewish Khazars,* 22–23; Frye, "The Political History of Iran under the Sasanians," 155–56.

392. See al-Ṭabarī, I, 874, pp. 112–13 and n. 290 above.

393. The episode briefly noted here reflects the fact that the Hepththalites were at this time squeezed between the growing might of the Sāsānids under Khusraw Anūsharwān and that of the Western Turks of Ishtemi or Istemi (see n. 394 below) and, subsequently, his son Tardu (Qaghan by 576). In the years from 560 to 563 the Qaghan of the Western Turks invaded Transoxania, seized Chāch (the later Tashkent) and defeated the Hephthalites near Bukhārā. The Hepththalite state in Transoxania thus came to an end, although minor Hephthalite principalities continued in Sogdia and the upper Oxus lands, with the main focus of the surviving Hepththalite power now in eastern and southeastern Afghanistan south of the Paropamisus mountains and the Hindu Kush, and in northwestern India. As a share of the spoils from operations contemporary with those of the Turks, Khusraw now received Bactria, but was to lose it to the Turks shortly afterward.

The name *W.r.z* (text, *W.z.r*) is probably to be connected with the Avestan name Varāza-, Middle Persian Warāz, Warāzān, frequent also in compound names in both Persian and Armenian, and meaning "boar, wild boar," especially as Ghirshman, *Les Chionites-Hephtalites,* 22–23, records an undated Hephthalite coin mentioning VRZ; whether this coin was issued by the *W.r.z* mentioned here is impossible to tell. See on the name Nöldeke, trans. 240 n. 1; Justi, *Namenbuch,* 348–50; Mayrhofer, *Die altiranischen Namen,* no. 355; Gignoux, *Noms propres sassanides,* nos. 940–44; Widengren, "Xosrau Anōšurvān, les Hephtalites et les peuples turcs," 93 n. 4; and for the compound name Shahrbarāz/Shahrwarāz, n. 749 below. Among the titles of the petty princes of Khurāsān at the time of the Arab

over the Abkhaz, the B.n.j.r and the Balanjar to his side, and they vouchsafed him their obedience. They informed him that the kings of Persia had always sought to ward them off by paying [896] tribute, thereby securing safety from their raids on their (sc., the Persians') lands. Khāqān now advanced with 110,000 warriors until he reached the fringes of the land of the Ṣūl. He sent a message to Kisrā, uttering threats and using peremptory language against him, to the effect that Kisrā must send to him treasure and to the Abkhaz, the B.n.j.r, and the Balanjar the tribute money the Persian kings had customarily paid before Kisrā came to power. [He further threatened] that, if Kisrā did not expedite the forwarding of all that he asked, he would enter his land and attack it. Kisrā paid no heed to his menaces and did not offer Khāqān a single item of what he had demanded, since he had strongly fortified the region of the gates of the Ṣūl and had blocked the ways and the tracks through defiles that the Khāqān Sinjibū would have to follow in order to reach him. He also knew the strength of his defensive forces in the frontier region of Armenia: five thousand warriors, cavalrymen, and infantry. The Khāqān Sinjibū got word of Kisrā's fortifying of the frontier regions of the Ṣūl, hence returned to his own land with all his troops and with his intentions frustrated. Those of the enemy who were massed against Jurjān were likewise, because of the fortifications Kisrā had built in its neighborhood, unable to mount any raids on it and to conquer it.[394]

---

invasions are mentioned Barāz-bandah in Gharchistān, '.b.rāz in Nasā, and Barāzān in Herat, Būshanj, and Bādhghīs, according to Ibn Khurradādhbih, *al-Masālik wa-al-mamālik,* 39–40. The last king of the northern Heptthalites, the one defeated and killed by the Western Turks, appears in the contemporary Greek sources as Katoulphos. See Christensen, *Sassanides,* 501; Ghirshman, *Les Chionites-Hephtalites,* 23, 94–95; Moravcsik, *Byzantinoturcica,* II, 156; Grousset, *The Empire of the Steppes,* 82–83; Litvinsky, "The Hephthalite Empire," 143–44.

394. Sinjibū is to be identified with the Turkish ruler mentioned by such Byzantine historians as Menander Protector (on whom see Moravcsik, *Byzantinoturcica,* I, 422–26) in their accounts of the diplomatic and commercial exchanges between the Greeks and the Western Turks from 563 onward as Sizaboulos, Silziboulos, etc. The reigning Western Turkish Qaghan at this time was Ishtemi or Istemi, the *Ištmi* or *Štmi* of the Orkhon inscriptions and the Stembischagan of Greek sources. Marquart, *Ērānšahr,* 216–17, identified him with Silziboulos, but this is linguistically difficult, and it is more likely that Silziboulos/Sinjibū, and his son Turkhath, mentioned by Menander, were lesser Turkish rulers in the southern, Transoxanian part of the extensive Türk empire. It has not so far been possible to recover the (presumably) Turkish original form of Silziboulos/Sinjibū; it seems to be rendered in the Chinese annals as *Shê-li čao-wu.* Marquart's analysis of the first

The people had recognized Kisrā Anūsharwān's excellent judgment, knowledge, intelligence, bravery, and resolution, combined with his mildness and clemency toward them.[395] When he was crowned, the great men of state and the nobles came into his presence, and with all their might and eloquence called down

---

element *Silz-* as connected with the *Sir* , the *Seres* of the Byzantine historian Jordanes, who located this people as living east of the Caspian Sea, and whose name seems to be enshrined in that of the Syr Darya river, is convincing, but his equation of the second element with *Yabghu,* the Turkish title of the leader holding the rank just below that of the Qaghan (*Ērānšahr,* loc. cit. and 247), is less so. This war between Khusraw and the Turks—who, after the defeat of the Hephthalites (see above), must have become uneasy neighbors in the Oxus region—is to be placed in the late 560s. See Nöldeke, trans. 158 n. 2, 159 n. 1; Grousset, *The Empire of the Steppes,* 82–83; Moravcsik, *Byzantinoturcica,* II, 275–76, 291; H. W. Haussig, "Die Quellen über die zentralasiatische Herkunft der europäischen Awaren," 31–32; Sinor, "The Establishment and Dissolution of the Türk Empire," 302–305; Sinor, "The Türk Empire. 1. The First Türk Empire (553–682)," 332–33.

The Khāqān's advance to "the fringes of the land of Ṣūl" (here, then, Arabic al-Ṣūl would correspond to the Armenian name for Darband, Č'or) is taken by Dunlop, *The History of the Jewish Khazars,* 24–25, as relating to Bāb al-Abwāb (the *bāb*s "gates" being the mouths of the river valleys running down from the mountains to the sea) or Darband, which commanded a particularly constricted point on the narrow route between the western Caspian shore and the easternmost spurs of the Caucasus. This would imply that the Western Turks were already operating in the South Russian steppes and the Kuban steppes north of the Caucasus, in the latter region perhaps through the agency of the tribal chief of the Khazars (if, again, as in al-Ṭabarī, I, 895, p. 151 above, one reads *al-Khazar* for *Abkhaz*). To Khusraw Anūsharwān is traditionally ascribed the building of the famous Wall of Darband, said to have been seven farsakhs long, to keep out the northern barbarians as part of his general plan of fortifying the Caucasus region and thereby protecting Caucasian Albania or Arrān and also Azerbaijan (impressive remains of fortifications are in fact still visible at Darband). However, many romantic and legendary elements were subsequently added to the story, e.g., in al-Balādhurī, *Futūḥ,* 195–96; Qudāmah b. Ja'far, *Kitāb al-kharāj,* 259–61; Yāqūt, *Buldān,* I, 304, s.v. Bāb al-Abwāb. See Minorsky, *A History of Sharvān and Darband,* 14, 86–88, 144; Dunlop, op. cit., 24–26; *EI*[1], s.v. Derbend (W. Barthold); *EI*[2], s.v. Bāb al-Abwāb (D. M. Dunlop).

395. Nöldeke, trans. 160 n. 2, notes that a new report on Khusraw's reign begins here, one which stems, on the basis of parallel reports in other sources, both Christian and Muslim, from Ibn al-Muqaffa'.

The image of Khusraw as a just, beneficent monarch, solicitous for the interests of rich and poor alike, while vigorous and powerful enough to defend the borders of his realm against the Greeks in the west and the Hepththalites and Turks in the east, and to extend Persian authority into lands as distant as Yemen, all contributed to the picture of an ideal ruler. Already, the Prophet Muḥammad is said to have praised him as a just king, although the prevalent Islamic image of the Kisrās, meaning the Sāsānid kings in general, came to be one of regarding them as examples of supreme royal pride and pomp. Nevertheless, for Khusraw Anūsharwān

blessings on his head. When they had concluded their speeches, he stood up and delivered an oration. He began by mentioning God's favors on His people when He had created them, and his own dependency on God for regulating their affairs and the provision of foodstuffs and the means of life for them. He left nothing [which ought to have been said] out of his oration. Then he told the people what they had suffered [through the spreading of Mazdak's teachings]; namely, the loss of their possessions, the destruction of their religion and the damage to their position regarding their children and their means of life. He further informed them that he was looking into ways and means of putting all that right and rendering affairs strong again, and urged the people to aid him in this. [897]

Next, he ordered the heads of the leaders of the Mazdakites to be chopped off and their possessions to be shared out among the poor and needy.[396] He killed a large number of those people who had

---

specifically, the image of him in the Islamic sources was in general positive, as can be discerned from anecdotes about him in *adab* works like the *Kitāb al-tāj* and the *Kitāb al-maḥāsin wa 'l-aḍdād* of Ps.-al-Jāḥiẓ, and the *Marzubān-nāmah* of Sa'd al-Dīn Warāmīnī, as also in the "Mirrors for Princes" such as Kay Kāwūs b. Iskandar's *Qābūs-nāmah* and Niẓām al-Mulk's *Siyāsat-nāmah;* often, he is linked with his supremely wise (semilegendary) vizier Buzurgmihr.

Even if there is truth in this picture—and certainly, the Sāsānid empire reached its apogee during his reign—it did not prevent Khusraw from being also a skillful exponent of *Realpolitik,* ready to use violence and terror to achieve his aims, and some of the later anecdotes about him stress his cunning and duplicity in dealing with opponents. The Christians of Persia had to endure some bouts of persecution during his time (although nothing as severe as that under Shābūr II), usually linked with resumption of Byzantine-Persian warfare. The Catholicos Mar Aba, a former Zoroastrian, survived imprisonment in Azerbaijan but died of the hardships he had suffered after Khusraw released him in 552. Clearly, the emperor must always have been careful to retain the support of the Zoroastrian priesthood. Yet, to be set against a natural feeling on the part of the Sāsānid authorities that Persian Christians must inevitably have a prime loyalty, through religion, to their co-religionists in the west, many of the Persian Christians seem, in fact, to have felt a strong attachment to their native land, Persia, and their own ethnos as Persians, and this counterbalanced any feelings of religious solidarity with the Greeks, especially as Byzantium stood for Chalcedonian orthodoxy as against the dominant Nestorianism and, to a lesser extent, Monophysitism, in the Persia empire. At least one high commander in the Persian army is known to have been a Christian. See for a detailed consideration of these attitudes, and the tensions between ethnos and faith which must often have been at work within the Persian Christian community, Asmussen, "Christians in Iran," 933–35, and Brock, "Christians in the Sasanian Empire," 10–17.

At all events, there was, on the whole, during Khusraw's reign, some amelioration of the Christians' lot. According to John of Ephesus, the king allowed the Monophysites to organize themselves within the realm and to choose a Catholicos

confiscated other people's possessions, and restored these possessions to their original owners. He commanded that every child concerning whom there was dispute before him about his or her origin should be attributed to that person in whose family the child was, when the real father was not known, and that the child should be given a [legal] share in the estate of the man to whom the child was now attributed, provided that the latter acknowledged the child. In regard to every woman who had been forced to give herself unwillingly to a man, that man was to be held to account and compelled to pay the bride price to her so that her family was thereby satisfied. Then the woman was to be given the choice between remaining with him or marrying someone else, except that if she had an original husband, she was to be restored to him. He further commanded that every man who had caused harm to another person in regard to his possessions, or who had committed an act of oppression against another person, should make full restitution and then be punished in a manner appropriate to the enormity of his offense. He decreed that, where those responsible for the upbringing of the children of leading families had died, he himself would be responsible for them. He married the girls among them to their social equals and provided them with their bridal outfit and necessities out of the state treasury; and he gave the youths in marriage to wives from noble families,

---

of their own. The peace treaty of 561 with Justinian promised freedom of worship for Christians in Persia, and for Zoroastrians in the Byzantine lands, provided that there was no proselytism between the two faiths (but the inference is that apostasy from Zoroastrianism had been tolerated till then). A certain amount of intellectual freedom and a spirit of enquiry seem to have characterized Khusraw's court, and this was an innovation among the Sāsānids. Some sources attribute to the emperor himself an interest in philosophical ideas and in the tenets of other faiths. There was indeed a movement for the translation of scientific, medical, and other works from languages like Greek and Sanskrit into Middle Persian. Translations from Sanskrit are especially attributed to the monarch's physician Burzōy. See Nöldeke, trans. 160 n. 3; Labourt, *Le Christianisme dans l'empire perse*, 177–90; Christensen, *Sassanides*, 372–73, 374–440; Frye, "The Political History of Iran under the Sasanians," 161–62; Asmussen, "Christians in Iran," 946; Wiesehöfer, *Ancient Persia*, 216–19; *EI*², s.v. Kisrā (M. J. Morony), and Tarḏjama. 2. Translations from Greek and Syriac (D. Gutas), 3. Translations from Middle Persian (Pahlawī) (F. C. de Blois).

396. According to Nöldeke, trans. 163 n. 1, other, later sources state that he merely banished the leaders of the Mazdakites from his land. And among these sources, Eutychius says that the confiscated goods and property were made into a charitable foundation for the common benefit.

presented them with money for dowries, awarded them sufficient riches, and ordained that they should be members of his court so that he might call upon them for filling various of his state offices. He gave the wives of his [dead] father the choice between staying with his own wives and sharing in their maintenance and provision, and enjoying the same income as these last, or alternatively, he would seek out for them husbands of the same social standing as themselves.[397]

He further ordained the digging of canals and the excavation of subterranean irrigation conduits (*al-qunī*), and provision of loans for the owners of agricultural lands and support for them. He likewise ordered the rebuilding of every wooden bridge or bridge of boats (*jisr*) that had been destroyed and of every masonry bridge (*qanṭarah*) that had been smashed, and further ordered that every village that had fallen into ruin should be restored to a better state of prosperity than previously. He made enquiries about the cavalrymen of the army (*al-asāwirah*), and those lacking in in [898]
resources he brought up to standard by allocating to them horses and equipment, and earmarked for them adequate financial allowances. He assigned overseers for the fire temples and provided good roads for the people. Along the highways he built castles and towers. He selected [good] administrators, tax officials, and governors, and gave the persons appointed to these functions stringent orders. He set himself to peruse the conduct, the writings, and the legal decisions of Ardashīr, and took them as a model to imitate, urging the people to do likewise.

Once he had a firm grip on the royal power and all the lands were under his control, and some years after he had been reigning, he marched against Antioch, where were stationed leading commanders of Qayṣar's army, and conquered it. He then gave orders that a plan should be made for him of the city of Antioch exactly to scale (literally, "according to its extent"), with the number of its houses, streets, and everything contained in it, and orders that a [new city] should be built for him exactly like Antioch but situated at the side of al-Madā'in. The city known as al-Rūmiyyah was built exactly on the plan of Antioch. He thereupon had the inhabitants of Antioch transported and settled in the new city; when

397. That is, the state of widowhood was, according to Persian custom, to be avoided as far as possible.

they entered the city's gate, the denizens of each house went to the new house so exactly resembling their former one in Antioch that it was as if they had never left the city.[398] Kisrā now attacked the town of Heraclea and conquered it, followed by Alexandria and the lands extending up to it. He left behind a detachment of

---

398. The attack on Antioch was part of the resumed war of 540–43. Khusraw had made peace with the Byzantines in 532, just after his accession, thus ending the war that had begun toward the end of Kawād's reign (see n. 362 above): the Persians had evacuated several fortresses in Lazica and the Byzantines had agreed to pay a very substantial annual tribute in return for "eternal peace," since the empire was being hard pressed by external enemies in the West; see Greatrex, *Rome and Persia at War, 502–532*, 213–24. The resumption of war resulted from a general Byzantine resentment at the inferior position which the paying of tribute implied, and from the sheer inability to keep up these payments at a time when the empire was being threatened on so many fronts, with military defense expenditure causing a disastrous drain on the Byzantine treasury. A considerable effort had been made in the early years of Justinian's reign (527–32) to continue the earlier work of Anastasius. Thus he improved Daras/Dārā or Anastasiopolis, founded by Anastasius in 505 at a strategic point some 25 km/15 miles southeast of Mārdīn and facing the Persian bastion of Niṣībīn, which lay further to its southeast (see on it Yāqūt, *Buldān*, II, 424; Le Strange, *Lands*, 96–97; *EIr*, s.v. Dārā (M. Weiskopf); Whitby, "Procopius' Description of Dara" (*Buildings* II, 1–3), 737–83, who describes and elucidates those of its buildings and defensive walls still visible), making it the single most important point in the Byzantine defensive system in Upper Mesopotamia. Justinian also strengthened the forward fortified points at such places as Circesium, Martyropolis, and Theodosiopolis. However, the "eternal peace" may have involved some restrictions on Byzantine frontier construction, and the emperor had in any case become involved in the defense of his western provinces. Hence when Khusraw marched against Antioch through the more weakly defended, more southerly middle Euphrates region, he found a city with deficiencies in its defenses, in part because of an earthquake some years previously. In June 540 he sacked it, a disastrous setback for the Greeks, in the course of which the overstretched Byzantine army was revealed as lacking the manpower really to protect this and other cities of northern Mesopotamia and northern Syria until troop reinforcements couild be brought up from further west and the military position in Mesopotamia stabilized. See Cameron, *Procopius and the Sixth Century*, 163–65; Whitby, "Procopius and the Development of Roman Defenses in Upper Mesopotamia," 726–29.

Meanwhile, Justinian had to agree to a truce on the basis of the Greeks paying an indemnity and arrears of tribute. The new city for the dispossessed citizens of Antioch on the Orontes was called by the Persian emperor Weh Andiyōg Khosrōy, "Khusraw [has built this] better than Antioch," and was popularly known by the Persians as Rūmagān "town of the Greeks" = al-Rūmiyyah; it formed part of the urban complex of al-Madā'in. See Nöldeke, trans., 165 nn. 2–4; Bury, *A History of the Later Roman Empire from Arcadius to Irene*, I, 420–27; idem, *History of the Later Roman Empire from the Death of Theodosius I to the Death of Justinian*, I, 91–112; Christensen, *Sassanides*, 386–87; Stein, *Histoire du Bas-Empire*, II, 486–92; Frye, "The Political History of Iran under the Sasanians," 154–55; Shahîd, *Byzantium and the Arabs in the Sixth Century*, I/1, 209–36.

his troops in the land of the Romans after Qayṣar had submitted to him and had paid him ransom money.[399]

He returned home from Rūm and then took the field against the Khazars, and sought revenge on them for the damage they had wrought on him by afflicting his subjects.[400] Next, he turned his atention to Aden. He blocked up part of the sea there which lay between two mountains and is adjacent to the land of Abyssinia (al-Ḥabashah), with large ships, rocks, iron columns, and chains, and he killed the great men of state of that land.[401] He then returned to al-Madā'in, having brought under his control all those regions of the land of Rūm and Armenia that are situated on this side of Heraclea plus the whole area between his capital and the sea,[402] in the region of Aden. He appointed al-Mundhir b. al-Nu'mān as king over the Arabs and loaded him with honors.[403] [899]
Then he took up residence in his own kingdom at al-Madā'in, and

399. The truce was denounced by Justinian because of Persian operations in 541 in the Black Sea region of Lazica, which was adjacent to Byzantine defense points in eastern Pontus and which had been recently Christianized, and because of what were regarded as unjustified exactions of Khusraw from the people of the Byzantine fortified points and towns in Upper Mesopotamia during the previous year, leading to Persian invasions of Upper Mesopotamia in 542, of Armenia in 543, and of Upper Mesopotamia again in 544. In the course of this last campaign, Edessa was strenuously besieged by the Persians (see on this event, J. B. Segal, *Edessa, 'The Blessed City'*, 105, 113, 158–60). There does not, however, seem to have been at any of these times a Persian advance into southern Anatolia as far as Heracleia (the Hiraqlah of later Islamic historians and geographers, modern Eregli, see on it Yāqūt, *Buldān*, V, 398–99; Le Strange, *Lands*, 149; *EI*², s.v. Eregli (J. H. Mordtmann-F. Taeschner), which, according to the contemporary church historian Evagrius Scholasticus, was not sacked by the Persians till much later, in the time of Justin II (r. 565–78). The mention of Alexandria (in Egypt!) must be a confusion with the Persian invasion of Egypt under Khusraw II Abarwēz some seventy years later in the imperial reign of Heraclius (see al-Ṭabarī, I, 1002, pp. 318–19 below). But as al-Ṭabarī says here, Edessa had been forced to pay an indemnity to the Persians after the final siege, and the peace or five years' truce of 545 beween Khusraw and Justinian involved the handing over by the Greeks of a substantial indemnity. See Bury, *A History of the Later Roman Empire from Arcadius to Irene*, I, 427–40; idem, *History of the Later Roman Empire from the Death of Theodosius I to the Death of Justinian*, I, 91–112; Stein, *Histoire du Bas-Empire*, II, 492–502; Frye, "The Political History," 155–56; Lang, "Iran, Armenia and Georgia," 521.

400. Presumably a repetition of the notice by al-Ṭabarī at I, 895, p. 151 above, of the emperor's Caucasian expedition.

401. An anticipatory mention of the South Arabian expedition, see al-Ṭabarī, I, 947ff., pp. 238ff. below.

402. Following the text's n. *f*, with the correct reading of the Sprenger ms. *al-baḥr* for the text's *al-Baḥrayn*.

403. See al-Ṭabarī, I, 899–900, p. 161 below.

turned his attention once more to affairs needing his personal care. After this, he led an expedition against the Hepththalites, seeking revenge for his grandfather Fayrūz. Previously, Anūsharwān had married Khāqān's daughter, so he now wrote to him before setting off on the expedition, informing him of his intentions and enjoining him to march against the Hephthalites. Anūsharwān came up against them, killed their king, and extirpated the whole of his family. He penetrated to Balkh and what lies beyond it and quartered his troops in Farghānah. He then returned home from Khurāsān.[404] When he got back to al-Madā'in, a deputation came to him seeking help against the Abyssinians. So he sent back with them one of his commanders heading an army of the men of Daylam and adjacent regions; they killed the Abyssinian Masrūq in Yemen and remained there.[405]

Thus Kisrā enjoyed an unbroken run of victories and conquests; all the nations were in awe of him; and numerous delegations from the Turks, the Chinese, the Khazars, and similar [distant] nations thronged his court. He lavished generosity on scholars. He reigned for forty-eight years. The birth of the Prophet fell within

404. In the account of these events at I, 895, p. 152 above, it is the Khāqān of the Turks who kills the Hephthalite king W.r.z/Warāz. The name of the Turkish princess whom Khusraw is said here to have married (the future mother of his successor Hormizd IV) is given by al-Mas'ūdī, *Murūj*, II, 211 = § 632 as the un-Turkish-looking Fāqum (thus vocalized by Pellat; the reading is dubious, but an Armenian author has Kaïēn, according to Nöldeke, trans. 264 n. 4). Although an Arabic geographer like Ibn Khurradādhbih, *al-Masālik wa-al-mamālik*, 30, says that Khusraw supposedly constructed the town of Farghānah, it seems most unlikely that Sāsānid power ever extended into the Farghānah valley of Central Asia. Marquart, *Ērānšahr*, 219–20, endeavored to make sense of this piece of information by relating it to a Wādī Farghānah south of Baghlān in the southern part of Ṭukhāristān, mentioned in the accounts of the Arab invasions of northern Afghanistan; but this seems very forced. See also Nöldeke, trans. 167 nn. 2–3.

405. See al-Ṭabarī, I, 948–50, 952–57, pp. 238–42, 244–50 below, for the story of the expedition to Yemen. The Daylamīs, mountaineers from the region of Daylam in the Elburz Mountains at the southwestern corner of the Caspian Sea, were often employed as mercenary infantrymen and alpine troops by the Sāsānids, and Procopius mentions *Dolomitae* in Khusraw's operations in Georgia and Lazica. See *EI*[2], s.v. Daylam (V. Minorsky). Khusraw's recourse to marginal peoples like the Daylamīs seems to have arisen from an increasing shortage of military manpower from the traditional Persian sources, i.e., the indigenous mailed cavalrymen of the *aswār* class (on whom see n. 258 above), during his reign, and part of what Zeev Rubin has called the "barbarization" of the Persian army at this time, a parallel to what happened in the Roman world. See Rubin, "The Reforms of Khusro Anūshirwān," 284–85.

the latter part of Anūsharwān's reign.[406] Hishām [Ibn al-Kalbī] has related that Anūsharwān's reign was (only) forty-seven years. He also related that 'Abdallāh b. 'Abd al-Muṭṭalib, the Messenger of God's father, was born during his reign [in the twenty-fourth year of this, and that he died] in the forty-second year of his dominion.[407]

Hishām also related: When Anūsharwān's position became assured, he sent a message to al-Mundhir b. al-Nu'mān the Elder (al-Akbar), whose mother was Mā' al-Samā', a woman of al-Namir [tribe], and appointed him as king over al-Ḥīrah and the lands over which the House of al-Ḥārith b. 'Amr Ākil al-Murār[408] used to rule, and al-Mundhir remained in this office continuously until he died.[409] He also related: Anūsharwān led an expedition against the [900]

406. This based on the traditional dating of the Prophet's birth to ca. 570. See al-Ṭabarī, I, 900, pp. 163–64 and nn. 414, 640 below.

407. The words between the parentheses supplied by Nöldeke, trans. 168, from other, parallel texts as necessary to complete the text where there is an obvious omission.

408. How Ḥujr, the essential founder of Kindī greatness in Najd at this time (see p. 122 and n. 312 above) and grandfather of al-Ḥārith (on whom, see Olinder, *The Kings of Kinda*, 51–69), gained the nickname *ākil al-murār,* "eater of bitter herbs," is unclear, although the Arabic sources give two not very convincing explanations (see Olinder, op. cit., 42; Robin, "Le royaume ḥujride," 3). But Arabic *murār* is virtually identical with Akkadian *murāru,* "bitter lettuce," and possibly connected with *irrū,* "a medical plant of the Cucurbilaceae family, possibly the colocynth" (see *The Assyrian Dictionary of the Oriental Institute of the University of Chicago, Letter M,* Part II, 218, *Letters I–J,* 182–83). R. Campbell Thompson thought that *irrū* was *Papaver,* probably *rhoeas* L., the poppy (*A Dictionary of Assyrian Botany,* 223–29). We are clearly dealing with bitter herbs used as a medicament, and possibly, in the light of Campbell Thompson's definition of *irrū,* with a pain-killing or narcotic drug.

409. Concerning Khusraw's apppointment (or more probably, confirmation; see pp. 140–41 and n. 362 above) of al-Mundhir III as his deputy on the fringes of Iraq and in northern and eastern Arabia, al-Ṭabarī records, at I, 958, p. 253 below, this time from Ibn Isḥāq, that, after thc peace treaty of 531 with Justinian, the Persian emperor appointed the Lakhmid as ruler over all the Arabian lands as far as Baḥrayn, 'Umān, Yamāmah, al-Ṭā'if, and Ḥijāz. See Smith, "Events in Arabia in the Sixth Century A.D.," 442, and al-Ṭabarī, I, 958, pp. 252–53 below). The rivalry of the houses of Lakhm and Kindah was thus bound to be intensified.

As well as Kindah's rivaling with Lakhm over control of Najd, the lands of Baḥrayn and Hajar in eastern Arabia were controled at this time by a subordinate branch of Kindah under Mu'āwiyah al-Jawn ("the dark colored one"), brother of 'Amr al-Maqṣūr and son of Ḥujr, which persisted there under Mu'āwiyah's descendants until the time of the Prophet (see Olinder, "Āl al-Ǧaun of the Family of Ākil al-Murār," 208–29). As noted at p. 122 n. 312 above, it certainly seems that there was a Kindī "kingdom," or rather, an assemblage of tribes ruled by a Kindī chief

Burjān, then turned back and built [the town of] al-Bāb and the Caspian Gates (al-Abwāb).[410]

## *[The History of al-Ḥīrah]*

Hishām related:[411] There reigned as king over the Arabs, as appointee of the Persian kings after al-Aswad b. al-Mundhir, his

---

centered on Najd and under the suzerainty of the Kings of Ḥimyar, a subordination explicit in two South Arabian inscriptions (Ry 445 and 446) from Ma'sal al-Jumḥ, 240 km/150 miles west-south-west of modern al-Riyāḍ and dating from the mid-fifth century and 631 Ḥimyarite era/A.D. 521–52, respectively. (De Blois is followed here for beginning the Sabaean or Ḥimyarite era in April 110 B.C. rather than 115 B.C., i.e., converting the South Arabian era to the Christian one by subtracting 110 years and not 115 years, the figure which has long been followed ever since Halévy propounded it a century and a quarter ago, since the disparity of only 110 years—a "short chronology"—causes fewer problems that that of 115 years. See de Blois, "The Date of the 'Martyrs of Nagrān,'" 119–20, and also Robin, who follows de Blois in this, in his *L'Arabie antique de Karib'īl à Mahomet,* 33, 151, and his "Le royaume ḥujride," 691; cf. also *EI*[2], s.v. Ta'rīkh. I, *Dates and Eras in the Islamic World,* 1. In the Sense of Date, Dating, etc. [de Blois].) The two inscriptions name Kindah and Ma'add as among the Arab auxiliaries and allies of the kings of Ḥimyar (see Robin, "Le royaume ḥujride," 675–95). Dating from some three decades after the second Ma'sal al-Jumḥ inscriptions, the inscription of the well of Muraygħān, situated to the north of Najrān and east of what is now now 'Asīr (Ry 506), records that the men of Kindah and Khindif fought in the army of the Abyssinian viceroy Abrahah when this last governor marched against the Lakhmid al-Mundhir III's son 'Amr (the later 'Amr III; see al-Ṭabarī, I, 900, p. 163 and n. 414 below) and his Bedouin allies. The main force under Abrahah himself engaged the Ma'add in a battle at Ḥulubān or Ḥalabān, not far to the south of Ma'sal al-Jumh (the name vocalized as Ḥulubān in al-Bakrī, *Mu'jam mā ista'jam,* I, 491, and Ḥalabān in Yāqūt, *Buldān,* II, 281–82; see on the place Thilo, *Die Ortsnamen in der altarabischen Poesie,* 53: a wadi arising in the Arwā chain and running into the Wādī Rikā', cf. his Map D). The Ma'add were decisively defeated and forced to give hostages, while another force, which included men of the tribes of Sa'd and Murād, operated in the territory of the Banū 'Āmir b. Ṣa'ṣa'ah and defeated the 'Āmir at Turabah, some 100 km/60 miles to the east-southeast of al-Ṭā'if. Al-Mundhir then had to sue for peace from Abrahah and send hostages to Yemen. The inscription dates these events to 662 Ḥimyarite era/A.D. 552–53. Much has been written on the inscription and the events it describes. Among all this, see Beeston, "Notes on the Mureighan Inscription," 389–92; Smith, "Events in South Arabia in the 6th Century A.D.," 435–37; M. J. Kister, "The Campaign of Ḥulubān. A New Light on the Expedition of Abraha," 425–36.

410. That is, against the Bulghārs of the Middle Volga; this must be a legendary touch, unless it is a reminiscence of the events already noted in al-Ṭabarī, I, 895–96, pp. 151–53 above. On Bāb al-Abwāb or Darband, see pp. 151, 153 and nn. 390, 394 above.

411. A continuation of Ibn al-Kalbī's narrative interrupted in al-Ṭabarī, I, 892, p. 146 above.

brother al-Mundhir b. al-Mundhir b. al-Nuʿmān, whose mother was Hirr bt. al-Nuʿmān, and who reigned for seven years. After him there reigned al-Nuʿmān b. al-Aswad b. al-Mundhir, whose mother was Umm al-Malik bt. ʿAmr b. Ḥujr, the sister of al-Ḥārith b. ʿAmr al-Kindī, who reigned for four years. Then there was appointed in his stead Abū Yaʿfur b. ʿAlqamah b. Mālik b. ʿAdī b. al-Dhumayl b. Thawr b. Asas b. Rab[412] b. Numārah b. Lakhm, who reigned for three years. Then there reigned al-Mundhir b. Imriʾ al-Qays al-Badʾ, i.e., Dhū al-Qarnayn. Hishām related: He was only thus called on account of two plaits made from his hair.[413] His mother was Māʾ al-Samāʾ, that is, Māriyah bt. ʿAwf b. Jusham b. Hilāl b. Rabīʿah b. Zayd Manāt b. ʿAmir al-Ḍaḥyān b. Saʿd b. al-Khazraj b. Taym Allāh b. al-Namir b. Qāsiṭ. He reigned for a total of forty-nine years. Then there reigned his son ʿAmr b. al-Mundhir, whose mother was Hind bt. al-Ḥārith b. ʿAmr b. Ḥujr Ākil al-Murār and who reigned for ten years.[414] He related: After ʿAmr b. Hind had been reigning for eight years and eight months, the Messenger of God was born; that was in the time of Anūshar-

---

412. Reading uncertain.

413. An unconvincing explanation for an appellation already well known as a by-name that was generally applied to Alexander the Great in Arabic lore, including in the Qurʾān; see n. 443 below. Its origin, if ever known, must have been forgotten by Ibn al-Kalbī's time.

414. Ibn al-Kalbī's filiation of the Lakhmid kings has come down to us in two slightly different versions, the one given here by al-Ṭabarī (and in part, in various other places in his *History*) and the other utilized by Ḥamzah al-Iṣfahānī, *Taʾrīkh*, 83–97, for his section on the Lakhmids. Sidney Smith thought that Ibn al-Kalbī derived information here from a Sāsānid register of years, "used with remarkable fidelity." The two versions are compared, together with others in the Arabic historical sources, and a harmonization attempted, by Rothstein, *Laḫmiden*, 50ff.; see now Smith, "Events in Arabia in the 6th Century A.D.," 429–30.

The accession of ʿAmr III b. al-Mundhir III, also called ʿAmr b. Hind after his mother, the Kindī princess, should be placed in 554, with what was apparently a smooth succession to his father, and the duration of his reign was sixteen years (as in Rothstein's table, 53, following the figure of sixteen in Ḥamzah al-Iṣfahānī, op. cit. 94, pace the one given here by al-Ṭabarī of ten years. This would place ʿAmr's death—as a result of being assassinated by the poet ʿAmr b. Kulthūm—in 569 or in 570, the traditional but impossible date given for the "Year of the Elephant" at Mecca. See for ʿAmr's reign (he had a reputation for firm rule and cruel behavior, seen in the celebrated affair of the "letter of al-Mutalammis," see n. 774 below), Nöldeke, trans. 170 n. 1, 172 n. 1; Rothstein, op. cit., 94–102; *EI*², s.v. ʿAmr b. Hind (A.J. Wensinck). See for the chronological difficulties involved in placing the Prophet Muḥammad's birth in the eighth year of ʿAmr's reign, Smith, op. cit., 434.

wān and the "Year of the Elephant" in which al-Ashram Abū
[901] Yaksūm led an attack on the Ka'bah.[415]

## *[The History of Yemen]* *Mention of the Rest of the Story of Tubba' in the Days of Qubādh and the Time of Anūsharwān and the Persians' Dispatch of an Army to Yemen in Order to Combat the Abyssinians, and the Reason for This Last.*[416]

There related to us Ibn Ḥumayd—Salamah—Muḥammad b. Isḥāq, who said: When Tubba' II (al-Ākhar), that is, Tubān As'ad Abū Karib, came back from the East, he traveled via Medina.[417] When he had passed by it at the beginning of his expedition (i.e., on his outward journey), he had not aroused any feelings of disquiet among its people, but had left behind there in their midst one of his sons, who had [subsequently] been treacherously slain.

---

415. See on this attack, al-Ṭabarī, I, 936–46, pp. 222–35 below. The patronymic Abū Yaksūm refers to the Abyssinian viceroy of South Arabia, Abrahah, also known as al-Ashram "the man with his nose-tip cut off," whose son Yaksūm was to succeed him as governor in South Arabia. See al-Ṭabarī, I, 931, p. 213, below, for the alleged occasion of this mutilation, and I, 945, pp. 235–36 below, for Yaksūm's reign. The actual name Yaksūm must stem from the toponym Aksum, the capital of the first Abyssinian kingdom, which lasted up to this sixth century

416. Nöldeke omitted from his translation the section beginning here at I, 901 l. 1, as far as 917 l. 17.

417. The following section, up to I, 917 l. 17, depends on the parallel account of Ibn Isḥāq, in essence only moderately different from that of Ibn al-Kalbī, but it must be taken as a later growth of legendary history of a type similar to that in the Alexander Romance, which may have influenced it. The section is reproduced substantially by Ibn Isḥāq in the *Sīrat al-nabī* of Ibn Hishām, ed. Wüstenfeld, 12ff. = ed. al-Saqqā et al. I, 19ff., trans., 6ff.; cf. Ibn Hishām, *Kitāb al-tījān,* 297–300, and F. Krenkow, "The Two Oldest Books on Arabic Folklore," 227–28.

Abū Karib As'ad himself was, however, a fully historical person, leaving aside the legendary accretions, the *'bkrb 's'd* of the Ḥimyaritic inscriptions. In the first half of the fourth century he expanded his territories from southwestern and southern Arabia into central Arabia. He inflated the royal title of the founder Shamir Yur'ish from that of "lord of Saba, Dhū Raydān, Ḥaḍramawt and *Ymnt*" to include "and of their Arabs (i.e., Bedouins) in *Ṭwd*$^{m}$ and Tihāmah," and succeeding Tubba' kings also used this fuller title (in Classical Arabic, *ṭawd* means "mountain"; for al-Hamdānī, *Ṣifat jazīrat al-'Arab,* 371, al-Ṭawd denoted the mountain range of the Sarāt, which divided Yemen between its coastland, *tihāmah,* and its inland plateau, *najd*). His fame ensured the later growth around him of a fantastic romance and epic similar to that of, and, as noted above, conceivably inspired by, that of Alexander the Great. See *EI*$^{2}$, s.v. Tubba' (A. F. L. Beeston).

Hence he now came to the town with the intention of reducing it to ruins, extirpating its people and cutting down its date palms. When they heard of his plans, this tribe (*ḥayy*) of the Anṣār banded together against him in order to defend themselves. Their chief at that time was ʿAmr b. al-Ṭallah, one of the Banū al-Najjār, and then of the Banū ʿAmr b. Mabdhūl.[418] They sallied forth to attack Tubbaʿ. When Tubbaʿ had encamped [with his troops] by the Medinans, one of the latter from the Banū ʿAdī b. al-Najjār, called Aḥmar, had killed one of Tubbaʿ's followers whom he had found cutting down the date clusters of a tree that belonged to him. He had therefore struck him with his reaping hook and killed him, saying, "The fruit belongs to the one who nurtures it and makes it grow!" After killing him, he had thrown the corpse into a well-known local well called Dhāt Tūmān (?); this naturally increased Tubbaʿ's rage against them, and the two sides became engaged in making war and fighting other. He related: The Anṣār assert that they used to fight Tubbaʿ by day but treat him as a guest each night. Tubbaʿ was amazed at this and used to say, "By God, these people of ours are generous of heart!"

While he was engaged thus, there came to him two rabbis from the Jews of the Banū Qurayẓah, learned scholars with firmly grounded knowledge, who had heard about Tubbaʿ's intention of destroying the town and its people.[419] They told him, "O King, don't do it, for if you persist in carrying out your plan, something will intervene to prevent you, and we fear that you will bring down on yourself speedy retribution." He said to them, "How can [902]

---

418. This is an anachronism, in that the designation of Anṣār "Helpers" was only given to his supporters in Medina by the Prophet after his *hijrah* of 622, and an inaccuracy in that it was not, of course, a tribal name. The Arabs inhabiting Yathrib, as it was mainly called in pre-Islamic times (see n. 370 above), were from the Banū Qaylah bt. Hālik, with its two branches of the Aws and the Khazraj. Al-Najjār were a clan of the Khazraj, and the ʿAmr b. Mabdhūl part of their subclan Māzin. The ʿAdī mentioned below were another subclan. See Ibn al-Kalbī-Caskel-Strenziok, *Jamharat al-nasab,* I, Tables 176–77, 185, II, 31, 34–35, 347: Robertson Smith, *Kinship and Marriage in Early Arabia,* 256; Montgomery Watt, *Muhammad at Medina,* genealogical table at 154.

419. Qurayẓah were one of the three main Jewish tribes in Medina, confederates of the Aws; they nevertheless suffered the massacre of their menfolk and the enslavement of their women and children by Muḥammad in 6/627 after the siege of Medina by Quraysh and their allies. See Buhl, *Das Leben Muhammeds,* 273–77; Watt, *Muhammad at Medina,* 193ff.; *EI*², s.v. Ḳurayẓa (W. M. Watt).

that be?" They replied, "It is the place to which a prophet, who will arise out of the tribe of Quraysh at the end of time, will migrate, and it will be his home and resting place." After having heard these words, Tubbaʿ desisted from what he had intended to do regarding Medina, perceiving that the two rabbis had special knowledge and being amazed at what he had heard from them. He departed from Medina, took them with him to Yemen, and embraced their religion. The names of the two rabbis were Kaʿb and Asad, both from the Banū Qurayẓah and paternal cousins of each other.[420] They were the most knowledgeable persons of their age, as Ibn Ḥumayd has mentioned to me—Salamah—Ibn Isḥāq—Yazīd b. ʿAmr—Abān b. Abī ʿAyyāsh—Anas b. Mālik—shaykhs from his people (sc., of Medina) who went back to the Jāhiliyyah.

A certain poet of the Anṣār, one Khālid[421] b. ʿAbd al-ʿUzzā b. Ghaziyyah b. ʿAmr b. ʿAbd b. ʿAwf b. Ghanm b. Mālik b. al-Najjār, recited these verses about the warfare between the Medinans and Tubbaʿ, vaunting ʿAmr b. al-Ṭallah and mentioning his merits and his resolute defense:

Has he relinquished youthful folly, or has its remembrance
ceased? Or has he obtained his fill of pleasure?
Or have you remembered youth? And what a memory of youth
or of its times you have![422]
For indeed, it was a young man's war (literally, the war of a
beast which sheds its two teeth next to the incisors at its
fourth or later year, *rubāʿī*, or of a young man similarly
shedding teeth, *rabāʿī*), whose like brings to a youth
experience and esteem.[423]

---

420 The names of the two rabbis as given here come from the Ibn Isḥāq version of this story, from an uncertain source; but Michael Lecker has recently pointed out that the late-period historian of Medina Nūr al-Dīn ʿAlī b. Aḥmad al-Samhūdī (d. 911/1506) cites an alternative tradition from the second/eighth-century historian of Medina Ibn Zabālah that the names of the two men were Suḥayt/Sukhayt and Munabbih, from the Medinan Jewish tribe of Hadl, who were actually clients of the more powerful Qurayẓah. See al-Samhūdī, *Wafāʾ al-wafā*, I, 190; Lecker, "The Conversion of Ḥimyar to Judaism and the Jewish Banū Hadl of Medina," 134–35.

421. The Cairo text, II, 106, has for this name *khāl* "the maternal uncle of. . . ."

422. An alternative translation of the second sentence in the line might be "And what is it that you remember? Youth or the passing of the whole span of life?"

423. Following *Addenda et emendanda*, p. DXCI, Thorbecke's reading *ātā*, "brings to," for the text's *atā*, "comes." One might also render the last word

[903]

So ask 'Imrān or ask Asd, then, at the time when [the army] came, when the morning star was still visible,[424]
An army headed by Abū Karib, with their bodies clad in long coats of mail and with pungent reek.
Then they said, Who is coming along with them, the Banū 'Awf or al-Najarah?
O Banū al-Najjār, indeed we have a burden of taking vengeance on them from long ago![425]
Then there went forth to encounter them in battle a body of lofty warriors (*'ashannaqah*),[426] whose extent was like that of a sheet of falling rain drops.[427]
A chief who is on a level of prestige with kings; whoever would make war on 'Amr does not realize his eminence.

A man of the Anṣār, mentioning their fierce resistance to Tubba', has said:

You impose upon me, among other duties in regard to it, [defense of] the date palm groves of al-Asāwīf and al-Manṣa'ah,[428]

---

*'ibarah* as "a moral example."

424. 'Imrān is not common in tribal genealogies, but may conceivably refer to the 'Imrān b. Hudhmah, a branch of the tribe of Muzaynah who lived to the south of Medina; see Ibn al-Kalbī-Caskel-Strenziok, *Jamharat al-nasab*, I, Table 88, II, 357; *EI*², s.v. Muzayna (F. M. Donner). Asd is, of course, the great tribe of Asd or Azd (*'sd* being the form in the South Arabian inscriptions), with its two branches originally centered on 'Umān and the Sarāt mountain chain in 'Asīr respectively; see *EI*², s.v. Azd (G. Strenziok).

425. The name 'Awf occurs in the genealogies of a large nuumber of Arab tribes, while al-Najjār b. Tha'labah were a subclan of the Medinan Khazraj; see Ibn al-Kalbī-Caskel-Strenziok, *Jamharat al-nasab*, I, Table 185, II, 442. What is unclear is whether the Najarah are identical with the Banū al-Najjār of the next line, the difficulty in identifying them as a single unit being that the 'Awf and the Najarah are apparently among the attackers, whereas one would expect the Banū al-Najjār to be among the defenders of their town.

426. Ibn Hishām, ed. Wüstenfeld, 14 = ed. Muṣṭafā al-Saqqā et al., I, 23, has *musāyifah,* "a body of swordsmen," for this rare word *'ashannaqah,* hence probably a *lectio facilior.*

427. Ibn Hishām, loc. cit., inserts here a line, "Among them is 'Amr b. Ṭallah; may God grant him long life for the welfare of his people!" which serves as a link between the preceding and following verses and elucidates the 'Amr who is subsequently praised.

428. Al-Asāwīf is the plural, used here for metrical purposes, one assumes, of al-Aswaf, a place outside Medina but regarded as coming within the Ḥaram estab-

Date palm groves the Banū Mālik have protected from the
terrifying cavalry hosts of Abū Karib.

He related: Tubbaʿ and his people were devotees of idols and worshiped them. He set out toward Mecca, this being on his route back to Yemen, until when he was at al-Duff in the district of Jumdān, between ʿUsfān and Amaj, a point along his way between Mecca and Medina,[429] a group of men from Hudhayl[430] met him and said, "O king, allow us to lead you to an ancient, largely obliterated treasury which previous monarchs have overlooked and which contains pearls, chrysoliths, rubies, gold, and silver." He replied, "Yes, indeed," and they went on to say, "[It is] a temple in Mecca which its people worship and pray by."[431] The Hudhalīs,
[904] however, intended by that Tubbaʿ's destruction, because they knew full well that if any king had any bad intentions concerning the Kaʿbah or acted deceitfully in regard to it, he would perish. When he had agreed to their proposal, he sent for the two rabbis

lished by the Prophet around the town. See Majd al-Dīn Ibn al-Athīr, *al-Nihāyah fī gharīb al-ḥadīth*, II, 422; al-Bakrī, *Muʿjam mā istaʿjam*, I, 151; al-Samhūdī, *Wafāʾ al-wafā*, IV, 1125–26. Al-Manṣaʿah, on the contrary, would be the singular of a place-name normally found in the plural, al-Manāṣiʿ, literally "places set apart," i.e., for purposes of fulfilling the needs of nature, outside Medina, specifically for the women of the town to use at night, and figuring as such in the famous *ḥadīth al-ifk*, "affair of the lie," involving ʿĀʾishah and her calumniators. See Majd al-Dīn Ibn Athīr, op. cit., V, 65; al-Samhūdī, op. cit., IV, 1313.

429. These places all lay to the north of Mecca, with ʿUsfān in the transition zone between the coastal plain, the Tihāmah, and the Ḥijāz mountain chain, the Sarāt, and the others on the road to Medina across the mountains. For al-Duff, see Yāqūt, *Buldān*, II, 458. For Jumdān, see al-Bakrī, *Muʿjam mā istaʿjam*, II, 391–92, and Yāqūt, op. cit., II, 162, respectively, describing it as a mountain in the territory of Sulaym and a mountain in the *ḥarrah*, or lava field, of Ḍariyyah. ʿUsfān is frequently mentioned in early Islamic sources as two stages from Mecca, and still exists as a village. See al-Bakrī, op. cit., III, 942–43, placing it in the territory of the Banū al-Muṣṭaliq of Khuzāʿah; Yāqūt, op. cit., IV, 120–21; Thilo, *Die Ortsmanen in der altarabischen Poesie*, 109 and Map C; Abdullah Al-Wohaibi, *The Northern Hijaz in the Writings of the Arab Geographers 800–1150*, 284–89. Amaj was an oasis settlement in the territory of Khuzāʿah. According to al-Bakrī, op. cit., I, 190–92, and according to Yāqūt, op. cit., I, 249–50, it was in the region of Medina; see also Al-Wohaibi, op. cit., 120–22, 186.

430. Hudhayl b. Mudrikah were a tribe, accounted North Arab in genealogy, from the Khindif branch of Muḍar, hence related to Quraysh of Mecca, whose territory was in the vicinity of Mecca and al-Ṭāʾif. See Ibn al-Kalbī-Caskel-Strenziok, *Jamharat al-nasab*, I, Tables 3, 58, II, 7, 286; *EI*², s.v. Hudhayl (G. Rentz).

431. That is, the Kaʿbah, regarded, as is stated below, as having been founded by Ibrāhīm (Abraham) and his son Ismāʿīl (Ishmael).

and asked them about it. They told him: "The sole intention of these people is to bring about your destruction and the destruction of your army. If you do what they are urging you to do, you and everyone with you will assuredly perish en bloc." Tubbaʿ said, "What then do you advise me to do when I get to the temple?" They replied, "When you get there, do as its devotees do: circumambulate it, venerate and honor it, shave your head in its presence and behave with humility until you leave its precincts." He asked them, "What is preventing you yourselves from doing that?" They retorted, "By God, it is indeed the temple of our forefather Abraham, and it is just as we have informed you; but the local people have interposed as obstacles, between us and the temple, various idols they have set up around it, and blood they shed there. They are unclean polytheists," or words to that effect.[432]

Tubbaʿ recognized the soundness of their advice and the veraciousness of their words. He had the group of Hudhalīs brought in, and cut off their hands and feet. Then he proceeded onwards till he reached Mecca. It was revealed to him in a dream that he should cover over the temple, so he covered it with sheets of woven palm leaves. Then in a second dream it was revealed to him that he should cover it with something better than that, so he covered it with Yemeni cloth (*al-maʿāfir*). Then in a third dream, that he should cover it with something even better than that, so he covered it with women's robes and pieces of finely woven Yemeni cloth joined together (*al-mulāʾah wa-al-waṣāʾil*). According to what they assert, Tubbaʿ was the first person to put a covering over the Kaʿbah.[433] He also ordered its guardians, from Jurhum,[434]

---

432. According to Muslim lore, the primitive monotheism of Abraham, the *millat Ibrāhīm,* became corrupted after his time by polytheistic practices such as are mentioned here, so that by Muḥammad's time it had become an idol temple. Whether the *ṭawāf* or circumambulation, and the requirement of shaving the head, part of the *iḥrām,* practices mentioned here, were part of the rites of the Kaʿbah in the two or three centuries before the coming of Muḥammad, the age of the Tubbaʿs, is unknown; but it seems quite likely that such taboos and ritual practices did exist well before their formalization under Islam as the *manāsik al-ḥajj.* See M. Gaudefroy-Demombynes, *Le pélerinage à la Mekke, étude d'histoire religieuse,* 30ff.; *EI*², s.v. Kaʿba (A. J. Wensinck).

433. For the *kiswah* or covering, see Gaudefroy-Demombynes, *Le pélerinage à la Mekke,* 33; idem, "Le voile de la Kaʿba," 5–21; *EI*², s.v. Kaʿba. 1. (A.J. Wensinck and J. Jomier).

434. Jurhum were an ancient tribe, accounted Yemeni in genealogy, who were said to have migrated northward to Ḥijāz and to have taken over Mecca and its

to look after it and to keep it in a state of ritual purity, not letting any blood, dead bodies, or *mīlāth,* that is, [cloth used for] menstruation, come near it, and he provided it with a door and a key. Then he set out for Yemen accompanied by his troops and the two rabbis. When he reached Yemen he summoned its people to enter into the same religion as he had done, but they refused until they were able to test it by means of ordeal by fire, which they had in Yemen.[435]

[905] Ibn Ḥumayd related to us—Salamah—Ibn Isḥāq—Abū Mālik b. Thaʿlabah b. Abī Mālik al-Quraẓī,[436] who said: I heard Ibrāhīm b. Muḥammad b. Ṭalḥah b. ʿUbaydallāh relate that, when Tubbaʿ drew near to Yemen in order to enter it, the Ḥimyarites blocked his way to it, telling him that he could not enter it because he had abandoned their religion. He invited them to accept his (new) faith, saying, "It is a better religion than yours." They retorted, "In that case, come and settle the matter with us by the ordeal of fire," and he agreed. He related: According to what the Yemenis assert, there was in Yemen a fire, by means of which they would settle matters in dispute among themselves; the fire would devour the wrongdoer but leave the one who had suffered injury unscathed. When they told this to Tubbaʿ, he replied, "You have made a fair proposition." So his people (i.e., the Ḥimyarites) went forth with their idols and with other sacred objects they were accustomed to utilize in their religion, while the two rabbis went forth with their sacred codices (*maṣāḥifihimā*)[437] hanging round their necks until they halted in front of the fire by the place where it blazed forth. The fire leapt out toward them, and when it neared them they withdrew from it in great fear. But those people present urged them onward and instructed them to stand firm. So they stood

---

shrine from the Amelekites before being themselves displaced by the local Ḥijāzī tribe of Khuzāʿah. Individuals with the *nisbah* of al-Jurhumī were still known in the time of Muḥammad. See *EI²*, s.v. Djurhum or Djurham (W. M. Watt).

435. This story is also in Ibn Hishām, ed. Wüstenfeld, 14–15 = ed. al-Saqqā et al., I, 237, trans. 8–9; idem, *Kitāb al-Tījān*, 294–96; al-Azraqī, *Akhbār Makkah*, I, 84–86.

436. Some male members of the Jewish tribe of Qurayẓah apparently survived the massacre mentioned in n. 419 above.

437. These *muṣḥafs* could have been made up of flat leaves, loose or sewn, or of rolled-up leaves, both procedures being apparently known in earliest Islam and doubtless before then. See *EI²*, s.v. Ṣaḥīfa (A. Ghédira).

their ground until the fire covered them and consumed the idols and the sacred objects they had brought along, together with the men of Ḥimyar who were bearing them. The two rabbis then went forth with their sacred codices round their necks, with their foreheads dripping with sweat but the fire did not harm them at all. At this, the Ḥimyarites agreed to accept Tubbaʿ's religion; from this time onward, and because of this episode, was the origin of Judaism in Yemen.

Ibn Ḥumayd related to us—Salamah—Ibn Isḥāq—one of his colleagues, that the two rabbis and the Ḥimyarites who went out with them at that same time only followed the track of the fire in order to repel it, for they said that whoever was able to drive it back was the most worthy of credence. When some of the Ḥimyarites came with their idols near to it in order to drive it back, the fire came on at them in order to consume them, hence they retreated and were unable to drive it back. But when the two rabbis drew near to it after that, and began to recite the Torah, the fire began to recede until they had driven it back to its place of origin. Thereupon, the Ḥimyarites adopted the two rabbis' [906] religion.

Now Riʾām was one of the temples they used to venerate and where they offered up slaughtered beasts and from which they used to speak under inspiration, this during the time when they were polytheists.[438] The two rabbis told Tubbaʿ that it was only a demon (*shayṭān*) that lured them into evil ways and made them its sport, and they asked him to let them deal with it how they would. He replied, "Just go ahead with it!." The Yemenis assert that the two rabbis drew out from it a black dog, which they

438. Al-Hamdānī, *Ṣifat jazīrat al-ʿArab*, 268, 365, describes Riyām/Riʾām as one of the fortresses and castles (*maḥāfid, quṣūr*; for the first term, sing. *maḥfad, maḥfid*, see C. Landberg, *Glossaire datînois*, I, 442–30) of Yemen and as one of the shrines of the Arabs (*mawāḍiʿ al-ʿibādah*), located in the territory of the Hamdān (i.e., in that part of northern Yemen between Ṣanʿāʾ and Ṣaʿdah). Ibn al-Kalbī, *Kitāb al-aṣnām*, ed. Aḥmad Zakī Pasha, in Klinke-Rosenberger, *Das Götzenbuch*, text, 7–8, Ger. trans. 35, comm. 87, Eng. trans. Faris, 10–11, states that it was a sanctuary of the Ḥimyarites at Ṣanʿāʾ and that there was an oracle there. The existence of both the place and the shrine at Rymᵘᵐ where the god Ta'lab was venerated, is confirmed by South Arabian inscriptions. See Fahd, *Le panthéon de l'Arabie centrale à la veille de l'hégire*, 141–43; W. W. Müller, "Ancient Castles Mentioned in the Eighth Volume of al-Hamdānī's Iklīl," 154.

slaughtered. They also tore down that temple; its remains, according to what has been mentioned to me, can still be seen today in Yemen at Ri'ām, with traces of the blood that used to be poured over it.[439]

Tubba' composed the following verses about that journey of his; what he had intended to do at Medina and the Ka'bah; how he dealt with the men of Hudhayl when they told him what they in fact told him; what he did regarding the Holy House when he came to Mecca, that is, putting a cover over it and purifying it; and what the two rabbis told him about the Messenger of God's future role:

Why [O my soul] is your sleep troubled, like that of one with
bleary, diseased eyes, suffering from sleeplessness, as if kept
awake incessantly?
Feeling rage against two Jewish tribes who settled at Yathrib,
who richly deserve the punishment of a day of violence![440]
When I made my dwelling place at Medina, my slumber there
was sweet and refreshing.
I made space for a dwelling place on a hill between al-'Aqīq and
[907] Baqī' al-Gharqad.[441]
We left behind its tract of dark-colored rocks and its plateaux,
and its salt flats extending on a bare plain,
And we descended to Yathrib, with our breasts raging with
anger at the killing of a slaughtered one (i.e., Tubba''s son).

---

439. This story is also in Ibn Hishām, *Sīrat al-nabī*, ed. Wüstenfeld, 17–18 = ed. al-Saqqā et al., I, 24–28, trans. 10–11, idem, *Kitāb al-tījān*, 37–38.

440. There were, of course, more than two Jewish tribes living in Medina at the time of the *hijrah* and almost certainly before then. Their presence there may even date to the diaspora from Palestine down the Wādī al-Qurā in western Arabia after such cataclysms for the Jewish people as the Roman emperor Titus's sack of Jerusalem in A.D. 70 and the suppression of the revolt of Bar Kokhba in A.D. 132; the question of the origins of the communities of Jews (or Judaised Arabs?) in such oases of western Arabia as Fadak, Khaybar and Medina has been much discussed, without finality having been reached. For Judaism in South Arabia, see n. 486 below.

441. The Wādī al-'Aqīq lay just to the west of Medina and is expressly lauded in Islamic tradition as "the blessed valley" because of the Prophet's fondness for it. See *EI²*, s.v. al-'Aḳīḳ (G. Rentz). Baqī' al-Gharqad was the first Muslim cemetery in Medina, much venerated in later times because so many of the Prophet's family, the Companions, and other notable figures of early Islam were buried there. See *EI²*, s.v. Baḳī' al-Gharḳad (A. J. Wensinck and A. S. Bazmee Ansari).

I have sworn a deliberate, binding vow, an oath which is, by your life, not to be rescinded,
"If I come to Yathrib, I will not suffer to remain in its central parts a single date cluster or any ripe dates."
Until there came to me a learned scholar of Qurayẓah, a rabbi to whom, by your life, the Jews accorded primacy.
He said, "Remove yourself from a settlement which is preserved [by God] for the prophet of Mecca from Quraysh, a divinely guided one."
So I forgave them without any reproach, and left them to the requital of an everlasting day (sc., the Day of Judgment).
And I left them to God, for whose forgiveness I hope on the Day of Reckoning, [escaping] from the stoked-up flames of Hell.
I left behind at Yathrib for him a group of men from our people, men of personal achievement and valor, whose deeds are praised,
A group of men who will bring victory in their train; I hope thereby a reward from the lord of one worthy of praise.[442]
I did not realize that there was a pure house, consecrated to God in the hollow of Mecca, where He is worshiped,
Until there came to me servile wretches from Hudhayl, at al-Duff of Jumdān above the ascent of the hill (*al-musnad*). [908]
They said, "[There is] at Mecca a house of ancient, forgotten wealth, with treasures of pearls and chrysoliths."
I wanted to get at them, but my Lord interposed between me and them, for God repels [profane ones] who would destroy the house of worship.
Hence I renounced my intentions against it and against the people of Yathrib, and left them as an example to the discerning.
Dhū al-Qarnayn before me submitted himself [to God], a king to whom the other kings became humble and thronged [his court].[443]

---

442. *rabbi muḥammadi,* which could be taken as presaging the coming of the Prophet Muḥammad.

443 "The man with the two horns" of Qur'ān, XVIII, 82–97/83–97, generally identified in Muslim lore with Alexander the Great, regarded by some authorities as a proto-Muslim because he spoke to the people of the West about God's punish-

He reigned over the Eastern and Western lands, yet sought the means of knowledge from a wise, rightly guided scholar.
He witnessed the setting of the sun in its resting place into a pool of black and foetid slime.
Before his time, Bilqīs was my paternal forebear (literally, "aunt") and ruled over them until the hoopoe came to her.[444]

There related to us Ibn Ḥumayd—Salamah—Ibn Isḥāq, who said: They assert that, in regard to this tribe (*ḥayy*) of the Anṣār, Tubbaʿ was only enraged at them because of the Jews who lived among them. Tubbaʿ intended to destroy them when he came to them at Medina, but the Anṣār restrained him from them until he then departed. This was the reason for his saying in his poem,

---

ment for the wicked and His reward for the righteous, though it was disputed whether he was a prophet. See *EI*², s.v. al-Iskandar (W. M. Watt). Tubbaʿ's citation here of Dhū al-Qarnayn as a predecessor no doubt reflects the elaboration in early Islamic times of South Arabian legends and folk-tales, which assigned to Alexander a place in the glorious past of Yemen, as a counterbalance to the North Arabs' glorying in the fact that it was from them that the Prophet Muḥammad had arisen. See Tilman Nagel, *Alexander der Grosse in der frühislamischen Volksliteratur,* 60ff.

444. This story is given in Ibn Hishām, *Sīrat al-nabī,* ed. Wüstenfeld, 12–18 = ed. al-Saqqā et al., I, 20–28, trans. 7–12, including the text of the whole poem. Guillaume wondered how Ibn Isḥāq came to insert so patently spurious a poem into a serious historical work. Bilqīs was the name given in Muslim lore to the Queen of Sheba (not actually given a personal name) in Qur'ān, XXVII, 15–45, to whom the hoopoe (*hudhud*) is said to have brought a letter from King Solomon. See *EI*², s.v. Bilḳīs (E. Ullendorff); J. Briend, in *Supplément au dictionnaire de la Bible,* s.v. Sheba. I. "Dans la Bible," cols. 1043–46.

It is quite possible that Solomon had some diplomatic contacts with some Arabian queen, though whether these really were with a monarch in South Arabia or whether the name of Saba, as being that of a well-known, mighty kingdom, was later attached to the story, is impossible to say. However, there was a historical Bilqīs, and the late Jacqueline Pirenne worked out from genealogical information in al-Hamdānī's *Iklīl* that her husband was in fact a *qayl* or local prince of Yemen called Baril or Barig Dhū Bataʿ, known from South Arabian inscriptions and to be placed in the mid-third century A.D., and that the monarch whom Bilqīs and her husband visited was an Arab king, the famous Odenathus/Udhaynah of Palmyra, ally of the Romans against the Persians. The identification of the king thus visited with Solomon would accordingly stem from the existing identification in Jewish lore and legend of the Old Testament monarch with the city-state of Palmyra. See Pirenne, "Who Was the Suleyman visited by al-Hamdani's Bilqis, Queen of Himyar?," 27–45.

Feeling rage against two Jewish tribes who settled at Yathrib,
who richly deserve the punishment of a day of violence! [909]

There related to us Ibn Ḥumayd—Salamah—Ibn Isḥāq, who said: Before this, there had come to Tubbaʿ Shāfiʿ b. Kulayb al-Ṣadafī, who was a soothsayer (*kāhin*). He stayed with Tubbaʿ, and when he signified his intention to say goodbye, Tubbaʿ said, "What does there remain of your learning?" Shāfiʿ replied, "An eloquent piece of historical lore—and a veracious item of knowledge."[445] He said, "Can you find a people with a kingdom equal in status to mine?" Shāfiʿ replied, "No, except that the king of Ghassān has numerous offspring (*najl*)." Tubbaʿ said, "Can you find any king superior to him in status?" He replied, "Yes." He said, "Who has such a kingdom?" He replied, "I find it belonging to a pious and God-fearing man—who has been made strong by conquests—and who has been described in the Scriptures (*al-zabūr*, literally "the Psalms of David")[446]—his community is given a superior status in the sacred books (*al-sufūr*)—and he will dispel darkness with light—Aḥmad the prophet—blessed be his community until he comes!—[He is] one of the Banū Lu'ayy—and then of the Banū Quṣayy."[447] Tubbaʿ sent for a copy of the scrip-

445. The *kāhin*'s utterance here is, as usual with such gnomic pronouncements, in assonantal, rhymed prose (*sajʿ*). See Fahd, *La divination arabe. Etudes religieuses, sociologiques et folkloriques sur le milieu natif de l'Islam*, 151–53; *EI*², s.v. Sadjʿ. i. As Magical Utterances in Pre-Islamic Arabian Usage (T. Fahd).

446. This term is used in the Qurʾān, in the singular, as here, for the Psalms, but in the plural *al-zubur* for written inscriptions in general; A. Jeffery, *The Foreign Vocabulary of the Qur'ān*, 148–49, see also *EI*¹, s.v. Zabūr (J. Horovitz), derived it from the Christian Orient. However, Mr. F. C. de Blois has pointed out to the present writer that a Sabaean verb *zbr*, "to write, inscribe," is now attested on the inscribed sticks that have been recently coming to light in Yemen, as described by W. W. Müller, "L'écriture *zabūr* du Yémen pre-islamique dans la tradition arabe," 35–39, who traces what appears to be the subsequent usage of the verb *zabara* in early Classical Arabic, perhaps influenced by Yemeni precursors and influences. It is accordingly possible that one should translate al-Ṭabarī's text here, *wa-wuṣifa fī al-zabūr*, as "and who has been described in the ancient written texts," and the subsequent mention of Tubbaʿ's sending for a copy of *al-zabūr* (here grammatically feminine, as if a collective) as simply for "ancient written documents."

447. Quṣayy was the semilegendary hero of the Banū Lu'ayy of Fihr or Quraysh who was an ancestor, separated by five generations, of Muḥammad/Aḥmad. He is said to have restored the Kaʿbah to the primitive monotheistic worship of the *millat Ibrāhīm* after the cult there had lapsed into pantheism under Jurhum (on whom see n. 434 above). See *EI*², s.v. Ḳuṣayy (G. Levi Della Vida).

tures and perused them; and lo and behold, he found there the Prophet's description!

There related to us Ibn Ḥumayd—Salamah—Ibn Isḥāq, to whom someone had transmitted from Sa'īd b. Jubayr—Ibn 'Abbās—others of the scholars of Yemen who relate traditions. Some of them transmitted part of the story, but all of that is gathered together in this present story, that there was a king from the Lakhm in Yemen among the Tubba's of Ḥimyar, called Rabī'ah b. Naṣr. Before his period of royal power in Yemen there had reigned Tubba' I, who was Zayd b. 'Amr Dhī al-Adh'ār b. Abrahah Dhī al-Manār b. al-Rā'ish b. Qays b. Ṣayfī b. Saba' the Younger b. Kahf al-Ẓulm b. Zayd b. Sahl b. 'Amr b. Qays b. Mu'āwiyah b. Jusham b. Wā'il b. al-Ghawth b. Qaṭan b. 'Arīb b. Zuhayr b. Ayman b. Hamaysa' b. al-'Aranjaj Ḥimyar b. Saba' the Elder b. Ya'rub b. Yashjub b. Qaḥṭān.[448] Saba''s name was (really) 'Abd Shams, and he was only called Saba', as they assert, because
[910] he was the first to take captives (*sabā*) among the Arabs.[449] This is the ruling house of the kingdom of Ḥimyar, among whom were the Tubba's.

After Tubba' I there came Zayd b. 'Amr and[450] Shamir Yur'ish b. Yāsir Yun'im b. 'Amr Dhī al-Adh'ār his paternal cousin.[451] It was

---

448. The genealogy is here taken back to Qaḥṭān, regarded as the progenitor of the South Arabs as 'Adnān was of the North ones, Ḥimyar being accounted, with Kahlān, as one of the two main subdivisions of Qaḥṭān. The name Qaḥṭān was connected by the Arab genealogists with the Old Testament name Yoqṭān/Joktan (cf. Gen. x. 28; I Chron. i. 20), but this seems phonologically hazardous. See Ibn al-Kalbī-Caskel-Strenziok, *Jamharat al-nasab,* I, Table 176, II, 31–33, 455; *EI*², s.v. Ḳaḥṭān (A. Fischer-A. K. Irvine).

449. The Sabaeans were reckoned by the Arab genealogists as stemming from Saba', called personally 'Āmir b. Yashjub. See Ibn al-Kalbī-Caskel-Strenziok, *Jamharat al-nasab,* I, Table 176, II, 491. In the Old Testament, Səbā figures in Gen. x. 7, as the son of Cush, son of Ham, and Shəbā in I Chron. i. 9, as a son of Joktan. Briend notes that Səbā (with initial *samekh,* occurring five times in the Old Testament) seems to have a different geographical connotation from Shəbā (with initial *shin,* occurring twenty-three times in the Old Testament), which seems definitely to be placed in southwestern part of Arabia. See *Supplément au dictionnaire de la Bible,* s.v. Sheba. I, col. 1046.

450. Supplying the "and" from the Cairo text, II, 111.

451. More correctly, Sh.m.r Yuhar'ish (on the form of the first element in the name, see n. 364 above), as the name appears in South Arabian inscriptions. He and his father Yāsir$^{um}$ Yuhan'im were ruling jointly in 385 Ḥimyarite era/A.D. 285–86 as founders of the Ḥimyarite line, since a decade or so before this Sh.m.r Yuhar'ish

Shamir Yur'ish who raided China, built Samarqand,[452] and laid out as an encampment (*ḥayyara*) al-Ḥīrah,[453] and it was he who recited the verses,

I am Shamir Abū Karib al-Yamānī; I urged on the horses from
Yemen and Syria,
In order that I might attack the slaves who had rebelled against
us, [when we were] in the lands beyond China, in 'Athm
and Yām,[454]
And then we shall inflict judgment in their lands with a just
decision, which not a single youth shall survive.

. . . and so on to the end of the ode.

He related: Then there came after Shamir Yur'ish the son of Yāsir Yun'im, Tubba' the Lesser; namely, Tubān As'ad Abū Karib b. Malkī Karib b. Zayd b. Tubba' I b. 'Amr Dhī al-Adh'ār.[455] It was he who came to Medina and who took back the two Jewish rabbis to Yemen, who venerated the Holy House and put a covering on it and who recited the poetry which is well known.[456] All these reigned before the royal power of Rabī'ah b. Naṣr al-Lakhmī, and

---

had taken over Yemen from the kings of Saba' and Ḥaḍramawt in order to consolidate the new united kingdom in South Arabia (see n. 314 above). See G. Ryckmans, *L'institution monarchique en Arabie méridionale avant l'Islam. Ma'în et Saba*, 210–12; Robin, in *Supplément au dictionnaire de la Bible*, s.v. Sheba. II, cols. 1102, 1139–40.

452. See for details of these legendary trans-Asian raids, al-Ṭabarī, I, 890–92, pp. 142–45 above.

453. Virtually nothing is known of the history of al-Ḥīrah before the Lakhmids built it up into their capital (see nn. 76–79 above), but this story of its foundation by the Tubba's is pure invention, conceivably influenced, however, by the fact that Lakhm were considered genealogically to be a South Arab tribe (see al-Ṭabarī, I, 834, p. 44 and n. 132 above).

454. The Yām b. Aṣbā were a component tribe of the South Arabian Hamdān living in the Najrān area and several times mentioned by al-Hamdānī in his geographical work. The Banū Yām gave their name to one of the districts (*mikhlāf*, pl. *makhālīf*, see n. 462 below) of Yemen, that around their home. See Ibn al-Kalbī-Caskel-Strenziok, *Jamharat al-nasab*, I, Table 229, II, 47, 590; *EI*², s.v. Yām (G. R. Smith). The reading 'Athm is uncertain, but al-Maqdisī, *Aḥsan al-taqāsīm*, 88, registers a place 'Asham in the *mikhlāf* of the Tihāmah; al-Hamdānī, *Ṣifat jazīrat al-'Arab*, 259, mentions this also as a mine (*ma'din*) in the Tihāmah of Yemen, while Yāqūt, *Buldān*, IV, 126, has an 'Ashm in the northern Tihāmah.

455. See n. 417 above, for his place as founder of the Tubba' line.

456. This tale is given in Ibn Hishām, *Sīrat al-nabī*, ed. Wüstenfeld, 12 = ed. al-Saqqā et al., I, 20, trans. 7; idem, *Kitāb al-tījān*, 294–96; cf. Krenkow, "The Two Oldest Books on Arabic Folklore," 227.

when the latter died, the whole of the royal authority in Yemen reverted to Ḥassān b. Tubān (or Tibān) As'ad Abī Karib b. Malkī Karib b. Zayd b. 'Amr Dhī al-Adh'ār.

There related to us Ibn Ḥumayd—Salamah—Ibn Isḥāq, from a
[911] certain scholar, that Rabī'ah b. Naṣr had a dream that alarmed him and that continued to disquiet him.[457] When he had this dream, he sent out enquiries among the people of his kingdom and gathered together in his presence every soothsayer, magician, drawer of omens from the flight of birds,[458] and astrologer. Then he informed them, "I have had a dream which has alarmed me and caused me disquiet, so tell me its interpretation." They replied, "Recount it to us, so that we might inform you of its meaning." He replied, however, "If I recount it to you, I shall have no confidence that you will be able to tell me its correct interpretation; the only person who will know its correct interpretation is the one who already knows about the dream without my telling him." When Rabī'ah had said all this to them, one of the assembled group of experts on dreams said, "If the king requires this, then he should send for Saṭīḥ and Shiqq, for there is no one more knowledgeable than these two, and they will certainly be able to tell you what you ask." Saṭīḥ's (real) name was Rabī' b. Rabī'ah b. Mas'ūd

457. What we have here is a story from the South Arabian tradition, meant to explain the presence of the (genealogically) South Arabian Lakhmids in Iraq and al-Ḥīrah. The story is traced back to the time of a generation after Shamir Yur'ish/Yuhar'ish, i.e., the first part of the fourth century, and Rabī'ah b. Naṣr al-Lakhmī is made the father of 'Adī, who in the Lakhmid king lists dependent upon Ibn al-Kalbī (see n. 414 above) is regarded as the progenitor of the line, the first figure in the royal genealogy, father of 'Amr I, the father of Imru' al-Qays I. At the end of the story of the dream, the Lakhmids are made to migrate from Yemen to al-Ḥīrah in order to escape the prophesied invasion of the Abyssinians, being allowed to settle at al-Ḥīrah by the Persian king Shāpūr I (see al-Ṭabarī, I, 913–14, p. 182 below, and Rothstein, *Laḫmiden*, 39–40, who states that we know, concerning the origins of the kingdom based on al-Ḥīrah, "so gut wie nichts").

458. See for this person, the *'ā'if*, al-Ṭabarī, I, 1058, p. 395 and n. 970 above. Concerning this series of persons skilled in various types of prognostication, cf. the series of "magicians, enchanters, sorcerers, and the Chaldaeans" whom Nebuchadnezzar summoned to interpret his dreams in Daniel ii. 2. For the practice of the interpretation of dreams, oneiromancy, a pseudo-science whose literature goes back through Classical Antiquity to Assyrian times and which in the Islamic period produced a considerable number of works on *ta'bīr al-ru'yā*, dream interpretation books, see Fahd, *La divination arabe*, 247–367, and *EI²*, s.v. Ru'yā (H. Daiber).

b. Māzin b. Dhi'b b. 'Adī b. Māzin b. Ghassān, and because of his genealogical connections with Dhi'b he was called al-Dhi'bī. Shiqq was the son of Ṣa'b b. Yashkur b. Ruhm b. Afrak b. Nadhīr b. Qays b. 'Abqar b. Anmār.[459]

When they told Rabī'ah that, he sent for the two men. Saṭīḥ came to him before Shiqq; there were no soothsayers (*kuhhān*) like them in their time. So when Saṭīḥ arrived, the king summoned him and said, "O Saṭīḥ, I have had a dream which has alarmed me and disquieted me, so tell me about it, for if you comprehend the dream correctly, you will know correctly its interpretation." Saṭīḥ replied, "I will do this. You saw in your dream a skull (*jumjumah*) (Abū Ja'far [al-Ṭabarī] says: I have found the rendering of it in other places as '. . . I saw blazing coals, *ḥumamah*')—which came forth from the darkness—and fell upon the lowlands descending to the sea—and devoured there everything with a skull!" The king said, "O Saṭīḥ, you have got it exactly right; so what, in your opinion, is the interpretation of it?" Saṭīḥ answered, "I swear by the serpent which is between the two *ḥarrahs*[460]—the Abyssinians (al-Ḥabash)[461] will certainly swoop down on your land —and will then rule over all the land from [912]
Abyan to Jurash."[462]

459. Saṭīḥ and Shiqq appear in Arabic lore as legendary personages, often described as barely human monsters, and they have roles in pre-Islamic history as diviners: here for the Lakhmid Rabī'ah but also (anachronistically) for al-Nu'mān (III) b. al-Mundhir (IV) and Khusraw Anūsharwān in predicting the fall of the Persian kingdom and the triumph of the Arabs (al-Ṭabarī, I, 981–84, pp. 285–89 below). See Rothstein, *Laḫmiden*, 39; *EI*², s.vv. Saṭīḥ b. Rabī'a (T. Fahd) and Shiḳḳ (B. Carra de Vaux and T. Fahd).

460. The geographers enumerate large numbers of *ḥarrah*s, basaltic lava fields, in the region between the Ḥawrān in southern Syria and Medina. See the long section in Yāqūt, *Buldān*, II, 245–50 (paraphrased and discussed by O. Loth, "Die Vulkanregionen von Arabien nach Yāḳūt," 365–82); *EI*², s.v. Ḥarra (ed.). Here the reference, if at all specific, is probably to two of the *ḥarrah*s in the vicinity of Medina, which included the Ḥarrat Wāqim, site of a famous battle in 63/683 when the Umayyad army under Muslim b. 'Uqbah al-Murrī defeated the Medinans there; see Loth, op. cit., 380.

461. This designates here the people of al-Ḥabashah, *ḥbs²t* of the later Sabaean inscriptions. See *EI*², s.v. Ḥabashat (A. K. Irvine). As observed by Irvine, there is no evidence for the statement in earlier authorities like Glaser and Rossini there that the *Ḥbs²t* may have been a South Arabian tribe in origin.

462. Abyan was a *mikhlāf* of the southernmost tip of Arabia, comrprising Aden and its eastward-stretching hinterland; see *EI*², s.v. Abyan (O. Löfgren). Jurash,

The king said to Saṭīḥ, "By your father! O Saṭīḥ, this is indeed distressing and painful for us; but when will this take place—in my own time, or subsequently?" Saṭīḥ replied, "Nay, indeed, a good while after it—more than sixty or seventy years will elapse." The king said, "Will that dominion of theirs endure, or will it be cut short?" he answered, "Nay, it will be cut short after seventy-odd years have gone by—and then all of them there will be slain or will be expelled from it as fugitives." The king said, "Who, then, will assume that task of killing and expelling them?" Saṭīḥ replied, "Iram of Dhū Yazan[463]—who will come forth against them from Aden—and not leave a single one of them in Yemen." The king enquired, "Will Iram's dominion there endure, or will it be cut short?" He replied, "It will indeed be cut short." The king said, "And who will cut it short?" He replied, "A prophet—a pure one—to whom the inspired revelation (*al-waḥy*) will come—from on high." The king asked, "Who will this prophet spring from?" He replied, "[He will be] a man from the progeny of Ghālib b.

---

frequently mentioned by al-Hamdānī, was an important town and a *mikhlāf* in mediaeval Islamic times, situated in northern Yemen to the northwest of Najrān. See al-Bakrī, *Mu'jam mā ista'jam*, II, 376; Yāqūt, *Buldān*, II, 126.

*Mikhlāf*, used in the early Islamic sources on Yemen in particular (although no longer used as an administrative term in modern Yemen), is said by the geographers to be the equivalent of *kūrah*. It may have a tenuous relationship to Sabaean *ḫlf* "vicinity of a town," but a form *mḫlf* has not so far been attested in the inscriptions. See Beeston *et alii*, *Sabaic Dictionary*, 60; *EI²*, s.v. Mikhlāf (C. E. Bosworth).

463. Muslim lore identified Iram with the Biblical Aram, son of Shem (Gen. x. 22–23; I Chron, I. 17), and made various peoples of Arabia his descendants. When the Qur'ān, LXXXIX, 6, speaks of Iram dhāt 'imād, it is probably referring to a tribe or people, here linked with the legendary giant race of 'Ād. See al-Hamdānī, *al-Iklīl. al-Juz' al-thāmin*, 33, trans. Faris, *The Antiquities of South Arabia*, 29–30; Nashwān al-Ḥimyarī, *Die auf Südarabien bezüglichen Angaben Našwāns im Šams al-'ulūm*, 2; *EI²*, s.v. Iram (W. M. Watt).

Dhū Yaz'an or Yazan was one of the Ḥimyarite kings of the first half of the sixth century, and father of Sayf b. Dhī Yazan who secured the help of Khusraw Anūsharwān to expel the Abyssinians from Yemen; see al-Ṭabarī, I, 946ff., pp. 236ff. and n. 585 below. The component *dhū* in his name is the South Arabian relative pronoun *ḏ*, often used to indicate clan or group affiliation, thence "the chief [of such a group]," as here. See Biella, *Dictionary of Old South Arabic, Sabaean Dialect*, 89–90; Beeston, *Sabaic Grammar*, §27:2. The Muslim Arabs regarded names thus compounded as so characteristic of South Arabian monarchical terminology that they used *dhū*, pl. *adhwā'*, as a generic term for South Arabian rulers. See Nashwān al-Ḥimyarī, *Die auf Südarabien bezüglichen Angaben Našwāns*, 39. 116; *EI²*, s.v. Adhwā' (O. Löfgren).

Fihr—son of Mālik b. al-Naḍr[464]—his dominion over his people shall last until the end of time." The king said, "O Saṭīḥ, will time (*al-dahr*) have an end?" He replied, "Yes, a day on which the first generations and the last generations wil be assembled—the righteous will be joyful on it—but the evildoers shall be made wretched." The king said, "Is what you are informing us true, O Saṭīḥ?" the latter replied, "Yes, by the redness of the dying sun at evening—and the beginning of the darkness of night—and the dawn when it is complete—what I have told you is undoubtedly true."

When Saṭīḥ had finished, Shiqq arrived, so the king summoned him. He said, "O Shiqq, I have had a dream that has alarmed and disquieted me, so tell me about it, for if you comprehend the dream correctly, you will know correctly its interpretation," just as he had said to Saṭīḥ. But he concealed from him what Saṭīḥ had said in order that he might see whether the two interpretations agreed or differed. Shiqq said, "Yes, you saw a skull—which came forth from the darkness—and fell upon all the land, meadows, and [913]
thickets—and devoured everything there with living breath." When that king perceived that the words of the two soothsayers agreed with each other totally, he said to Shiqq, "O Shiqq, you have got it exactly right, so what, in your opinion, is the interpretation of it?" Shiqq replied, "I swear by the men living between the two *ḥarrah*s—the blacks will certainly come down on your land—and will seize custody of every tender one from your hands—and will then rule over all the land from Abyan to Najrān."[465]

The king exclaimed, "By your father! O Shiqq, this is indeed distressing and painful for us; but when will this take place—in my own time, or subsequently?" Shiqq answered, "Nay indeed, a stretch of time after you—then a mighty one, lofty of status, shall rescue you from it—and will make them taste the deepest abasement." The king said, "Who is this person mighty of status?"

---

464. That is, from Quraysh, these being persons figuring in the genealogy of the tribe back to Ma'add b. 'Adnān. See Ibn al-Kalbī-Caskel-Strenziok, *Jamharat al-nasab*, I, Table 4; *EI*², s.v. Ḳuraysh (W. M. Watt).

465. Again implying the whole length of Yemen, since Najrān lay on its north-eastern fringes. See al-Bakrī, *Mu'jam mā ista'jam*, IV, 1298–99; Yāqūt, *Buldān*, V, 266–71; *EI*², s.v. Nadjrān (Irfan Shahîd).

Shiqq retorted, "A youth neither base nor inadequate for what he attempts—he will issue forth from the house of Dhū Yazan." The king said, "Will his dominion endure, or will it be cut short?" He replied, "Indeed, it will be ended by a prophet who will be sent—who will come with right and justice—among the people of religion and virtue—the dominion will remain among his people until the Day of Separation. One may ask, 'What is the Day of Separation?'[466] —The reply is, the day on which those near to God will be recompensed—invocations from the heavens will be made—which both the quick and the dead shall hear—and on which the people will be gathered together at the appointed place[467]—on which there will be salvation and blessings for those who fear God." The king said, "Is what you say true, O Shiqq?" The latter replied, "Yes, by the lord of heaven and earth—and the highlands and the lowlands which lie between them—what I have communicated to you is indeed the truth, in which there is no dissimulation."

When the king had finished questioning the two men, there came into his mind that what the two of them had told him regarding the invasion of the Ethiopians was really going to take place, so he fitted out his sons and other members of his house for the journey to Iraq, together with what they needed, and wrote on their behalf to one of the kings of Persia called Shābūr, son of Khurrazād,[468] who allowed them to settle at al-Ḥīrah. Al-Nuʿmān b. al-Mundhir, the king of al-Ḥīrah, was a descendant of Rabīʿah b.
[914] Naṣr; he is al-Nuʿmān b. al-Mundhir— b. al-Nuʿmān b. al-Mundhir b. ʿAmr b. ʿAdī b. Rabīʿah b. Naṣr, that same king in the genealogy and the lore of the scholars (*ahl*) of Yemen.[469]

466. Echoing the Qurʾānic usage of the eschatological concept of the *yawm al-faṣl*, the day of separation or distinction between those who will be saved and those who will be damned, as expounded n XXXVII, 21, etc., and especially in LXXVII, 13, 14, 38.

467. That is, the *ḥashr* or "crowding together" for the Last Judgment. See *EI*², s.v. Ḳiyāma (L. Gardet).

468. Presumably the reference is to Shābūr I, since his father Ardashīr I's mother was Khurrazād. See Justi, *Namenbuch*, 96–97.

469. This story is in Ibn Hishām, *Sīrat al-nabī*, ed. Wüstenfeld, 9–12 = ed. al-Saqqā et al., I, 15–19, trans. 4–6, and Ibn al-Athīr, *Kāmil*, I, 418–20, and cf. Fahd, *La divination arabe*, 250–52. As noted in n. 457 above, the dream described thus becomes an explanation for the movement of a South Arabian group like the

There related to us Ibn Ḥumayd—Salamah—Ibn Isḥāq, who said: When Saṭīḥ and Shiqq told that to Rabī'ah b. Naṣr, and Rabī'ah did with regard to his sons and other members of his house what he in fact did, the mention of all this spread among the Arabs, and they talked about it extensively until his fame and his reputation for knowledge became widely disseminated among them. Hence when the Ethiopians occupied Yemen, and the events which they had previously been talking about, including the interpretations of the two soothsayers, came to pass, al-A'shā—that is, al-A'shā of the Banū Qays b. Tha'labah al-Bakrī[470]—said in some of the poetry he recited, mentioning the events involving those two soothsayers Saṭīḥ and Shiqq:

A woman with her eyelids never looked forth like with a look
full of penetration, as when al-Dhi'bī made
pronouncements when he spoke in *saj'*.

Saṭīḥ used only to be called al-Dhi'bī by the Arabs because he came from the progeny of Dhi'b b.'Adī. When Rabī'ah b. Naṣr died and the royal power in Yemen became concentrated into the hands of Ḥassān b. Tubān As'ad Abī Karib b. Malkī Karib b. Zayd b. 'Amr Dhī al-Adh'ār,[471] one of the factors involving the eruption of the Ethiopians, the transfer of the royal power from Ḥimyar, and the ending of their period of dominion—and there is a cause for everything—was that Ḥassān b. Tubān As'ad Abī Karib led an expedition with the army of Yemen, aiming at overrunning the land of the Arabs and the land of the Persians, just as the Tubba's had been wont to do previously. But when the expedition reached

---

Lakhmid family from Yemen to Iraq.

470. The celebrated poet al-A'shā Maymūn b. Qays, often ranked for his poetic genius with the authors of the Seven *Mu'allaqāt,* came from the Qays b. Tha'labah of Bakr b. Wā'il (d. after 3/625), grew up in the Christian environment of al-Ḥīrah and eulogized *inter alios* Iyās b. Qabīṣah, the appointee of the Persians to the governorship of al-Ḥīrah after the deposition and death of al-Nu'mān V b. al-Mundhir II (see al-Ṭabarī, I, 1029–30, p. 359 below). His life was much bound up with political and military events along the desert frontiers of Iraq. The verse is from his *qaṣīdah* beginning with the formulaic hemistich *Bānat Su'ād wa-amsā ḥabluhā inqaṭa'a,* in *Dīwān,* ed. Geyer, *Gedichte von 'Abû Baṣîr Maimûn ibn Qais al-A'šâ,* 74, no. 13, v. 16. See on the poet Blachère, *Histoire de la littérature arabe,* II, 321–25; *EI²,* s.v. al-A'shā, Maymūn b. Ḳays (W. Caskel).

471. Nashwān al-Ḥimyarī, *Die auf Südarabien bezüglichen Angaben Našwāns,* 38, has a fanciful explanation for the princely name Dhū al-Adh'ār.

a certain spot in the land of Iraq, Ḥimyar and the tribes of Yemen refused to go on further with him and wanted to return to their own homeland and families. Hence they approached and spoke with one of Ḥassān's brothers, who was with him in the army, called ʿAmr, saying, "Kill your brother Ḥassān, and we will make you king over us in his stead and you can lead us back to our homeland." He agreed to their plan, and Ḥassān's brother and his followers from Ḥimyar and the tribes of Yemen agreed to kill
[915] Ḥassān, except for Dhū Ruʿayn al-Ḥimyarī, who forbade ʿAmr to do this and told him, "You are the ruling house of our kingdom; do not kill your brother and thereby dissolve the uniting bonds of our house," or something like that. But ʿAmr rejected his words, although Dhū Ruʿayn was a leading noble of Ḥimyar.[472] Hence Dhū Ruʿayn obtained a leaf of writing material and inscribed on it:

O who would buy sleeplessness for sleep? The one who passes
his nights in a calm and peaceful state is indeed fortunate.
And although Ḥimyar has acted treacherously and faithlessly,
God will hold Dhū Ruʿayn blameless.

Then he sealed the piece of writing and gave it to ʿAmr, telling him, "Keep this document by you on my behalf, for there is in it something which I desire earnestly and have need of" (i.e., for his eventual exculpation), so ʿAmr did that. When Ḥassān got news of what his brother ʿAmr, Ḥimyar, and the tribes of Yemen had resolved upon, that is, his death, he recited to ʿAmr:

O ʿAmr, do not hasten my deathly fate, but take the royal
power without using armed force.

But ʿAmr was set on killing him, and in fact did the deed. He then returned to Yemen with his accompanying army. A certain poet of Ḥimyar recited:

When, [I pray] to God, has anyone ever seen, in previous long
spans of years, the like of Ḥassān, as a slain one?

---

472. That Dhū Ruʿayn were a noble family of Ḥimyar is confirmed by Nashwān al-Ḥimyarī, *Die auf Südarabien bezüglichen Angaben Našwāns*, 46, cf. 41, apparently claiming a connection for them with the previous ruling house of Sabaʾ.

The princelets (*aqyāl*) slew him out of fear lest they be kept at military service, while assuring him, "No harm, no harm!" (*labābi labābi*).[473]
Your dead one was the best of us and your living one is lord over us, while all of you are chiefs.

When ʿAmr b. Tubān Asʿad Abī Karib established himself in Yemen, he was unable to sleep and suffered permanent insomnia, according to what they assert. He found it impossible to sleep. It reduced him to a state of exhaustion, so he set about asking the physicians, and the soothsayers and diviners who work by examining physiognomy, what was the matter with him, saying, "I am deprived of sleep, and can get no rest, and insomnia has reduced me to a state of exhaustion." One of them told him, "By God, no [916]
man has ever killed his brother or a blood relation wrongfully, as you killed your brother, without losing his sleep and incurring sleeplessness." On being told this, ʿAmr set about killing all those members of the nobles of Ḥimyar and tribes of Yemen who had urged him to kill his brother Ḥassān, until finally he came to Dhū Ruʿayn. When ʿAmr expressed his intention of killing him, Dhū Ruʿayn said, "You have in your possession a document exonerating me from what you propose to do with me." ʿAmr said, "What is this exculpating document in my possession?" He replied, "Fetch out the paper which I entrusted to you and left with you." The king fetched out the paper, and lo and behold, there was written on it those two verses of poetry:

O who would buy sleeplessness for sleep? The one who passes his nights in a calm and peaceful state is indeed fortunate.

---

473. Nashwān b. Saʿīd, *Die auf Südarabien bezüglichen Angaben Našwāns*, 89, defines *qayl* as meaning "king" among the Ḥimyarites. It seems to have a fairly late usage in South Arabia in the explicit form *qyl*, mainly in the fifth and sixth centuries, and to bear the meaning "prince," a potentate subordinate to a *malik* or king, as well as the meaning of "tribal chief." See G. Ryckmans, "Le Qayl en Arabie méridionale préislamique," 144–55; Biella, *Dictionary of Old South Arabic, Sabaean Dialect*, 453–54; *EI*², s.v. Ḳayl (A. F. L. Beeston).
The word *labābī/labāb*$^{in}$ is said by Ibn Isḥāq, in Ibn Hishām, *Sīrat al-nabī*, ed. Wüstenfeld, 19 = ed. al-Saqqā et al., I, 29, trans. 13, to mean in the Ḥimyarite language *lā ba's*.

And although Ḥimyar has acted treacherously and faithlessly,
God will hold Dhū Ruʿayn blameless.

When ʿAmr read these two verses, Dhu Ruʿayn told him, "I forbade you to kill your brother, but you would not listen to me; so when you refused thus to listen to me, I left this paper with you as proof of my innocence in regard to you and as exoneration of me vis-à-vis you. I feared that, if you killed him, you would be afflicted as you have in fact been afflicted; and if you intend to inflict on me what I see you have inflicted on those who urged you to kill your brother, this paper will serve as a means of preserving me from your intentions." Hence ʿAmr b. Tubān Asʿad left him alone and did not include him among the nobles of Ḥimyar whom he executed; he recognized that Dhū Ruʿayn had given him wise counsel, if only he had followed it.

ʿAmr b. Tubān Asʿad recited, when he executed those guilty men of Ḥimyar and the people of Yemen who had urged him to kill his brother Ḥassān:

We purchased sleep, when tendons in the neck were drawn
tight with what causes sleeplessness and knotting of sinews
which will not go away.
They called out together at the time of their treacherous action,
"No harm!" when the exculpation of Dhū Ruʿayn had
[917] already been expressed.
We have now executed those responsible for this betrayal, as an
act of retaliation for Ibn Ruhm, which does not entail
responsibility for a blood feud.
We have executed them in requital for Ḥassān b. Ruhm, for
Ḥassān was the one murdered by the ones who stirred up
trouble.
We have executed them, so that none of them now remains,
and every eye feels refreshed at their fate.
The eyes of the lamenting women are weeping with grief for the
noble women, women of the two armies.
Gentle maidens at nightfall, who are dark eyed when the upper
parts of Sirius and Procyon rise.
Hence we are known by our fidelity when our lineage is traced
back, and we disassociate ourselves strongly from the one
who acts treacherously.

We surpass in eminence all other people, just as pure gold is superior to silver.
We exercise royal power over all other peoples; we have the connections of nobility and power, after the two Tubbaʿs.
We assumed royal power after Dāwūd (David) for a lengthy period, and we made the kings of East and West our slaves.[474]
We wrote down in Ẓafār the ancient writings of glory, so that the chiefs of the two towns (*al-qaryatān*, sc., Mecca and al-Ṭā'if)[475] might read them.
We are the ones who pursue every burden of revenge when the eloquent ones cry out, "Where, O where [is vengeance to be taken]?"
I shall quench my thirst of [the blood of] the treacherous ones, for treachery has entailed perdition for them and for me (i.e., through his brother's murder).
I obeyed them (i.e., in their evil counsels) and was not well guided; they were seducers into evil ways, who have destroyed my noble reputation and handsome qualities.

He related: Not long afterward, ʿAmr b. Tubān died.[476]

Hishām b. Muḥammad related: This ʿAmr b. Tubbaʿ was called Mawthabān because he sprang upon (*wathaba*) his brother Ḥassān

---

474. The king and prophet Dāwūd/David (whose reign over the Children of Israel is given by al-Ṭabarī in I, 554–72 above, trans. W. M. Brinner, *The History of al-Ṭabarī. III. The Children of Israel,* 135–51) is presumably adduced here to connect the Tubbaʿs with early prophetic history. For David in Islamic lore, see *EI*², s.v. Dāwūd (R. Paret).

475. The royal city and capital of the Ḥimyarites appears in South Arabian inscriptions as *ẓfr,* but was known as such to classical authors from the time of Pliny the Elder (his *regia Sapphar*) onward. Its ruinous site now lies to the southwest of Yarīm in southern Yemen. It remained of some significance into early Islamic times, and al-Hamdānī describes it both in his *Iklīl,* 25–29, trans. Faris, 20–26, and in his *Ṣifat jazīrat al-ʿArab,* 365, as one of the great fortresses of Yemen. See Yāqūt, *Buldān,* IV, 60; Shahîd, "Byzantium and South Arabia," 29, 43–47; *EI*¹, s.v. Ẓafār (J. Tkatsch).

Mecca and al-Ṭā'if are usually taken as the referents of "the two towns" in the Qur'ānic passage that this echoes, XLIII, 30/31, speaking of a *rajul min al-qaryatayn*ⁱ *ʿaẓīm,* "a man of the two towns, a respected one," but the context is somewhat obscure and the identification by no means certain. See for this question of the "two towns," Buhl, *Das Leben Muhammeds,* 114–15.

476. This story appears in Ibn Hishām, *Sīrat al-nabī,* ed. Wüstenfeld, 26–28 = ed. al-Saqqā et al., I, 28–30, trans. 12–13. Cf. also idem, *Kitāb al-tījān,* 297–98.

at the gap of Nuʿm and killed him.[477] He related: The "slope of Nuʿm (*furḍat Nuʿm*)" was the desert tract of Ṭawq b. Mālik; Nuʿm was the concubine of the Tubbaʿ Ḥassān b. Asʿad.[478]

The narrative returns to that of Ibn Isḥāq.[479]

He related: The affairs of Ḥimyar fell into disorder at this point, and the people became split up. A man of Ḥimyar who did not stem from the royal house of Ḥimyar, called Lakhīʾathah (?) Yanūf Dhū Shanātir, rose up against them, seized power over them,
[918] killed the choicest men of Ḥimyar, and treated with scorn the ruling families of the kingdom.[480] Hence a certain man of Ḥimyar

---

477. Other Arabic sources give an alternative etymology for the cognomen *Mawthabān:* that rulers were thus called in the language of Ḥimyar because they "sat down" and did not engage in raiding and warfare. See Ibn Hishām, *Kitāb al-tījān,* 298–99 (with a brief version of the preceding story), and Nashwān al-Ḥimyarī, *Die auf Südarabien bezüglichen Angaben Našwāns,* 113. The confusion stems from the fact that in South Arabian, the prime signification of *wṯb* was, as in Hebrew, "to sit down," with *mwṯb(n)* thus meaning "seat, shrine of a god," as opposed to Classical Arabic *wathaba* "to rise, spring up," although another range of meanings for South Arabian *wṯb* does exist, "to attack, assault," to which the cognomen given here by al-Ṭabarī of *Mawthabān* could be attached. See Beeston et al., *Sabaic Dictionary,* 165–66; Biella, *Dictionary of Old South Arabic, Sabaean Dialect,* 153–54. The confusion that could arise out of the two opposing senses of the root forms the basis of favorite anecdotes in the sources in which a man dies or is killed through misunderstanding the South Arabian sense of the word. See al-Hamdānī, *Iklīl,* 32, trans. Faris, 28; Nashwān al-Ḥimyari, loc. cit.; Robin, in *L'Arabie antique de Karib'îl à Mahomet. Nouvelles données sur l'histoire des Arabes grâce aux inscriptions,* 108.

478. According to the geographers, the *furḍat Nuʿm* lay in Jazīrah, in the tract of land along the Euphrates, where, so Yāqūt says, Ḥassān b. Tubbaʿ had built a palace for this *umm walad* of his. See al-Bakrī, *Muʿjam mā istaʿjam,* IV, 1211; Yāqūt, *Buldān,* IV, 251.

479. Nöldeke's translation resumes here. He regarded the following material as still essentially legendary and fabulous, but considered that it was connected with such historical events as the persecution of the Christians of Yemen, the resultant Abyssinian occupation, and the eventual Persian conquest, hence as such worthy of translation; see his trans. 172 n. 4.

480. The episode of Lakhīʿathah or Lakhnīʿathah is somewhat mysterious. The name is variously written in the Arabic sources, e.g., Lakhnīʿah in Ibn Hishām, *Sīrat al-nabī,* ed. Wüstenfeld, 19 = ed. al-Saqqā et al., I, 30), but Nöldeke, trans. 173 n. 1, suggested the form Lakhīʿathah on the basis of its form in the South Arabian inscriptions known at that time, in which *Ynf* is likewise attested. Professor Christian Robin has suggested (personal communication) that it is a corruption of a very common personal name *Lḥy ʿṯt,* often shortened to *Lḥyʿt,* which would mean "ʿAtht[ar] illuminates" (after Geʿez *laḥaya* "to be shining, to gleam"); it would seem that *ḥ* was only feebly aspirated in Ḥimyaritic speech, since the name passed

mentioned what was destroying the fabric of Ḥimyar, rending apart its unity and getting rid of its choicest men:

Ḥimyar is massacring its own sons and expelling its own
princes, and creating humiliation for itself with its own
hands.
Destroying its own worldly prosperity with light-headed
fantasies of its own, but what it destroyed of its religion
was even greater.
In the same way, earlier generations brought down evil on
themselves, through their oppression and profligacy, and
then perished.[481]

Lakhī'athah Yanūf Dhū Shanātir brought about all that for them. He was an evildoer, being allegedly a practitioner of sodomy. In addition to the killing and oppression he inflicted upon them, when he heard that a youth from the royal family had reached the age of puberty, he sent for him and ravished him in an upper chamber he had had constructed for this purpose, so that the youth could never rule after him (i.e., because of the dishonor). He would then go out from that upper chamber to his guards and those of his army who were present—these people being at a lower level—with a toothpick (*siwāk*) he had placed in his mouth,[482]

---

into Classical Arabic as Lahīʿah.

Maʿdī Karib, probably the last of the Tubbaʿs (al-Ṭabarī's "the royal house of Ḥimyar") is attested in inscriptions as ruling in 631 Ḥimyarite era/A.D. 521–22. We have therefore only a year or so for Lakhīʿathah's inscription and the accession of Dhū Nuwās. One suggestion for resolving this tight chronology was put forward by Altheim and Stiehl, *Die Araber in der Alten Welt*, V/1, 377–78: that the title Maʿdī Karib Yaʿfur was the throne-name assumed by the usurping Lakhīʿathah, just as his successor Dhū Nuwās was to assume the throne-name of Yūsuf As'ar Yath'ar (see n. 488 below). But this suggestion does not seem to have found much favor. At all events, one can only treat the tale of Lakhīʿathah's sodomitical proclivities as a pretext for his murder with caution.

Concerning Lakhīʿathah's nickname or cognomen, Nashwān al-Ḥimyarī, *Die auf Südarabien bezüglichen Angaben Našwāns*, 58, says that *shuntur* means "finger" in the Ḥimyarī language. But when linked with *dhū*, one would more naturally expect a place-name; none like Shanātir is, however, so far attested.

481. As noted by Nöldeke, trans. 174 n. 1, the wording of the poem, with such words in it as *ḍayyaʿat, ẓulm, isrāf, takhsaru*, etc., is very reminiscent of Qur'ānic phraseology and concepts.

482. That is, a piece of wood with the end incised for use as a toothbrush. It has been suggested that the use by the Arabs of such a primitive toothbrush or tooth-

that is, in order to let them know that he had acomplished his purpose with the youth. Then he would release the youth and go forth and appear before the guards and the people, having completely disgraced the youth.

At last it was the turn of the last of the youths from that line of kings, Zur'ah Dhū Nuwās b. Tubān As'ad Abī Karib b. Malkī Karib b. Zayd b. 'Amr Dhī al-Adh'ār the brother of Ḥassān.[483] Zur'ah had been only a small boy when his brother was killed, and had grown up into a fine and handsome youth, with an attractive appearance and intelligence. Lakhī'athah Yanūf Dhū Shanātir sent for him in order to do with him as was his wont with the princes of the royal house before him. When the messenger came to Zur'ah, he realized what Lakhī'athah intended to do, so he took a slim-bladed, sharp knife and placed it between his sandal and the sole of his
[919] foot. Then he set out to Lakhī'athah with the latter's envoy. When Lakhī'athah was alone with Zur'ah in that upper chamber of his, he locked the door on the two of them and pounced upon Zur'ah. But Dhū Nuwās leaped on him first with the knife and stabbed him with it until he had killed him. Then he cut off his head and stuck it in the window niche of that upper chamber of Lakhī'athah's, from where he was accustomed to show himself to his guards and troops. He took that toothpick of Lakhī'athah's and stuck it in the latter's mouth, and went forth to the people. They said to him, "Dhū Nuwās—was it wetness or dryness?" He an-

---

pick was influenced by the similar Persian religious custom, and that the Arabic term may stem from MP **sawāk*, "scraper," from the verb *sūdan*, "to scrape, rub." See Shaked, "Some Iranian Themes in Islamic Literature," 149 and n. 35, citing Goldziher; *EI*[2], s.v. Miswāk (A. J. Wensinck).

483. Unlike Lakhī'athah, Dhū Nuwās is a fully historical figure, mentioned in Byzantine sources, e.g., in the Greek of the *Martyrium Arethae* as *Dounaas*. An Arabic etymology for his name is given in the Arabic sources, e.g., Abū al-Faraj al-Iṣfahānī, *Aghānī*[3], XXII, 318, and Nashwān al-Ḥimyarī, *Die auf Südarabien bezüglichen Angaben Našwāns*, 106, as "the man with the dangling forelock, long hair," but again is more likely to relate to a place name, or possibly to a deity. See on him further, nn. 486, 488, 506 below, and Nöldeke, trans. 174 n. 3, who also notes that Zur'ah is likewise a historically-attested name, since one of the local princes of Yemen who sent to the Prophet in autumn of the year 9/630 offering their acceptance of Islam, was Zur'ah Dhū Yazan, quite possibly a descendant of Dhū Nuwās; it was to him that Muḥammad sent a group of *ṣadaqah* collectors headed by Mu'ādh b. Jabal. See Ibn Hishām, *Sīrat al-nabī*, ed. Wüstenfeld, 955–57 = ed. al-Saqqā et al., IV, 235–36, tr. 642–44.

swered, "Ask n.kh.mās[484]—'s.t.r.ṭ.bān Dhū Nuwās—'s.t.r.ṭ.bān Dhū Nuwās—[he is] unharmed (*lā ba's*)." They went off to look when he called to them in these terms, and lo, there was the severed head of Lakhī'athah Yanūf Dhū Shanātir in the window niche, with his toothpick in his mouth, which Dhū Nuwās had jammed there! Ḥimyar and the guards went off after Dhū Nuwās until they caught up with him and told him, "The only fitting person to rule over us is yourself, since you have rid us of this abominable fellow." They therefore made him king, and Ḥimyar and the tribes of Yemen rallied round him.[485] He was the last of the kings of Ḥimyar. He became a convert to Judaism (*tahawwada*), and the Ḥimyarites followed him in this path. He adopted the name of Yūsuf (i.e., Joseph) and reigned for a considerable time.[486]

---

484. According to Ibn Hishām's gloss, *Sīrat al-nabī*, ed. Wüstenfeld, 20 = ed. al-=Saqqā et al., I, 31, tr. 14, *n.khmās* was a Ḥimyarī word for "head." The rest of this puzzling saying clearly has an obscene reference, as the word seemingly figuring in it—*ist*, "anus"—implies, explicit in Abū al-Faraj al-Iṣfahānī, *Aghānī*[3], xxii, 319.

485. This story comes also in Ibn Hishām, *Sīrat al-nabī*, ed. Wüstenfeld, 19–20 = ed. al-Saqqā et al., I, 30–31, tr. 13–14; idem, *Kitāb al-tījān*, 300–301; Abū al-Faraj al-Iṣfahānī, *Aghānī*[3], xxii, 318–19.

486. The questions of the date of the appearance of Judaism in Yemen, the extent of that faith's spread from the ruler and nobles downward to the generality of the population, and the nature and quality of that Judaism, have excited much discussion.

There seems no reason to doubt the reports (al-Ṭabarī, I, 892, 902, 905, pp. 145, 165–66, 170–71 above: one of Ibn Isḥāq's informants for these seems to have been Abū Mālik b. Tha'labah b. Abī Mālik al-Quraẓī, whose grandfather had been a Jewish client of Kindah and who had migrated from Yemen to Yathrib; see M. Lecker, "Abū Mālik 'Abdallāh b. Sām of Kinda, a Jewish convert to Islam," 280–82) that Abū Karib As'ad accepted the Jewish faith in some form or other when he was at Yathrib in the first half of the fifth century and that the faith was already known at the Ḥimyarite court in the time of his father Malkī Karib, i.e., the end of the fourth century, when paganism was abandoned for monotheism. The implantation of a genuine Judaism there around that time would be parallel to the contemporaneous consolidation of the Christian community at Najrān, for which see n. 487 below. See Smith, "Events in South Arabia in the 6th Century A.D.," 462–63; J. Ryckmans, "Le Christianisme en Arabie du Sud préislamique," 417–19. 426–28, 447; Lecker, "The Conversion of Ḥimyar to Judaism and the Jewish Banū Hadl of Medina," 129–36.

There is epigraphic evidence for the existence of adherents of Judaism in Yemen proper during the later fifth century, in that the Bayt al-Ashwal I inscription was erected at Ẓafār by a man called *Yhwd' Ykf*/Yehūdā Yakkuf (for Yankuf), clearly a native South Arabian, who invokes "the Lord of Heaven and Earth" and "His

There were in Najrān remnants of people who adhered to the religion of ʿĪsā (Jesus), followers of the Gospel, virtuous and upright.[487] They had a head, of this same faith, called ʿAbdallāh b. al-Thāmir. The place where that faith originally took root was Najrān, which at that time was in the center of the land of the Arabs;

---

people ($s^{2}$ʿ$b$) Israel" and who mentions the king Dharaʾ ʾamar Ayman (II), who ruled in the later fourth century. See Müller, "Eine hebraeisch-sabaeische Bilinguis aus Bait al-Aśwal," 117–23; Robin, in *L'Arabie antique de Karib'îl à Mahomet,* 145–46. Judaism seems to have made rapid advances at the Ḥimyarite court, with three of the leading noble families, those of Hamdān, Yaz'an, and Haṣbaḥ, becoming converts. There was in the later fifth and early sixth centuries an important Jewish trading community on the island of Yotabē (not yet specifically located, but somewhere near the mouth of the Gulf of ʿAqabah; see Smith, "Events in South Arabia in the 6th Century A.D.," 428–29; Z. Rubin, "Byzantium and Southern Arabia—the Policy of Anastasius," 388–89), which was controlled by a local chief called Amorcesos and which probably served as a base for mercantile activities down the Red Sea as far as the shores of Yemen.

We cannot judge how far below the level of the royal family and that of the great nobles this adherence to Judaism may have penetrated; but more controversial is the nature and quality of the faith as implanted in South Arabia—was it recognizably Rabbinical Judaism or was it an aspect of the monotheistic faith "Raḥmānism," another aspect of which may have been the ascetic monotheism of the *ḥanīf*s during the period just before Muḥammad's call to prophethood? After ca. A.D. 450–60 the South Arabian inscriptions begin to give the "Lord of Heaven and Earth" the proper name of Raḥmānān, one equally used by the Christian monotheists and, in the early seventh century, by Muḥammad's rival among the Banū Ḥanīfah of al-Yamāma, Musaylimah. It does seem that, sixty or so years later, a ruler like Yūsuf As'ar Dhū Nuwās was an enthusiastic Jewish believer. Jacques Ryckmans stressed that the name Raḥmānān in South Arabia must have come originally from a Jewish milieu, almost certainly the Jewish communities of Medina and the settlements of the Wādī al-Qurā, since the term stems from the Aramaic Raḥmānā, frequent in the Babylonian Talmud and sporadically found in the Jerusalem one, while rare in Christian texts of the time. But he went on to suggest that Raḥmānān became generalized in South Arabian monotheistic usage, not least among Christians, via the Christian community in Najrān, by the end of the fifth century, since it appears in an inscription of the Christian king Sumu-yafaʿ Aśwaʿ, installed by the Ethiopians after the death of Dhū Nuwās (see n. 518 below), for the first person of the Trinity. See Ryckmans, "Le Christianisme en Arabie du Sud préislamique," 436–40; Shahîd, Byzantium and the Arabs in the Fourth Century, 100–06; Beeston, "Judaism and Christianity in Pre-Islamic Yemen," 271–78; idem, "Himyarite Monotheism," 149–54; Rubin, op. cit., 387–88; Robin, in op. cit., 145–47; idem, in *Supplément au dictionnaire de la Bible,* s.v. Sheba. II, cols. 1115–16, 1190–92.

Concerning the length of Dhū Nuwās's reign, tradition gives him one of thirty-eight years, a vastly exaggerated number; see n. 488 below.

487. In Muslim eyes, Christianity had in general degenerated by the time of the Prophet's coming, leaving only "remnants" such as those mentioned here. Cf. Nöldeke, trans. 177 n. 2.

Shahîd has propounded that Najrān at this time came definitely within the

its people, like all the rest of the Arabs, were (originally) idol worshipers. At that point, a man called Faymiyūn, from the rem-

---

Arabic cultural and liguistic sector of the Arabian Peninsula rather than the Sabaean-Ḥimyarite one, on the basis of the Arabic names of the Martyrs of Najrān and the existence there in the sixth century of a school of Arabic poets; but this suggestion is rejected by such experts on South Arabian languages as W. W. Müller.

The advent of Christianity to Najrān was part of a general percolation of monotheistic religions, specifically Judaism and Christianity, into the Arabian Peninsula (for Judaism in western and southern Arabia, see n. 486 above, and for Judaism at Najrān specifically, where the community seems to have been an old, established one, see Lecker, "Judaism among Kinda and the *Ridda* of Kinda," 635–36). Already in the mid-fourth century, the king of Ḥimyar had received a diplomatic mission sent by the Byzantine emperor Constantius II (r. 337–61) under Theophilus "the Indian" (who was actually from the island of Socotra, the whole region of South Arabia and the Gulf of Aden shores being often referred to vaguely in Byzantine sources as "India"), an Arian in faith like his master, and the king had undertaken to build three churches within his dominions. Later in that same century, Abū Karib As'ad and others of his family adopted a monotheism that involved some form of Judaism (see n. 486 above). There may well have been some political factors at work here, since the Abyssinian kingdom of Axum was at this time adopting Christianity and the faith was also spreading among the Arabs of the northern and eastern fringes of the Peninsula. The Ḥimyarite rulers may have wished to counter a possible threat of intervention on religious grounds from outside—intervention which was, indeed, to materialize when the power of the Ḥimyarite monarchy went into decline in the early sixth century. J. Ryckmans opined that both Nestorianism and Monophysitism were represented within the Najrān Christian community, but that the former was likely to have been more favorably regarded by the Jewish or Judaizing Ḥimyarite kings of the eighty years or so before the Abyssinian intervention in favor of Monophysitism, and that the celebrated persecutions at Najrān were essentially of the Monophysites there, with the Nestorians merely looking on, if not actively encouraging the Himyarite rulers; see his "Le Christianisme en Arabie du Sud préislamique," 448, 450–52. Through Abyssinian enthusiasm for Monophysitism, and a distinct Byzantine preference for it over Nestorianism (see n. 511 below), Najrān itself became the focus in the sixth century for something like an Arabian national church, Monophysite in theology. From the time of the Byzantine emperor Anastasius I (r. 491–518), the Ḥimyarites had a bishop of their own, probably a Syrian and Monophysite in theology, called Silvanus, and we know the names of two Monophysite bishops, both named Paul, consecrated for Najrān itself around this time (see below). During the early Islamic period, despite the deportations of Christians from Najrān to Iraq by the second caliph 'Umar b. al-Khaṭṭāb, the faith was to survive there (as also in the island of Socotra, in the Gulf of Aden) into mediaeval Islamic times. The Nestorian Church in Iraq had contacts with Christians in southwestern Arabia for some three centuries after the advent of Islam: the Patriarch Timothy ordained a bishop for Yemen and Ṣan'ā' in ca. 800, and John IV answered questions from a priest "of the people of Yemen" in ca. 900. See Fiey, *Assyrie chrétienne,* III, 230; Beaucamp and Robin, "Le Christianisme dans la péninsule arabique d'après l'épigraphie et l'archéologie," 56–57; *EI*², s.v. Nadjrān (Irfan Shahîd).

But before the consolidation of Christianity in Najrān under Byzantine and Abyssinian influence came about, the desire of the Ḥimyarite ruling strata to

nants of the adherents of that faith had come among them; he summoned them to his religion and they adopted it.

Hishām related: [He was] Zur'ah Dhū Nuwās, but when he be-
[920] came a convert to Judaism, he assumed the name of Yūsuf.[488] It

---

preserve their national identity and culture between the two powerful Christian realms of Byzantium and Abyssinia, had inevitably entailed a growing hostility toward the indigenous Monophysite Christian community, even if for political rather than strictly religious reasons. There was persecution under Sharaḥbi'īl Yakuf (known to have been reigning in 472), when we know from an Ethiopic hagiographical work that the missionary Azqīr (whose name Ryckmans linked, through deformed transcriptions, with the Yazdīn of a Persian romance centered round one of the Persian Christian martyrs; Beeston suggested a possible connection with Arabic al-Dhakīr "the famed, reputed one") was killed, possibly for proselytizing but certainly with some sort of Jewish involvement in the deed (see Ryckmans, op. cit., 441–43; Beeston, "The Martyrdom of Azqir," 5–10; Rubin, "Byzantium, and Southern Arabia—the Policy of Anastasius," 387–88); and Paul, the first bishop of Najrān, was martyred at the Ḥimyarite capital Ẓafār, stoned by the Jews there, at an unknown date before 521 but possibly before 504, as is known from the Syriac martyrological literature. Intervention by Abyssinia was not long in coming, and it seems that Yūsuf As'ar Dhū Nuwās's predecessor Ma'dī Karib Ya'fur was placed on the throne of Ḥimyar by the Abyssinians in late 518 or early 519, as part of a direct extension of Abyssinian influence into Yemen, involving even a permanent mission in Ẓafār, where (judging from their names) Abyssinian representatives built a palace for themselves during the reign of Ma'dī Karib Ya'fur's predecessor Marthad 'ilān Yanūf. The stage was thus set for the culmination of what had probably been a series of persecutions of the Christians of Najrān, the most notorious being that in the proto-nationalist, pro-Jewish reaction, which intensified under Yūsuf As'ar Dhū Nuwās; see the following note. On the vestiges Arabian Christianity has left in the epigraphy and archaeology of the peninsula, see Beaucamp and Robin, op. cit., 45–61; on the position of Christianity in the politics and diplomacy of southwestern Arabia at this time, Robin, "Le royaume ḥujride," 699–702; and on the faith there in general, the references in the following note.

Nöldeke, trans. 177 n. 3, thought that Faymiyūn was most likely a shortened form of Euphemion, so that this Greek name would point to a man coming from the Byzantine lands. But since his time there has been further investigation of the origins of this story of the introduction of Christianity to Najrān, in particular, by A. Moberg. Moberg traced the story of the Arabic sources, with its theme of the wandering ascetic from Syria, to Persian Christian romantic legends of Yazdīn-Pethion, involving the martydom in Persia in 447 of Pethion, whose name yielded the Arabic form Faymiyūn. See the discussion of his views in J. Ryckmans, op. cit., 441–42.

The story of 'Abdallāh b. al-Thāmir is given in al-Ṭabarī, I, 923–25, pp. 200–202 below.

488. The actual name of Dhū Nuwās (this being a nickname or cognomen, see n. 483 above), of the family of Yaz'an, emerges from an inscription dating from the month of Dhū Madhra'ān 633 of the Ḥimyarite era/June–July 523. His name is given in the inscription as Yusuf/Yūsuf (replacing Yanūf ?) As'ar Yath'ar, with the title "king of all the tribes, *'s²'bⁿ*," a much more modest one than the usual

was he who had the trench (*al-ukhdūd*) dug out at Najrān and killed the Christians.[489]

There related to us Ibn Ḥumayd—Salamah—Muḥammad b. Isḥāq—al-Mughīrah b. Abī Labīd, a freedman of al-Akhnas—Wahb b. Munabbih al-Yamānī,[490] who related to them that the

---

grandiloquent ones of the Ḥimyarite kings, such as "king of Saba', Dhū Raydān, Ḥaḍramawt, and Yamanat, together with the Arabs of the Ṭawd and the Tihāmat" (see nn. 314, 417 above) and one which seems to reflect the fact that, as an usurper, his rule was illegitimate.

Dhū Nuwās replaced the last Tubba' ruler Ma'dī Karib Ya'fur between June 521 and June 522, and was defeated by the Abyssinians soon after Pentecost 525, killing himself shortly afterward (see al-Ṭabarī, I, 927–28, p. 207 below). Whatever the nature of his commitment to Judaism (see n. 486 above)—and Shahîd has suggested that he may well have started off as a Christian and as the designated successor of Ma'dī Karib (but see above)—he embarked in 523 on his campaign to eliminate the Abyssinians and the indigenous Christians of southwestern Arabia. The eight hundred-strong Abyssinian community in Ẓafār was put to death and the Abyssinian-held fortresses in Shamir taken. Tihāmah was conquered, and Najrān compelled to give hostages and to endure a blockade. Then in November of that same year 523, Najrān was attacked and occupied, its Christian population massacred, the churches burned down, and Greek and Abyssinian traders there killed. See R. Bell, *The Origin of Islam in Its Christian Environment,* 33–63; Smith, "Events in South Arabia in the 6th Century A.D.," 459–60; G. Ryckmans, "Le Christianisme en Arabie du Sud préislamique," 413–53; Altheim and Stiehl, *Die Araber in der Alten Welt,* V/1, 373–85; idem, *Christentum am Roten Meer,* I, 442–43; Shahîd, *The Martyrs of Najrân. New Documents,* 266–68; Trimingham, *Christianity among the Arabs in Pre-Islamic Times,* 297–99; Müller, "Survey of the History of the Arabian Peninsula," 129; Robin, in op. cit., 151–52; *EI*², s.vv. Dhū Nuwās (M. R. Al-Assouad), Mathāmina (Chr. Robin); n. 506 below.

The chronology adopted here for these events, including the actual martyrdoms at Najrān and the happenings following on from them, is that put forward, after a very thorough sifting of the evidence (from Byzantine Greek and Syriac sources and from contemporary South Arabian inscriptions) by François de Blois, that the martyrdoms took place at the traditional date of 523 and not in 518, as argued by, e.g., Rubin and Shahîd. See de Blois, "The Date of the "Martyrs of Nagrān," 110–27.

489. Traditional Qur'ānic exegesis regarded the *aṣḥāb al-ukhdūd,* "companions of the trench," of LXXXV, 4–8, as being the Christian martyrs of Najrān, praised for their steadfastness in the face of immolation or, occasionally, connected with the three men in Nebuchadnezzar's fiery furnace of Daniel, iii. 13ff. Joseph Halévy, on his pioneer expedition into Yemen in 1869–70 sponsored by the Académie des Inscriptions et Belles-Lettres, found that the Najrān of that time was called Madīnat al-Khudūd (< Ukhdūd); see his "Rapport sur une mission archéologique dans le Yémen," 37–40. The connection with the martyrs of Najrān was upheld by older generations of Western scholars, e.g., Nöldeke, in his *Geschichte des Qorāns,* I, 97 n. 3, and (originally) Richard Bell in his *The Origin of Islam in Its Christian Environment,* 38, 68. But it is now generally recognized as being not a specifically historical reference but, rather, an eschatological one, the "companions of the trench" being unbelievers destined for Hell Fire because of what they had done to

implantation of that religion (sc., Christianity) in Najrān arose from the fact that there was a man from the remnants of the followers of the faith of ʿĪsā b. Maryam called Faymiyūn,—a pious man, a zealous fighter for the faith and an ascetic, one whose prayers were answered by God.[491] He used to wander forth, staying in villages. As soon as he became known in one village (sc., as a holy man and wonder worker), he would leave it for another village where he was not known. He lived entirely off what his own hand gained; he was a builder, who worked with mud brick. He used to keep Sunday holy, and when this day came round would do no work but would go out into a desert place and pray and worship there until it was evening. He was once in one of the villages of Syria, performing those rites of his away from human gaze, when a local man called Ṣāliḥ realized what sort of an exalted religious state Faymiyūn had attained and felt a love for him such as he had never felt for anything previously.[492] He followed Faymiyūn around wherever he went, unperceived by Faymiyūn, until on one occasion Faymiyūn went forth into the desert on Sunday, as was his custom, followed by Ṣāliḥ, unbeknown to Faymiyūn. Ṣāliḥ sat down in a place where he could see

---

the believers (v. 7). See Bell, ed. Bosworth and M. E. J. Richardson, *A Commentary on the Qur'ān*, II, 517; *EI*², s.v. Aṣḥāb al-ukhdūd (R. Paret).

490. The *Tābiʿ* or Successor Abū ʿAbdallāh Wahb b. Munabbih (b. ca. 34/654–55, d. 110/728 or 114/732) was one of the most knowledgeable of Umayyad period historians, especially regarding the "Stories of the Prophets" and regarding South Arabian lore, having been himself born, of Persian stock, at Dhimār to the north of Ṣanʿāʾ. He seems to have been able to draw on both Jewish and Christian traditions (in the latter case, notably for the story of the events here at Najrān); it is regrettable that his *Kitāb al-mulūk al-mutawwajah min Ḥimyar wa-akhbārihim wa-qiṣaṣih wa-qubūrihim wa-ashʿārihimm* is only known through later citations, including extensively in the first part of Ibn Hishām's *Kitāb al-tāj*, which depends heavily on Wahb. See Krenkow, "The Two Oldest Books on Arabic Folklore," 56ff.; Sezgin, *GAS*, I, 305–307; *EI*², s.v. Wahb b. Munabbih (R. G. Khoury).

491. Nöldeke, trans. 177 n. 3, regarded the following tale of Faymiyūn and Ṣaliḥ, and its sequel, the tale of ʿAbdallāh b. al-Thāmir, as nothing but pious legend, but Trimingham, *Christianity among the Arabs in Pre-Islamic Times*, 294–95, thought that they should not be discounted as complete inventions but should be considered as reflections of later Islamic attempts to iluminate the background of the Prophet's life and to elucidate supposed Qur'ānic references to events in Najrān (but see on these references, n. 489 above).

492. The name Ṣāliḥ has connotations of "piety, God-fearingness," and also evokes the name of the Qur'ānic native Arabian prophet sent to warn Thamūd. As a personal name, it seems to be very rare in pre-Islamic usage. See *EI*², s.v. Ṣāliḥ (A. Rippin).

Faymiyūn, but in a place concealed from Faymiyūn, not wishing the latter to know where he was. Faymiyūn started praying, but while he was preoccupied with this, a *tinnīn,* a serpent with seven heads, slid up to him.[493] On seeing it, Faymiyūn called down a curse on it, and it died. Ṣāliḥ saw the *tinnīn,* but did not know what had happened to it, and feared for Faymiyūn's safety. Hence he was overcome with concern for him and cried out, "O Faymiyūn, a *tinnīn* has just come up to you!" But Faymiyūn paid no attention to him and kept on with his worship and prayers until he had completed them. Evening having come on, he returned, knowing that he had been recognized; Ṣāliḥ likewise knew that Faymiyūn had seen where he was. Ṣāliḥ addressed him, saying, "O Faymiyūn, God knows that I have never loved anything as [921]
much as I love you; I want to accompany you and be with you wherever you may go." Faymiyūn replied, "As you wish. You see what my work is, but if you believe that you are strong enough to undertake it yourself, well and good." Ṣāliḥ accordingly remained with him closely, but the people of the village were on the verge of discovering Faymiyūn's real nature. For when one of God's servants with some disease suddenly crossed his path, Faymiyūn prayed for him, and he was cured; but when he was summoned to a sick person, he refused to go. Now one of the people of that village had a son who had some affliction (*ḍarīr*),[494] and he asked about Faymiyūn's conduct. He was told that he never came when expressly summoned but that he was a man who did building work for people in return for his hire. So the man went along to that son of his, and put him in his room and threw a garment over him. Then he went to Faymiyūn and asked him, "O Faymiyūn, I want some building work done in my house, so come back with me and have a look at it, so that I can discuss conditions with you." Faymiyūn went back with him and entered the room. He next said, "What do you want done in your house?" The man replied, "So-and-so," and whisked away the garment from of the lad, saying, "O Faymiyūn, one of God's servants has been afflicted as you can see; so pray to God for him!" Faymiyūn exclaimed

493. The *tinnīn* appears as a seven-headed dragon in Jewish Haggadic lore, taken over subsequently into the Islamic *qiṣaṣ al-anbiyā'* stories; see, e.g., W. M. Thackston Jr., *The Tales of the Prophets of al-Kisa'i,* Boston 1978, 201.

494. Thus in the context, rather than "blind."

when he saw the boy, "O God, Your enemy has entered into the sound health which You bestowed on one of your servants in order to destroy it, so cure him, restore him to health and protect him from the Devil!" The boy thereupon got up and was completely free of any defect.

Faymiyūn now realized that he was recognized, so departed from the village, with Ṣāliḥ accompanying him. On one occasion, he was walking somewhere in Syria and passed by a large tree. A man called down to him from the tree, saying, "Is that Faymiyūn?" The latter replied, "Yes." The man said, "I have been continuously awaiting you and have kept saying, 'When is he coming?' until I heard your voice and knew that you were its owner. Don't go away until you have prayed over my grave, for I am now at the point of death." He related: He did die at that moment, and Faymiyūn prayed over him and buried him.[495] Then
[922] he departed, accompanied by Ṣāliḥ, until the two of them set foot in part of the land of the Arabs. But the Arabs swept down on them, and a caravan of some Arab group snatched them up, carried them off, and finally sold them in Najrān.

At that period, the people of Najrān followed the religion of the Arabs, worshiping a lofty date palm in their midst. Every year they had a festival, when they hung on that tree every fine garment they could find and also women's ornaments. Then they went forth and devoted themselves to worship of it for the whole day.[496] One of the nobles of Najrān purchased Faymiyūn, and another man purchased Ṣāliḥ. Now one night Faymiyūn stood up in a hut (*bayt*) his master had allotted to him, praying, when the whole hut

---

495. The man in the tree was presumably a dendrite, a tree-dwelling ascetic, with a way of life analogous to that of a stylite or pillar dweller.

496. The worship of sacred trees was a standard feature of ancient Semitic religion, attested among the Canaanites, Phoenicians, etc. In Arabia, as well as this date palm at Najrān, there was the acacia tree (*samurah*) at al-Nakhlah, between Mecca and al-Ṭā'if, embodiment of the goodess al-'Uzzā, and the great tree at Ḥunayn called *dhāt anwāṭ* "[tree] on which date baskets, etc., are hung," to which the people of pre-Islamic Mecca used to resort and bring gifts. See Robertson Smith, *Lectures on the Religion of the Semites. First Series. The Fundamental Institutions*, 185ff; J. Wellhausen, *Reste arabischen Heidentums*², 36, 104–105; H. Lammens, *Le berceau de l'Islam*, 7–72; Buhl, *Das Leben Muhammeds*, 79–80; Fahd, *Le panthéon de l'Arabie centrale à la veille de l'hégire*, 31–32, 58. Nöldeke, trans. 181 n. 1, attributed the hanging of women's ornaments on the tree to the fact that the word for date palm, *nakhlah*, is of feminine gender in Arabic.

was filled with light as if from a lamp, until it was completely illuminated but without the presence of any lamp. Faymiyūn's master saw this, and the sight filled him with wonder. He asked Faymiyūn about his religion, and the latter told him about it. Faymiyūn explained to him: "You people are completely in error; this date palm can neither harm nor benefit, and if I were to invoke against it the One whom I worship, He would destroy it. He is God, the One, without any partner."[497] He related: His master told him, "Do that, and if you can bring that to pass, we will embrace your religion and abandon the one we used to hold." He related: Faymiyūn arose, purified himself, prayed two *rakʿah*s,[498] and then invoked God's curse on the date palm. God sent a wind that tore it up from its roots and cast it down. At that, the people of Najrān followed Faymiyūn and adopted his religion. He instructed them in the law (*sharīʿah*) of the faith of ʿĪsā b. Maryam. But after that, various innovations (*aḥdāth*)[499] came into their faith, as into that of their coreligionists in every land. From this center, the Christianity of Najrān spread in the land of the Arabs—all this being the report of Wahb b. Munabbih concerning the people of Najrān.[500]

There related to us Ḥumayd—Salamah, who said: There related to us Muḥammad b. Isḥāq—Yazīd b. Ziyād, a freedman of the Banū Hāshim—Muḥammad b. Kaʿb al-Quraẓī.[501] He said: There related to us also Muḥammad b. Isḥāq from a man of the people of [923]

---

497. Anticipating, in its Qur'ānic phraseology regarding God's unity, *tawḥīd*, Muḥammad's denunciation, in his later years at Mecca, of the "Daughters of Allāh," the three pagan goddesses worshiped by Quraysh, as having no spiritual efficacity, either positive or negative. See on this last episode, involving the so-called Satanic verses, Watt, *Muhammad at Mecca*, 100–109.

498. Looking forward to the *rakʿah*, the act of bowing and bending, which forms part of the Muslim *ṣalāt*.

499 This seems to be the sense here of *aḥdāth*, rather than the general one of "events, happenings."

500. This tale, of no direct relevance to the drama of political and military events in South Arabia that swirled around such figures as Dhū Nuwās and Abrahah, is given in Ibn Hishām, *Sīrat al-nabī*, ed. Wüstenfeld, 20–22 = ed. al-Saqqā et al., I, 32–35, tr. 14–16.

501. Muḥammad b. Kaʿb (d. 118/736), descended from the Medinan Jewish clan of Qurayẓah, was a Successor famed both as an early Qur'ān commentator and as a retailer of *akhbār*, historical traditions, and in this last utilized by Ibn Isḥāq. See Sezgin, *GAS*, I, 32.

Najrān: The people of Najrān were polytheists who worshiped idols. In one of their villages near Najrān—Najrān being the major urban center there, in which the people of that region used to come together—there was a sorcerer who used to teach magic to the Najrān youths. When Faymiyūn took up residence in Najrān (He related: They did not call him by the name which Wahb b. Munabbih gives him, but they simply said "a man took up residence there"), he put up a tent between Najrān and that village where the sorcerer lived. The people of Najrān began to send their boys to that sorcerer, who then taught them magic. Hence al-Thāmir sent his son ʿAbdallāh b. al-Thāmir, together with the other youths of the people of Najrān. When ʿAbdallāh b. al-Thāmir passed by the man in the tent, he was astonished by what he saw of the man's praying and acts of devotion, and began to sit with him and listen to him, until he surrendered himself to God (*aslama*), acknowledged God's unity, and worshiped Him. He set about asking the man about the Greatest Name (of God), but although the man knew it, he concealed it from him with the words, "O my nephew, you will not be able to bear it; I fear you are too weak for it."[502] He therefore refused to tell him. Meanwhile, al-Thāmir, the father of ʿAbdallāh, had no idea that his son ʿAbdallāh was not going along [regularly] to the sorcerer just as the other youths were doing. When ʿAbdallāh saw that his master had kept the knowledge [of God's Greatest Name] from him and was afraid for his weakness, he took a number of arrows and gathered them together.[503] Every name of God that he knew he wrote on an arrow, every name on a single arrow. When he had counted all the

502. This is what became the Islamic equivalent of the Jewish name of God, the tetragrammaton *yhwh, ha-shem ha-məfōrāsh,* known only to the High Priest, who was only allowed to pronounce it once a year. In Islam, the secret name of God becomes a word of power, whose possessor can wreak with it mighty, supernatural deeds. See Nöldeke, trans. 183 n. 1.

503 Arrows were used for oracular and divinatory purposes in some sectors at least of ancient Semitic religion, as in Ezek. xxi. 21, where the king of Babylon consults his divining arrows. In Qur'ān, V, 4/3, *al-istiqsām bi-al-azlām,* "division [of a sacrificial offering] by means of arrows," which is said to have been practiced in the Kaʿbah of pre-Islamic times before the image of the god Hubal (see Ibn al-Kalbī, *Kitāb al-aṣnām,* 17, tr. Klinke-Rosenberger, 44 and 114–15 n. 256, tr. Faris 23–24; al-Ṭabarī, I, 1075–78), is denounced as a relic of paganism. See Fahd, *La divination arabe,* 181–82; *EI*², s.v. Istiḳsām (T. Fahd).

names,[504] he lit a fire for this special purpose and began to throw the arrows on it one by one, until he finally reached the arrow with the Greatest Name of God [on it]. He threw it on the fire, but it immediately sprang out completely undamaged. He went up to it and grasped it, and then went to his master and informed him [924] that he had now come to know the name his master had concealed from him. His master questioned him about it, and the youth replied that it was such-and-such. His master said, "How did you come to know it?" The boy told him how he had set about discovering it. He related: He then said, "O my nephew, you have got it correctly, but keep it to yourself—yet I don't think you actually will."

Thereafter, whenever ʿAbdallāh b. al-Thāmir came to Najrān and met any sick person there he would invariably say, "O servant of God, will you confess the unity of God and adopt my religion, so that [if you do], I may invoke the blessing of God and He will cure you of your affliction?" The sick person would assent. ʿAbdallāh would thereupon proclaim God's unity, submit himself to God, and pray to Him, so that the man was then healed. In the end, there was no sick or maimed person left in Najrān who did not come to him and then followed him in his faith; ʿAbdallāh invoked God's blessing on the sick person and he was healed. Ultimately, the news of his activity reached the king of Najrān. He sent for ʿAbdallāh and accused him: "You have corrupted the people of my town and have set yourself against my religion and that of my forefathers; I shall inflict exemplary punishment on you!" ʿAbdallāh replied, "You have no power to do that." The king set about dispatching him to a high mountain, from whose summit he was hurled down; but he fell to the ground totally unhurt. Next, the king had him consigned to some waters at Najrān, [deep] stretches of water out of which nothing had ever emerged alive. He was thrown into them, but again came out unharmed.

Having thus triumphed over the king, ʿAbdallāh b. al-Thāmir told him, "By God, you will never be able to kill me until you confess the unity of God and believe in my own system of belief; but if you do that, you will be given power over me and will be able

504. A total formalized in later Muslim piety as the "Ninety-nine Most Beautiful Names" of God. See *EI*², s.v. al-Asmāʾ al-ḥusnā (L. Gardet).

to kill me." That king thereupon confessed the unity of God and bore witness to the creed of ʿAbdallāh b. al-Thāmir. He then struck him with a staff he had in his hand, striking his head with a blow of only moderate violence, thereby killing him; but the king himself then dropped dead on the spot. The people of Najrān accepted the faith of ʿAbdallāh b. al-Thāmir en masse, and henceforth held fast to the gospel and the law that Jesus son of Mary had
[925] brought. Subsequently, they were affected by the events that also affected their coreligionists. This was the origin of Christianity at Najrān.[505]

Such is the report of Muḥammad b. Kaʿb al-Quraẓī and another scholar of Najrān knowledgeable about that event; but God is the most knowledgeable [about all this].

He (i.e., Ibn Isḥāq) related: Dhū Nuwās marched against them with his forces of the Ḥimyarites and the tribes of Yemen. He gathered the people of Najrān together, and summoned them to the Jewish faith, offering them the choice between that and being killed. They chose being killed, so he dug out for them the trench (*al-ukhdūd*). He burnt some of them with fire, slew some violently with the sword, and mutilated them savagely until he had killed nearly twenty thousand of them.[506] Out of them there es-

505. There was pointed out to Halévy, at the ruins of the old town of Najrān, a mosque built at the tomb of ʿAbdallāh b. Ṭāmir (*sic*), described to him as the first Muslim apostle to the district, although scholars in Najrān attributed the tomb to a saint of pre-Islamic times; see his "Rapport sur une mission archéologique dans le Yémen," 39–40. Today, there is a police post in the Wādī Najrān named Qaṣr ʿAbdallāh b. Thāmir after the nearby supposed tomb of the *walī* of this name, see Beaucamp and Robin, "Le Christianisme dans la péninsule arabique d'après l'épigraphie et l'archéologie," 53–54 and n. 49.

506. Ibn Isḥāq has more detail here than Ibn al-Kalbī on the actual martyrdom of the Christians. Although the Syriac *Book of the Himyarites*, composed in the second quarter of the sixth century and therefore very close to the time in question, i.e., 523, mentions nothing about the Christians being put in a pit, the recently discovered Syriac "new" letter of Simeon of Bēth Arshām specifically says that two thousand Christians were immolated when their church was burned. See Shahîd's edition, translation, and study, *The Martyrs of Najrân. New Documents.*

Dhū Nuwās's policy here may not have been one that he conceived and pursued entirely of his own accord, in isolation from outside considerations, given the possible background of his conversion to some form of Judaism (see n. 486 above). That it was aimed at countering an extension of Christian Abyssinan influence in Yemen is clear, but Dhū Nuwās may have looked for support in another quarter of Arabia. M. J. Kister has suggested, with impressive documentation, that the

caped only one man, called Daws Dhū Thaʿlabān, on one of his horses, who traveled through the sands until he threw his pursuers off.[507]

He related: I have heard a certain man from the people of Yemen say that the man who escaped from them was a man of Najrān called Jabbār (var. Ḥayyān) b. Fayḍ. He related: In my view, the more authentic of the two reports is that of the man who narrated to me that it was Daws Dhū Thaʿlabān.

Dhū Nuwās returned with his forces to Ṣanʿāʾ in the land of Yemen.[508] Concerning Dhū Nuwās and his troops, there narrated

---

Lakhmid king of al-Ḥīrah al-Mundhir III (on whom see nn. 362, 409 above) exerted a measure of control across Najd as far as Medina, with the backing of his suzerains the Sāsānids, for whom an *ʿāmil* collected taxes in Medina at this time; see his "Al-Ḥīra. Some Notes on Its Relations with Arabia," 144–49. From this possibility of an alliance between the pagan Lakhmid rulers with the Jewish tribes in Medina, who were still dominant over the local Arabs of the Yathrib oasis during the first half of the sixth century, Shahîd and Altheim and Stiehl have gone on to suggest that Dhū Nuwās, in his anti-Abyssinian and anti-Christian policies at Najrān and in Yemen, looked to al-Mundhir for at least moral and perhaps diplomatic backing, given the apparent connection of the later Ḥimyarite kings' Jewish tendencies or sympathies with Medina (cf. the tale, in al-Ṭabarī, I, 901–905, pp. 164–70 above, of Tubān Asʿad Abū Karib's espousal of Judaism when passing through Medina, and also n. 486 above). Furthermore, Ḥamza al-Iṣfahānī, *Taʾrīkh*, 113, states that "Dhū Nuwās halted at Yathrib when once he was passing through, and was favorably impressed by the Jewish faith. Hence he adopted it for himself, and the Jews of Yathrib incited him to attack Najrān and to inflict trials and tribulations on the Christians there." Al-Mundhir, for his part, would have welcomed an opportunity to counteract Abyssinian power over southwestern Arabia. See Nöldeke, trans. 183 n. 1; Bell, *The Origin of Islam in Its Christian Environment*, 36–39; Altheim and Stiehl, *Die Araber in der Alten Welt*, V/1, 359–61; eidem, *Christentum am Roten Meer*, I, 440–41; Shahîd, *The Martyrs of Najrân*, 266–68; Trimingham, *Christianity among the Arabs in Pre-Islamic Times*, 297; Rubin, "Byzantium and Southern Arabia—the Policy of Anastasius," 401–402.

However, by the time the Abyssinians appeared in Yemen in 525 in order to avenge the Martyrs of Najrān and the Abyssinians slain in southwestern Arabia, al-Mundhir was in no position to offer any military help, being hard pressed by his rivals of Kindah and being shortly afterward ejected, albeit temporarily, from his own capital al-Ḥīrah by the Kindī al-Ḥārith b. ʿAmr (see n. 362 above).

507. Dhū Thaʿlabān was the name of one of the eight great noble families of Ḥimyar, influential either during the period of independent Ḥimyarite royal power or during that of Abyssinian and then Persian domination over southwestern Arabia that followed the extinction of the Ḥimyarite ruling dynasty, Thaʿlab being apparently a tribal name. Epigraphic evidence does support the fact that the Dhū Thaʿlabān came from the Najrān area. See Nöldeke, trans. 186 n. 1; *EI*², s.v. al-Mathāmina (Chr. Robin).

508. Ṣanʿāʾ emerges into prominence only in the inscriptions of the third cen-

to us Ibn Ḥumayd—Salamah b. al-Faḍl—Muḥammad b. Isḥāq, who said: God sent down to His Messenger the words "Slain were the Men of the Trench, with the fire abounding in fuel," to His words ". . . and God, the Mighty, the Praiseworthy."[509] It is said that ʿAbdallāh b. al-Thāmir, their leader and imām, was among those whom Dhū Nuwās killed, but it is also said that ʿAbdallāh b. al-Thāmir was killed before that event, killed by a previous ruler. He was the founder of that faith [at Najrān], and Dhū Nuwās only slew adherents of ʿAbdallāh's religion who came after him.

As for Hishām b. Muḥammad, he says that the royal power in
[926] Yemen was handed down continuously, with no one venturing to contest it until the Abyssinians (*al-Ḥabashah*) seized control of their land in the time of Anūsharwān. He related: The reason for their conquest was that Dhū Nuwās the Ḥimyarite exercised royal power in Yemen at that time, and he was an adherent of the Jewish faith. There came to him a Jew called Daws from the people of Najrān, who told him that the people of Najrān had unjustly slain his two sons;[510] he now sought Dhū Nuwās's help against

tury A.D., although it doubtless had a history before that time. It was a *hgr*/*hajar* or town in what was at that time the petty kingdom of Samay, which was seemingly linked in some sort of federal arrangement with Saba'. It was a military center, as the probable connection of its name with the Sabaean root *ṣ.n.'*, "to fortify [a place]," indicates (al-Hamdānī, *Ṣifat jazīrat al-ʿArab*, 81, states however that the town's ancient name was Azāl). Ṣanʿā' seems to have reached a peak of importance within the wider Sabaean state at this time, with one of its kings, Ilisharaḥ Yaḥḍab, named in Islamic sources (e.g., Yāqūt, *Buldān*, IV, 210). As builder of the famous castle of Ghumdān (see al-Ṭabarī, I, 928, p. 209 and n. 520 below). After this, Ṣanʿā' suffered a temporary eclipse when power shifted to the Ḥimyarite dynasty of the Tubbaʿs, with their capital at Ẓafār (see n. 475 above). Neither Ṣanʿā' nor Ghumdān figure in inscriptions dating from the fourth to the sixth centuries. The town does nevertheless seem to have had within it during pre-Islamic times a *mḥrm*/*maḥram*, a place to which access was prohibited or restricted, usually for religious or cultic reasons, and R. B. Serjeant suggested that the pre-Islamic *hijrah* or sacred area of Ṣanʿā' may have existed in parallel with the Ḥaram of Mecca. One can therefore easily comprehend that the profanation of the Christian church built at Ṣanʿā' by Abrahah (see al-Ṭabarī, I, 934, 943, pp. 217, 232–33 below) was a particularly heinous action if, as seems possible, the church was situated in the *maḥram* area. See Shahîd, "Byzantium and South Arabia," 81–83; Beeston, "Pre-Islamic Ṣanʿā'," 36–38; Serjeant, "Ṣanʿā' the 'Protected', Hijrah," 39–40; *EI*², s.v. Ṣanʿā' (G. R. Smith).

509. See n. 489 above.

510. Nöldeke thought that, given the deeply rooted hostility of Eastern Christians toward Jews, this incident was perfectly possible.

them. The people of Najrān were Christians. Dhū Nuwās was a fervent partisan of the Jewish faith, so he led an expedition against the people of Najrān, killing large numbers of them. A man from the people of Najrān fled and in due course came to the King of Abyssinia. He informed the king of what the Yemenis had committed and gave him a copy of the Gospels partly burned by the fire. The King of Abyssinia said to him: "I have plenty of men, but no ships [to transport them]; but I will write to Qayṣar (i.e., the Byzantine Emperor) asking him to send me ships for transporting the soldiers." Hence he wrote to Qayṣar about this matter, enclosing the [partly] burned copy of the Gospels, and Qayṣar dispatched a large number of ships.[511]

---

511. Refugees from Najrān and the other places in Yemen and Ḥaḍramawt where there had been persecutions (the Syriac *Book of the Ḥimyarites* mentions that these occurred in five towns, Ẓafār, Najrān, "the town of Ḥaḍramawt," Mārib, and [Ha]jjarēn; see Shahîd, "Byzantium in South Arabia," 38) probably managed to escape to Abyssinia and possibly to Byzantine territory at the head of the Red Sea. At all events, the news speedily reached the Christian kingdoms of Axum and Byzantium, and the sufferings of the Najrānites entered their martyrologies (the Ethiopian Church adopted into its calendar the commemoration of the *samā'tāta Neğrān,* "witnesses of Najrān," on 26 November; see H. M. Hyatt, *The Church of Abyssinia,* 32). The martyrdoms at Najrān involved essentially, as noted in n. 487 above, the local Monophysites, and the Church of Abyssinia was also Monophysite. Byzantium was Melkite, and persecuted Monophysites within the empire's boundaries, but southwestern Arabia was sufficiently far from the imperial heartlands for theological niceties not to count in the face of a Judaizing ruler and his persecution of Christians. Justin halted his own persection of the Monophysites within his dominions, and utilized the Monophysite Patriarch of Alexandria as his intermediary with the Abyssinian Najāshī or Negus in Axum.

Eventually, a fleet of some sixty merchant ships commandeered by the Byzantine authorities set out from Adulis, the port of Axum on what is now the Eritrean coast under the leadership of the king in Axum, Kālēb, who had the regnal name of Ĕlla Aṣbĕḥa (rendered by Procopius, *The Persian War,* I.xx.1–13, as Hellēsthaios for Hellesbaios; in a South Arabian inscription *'l'ṣbḥ*). This was probably in the spring or summer of 525. Kālēb's activities as the restorer of Christianity in South Arabia were to earn him great renown within the church. After disposing of Dhū Nuwās, Ĕlla Aṣbĕḥa seems to have erected a victory inscription in Ge'ez, one which is unfortunately only fragmentarily legible, at Mārib. He very probably engaged in a campaign of revenge, slaughtering great numbers of Ḥimyarites and destroying their idols and temples. He certainly embarked upon an extensive program of church building in southwestern Arabia, details of which are given in the Greek—possibly with a Syriac *Vorlage*—hagiographical *Vita Sancti Gregentii,* whose extensive information here has been made the subject of a close study by Irfan Shahîd. See Nöldeke, trans. 188 n. 1; Smith, "Events in South Arabia in the 6th Century A.D.," 454–55; Murad Kamil, "An Ethiopian Inscription found at

The narrative returns to that of Ibn Isḥāq. There related to us Ibn Ḥumayd—Salamah—Muḥammad b. Isḥāq—'Abdallāh b. Abī Bakr b. Muḥammad b. 'Amr b. Ḥazm, who related that there was a man from the people of Najrān in the time of 'Umar b. al-Khaṭṭāb[512] who dug up one of the ruined sites of Najrān intending to utilize it, and found [the body of] 'Abdallāh b. al-Thāmir inside a hollow there that had become filled with sand (*dafn, difn*). He was in a sitting position, with his hand covering the wound from the blow to his head, holding it firmly with that hand. When his hand was lifted off, the wound began to flow with blood, but when his hand was released, he placed it back on the wound and the flow of blood ceased. On [the finger of] his hand was a seal ring, with the inscription "My lord is God." A report was sent to 'Umar telling him the story, and he wrote back to them: "Leave him
[927] alone, and replace the grave that was over him," so they did that.[513]

When Daws Dhū Tha'labān threw off his pursuers in this manner, he pressed onward until he came to Qayṣar, the ruler of al-Rūm.[514] He requested his help against Dhū Nuwās and his troops, and told him what his people had suffered from them. Qayṣar replied, however, "Your land is distant from our own and too remote for us to be able to reach it with our own armies, but I will write on your behalf to the king of Abyssinia, for he is a Christian also. He is nearer than us to your land, hence can give you aid, protect you, and exact vengeance on your behalf from those who oppressed you and who violently shed the blood of you and your coreligionists."

Qayṣar sent back Daws with a letter to the king of Abyssinia in which was mentioned Daws's moral entitlement to help and what he and his coreligionists had endured, and Qayṣar commanded the king of Abyssinia to provide Daws with succor and the means for

---

Mareb," 56–57; Altheim and Stiehl, *Die Araber in der Alten Welt*, V/1, 385–91; eidem, *Christentum am Roten Meer*, I, 445–57; Shahîd, "Byzantium in South Arabia," 23–94.

512. That is, in the later 630s or early 640s.

513. This same story of the discovery of 'Abdallāh b. al-Thāmir's corpse is found in al-Hamdānī, *Iklīl*, 134–35, tr. 80–81.

514. Here the narrative returns to the account of Ibn al-Kalbī broken off by this parenthesis from Ibn Isḥāq.

him to exact vengeance for these who had treated him and his fellow Christians wrongfully.

When Daws Dhū Thaʿlabān presented Qayṣar's letter to the Najāshī,[515] ruler of Abyssinia, the latter sent a force with Daws of seventy thousand Abyssinian troops, appointing as commander over them one of their number, an Abyssinian called Aryāṭ (? Arethas).[516] He laid upon him the following charge: "If you secure the victory over (i.e., Dhū Nuwās and the Yemenis), kill a third of their menfolk, lay waste a third of their land, and capture and enslave a third of their women and children." Aryāṭ set out with his troops. Among these last was Abrahah al-Ashram ("the man with a cut-off nose tip").[517] He crossed the sea with Daws Dhū Thaʿlabān until they landed on the coast of Yemen. Dhū Nuwās heard of their approach, and he collected together at his side Ḥimyar and those tribes of Yemen owing him obedience, but there were many dissensions and divisions in their ranks on account of the approaching end of the period [appointed by God], the suffering of hardships, and the coming down of punishment. There ensued no real battle and Dhū Nuwās was only able to engage in a certain amount of skirmishing, and then his troops were put to flight and Aryāṭ overran the land with his forces. Hence when Dhū Nuwās saw what had befallen him and his supporters, he headed his horse toward the sea; he whipped it onward and it went into the sea, bearing him through the shallows until it carried him into the [928]
deep water. He urged it onward into the open sea, and that was the last ever seen of him.[518]

---

515. An accurate rendering of Ethiopic Nägāsī, "ruler, king," used also as a regnal title (and Anglicized as Negus). The Najāshī figures extensively in the *Sīrah* of the Prophet, in the first place in connection with the two *hijrahs* of the first Muslims from Mecca to Abyssinia. See *EI²*, s.v. al-Nadjāshī (E. van Donzel).

516. The reading of this name is uncertain; the manuscripts have Aryāṭ and Arbāṭ, but other renderings are possible. See the detailed discussion of the evidence from parallel Greek sources in Nöldeke, trans. 190 n. 3.

517. Abrahah is the Arabic form of Ethiopic Abrĕha.

518. Dhū Nuwās seems in reality to have been killed by the Abyssinians in battle; this final touch about the mode of his death must be a romanticizing, South Arabian one, as remarked by Nöldeke, trans. 191 n. 2.

The events of the years immediately after Dhū Nuwās's death are somewhat obscure. De Blois has suggested that the Abyssinian invaders, having disposed of Dhū Nuwās, set up a puppet Christian king called Abraham (not to be confused with the subsequent Abrahah) and then withdrew the bulk of their troops back

Aryāṭ marched across Yemen with the Abyssinian army, killing a third of its menfolk, devastating a third of the countryside, and sending back to the Najāshī (the Negus) a third of the captured women and children. He remained there, imposing firm control over the land and reducing it to submission. A certain poet of the Yemenis has said, recalling how Daws Dhū Tha'labān had imposed upon them the yoke of the Abyssinians:

[Do not let anyone act] like Daws, and not like what he has
fastened on his saddlebag [for us] (i.e., the yoke of the
Abyssinians),

that is, what he brought down on them in the shape of the Abyssinians; this has remained a proverbial saying in Yemen up to this day.

Dhū Jadan al-Ḥimyarī[519] recorded the following lines, mentioning Ḥimyar and the humiliations it now suffered after its former

---

across the Bāb al-Mandab. But the Ethiopian hold in Yemen was clearly a precarious one, for within a short time, the anti-Abyssinian party in Yemen apparently got the upper hand once more, necessitating a second Abyssinian invasion at the end of 530 or the beginning of 531 on the pretext of Jewish persecution of the Christians there. This was once more successful. Procopius records the expedition, and his information is confirmed by the Ḥiṣn al-Ghurāb inscription (CIH 621) of 640 Ḥimyarite era/A.D. 530–31, in which a local potentate, the Christian Sumuyafa' Ašwa', records the killing of a local king of the Ḥimyarites and his own subordination to the *Ḥbšt:* This local potentate is Procopius's Esimiphaios, now appointed king of Yemen under Abyssinian suzerainty. In any event, Sumu-yafa' Ašwa' cannot long have reigned before the usurpation of the former slave Abrahah (see al-Ṭabarī, I, 930ff., pp. 212ff. below). All this implies that there were in fact three Abyssinian invasions of South Arabia within two decades: one ca. 518; a second one between 525 and 527, resulting in the overthrow of Dhū Nuwās and the setting-up of Abraham; and a third one at the end of 530 or beginning of 531 after Abraham's death and the temporary resurgence of the anti-Abyssinian party, resulting in the establishment of Esimphaios. See de Blois, "The Date of the 'Martyrs of Nagrān,'" 119–20. For other reconstructions of events at this time, see Smith, "Events in South Arabia in the 6th Century A.D.," 455–56; Altheim and Stiehl, *Christentum am Roten Meer,* I, 446–47; Robin, in *Supplément au dictionnaire de la Bible,* s.v Sheba. II, col. 1143; *EI*², s.v. Abraha (A. F. L. Beeston).

The story of the persecutions of Najrān and the Abyssinian invasion appears also in Ibn Hishām, *Sīrat al-nabī,* ed. Wüstenfeld, 24–26 = ed. al-Saqqā et al., I, 37–39, tr. 17–18; idem, *Kitāb al-tījān,* 301–02; Abū al-Faraj al-Iṣfahānī, *Aghānī*³, XVII, 303–305.

519. This poet, much cited by al-Hamdānī in his *Iklīl,* appears in Nashwān al-Ḥimyarī, passim, as 'Alqamah Dhū Yazan and 'Alqamah b. Dhī Jadan. This name would connect him with Dhū Jadan, one of the eight leading noble families of Ḥimyar (see n. 507 above and n. 585 below), specifically from the Mārib region. See

glory, and [recalling] the fortresses of Yemen Aryāṭ had destroyed, in addition to his devastation of the countryside, that is, Silḥīn, Baynūn, and Ghumdān, castles without parallel among mankind:[520]

Gently, [O woman!]. Tears cannot bring back what has gone by,
and do not destroy yourself out of grief, recalling those who are dead.
After Baynūn, of which there is no visible trace and vestige, and
after Silḥīn, shall men ever construct [such] buildings again?

Dhū Jadan al-Ḥimyarī further said in this connection:

Leave me alone [O woman], may you be deprived of your father!
You will not be able to deflect me from my resolve—may God heap shame on you, you have dried up my spittle!
When, to the music of singing girls, we became exhilarated by
wine, and when we were given to drink the finest vintage, [that was indeed good].
Consuming wine is no shame for me, since my drinking
companion does not reproach me at all for it.

---

al-Hamdānī, *Iklīl*, index s.v. (usually cited simply as "ʿAlqamah"); O. Löfgren, "ʿAlqama b. Dī Ǧadan und seine Dichtung nach der Iklīl-Auswahl in der Biblioteca Ambrosiana," 199–209; *EI*², s.v. al-Mathāmina (Chr. Robin).

520. These were former castles of pre-Islamic Yemen, and are mentioned as such by authors like al-Hamdānī in the eighth book of his *Iklīl* devoted to the castles and fortresses of South Arabia, and Nashwān al-Ḥimyarī. Silḥīn or Salḥīn, in South Arabian inscriptions *slḥm*, was the royal palace of the kings of Sabaʾ at Mārib, the minting center for Sabaean coins and the building in South Arabia most frequently mentioned in the inscriptions. Ghumdān (*ǧndn, ǧmdn*) was originally the royal residence at Ṣanʿāʾ of the Dhū Gurat family, and is particularly frequently cited by the post-Islamic poets as an example of the transience of human achievement; in fact, although allegedly destroyed by the Abyssinian viceroy Abrahah or the Islamic caliph ʿUthmān, it was several times refortified in the early Islamic centuries. Baynūn is located by al-Hamdānī in the eastern part of the lands of the Banū ʿAns. See al-Hamdānī, *Iklīl*, 3–5, 12–21, 48–51,54–57, tr. 8–9, 14–19, 36–38, 40; Nashwān al-Ḥimyarī, *Die auf Südarabien bezüglichen Angaben Našwāns*, 10, 50, 81; Yāqūt, *Buldān*, I, 535–36, III, 235, IV, 215–16; Müller, "Ancient Castles Mentioned in the Eighth Volume of Al-Hamdānī's Iklīl and Evidence of Them in Pre-Islamic Inscription," 141–43, 145–47; Serjeant and R. Lewcock, "The Church (al-Qalīs) of Ṣanʿāʾ and Ghumdān Castle," 44; *EI*², s.v. Ghumdān (O. Löfgren).

No one can hold back the onslaught of death, even though he
were to drink a healing remedy together with sniffing a
perfumed medicament.
Nor can any monk in a cell (*usṭuwān,* literally, doorway,
portico)[521] whose walls [are so lofty that they] abut on to
[929] the nests (literally, "eggs") of the vulture.
Ghumdān, of which you have been told, and which they
constructed with a high roof[522] on a mountain top,
With skilled carpenter's (or smith's) work, and its lower part of
hewn stone and choicest damp and smooth clay.
Lamps filled with oil shine forth within it at eventide, like the
gleaming of lightning flashes,
Its date palms are planted up against it, and the fresh dates
almost bend the branches down to earth with their clusters.
Yet this once-new fortress has now become a pile of ashes, and
the consuming flames have transformed its former beauty.
Dhū Nuwās gave himself over to impending death, and he
warned his people of the afflictions that were to come upon
them.[523]

Ibn Dhi'bah al-Thaqafī[524] recited, remembering Ḥimyar when the black troops swept down on it and what the Ḥimyarite people suffered from them:

By your life, there is no escape for a man when death and old
age overtake him!
By your life, a man has no open space to which he can flee, nor
indeed, any refuge!
What moralizing example can there be, after what came upon
Ḥimyar's tribes one morning,[525]

---

521. For this word (< Greek *stōa*), see Dozy, *Supplément,* I, 22.

522. Reading, with al-Azraqī, *Akhbār Makkah,* I, 87, *musmak^an* (= text, n. *a*).

523. As Nöldeke observed, trans. 194 n. 1, the poet seems to echo the implication of the prose accounts by Ibn al-Kalbī and Ibn Isḥāq, that Dhū Nuwās was inadequately supported by his own followers, hence willingly sought his own death.

524. Ibn Hishām's gloss in his *Sīrat al-nabī,* ed. Wüstenfeld, 27 = ed. al-Saqqā et al., I, 41, tr. 695, says that Dhi'bah was this poet's mother's name and that his own name was Rabī'ah b. 'Abd Yālīl b. Sālim . . . Nothing seems to be known about this poet of al-Ṭā'if.

525. One could alternatively translate, "Can there be anything after there came

Namely, a swift-moving gathering of warriors[526] and spearmen,
[gleaming in the sun] like the heavens just after rain,
With battle cries deafening the charging horses, and with their
putting to flight the warriors with their stink,[527]
Witches,[528] like the very grains of sand in number, who make
the tender branches of trees dry up [at their approach].

As for Hishām b. Muḥammad, he asserts that when the ships sent by Qayṣar reached the Najāshī, the latter transported his army by means of them, and the troops landed on the coast of al-Mandab.[529] He related: When Dhū Nuwās heard of their approach, he wrote to the local princes (*maqāwil*)[530] summoning them to [930] provide him with military support and to unite in combating the invading army to repel it from their land. But they refused, saying, "Let each man fight for his own princedom (*maqwalah*) and re-

upon Ḥimyar's tribes one morning a cause for bitter tears,," reading, with the Cairo edition, II, 127, *dhāt al-ʿabar* for the text's *dhāt al-ʿibar.*

526. Following the emendation *bi-alb*[in] *ulūb*[in] of *Addenda et corrigenda,* p. DXCI, cf. *Glossarium,* p. CLXXXVII.

527. Following the *bi-al-dhafar* of text, n. *e,* as also in al-Azraqī and Ibn Hishām; the black Abyssinian warriors are depicted, as often in early Islamic writings on blacks, as stinking.

528. *saʿālā, saʿāl*[in], pl. of *siʿlāt,* often regarded as the female counterpart of the *ghūl,* a malevolent, demonic being, hence with the characteristics of a succubus or sometimes as a *sāḥirah* or witch, enchantress. See G. van Vloten, "Dämonen, Geister und Zauber bei den altern Arabern. Mitteilungen aus Djâhitz' Kitâb al-haiwân," Part I, 179–80; Wellhausen, *Reste arabischen Heidentums*², 152; *EI*², s.v. Ghūl (D. B. Macdonald-Ch. Pellat).

529. That is, in the neighborhood of the Bāb al-Mandab, the straits connecting the Red Sea with the Gulf of Aden and the Arabian Sea. South Arabian inscriptions speak of *mdbn* and its $s^1s^1lt$ or $s^1s^3lt$ = *silsilah* (a chain across an inlet or harbor?) in connection with the events of this period. Al-Hamdāni mentions only the Bāb al-Mandab as a headland dangerous for seamen but locates a town of al-Mandab on or near the Tihāmah coast at an unidentified spot between Farasān and the territory of the Banū Majīd b. Ḥaydān; see his *Ṣifat jazīrat al-ʿArab,* 67, 72, 205, 258, and cf. *EI*², s.v. Bāb al-Mandab (G. Rentz). Beeston, "The Chain of al-Mandab," 1–6, discussed the passages of the Arabic historians and al-Hamdānī, and the mentions in the Byzantine Greek *Martyrion Aretha,* regarding the chain of al-Mandab and the landing(s) of the Abyssinians (since the latter source speaks of two landings, at spots widely apart). He concluded that the reports of an actual chain are fully historical, and thought that its location was at the Khōr Ghurayrah, the inlet immediately behind the Cape of al-Mandab; see his map at p. 4.

530. Sing. *miqwal,* reflecting the *mqwl* of South Arabian inscriptions, with the sense "prince, minor ruler," or the residence of such a ruler, and cognate with *qayl* (on which see n. 473 above). See Beeston et al., *Sabaic Dictionary,* 110; Biella, *Dictionary of Old South Arabic, Sabaean Dialect,* 449.

gion." When Dhū Nuwās saw that, he had a large number of keys made, and then loaded them on to a troop of camels and set out until he came up with the [Abyssinian] host. He said: "These are the keys to the treasuries of Yemen, which I have brought to you. You can have the money and the land, but spare the menfolk and the women and children." The army's leader said, "I will write to the king," so he wrote to the Najāshī. The latter wrote back to the leader ordering him to take possession from the Yemenis of the treasuries. Dhū Nuwās accompanied them until, when he brought them into Ṣan'ā', he told the leader, "Dispatch trusted members of your troops to take possession of these treasuries." The leader divided up his trusted followers into detachments to go and take possession of the treasuries, handing over the keys to them. [Meanwhile,] Dhū Nuwās's letters had been sent to every region, containing the message "Slaughter every black bull within your land." Hence they massacred the Abyssinians so that none were left alive except for those who managed to escape.

The Najāshī heard what Dhū Nuwās had done and sent against him seventy thousand men under the command of two leaders, one of them being Abrahah al-Ashram. When they reached Ṣan'ā' and Dhū Nuwās realized that he had not the strength to withstand them, he rode off on his horse, came to the edge of the sea amd rushed headlong into it; this was the last ever seen of Dhū Nuwās.

Abrahah set himself up as ruler over Ṣan'ā' and its dependent districts (*makhālīf*),[531] but did not send any tribute or captured plunder back to the Najāshī. The latter was informed that Abrahah had thrown off his obedience and now considered himself an independent potentate. Hence the Najāshī sent against him an army commanded by one of his retainers called Aryāṭ. When Aryāṭ reached his camping place, Abrahah sent a message to him in these terms: "We are linked together by both the same homeland and the same faith, so we ought to look to the interests of our fellow countrymen and coreligionists who make up the troops who are with us respectively. So if you are agreeable, engage me in single combat, and whichever of us overcomes his opponent shall have the kingship, and the Abyssinians will not be killed because

531. For *mikhlāf,* see n. 462 above.

of our quarrel." Aryāṭ agreed to this, but Abrahah planned to act deceitfully with him. They appointed a place where the two of them were to meet [for the fight], but Abrahah placed in an ambush for Aryāṭ one of his slaves called '.r.n.j.d.h (?), in a depression [931]
in the ground, near the spot where they were to fight. When they met together, Aryāṭ moved forward first and lunged at Abrahah with his spear; but the spear slipped from off Abrahah's head and sliced off the end of his nose, hence his nickname of al-Ashram. Then '.r.n.j.d.h rose out from the depression and lunged with his spear at Aryāṭ, piercing his body and killing him. Abrahah said to '.r.n.j.d.h, "Name your own reward!" The latter said, "I claim the right to sexual intercourse with every women of Yemen before her marriage with her husband." Abrahah replied, "I concede that to you." '.r.n.j.d.h continued to enforce this right[532] for a long period, until the people of Yemen rose up against him and killed him. Abrahah said, "The time has at last come for you to act as free men."[533]

News of the killing of Aryāṭ reached the Najāshī, and he therefore swore that he would not rest in his mind until he had shed Abrahah's blood and overrun his land. News of the Najāshī's oath reached Abrahah, and he accordingly wrote back to him, "O king, Aryāṭ was merely your slave, and I am your slave also, He advanced against me with the intention of weakening your royal power and of slaughtering your troops. I asked him to stop fighting me until until I might send an envoy to you; if, then, you should order him to desist from attacking me, [all right,] but if not, I would hand over to him all my power and possessions. However, he refused to accept anything except to make war on me. I thus attacked him and gained the upper hand over him. Any power that I possess is yours, but I have heard that you have sworn not to stop until you shed my blood and overrun my land. Hence I have now forwarded to you a phial of my blood and a leather bag of soil from my territory. By means of these, you will be able to secure release

---

532. Reading, with *Addenda et emendanda,* p. DXCI, *fa-ghabara* for the text's *fa-ʿabara.*

533. That is, for them no longer to support the dishonoring of their womenfolk. On the military struggle beween Aryāṭ and Abrahah, see al-Ṭabarī, I, 943, p. 232 and n. 571 below.

from your oath. I ask for the completion of your favor upon me, O king, for I am merely your slave; any power and splendor which I have is your power and splendor." The Najāshī regarded him [once more] with favor, and confirmed him in his office.[534]

The narrative returns to that of Ibn Isḥāq. He related: Aryāṭ remained in Yemen for several years in the course of that period of his rule. Then Abrahah the Abyssinian, who was one of his troops,
[932] fought with him over the Abyssinian dominion in Yemen until the Abyssinians became split into two groups, with one faction joining up with each contender. Then one of them marched against the other. When the troops drew near and approached each other, Abrahah sent a message to Aryāṭ: "You will not wish to cause the Abyssinians to encounter each other in battle to the

534. As described in n. 518 above, the invading Abyssinians set up in Yemen a ruler, Sumu-yafa' Ašwa', Procopius's Esimphaios, who was now subordinate to the Abyssinian king Ẽlla Aṣběḥa, Procopius's Hellesthaios. Abrahah, originally the slave of a Greek merchant in Adulis, led a revolt of malcontent Abyssinian troops against Sumu-yafa' in ca. 533, and replaced him as ruler in Yemen; subsequent expeditions sent in the next year or so by Ẽlla Aṣběḥa, which must be the ones led by Aryāṭ in al-Ṭabarī's account here, were unable to dislodge Abrahah. After the Abyssinian king's death in ca. 536, the fait accompli of Abrahah's dominion in South Arabia was recognized by Ẽlla Aṣběḥa's successors in Axum, but Abrahah would only agree to pay tribute to the Byzantine emperor Justinian I, as a remote suzerain unlikely to interfere in Yemeni affairs and trouble his untrammeled power there, rather than to the much closer Abyssinian king. In 657 Ḥimyarite era/A.D. 547–48, the celebrated inscription of Abrahah recording repairs to the Mārib dam mentions that he quelled a rebellion by a son of Sumu-yafa'. See Smith, "Events in South Arabia in the 6th Century A.D.," 459; Altheim and Stiehl, *Christentum am Roten Meer*, I, 449–51; Trimingham, *Christianity among the Arabs in Pre-Islamic Times*, 300–301; *EI*², s.v. Abraha (A. F. L. Beeston).

The circumstantial detail in the accounts both of Ibn Isḥāq and Ibn al-Kalbī regarding Abrahah's dealings with Aryāṭ and 'Atwadah/'Atūdah must be legendary additions to the basic fact of Abrahah's assumption of power in Yemen. Al-Azraqī, *Akhbār Makkah*, 88, in his account of these events, has some additional touches, such as the fact that the Najāshī's residence was in *arḍ Aksūm* in the land of the Ḥabash. Even by early Islamic times, the name of Axum had virtually disappeared from Arab consciousness. It is mentioned in poetry written about Abrahah's "Expedition of the Elephant" against Mecca, with Abrahah called Abū Yaksūm, and 'Adī b. Zayd speaks of the *āl Barbar wa-al-Yaksūm* = the Abyssinians, but when al-Hamdānī and Nashwān b. Sa'īd mentioned it, it must have been a term from the remote past. See 'Adī b., Zayd, *Dīwān*, 47 no., 5; Ibn Hishām, *Sīrat al-nabī*, ed. Wüstenfeld, 39–40, 45 = ed. al-Saqqā et al., I, 61, 70, tr. 29, 33. Nöldeke, trans. 198 n. 2, took Barbar as a place name, the ancient form of modern Berbera = the coasts of Somaliland and Eritrea in general, and the name *Barbaria* for this is certainly found in the *Periplus of the Erythraean Sea*.

point that you destroy part of them, so come out against me and fight, and I will come out against you and fight, and whichever of us is able to smite his opponent, the latter's troops will come over and join the victor." Aryāṭ sent a reply: "You have proposed a just procedure, so come forth [against me]." Abrahah went forth; he was short, fleshy, and with a stout body, and held fast to the Christian faith. Aryāṭ marched out against him; he was a powerful, tall, and handsome man, and bore a spear in his hand. Behind Abrahah was a hillock that protected his rear, and concealed behind it was one of his slaves called ʿAtwadah (ʿAtūdah). When the two contestants drew near to each other, Aryāṭ raised his spear and struck Abrahah's head with it, aiming at the top of his skull. But the spear-blow fell across Abrahah's forehead and split his eyebrow, eye, nose, and lip; for this reason, Abrahah was called al-Ashram. Abrahah's slave boy ʿAtwadah sprang upon Aryāṭ from behind Abrahah and killed him. Aryāṭ's troops then went over to Abrahah, so that all the Abyssinians in Yemen rallied to his side. ʿAtwadah said concerning the killing of Aryāṭ: "I am ʿAtwadah—from a base stock—without a noble father or mother," meaning, "Abrahah's slave has killed you."

He related: Al-Ashram at this point said to ʿAtwadah, "Choose what you wish, O ʿAtwadah . . .[535] even though you have killed him; we have only now the responsibility for paying Aryāṭ's blood money." ʿAtwadah replied, "My choice is that I should have the [933] first opportunity for sexual intercourse with every bride from the people of Yemen before she enters the possession of her husband," and Abrahah granted him this. He then handed over the blood money for Aryāṭ. Everything Abrahah did was without the knowledge of the Najāshī, king of the Abyssinians.

When news of all that reached the latter, he became filled with rage and said, "He has attacked my own commander and killed him without any instruction from me!" He swore an oath that he would not leave Abrahah in power until he had overrun his land and cut off his forelock. When Abraham heard this, he shaved his head and filled a leather sack with the soil of Yemen, and then sent it to the Najāshī with the message: "O King, Aryāṭ was only

535. According to the editor of the Cairo text, II, 129 n. 4, something has dropped out here.

your slave, and I am your slave too. We disputed about your command; both of us owed you obedience, but I was stronger in directing the affairs of the Abyssinians, firmer and more skillful in statesmanship regarding them. When I heard about the king's oath, I shaved my head completely, and I have dispatched to him a sack of the earth of Yemen in order that the king may put it under his feet and thus fulfill his oath." When this message reached the Najāshī, he showed Abrahah his favor [once more] and wrote back to him: "I confirm you in your office in the land of Yemen until such time as a further command of mine reaches you."

When Abrahah perceived that the Najāshī had shown him favor and had appointed him viceroy over the Abyssinian troops and the land of Yemen, he sent to Abū Murrah b. Dhī Yazan and took from him his wife Rayḥānah bt. ʿAlqamah b. Mālik b. Zayd b. Kahlān. The father of Rayḥānah was Dhū Jadan. Abū Murrah had a son by her, Maʿdī Karib b. Abī Murrah. She now had a son by Abrahah, after Abū Murrah, Masrūq b. Abrahah and a daughter by him, Basbāsah. Abū Murrah fled from him. Abrahah remained in Yemen, while his slave ʿAtwadah was for a long time exercising there the right Abrahah had conceded to him as ʿAtwadah's chosen reward; but then a man of Ḥimyar or of Khathʿam[536] attacked ʿAtwadah and killed him. When Abrahah received the news of his death—and Abrahah was a magnanimous, noble leader, piously
[934] attached to his Christian religion[537]—he exclaimed, "The time is nigh for you, O people of Yemen, to have over you a man of solid judgment who is able to exercise the self-control appropriate to men of character. By God, if I had known, when I let ʿAtwadah choose his own reward, that he would ask what he did, I would

---

536. Khathʿam b. Anmār were an Arab tribe of the Sarāt mountain region between al-Ṭāʾif and Najrān, i.e., the hinterland of the modern province of ʿAsīr, although the tribe is not mentioned as such in the South Arabian inscriptions (personal communication from Professor Chr. Robin). As al-Ṭabarī relates, I, 936–37, pp. 221–23 below, Abrahah is said to have marched into their territory en route for Mecca at the time of the "Expedition of the Elephant," defeated the Khathʿam, and compelled their chief to guide him along the road to Mecca as far as al-Ṭāʾif. See Ibn al-Kalbī-Caskel-Strenziok, *Jamharat al-nasab,* I, Table 234, I, 45, 345; *EI*², s.v. Khathʿam (G. Levi Della Vida).

537. As Nöldeke remarked, trans. 200 n. 3, such an encomium hardly squares with Abrahah's long tolerance of ʿAtwadah's behavior or with his own appropriation of Abū Murrah b. Dhī Yazan's wife.

never have allowed him the choice and would never have heaped favors on him in any way. I swear by God, there shall be no blood price exacted from you for his death, and you will not receive any untoward retribution from me for his death."[538]

He (Ibn Isḥāq) related: Abrahah now built the cathedral church (*qalīs, qullays*) at Ṣan'ā'—such a church as had never been constructed on earth in its time. He then wrote to the Najāshī, king of the Abyssinians: "O king, I have constructed for you a church whose like has never been built for any monarch before you. I shall not give up until I have diverted the Arab pilgrims to it."[539] When

538. Al-Ṭabarī has thus given two versions of Abrahah's rise to power and fame, those of Ibn al-Kalbī and of Ibn Isḥāq, the two accounts being substantially in agreement. But in Abū al-Faraj al-Iṣfahānī, *Aghānī*[3], XVII, 304–307, a fuller form of what was given by al-Dīnawarī in his *al-Akhbār al-ṭiwāl*, 62, there is a third account, in which Abrahah is a subordinate commander of 'Aryāṭ's, of low birth (*lā bayta lahu*), who kills Aryāṭ with a poisoned dagger. Abrahah's lowly birth may be the origin of Procopius's tale that Abrahah was originally a slave in Adulis. See Nöldeke, trans. 200 n. 4.

539. *qalīs, qullays,* via Syriac *qəlēsā,* from Greek *ekklēsia.* The site of this famous church is still shown in Ṣan'ā' as a large, shallow pit lined with courses of rubble masonry and called Ghurqat al-Qalīs/al-Qullays, and Serjeant and Lewcock saw no reason to doubt that this site, near the citadel, is indeed that of Abrahah's building, which had a west-east orientation like that of the Axumite churches of Abyssinia. Al-Azraqī, *Akhbār Makkah,* 88–90, citing information from "trustworthy Yemeni shaykhs at Ṣan'ā'," provides a highly detailed and plausible account of the structure, stating that building stone for it was taken from the "palace of Bilqīs" at Mārib, and giving copious measurements of its various features. He further mentions a dome at what would have been the east end of the church, and in this last were two ornamented beams of teak (*sāj*) called Ku'ayb al-Aḥ.w.zī (this latter component of the name said to mean al-Ḥurr, "the free one," "in their language") and his wife, respectively, which were considered as objects of superstitious reverence. Shahîd has plausibly suggested that the dome covered a *martyrium* or shrine and that the images of Ku'ayb, and his wife were originally those of saints and martyrs, very probably those of Najrān: Ku'ayb's name might be a reminscence of the Najrān martyr al-Ḥārith b. Ka'b and his wife could be the most celebrated women martyr of Najrān, Ruhaymah. Around the church was a large, open area to accommodate pilgrims and visitors, and corresponding to the Ḥaram around the Meccan Ka'bah. Al-Azraqī, op. cit., 91–92, further describes how the church continued in use by the Christian community of Ṣan'ā' (which may have persisted up to the fourth/tenth century or beyond) until the 'Abbāsid caliph al-Manṣūr ordered his governor in Yemen al-'Abbās b. al-Rabī' al-Ḥārithī to demolish it, a process that was accomplished but resented by the Ṣan'ānīs, both Christian and Muslim, because of their reverence for Ku'ayb and his wife. Hence Nöldeke's comment, trans. 201 n. 1, that Christianity put down only weak roots in Yemen and at the time of the coming of Islam to the province had left hardly any trace, is clearly wrong. See Bell, *The Origin of Islam in Its Christian Environment,* 39–41;

the Arabs fell to talking about Abrahah's letter to the Najāshī, one of the men charged with intercalating the calendar (*al-nasa'ah*) flew into a rage. He was one of the Banū Fuqaym, part of the larger tribal group of the Banū Mālik.[540] He set out until he came to the cathedral church and then defecated (*qa'ada*) in it, and then departed and reached his own land. Abrahah was informed about the incident and demanded, "Who perpetrated this deed?" They told him, "A man from that House at Mecca, to which the Arabs make pilgrimage, did it, because he had heard your words 'I shall divert the Arab pilgrims to it (i.e., the new cathedral).' He became enraged, came here, and defecated in it, aiming to show that it was not worthy of that purpose." Abrahah himself became full of ire and swore that he would march against the House and demolish it.[541]

Now Abrahah had in his retinue some men of the Arabs who had come to him seeking his bounty, including Muḥammad b. Khuzā'ī b. Ḥuzābah of the Banū Dhakwān and then of the larger tribal group of the Banū Sulaym,[542] together with a group of his

---

Trimingham, *Christianity among the Arabs in Pre-Islamic Times*, 304; Shahîd, "Byzantium in South Arabia," 81–83; Serjeant and Lewcock, "The Church (al-Qalīs) of Ṣan'ā' and Ghumdān Castle," 44–48; Robin, in *Supplément au dictionnaire de la Bible*, s.v. Sheba. II, cols. 1192–93.

540. The Fuqaym b. 'Adī were a branch of Mālik of Kinānah, a Ḥijāzī tribe who dwelt in the vicinity of Mecca and from whom sprang Quṣayy, founder of Quraysh's fortunes in Mecca. They were said to have been entrusted, in pre-Islamic times, with the periodic intercalation of an extra month in the lunar calendar in order to make the *Ḥajj* or Pilgrimage coincide with the fairs and markets that accompanied it. If it had been true that Abrahah had planned to build up Ṣan'ā' into a pilgrimage center rivaling Mecca, the Banū Fuqaym's function as *nasa'ah* or intercalators would have become otiose. See Ibn Hishām, *Sīrat al-nabī*, ed. Wüstenfeld, 30 = ed. Saqqā et al., I, 44–47, tr. 21–22; Muḥammad b. Ḥabīb, *Kitāb al-muḥabbar*, 156–57; Ibn al-Kalbī-Caskel-Strenziok, *Jamharat al-nasab*, I,. Table 47, II, 6, 247; al-Azraqī, *Akhbār Makkah*, 125; *EI²*, s.v. Kināna (W. M. Watt), Nasī' (A. Moberg).

541. The Arabic sources have differing information on the location of Abrahah's church (Ṣan'ā', Najrān, or a place on the seashore) and on the person(s) desecrating it (Nufayl b. Ḥabīb al-Khath'amī, a man or men from Kinānah, etc.), but all of them point to Quraysh of Mecca being the real instigators of the desecration or burning of the church, Kinānah being of course closely connected with Quraysh. See Kister, "Some Reports Concerning Mecca. From Jāhiliyya to Islam," 63–65 (utilizing information from Ps.-al-Aṣma'ī, *Nihāyat al-arab fī akhbār al-Furs wa-al-'Arab*; see on this work n. 624 below).

542. Dhakwān b. Tha'labah were one of the three great subdivisions of the

fellow tribesmen, including his brother, Qays b. Khuzāʿī. While they were at Abrahah's court, there came round unexpectedly for them one of Abrahah's festivals. He sent along to them on that [935] feast day some of his morning meal. Abrahah used to eat [animals'] testicles. When Abrahah's food was brought to them, they protested, "By God, if we eat this the Arabs will never stop blaming us for it as long as we live!"[543] Muḥammad b. Khuzāʿī arose and went to Abrahah, saying, "O king, today is our festival when we eat only the flank and forelegs [of beasts]." Abrahah replied, "We will send you what you like; I was only showing honor to you with food from my morning meal because of your high status in my eyes." He then crowned Muḥammad b. Khuzāʿī and appointed him governor over Muḍar. He further commanded him to go out among the [Arab] people and summon them to make pilgrimage to the cathedral, the church he had built. So Muḥammad b. Khuzāʿī went off until he reached a spot in the territory of the Banū Kinānah. Meanwhile, the people of Tihāmah[544] had received information about Muḥammad's mission and what he was aiming to do, so they dispatched against him a man of Hudhayl called

---

powerful North Arab tribe of Sulaym b. Manṣūr, whose territories in Ḥijāz lay between Mecca and Medina, but bordered closely on Mecca; in both the pre-Islamic and the post-Islamic periods, Dhakwān were the closest Sulamī allies of the Meccans, intermarrying with some of the leading clans of Quraysh, including Umayya. Muḥammad b. Khuzāʿī b. ʿAlqama b. Ḥuzābah, who is said here to have been appointed chief over the tribes of Muḍar for Abrahah and who, according to Ibn Saʿd, was actually crowned by Abrahah, has a certain fame through being one of the few people who bore the name Muḥammad in the Jāhiliyyah. See Ibn al-Kalbī-Caskel-Strenziok, *Jamharat al-nasab*, I, Table 125, II, 18–19, 235, 517; Muḥammad b. al-Ḥabīb, *Kitāb al-muḥabbar*, 130; idem, *Kitāb al-munammaq*, 68–72; M. J. Kister, "Some Reports Concerning Mecca. From Jāhiliyya to Islam," 72; Lecker, *The Banū Sulaym. A Contribution to the Study of Early Islam*, 91–98, 108–19; *EI*², s.v. Sulaym (Lecker).

543. The Arabs are reported to have been repelled by certain of the customs and food practices of the Abyssinians; cf. the poet of Hudhayl's revulsion from his Abyssinian wife cited by Nöldeke, trans. 203 n. 2. But it seems strange that the Arabs of that time should have objected to eating animals' testicles when, at the present day, they are eaten as a delicacy all over the Middle East.

544. That is, the lowland strip along the Red Sea shores, running the length of what was in later times the provinces of Ḥijāz, ʿAsīr and Yemen. See Yāqūt, *Buldān*, II, 63–64; *EI*², s.v. Tihāma (G. R. Smith; and for its pre-Islamic history, Robin, "La Tihāma yéménite avant l'Islam: Notes d'histoire et de géographie historique," 222–33.

'Urwah b. Ḥayyāḍ al-Milāṣī[545] who shot Muḥammad with an arrow and killed him. Muḥammad's brother Qays was with him, and when Muḥammad was killed, he fled and went to Abrahah, informing him of Muḥammad's death. This sent Abrahah into an even greater rage and fury, and he swore that he would lead an expedition against the Banū Kinānah and tear down the House [at Mecca].[546]

Hishām b. Muḥammad related, however, as follows: After the Najāshī had restored Abrahah to favor and had confirmed him in his charge, the latter built the church at Ṣan'ā'. He made it a marvelous building, whose like had never been seen before, using gold and remarkable dyestuffs and stains. He wrote to Qayṣar

545. The Milāṣ b. Ṣāhilah were a subdivision of Hudhayl. See Ibn al-Kalbī-Caskel-Strenziok, *Jamharat al-nasab,* I, Table 58, II, 407.

546. Abrahah's appointment of Muḥammad b. Khuzā'ī and then his invasion of Ḥijāz, which later Meccan lore may have transformed into the "Expedition of the Elephant," seems to have been part of a far-reaching policy of extending Abrahah's dominion into central and even northern Arabia, confronting there Persia and its allies, through alliances with and favors to the Bedouin tribes of those regions. This was clearly the case with the expedition which he led into central Arabia in ca. 552, which included contingents from Kindah and Ma'add and which defeated the Lakhmid al-Mundhir III at Ḥulubān or Ḥalabān (see n. 409 above). The poet of al-Ṭā'if, Umayyah b. Abī al-Ṣalt, an older contemporary of the Prophet Muḥammad, speaks of "kings of Kindah, heroic warriors, fierce in battle, falcons" around Abrahah's elephant in the expedition of that name (*Sharḥ dīwān Umayyah,* ed. Sayf al-Dīn al-Kātib and Aḥmad 'Iṣām al-Kātib, 65; Bahjah 'Abd al-Ghafūr al-Ḥadīthī, *Umayyah b. Abī al-Ṣalt, ḥayātuhu wa-shi'ruhu,* 337–38 no. 154; Ibn Hishām, *Sīrat al-nabī,* ed. Wüstenfeld, 40 = ed. al-Saqqā et al., I, 62, tr. 30). Procopius states that the Byzantine emperor tried to bring together in an alliance "Qays," specified in a parallel source as "the prince of Kindah and Ma'add," with the viceroy of the Abyssinians (cited by Nöldeke, trans. 204 n. 2).

It is clear that Abrahah's expedition to Mecca, whatever its place in the history and chronology of events at that time (see regarding this, n. 563 below), contained substantial bodies of Arab tribesmen as well as a core of Abyssinian troops, even though the account of Ibn Isḥāq, in al-Ṭabarī, I, 936, p. 222 below, speaks—for obvious reasons of Arab-Islamic national pride—of the attackers as being wholly Abyssinians and of the Arabs as solidly united against them in defense of the Holy House in Mecca. Abrahah received a welcome in al-Ṭā'if and assistance to find his way to Mecca (al-Ṭabarī, I, 937, p. 223 below), and varying traditions on the expedition speak of participation in Abrahah's army by South Arab tribes like 'Akk, Ash'ar, Khath'am, Balḥārith, and Khawlān, and by North Arab tribes like Sulaym of Muḍar. Muḥammad b. Ḥabīb in his *Munammaq,* 70, refers to the incident of the Muḍarī troops recoiling from eating animals' testicles and implies that the food habits of North and South Arabs were different. See Kister, "Some Reports Concerning Mecca. From Jāhiliya to Islam," 67–73.

telling him that he intended to build a church at Ṣanʿāʾ whose traces and whose fame would last forever and asked for the emperor's aid in this. Qayṣar accordingly sent back to him skilled artisans, mosaic cubes, and marble.[547] When the building was completed, Abrahah wrote to the Najāshī that he planned to divert to it the pilgrims of the Arabs. When the Arabs heard that, they [936]
regarded it with perturbation and it assumed momentous proportions in their eyes. A man from the Banū Mālik b. Kinānah went off until he reached Yemen, entered the temple, and defecated in it. Abrahah's wrath was aroused, and he resolved to lead an expedition against Mecca and to raze the House to the ground. He set off with the Abyssinian army, including the elephant.[548] Dhū Nafar al-Ḥimyarī encountered him in battle. Abrahah fought with him and captured him. Dhū Nafar pleaded, "O king, I am nothing but your slave, so spare me, for keeping me alive will be more useful to you than killing me"; so he spared him. Abrahah marched onward. Nufayl b. Ḥabīb al-Khathʿamī opposed him, but Abrahah engaged him in battle, putting his supporters to flight and capturing him. Nufayl asked Abrahah to spare him; Abrahah agreed, and made him his guide in the land of the Arabs.

547. This seems perfectly feasible, given that, in early Islamic times, the Umayyad caliph al-Walīd I asked the Byzantine emperor (presumably Justinian II) to send skilled artisans and mosaic cubes (*al-fusayfisāʾ*, from Greek *psēphos*, the word used here in al-Ṭabarī's text) for the decoration of the Umayyad Mosque at Damascus and the Prophet's Mosque at Medina. See H. A. R. Gibb, "Arab-Byzantine Relations under the Umayyad Caliphate," 51–56. As mentioned in n. 539 above, we have highly detailed descriptions of the interior decoration of Abrahah's church, which included a lavish use of tropical hardwoods, gold, silver, mosaic cubes, jewels, etc., in both the portico (*aywān*) of the church and the part of the basilica beneath the dome (*qubbah*). It is improbable that all this could have been achieved without outside assistance. The completed building must indeed have seemed like a wonder of the world, and explains the attachment of the local people, both Christian and Muslim, to it (see n. 539 above). As well as the account by al-Azraqī referred to in the above-mentioned note, see also the account of the church by the thirteenth-century Egyptian Coptic author Abū Ṣāliḥ al-Armanī (one which may possibly have been influenced by the author's knowledge of Egyptian church interiors), *The Churches and Monasteries of Egypt*, trans. B. J. A. Evetts, 300–302; Serjeant and Lewcock, "The Church (al-Qalīs) of Ṣanʿāʾ and Ghumdān Castle," 47.

548. Nöldeke, trans. 206 n. 1, cites the Byzantine historian John Malalas that the Abyssinian king rode one of the four elephants pulling the royal coach or cart. Whether Abrahah actually rode on the elephant here is not explicit.

The narrative returns to the account of Ibn Isḥāq. He said: When Abrahah decided on an expedition against the House [at Mecca], he ordered the Abyssinians to prepare for the campaign and put themselves in a state of readiness, and he set out with the army and with the elephant. He related: The Arabs heard about this; they found the news alarming and were filled with fear at it. They regarded fighting in defense of the Ka'bah, God's Holy House, as a duty laid upon them when they heard of Abrahah's intention to tear it down. A man who was one of the nobles of the Yemenis called Dhū Nafar rose up against him and summoned his people, and those of the Arabs who responded to his call, to make war on Abrahah and oppose him strenuously in defense of God's House and in the face of Abrahah's intention of demolishing and reducing it to a pile of ruins. A certain number rallied to his side. He confronted Abrahah, but Abrahah attacked him, and Dhū Nafar and his followers were put to flight. He himself was taken prisoner and brought before Abrahah. The latter was on the point of killing him when Dhū Nafar said to him: "O king, don't put me to death, for it may be that my presence at your side could be more advantageous for you than killing me." Abrahah therefore desisted from killing him, but kept him in captivity by him, loaded with fetters; Abrahah was a magnanimous man.

After this, Abrahah continued onward in accordance with his plan, intending to do what he had set out to do, until when he reached the territory of the Khath'am, he was opposed by Nufayl
[937] b. Ḥabīb al-Khath'amī with a force from the two component tribes of Khath'am, Shahrān, and Nāhis,[549] and others from the tribes of the Arabs who followed him. He attacked Abrahah, but the latter routed him. He was taken prisoner and brought before Abrahah. Abrahah intended to put Nufayl to death, but he pleaded with him: "O king, don't kill me, for I will act as your guide through the land of the Arabs; these two hands of mine are your sureties for the obedience and good behavior of the two tribes of Khath'am, Shahrān, and Nāhis." Hence Abrahah spared him and released

549. In the genealogy of Khath'am, these two subdivisions were the descendants of two of the great-grandsons of Khath'am b. Anmār; the name of Shahrān survives today. See Ibn al-Kalbī-Caskel-Strenziok, *Jamharat al-nasab*, I, Tables 124–25, II, 345.

him. Abrahah went forth with Nufayl, the latter acting as his guide along the road until they reached al-Ṭā'if.[550] Mas'ūd b. Mu'attib came out with the men of Thaqīf,[551] and addressed Abrahah: "O king, we are your servants, obedient and submissive to you, and you will not find us offering any resistance to you. This house of ours (they meant [the house of] Allāt) is not the House which you seek. You want the House which is at Mecca (they meant the Ka'bah), and we will send a man with you who will guide you." He therefore passed them over and did not molest them.

They sent with him Abū Righāl [as guide], and Abrahah departed, accompanied by Abū Righāl, until the latter brought him as far as al-Mughammis. As soon as he had conducted Abrahah thither, Abū Righāl died at that very place. The Arabs subsequently hurled stones at his grave; it is this grave at which people hurl stones at al-Mughammis [today].[552] When Abrahah en-

---

550. Muḥammad b. Ḥabīb, *Munammaq,* 68, says that Abrahah gathered together a force, "a motley crew of the evildoers of the Arabs" (*fussāq al-'Arab wa-ṭakhārīrihim*), mainly from Khath'am and the Banū Munabbih b. Ka'b b. al-Ḥārith b. Ka'b, said to have been traditionally hostile to the Ka'bah, and all under Nufayl's leadership. This author, at least, does concede that, *pace* Ibn Isḥāq (see n. 546 above) Arabs were included in Abrahah's army.

551. As Mas'ūd b. Mu'attib says here, the shrine of the pre-Islamic goddess Allāt was located at al-Ṭā'if, and the popularity of its cult made it a considerable rival to that of Allāh in the Ka'bah of Mecca during pre-Islamic times, until the shrine was despoiled and destroyed at the surrender of al-Ṭā'if in 8/630.

'Urwah b. Mas'ūd was one of the leaders of the Aḥlāf group of Thaqīf during the time of the Prophet's career; Aḥlāf were more inclined toward conciliation with the Prophet than the other group of Thaqīf, the Banū Mālik. 'Urwah was in fact assassinated on his return from the Prophet's side in Medina, allegedly having become a secret Muslim working for the surrender of his town to the Muslims; he thereby earned the Islamic designations of *shahīd,* "martyr," and of *ṣaḥābī,* Companion of the Prophet. See Watt, *Muhammad at Medina,* 102–04; *EI*², s.v. 'Urwa b. Mas'ūd (C. E. Bosworth).

552. Abū Righāl is at best a semilegendary figure, the story of whose guiding Abrahah to Mecca may have been elaborated as part of the anti-Thaqafī bias of pietistic Muslim circles hostile to the role of prominent men of al-Ṭā'if within the Umayyad caliphate like 'Ubaydallāh b. Ziyād b. Abīhi and al-Ḥajjāj b. Yūsuf. However, the practice of stoning Abū Righāl's alleged burial place must have developed early, as attested to by mention of it in a verse of the Umayyad poet Jarīr (d. 110/728–29 or shortly thereafter) cited by al-Azraqī, *Akhbār Makkah,* 93. Al-Mughammis or al-Mughammas was a valley just off the Mecca to al-Ṭā'if road on the edge of the Ḥaram of Mecca. See al-Bakrī, *Mu'jam mā ista'jam,* III, 1248; Yāqūt, *Buldān,* V, 161–62; *EI*², s.vv. Abū Righāl (S. A. Bonebakker) and al-Mughammas

camped at al-Mughammis, he sent forward one of the Abyssinians called al-Aswad b. Maqṣūd (or Mafṣūd) with a troop of cavalry until al-Aswad reached Mecca, from where he sent back to Abrahah captured beasts taken from the people of Mecca, Quraysh, and others. Among these, Abrahah acquired two hundred camels belonging to 'Abd al-Muṭṭalib b. Hāshim, at that time the paramount chief and lord of Quraysh.[553] Quraysh, Kinānah, Hudhayl, and all the rest of the people who dwelled in the Holy Enclosure (*al-Ḥaram*) contemplated giving fight to Abrahah's forces, but then realized that they lacked the power to resist him, so renounced the idea.

[938] Abrahah sent Ḥunāṭah al-Ḥimyarī to Mecca and instructed him: "Ask who is the lord and noble leader of this territory, and then inform him that the king tells them, 'I have not come to make war on you, but have merely come to destroy the House. If you do not wish to defend it by force of arms, then there will be no need for us to shed your blood; and if he (i.e., 'Abd al-Muṭṭalib) does not intend to oppose us by fighting, then bring him back to me.'" Now when Ḥunāṭah entered Mecca, he asked who was the lord and noble leader of Quraysh, and was told that this was 'Abd al-Muṭṭalib b. Hāshim b. 'Abd Manāf b. Quṣayy; so he went to him and delivered the message Abrahah had commanded him to communicate. 'Abd al-Muṭṭalib replied, "By God, we don't want to fight with him, for we have no power to do so. But this is the Holy House of God and the House of His friend Ibrāhīm (Abraham)," or words to that effect, "and if He defends it against him, well, it is

(ed.). The custom of stoning Abū Righāl's grave bears an obvious resemblance to the ritual stoning of Satan at Minā in the course of the Pilgrimage ceremonies. See *EI*², s.v. Djamra (F. Buhl-J. Jomier).

Nöldeke, trans. 208 n. 1, citing the anthology *al-Kāmil* of al-Mubarrad, noted that in post-Islamic times Hudhayl were still reviled for having guided the Abyssinians against the Ka'bah, but he considered this to be really an echo of the alleged role of Hudhalīs in guiding Tubba' Tubān As'ad Abū Karib against the Ka'bah, see al-Ṭabarī, I, 903–904, pp. 168–69 above.

553. The importance of the figure of 'Abd al-Muṭṭalib, great-grandson of Quṣayy and grandfather of the Prophet, has doubtless been inflated by Islamic tradition. At the time of Abrahah, he was clan chief of Hāshim and probably the de facto leader of a group of Meccan clans who tried to negotiate with Abrahah if only to gain some advantage over their rivals within Mecca, but we have no solid information about his role here, and Nöldeke, 209 n. 1, was justly skeptical. See Buhl, *Das Leben Muhammeds*, 113–16; Watt, *Muhammad at Mecca*, 30–33; *EI*², s.v. 'Abd al-Muṭṭalib (W. M. Watt).

His House and His sanctuary; whereas if He allows Abrahah to get possession of it, then, by God, we have no one who can defend it from him," or words to that effect. Ḥunāṭah told him, "You must come back [with us] to the king, for he has ordered me to bring you to him."

Ḥunāṭah accordingly set off with ʿAbd al-Muṭṭalib, the latter accompanied by one of his sons, until they reached the army camp. ʿAbd al-Muṭṭalib enquired after Dhū Nafar, who was a friend of his, and was directed to him, Dhū Nafar being however in confinement. ʿAbd al-Muṭṭalib said, "O Dhū Nafar, have you any means of relief for the trouble which has come upon us?" The latter replied, "What relief is possible from a man held captive at the king's hand, one who expects to be killed at any moment (literally, "in the morning or evening")? I can't avail at all in regard to your misfortune, except that Unays, the keeper of the elephant, is a friend of mine. I will send a message to him and will commend you to him, put the case to him for helping you as strongly as possible, and ask him to try to arrange an audience for you with the king. So make your request to him, and Unays will intercede with him on your behalf as skillfully as possible for him." ʿAbd al-Muṭṭalib responded, "That's as much as I can hope." Dhū Nafar accordingly sent a message to Unays, and came to him[554] saying, "O Unays, ʿAbd al-Muṭṭalib is the chief of Quraysh and master of the Meccan caravan (*ʿīr*);[555] he feeds the people on the plains and the wild beasts on the mountain peaks.[556] The king has seized two [939]
hundred of his camels, so I ask permission for him to come before

554. Following the suggested emendation of text, n. *e*, *fa-jāʾahu*.

555. Thus in text, in Ibn Hishām, *Sīrat al-nabī*, ed. al-Saqqā et al., I, 51, and in al-Azraqī, *Akhbār Makkah*, 94, but Ibn Hishām, op. cit., ed. Wüstenfeld, 33, trans. 25, has *ʿayn*, "well," i.e., the well of Zamzam in Mecca.

556. An allusion to the *rifādah*, the supplying of provisions to pilgrims and traders coming to Mecca for the *Ḥajj* and its attendant fairs. It was linked to another service, that of *siqāyah*, the supplying of water, *nabīdh* or date wine, and the semiliquid foodstuff *sawīq* to the pilgrims also. Both of these were said to have been established in Mecca by Quṣayy for the ʿAbd al-Dār clan but usurped by the ʿAbd Manāf clan, of whom Hāshim were a component. These rights are adduced by later Islamic authors as showing the nobility of the Prophet's clan in pre-Islamic times, but in reality must have been not so much philanthropic or social services as much as lucrative sources of revenue for the holders Hāshim. See Gaudefroy-Demombynes, *Le pélerinage à la Mekke*, 89–101; Bosworth, "The Terminology of the History of the Arabs in the Jāhiliyya According to Khwārazmī's 'Keys of the Sciences,'" 31–33.

the king, and be as useful as possible on his behalf." Unays replied, "I'll do that." Unays spoke to Abrahah, saying, "O king, this is the chief of Quraysh, now in your court, who is seeking an audience of you. He is master of the Meccan caravan, and feeds the people on the plain and the wild beasts on the mountain peaks. So grant him permission to come before you, so that he may tell you his request, and treat him kindly!"

He related: Abrahah granted ʿAbd al-Muṭṭalib an audience. Now ʿAbd al-Muṭṭalib was an impressive, handsome, and well-built man. When Abrahah beheld him, he treated him with too great a respect and kindness to allow ʿAbd al-Muṭṭalib to sit below him. Abrahah did not, however, want the Abyssinians to see him letting ʿAbd al-Muṭṭalib sit at his side on his royal throne, so he came down from his throne and then sat on his carpet, bidding ʿAbd al-Muṭṭalib sit on it also by his side. He then told his interpreter to ask him what was his request of the king. The interpreter passed these words on to ʿAbd al-Muṭṭalib, and the latter said, "My request of the king is that he should give me back the two hundred camels of mine which he has seized." When the interpreter informed Abrahah of this, Abrahah told him through the interpreter, "You impressed me favorably when I saw you, but I went off you (*zahidtu fīka*) when you spoke to me. Do you speak to me about the two hundred camels which I seized, and brush aside a House that enshrines your religion and the religion of your forefathers, and which I have come to destroy, and say nothing to me about it?" ʿAbd al-Muṭṭalib replied: "I am the owner of the camels; the House has a lord of its own who will defend it." Abrahah said, "He won't be able to defend it against me!" But ʿAbd al-Muṭṭalib retorted, "That's your own affair; just give me back my camels!"

A certain learned scholar has asserted that ʿAbd al-Muṭṭalib had gone to Abrahah, when the latter sent Ḥunāṭah to him, accompanied by Yaʿmar[557] b. Nufāthah b. ʿAdī b. al-Duʾil b. Bakr b. ʿAbd Manāt b. Kinānah, who was at that time chief of the Banū Kinānah, and Khuwaylid b. Wāthilah al-Hudhalī, chief of Hudhayl at the time. They offered Abrahah a third of the wealth (*amwāl*) of
[940] Tihāmah if he would go back home and not destroy the House, but

557. Following the correct reading for this name in Ibn Hishām, *Sīrat al-Nabī*, ed. Wüstenfeld, 34 = ed. al-Saqqā et al., I, 52, trans. 25, and in al-Azraqī, *Akhbār Makkah*, 95, against the ʿ*Amr* of the text.

he refused. But God is more knowing [about the truth of this]. At any rate, Abrahah had meanwhile restored to ʿAbd al-Muṭṭalib the camels he had seized.

When they left him, ʿAbd al-Muṭṭalib went back to Quraysh and told them the news. He ordered them to go forth from Mecca and seek refuge on the mountain tops and in the defiles, fearing violent behavior from the [Abyssinian] army. ʿAbd al-Muṭṭalib then arose and took hold of the door-ring, that of the door of the Kaʿbah, and a group of Quraysh stood with him praying to God and imploring His help against Abrahah and his troops. ʿAbd al-Muṭṭalib recited at the time when he took hold of the door-ring of the Kaʿbah:

O Lord, I don't hope for any one but you against them!
O Lord, defend your sacred area (*ḥimā*) from them![558]
Indeed, the enemy of the House is the one who is attacking you!
Repel them lest they lay waste Your settlements!

Then he further recited:

O God, a servant [of God] defends his dwelling, so protect Your dwelling places and their people (*ḥilālak*)![559]
Let not their cross and their cunning craft (*miḥāl*) prevail over Your cunning craft on the morrow![560]
But if You do that (i.e., abandon them), then it may be something which seems most appropriate [for You] and an affair which appears best to you.

558. In pre-Islamic Arabia, *ḥimā*, "protected area," denoted a stretch of pasture or hunting or other desirable land set aside for the use of a particular group and protected by that group. Many *ḥimā*s gradually acquired taboos and a religious aura from tribal deities, hence by the time of the coming of Islam, the Ḥaram of Mecca had become the protected area par excellence. See Wellhausen, *Reste arabischen Heidentums*², 105–09; Lammens, *Le berceau de l'Islam*, 60–64; *EI*², s.v. Ḥimā (J. Chelhod).

559. Reading thus for the text's *ḥalālak* (*ḥilāl* = pl. of *ḥillah*), following *Addenda et emendanda*, p. DXCII, and *Glossarium*, p. CXCIX, but with more or less the same meaning anyway.

560. Reading *ghadw*ᵃⁿ for the text's ʿ*adw*ᵃⁿ, following *Addenda et emendanda*, p. DXCII. The verse echoes the Qurʾānic use of *miḥāl* "the cunning craft and force [of God]" in sūrah XIII, 14/13, God being depicted elsewhere in the Qurʾān (II, 47/54. VIII, 30) as "the best of those who use craft and guile, *makr*."

And if You do that, well, it is an affair which will complete
your [divine] plan of action.
When some person comes to you seeking peace, we hope that
[941] You will act toward us in a like manner.
Then they turned back, having gained nothing but humiliation;
perdition was coming upon them there.
I never heard of the most reprobate of men who desired glory
and who then violated the sanctity of Your sacred enclosure
(*ḥarām*).
They brought into action the assembled host of their land and
the elephant, in order to capture and enslave members of
your families.
They attacked your sacred area (*ḥimā*) with their cunning, out
of sheer savagery (*jahlan*), and paid no heed to Your
exaltedness.[561]

Then ʿAbd al-Muṭṭalib let go of the ring of the door, the door of the Kaʿbah, and set off with his companions of Quraysh to the mountain tops and sought refuge there, in expectation of what Abrahah was going to do in Mecca when he entered it. Next morning, Abrahah prepared to enter Mecca, got ready his elephant (whose name was Maḥmūd), and drew up his army. Abrahah was determined upon destroying the House and then returning to Yemen. When they drove the elephant forward, Nufayl b. Ḥabīb al-Khathʿamī came up and stood by its flank. He then got hold of its ear and said, "Kneel, O Maḥmūd, and go [then] straight back whence you came, for you are in God's sacred territory!" Then he let go its ear; the elephant knelt down,[562] while Nufayl b. Ḥabīb made off at top speed and clambered up the mountain. The soldiers beat the elephant to make it get up, but it refused. They beat its head with a battle axe to make it get up, but it still refused. They stuck hooks into its soft underbelly and scarified it to make it rise, and yet again it refused. But then they turned it round to face back to Yemen (i.e., southward); it got up and trotted off. They

561. Nöldeke notes in text, n. *d*, that the last three verses of this poem are in a different meter (*wāfir*) from the rest of it (*kāmil*) and that some manuscripts have rearranged the wording of these three verses to make them fit the *kāmil* meter of the whole poem. Otherwise, one must assume that we have here verses from two separate poems, even though they share the same rhyme in *-ak*/*-ik*.

562. As pointed out by Nöldeke, trans. 213 n. 1, elephants do not kneel down like camels, a fact already recognized by one of the scholiasts of Ibn Hishām.

pointed it in the direction of Syria (i.e., northwards), and it behaved exactly the same. They pointed it in the direction of the east, and it again did likewise; but when they made it face Mecca, it knelt down.

God now sent down on them a flock of birds, like swallows, each bird bearing three stones like chick peas and lentils, one stone in its beak and two in its claws. Everyone whom the birds hit [with the stones] perished, although not all of them were in fact hit.[563] They retreated in haste along the road they had come, [942]

---

563. The description of the divine visitation on Abrahah's impious forces is connected, as here, by the compilers of the *Sīrah* of the Prophet and subsequent commentators with Qur'ān, CV, Sūrat al-Fīl. But as both Gordon Newby and Irfan Shahîd have noted, the connection is by no means explicit in the Qur'ān. There is no mention in the sūrah of place or time, the object of the attack or the identity of the attackers themselves. Moreover, Shahîd adds that the agents of the destruction of the *aṣḥāb al-fīl* are by no means clearly the birds of vv. 3–4, described there as sweeping down in flocks (*abābīl*) bearing *sijjīl.* These last have been traditionally interpreted as "stones of baked clay," and this meaning fits the context here and in the other two Qur'ānic attestations of the word, cf. *EI*², s.v. Sidjdjīl (V. Vacca-Ed.); but F. de Blois now suggests that *sijjīl* stems ultimately from the pre-Islamic religious tradition of North Arabia and may even have been in origin the name of a local deity, see his forthcoming "Ḥijāratun min sijjīl." The birds may have been scavengers after the work of destruction wrought by God Himself, if one follows the variant reading *yarmīhim,* "[He] pelted them," for the accepted text *tarmīhim,* "[they, i.e., the birds] pelted them." Shahîd doubts whether Muḥammad's Meccan audience could have been misled by assumptions about an event that had taken place only two generations previously. Instead, we must regard the later Islamic tradition as supplying a specific reference for what was, at the time of its revelation in Mecca, rather, an eschatological description of the imminence of punishment for unbelieving peoples. See G. H. Newby, "Abraha and Sennacherib: A Talmudic Parallel to the *Tafsīr* on *Sūrat al-Fīl,*" 433–34; I. Shahîd, "Two Qur'ānic Sūras: *al-Fīl* and *Qurayš*," 431, 433–44; and cf. R. Paret, *Der Koran. Kommentar und Konkordanz*², 522.

Whatever the original significance and message of *Sūrat al-Fīl,* rationalizing interpretations of the story of Abrahah's abortive expedition against Mecca arose early, mainly involving the explanation that the attacking forces were struck down by mass disease or by an epidemic, such as measles or smallpox mentioned by al-Ṭabarī, I, 945, p. 235 below, reducing Abrahah's combatant power and compelling a withdrawal. An explanation from smallpox was put forward in *ḥadīth*s going back to the Successor ʿIkrimah (d. 105/723–24), and in one line of poetry cited by Ibn Isḥāq from the verse written on the "Expedition of the Elephant" by Muḥammad's opponent in Mecca, ʿAbdallāh b. al-Zibaʿrā al-Sahmī (on whom, see Abū al-Faraj al-Iṣfahānī, *Aghānī*³, XV, 139–84), "Sixty thousand men (i.e., Abrahah's forces) did not return to their land, and their sick ones did not survive after the return home." See Ibn Hishām, *Sīrat al-nabī,* ed. Wüstenfeld, 39 = ed. al-Saqqā et al., I, 59, tr. 28; *EI*², s.v. al-Fīl (A. F. L. Beeston).

The historicity of some move by Abrahah against Mecca seems likely, given the undoubted fact that his sphere of military activity extended as far as central Ara-

asking Nufayl b. Ḥabīb to guide them along the way to Yemen. When Nufayl b. Ḥabīb saw what God had sent down on them as punishment, he said:

Where can a man flee, when God is pursuing [him]? Al-Ashram (i.e., Abrahah) is the conquered one, not the conqueror!
Ho, Rudaynah,[564] may greetings be upon you! When we went forth this morning, our eyes rejoiced at you!
A seeker after fire from among you came to us yesterday evening, but he was unable to get anything from us.
If you had been able to see, O Rudaynah—but you were not able to see it—what we saw in the vicinity of al-Muḥaṣṣab,[565]

---

bia, where he aimed at countering an extension of Lakhmid power and, behind that, Persian influence, on the evidence of the well of Murayghān inscription dating from 662 Ḥimyarite era/A.D. 552–53 (a *terminus ad quem* for dating this campaign being, in any case, Abrahah's opponent al-Mundhir III of al-Ḥīrah's death in 554; see further on this episode, n. 409 above). How much later than this date Abrahah could have mounted the "Expedition of the Elephant" is uncertain, but must have been very soon afterward. The inscription commemorating Abrahah's repair of the Dam of Mārib has the date 658 Ḥimyarite era/A.D. 548–49 (Smith, "Events in South Arabia in the 6th Century A.D.," 437–41), but Abrahah had to die and be succeeded in South Arabia by his two sons Yaksūm and Masrūq before the appearance of the Persians in Yemen in 570 (see al-Ṭabarī, I, 945–46, pp. 235–36 below). It has been suggested that the campaign of Abrahah, with its victories over Ma'add and other tribes at Ḥulubān/Ḥalabān, and the victory of his Kindah and Sa'd-Murād confederates over the 'Āmir b. Ṣa'ṣa'ah at Turabah, were either a preparation for an expedition against Mecca shortly afterward or the basis for a later tradition growing out of an Abyssinian expedition against Mecca. Going a step further, Altheim and Stiehl have very plausibly suggested that the Meccan expedition was actually part of the general operations of Abrahah in central Arabia during the course of 552. The chronological differences arising out of the fact that the Islamic tradition generally placed the Prophet's birth in the "Year of the Elephant," conventionally taken as A.D. 570, may not be unresolvable, since M. J. Kister, following H. Lammens, has pointed out the existence of traditions giving a different birth date for Muḥammad, including one in Ibn al-Kalbī that he was born twenty-three years after the "Expedition of the Elephant" and one going back to al-Zuhrī which, by a computation involving the dates of various events mentioned in the *ḥadīth,* would fix the "Year of the Elephant" in 552, i.e., precisely the year the Ry 506 inscription records for Abrahah's military operations. See Lammens, "L'âge de Mahomet et la chronologie de la Sîra," 211–12, and the full discussion in Kister, "The Campaign of Ḥulubān," 426–28.

564. That is, the poet is, in accordance with poetic convention, addressing a real or imaginary beloved, Rudaynah.

565. Literally, "ground strewn with pebbles," a valley near Minā through which the pilgrims pass on the return from Minā to Mecca at the end of the *Ḥajj.* On halting there, *taḥṣīb,* the act of throwing pebbles, is a recommended (*mustaḥabb*)

You would have exonerated me and praised my good judgment,
and not have grieved over what has passed and gone between us.[566]
I praised God when I saw with my own eyes the birds, but
feared that the stones might be rained upon us.
All the people are asking for Nufayl, as though I owed the
Abyssinians a debt.[567]

As they retreated, the Abyssinian troops were continually falling by the wayside and perishing at every watering place (or halting place, *manhal*). Abrahah was smitten in his body; they carried him with them, with his fingers dropping off one by one. As each finger dropped off, there followed a purulent sore in its place, which exuded pus and blood, until they brought him to Ṣan'ā', with him looking like a newly born chick (i.e., plucked and emaciated). They allege that, as he died, his heart burst out from his breast.[568]

Al-Ḥārith related to me, saying: There related to us Muḥammad b. Sa'd—Muḥammad b. 'Umar[569]—'Abdallāh b. 'Uthmān b. Abī Sulaymān—his father. There also related to us from Muḥammad

---

action, and this may be a reminiscence of a pre-Islamic rite, perhaps one of lapidation. See al-Bakrī, *Mu'jam mā ista'jam*, IV, 1192; Yāqūt, *Buldān*, V, 62; Gaudefroy-Demombynes, *Le pélerinage à la Mekke*, 303–304.

566. Taking *baynā* as standing for *baynanā*.

567. Nöldeke, trans. 214 n. 2, commented that these verses are ostensibly part of a longer poem but contain many details and features have no connection with the supposed circumstances of their composition. In fact, they correspond in verse form, rhyme, and, to some extent, in wording, to an old poem in the *Ḥamāsah* anthology of the 'Abbāsid poet Abū Tammām, demonstrating that the verses have been modeled on this latter poem.

568. This tale of the manner of Abrahah's death is perhaps a transference to him of the army's being afflicted by disease, see n. 563 above. It is also given in Ibn Hishām, *Sīrat al-nabī*, ed. Wüstenfeld, 36 = ed. al-Saqqā et al., I, 55–56, tr. 27, and al-Azraqī, *Akhbār Makkah*, 97–98, the latter author adding that some stragglers and deserters from the Abyssinian army, and other elements had been attached to it, came into Mecca and stayed there, working as laborers and camel herders. This seems quite feasible, but less so the *khabar* going back to 'Ā'ishah (born ca. 614) quoted by al-Azraqī, op. cit., 98, 103, according to which she saw the elephant's conductor and its groom as blind beggars for food in the center of Mecca. See Nöldeke, trans. 219 n. 1; also Muḥammad b. Ḥabīb, *Munammaq*, 73–76.

569. That is, the *khabar* here goes back to Muḥammad b. 'Umar al-Wāqidī (d. 207/823), a member of the Medinan historical school who worked in Baghdad, and to his secretary and transmitter, Ibn Sa'd (d. 230/845). See Sezgin, *GAS*, I, 294–97, 300–301; *EI*[2], s.vv. Ibn Sa'd (J.W. Fück) and al-Wāḳidī (S. Leder).

b. ʿAbd al-Raḥmān b. al-Salmānī—his father. There also related to
[943] us ʿAbdallāh b. ʿUmar b. Zuhayr al-Kaʿbī—Abū Mālik al-Ḥimyarī—ʿAṭāʾ b. Yasār. There also related to us Muḥammad b. Abī Saʿīd al-Thaqafī—Yaʿlā b. ʿAṭāʾ—Wakīʿ b. ʿUdus—his paternal uncle Abū Bazīn al-ʿUqaylī. There also related to us Saʿīd b. Muslim—ʿAbdallāh b. Kathīr—Mujāhid—Ibn ʿAbbās. Parts of some narratives are combined with others. They say: Al-Najāshī had dispatched Aryāṭ Abū Ṣaḥam[570] with a force of four thousand men to Yemen. He subjugated and conquered it. He gave rewards to the local kings but treated the poor with contempt. There arose a man from among the Abyssinians called Abrahah al-Ashram Abū Yaksūm. He invited the people to give him allegiance, and they responded, so he then killed Aryāṭ and seized control of Yemen.[571] He observed the local people getting ready, at the time of the festival, for pilgrimage to the Holy House [in Mecca], and asked, "Where are the people going?" They told him that they were making pilgrimage to God's House at Mecca. He enquired, "What is it made of?" They replied, "Of stone." He said, "What is its covering (*kiswah*)?" They responded, "The striped Yemeni cloth (*al-waṣāʾil*), which comes from here."[572] Abrahah swore, "By the Messiah! I will certainly build for you something better than that!" So he built for them a house constructed from white,

---

570. Thus in the text; the *Addenda et emendanda*, p. DXCII, prefer the reading Aṣḥam (which would mean "dust-colored, yellowish, tinged with black"). However, Nöldeke, trans. 215 and n. 2, states that Ḍaḥam or Ṣaḥam is the correct reading, as in the name of the Ethiopian king Ĕlla Ṣaḥam.

571. What Ibn Saʿd says here of Aryāṭ's discriminatory policy as a cause of his downfall is confirmed by extra details in the *Nihāyat al-irab* (see for this n. 624 below): that Aryāṭ, a noble and nephew of the Najāshī, appropriated captured booty and other wealth for himself, the nobility, and chiefs of the Abyssinians. Abrahah, himself of servile origin, was thus able to champion the cause of the excluded rank and file and the lower classes, and was able to lead an uprising against Aryāṭ in the name of equality of treatment. See von Gutschmid, "Bemerkungen zu Tabari's Sasanidengeschichte, übersetzt von Th. Nöldeke," 738–40; Kister, "Some Reports Concerning Mecca. From Jāhiliyya to Islam," 61–63 n. 5.

572. For the *kiswah*, see al-Ṭabarī, I, 904, p. 169 and n. 433 above, where the Tubbaʿ Asʿad Abū Karib is said first to have covered the Kaʿbah with Yemeni *maʿāfirī* cloth, Yemen being traditionally famed for its textiles. There seems to have been an ancient tradition in Arabia of covering *qubbahs*, i.e., tents and similar structures housing sacred objects, with materials like skins and cloth, according to H. Lammens, "Le culte des bétyles et les processions religieuses chez les Arabes préislamiques," 130–32, 138–42.

red, yellow, and black marble, and adorned it with gold and silver, and encompassed it with jewels. He provided it with doors made with sheets of gold and with golden nails, and set the space between them with jewels, which included an enormous ruby. He provided it with a covered sanctuary (*ḥijāb*), in which sweet-smelling aloes wood was continually burnt, and its walls were smeared with musk, thereby darkening the walls until the jewels [encrusted on them] appeared sunken. He gave orders to the people, and they made pilgrimage to it, as did a large number of the tribes of the Arabs over a period of years. There lived permanently within this temple men who made perpetual adoration and service to God there, and who devoted themselves to worshiping Him in it.

Nufayl al-Khathʿamī was planning to do by stealth something unpleasant to it.[573] One night, when he saw no one moving around, he got up and took some excrement and smeared the apse of the high altar (*qiblah*)[574] of the temple with it, and he gathered together some putrefying animal carcases and threw them into it. Abrahah was told about this; he became extremely angry and exclaimed, "The Arabs have only done this out of vexation on account of their own House; I shall certainly destroy it stone by stone!" He wrote to the Najāshī informing him of that and asking the Najāshī to send him his elephant Maḥmūd—this being an elephant unparalleled in the whole earth for its size, stout body, and strength. The Najāshī accordingly dispatched it to him. [944]

Once the elephant had arrived, Abrahah set out with his army, accompanied by the king of Ḥimyar[575] and Nufayl b. Ḥabīb al-Khathʿamī. When he reached the Sacred Enclosure (*al-ḥaram*), he commanded his troops to raid the beasts of the local people. They captured some camels belonging to ʿAbd al-Muṭṭalib. It happened

573. *kāna yu'arriḍu lahu;* for *arraḍa,* see *Glossarium,* p. cxi. Here we have a variation from the man of the Banū Fuqaym who is responsible for the desecration of the church in Ibn Isḥāq's account given by al-Ṭabarī, I, 934, p. 218 above, and, since Nufayl is said at I, 937, p. 223 above, to have guided Abrahah to al-Ṭā'if, a confusion also. Al-Dīnawarī, *al-Akhbār al-ṭiwāl,* 62–63, has "a man from the people of al-Tihāmah" as the perpetrator of the deed.

574. The use here of the technical term *qiblah,* literally, "direction to be faced [in the Muslim worship]," is an anachronism.

575. The *malik Ḥimyar* must be Dhū Nafar, called at I, 936, p. 222 above, "one of the nobles of Ḥimyar."

that Nufayl was a friend of ʿAbd al-Muṭṭalib's, so the latter spoke to Nufayl about his camels. Nufayl, therefore, spoke to Abrahah, saying, "O king, there has come to you the lord of the Arabs, the most distinguished of them in status and the foremost of them in nobility—he gives people swift horses as mounts, bestows largesse, and feeds whatever the wind blows along." He brought him into Abrahah's presence, and the latter said [to ʿAbd al-Muṭṭalib], "What's your request?" ʿAbd al-Muṭṭalib replied, "That you should give me back my camels." Abrahah retorted, "I consider what I have just heard from you nothing but fraud. I had expected that you would speak to me about your House, which is your source of nobility and pride." But ʿAbd al-Muṭṭalib merely said, "Give me back my camels and do what you like with the House, for it has a lord who will protect it." So Abrahah ordered the camels to be returned to him.

When ʿAbd al-Muṭṭalib took possession of them, he draped the soles of sandals round their necks, marked them as intended sacrifices, offered them as gifts [to the Sacred Enclosure], and let them scatter throughout the sacred enclosure. [He did that] so that if anyone of them should be seized [by the Abyssinians], the lord of the Sacred Enclosure would thereby become angered.[576] ʿAbd al-Muṭṭalib, accompanied by ʿAmr b. ʿĀʾidh b. ʿImrān b. Makhzūm, Muṭʿim b. ʿAdī and Abū Masʿūd al-Thaqafī, went up to Mount Ḥirāʾ[577] and recited:

O God, a man defends his dwelling, so protect your dwelling
places and their people (*ḥilālak*).
Let not their cross and their cunning craft overcome Your
cunning craft on the morrow.

---

576. Qurʾān, V, 2, refers to the *qalāʾid*, necklets hung round the necks of animals destined for sacrifice, *budn*, part of the *shaʿāʾir Allāh* mentioned in XXII, 37/36. There is also reference in V, 102/103, to various types of camel, including the *sāʾibah*, the *waṣīlah* and the *ḥāmī*, left to roam freely after dedication to God. See Wellhausen, *Reste arabischen Heidentums*², 112ff.; *EI*², s.v. Baḥīra (A. J. Wensinck). Seizure by the Abyssinians of the camels released by ʿAbd al-Muṭṭalib would thus incur Allāh's wrath.

577. Ḥirāʾ or Ḥarāʾ was a mountain outside Mecca mentioned later in the *Sīrah* as a place where Muḥammad, in the period before his public ministry, would spend time in *taḥannuth*, pious and ascetic exercises. See Buhl, *Das Leben Muhammeds*, 132; Watt, *Muhammad at Mecca*, 40, 44; *EI*², s.v. Ḥirāʾ (T. H. Weir-W. M. Watt).

But if You do abandon them and our *qiblah,* then it may well
be something which seems best to You. [945]

He related: The birds flew in from the sea successively. Each bird had three stones, two in its claws and one in its beak. They hurled down the stones upon the Abyssinian troops, and everyone who was hit suffered either a severe wound or else that spot erupted into blisters and pustules. (That was the first time that smallpox and measles and bitter shrubs appeared [in the land].) Thus the stones snuffed them out completely, and God sent a torrential flow of water, which swept them all away and hurled them into the sea.[578] He related: Abrahah and the survivors who were with him took to flight. Abrahah's limbs began to drop off one by one. As for Maḥmūd, the Najāshī's elephant, it lay down and would not venture[579] into the Sacred Enclosure and was thus preserved in safety; but regarding the other elephant, it ventured into the Sacred Enclosure and it suffered a hail of stones.[580] It is also said that there were thirteen elephants. ʿAbd al-Muṭṭalib went down from Mount Ḥirāʾ and two of the Abyssinians came up to him, kissed his hand and said, "You were more knowledgeable [than us]."

There related to us Ibn Ḥumayd—Salamah—Ibn Isḥāq—Yaʿqūb b. ʿUtbah b. al-Mughīrah b. al-Akmas, who said that the first time measles and smallpox were seen in the land of the Arabs was in that year, as also the first tme for bitter shrubs like rue, colocynth, and gigantic swallow-wort[581] to be seen.

Ibn Isḥāq says: On Abrahah's death, there succeeded to power in Yemen over the Abyssinians his son Yaksūm b. Abrahah. Abrahah's patronymic[582] was from him. Ḥimyar and the tribes of the Arabs submitted, and the Abyssinians treated them oppressively,

578. That is, a *sayl,* the torrent from a sudden rainstorm, typical of the erratic weather conditions in the mountains in the western part of the Arabian Peninsula. In Arabic lore, the sweeping away of peoples by such inundations is not infrequent; cf. the *sayl al-ʿarim,* "bursting of the dam by a torrent," in Qurʾān, XXXIV, 15/16. See Lammens, *Le berceau de l'Islam,* 23–25.

579. *wa-lam yashjaʿ ʿalā . . . ;* for this verb, see *Glossarium,* p. CCCVI.

580. Following the text's *fa-ḥuṣiba;* one might also read *fa-ḥaṣaba* "and it suffered blisters and pustules," as taken by Nöldeke in his trans. 209.

581. That is, *Asclepias gigantea* L.

582. That is, Abū Yaksūm. According to Nöldeke, trans. 219 n. 3, there exists a coin minted by Yaksūm.

taking their women as sexual partners, killing their menfolk, and employing their sons as interpreters between themselves and the Arabs.[583] He related: After God hurled back the Abyssinians from Mecca, and the latter received the punishment described above, the Arabs treated Quraysh with great honor, saying, "[They are] the people of God; God fought on their behalf and relieved them of the burden of their enemies.

He related: On Yaksūm b. Abrahah's death, there succeeded to power in Yemen his brother Masrūq b. Abrahah. The burden of oppression on the people of Yemen became protracted. The Abyssinian dominion in Yemen extending from the time when
[946] Aryāṭ came to Yemen until the Persians killed Masrūq and expelled the Abyssinians from the land, was seventy-two years. During that period, four kings ruled there successively: Aryāṭ, then Abrahah, then Yaksūm b. Abrahah, and finally, Masrūq b. Abrahah.[584]

Sayf b. Dhī Yazan al-Ḥimyarī, whose patronymic was Abū Murrah, went forth until he reached the court of Qayṣar, king of al-Rūm.[585] He complained to Qayṣar about what they were suffer-

583. According to al-Dīnawarī, *al-Akhbār al-ṭiwāl*, 63, Yaksūm was worse and more malevolent than his father, and his brother Masrūq yet more so. Yaksūm's tenure of power is very summarily treated in Ibn Hishām, *Sīrat al-nabī*, ed. Wüstenfeld, 41 = ed. al-Saqqā et al., I, 63, tr. 30; see also idem, *Kitāb al-tījān*, 303, cf. Krenkow, "The Two Oldest Books on Arabic Folklore," 229.

584. The seventy-two years given here for the Abyssianian domination must be a considerable exaggeration, since this rule extended in reality only from 525 to ca. 570, i.e., forty-five years. In Abū al-Faraj al-Iṣfahānī, *Aghānī*[3], XVII, 311, the respective reigns of the Abyssinian governors are given: Aryāṭ, twenty years; Abrahah, twenty-three years; Yaksūm, nineteen years (thus also in al-Dīnawarī); Masrūq, twelve years; total, seventy-four years. Of these, that of Aryāṭ is much exaggerated; Abrahah was certainly still alive in 552, the date of the well of Muraygh̄an inscription, itself five years after his Dam of Mārib inscription. This would leave eighteen years at most for the combined reigns of Yaksūm and Masrūq. Cf. Nöldeke, trans. 220 n. 3.

585. Yazan was one of the great families of South Arabia, accounted one of the Mathāminah, influential in Ḥaḍramawt and known (as *Yz'n*) in inscriptions from the mid-fifth century A.D. onward. It appears that their original center was in the Wādī 'Amāqīn area near al-Ḥawṭah in what became in modern times the hinterland of al-Mukalla. The family or clan appears in early times in association with the ancient Sabaean family or clan of Gadan or Dhū Gadan. By the early sixth century, the Yazan probably dominated all the Ḥaḍramawt and the Ẓufār coastlands as well as the island of Socotra, whence their title of *Dhū* implying lordship. Members of the family served the last Tubba' Ma'dī Karib and then Dhū Nuwās as

ing, and asked hm to expel the Abyssinians and take over the rule there personally.[586] [He asked him to] send what forces he pleased of the Byzantines, and then the rule over Yemen would be his; but Qayṣar would not satisfy his plea, and he got none of the satisfaction he sought from Qayṣar.

So he set out again until he arrived at al-Nuʿmān b. al-Mundhir's court at al-Ḥīrah. Al-Nuʿmān was Kisrā's governor over al-Ḥīrah and adjacent parts of Iraq in the land of the Arabs.[587] Sayf b. Dhī Yazan now complained to al-Nuʿmān about the oppression and humiliation the people of Yemen were suffering. Al-Nuʿmān replied, "I have the obligation of paying a formal visit to Kisrā every year, so stay with me until the time for it comes round, and I will take you with me." He related: So he remained with al-Nuʿmān until the latter set off on his visit to Kisrā, accompanied by Sayf b. Dhī Yazan. When al-Nuʿmān came into Kisrā's presence and had completed his own business with the king, he mentioned to him Sayf b. Dhī Yazan and the reason for his coming to him, requesting an audience for him; Kisrā granted this. Kisrā was in his throne chamber (*aywān majlisihi*), where his crown was kept. This crown was like a huge grain measure (*qanqal*),[588] and set with rubies, emeralds, pearls, gold, and silver, and was suspended by a

---

military commanders, and it was perhaps the connection with the latter that led to a tradition, given by al-Dīnawarī, *al-Akhbār al-ṭiwāl*, 63, that Sayf b. Dhī Yazan was a descendant of Dhū Nuwās. Little is in fact known about Sayf, whose activities as leader of the "patriotic" reaction against the Abyssinians in 570 fall outside the period for which we have epigraphic evidence; his role in later Arabic popular epic literature has no known historical basis. See M. A. Bafaqih, "New Light on the Yazanite Dynasty," 5–6; *EI*², s.vv. Mathāmina (Chr. Robin), Sayf b. Dhī Yazan (J. P. Guillaume: entirely on the romance) and Yazan (A. F. L. Beeston).

586. The Byzantine emperor at this time was Justin II (r. 565–78). There is no record in Byzantine sources of this alleged embassy from South Arabia.

587. This is a patent confusion with the last Lakhmid, al-Nuʿmān III b. al-Mundhir IV (r. ca. 580–602); the ruler in al-Ḥīrah at this time must have been ʿAmr II b. al-Mundhir III (b. Hind) or his brother and successor Qābūs b. al-Mundhir III. See Rothstein, *Laḫmiden*, 96–105. In Ibn al-Kalbī's version of these events (al-Ṭabarī, I, 950, p. 242, cf. n. 596 below), the conjecture is expressed that it was ʿAmr b. Hind.

588. In al-Khwārazmī's *Mafātīḥ al-ʿulūm*, 67, the *qanqal* is a large measure of capacity used in Iraq and equalling three thousand *raṭl*s, i.e., two "equalised" *kurr*s, but the latter measure itself varied considerably even within the Sawād of Iraq. See Bosworth, "Abū ʿAbdallāh al-Khwārazmī on the Technical Terms of the Secretary's Art," 148–49.

golden chain from the top of the dome of that chamber. The crown was too heavy for his neck to bear, so he concealed himself in robes until he sat down on that throne; his head was inserted into the crown, and when he had settled down comfortably on his throne, the robes were whisked away from him. Everyone who saw him for the first time fell down on his knees out of awe for [947] him, hence Sayf b. Dhī Yazan sank down on his knees when he entered his presence.

Then he addressed Kisrā, "O king, ravens have seized control over our land," and when Kisrā asked him, "Which ravens, those from Abyssinia or those from Sind?"[589] he replied: "The Abyssinians, and I have come to you imploring help against them and for you to expel them from our midst. You can then assume the royal power in my land, for you are more loved by us than them." Kisrā retorted, "Your land is far away from our own one, and your land is poor in resources: nothing there but sheep and camels, which are no use to us. I am not prepared to commit a Persian army to the land of the Arabs; there is no good reason why I should do this." However, he ordered Sayf b. Dhī Yazan to be given ten thousand dirhams of full weight, and gave him a fine robe of honor. Sayf b. Dhī Yazan took the money, went forth, and began distributing it wholesale among the people, so that boys, slave boys, and slave girls seized it avidly. Very soon, this was reported to Kisrā, who was told, "The Arab to whom you gave a sum of money is scattering the dirhams among the people, and slave boys, boys, and slave girls are scrambling for them." Kisrā said, "There is something strange about this man, bring him back to me!" When Sayf b. Dhī Yazan came into his presence, Kisrā said, "This is what you do with a royal gift! You distribute it among the people?" Sayf b. Dhī Yazan responded, "And what exactly should I do with the king's gift, when the mountains of the land from which I have come are composed wholly of gold and silver?"[590] [He said this] in order to excite the emperor's cupidity, when the latter saw how little Sayf

589. Since the ancient Persians tended to classify all blacks as "Indians," a usage taken over by Greek and Syriac writers, there arose uncertainty over the geographical extent of "India," which could cover South Arabia and the Horn of Africa. Cf. Nöldeke, trans. 222 n. 2.

590. Sayf b. Dhī Yazan's boast reflects the ancients' belief that South Arabia was a land of famed wealth, with its precious metals, perfumes and aromatic substances, etc.

was concerned about the money. [He continued] "I have only made my way to the king that he might preserve me from tyranny and relieve me of humiliation." Kisrā said to him, "Remain here with me while I consider your case;" so he remained at Kisrā's court.

Kisrā assembled his Marzbāns and the sagacious advisers he was wont to consult, and said, "What do you think about this man and the proposition he has made?" One of them said, "O king, you have in your prisons various men whom you have incarcerated in [948] preparation for killing them. Why don't you send them back with Sayf? If they perish, well, that is the fate you ordained for them, and if they gain control of his land it will be an additional kingdom to your own." Kisrā exclaimed, "That's a good idea. Count for me how many men there are in my prisons." These men were counted up, and they found a total of eight hundred men in the prisons. Kisrā then ordered, "Find out the man among them with the best achievements and lineage, and make him the commander over them." They found that the best person qualified in these respects was Wahriz, who was a man of mature years.[591] Kisrā accordingly sent him with Sayf and appointed him commander of his troops.

---

591. In the Arabic sources, noble birth from various origins is attributed to Wahriz, e.g., in Ibn Hishām, *Sīrat al-nabī,* ed. Wüstenfeld, 43 = ed. al-Saqqā et al., I, 65, trans. 31, that he was of advanced age and of good, unspecified, family; in al-Dīnawarī, *al-Akhbār al-ṭiwāl,* 63–64, that he was a centenarian (!) and the son of Kānjār, of noble stock but imprisoned because he had taken to highway robbery; in al-Mas'ūdī, *Murūj,* III, 163 = § 1016, that he was the Ispabadh of Daylam; and in Ḥamzah al-Iṣfahānī, *Ta'rīkh,* 52, that he was from the progeny of Bihāfarīdūn, son of Sāsān, son of Bahman, son of Isfandiyār. It would be usual for the commander of an expedition to be of high rank and birth, but unlikely that his troops, if they had been rescued from incarceration and the threat of death, to have been of good stock also, as is asserted by a poet of Ḥaḍramawt cited by al-Mas'ūdī, op. cit., III, 164 = § 1017 (". . . from the clan of Sāsān and the clan of Mahrasan") and by Ḥamzah al-Iṣfahānī, loc. cit. Such claims to exalted origins were doubtless fabricated by or for the descendants of the Persians in Yemen, the so-called Abnā', the children of unions between Persians and Arabs in Yemen. Cf. Nöldeke, trans. 223 n. 2. But in any case, these reports from Ibn Isḥāq and Ibn al-Kalbī (for the latter report, see al-Ṭabarī, I, 952–53, pp. 244–45 below) that Yemen was conquered by a force of gaolbirds and desperadoes must be regarded as romantic accretions to the real story of the Persian expeditionary force to Yemen as mentioned at I, 899, p. 160 above: that Wahriz's force was composed of tough Daylamī mountaineers, recruited as mercenaries for the specific task, see n. 405 above.

Wahriz/Wahrīz is presumably MP *Weh-rēz,* "having a good abundance," see Justi, *Namenbuch,* 340. It seems, however, to have been in origin a title rather than a personal name; Procopius, describing an expedition sent by the emperor Kawād I into Georgia and Lazica, calls its commander a "Persian" named Boēs, who had the

He provided them with eight ships, each one carrying a hundred men plus equipment and supplies for the sea voyage. However, when they got out into the open sea, two of the ships foundered with everyone and everything in them. But six ships safely reached the coast of Yemen in the region of Aden, and these contained six hundred men, including Wahriz and Sayf b. Dhī Yazan. When they were safely on dry land in the land of Yemen, Wahriz said to Sayf, "What resources do you have?" Sayf replied, "As many Arab soldiers and Arab horses as you wish; I will put my leg on your leg [over this], so that we either die together or conquer together." Wahriz said, "You have spoken fairly and eloquently." Sayf now brought to Wahriz's standard those of his people who were in his obedience.

Masrūq b. Abrahah heard about their arrival. He assembled round himself the Abyssinian army and marched against them. The two armies moved close to each other and encamped in close proximity to each other. Wahriz now sent one of his sons called Nawzādh[592] with a cavalry detachment and instructed him, "Engage in skirmishing with the enemy army, so that we may get to know their mode of fighting." Nawzādh sallied forth and engaged in some skirmishing with them, but then got himself into a spot from which extrication was impossible, and the enemy killed him. This aroused Wahriz to a frenzy of rage and made him more determined to fight them. When the opposing troops were drawn
[949] up in ranks against each other, Wahriz said, "Point out their king for me." They replied, "Do you see a man on an elephant, with a crown on his head and a red ruby on his forehead?" He said, "Yes," and they retorted, "That's their king!" He said, "Leave him alone for the present," and they waited a long time. Then he said, "What's he riding?" They replied, "He has mounted a horse now." He said, "Leave him alone," and again they waited a long time. He said, "What's he riding now?" They replied, "He has mounted a mule now." Wahriz said, "A wild ass's filly! He is a weak individual, and so is his kingdom! Are you listening to me properly? I am going to shoot at him. If you observe his guards still standing

title Ourazēs, which would appear to be *Wahriz. See *EI*[2], s.vv. Daylam (V. Minorsky), and Wahriz (C. E. Bosworth).

592. That is, "the newborn." See Justi, *Namenbuch*, 227.

around and not moving, then stand fast until I give you the command [to advance], for I shall have missed him. But if you see the enemy troops crowding round him and sticking close to him, I shall have hit the man, so launch an attack on them!" Then he strung his bow (according to what has been asserted, none but Wahriz himself could bend it because of its strength). He ordered his eylids to be fastened up,[593] placed an arrow in his bow, braced the bow as widely as possible until, when it was fully extended, he released it. The arrow struck the ruby on Masrūq's forehead, and penetrated through his head, coming out at the nape of the neck. Masrūq was thrown backward from his mount, and the Abyssinians crowded round him closely. The Persians charged at them, and the Abyssinians were defeated. The Persians made great slaughter, and groups of the Abyssinians fled in all directions.[594] Wahriz advanced against Ṣanʿāʾ with the intention of entering it, but when he reached the city gate, he said, "My banner shall never enter [a town] lowered! Break down the gateway!" The gateway of Ṣanʿāʾ was accordingly demolished, and he then entered it with his banner raised high and borne in front of him.

Once he had secured dominion over Yemen and had expelled the Abyssinians from it, Wahriz wrote to Kisrā, "I have subdued Yemen for you and have driven out those Abyssinians who occupied it," and he forwarded to him wealth. Kisrā wrote back ordering him to set up Sayf b. Dhī Yazan as ruler of Yemen and its territories, and he imposed on Sayf the responsibility for the poll

---

593. That is, because the muscles of his eyelids were relaxed with old age and drooped over his eyes. A similar explanation is given for the name of a Persian commander in the fighting with the Arabs during the caliph ʿUmar I's reign, one Dhū al-Ḥājib ("the man with the eyelid") Mardānshāh; see al-Balādhurī, *Futūḥ*, 251. This seems to have been something of a topos in early Arabic, since a leader of the Banū ʿĀmir b. Ṣaʿṣaʿah at the late sixth-century "Day of Jabalah" (see *EI*², s.v. Djabala [F. Buhl-R. H. Headley]) is likewise said to have had his eyelids falling into his eyes. See *Naqāʾiḍ Jarīr wa-al-Farazdaq*, II, 657, 1062, and cf. Caskel, *Aijām al-ʿarab. Studien zur altarabischen Epik*, 36.

594. As noted by Nöldeke, trans. 226 n. 2, the story of Wahriz's battle with Masrūq is also given by Ibn Qutaybah, *ʿUyūn al-akhbār*, I, 149, from "the books of the Persians." In his account, Wahriz has drawn from his quiver an arrow of good omen with his wife's name inscribed on it, which he interprets as Persian *zanān*, "women," and then as the exhortation *zan ān*, "strike that [person]," hence he launches the arrow at Masrūq and kills him, as al-Ṭabarī relates. Cf. also Siddiqi, *Studien über die persischen Fremdwörter*, 81.

[950] tax and the land tax, which he was to send to Kisrā annually as fixed sums. He also ordered Wahriz to return to him, and Wahriz did this. Sayf b. Dhī Yazan was thus appointed as ruler over Yemen as his father Dhū Yazan, one of the kings of Yemen, had been [before him]. This is what Ibn Ḥumayd transmitted to us—Salamah—Ibn Isḥāq concerning the affairs of Ḥimyar, the Abyssinians and their rule, and Kisrā's dispatch of an expedition to attack the Abyssinians in Yemen.[595]

As for Hishām b. Muḥammad, he relates as follows. After Abrahah, there reigned Yaksūm and then Masrūq. He related: It was this last whom Wahriz killed in the reign of Kisrā, son of Qubādh, and then expelled the Abyssinians from Yemen. He related: Among what he related is that Abū Murrah al-Fayyāḍ Dhū Yazan was one of the nobles of Yemen. He had a wife Rayḥānah bt. Dhī Jadan, and she presented him with a boy, whom he called Ma'dī Karib. She was beautiful, hence al-Ashram took her away from Abū Murrah and forced her to marry him. Abū Murrah departed from Yemen and came to one of the kings of the house of al-Mundhir—I think it was 'Amr b. Hind[596]—and asked him to write on his behalf to Kisrā, asking him to tell Kisrā about his high worth, his nobility, and his aid and support for Kisrā in any affair in which he could help the emperor. [The ruler in question from the house of al-Mundhir] replied, "Don't act rashly; I am obliged to visit Kisrā each year, and the time for this is so-and-so." Hence Abū Murrah remained at his court until he accompanied the ruler on his visit to Kisrā. 'Amr b. Hind went into Kisrā's presence; he mentioned to him Dhū Yazan's nobility and lofty estate, and sought permission for him to have an audience of the emperor. Dhū Yazan went in, and 'Amr made space for Dhū Yazan to go before him. When Kisrā observed that, he realized that 'Amr could have treated Dhū Yazan thus in his presence only out of regard for his nobility. When Dhū Yazan went up to the emperor, the latter treated him kindly and questioned him in a friendly way, saying to

595. The story of Sayf b. Dhī Yazan's appeal to Kisrā and the Persian conquest of Yemen by Wahriz and his force is given by Ibn Hishām, *Sīrat al-nabī*, ed. Wüstenfeld, 41–45 = ed. al-Saqqā et al., I, 64–70, tr. 30–33; idem, *Kitāb al-tījān*, 306–309, cf. Krenkow, "The Two Oldest Books on Arabic Folklore," 229.

596. As noted in n. 587 above, Ibn al-Kalbī's conjecture here is probably correct.

him, "What has brought you here?" Dhū Yazan replied, "O king, the blacks have seized from us power over our own land, and have committed things so frightful that my respect for the king makes [951] me shrink from mentioning them. If the king were to offer us help without our having to ask for it [formally], that would be appropriate for him because of his excellence, nobility, and preeminence over the rest of monarchs; why should this not be so, when we have made our way toward him, full of expectations regarding him, hoping that God will smash our enemies, aid us against them, and procure for us revenge over them? If the king sees fit to make our speculations come true, fulfill our hopes and send back with me an army that will eject this enemy from our land so that he may add it to his own kingdom—for it is one of the most fertile of lands and most amply endowed with resources, not like the region of the Arabian peninsula bordering on his empire [at present]—he may do all this."

Kisrā replied. "I know well that your land is as you describe it; but which blacks are they who have conquered it, the Abyssinians or the Sindīs?" Dhū Yazan said, "The Abyssinians." Anūsharwān said, "I would certainly like to make your speculations come true, and would like to enable you to go back home with your request fulfilled; but the way to your land is difficult for the army, and I would not like rashly to commit my troops. But let me think about your request. Meanwhile, you can stay here with whatever you like." He ordered Dhū Yazan to be given suitable lodging and to be treated hospitably. He remained at Kisrā's court until he died. Abū Murrah had composed an ode in the Ḥimyaritic language in which he eulogised Kisrā. When it was translated for him, he was delighted with it.[597]

597. The South Arabian language had, in fact, been in steep decline long before this time, and the story of Abū Murrah being able to compose a poem in the "Ḥimyaritic language" must be apocryphal. Chr. Robin, basing himself on such indications as a perceptible decline in the quality and correctness of the Sabaean language in the later inscriptions, believes that it had yielded place, as a spoken tongue, to early (North) Arabic by the fourth century A.D. Hence after ca. 400 it was only a learned language, increasingly poorly known, although still used epigraphically for a further century and a half. The latest dated inscription so far discovered, CIH 325, comes from 669 of the Ḥimyarite era, hence A.D. 559–60, although some graffiti found in northern Yemen at Umm Laylā north of Ṣaʿdah, in North Arabic language and South Arabian script, probably date from the beginning

Rayḥānah bt. Dhī Jadan gave birth to a son of Abrahah al-Ashram's, whom he called Masrūq. Ma'dī Karib b. Dhī Yazan grew up with his mother Rayḥānah in Abrahah's house. One of Abrahah's sons satirized him, and said to him, "May God curse you! And may God curse your father!" Ma'dī Karib had never realized that al-Ashram was anyone but his own father. He went along to his mother and said to her, "Who is my father?" She replied, "Al-Ashram." He retorted, "No, by God, he is not my father; if he were really my father, so-and-so would not have satirized me." So she told him that his father was [in reality] Abū Murrah al-Fayyāḍ, and communicated to him the whole story. All this had a profound
[952] effect on the lad's mind, but he bided his time for a long period.

Then al-Ashram died, followed by the death of his son Yaksūm. Dhū Yazan's son set out, making for the king of the Byzantines' (*al-Rūm*) court, avoiding Kisrā because he had delayed so long in helping his father. But he did not get what he wanted from the king of the Byzantines, and found him taking the side of the Abyssinians because they shared a common religious allegiance. Hence he turned away from the Byzantine court and made for the court of Kisrā. He presented himself before Kisrā one day, when he was on horseback, and called out to him, "O king, my future heritage lies in your hands!" Kisrā summoned him when he had dismounted and asked him, "Who are you, and what is this heritage of yours?" Dhū Yazan's son replied, "I am the son of the senior chief (*shaykh*) of the Yemenis, Dhū Yazan, whom you promised to aid, but then [in the end] he died at your court and in your entourage. That promise is my rightful due, and a heritage which you have an obligation to fulfill for me." Kisrā relented toward him and ordered him to be given a sum of money. The lad went out and began to scatter the dirhams about, and the people scrambled for them. Kisrā sent a message to him, "What has led you to do what you have done?" The lad replied, "I didn't come to

---

of Islam. See Robin, "Résultats épigraphiques et archéologiques de deux brefs séjours en République arabe du Yémen," 188–93.

In the fourth/tenth century, al-Ḥasan al-Hamdānī was able in his *Iklīl*, Book VIII, 122–23, tr. 72–73, to give the values of the letters of the South Arabian script (*musnad*), but was only able with difficulty to read a few names of the inscriptions. See Robin, *L'Arabie antique de Karib'īl à Mahomet*, 15, 19–20, 134–35; idem, in *Supplément au dictionnaire de la Bible*, s.v. Sheba. II, cols. 1216–17.

you seeking money, but rather, I came to you seeking men and that you should preserve me from humiliation." Kisrā was pleased with this rejoinder and sent back a message to him, "Stay here while I look into your case."

Kisrā then sought counsel from his ministers concerning sending an army back with him. The [Chief] Mōbadh said to him, "This lad has a just claim upon us, through his journey here and the death of his father at the king's court and in his entourage, and because of the promises made by the king to him previously. Now in the king's prisons are men of valor and martial strength. Let the king send these men with Dhū Yazan's son; if they secure a victory, it will be a triumph for the king; if they all perish, he will have secured his own peace of mind [from the threat of them] and will have relieved the citizens of the kingdom of them. That would not be far from the correct line of action." Kisrā said, "This is a sound piece of advice," and he gave orders for the men of this description in the prisons to be counted. They extended to eight hundred men. He appointed as commander over them a com- [953]
mander from among his cavalrymen (*asāwiratihi*) called Wahriz, whom Kisrā accounted the equal of a thousand cavalrymen. He supplied them with weapons and equipment and ordered them to be transported in eight ships, each one containing a hundred men.

They set forth on the seas, but two ships out of the eight foundered, leaving six safe and sound. They landed on the coast of Ḥaḍramawt.[598] Masrūq marched out against them with an army of one hundred thousand men, including Abyssinians, Ḥimyarites, and Bedouins. [However,] a considerable number of people joined the son of Dhū Yazan. Wahriz encamped on the sea coast, placing the sea at his back. When Masrūq saw how few were their numbers, he became eager to engage them. He sent a mes-

598. It seems likely that the ships, buffeted by storms, would come up on the Ḥaḍramawt coast, and apparently the landing was in the vicinity of al-Shiḥr. The Ḥaḍramī poet cited by al-Mas'ūdī, *Murūj*, III, 164 = § 1017, says that the ships were washed up at *M.th.w.b*, read by Pellat as Mathwab but read by Nöldeke, trans. 230 n. 2, as Manūb. A Manūb cerainly existed in Ḥaḍramawt in Islamic times, and it is mentioned by al-Hamdānī, *Ṣifat jazīrat al-'Arab*, 172 and n. 2, 215, but described by him as a wadi with villages in the territory of Kindah and in the Shibām/al-Qārah region, i.e., well inland and away from the coast. Al-Bakrī's listing of Manūb, in his *Mu'jam mā ista'jam*, I, 316–17, IV, 1273, is vague and unhelpful.

sage to Wahriz, "What has brought you here? You have only the [few] men whom I can see, while I have [the large number] whom you can see. You have recklessly put yourself and your followers at risk, but if you like, I will allow you to return to your homeland; I shall not hurl satires at you, nor will there be inflicted upon you any unpleasant action on my part or on that of my troops. Or if you wish, I will march out against you immediately. Or yet again, if you wish, I will allow you a period of respite (*ajal*) so that you may consider your position and take counsel with your followers." Wahriz realized how strong they were and perceived that he could not match their strength. So he sent to Masrūq the message, "All right, grant a period of respite for us both; give me an engagement and compact, and receive in return the same promises from me, that neither side should fight with the other until the period of truce is up and until we can see our [correct] course of action." Masrūq agreed to that.

Each side remained within its encampment. Then, when ten days had elapsed of the standstill in hostilities, Wahriz's son set off on one of his horses and went forward until he drew near to the enemy's encampment. But his horse carried him onward into the midst of their encampment, and they killed him, Wahriz being unaware of all this. When the news of the killing of his son reached him, he sent a message to Masrūq, "There has been, as you well know, a compact between us, so why did you kill my son?" Masrūq sent a message back, "Your son charged into the
[954] midst of our encampment, and some irresponsible elements of our army sprang up and killed him. I myself strongly disapprove of his killing." Wahriz said to the messenger, "Tell him that he was not my son, but only the son of a whore (*zāniyah*); if he had been my son, he would have patiently waited and not broken the truce between us until it had come to an end."[599] Then he ordered the corpse to be thrown down on to the ground, where his body could be seen, and he swore an oath that he would not drink wine nor

599. Nöldeke, trans. 232 n. 1, explained that Wahriz disowns his son and refuses any responsibility for him because he does not wish to have to accept blood money for him from the Abyssinians; the blood money will be their own blood. Also, the killing of the Persian, though half-justified, will incur divine retribution for the breach of the oath-protected truce.

rub his head with any scented oil until the truce should come to its end.

When there was just one day left of the truce, Wahriz gave orders for the ships in which they had sailed to be set on fire, and likewise with regard to all superfluous clothing they had with them, leaving his men only with what they had on their backs. Next, he ordered all their provisions to be brought out and instructed his men, "Eat up this food!" So they ate up [as much as they could]. When they had finished, he ordered what remained to be thrown in the sea. At that point, he stood up in their midst and made a speech, saying to them, "Regarding the ships of yours which I caused to be burned, I wanted you to realize that there is no way for you ever to return home. Concerning your clothing which I had burned, it was arousing my ire that, should the Abyssinians gain the victory over you, it should fall into their hands. As for your food which I caused to be thrown into the sea, I would not wish any of you to have food for himself to exist on for a single day [if we should be defeated]. If you are people who will fight alongside me and endure the heat of battle, let me know this now; but if you will not do this, I shall fall upon this sword of mine until it comes out of my back, for I have no mind ever to let the Abyssinians gain power over me alive. So consider you own position now, since I, your commander, have chosen this course for myself." They responded, "Indeed, we will fight alongside you, until either we are dead to the last man or we are victorious!"

On the morn of the day when the truce ended, Wahriz arranged his troops for the fight, with the sea at their rear. He went up to [955] them and exhorted them forcefully to remain steadfast in battle, and told them that they had two possible ways forward: either to be victorious over their enemy or to die gloriously. He ordered them to have their bows bent and strung, and said, "When I give you the order to shoot, let fly at them swiftly with a five-arrow volley (*bi-al-banjakān*)."[600] The people of Yemen had never seen

600. This seems to be the meaning here, since Persian *panj*, "five," is clearly an element of the word, presumably *panjagān*, "five-fold," in origin. It is presumably related to the *banjakiyyah* of al-Jawālīqī, *al-Mu'arrab*, 71: a volley of five arrows, mentioned in a context which speaks of the Khurāsānians. Siddiqi, *Studien über die persischen Fremdwörter*, 81 n. 7, less plausibly interprets *banjakān* as referring to five-pointed or five-barbed arrows ("fünfzackige [Pfeile]").

war arrows before this occasion. Masrūq advanced with a host that appeared limitless, on an elephant, wearing a crown on his head and with a ruby the size of an egg on his forehead; he could not conceive the possibility of anything except victory. Wahriz's sight had become poor through old age, and he said, "Show me their leader." He was informed, "It's the man on the elephant," but then very soon afterward Masrūq got down from the elephant and mounted a horse. So they exclaimed, "He's now mounted a horse." Wahriz said, "Prop open my eyelids"—they had fallen down over his eyes on account of his age[601]—so they held them up with a bandage. He then took out an arrow, placed it in the center (*kabid*)[602] of his bow and said, "Point out for me Masrūq." They did that for him, until Wahriz was sure of him, and then he gave the order "Shoot!" He himself pulled on his bow until, when he had drawn it to its utmost, he released the arrow. It sped forward as if it were a tightly stretched rope, and struck Masrūq's forehead. He fell from his mount. A great number of men were killed by that rain of arrows. When they saw their commander felled to the ground, their front rank crumbled, and there was nothing for it but flight.

Wahriz immediately gave orders for the burial of his son's corpse, and ordered that Masrūq's corpse be thrown down in its place. Booty was found in the defeated army's encampment in quantities beyond measure and beyond enumeration. Each individual Persian cavalryman got fifty or sixty Abyssinians, Ḥimyarites, or Bedouin as captives, and drove them along, unresisting, before him in bonds. Wahriz said, "Leave the Ḥimyarites and Bedouin alone, just hunt down the blacks and don't leave a single one alive." The Abyssinians were massacred on that day
[956] until not a single one of their host remained. A Bedouin managed to flee on his camel and galloped onward day and night. Then he happened to turn round and saw an arrow stuck in his provision bag behind the saddle. He exclaimed, "The devil take it! (literally, "Woe to your mother!")—has it traversed such a wide distance or

601. See al-Ṭabarī, I, 949, p. 241 above.
602. For the technical term *kabid al-qaws* (*kabid*, literally "liver" "center, heart of a thing"), see J. D. Latham and W. F. Paterson, *Saracen Archery*, 161, 184: exactly, "the point the arrow passes when shot," i.e., the arrow pass.

traveled so far!" He thought that the arrow had caught up with him!

Wahriz advanced until he entered Ṣan'ā' and reduced to submission the whole land of Yemen. He sent out governors to the provincial districts (*makhālīf*). Abū al-Ṣalt, the father of Umayyah b. Abī al-Ṣalt al-Thaqafī,[603] says concerning the son of Dhū Yazan, his adventures, and those of Wahriz and the Persians, the following verses:

Let those who are like the son of Dhū Yazan seek vengeance, a man who spent several years traveling across the seas on account of his enemies.
He came to Heraclius, at a time when his enemies were already falling into discord and perturbation, but he did not secure from him any part of what he sought.
Then after seven years he turned toward Kisrā; how far away did you have to travel!
Until at last he brought with him the Free Ones (*Banū al-Aḥrār*, i.e., the Persians),[604] whom he bore along; by my life, you spent long in strenuous activity!

---

603. Ibn Hishām's scholion to Ibn Isḥāq's text here, *Sīrat al-nabī*, ed. Wüstenfeld, 44 = ed. al-Saqqā et al., I, 67–68, tr. 698, states that some authorities ascribe the poetry to the son Umayyah, who was a contemporary of the Prophet but, on account of the links between al-Ṭā'if and Quraysh, was a supporter of Muḥammad's opponents; he seems to have been dead by the time of the *fatḥ*, the conquest of Mecca, in 8/630. See *Sharḥ dīwān Umayyah*, 65; al-Ḥadīthī, *Umayyah b. Abī al-Ṣalt, ḥayātuhu wa-shi'ruhu*, 344 n. 158; Blachère, *Histoire de la littérature arabe*, II, 304–306; Sezgin, *GAS*, II, 298–300, IX, 277; *EI*², s.v. Umayya b. Abi 'l-Ṣalt (J. E. Montgomery).

Ibn Hishām's text has for the name *Hiraql* in v. 2 the more general *Qayṣar*, "emperor," and if this is the older and better reading, it would point to the poem's being either contemporaneous with the events described or at least written not long afterward, by Abū al-Ṣalt rather than by his son Umayyah. If the reading *Hiraql* should be correct, then the poem would date from at least one or two generations after the events, since Heraclius reigned 610–41, The reading *Hiraql* would certainly appear to predate al-Ṭabarī, since it is the one found in the *Kitāb al-shi'r wa-al-shu'arā'*, 281, of Ibn Qutaybah (d. 276/889), repeated also in al-Azraqī, *Akhbār Makkah*, 99.

604. *Banū al-aḥrār* is a frequent designation in early Arabic usage for the Persians encountered by them along the borders of Iraq and during the conquest of Iraq and Persia, e.g., at the engagements of Dhū Qār (see al-Ṭabarī, I, 1036, p. 367 below) and al-Qādisiyyah. We find the equivalent *eleutheroi* used by Josephus for the Parthians as the equivalent of the social-military Persian term underlaying the Arabic expression, i.e., *āzādhagān* (in origin, Avestan *āzāta*-"agnate, born into a clan" "freeman (as opposed to a slave)" and, in a narrower sense, "noble," "free"),

Who is like Kisrā, the supreme king (*shahanshāh*) over the
dependent kings, or like Wahriz on the day of the army,
when he attacked furiously!
What a remarkable band went forth! You will never see among
men their likes again!
Outstanding warriors, noble chiefs, gleaming ones, marzbāns,
[957] lions who train their cubs in the thickets,
Who shoot from highly bent bows, as if they were camel
saddles, with long, slim arrows which bring the one who is
hit to a speedy death.
You loosed lions against black dogs, and their scattered
fugitives have spread through the land in full flight.
So drink with full peace of mind, wearing your crown and
reclining high on Ghumdān in a house which you have
made [once more] frequented.
Indulge freely in the use of musk, for they (i.e., your enemies)
are in complete disarray, and on this day let your two
luxurious robes trail freely!
These are noble deeds! Not two wooden bowls of milk mingled
with water, which subsequently turned to urine.[605]

---

i.e., noble ones," the class of great and lesser landowners, i.e., aristocrats and gentry, who supplied the military commanders and the élite cavalrymen of the army and upon whom the Persian kings had depended since Achaemenid times. De Blois has suggested that the expression *Banū al-aḥrār*, with its apparently otiose use of the component *banū*, reflects Aramaic usage and that the Arabs may have adopted it from Aramaic-speaking population of the Sāsānid empire in Mesopotamia. See Nöldeke, trans. 235 n. 2; De Blois, "'Freemen' and 'Nobles' in Iranian and Semitic Languages," 5–15; *EIr*, s.v. Aḥrār or Banu 'l-Aḥrār (C. E. Bosworth); and cf. n. 258 above.

605. This last verse has the ring of a proverbial saying. According to the scholion of Ibn Hishām, *Sīrat al-nabī*, ed. Wüstenfeld, 44 = ed. al-Saqqā et al., I, 68–69, tr. 698, the poem was correctly transmitted by Ibn Isḥāq except for the last verse, actually by the *mukhaḍram* poet and Companion of the Prophet al-Nābighah al-Ja'dī (died toward the end of the seventh century?), on whom see Blachère, *Histoire de la littérature arabe*, III, 477–79; Sezgin, *GAS*, II, 245–47, IX, 274; *EI*², s.v al-Nābigha al-Dja'dī (A. Arazi).

For other sources on Sayf b. Dhī Yazan's appeal for help and Khusraw Anusharwān's despatch of Wahriz and his army, see al-Ya'qūbī, *Ta'rīkh*, I, 187, 226–27; al-Dīnawarī, *al-Akhbār al-ṭiwāl*, 64; Ḥamzah al-Iṣfahānī, *Ta'rīkh*, 52–53, 114–15; Abū al-Faraj al-Iṣfahānī, *Aghānī*³, XVII, 308–13; al-Azraqī, *Akhbār Makkah*, 98–99. See also Christensen, *Sassanides*, 368–69, 373; Frye, "The Political History of Iran under the Sasanians," 158; Bosworth, "Iran and the Arabs before Islam," 606–607. Two further verses of the poem are given by al-Azraqī and Nashwān al-

The story returns to the narrative of Ibn Isḥāq.

He related: Wahriz went back to Kisrā, having appointed Sayf as king of Yemen. The latter now fell upon the Abyssinians and began to kill them, ripping open the pregnant womenfolk to tear out the fetuses, until he had exterminated the Abyssinians, apart from an insignificant, wretched few whom he took into his service as slaves. Some of these he employed as runners to go before him with their spears. Sayf carried on thus only for a short while before he went forth one day, with the Abyssinians running before him with their spears, until suddenly he found himself surrounded by them, and they attacked him with their spears, killing him. One of the Abyssinians assumed power over them, and carried out a policy of killing the Yemenis, creating havoc and wreaking all manner of evil. When news of this reached Kisrā, he dispatched Wahriz against them with four thousand Persian troops and ordered him not to leave alive in Yemen a single black, nor the child of an Arab woman by a black, whether young or old, nor to leave alive a single man with crisp and curly hair in whose generation the blacks had been involved. Wahriz advanced until he entered [958] Yemen, and did all that, killing every Abyssinian he could find. Then he wrote to Kisrā informing him of what he had done. Kisrā appointed him as viceroy over Yemen. He ruled over it, and levied taxation on it for Kisrā until he died.[606]

After him, Kisrā made his son al-Marzubān, son of Wahriz, viceroy, who governed the land until he died. Then Kisrā appointed al-

---

Ḥimyarī; see Nöldeke, trans. 235 nn. 4–5.

Frye, loc. cit., makes the point that, by the time of the invasion, the pro-Byzantine attitude of the Monophysite Christians in South Arabia, so decisive at the time of the Najrān persecutions and the first Abyssinian intervention in Yemen, changed (i.e., by 570). But in fact, Justin continued his predecessors' policy of tolerance toward religious dissidents during the first five or six years of his reign, and only in 572, i.e., after the Persians had appeared in Yemen, did he start to persecute the Samaritans and Christian Monophysite dissidents under the influence of the Chalcedonian Patriarch of Constantinople, John Sirimis. See Bury, *A History of the Later Roman Empire from Arcadius to Irene,* II, 76.

606. According to al-Dīnawarī, *al-Akhbār al-ṭiwāl,* 64, Wahriz governed Yemen for five years. On his deathbed, he shot an arrow, which fell at the spot where his tomb was to be; "to this day," says the historian, "the place is called the *maqbarat Wahriz.*" This same tale is given later by al-Ṭabarī, I, 988, p. 294 below, as part of Ibn al-Kalbī's narrative.

Bīnajān (?), son of al-Marzubān,[607] son of Wahriz, until he also died. Then Kisrā[608] appointed after him Khurrakhusrah, son of al-Bīnajān, son of al-Marzubān, son of Wahriz. The latter governed Yemen, but then Kisrā grew angry with him and swore that the Yemenis should bring Khurrakhusrah to him at his court borne on their shoulders. This they did. When Khurrakhusrah came before Kisrā, one of the Persian great men went right up to him and laid across him a sword that belonged to Kisrā's father. Kisrā therefore granted him security from being killed, but dismissed him from his post and sent Bādhān[609] to Yemen [as governor] instead. Bādhān remained in that office until the time when God sent His Messenger Muḥammad.[610]

## *[Resumption of the History of Kisrā Anūsharwān]*

It is related that there was a peace accord and a truce between Kisrā Anūsharwān and Yakhṭiyānūs (Justinian), king Byzantines. Discord and emnity arose between a man of the Arabs called Khālid b. Jabalah,[611] whom Yakhṭiyānūs had appointed over the

607. In Ibn al-Kalbī's version of these events, i.e., in al-Ṭabarī, I, 988, p. 294, and cf. n. 693 below, al-Marzubān appears as *al-M.r.w.zān*, a better reading, probably to be vocalized as al-Marūzān. Likewise, al-Bīnajān appears as *Z.y.n*, perhaps for *W.y.n*, according to the suggestion of Marquart in *Addenda et emendanda*, p. DXCII, whereas Nöldeke thought it more likely that this consonant ductus contained the names of two persons, *W.y.n* and *W.y.n.jān*. But in the version of Ibn Isḥāq at I, 958 n. *d*, Nöldeke adduced the name of a commander mentioned by the contemporary Byzantine historian Menander Protector, one Binganēs.

608. The Kisrā in question must be, of course, Khusraw II Abarwēz (r. 591–628).

609. Perhaps originally Bādhām, in which case the etymology would be presumably from *bādām*, "almond." The name is in fact attested in Middle Persian as *w'd'm*. See Justi, *Namenbuch*, 56, connecting it with NP *bād*, Avestan *vāta-*, the spirit of the wind; Gignoux, *Noms propres sassanides*, no. 914; *EI*² Suppl., s.v. Bādhām, Bādhān (C. E. Bosworth).

610. This marks the end of this extended section on the history of Yemen, and the narrative now resumes from Persian sources as a parallel to that already given by al-Ṭabarī at I, 898–99, pp. 157–59 above.

611. That is, the Jafnid/Ghassānid ruler, the greatest of his line, correctly, al-Ḥārith b. Jabalah or Arethas (r. 529–69). (Nöldeke, trans. 238 nn. 2–3, pointed out that al-Ṭabarī's form Khālid arises from the ambiguities of the Pahlavi script, as does the *kh* for *st* in Yakhṭiyānūs = Justinian, showing that al-Ṭabarī's ultimate source here must have been a Persian one.) Al-Ḥārith was a redoubtable *foederatus* or ally of the Byzantines, stemming as he did from a fervently Christian, albeit Monophysite, Arab family. He fought at the side of the Greeks in two major wars,

Arabs of Syria, and a man from Lakhm called al-Mundhir b. al-Nu'mān,[612] whom Kisrā had appointed over the lands extending from 'Umān, al-Baḥrayn and al-Yamāmah to al-Ṭā'if and the rest of Ḥijāz and all the Arabs of the intervening lands. Khālid b. Jabalah raided al-Mundhir's territory and wrought great slaughter among his subjects and seized as plunder extensive lands of his. Al-Mundhir laid a complaint about this before Kisrā, and asked him to write to the king of the Byzantines requesting the latter to secure justice for him against Khālid. Kisrā therefore wrote to [959] Yakhṭiyānūs mentioning the agreement regarding the truce and peace between the two sides and informing him of what al-Mundhir, his governor over the Arabs [within the Persian sphere of influence], had suffered at the hands of Khālid b. Jabalah, whom Yakhṭiyānūs had appointed governor over the Arabs within his dominions. He further asked him to command Khālid to return all the plunder he had driven off from al-Mundhir's territory and lands and [to command Khālid] to hand over the blood price for the Arabs whom he had killed and who were in al-Mundhir's jurisdiction and to furnish justice to al-Mundhir against Khālid. Yakhṭiyānūs was not to treat what Kisrā had written lightheartedly and contemptuously; [if he were to do so, ] then this would be the cause of the rupturing of the agreement and truce between them. Kisrā sent a stream of letters to Yakhṭiyānūs urging him to furnish justice to al-Mundhir, but Yakhṭiyānūs paid no heed.

Hence Kisrā got ready his forces and led an expedition of some ninety thousand warriors against Yakhṭiyānūs's lands.[613] He cap-

including at the battle of Callinicum (the Arabic al-Raqqah) in 531, and himself defeated and in 554 killed the Lakhmid al-Mundhir III at the battle of al-Ḥiyār at Chalcis (the Arabic Qinnasrīn) (possibly the *yawm Ḥalīmah*—Ḥalīmah being al-Ḥārith's daughter—of the Arabic *ayyām al-'Arab* literature), a decisive victory not merely as an intra-Arab clash but an event which gave the Ghassānids the preponderance over the Lakhmids for a long time to come. See on al-Ḥārith and the battle of Chalcis, Nöldeke, *Die Ghassânidische Fürsten*, 17–19; Rothstein, *Laḫmiden*, 83–87; Shahîd, *Byzantium and the Arabs in the Sixth Century*, I/1, 63–82, 134ff., 236–66; *EI*², s.vv. Ghassān and al-Ḥārith b. Djabala (I. Shahîd).

612. That is, al-Mundhir III, who played this leading rôle in the extension of Persian power into eastern and central Arabia and, indeed, as far as Ḥijāz. See nn. 409, 563 above.

613. This is the renewed, second war of the Persian emperor with Justinian, spanning 540–45, with the campaign against Antioch already described at I, 898, p. 157 and nn. 398–99 above. The events in question form the very detailed narrative

tured by force of arms the towns of Dārā, al-Ruhā (Edessa), Manbij, Qinnasrīn, Aleppo, Antioch (which was the finest town in Syria), Fāmiyah (Apamea), Ḥimṣ (Homs), and numerous other towns in the neighborhood of these towns;[614] he appropriated all the wealth (or: beasts, *al-amwāl*) and moveable goods in them; and he took captive all the inhabitants of Antioch, deported them to the Sawād, and gave orders for a town to be built for them at the side of Ctesiphon exactly on the pattern of the original Antioch, as I have already mentioned previously. He resettled the people of Antioch there; this is the town called al-Rūmiyyah. He erected this district into an administrative division (*kūrah*), which was to comprise four subdistricts (*ṭassūj*s): that of Upper Nahrawān, that of Lower Nahrawān, that of Bādarāyā, and that of Bākusāyā.[615] He allotted

---

of Procopius in the later part of Book I and then Book II of *The Persian War,* in which the historian highlights the deeds of the general Belisarius, first appointed *Magister Militum per Orientem* in 529 and whom Procopius himself served as *symboulos,* i.e., as legal adviser and secretary. See Cameron, *Procopius and the Sixth Century,* 8, 157–70.

614. Of these towns of Upper Jazīrah and northern and central Syria, Nöldeke, trans. 239 n. 2 noted that Aleppo, Antioch, and Apamea (situated on the Orontes, to the northwest of Ḥamāt: see Yāqūt, *Buldān,* I, 227; Le Strange, *Palestine,* 384–85; *EI*², s.v. Afāmiya [H. A. R. Gibb]) were conquered by the force of Persian arms, while Daras/Dārā (see for this n. 398 above), Edessa, Manbij (the classical Hierapolis, an important military post commanding crossings of the upper Euphrates: see Yāqūt, op. cit., V, 205–207; Le Strange, op. cit., 107; *EI*², s.v. Manbidj [N. Elisséff]), and Qinnasrīn (the classical Chalcis to the south of Aleppo: see Yāqūt, op. cit., IV, 403–404; Le Strange, *Palestine,* 486–87; *EI*², s.v. Ḳinnasrīn [Elisséff]) purchased their safety from the Persians by handing over substantial indemnities. Emesa or Ḥimṣ also suffered badly.

615. Nahrawān was the district containing an extensive canal system to the east of the Tigris and in the region of the lower Diyālā river, with its center at the town of Nahrawān, which lay to the northeast of where the later Baghdad was to be situated. The canal system doubtless dates in some form from ancient times, but Khusraw Anūsharwān developed it extensively and caused to be dug a lengthy feeder channel, al-Qāṭūl al-Kisrawī, "the Imperial cut," from the Tigris near the later Sāmarrā to the Diyālā below Ba'qūbā. At various places, there were *shādhurwāns* or weirs (see for these, n. 94 above) dating from Sāsānid times. The *kūrah* mentioned here was one created with the city of Weh-Antioch-i Khusraw/Rūmiyyah where the people deported from Antioch in Syria were settled ca. 540. The Arabic sources actually list five *ṭassūj*s of the Nahrawān *kūrah,* the additional one being that of Middle Nahrawān. Bādarāyā and Bākusāyā (Aramaic Bēth Darāyā and Bēth Kosāyā) formed the region of Bandanījīn, stretching from the east of Nahrawān to the fringes of the Zagros range and the border with the province of Media or Jibāl. See Yāqūt, *Buldān,* I, 317–18, 327, V, 324–27; Le Strange, *Lands,* 57–61; Fiey, *Assyrie chrétienne,* III, 245–49; Morony, *Iraq after the Muslim Con-*

living allowances for the people whom he had transported from Antioch to al-Rūmiyyah, and appointed as overseer of their affairs [960] a man from the Christian community of Ahwāz called Barāz,[616] whom he had earlier made head of the the artisans and craftsemen working for him. This Kisrā did out of tenderness and sympathy for those captives, and also with the administrative aim of causing them to feel at home with Barāz, because he was their coreligionist, and making them regard him with trust. As for the remainder of the towns of Syria and Egypt,[617] Yakhṭiyānūs bought Kisrā off from them with a very large sum, which he handed over to the Persian king, and he undertook to pay ransom money to him each year in return for Kisrā's undertaking not to raid his lands. He wrote for Kisrā a document enshrining these terms, which he and the Byzantine great men of state sealed officially. They accordingly paid this sum annually.[618]

The rulers of Persia before Kisrā Anūsharwān used to levy land tax (*kharāj*) on the administrative divisions (*kuwar*), a third or quarter or fifth or sixth [of their produce], according to the water supply and the degree of cultivation; and poll tax (*jizyat al-jamājim*) according to a fixed sum.[619] King Qubādh, son of Fayrūz

---

*quest*, 138–40; *EI*², s.vv. Badra (S. H. Longrigg) and al-Nahrawān (M. J. Morony).

616. As explained in n. 393 above, this is the New Persian form of MP Warāz, etc., meaning literally "boar, wild boar," an animal admired for its strength and tenacity; see on it the references in that note.

617. Again, as in al-Ṭabarī, I, 898, p. 158 above, a confusion with the campaign early in the seventh century of Khusraw II Abarwēz.

618. Nöldeke, trans. 240 n. 4, noted that al-Dīnawarī, *al-Akhbār al-ṭiwāl*, 69, names a certain Sharwīn of Dastabā as *wakīl* or overseer of payment of the tribute, but that there is uncertainty in other sources regarding this personage.

619. Since *jumjumah* means "skull," its plural use in *jizyat al-jamājimah* conveys literally the idea of a poll tax. Al-Khwārazmī, *Mafātīḥ al-ʿulūm*, 58, equates *māl al-jamājim* with *māl al-jawālī*, that money paid in the first place by non-Muslims expelled from the Arabian peninsula by the caliph ʿUmar I but then applied to all Dhimmīs, "Protected peoples," liable to poll tax, whether émigrés or not; see Bosworth, "Abū ʿAbdallāh al-Khwārazmī on the Technical Terms of the Secretary's Art," 132. It has been known for some time, including from Talmudic references to it, that the Sāsānids levied a poll tax (the *kargā, kərāgā*) as well as a land tax (*ṭasqā*) and a further land tax (*mənātā də malkā*, "the king's share"; different from the *ṭasqā*?), but much remains obscure about this fiscal system. See Grignaschi, "La riforma tributaria di Ḫosrō I e il feudalesimo sassanide," 113–15; Rubin, "The Reforms of Khusro Anūshirwān," 231–32). Whether there was any continuity between this Sāsānid poll tax and the early Islamic *jizyah* on the Dhimmīs, is unclear; it may have been just one among several contributory strands in

ordered, toward the end of his reign, a cadastral survey (*masḥ al-arḍ*), comprising plains and mountains alike, so that the correct amount of land tax could be levied on the lands.[620] This was carried out, except that Qubādh's death supervened before that survey could be completed. Hence when his son Kisrā succeeded to power, he gave orders for it to be carried through to its end and for an enumeration to be made of date palms, olive trees, and heads (i.e., of those liable to the poll tax). He then ordered his secretaries to calculate the grand total of that, and he issued a general summons to the people. He commanded the secretary responsible for the land tax to read out to them the total tax liabilities from the land and the numbers of date palms, olive trees, and heads. The secretary read all this out to them, after which Kisrā said to them, "We have judged it advisable to establish the rates of taxation (*waḍā'i'*) on the basis of what has been enumerated of the various *jarīb*s of this cadastral survey[621]—date palms, olive trees, and heads—and we ordain that the taxation
[961] should be paid in installments spread over the year, in three installments. In this way, sums of money will be stored in our treasuries so that, should any emergency arise along one of our vulnerable frontiers or on any one of our distant boundaries, a breach of the borders or anything else untoward, and we have a need to deal with it and to nip it in the bud, involving the expenditure of money on this, we shall have money stored up here, ready and to

---

the emergence of this Islamic tax. See Nöldeke, trans. 241 n. 1; Løkkegaard, *Islamic Taxation in the Classic Period,* 15, 132, 141.

620. Such surveys were frequently used by later, Islamic rulers as the bases for new tax assessments, involving the assessment of growing crops (*takhmīn*) and the sharing out of the harvested crop between the tax collector and the cultivator (*muqāsamah*), the technique of surveying being called *misāḥah.* See *EI*², s.vv. Ḳānūn. ii. Cadaster (Cl. Cahen), Kharādj. I. In the Central and Western Islamic Lands (Cahen) and Misāḥa. 1. In the Central Islamic Lands (C. E. Bosworth).

621. Al-Khwārazmī, *Mafātīḥ al-'ulūm,* 66, 67, tr. in Bosworth, "Abū 'Abdallāh al-Khwārazmī on the Technical Terms of the Secretary's Art," 148–49, states that the *jarīb* was a measurement of surface area equaling thirty-six hundred square *dhirā'*s or cubits, although of a fluctuating equivalence in Khurāsān. The *jarīb* was, in fact, the basic measurement for area in early Islamic times, still in use today in Persia, officially equaling one hectare, as well as being a measure of capacity for grain, etc.; but in origin it was the amount of agricultural land which could be sown with a *jarīb*'s measure of grain. See Nöldeke, trans. 242 n. 2; *EI*², s.v. Misāḥa. 1.

hand, since we do not wish to have to levy a fresh installment of taxation for that emergency. So what do you think about the procedure we have envisaged and agreed upon?"

None of those present offered him any further advice or uttered a single word. Kisrā repeated these words to them three times. Then a man stood up from out of the expanse of persons present and said to Kisrā, "O king—may God grant you long life!—are you estabishing a perpetual basis for this land tax on transient foundations: a vine that may die, land sown with corn that may wither, a water channel that may dry up, and a spring or qanāt whose water supply may be cut off?" Kisrā replied, "O troublesome, ill-omened fellow, what class of people do you come from?" The man said, "I am one of the secretaries." Kisrā gave orders, "Have him beaten with ink holders (*al-dawā*) until he dies."[622] Hence the secretaries in particular beat him with their ink holders, seeking to disassociate themselves, in Kisrā's eyes, from the man's views and utterance, until they killed him. The people said, "O king, we are in full agreement with the land tax which you are imposing on us."

Kisrā chose some men of sound judgment and wise counsel, and ordered them to investigate the various types of crops the cadastral survey had revealed for him, the numbers of date palms and olive trees, and the numbers of heads of those liable for the poll tax. On that basis, they were to fix the rates of taxation by the yardsticks of what they perceived would ensure the well-being of his subjects and ample means of sustenance for them. They were to report the results of this to him. Each man of them now spoke, according to the measure of his perception, regarding those rates [962]
of taxation which were to be fixed. They discussed the matter among themselves at length, and finally agreed to base the land tax on the products that maintained alive men and beasts, these being: wheat, barley, rice, grapes, trefoil and clover (*riṭāb*),[623] date

622. These would be ink holders of what later became the typical Islamic pattern, with a heavy head to hold the actual ink and with a handle. This secretary courageous enough to protest against Khusraw's measures is making the point adumbrated in n. 624 below: that fixed rate taxes will leave the cultivator at the mercy of crop failures or natural disasters, which will make him unable to find the money demanded.

623. As Nöldeke, trans. 244 n. 1, notes, al-Mas'ūdī in his *Murūj*, II, 204–205 = § 627, specifies that Anūsharwān's land-tax measures were only for Iraq, the richest

palms, and olive trees. They fixed the land tax rate for every *jarīb* of land planted with trefoil and clover, seven dirhams; on every four Persian date palms, one dirham; on every six date palms of lesser quality (*daqal*), the same figure; and every six olive tree stacks, the same figure. They only levied tax on date palms planted in enclosures or grouped together, not those growing as isolated trees. Everything apart from these seven types of crops from the earth they left tax free, and the people were to have a satisfactory standard of life from them.[624]

---

province of the empire. He also explains the stress on the annual fodder plants trefoil and clover (*raṭbah,* pl. *riṭāb* = Persian *aspist*) from the outstanding importance of horses in an army composed essentially of cavalrymen.

624. This land-tax reform was really begun by Kawād I but completed by Khusraw Anūsharwān. Previously, the land tax had been proportional to the harvest, but this basis, though apparently fair, had the disadvantage that the cultivators' harvested crop might rot before the state's assessor could arrive and extract the ruler's share. Hence a fixed unit of the land, the *jarīb,* was now taken as the basis for assessment, and from the ruler's point of view, such a reform was highly advantageous since it gave promise of a fixed and predictable income from taxation. It was, however, less advantageous to the cultivator (despite what could be said, as noted above, about the possibility of the crop rotting or failing before the state's assessor arrived). Whatever the yield from his crops, he was obliged to pay the fixed sum stipulated, might have to sell his harvest at a time of glut and low prices, or borrow money at excessive interest, and could thus be left either starving or burdened with debt. See D. C. Dennett, *Conversion and the Poll Tax in Early Islam,* 14–15; Løkkegaard, *Islamic Taxation in the Classic Period,* 110, 117, 119; Crone, "Kavād's Heresy and Mazdak's Revolt," 33–34.

The topic of Anūsharwān's land-tax reforms, involving such questions as the stimulus for them (did the Mazdakite movement play any rôle here?), the precise nature of the reforms, and their social effects, has been long recognized as a crucial episode in Sāsānid history, one with repercussions that continued into the early Islamic period for the land and fiscal systems in the Persian lands and Iraq.

Al-Ṭabarī's account is basic, and is largely corroborated by the poetic one in Firdawsī's *Shāh-nāmah;* the ultimate source must have been the *Khwadāy-nāmag,* as also for al-Dīnawarī, *al-Akhbār al-ṭiwāl,* 71–72, in his parallel section on the land tax in the time of Anūsharwān. But the Italian scholar Mario Grignaschi has, in a series of publications, drawn attention to several other little-known but relevant sources. These include the anonymous *Nihāyat al-arab fī akhbār al-Furs wa-al-ʿArab,* in the past attributed to the philologist al-Aṣmaʿī but in fact by some unknown author of the third/ninth century, still substantially unpublished (but see below), and rejected by Nöldeke, trans. 475–76, as an inferior version of al-Dīnawarī's *Long Histories.* See Grignaschi, "La *Nihāyatu l-'arab fī aḫbāri-l-Furs wa-l-ʿArab* (première partie)," 15–67; idem, "La *Nihāyatu 'l-arab fī aḫbāri l-Furs wa-l-ʿArab* et les *Siyaru mulūki l-ʿAǧam* du Ps. Ibn al-Muqaffaʿ," 83–102. There is further a *Sīrat Anūshirwān,* which claims to be the emperor's autobiography and which is preserved within the text of the Būyid historian Mis-

They imposed the poll tax on everyone except for people from noble families, great men, warriors, hērbadhs, secretaries, and those in the king's service, and made them liable for it according to four levels, of twelve, eight, six, and four dirhams according to the richness or poverty of the person in question.[625] The poll tax

---

kawayh's *Tajārib al-umam.* See Grignaschi, "Quelques spécimens de la littérature sassanide conservée dans les bibliothèques d'Istanbul," 16–45.

Grignaschi used these sources in his closely argued article "La riforma tributaria di Ḫosrō I e il feudalesimo sassanide," 87–138, to which he appended the texts of relevant extracts from the above-mentioned *Sīrat Anūshirwān* and the *Nihāyat al-arab* bearing on Khusraw's reforms. The topic has been recently subjected to a thoroughgoing analysis by Zeev Rubin in his "The Reforms of Khusro Anūshirwān," 227–97. Rubin compares the relevant sections of al-Ṭabarī, the *Nihāyah,* and al-Dīnawarī and notes that the account of the *Nihāyah* is perceptibly less favorable to Khusraw than al-Ṭabarī's: instead of the vigorous, single-minded monarch of the latter historian, the *Nihāyah*'s Khusraw emerges as a somewhat hesitant person who has to explain and justify his proposed reforms. All three accounts neverthless seem to go back to a common tradition put together in early ʿAbbāsid times within Shuʿūbī circles.

The social and political chaos of the decades before Khusraw's accession were obviously a stimulus for the fiscal reforms begun by Kawād and carried through by his son. Rubin also avers that we should examine the reforms against the background of the general economic situation of the Sāsānid state. First, it benefited from the commerce of the Orient, which had largely to pass through its territories or through Indian Ocean and Arabian Sea waters which the Persian could controled en route for the Mediterranean world. Nor were the financial subsidies that the Byzantine empire had to pay as the price of peace in the Near East negligible contributions to the economic health of Persia. Second, the fiscal reforms should be considered together with Khusraw's military reforms, already examined by Geo Widengren as part of his general survey of the Persian army as a feudal force from Achaemenid to Sāsānid times (see his "Recherches sur le feudalisme iranien," 152–74. There is also particular detail on military affairs in the *Sīrat Anūshīrwān,* see Grignaschi, "Quelques spécimens de la littérature sassanide conservée dans les bibliothèques d'Istanbul," 20–21). Despite the envisaged rise in revenue yields envisaged by the reforms, there does not seem ever to have been enough money available to finance a large, professional army of mailed cavalrymen directly recruited and paid by the monarch and freeing him from dependence on the military services of the great noble families of Persia and their retinues. Hence there seems to have evolved the practice of bringing in manpower from non-Persian, mercenary sources, such as Turks and Hephthalites from Central Asia and Bactria, Daylamīs from the Elburz mountain region, and Arabs from the desert fringes of Iraq. Khusraw was here continuing a process already begun under Kawād, who had regained his throne and been kept in power by the backing of Hephthalite mercenaries, links with the Hephthalites having been forged during his enforced exile within their lands in the 490s.

Finally, the course and development of Khusraw's fiscal system are briefly touched upon by Rubin. The system must have changed even within the course of his long reign, and was already showing signs of decay by the end of that time. The

was not to be levied on those below twenty or above fifty years of age. They brought their tax assessments before Kisrā; he approved them and ordered them to be put into force and for tax collecting to be done on their basis annually, in three installments each of four months. These he called *'.b.rās.yār* (?), meaning "an arrangement mutually agreed upon by all."[626] It was these tax assessments 'Umar b. al-Khaṭṭāb followed when he conquered the Persian lands and levied taxation on the "protected peoples" (*ahl al-dhimmah*) there, except that he levied taxation on every uncultivated (*ghāmir*) piece of land according to its potential yield, at the same rate as he levied on sown land. Also, he levied on every *jarīb*
[963] of land growing wheat or barley from one to two additional *qafīz*s

---

control system of the provincial judges, in fact district mōbadhs of the Zoroastrian state church (see al-Ṭabarī, I, 963, p. 261 below) probably proved no less susceptible to corrupt practices than any other officials in a similar situation. Under Khusraw's son and successor Hormizd IV, the great military families of the provinces gained excessive opportunities for exploiting the peasantry, and Rubin speculates that Hormizd's reputed violence against the military aristocracy (see al-Ṭabarī, I, 988–89, p. 295 below) may have been a desperate attempt to stem corruption and oppression and to salvage something of Khusraw's sytem. The cataclysmic events toward the end of Khusraw II Abarwēz's reign must have plunged the system into deeper malfunction. It nevertheless survived intact enough to be taken over by the Muslims when they overran Iraq and Persia, basically as the *misāḥah* system, but was at least in part converted into *muqāsamah* in the early 'Abbāsid period, a reversion to the system before the reforms of Kawād and Anūsharwān. See Løkkegaard, *Islamic Taxation in the Classic Period,* 109–13.

625. The poll tax (see n. 619 above) had previously been a fixed sum that the assessors and collectors had had to divide out as best they could. The exemptions for the royal family, aristocracy, soldiers (al-Dīnawarī, *al-Akhbār al-ṭiwāl,* 71, specifies here *marāzibah* and *asāwirah* [al-Ṭabarī has, less specifically, for these two classes *'uẓamā'* and *muqātilah*] and *kuttāb*), secretaries, and the Zoroastrian priests increased their position as privileged castes. While the tax liabilities of the middle and lower classes were theoretically meant to compensate for the royal service and religious duties that they were unable to perform, in practice, payment of these taxes amounted to an acknowledgment of social inferiority. As mentioned in n. 619 above, the existence of this Sāsānid institution may have been a contributory factor when the nascent Islamic state evolved the poll tax (*jizyah*) and applied it to the Dhimmīs as a mark of their social and religious degradation and second-class citizenship compared with the Muslim Arabs, but this is speculative.

626. This term is wholly obscure. Al-Dīnawarī, *al-Akhbār al-ṭiwāl,* 71, says that the warehouses where the three installments of collected produce were stored were called *sarāy simarrah* (text, *shimarrah*), i.e., "house for the three (*sic*) times (*marrah*) [of collection]"; cf. the loan word in Arabic *samarjā* or *samaraj,* see Asya Asbaghi, *Persische Lehnwörter im Arabischen,* 165: "Steuer in drei Stufen."

of wheat; this he used for feeding his army.[627] But in the specific case of Iraq, 'Umar did not make any arrangements contrary to those of Kisrā regarding the *jarībs* of land and regarding the date palms, olive trees, and the heads [of those liable to the poll tax], and he excluded from liability to taxation the people's means of daily sustenance, as Kisrā had done.[628]

Kisrā ordered the new tax assessments to be written down in several copies. One copy was to be kept in his own chancery close at his hand; one copy was sent to the land-tax collectors (*'ummāl al-kharāj*) for them to collect taxation on its basis; and another copy was sent to the judges of the administrative divisions (*quḍāt al-kuwar*). The judges were charged with the duty of intervening between the tax collectors and the people if the tax collectors in the administrative districts attempted to raise an additional sum above the amount laid down in the master copy of the tax assessment in the chancery, of which they had received a copy. Also, the judges were to exempt from land tax those whose tillage or other tax-attracting produce had been damaged or badly affected in any way, according to the seriousness of that damage or defect. Regarding those persons liable for the poll tax who had died, or who had passed the age of fifty, collecting the taxation was likewise suspended; the judges were to write back to Kisrā about the tax exemptions here, which they had granted so that Kisrā might issue appropriate instructions to his tax collectors. Furthermore,

---

627. As with the *jarīb*, the *qafīz* was a measure both of surface area (one-tenth of a *jarīb*, i.e., 360 square *dhirā*'s or cubits, according to al-Khwārazmī, *Mafātīḥ al-'ulūm*, 66) and also one of capacity (ibid. 67–68, giving the varying equivalences of the basically Iraqi *qafīz* for different parts of the Persian lands, where the *manā* was the normal measure for capacity). See Nöldeke, trans. 246 n. 6; Bosworth, "Abū 'Abdallāh al-Khwārazmī on the Technical Terms of the Secretary's Art," 148–50, citing information from W. Hinz, *Islamische Masse und Gewichte umgerechnet ins metrische System*, 16–23.

628. On 'Umar's *misāḥah*, see Dennett, *Conversion and the Poll Tax in Early Islam*, 22ff., and Løkkegaard, *Islamic Taxation in the Classic Period*, 119–20. Regarding 'Umar's procedure over the land tax, there are actually contradictory reports in the Arabic sources concerned with the postconquest Sawād of Iraq. Thus according to al-Māwardī, 'Umar imposed on the Sawād a flat rate of one dirham and one *qafīz* of produce for the provisioning of the Arab warriors (but in other parts of Iraq, the rate varied according to the crop); but according to Abū Yūsuf, 'Umar taxed land according to the crop grown there. In reality, the disparity only arises, suggested Dennett, because the two viewpoints reflect changes in 'Umar's prescriptions here.

the judges were not to let the tax collectors levy taxation on persons aged less than twenty.[629]

Kisrā had appointed over the department of the warriors (*dīwān al-muqātilah*) a man from the secretarial class who was outstanding for his noble birth, martial virtues, sufficiency, and capability, called Bābak, son of '.l.y.r.wān (?).[630] This last said to Kisrā, "My function cannot properly be carried out unless I have a free hand at putting into practice what seems best to me for the good conduct of the king's affairs in regard to his army." Kisrā granted Bābak this. Bābak now gave orders for the construction of a platform in the place where army reviews were customarily held, carpets from Sūsanjird and woolen rugs were laid on it, and cushions provided for him to lean back upon. He then took up his place on all those coverings.

Bābak's herald now proclaimed throughout those troops present
[964] in Kisrā's army camp that the cavalrymen were to present themselves before him for inspection on their mounts and with their weapons, and the infantrymen with their requisite weapons. The troops massed together in front of him in the manner Bābak had stipulated they were to parade, but he did not see Kisrā present in their ranks, so he told them to go back. His herald made the same proclamation on the next day, and the troops gathered round him again; but when he still could not discern Kisrā among them, he told them to go back and reappear before him next morning. He instructed his herald to proclaim on the third day, "Let no one present in the army camp lag behind, even if he is honored by possessing a crown and a throne," for Bābak had resolved that there should be no exception in his favor and no partiality shown to him (i.e., to Kisrā). The message reached Kisrā, and he placed the crown on his head, girded on the weapons of a soldier, and then went along to Bābak so that he might present himself for inspection by him.

The equipment that a cavalryman of the army had to take along with him comprised horse mail, soldier's mailed coat, breastplate,

629. These judges from the religious institution were presumably mōbadhs who administered the Zoroastrian church law; here they are charged with protecting the taxpayers from tyranny and exploitation by the taxcollectors.

630. Nöldeke, trans. 247, though that this name might be Bīrawān (?); it is equally corruptly written in al-Dīnawarī's passage on the Sāsānid army review, *al-Akhbār al-ṭiwāl*, 72–73, as al-Nahrawān.

leg armor plates, sword, lance, shield, mace, and, fastened at his waist, a girdle, battle axe, or club, a bow case containing two bows with their strings, thirty arrows, and finally, two plaited cords, which the rider let hang down his back from his helmet.[631] Kisrā presented himself for inspection before Bābak with his weapons all complete except for the two cords he was supposed to tie on his back. Bābak did not pass over his name, but said to him, "O king, you are standing in such a place where all are treated equally, where no partiality on my part can be shown nor any relaxation! So step forward with all the requisite kinds of weapons!" At that point, Kisrā remembered the matter of the two cords, so he let them hang down.

Bābak's herald now sang out in a loud voice, saying, "For the brave warrior, lord of brave warriors, four thousand and one dirhams,"[632] and Bābak passed over his name. Then the king returned home. Now Bābak used to give the king a pay rate superior to that of the rest of the soldiers by one dirham. When Bābak got [965] up from his seat [on the platform], he went to Kisrā and told him, "The lack of consideration that I showed you today, O king, was only so that the function with which you charged me could be thereby properly discharged, because the most secure way of achieving the king's aim is his making my office as firmly based as possible." Kisrā replied, "We don't regard as any lack of consideration for us a procedure that I desire for the furtherance of the welfare of my subjects and by means of which the injury of an injured person may be set right."[633]

---

631. Nöldeke, trans. 248 n. 2, noted that Firdawsī adds to the list the lassoo, characteristic of steppe-dwelling herdsmen, and mentioned by Herodotus, VII. 85, as a weapon of the Iranian tribe of the Sagartians, possibly to be located in northeastern Persia.

632. The "and one" is supplied from the parallel passage in al-Dīnawarī, *al-Akhbār al-ṭiwāl,* 73, as done by Nöldeke in trans. 249, cf. n. 1, and noted in text, n. *e;* without this amendment, the point made just afterward is lost.

633. Bābak's rôle as head of the military department corresponds to that of the *'āriḍ* who presided over the department of the army, *dīwān al-jaysh, dīwān al-jund,* in the 'Abbāsid caliphate and the *dīwān al-'arḍ* in such successor states to it in the Persian lands as those of the Sāmānids, Ṣaffārids, Būyids, and Ghaznavids. The institution of regular inspections of troops was probably an ancient one in Persia. According to Widengren, in Achaemenid times, the Persian army had a rallying point, apparently termed the **handaisa-* < *handēz,* corresponding to Xenophon's *exetasis,* and there was a secretary, the *rēš dupšarri ša ūqu* who fulfilled the rôle of Bābak here. From the evidence of the Bablyonian Talmud, the

Kisrā now dispatched to Yemen an army under the command of a man from the people of Yemen called Sayfān b. Ma'dī Karib—some authorities aver, however, that he was called Sayf b. Dhī Yazan—which killed the blacks there (i.e., the Abyssinians) and conquered the land.[634] Having secured the submission of the land of Yemen, Kisrā sent one of his commanders, with a numerous army, against Sarandīb, the land of precious stones, in the land of India.[635] The commander attacked its king, killed him, and seized control of it, sending back from there to Kisrā abundant wealth and many jewels.

In the land of Persia there were no jackals (*banāt āwā*),[636] but

---

related term *andesaq* seems to have been used in Arsacid times. The account given here by al-Ṭabarī and also by al-Dīnawarī of the Sāsānid army inspection is distinctly imaginative in its details, and can hardly be accepted as firm evidence for detailed Sāsānid practice here. Yet it is likely that there was some department of the bureaucracy concerned with the army and its standard of effectiveness, and precampaign inspections of the Persian army, in the presence of the monarch and the commanders appointed to lead that expedition, are mentioned by Procopius (Christensen, *Sassanides*, 213–14). The *Sīrat Anūshirwān* mentions these reviews held by the emperor, and says that they took place in the presence of the *qā'id* or commander, the *pādhguspān* or commander-in-chief of the force (the later *ispahbadh*), the *qāḍī* or judge, and a trusty secretary appointed directly by the king (*amīn min qibalinā*). See Widengren, "Recherches sur le feudalisme iranien," 152ff.; Grignaschi, "Quelques spécimens de la littérature sassanide conservée dans les bibliothèques d'Istanbul," 20 and n. 48.

For the Islamic period, we have a detailed account of the *'arḍ* as practiced in the Ṣaffārid army under 'Amr b. al-Layth (r. 265–87/879–900) in which the Amīr, like Khusraw Anūsharwān, had to be inspected by the *'āriḍ* and passed fit for service just like every other soldier. The authority for this is al-Sallāmī, author of a lost history of the governors of Khurāsān, cited in Ibn Khallikān's *Wafayāt al-a'yān*. Ibn Khallikān juxtaposes this with al-Ṭabarī's account of the Sāsānid inspection in the time of Anūsharwān (actually cited via the historian of Aleppo Ibn al-'Adīm), and notes the similarity between the two procedures. A modern historian like Barthold observed that the resemblances could hardly be coincidental. See Ibn Khallikān, *Wafayāt*, VI, 421–23, tr. de Slane, IV, 322–24; W. Barthold, *Turkestan Down to the Mongol Invasion*$^3$, 221; Bosworth, "The Armies of the Ṣaffārids," 549–50.

634. This seems to be a purely Persian piece of historical information, perhaps compressed by al-Ṭabarī because of its contradictions with the story of Wahriz's South Arabian expedition given by him at considerable length in I, 952–58, p. 245–51 above. According to Nöldeke, trans. 250 n. 1, we should correct the text's Sayfān (which in Persian would mean "son of Sayf") to Sayf b. Dhī Yazan.

635. Sarandīb was the name given to the island of Ceylon in mediaeval Islamic geographical and historical literature; see *EI*$^2$, s.v. Sarandīb (C. E. Bosworth). It was famed in Islamic lore for its supposed wealth. The story of a Sāsānid conquest of Ceylon is, of course, pure legend.

636. The jackal (*canis aureus* or *anthus*, in Persian, *shaghāl*) is in fact widely distributed today in Persia. See Naval Intelligence Division. Admiralty Handbooks, *Persia*, 209–10.

some of them infiltrated into Persia from the land of the Turks during the reign of Kisrā Anūsharwān. News of this reached Kisrā, and caused him anguish. He summoned the Chief Mōbadh and told him, "We have heard about the appearance of those wild beasts in our land, and it has distressed the people. We are, however, astonished that they consider such an insignificant occurrence as so portentous; tell us what you think about all this." The Chief Mōbadh replied, "O king—may God grant you long life—I have heard our scholars learned in the divine law say that, so long as justice does not overlay tyranny in a land and itself becomes obliterated, the people of that land will be afflicted by incursions of their enemies against them, and all sorts of unpleasant things will gradually come upon them. I have become afraid lest the infiltration of these wild beasts into your land is connected with what I have just told you." Very soon afterward, the news reached [966] Kisrā that a band of Turkish youths had raided the furthest boundaries of his land. He ordered his ministers and provincial governors not to go beyond what was just in the course of their official duties and not to act in any way during the course of those duties except justly. Because of this policy of acting justly, God deflected that enemy from Kisrā's land without his having to make war on them or to undertake great trouble in repelling them.[637]

Kisrā had several handsomely educated sons. From out of those, he appointed as his successor to the throne Hurmuz, whose mother was the daughter of Khātūn and Khāqān,[638] because he knew Hurmuz to be a person who would act with circumspection and fidelity to his word, and because he hoped through this appointment that Hurmuz would keep the kingdom in order and would show strength in directing the government of the land and in ruling over the subjects and treating them suitably.[639]

637. The story of an invasion of jackals into Iraq appears in al-Dīnawarī, *al-Akhbār al-ṭiwāl,* 74, but with no mention of an incursion of Turkish youths; here, the depredations of the jackals are attributed to the existence of tyranny and injustice within Anūsharwān's lands, remedied by his appointing a commission of thirteen agents to enquire into the matter, as a result of which the king executed ninety evil officials *pour décourager les autres.* Cf. Nöldeke, trans. 251 n. 1.

638. See al-Ṭabarī, I, 899, p. 160 above.

639. Anūsharwān's designation of Hormizd (IV) sprang no doubt from his mother's royal birth. According to such sources as al-Dīnawarī, *al-Akhbār al-ṭiwāl,* 74–75, and al-Ya'qūbī, *Ta'rīkh,* I, 187, the king passed over his other sons because they had mothers of lowly origin and were only *awlād sūqah,* and chose Hormizd after

The birth of the Messenger of God took place during the reign of Kisrā Anūsharwān, in the year when Abrahah al-Ashram Abū Yaksūm marched against Mecca with the Abyssinians, bringing with him the elephant, having the intention of demolishing the Holy House of God. It happened after forty-two years of Kisrā Anūsharwān's reign had elapsed.[640] In this same year also was the

---

carefully observing his worthy behavior. Cf. Nöldeke, trans. 252 n. 3.

640. This would make it the year 573. The question of the birth date of Muḥammad is unusually speculative and controversial. A key point is what al-Ṭabarī mentions here, i.e., the date of Abrahah's expedition against Mecca in the "Year of the Elephant," with which the Prophet's birth date is held to coincide. But since the early Islamic historical tradition does not date this expedition, a date of 570 has been calculated backward from the fact that Muḥammad's first call to prophethood, the *mabḥath,* fell approximately in 610 and from the saying that he was about forty years old when he received this call.

However, this date of 570, while repeated in many of the biographies of Muḥammad, is contradicted both by evidence outside the Islamic tradition, principally from what we know about South Arabian history in the mid-sixth century, and by some reports within the Islamic tradition, which give widely differing dates up to twenty years after the "Year of the Elephant." Already more than 120 years ago, Nöldeke, trans. 204 n. 2, saw that the traditional dating was untenable, adducing among other things Ibn al-Kalbī's assertion that Muḥammad's birth was twenty-three years after Abrahah's expedition (also in his *Geschichte des Qorāns,* I, 67–70). Lammens pointed out that, if one takes ten years off the traditional birth date of 570, i.e., placing Muḥammad's birth in 580 so that he was fifty-two years old when he died, there is a correspondence with the date for the Prophet's death given by Barhebraeus in his *Mukhtaṣar Ta'rīkh al-Duwal,* ed. A. Ṣāliḥānī, Beirut 1890, 160, i.e., 892 of the Seleucid era = A.D. 580 (unfortunately Barhebraeus does not say how he acquired this date); see Lammens, "L'âge de Mahomet et la chronologie de la Sîra," 239–40. Various Islamic traditions stating that Muḥammad was not born in the "Year of the Elephant" have been listed by Kister, see n. 563 above. What we know of Abrahah's policy in pushing his dominion northward from Yemen into Ḥijāz and central Arabia places his activities in the 550s, as attested by the well of Murayghān inscription from 552–53. Whether an attack on Mecca was part of the campaign of Abrahah to Ḥulubān or another campaign mounted into Ḥijāz shortly afteward is discussed in n. 563 above. All in all, it does not seem feasible to uphold the date of 570 as being that of the Prophet's birth. Furthermore, L. I. Conrad, in a detailed discussion of the whole topic, has pointed out how little interested were the Arabs of north and central Arabia in questions of firm dating and chronology, seen in the vagueness and confusedness over the chronological order and relationship to each other of the *ayyām al-ʿArab,* the battles of the pre-Islamic Arabs. Hence the figure of forty years for Muḥammad's life before his call to *nubuwwah*—apart from the fact that "forty" is a literary topos in both ancient and mediaeval times for a number with connotations of perfection, completion, and culmination—must be regarded as a symbolic rather than a chronologically exact one. See his "Abraha and Muḥammad. Some Observations Apropos of Chronology and Literary Topoi in the Early Arabic Historical Tradition," 225–40.

"Day of Jabalah," one of the celebrated "days" (i.e., battles) of the Arabs.[641]

641. Jabalah, an isolated mountain in Najd some 150 km/90 miles south of 'Unayzah (al-Bakrī, *Mu'jam mā ista'jam*, II, 365–66; Yāqūt, *Buldān*, II, 104), was the scene of the *yawm [shi'b] Jabalah* or *yawm al-Nūq* between 'Āmir b. Ṣa'ṣa'ah and 'Abs on one side, and Tamīm, supported by Dhubyān, Asad, a contingent from al-Ḥīrah and men of Kindah from the Āl Jawnah then ruling in Baḥrayn (see n. 312 above), accounted as one of the most celebrated battles of the Arabs. 'Āmir and their allies were victorious, and one result was the shattering of Kindī power in Najd (see Olinder, "Āl al-Ǧaun of the Family of Ākil al-Murār," 214–25; because two members of the line of Jawn took part in the battle, the encounter is also known as the *yawm al-Jawnayn*). The historical traditions vary concerning the date of the "Day of Jabalah"; some place it in the year of Muḥammad's birth, others seventeen or nineteen years before that. In reality, if the Lakhmid king who sent a contingent was, as the historical traditions say, al-Nu'mān (III) b. al-Mundhir (IV), then the date cannot be before 580, the year of his accession. See Caskel, *Aijām al-'Arab. Studien zur altarabischen Epik*, 11, 34, 36–37, 62, translating at 95–97 part of the *Naqā'iḍ Jarīr wa-al-Farazdaq*, II, 654ff., describing the "Day"; *EI*[2], s.vv. Djabala (F. Buhl-R. L. Headley), Shi'b Djabala (I. Shahîd).

# Mention of the Birth of the Messenger of God

There related to us Ibn al-Muthannā—Wahb b. Jarīr—his father, who said: I heard Muḥammad b. Isḥāq—al-Muṭṭalib b. ʿAbdallāh b. Qays b. Makhramah—his father—his grandfather, who said:
[967] The Messenger of God and myself were born in the Year of the Elephant.

He related: ʿUthmān b. ʿAffān asked Qubāth b. Ashyam, a member of the Banū ʿAmr b. Layth, "Who is the greater in build (*akbar*), you or the Messenger of God?" He replied, "The Messenger of God is greater in build than I, although I preceded him in date of birth (*anā aqdam minhu fī al-mīlād*); I saw the elephant's dung, dark colored and reduced to a powdery form, one year after the beast's appearance. I also saw Umayyah b. ʿAbd Shams as a very old man being led around by his slave." His son said, "O Qubāth, you have the best knowledge; what do you say?"

There related to us Ibn Ḥumayd—Salamah—Ibn Isḥāq—al-Muṭṭalib b. ʿAbdallāh b. Qays b. Makhramah—his father—his grandfather Qays b. Makhramah, who said: The Messenger of God and myself were born in the Year of the Elephant, and we were coevals of each other.

There was narrated to me a narrative going back to Hishām b. Muḥammad, who said: ʿAbdallāh b. ʿAbd al-Muṭṭalib, the Messenger of God's father, was born in the twenty-fourth year of Kisrā Anūsharwān's period of power, and the Messenger of God was born in the forty-second year of his period of power.[642]

642. That is, ʿAbdallāh would have been born, on this reckoning, in 555 and his son Muḥammad in 573.

I was informed by Yūsuf b. Muʿīn—Ḥajjāj b. Muḥammad—Yūnus b. Abī Isḥāq—Saʿīd b. Jubayr—Ibn ʿAbbās, who said: The Messenger of God was born in the Year of the Elephant.

I was informed by Ibrāhīm b. al-Mundhir—ʿAbd al-ʿAzīz b. Abī Thābit—al-Zubayr b. Mūsā—Abū al-Ḥuwayrith, who said: I heard ʿAbd al-Malik b. Marwān say to Qubāth b. Ashyam al-Kinānī al-Laythī, O Qubāth, who is the greater in body, you or the Messenger of God?" He replied, "The Messenger of God was greater in body than me, but I am older than him. The Messenger of God was born in the Year of the Elephant, and my mother stood with me by a pile of the elephant's dung, when it was crumbling away to powder, at a time when I was nevertheless able to understand what it was."

There related to us Ibn Ḥumayd—Salamah—Ibn Isḥāq, who said: The Messenger of God was born in the Year of the Elephant, [968] on Monday, the twelfth of the month of Rabīʿ I. It is said that he was born in the house known as that of Ibn Yūsuf. It is further said that the Messenger of God gave this house to ʿAqīl b. Abī Ṭālib, who retained ownership of it until he died, when his son sold it to Muḥammad b. Yūsuf, brother of al-Ḥajjāj b. Yūsuf. Muḥammad rebuilt the house called that of Ibn Yūsuf, and incorporated that new part into the house as a whole. Later, al-Khayzurān separated the new part from the house as a whole and made it into a mosque, which then came into use for public worship.[643]

There related to us Ibn Ḥumayd—Salamah—Ibn Isḥāq, who said: Among what people relate is the assertion—but God is the most knowing [about the truth]—that Āminah bt. Wahb, the Messenger of God's mother, used to relate that when she became pregnant, people came to her and said, "You are bearing the lord of this community (*sayyid hādhihi al-ummah*), and when he drops to the ground [from you], exclaim, 'I seek refuge in the One God—from the evil of every envious one,' and then name him Muḥammad." When she was pregnant with him, she dreamed that there came forth from her a light, by which she could discern the for-

643. Muḥammad had made this house over to ʿAlī's half-brother ʿAqīl b. Abī Ṭālib when he left Mecca on the Hijrah to Medina; with al-Khayzurān's purchase of it, the house returned to the family of Hāshim. See al-Azraqī, *Akhbār Makkah*, 422; Nabia Abbott, *Two Queens of Baghdad, Mother and Wife of Hārūn al-Rashīd*, 118–19.

tresses (*quṣūr*) of Buṣrā in the land of Syria.[644] When she actually gave birth to him, she sent a message to the child's grandfather ʿAbd al-Muṭṭalib: "A baby boy has been born for you, so come and see him." He indeed came along and saw the child, and she told him about the dream she had had while pregnant with the child, what had been told her regarding him and what she had been commanded to call the child.[645]

There related to us Muḥammad b. Sinān al-Qazzāz—Yaʿqūb b. Muḥammad al-Zuhrī—ʿAbd al-ʿAzīz b. ʿImrān—ʿAbdallāh b.

644. Buṣrā or Boṣrā was an ancient town of the Ḥawrān in southern Syria, to the south of the modern Jabal al-Durūz. At the time of Muḥammad's birth it was an important center of Byzantine power and of Eastern Christianity. Muslim legend later made the Arabs' capture of Buṣrā, the first town of the Byzantines to fall into their hands, into a sign of divine favor for Muḥammad's mission. It also had a continued fame as the place to which the youthful Muḥammad is said to have journeyed in the company of his uncle Abū Ṭālib and where he is said to have met the Christian monk Baḥīrā or Buḥayrā, who foretold the boy's coming greatness as a prophet. See Yāqūt, *Buldān*, I, 441–42; Le Strange, *Palestine*, 425–26; T. Andrae, *Die Person Muhammeds in Lehre und Glauben seiner Gemeinde*, 38; M. Lings. *Muhammad, His Life based on the Earliest Sources*, 29–30; *EI*², s.vv. Baḥīrā and Boṣrā (A. Abel).

645. Āminah bt. Wahb b. ʿAbd al-Manāf was from the Meccan clan of Zuhrah. Her apparently uxorilocal marriage with ʿAbdallāh b. ʿAbd al-Muṭṭalib was ended by the latter's premature death (see n. 662 below), and she herself died when Muḥammad was only six years old, leaving him to his paternal grandfather's care. See *EI*², s.v. Āmina (W. M. Watt). Popular belief and lore in early Islam attributed various supernatural details to Aminah's pregnancy and the birth of Muḥammad, including the story of the dream of divine radiance, "the light of prophethood," the averring that she was bearing "the lord of this community," and the remarkable ease of her giving birth to him, clean, with cut umbilical cord and circumcised, after which the infant placed his hands on the ground and gave thanks to heaven. See Ibn Hishām, *Sīrat al-nabī*, ed. Wüstenfeld, 102, 106 = ed. al-Saqqā et al., I, 166–67, 175, tr. 69, 72; Ibn Saʿd, *Kitāb al-Ṭabaqāt al-kabīr*, I/1, 60–61, 63–64. On the topic of Muḥammad's being born circumcised and the fact that, according to some traditions, Muḥammad was only one of a series of prophets born circumcised, see Kister, ". . . And he was born circumcised. . . .' Some Notes on Circumcision in Ḥadīth," 10–30 and esp. 13–16.

Modern scholars have pointed out the resemblance of many of these details to the stories of the birth and early life of other great religious leaders. Thus the *nūr muḥammadī* parallels the old Iranian idea of the divine fortune or glory of kings, *xvarənah*, MP *farrah*, NP *farr* (see n. 232 above), which manifested itself, according to the account in the *Dēnkard*, at the time of Zoroaster's birth, and the light at the births of Krishna and the Buddha, while the announcement of Aminah's forthcoming delivery of a child is like that of Mary glorying in her conception of Jesus in the Magnificat. See I. Goldziher, "Neuplatonische und gnostische Elemente im Ḥadīt," 328–30; Andrae, *Die Person Muhammeds*, 28–33, 319–21; idem, *Mohammed, sein Leben und Glaube*, 28–29

'Uthmān b. Abī Sulaymān b. Jubayr b. Muṭ'im—his father—Ibn Abī Suwayd al-Thaqafī—'Uthmān b. Abī al-'Āṣ—his mother, who said that she was present at the Messenger of God's mother [969] Āminah bt. Wahb's giving birth, this being during the night, and Āminah said, "What is this thing which I can see from the house, lighting everything up, and I can also see the stars drawing near me to such a point that I can say that they are falling on top of me."

Ibn Ḥumayd—Salamah—Ibn Isḥāq, who said: People assert that 'Abd al-Muṭṭalib picked up the child and took it along to Hubal,[646] in the heart of the Ka'bah, and stood by him, praying to God and giving thanks for what He had vouchsafed him. Then he went forth with the child and handed him over to his mother. He sought out for the child foster mothers,[647] and asked a woman to foster him, one from the Banū Sa'd b. Bakr called Ḥalīmah bt. Abī Dhu'ayb, Abū Dhu'ayb being 'Abdallāh b. al-Ḥārith b. Shijnah b. Jābir b. Rizām b. Nāṣirah b. Quṣiyyah b. Sa'd b. Bakr b. Hawāzin b. Manṣūr b. 'Ikrimaha b. Khaṣafah b. Qays b. 'Aylān b. Muḍar. The name of the Messenger of God's foster father was al-Ḥārith b. 'Abd al-'Uzzā b. Rifā'ah b. Mallān b. Nāṣirah b. Quṣiyyah b. Sa'd b, Bakr b. Hawāzin b. Manṣūr b. 'Ikrimah b. Khaṣafah b. Qays b. 'Aylān b. Muḍar. The names of his foster brother and sisters were 'Abdallāh b. al-Ḥārith, and Unaysah bt. al-Ḥārith and Judhāmah[648] bt. al-Ḥārith, respectively. The latter was in practice called al-Shaymā',[649] a name that prevailed over her proper name so that,

646. The cult of the god Hubal was said to have been introduced into Mecca by a man of Khuzā'ah, 'Amr b. Luḥayy. He became an especially popular god in the pantheon of the Ka'bah, before whom divination by means of arrows (cleromancy, the *istiqsām bi-al-azlām* of Qur'ān, V, 4/3), so that Wellhausen speculated (*Reste arabischen Heidentums*², 75) whether the worship of Hubal was not identical with, or paved the way for, the worship of Allāh there. This seems, however, unlikely, especially as, at the battle of Uḥud in the course of the warfare between Quraysh of Mecca and the Muslims in Medina, the clash between the Meccans' god Hubal and the Muslims' Allāh is stressed. See Fahd, *Le panthéon de l'Arabie centrale à la veille de l'Hégire,* 95–103; *EI*², s.v. Hubal (T. Fahd).

647. *ruḍa'ā'*, literally "children suckling at the breast," sing. *raḍī'*, hence used here by metonymy for "foster mothers" or for some expression like *dhawāt* or *ulāt/ūlāt al-raḍā'ah.*

648. In parallel sources we have the variants Khidhāmah and Ḥudhāfah for this name.

649. Literally, "the woman marked by a mole (*shāmah*)."

among her people, she was known exclusively by it. [The mother of these foster siblings was] Ḥalīmah bt. ʿAbdallāh b. al-Ḥārith, (foster) mother of the Messenger of God. It is asserted that al-Shaymāʾ used to carry the Messenger of God in her bosom, as also did her own mother while the boy was in her care.[650]

As for the report from an authority other than Ibn Isḥāq, he relates concerning that: There related to me al-Ḥārith—Ibn Saʿd—Muḥammad b. ʿUmar—Mūsā b. Shaybah—ʿUmayrah bt. ʿUbaydallāh b. Kaʿb b. Mālik—Barrah bt. Abī Tujzaʾah, who said:
[970] The first person who suckled the Messenger of God for a few days was Thuwaybah, with milk for a son of hers called Masrūḥ, before Ḥalīmah was put forward; she had previously suckled Ḥamzah b. ʿAbd al-Muṭṭalib, and after him she suckled Abū Salamah b. ʿAbd al-Asad al-Makhzūmī.

There related to us Ḥumayd—Salamah—Ibn Isḥāq, also Hannād b. al-Sarī—Yūnus b. Bukayr—Ibn Isḥāq, also Hārūn b. Idrīs al-Aṣamm—al-Muḥāribī—Ibn Isḥāq, also Saʿīd b. Yaḥyā al-Umawī—his paternal uncle Muḥammad b. Saʿīd—Muḥammad b. Isḥāq—al-Jahm b. Abī al-Jahm, a mawlā of ʿAbdallāh b. Jaʿfar—ʿAbdallāh b. Jaʿfar b. Abī Ṭālib, who said: Ḥalīmah bt. Abī Dhuʾayb al-Saʿdiyyah, the Messenger of God's (foster) mother who suckled him, used to relate that she went forth from her land, accompanied by her husband and an infant son of hers whom she was nursing, with a group of women from the Banū Saʿd b. Bakr, seeking for babies whom they could foster. This was, she related, in a year of severe drought, which had left nothing. [She related:] I set out on a greyish-white she-ass of mine, together with an old she-camel which was not, by God, yielding a drop [of milk]. We could not sleep the whole night because of our child's crying from hunger. There was nothing in my breasts to satisfy him, and nothing in our she-camel to provide him with nourishment, but we were hoping for rain and for relief.

---

650. Ḥalīmah's tribe Saʿd b. Bakr were part of the Hawāzin confederation, who lived in Ḥijāz in the vicinity of Mecca and al-Ṭāʾif. When women of Saʿd b. Bakr were captured by Muḥammad on his defeat of Hawāzin at the battle of Ḥunayn in 8/630, he honored Ḥalīmah's daughter al-Shaymāʾ and responded favorably to appeals by the menfolk of the tribe on the basis of their foster relationship. See *EI*², s.vv. Ḥalīma bint Abī Dhuʾayb and Saʿd b. Bakr (W. M. Watt).

I set off on that she-ass of mine, but through weakness and emaciation it was jaded, and lagged behind the rest of the group until that became an irritation for them. Finally, we reached Mecca, where we sought for children to foster. The Messenger of God was offered to every one of the women, but each one rejected him when told that he was an orphan, since we hoped for the customary payment from the child's father. We would say, "An [971] orphan! And what are his mother and grandfather likely to do?" Hence for that reason we spurned him. Every woman in the group that had come with me had found a child to foster except myself. When we decided to depart, I said to my husband, "I dislike the idea of returning with my group of women companions without having taken a foster child; by God, I shall go back to that orphan and take him." My husband said, "You are free to do as you wish; perhaps God will send us a blessing on his account." She related: I took him up and brought him back to my traveling baggage. When I placed him in my bosom, my breasts immediately began to flow for him with all the milk he desired. He sucked until he was full up, as did also his (foster) brother. Then they both slept, whereas previously he had not been able to sleep. My husband arose and went to that old she-camel of ours and looked at it, and lo and behold, her udders were full. He milked it, and we both drank of the milk until we were finally refreshed and replete, and we passed a happy night. She related: When it was morning, my husband said to me, "By God, O Ḥalīmah, do you realize that you have taken a blessed creature?" I replied, "By God, I hope so." She related: Then we set off. I rode that she-ass of mine and carried him with me, and by God, she went ahead through the party of riders so that none of their other male asses could keep up with it, to the point that my women companions were saying to me, "O Ibnat Abī Dhu'ayb! Wait for us! Isn't this she-ass of yours the one on which you started out?" and they commented, "By God, there is something extraordinary about it!" She related: We then reached our camping grounds in the country of the Banū Sa'd; and [972] I do not known any of God's lands more barren than that.

[She related:] When we had him with us, my flock used to come back to us in the evening satiated and full of milk. We would milk them and drink the milk, while other people could not draw a drop or find anything in their beasts' udders, until those of our tribes who had fixed dwelling places (*al-ḥāḍir min qawminā*) used to tell their shepherds, "Woe to you! Send your flocks to pasture where Ibnat Abī Dhu'ayb's shepherd sends his flock!" But their flocks nevertheless would come back in the evening hungry, not yielding a drop of milk, while my flock would come back satiated and full of milk. We kept on recognizing increased bounty from God through the child, until two years had gone by, when I weaned him. He was growing up into a boy such as none of the other lads were, so that by the time he was two years old, he was a well-formed child beyond the age of suckling. We brought him to his [real] mother, although we were very eager for him to continue staying with us because of the blessing we observed he had brought us. So we talked with his mother and said to her, "O wet nurse (*ẓi'r*),[651] I should like you to leave my little boy with me [for a further period], until he becomes big and sturdy, for I fear his succumbing to the plague in Mecca." She related: We kept on at her until she sent him back with us.[652]

She related: We brought him back, and by God, a few months after our return with him, he and his (foster) brother were with some lambs of ours, behind our tents, when his (foster) brother came running toward us and told me and his (foster) father, "Two men wearing white robes have come to that Qurashī brother of mine, and have laid him down on the ground and slit open his belly and are at this moment stirring it up." She related: His (foster) father and I ran swiftly out and found him standing there with a livid face. She related: His father and I rushed to his side and said to him, "What's the matter, my dear son?" He replied, "Two men wearing white robes came up to me, laid me down on the

---

651. As Guillaume observed, Ibn Hishām, *Sīrat al-nabī*, trans. 71 n. 1, the implication that Āminah was not Muḥammad's biological mother is rather strange.

652. These miraculous events attending Ḥalīmah's suckling of the infant Muḥammad, the abundance of milk from the animals in time of dearth, and the revival of the flagging donkey, are part of the traditional *Sīrah* of the Prophet. See Ibn Hishām, *Sīrat al-nabī*, ed. Wüstenfeld, 103–105 = ed. al-Saqqā et al., I, 171–73, tr. 70–71; Ibn Sa'd, *Kitāb al-Ṭabaqāt al-kabīr*, I/1, 69–70; and cf. Lings, *Muhammad*, 25–26. See for modern discussions of these miraculous details, Andrae, *Die Person Muhammeds*. 28ff.; Buhl, *Das Leben Muhammeds*, 117–17; Watt. *Muhammad at Mecca*, 33–36; Annemarie Schimmel, *And Muhammad Is His Messenger. The Veneration of the Prophet in Islamic Piety*, 10.

ground, slit open my belly, and searched within it for something I know not what." She said: We took him back with us to our tent. She related: His (foster) father said to me: "O Ḥalīmah, by God, I fear that this child may have been struck by some malady, so take [973] him back to his family before the results of the attack become manifest." She related: So we picked him up and bore him back to his mother. She asked, "What has made you bring him back, O wet nurse, when you were formerly so anxious for his welfare and for his remaining with you?" She related: I said, "God has allowed my (foster) son to grow up so far, and I have fulfilled the duties incumbent upon me. I now fear that something untoward may afflict him, so I have handed him back to you as you desire." Āminah asked me, "What's all this that has happened to you? Tell me the truth!" She related: She would not leave me alone until I had told her the whole story. She asked, "Were you then afraid a demon (*al-shayṭān*) had possessed him?" She related: I replied, "Yes." She exclaimed, "By God, indeed no! No demon has power over him. My dear son has a great future before him; shall I not tell you his story?" She related: I answered, "Yes, please." Āminah said, "When I became pregnant with him, a light went forth from me which illuminated all the fortresses of Buṣrā in the land of Syria for me, and thereafter I bore him, and by God, I never had a pregnancy that was easier and smoother than the one with him. Then when I gave birth to him, he slid out, and placed his hands on the ground and raised his head toward the heavens. Leave him now, and go back with your task honorably fulfilled."

There related to us Naṣr b. ʿAbd al-Raḥmān al-Azdī—Muḥammad b. Yaʿlā—ʿUmar b. Ṣubayḥ—Thawr b. Yazīd al-Shaʾmī—Makḥūl al-Shaʾmī—Shaddād b. Aws, who said: Once, while we were sitting with the Messenger of God, there approached a shaykh of the Banū ʿĀmir, who was the leading chief and sayyid of his tribe and descendant of a great shaykh, leaning upon a staff, and appeared before the Messenger of God, standing here, and attributed the latter genealogically to his grandfather, saying thus, "O Ibn ʿAbd al-Muṭṭalib, I have been informed that you claim to be the Messenger of God to the people (*al-nās*) and that [you claim that] God has sent you with the message which He entrusted to Ibrāhīm (Abraham), Mūsā (Moses), ʿĪsā (Jesus), and

[974] other prophets. [I am further informed] that you have pronounced a momentous message (*fawwahta bi-ʿaẓīm*[in]).[653] But the prophets and the representatives of God (*al-khulafāʾ*) have stemmed only from two houses of the Children of Israel, whereas you come from a people who worship these stones and idols. So what connection have you with prophethood? Nevertheless, every utterance has its core of truth, so tell me about the truth of your words and the beginnings of your claim to prophethood." He related: The Prophet was pleasurably impressed by his question, and replied, "O brother of the Banū ʿĀmir, this affair you are asking me about has indeed its own story and place (or: occasion) where (or: when) it should be recounted, so sit down!"

The man bent his legs and then knelt down just as a camel does, and the Prophet faced him and began to speak. He said: "O brother of the Banū ʿĀmir, the truth of my words and the beginnings of my claim to prophethood lie in the fact that I am what my forefather Abraham prayed for and the good news of my brother Jesus, son of Mary. I was my mother's first born, and she conceived and bore me as the heaviest burden she had ever borne and began to complain of the weight she felt to her fellow wives (or: fellow womenfolk, *ṣawāḥibihā*). Then my mother saw in a dream that what she bore in her womb was a light, and she said, "I began to follow the light with my gaze, and the light went before my gaze until it lit up for me the whole eastern and western limits of the earth." Then she gave birth to me, and I grew up. When I grew up, the idols of Quraysh were rendered hateful to me, as was also poetry.[654] I was offered for suckling among the Banū Layth b. Bakr.[655]

---

653. This seems to be the sense here of *fawwaha,* although the lexica only give the meaning for this form II verb of "[God] created someone with a wide mouth."

654. In the years at Mecca before his call to prophethood, Muḥammad is said to have recoiled from swearing by Allāt and al-ʿUzzā, but this premature rejection of polytheism may be a retrojection of subsequent attitudes. Also, Muḥammad's rejection of poetry was not presumably from lack of interest or for aesthetic reasons but, as is clear from Qurʾān, XXVI, 221–26, cf. LXIX, 40–43, because the themes of poetry were the expression par excellence of the old pagan order, with its violence, its emphasis on revenge, and its proclamation of trust in human effort as a major factor in life, attitudes which the new faith of Islam aimed at countering or transforming.

655. In al-Ṭabarī, I, 969, p. 271 above, Ḥalīmah's tribe is the Banū Saʿd b. Bakr. Layth b. Bakr b. ʿAbd Manāt were one of the main branches of Kinānah; see Ibn al-Kalbī-Caskel-Strenziok, *Jamharat al-nasab,* I, Table 36, II, 6, 376.

One day, I was away from the rest of my people in the bottom of a wadi, with a group of children of my own age, and we were playing at throwing between us pieces of camels' dung. Suddenly, a group of three men approached us, bearing a gold pitcher filled with snow. They took me out of the group of my friends, and the latter fled until they reached the edge of the wadi. Then they came back to the group of three and said, "What do you intend to do with this lad? He is not one of us but is the son of the lord of Quraysh, and is an orphan, for whom a wet nurse was sought among us; he has no father. What good will killing him bring you, [975] and what will you gain from that? But if you are determined ineluctably on killing him, then choose one of us, whichever you like; let him come to you in his stead, and then kill him; but leave this lad alone, he is an orphan." However, when the children saw the group of three men returning no answer to them, they fled at top speed back to the tribe, telling them what had happened and imploring help against the men.

One of the three men came up to me and laid me gently on the ground, and then split open my body from the division of my rib cage (*mafraq ṣadrī*) to the end of the pubic hair, while I was watching all this but not feeling any touch at all. He then took out the viscera from my abdomen and washed them with that snow. He washed them carefully and replaced them. Then the second man stood up and said to his companion, "Stand aside," and he drew him away from me. He then put his hand into my insides and brought forth my heart, with me watching all the time. He split it asunder, extracted a black drop and threw the drop aside. He went on to say: In his hand, at his right side, there was as if he were holding something, and lo and behold, just by me was a seal ring in his hand, emitting light that dazzled anyone looking at it, and by means of which he sealed my heart so that it became filled with light; this was the light of prophethood and wisdom. Then he returned it to its place. I felt the coolness of that seal ring in my heart for a long time afterward. The third man now said to his companion, "Stand aside from me," and he passed his hand over my body from the division of my rib cage to the end of the pubic hair, and that slit was henceforth healed together, by God's permission. He now took my hand and gently made me get up from my resting place, and said to the first man, who had slit open my

body, "Weigh him against ten of his community!" They weighed me against them, and I outweighed them. Next he said, "Weigh him against a hundred of his community!" They weighed me against them, and I outweighed them. Finally he said, "Weigh him against a thousand of his community!" They weighed me against them, and I outweighed them. He then said, "Let him be; even if you were to weigh him against the whole of his community, he would outweigh them all!" He related: They then clasped me to
[976] their breasts, and kissed my head and the place between my eyes. They said to me, "O my dear one, you have not been rendered terrified. If only you knew the goodness and benefit that is intended through you, you would rejoice and be refreshed."

He related: While we were engaged thus, behold, I found the tribe at my side, who had come in their entirety, and there was my mother, who was [really] my wet nurse, in the forefront of the tribe, crying out at the top of her voice and saying, "Alas for a poor, weak one!" He related: They crowded round me and fell upon me, kissing my head and the place between my eyes, and said, "Good for you O poor, weak one!" Then my wet nurse lamented, "Alas for a solitary one!" at which they crowded round and fell upon me and clasped me to their breasts, kissing my head and the place between my eyes, and said, "Good for you, O solitary one, for you are not a solitary one—indeed God, His angels, and all the believers of the people of the earth are with you!" But my wet nurse still lamented, "Alas for an orphan, treated as a weak one among your companions and then killed because of your weakness!" at which they crowded round and fell upon me and clasped me to their breasts, kissing my head and the place between my eyes, and said, "Good for you, O orphan, how noble you are in the sight of God! If you only knew what goodness and blessing is intended through you!" He related: They (i.e., the three miraculous visitants) brought me to the edge of the wadi. When my mother, who was [really] my wet nurse, saw me, she cried out, "O my dear son! Do I really see you still alive?" and she came up to me, fell upon me and clasped me to her breast. And by Him in whose hand is my soul, I was within her bosom, she having clasped me to her, while my hand was still in the hand of one of the three men. I began to turn toward them, imagining that the members of the tribe could see them [also], but they could not in fact see them. One of the members of the tribe commented, "Some touch of madness or a visitation of the jinn has affected this lad; let us take him along to our soothsayer and medicine man (*kāhin*), so that he may examine him and cure him." I said to him, "O so-and-so, nothing such as you mention has affected me; my mental faculties are intact and [977] my heart is sound; I am not afflicted by any malady."[656] My father said—he being the husband of my wet nurse—"Do you not perceive that what he says is the speech of a perfectly sound person? I fully expect that no affliction will permanently affect my son." They nevertheless agreed upon taking me along to the soothsayer, and they carried me until they came to him. When they related to him the story of what had happened to me, he told them, "Shut up, until I hear from the child himself, for he knows more about what happened to him than you do." He questioned me, and I told him my story, from beginning to end. When he had heard my words, he sprang up and clasped me to his breast, and then called out in the loudest possible voice, "O Arabs, O Arabs, forward! Kill this lad, and kill me with him, for by Allāt and al-ʿUzzā, if you let him be and he reaches the age of puberty, he will most certainly subvert your religion, declare your minds and those of your forefathers to be deluded, oppose your way of life, and bring forward for you a religion of whose like you have never heard." I made for my foster mother, and she snatched me away from his bosom, saying, "You yourself are certainly more deranged and more possessed by the jinn than this son of mine, and if I had only known that you would have made such a pronouncement as this, I would not have brought him along to you. Seek out for yourself someone who will kill you, for I am not going to kill this lad!" Then they bore me along and handed me back to my family. I subsequently lost all fear of what had been done to me, and the traces of that cut from my breast to the end of the pubic hair became just a faint line. This, O brother of the Banū ʿĀmir, is the truth of my words and the beginnings of my claim to prophethood.[657]

---

656. *qalabah*, literally "a condition or malady for which the afflicted one should be turned over and examined," apparently a disease of camels and horses; according to the lexicographers, it was only used in negative contexts, as here. See Lane, *Lexicon*, 2554b–c.

657. The story of the opening of Muḥammad's breast has been first given by al-

The 'Āmirī exclaimed, "I call to witness God, than whom there is no other god, that your calling is a true one, so give me information about various things I am going to ask you." The Prophet replied, "Ask what you want (*sal 'anka*)" (before this, the Prophet always used to say to a questioner, "Ask whatever you wish and about what seems good to you," *sal 'ammā shi'ta wa-'ammā badā laka;* he only said to the 'Āmirī on that particular day *sal 'anka* because that was a dialectical peculiarity [*lughah*] of the Banū 'Āmir). The Prophet spoke to him concerning what he knew.

[978] The 'Āmirī said, "Tell me, O Ibn 'Abd al-Muṭṭalib, about that which increases one's knowledge." The Prophet re-

---

Ṭabarī at I, 972–73, pp. 274–75 above, on the basis of four *isnād*s all going through Ibn Isḥāq and in a fairly brief form. It is now given in greater detail in a *khabar* going back to Shaddād b. 'Amr b. Thābit (nephew of the poet of Medina Ḥassān b. Thābit, died 58/678; see Ibn Sa'd, *Kitāb al-ṭabaqāt al-kabīr,* VII/2, 124). Then thirdly, we have at I, 979, p. 282 below, a briefer version in a *khabar* going back to Khālid b. Ma'dān al-Kalā'ī (known as an ascetic and as a trustworthy authority, *thiqah,* for *ḥadīth* transmission, died 103/721–22; see Ibn Sa'd, op. cit., VII/2, 162). Ibn Hishām, *Sīrat al-nabī,* ed. Wüstenfeld, 105–06 = ed. al-Saqqā et al., I, 173–76, tr. 71–72, gives, of course, the first version, that through Ibn Isḥāq, as does Ibn Sa'd, op. cit., I/1, 70.

Again, this story can be paralleled in the lore and legend of many other human societies. The visitation by angels or spirits, the slitting open of Muḥammad's belly, the removal of the black spot of sin and purification by washing with snow, all suggest ritual cleansing and the communication of extraordinary powers. In the Jāhiliyyah, it was often held that the *jinn* could communicate poetic inspiration to a man by similar means. Goldziher, in his *Abhandlungen zur arabischen Philologie,* I, 213, cited as a parallel to the history of the opening of Muḥammad's breast what the sister of the poet of al-Ṭā'if, Umayyah b. Abī al-Ṣalt (on whom see n. 603 above) is said to have told the Prophet that a *jinnī* in the form of a vulture opened the breast of the sleeping Umayyah, filled his breast with something unspecified and then closed it up. This gave the prophet Umayyah the inspiration for introducing wise aphorisms (*ḥikmah*) into his poems and also the idea of divine unity (*tawḥīd*).

What connection the story of Muḥammad and his supernatural visitants has with the words of Qur'ān, XCIV, 1–2, "Did We not open your breast, And removed from you your burden?" is unclear. The Qur'ān commentators take this figuratively rather than literally (i.e., with the verb *sharaḥa* in *a-lam nashraḥ ṣadraka* taken as meaning "to remove, lift away" rather than "to cut open": see Paret, *Der Koran. Kommentar und Konkordanz,* 515–16; Bell, *A Commentary on the Qur'ān,* II, 554), that God opened up thereby Muḥammad's awareness of the spiritual world; but there is always the possibility that the story of the opening of Muḥammad's breast may have evolved to explain the Qur'ānic passage in a literal sense. See Andrae, *Die Person Muhammeds,* 32–34; Watt, *Muhammad at Mecca,* 35–36; H. Birkeland, *The Legend of the Opening of Muhammad's Breast,* passim; Schimmel, *And Muhammad Is His Messenger,* 67–69.

plied, "The process of learning." The 'Āmirī asked, "Tell me what points toward knowledge." The Prophet replied, "Asking questions." The 'Āmirī asked, "Tell me about that which increases in evil." The Prophet replied, "Persistence [in evil ways]." The 'Āmirī asked, "Tell me, is piety of any avail after evil doing?" The Prophet replied, "Yes, repentance (*tawbah*) cleanses from sin, and good deeds sweep away evil deeds. If a servant [of God] mentions his Lord's name when he is enjoying ease of life, God will aid him in times of distress." The 'Āmirī said, "How can that be, O Ibn 'Abd al-Muṭṭalib?" The Prophet replied, "This is because God says, 'No, by my power and exaltedness, I shall not gather together for My servant two causes of security, nor shall I ever gather together for him two causes of fear. If he shows fear toward Me in this present world, he will feel secure from Me (i.e., from my wrath) on the Day when I shall gather together all my servants in the sacred enclosure (*ḥaẓīrat al-quds*).[658] This feeling of security will remain with him perpetually and I shall not withhold my blessings from him when I do deny blessings [from others]. But if he feels secure from Me (i.e., self-sufficient) in this present world, he will fear Me on the day when I shall gather together all my servants at a specified time on an appointed day, and his fear will remain with him perpetually.'"

The 'Āmirī said, "Tell me, O Ibn 'Abd al-Muṭṭalib, to what are you summoning people?" The Prophet replied, "I am summoning people to worship the One God, who has no partners, and that you should throw off allegiance to idols, proclaim your disbelief in Allāt and al-'Uzzā, affirm your belief in the Book or the prophets which have come from God, perform the five acts of worship with all their significant details, fast for a month in each year, and hand over poor tax on your wealth, [for if you do so,] God will purify you by means of it and render your wealth wholesome for you. Also, that you should perform the Pilgrimage to the [Holy] House when you are able to do this, perform the major ablution (*ghusl*) after

658. The Cairo text of al-Ṭabarī, II, 164, has *ḥaẓīrat al-firdaws* "enclosure of Paradise," as in ms. P. of the Leiden text, see n. *e*. The reference is to the gathering together of the saved after the Last Judgment, as foretold in Qur'ān, XIX, 85/88, and their admittance to Paradise. See *EI*², s.v. Ḳiyāma (L. Gardet).

major bodily pollution (*janābah*),[659] and believe in death and the resurrection after death, and in the Garden and Hell Fire." The ʿĀmirī said, "O Ibn ʿAbd al-Muṭṭalib, if I do all that, what will be
[979] my reward?" The Prophet replied, "The Garden of Eden, from below which springs of water flow, in which [those who are saved] will remain forever, that is the reward of those who aim at righteousness."[660] The ʿĀmirī said, "O Ibn ʿAbd al-Muṭṭalib, is there, as well as all that, any advantage for this present life, for I find ease and pleasantness of daily life attractive?" The Prophet replied, "Yes, indeed, success and a firm place in the land."[661] He related: The ʿĀmirī responded to the Prophet's call and turned to God.

There related to us Ibn Ḥumayd—Salamah—Muḥammad b. Isḥāq—Thawr b. Yazīd—Khālid b. Maʿdān al-Kalāʿī, who said: A group of the Messenger of God's followers asked, "O Messenger of God, tell us about yourself!" He replied, "Yes, I will. I am what my forefather Abraham prayed for and the good news of Jesus. My mother saw in a dream when she bore me within her womb that there came forth from her a light which illuminated for her the fortresses of Buṣrā in the land of Syria. I was offered for suckling to the women of the Banū Saʿd b. Bakr. Once when I was with one of my (foster) brothers, behind our tents, tending our lambs, there came to me two men wearing white robe and bearing a golden pitcher filled with snow. They took hold of me, split open my belly and then extracted from it my heart, which they split open, taking out from it a black blood clot. They threw it aside, and then washed my belly and my heart with that snow, until they had cleansed it. Then one of them said to his companion, 'Weigh him with ten of his community,' so he weighed me with them, and I was equal to them in weight. Then he said, 'Weigh him with a hundred of his community,' so he weighed me with them, and I was equal to them in weight. Then he said, 'Weigh him with a

659. That is, the major ablution required after such polluting events as sexual intercourse, contact with menstrual blood, etc. See *EI*², s.v. Ghusl (G. H. Bousquet).

660. Qurʾān, XX, 78/76. For this interpretation of *tazakkā* in a late Meccan-early Medinan context, see Watt, *Muhammad at Mecca*, 165–66.

661. Again echoing Qurʾānic phraseology, in which *al-tamakkun fī al-arḍ*, "establishing a firm place in the land," is often a reward for the righteous.

thousand of his community,' so he weighed me with them, and I was equal to them in weight. Finally, he said, 'Leave him alone, for even if I were to weigh him with [the whole of] his community, he would be equal to them.'"

Ibn Isḥāq says: ʿAbd Allāh b. ʿAbd al-Muṭṭalib, the Messenger of God's father, died at a time when the Messenger of God's mother, Āminah bt. Wahb b. ʿAbd Manāf b. Zuhrah, was pregnant with him.

As for Hishām [b. Muḥammad], he says: ʿAbdallāh, the Messenger of God's father, died when the Messenger of God was [980] twenty-eight months old.[662]

There related to me al-Ḥārith—Ibn Saʿd, who said: Muḥammad b. ʿUmar al-Wāqidī stated that the firmly accepted belief, from which none of our companions differ, is that ʿAbdallāh b. ʿAbd al-Muṭṭalib came back from Syria in a caravan of Quraysh's and encamped at Medina, and he remained there until he died. He was buried in the building (*dār*) of al-Nābighah, in the small hut (*al-dār al-ṣughrā*), [which is], when you go into the building, on your left, within the house (*bayt*).[663]

There related to us Ibn Ḥumayd—Salamah—Ibn Isḥāq—ʿAbdallāh b. Abī Bakr b. Muḥammad b. ʿAmr b. Ḥazm al-Anṣārī, who said that the Messenger of God's mother Āminah died at al-Abwāʾ between Mecca and Medina when the Messenger of God

662. Ibn Isḥāq preferred the view that 'Abdallāh died before Āminah gave birth to Muḥammad, although one line of transmission adds that he died when Muḥammad was twenty-eight months old. Other authorities mentioned, such as Ibn al-Kalbī cited here, give figures like twenty-eight months or seven months for Muḥammad's age at his father's death. Half-a-century later than Ibn Isḥāq, however, the historian al-Wāqidī (on whom see n. 1020 below) had much more circumstantial detail about the time and place of 'Abdallāh's death (cf. below and n. 663). See Ibn Hishām, *Sīrat al-nabī*, ed. Wüstenfeld, 102 = ed. al-Saqqā et al., I, 167, tr. 69; Ibn Sa'd, *Ṭabaqāt*, I/1, 61–62; and the detailed discussion of the varying reports on 'Abdallāh's death in Lecker, "The Death of the Prophet Muḥammad's Father: Did Wāqidī Invent Some of the Evidence?" 9–27.

663. Ibn Saʿd, *Ṭabaqāt*, I/1, 61, following reports used by al-Wāqidī, says that ʿAbdallāh was taken ill on the way back from Syria, was unable to carry on the journey to Mecca and died at Medina among his maternal kinsmen, the Banū ʿAdī b. al-Najjār (his grandfather Hāshim having married Salmā bt. ʿAmr from this Medinan clan, see Ibn Hishām, *Sīrat al-nabī*, ed. Wüstenfeld, 88 = ed. al-Saqqā et al., I, 144–45, tr. 59; Ibn Saʿd, op. cit., I/1, 46).

was six years old, She had brought him to Medina to let him visit his maternal uncles of the Banū ʿAdī b. al-Najjār, but she died on the way back to Medina with him.[664]

Al-Ḥārith related to me—Muḥammad b. Saʿd—Muḥammad b. ʿUmar—Ibn Jurayj—ʿUthmān b. Ṣafwān, who said that Āminah bt. Wahb's grave is in the ravine of Abū Dharr at Mecca.

There related to us Ibn Ḥumayd—Salamah—Ibn Isḥāq—al-ʿAbbās b. ʿAbdallāh b. Maʿbad b. al-ʿAbbās—some member of his family, who said that ʿAbd al-Muṭṭalib died when the Messenger of God was eight years old. But another authority says that ʿAbd al-Muṭṭalib died when the Messenger of God was ten years old.

There related to us Ibn Ḥumayd—Salamah—Ṭalḥah b. ʿAmr al-Ḥaḍramī—ʿAṭāʾ b. Abī Rabāḥ—Ibn ʿAbbās, who said: The Prophet
[981] was in the care of Abū Ṭālib after his grandfather ʿAbd al-Muṭṭalib, and became the latter's child as if he were part of himself.[665]

The story returns to the completion of the reign of Kisrā Anūsharwān.

---

664. Ibn Hishām, *Sīrat al-nabī*, ed. Wüstenfeld, 107 = ed. al-Saqqā et al., I, 177, tr. 73, and Ibn Saʿd, *Ṭabaqāt*, I/1, 73–74, confirm that Āminah died at al-Abwāʾ when Muḥammad was six years old, and state that the Prophet visited and tended her grave and mourned over her when he was en route for al-Ḥudaybiyah in 6/628. Al-Abwāʾ lay just north of Mecca along the Medina road; it was said to be the goal of Muḥammad's first *ghazwah* or raid against the Banū Ḍamrah and the Banū Bakr b. ʿAbd Manāt of Kinānah only twelve months after the Hijrah. See al-Bakrī, *Muʿjam mā istaʿjam*, I, 102; Yāqūt, *Buldān*, I, 79–80; Watt, *Muhammad at Medina*, 84, 340; Al-Wohaibi, *The Northern Hijaz*, 35–40.

665. *ghumṣ$^{an}$ rumṣ$^{an}$ . . . saqīl$^{an}$ dahīn$^{an}$*, literally, "like the wet and dry dirty matter which collects in the inner corner of the eye . . . and like something smooth and anointed with oil."

# [The Remainder of Kisrā Anūsharwān's Reign and the Last Sāsānid Kings]

There related to us ʿAlī b. Ḥarb al-Mawṣilī—Abū Ayyūb Yaʿlā b. ʿImrān al-Bajalī—Makhzūm b. Hāni' al-Makhzūmī—his father, who was a hundred and fifty years old. He said: When it was the night in which the Messenger of God was born, the Aywān of Kisrā was shaken and fourteen pinnacles of it fell down;[666] the [sacred] fire of Fārs, which had not previously been extinguished for a thousand years, was extinguished;[667] the waters of the lake of Sāwah sank into the earth;[668] and the Chief Mōbadh saw in a dream refractory camels running before noble Arab horses which had crossed the Tigris and had spread through those districts of it.[669] The next morning, Kisrā was affrighted by what he had seen. He resolutely held himself back in patience, but then he considered that he ought not to conceal it from his ministers and Marzbāns. He put on his crown and seated himself on his throne,

666. That is, the Aywān or Ṭāq-i Kisrā, the great Sāsānid palace in the district of Aspānbār at al-Madā'in, on the east bank of the Tigris, where its ruinous partial shell still exists. See Le Strange, *Lands*, 34; Herrmann, *The Iranian Revival*, 126–28; *EI²*, s.v. al-Madā'in (M. Streck-M. J. Morony).

667. Presumably the great fire temple at Iṣṭakhr, i.e., at Persepolis, at whose ruins al-Masʿūdī marvelled. See his *Murūj*, III, 76–77 = § 1403; *EIr*, s.v. Ātaškada (M. Boyce).

668. Sāwah is a town of northwestern Persia, in the mediaeval Islamic province of Jibāl, not however known to have existed in pre-Islamic times. It was nevertheless made the site of one of these tales of portents announcing the Prophet's birth. See Yāqūt, *Buldān*, III, 179–80; Le Strange, *Lands*, 211–12; Schwarz, *Iran*, 339–42; *EI²*, s.v. Sāwa (C. E. Bosworth-H. H. Schaeder).

669. These portents are mentioned also by al-Masʿūdī, *Murūj*, I, 217, II, 228 = §§ 231, 649.

and gathered them around him. When they were all gathered together around him, he told them why he had sent for them and what he had summoned them for. While they were engaged in all this, a letter arrived bringing news of the extinguishing of the [sacred] fire, so that his distress of spirit increased. The Chief Mōbadh said, "I too—may God grant the king righteousness—had a dream that same night," and he recounted to him his dream about the camels. The king said, "What is this thing, O Chief Mōbadh," although he himself was the most knowing about the real meaning of that. The Chief Mōbadh replied, "An event which is issuing from the Arabs."

On hearing that, Kisrā wrote a letter, as follows: "From Kisrā, the king of kings, to al-Nuʿmān b. al-Mundhir. As follows: Send to me a man who is knowledgeable about what I wish to ask him," so al-Nuʿmān dispatched to him ʿAbd al-Masīḥ b. ʿAmr b. Ḥayyān b. Buqaylah al-Ghassānī.[670] When the letter reached Kisrā, Kisrā asked him, "Do you know what I wish to ask you?"
[982] He replied, "Let the king tell me about it; and if I am knowledgeable about it, [well and good], but if not, I can tell him about someone who will know it for him." Kisrā accordingly told him about his dream. ʿAbd al-Masīḥ said, "A maternal uncle of mine who lives in the elevated regions of Syria, called Saṭīḥ, will have knowledge about it."[671] Kisrā said, "Go to him, and ask him what I have just asked you, and bring me back his answer." ʿAbd al-Masīḥ rode off on his mount until he came to Saṭīḥ, who was, however, on the verge of death. He greeted him and wished him long life, but Saṭīḥ returned no answer. Hence ʿAbd al-Masīḥ began to recite:[672]

---

670. This member of the Christian ʿIbād of al-Ḥīrah seems to have been a historical person, although his role in these events and the attribution to him of an age of 350 years are clearly embellishments. He is said to have negotiated with Khālid b. al-Walīd for the surrender of al-Ḥīrah to the incoming Muslim Arabs. See al-Balādhurī, *Futūḥ*, 243; al-Masʿūdī, *Murūj*, I, 217–22 = §§ 231–33; Abū al-Faraj al-Iṣfahānī, *Aghānī*³, XVI, 194–95.

Buqaylah was one of the clans of al-Ḥīrah, of Ghassānid tribal origin, as appears also from al-Ṭabarī, I, 1023, p. 349 below, which had a castle (*qaṣr*) of its own. See al-Yaʿqūbī, *Kitāb al-buldān*, 309, tr. G. Wiet, 140–41; Nöldeke, trans. 254 n. 2; Rothstein, *Laḫmiden*, 114 n. 2.

671. For Saṭīḥ, see al-Ṭabarī, I, 911ff., pp. 178ff. above.

672. Nöldeke noted, trans. 255 n. 1, that the manuscripts have considerable variation in the readings of various words and in the order of these *rajaz* verses,

Is the proud lord of Yemen deaf, or does he hear? Or has he gone away, and has the course of untimely death made away with him?
O you who are able to give the interpretation of an affair which was too difficult for this man and that, the shaykh of the tribe, from the house of Sanan, has come to you,
Whose mother is from the house of Dhi'b b. Ḥajan, a blue-eyed one, with sharpened fang, whose ears are ringing,[673]
A shining white one, with an ample cloak and corselet of mail, the envoy of the prince (*qayl*) of the Persians, who journeys onward during the time for sleeping. [983]
A stout, compactly built she-camel travels through the land, which conveys me up a rocky slope at one time and down it the next,
Fearing neither thunderbolts nor the misfortunes of time, until it becomes lean and emaciated in the breast and the part between the thighs (i.e., from traveling continuously).
The fine dust of the deserted encampments' traces swirls round it in the wind, as if it were galloping vigorously from the two slopes of Thakan.[674]

When Saṭīḥ heard the verses, he raised his head and said: ʿAbd al-Masīḥ—traveling on a camel—to Saṭīḥ—who is already on the brink of the tomb—the king of the sons of Sāsān has sent you—because of the Aywān's being shaken—and the extinguishing of the fires—and the dream of the Chief Mōbadh—of refractory camels running before noble Arab horses—which had crossed the Tigris and spread through those districts of it—O ʿAbd al-Masīḥ,

---

with interchanging of hemistichs, and that the text and interpretation of the poem is uncertain in parts. Older poets, as here ʿAbd al-Masīḥ, use the *mashṭūr* form of the *rajaz* meter in which, in each *bayt,* every *shaṭr* rhymes with the following hemistich and not just with regard to the two hemistichs of the first *bayt;* with a common rhyme for the whole poem, hemistich by hemistich, interchange of hemistichs within *bayts* is easy. See Wright, *A Grammar of the Arabic Language,* II, 362A–B.

673. Sanan and Dhi'b b. Ḥajan must be tribal groups of Yemen, but do not figure in such works as Ibn al-Kalbī's *Jamharat al-nasab* or al-Hamdānī's *Ṣifat jazīrat al-ʿArab.*

674. Thakan is listed by al-Bakrī, *Muʿjam mā istaʿjam,* I, 342, and Yāqūt, *Buldān,* II, 82, but with no mention of its location and with this verse as the only *shāhid* for it.

when there has been much recounting of stories—and the man with the staff has been sent[675]—and the valley of al-Samāwah[676] has overflowed (i.e., with invading troops)—and the waters of the lake of Sāwah have sunk into the earth—and the [sacred] fire of Fārs has been extinguished—then Syria is no longer for Saṭīḥ Syria—kings and queens from amongst them (i.e., the last Sāsānids) shall reign—according to the number of pinnacles (i.e., those fallen from the Aywān)—and everything whose coming is decreed will come." Then Saṭīḥ expired on the spot. 'Abd al-Masīḥ now mounted his steed and recited:

Gird yourself for action, for you are keen in resolution,
vigorous! Let not separation and mutability affright you!
If the dominion of the sons of Sāsān escapes from their hands,
well, time is made up of different evolutions and lengthy periods.
How oft, O how oft did they reach a lofty stage in which lions
[984] which tear their prey were afraid of their mighty onrush!
To them belongs Mihrān, the man of the lofty tower,[677] and his
brothers, the two Hurmuzs, Sābūr and [the other] Sābūr.
The people are all half brothers and sisters of each other; when
one of them comes to realize that another one has become lacking in some way, that person is cast aside and treated with contempt.
But they are also brothers from the same mother; when they see
some item of property, that item is protected and supported in the owner's absence.
Good and bad fortune are closely linked together like a rope
binding two camels; good fortune is sought after, but bad fortune is avoided.

When 'Abd al-Masīḥ arrived back to Kisrā, he informed him of Saṭīḥ's words. Kisrā commented, "Once fourteen of us have re-

675. That is, 'Umar b. al-Khaṭṭāb, the second caliph, mentioned here as bearing his staff of office (*hirāwah*, the equivalent of the *qaḍīb* or *'aṣā*), with which the stern 'Umar trounced malefactors and which became one of the insignia of the caliphal office. See *EI*², s.v. Ḳaḍīb (D. Sourdel).

676. That is, "the elevated land," the desert region between the Euphrates and Syria. See *EI*², s.v. al-Samāwa (C. E. Bosworth).

677. See al-Ṭabarī, I, 885, p. 131 and n. 340 above.

igned, things will happen!" Ten of them, however, reigned for a total of four years only, and the rest of them held power until the reign of 'Uthmān b. 'Affān.[678]

I received reports going back to Hishām b. Muḥammad,[679] who said: [On one occasion,] Wahrīz dispatched wealth and valuable specialities of Yemen to Kisrā. When these reached the territory of the Banū Tamīm, Ṣa'ṣa'ah b. Nājiyah b. 'Iqāl al-Mujāshi'ī[680] summoned the Banū Tamīm to fall upon the caravan, but they refused. When the caravan reached the territory of the Banū Yarbū',[681] Ṣa'ṣa'ah summoned these last to do that, but they were fearful of doing it. He said, O Banū Yarbū', I can foresee that this caravan will pass into the territory of the Banū Bakr b. Wā'il and they will attack it, and they will then use the wealth acquired hereby to make war on you!"[682] When they heard that, they plundered the caravan. A man of the Banū Salīṭ called al-Naṭif seized a saddle bag filled with jewels, hence people said, "He has seized the treasure of al-Naṭif," and this became proverbial. Ṣa'ṣa'ah acquired a palm-leaf basket containing silver ingots. The people of the caravan went to Hawdhah b. 'Alī al-Ḥanafī in al-Yamāmah,[683] who pro-

678. The ten ephemeral rulers mentioned here would presumably be those transient rulers, pretenders, and usurpers who filled the four years or so after Heraclius's invasion of Mesopotamia in 627 had left a legacy of chaos and confusion within the Persian ruling classes; see al-Ṭabarī, I, 1045–66, pp. 381–409 below. Of the kings after Anūsharwān, only three persons, Hormizd IV, Khusraw II Abarwēz, and Yazdagird III, could be said to have enjoyed reigns of reasonable duration.

679. Nöldeke, trans. 257 n. 3, noted that the Arabic sources on the conflict of the Persians with the Arabs of Tamīm give considerably varying stories but fall substantially into two versions, the one largely agreeing with the account here, the other, however, quite aberrant; and he stressed the vivacity and generally realistic nature of the Arabic narratives on this topic.

680. Grandfather of the famous Umayyad poet al-Farazdaq, and called *muḥyī al-maw'ūdāt* "he who restores to life those female children meant for killing," because he ransomed—allegedly as many as three or four hundred—girls about to be slaughtered by their destitute parents. See Abū al-Faraj al-Iṣfahānī, *Aghānī*[3], XXI, 276–77.

681. An important group of the Tamīm b. Murr, as were the Mujāshi'. The Salīṭ mentioned below were a subgroup of them. See Ibn al-Kalbī-Caskel-Strenziok, *Jamharat al-nasab*, I, Tables 68–71, II, 9, 591; *EI*[2], s.v. Yarbū', Banū (G. Levi Della Vida).

682. The Bakr and the Tamīm were ancient enemies, as was to be seen at the "Day of Dhū Qār," see al-Ṭabarī, I, 1015ff., pp. 338ff. below.

683. Hawdhah was one of the leading men of the Ḥanīfah b. Lujaym, a component tribe of the Bakr and occupiers of the rich eastern Arabian province of al-

vided them with clothing, food supplies, and mounts, and personally accompanied them until he reached Kisrā's presence. Hawdhah was a handsome and eloquent man, and Kisrā was favorably impressed by him and accounted to his credit what he had done. He called for a circlet of pearls, and it was placed on
[985] Hawdhah's head [as a diadem], and he gave him a brocade coat of honor and many other items of clothing; because of all that, Hawdhah was called "the man with the crown." Kisrā said to Hawdhah, "Do you know whether these fellows, who have done this deed, are from your own tribe?" He answered, "No." Kisrā said, "Is there a peace agreement between you and them?" He replied, "[No,] there is death between us." Kisrā said, "Your requirement is now about to be fulfilled," and he resolved to send a force of cavalry against the Banū Tamīm.

He was informed, however, "Their land is a bad land, made up of deserts and wastes, with tracks that cannot be followed. Their water comes from wells, and one cannot be sure that they will not block them up, with the result that your troops will perish." He was advised to write to his governor in al-Baḥrayn, Āzādh Firūz, son of Jushnas, whom the Arabs called al-Muka'bir ("the Mutilator"), because he used to cut off hands and feet.[684] He had sworn not to leave, among the Banū Tamīm, a single eye that could flow with tears. Kisrā followed this advice, and sent an envoy to him. He also summoned Hawdhah again, and gave him a further, fresh lot of honors and presents, and told him, "Travel back with this envoy of mine, and secure a satisfactory solution (i.e., secure re-

---

Yamāmah (see on the Ḥanīfah, Ibn al-Kalbī-Caskel-Strenziok, *Jamharat al-nasab*, I, Table 156, II, 25, 297). It was to Hawdhah (who was, as emerges from the poem cited by al-Ṭabarī, I, 987, p. 293 below, penultimate verse, a Christian, like much of the Banū Ḥanīfah at this time), together with Thumāmah b. Uthāl, that Muḥammad sent an envoy with a letter for "the king of al-Yamāmah" inviting him to become a Muslim, and Hawdhah was allegedly at one point in correspondence with Muḥammad offering to become a Muslim if he could have the succession to the Prophet's office after Muḥammad's death; but Hawdhah himself died shortly afterward and before the Prophet, probably in 8/630. See Ibn Hishām, *Sīrat al-nabī*, ed. Wüstenfeld, 971–2 = ed. al-Saqqā et al., IV, 254, tr. 653, 789; al-Balādhurī, *Futūḥ*, 86–87; *EI²*, s.v. Musaylima (W. Montgomery Watt).

684. After his operations against Tamīm, al-Muka'bir apparently remained in eastern Arabia, since he later led the Persian forces there together with their allies against Abū Bakr's commander al-'Alā' b. al-Ḥaḍramī during the opening years of 'Umar's caliphate, but he eventually submitted and became a Muslim. See al-Balādhurī, *Futūḥ*, 85–86.

venge) for both myself and yourself." Hawdhah and the army reached al-Muka'bir just before the time for gleaning. Meanwhile, at that moment the Banū Tamīm had moved to Hajar in order to get provisions and gleanings. Al-Muka'bir's herald proclaimed, "Let those of the Banū Tamīm who are here, come forward, for the king has decreed that provisions and food should be made available for them and divided out among them." They came forward, and he brought them into al-Mushaqqar, which is a fortified place facing another fortress called al-Ṣafā and separated from it by a river called the Muḥallim.[685]

The builder of al-Mushaqqar was one of Kisrā's cavalry troops called Basak (?), son of Māhbūdh,[686] whom Kisrā had sent expressly for its construction. When he began work on it, he was told, "These workmen will not remain in this place unless they are provided with womenfolk; but if you do that, the construction [986] work will be completed, and they will remain working on it until they have finished it." So he had brought for them whores from the regions of the Sawād and al-Ahwāz, and had skins of wine for them, from the land of Fārs, conveyed across the sea. The workmen and the women married each other and begat children, and soon comprised the greater part of the population of the town of Hajar. The people spoke Arabic and claimed kinship with the 'Abd al-Qays. When Islam came, they said to the 'Abd al-Qays, "You know well our numerical strength, our formidable equipment and

685. The port and fortress of al-Mushaqqar was the seat of Persian military power in the region of Hajar or the eastern Arabian shorelands, with the place's foundation variously attributed to the rulers of Kindah, the Persian commander mentioned below, etc. It lay in the territory of the 'Abd al-Qays tribe (on whom see al-Ṭabarī, I, 836, p. 51 and n. 150 above), but its exact site is unknown. See *EI²*, s.v. al-Mushakkar (C. E. Bosworth). At all events, it became a notable center for the extension of Sāsānid political control over the western shores of the Persian Gulf. By the mid-sixth century, the Arab poet of Bakr, Ṭarafah b. 'Abd, could call the Arabs of Baḥrayn, with a distinct note of contempt, *'abīd Asbadh* (where Asbadh stems from *asb*, "horse," + *ped*, "chief, commander," *pace* Nöldeke's etymology, trans. 260 n. 1, from *ispabadh*) "slaves of the commander of mounted warriors," i.e., of the Persian mailed cavalrymen, while other poets refer to the Persians settled in eastern Arabia as *Asbadhīs*. See Siddiqi, *Studien über die persischen Fremdwörter*, 78–79.

686. On these two names (the second of which is, however, uncertain), see Nöldeke, trans. 260 n. 3, and Justi, *Namenbuch*, 185 (Māhbōdh), 357–58 (*Wasaka, Vasaces). For the father Māhbūdh, Māhbōdh, who played a great role as commander in fighting between the Persians and Byzantines during Hormizd's reign, see Nöldeke, trans. loc. cit. and 438 n. 4, and n. 703 below.

weapons, and our great proficiency, so enroll us formally among your tribe and give us your daughters in marriage." They responded, "No, but remain here as you were as our brothers and clients (*mawālī*)." One man of ʿAbd al-Qays said, "O tribesmen of ʿAbd al-Qays! Follow my suggestion and enroll them as full members of the tribe, for the likes of those people are very much to be desired." But another member of the tribe said, "Aren't you ashamed of yourself? Are you telling us to take into our midst people who, as you know, have such beginnings and origins?" The first man replied, "If you don't adopt them into the tribe, other Arabs will." The second man answered, "In that case, we shan't worry about them in future!" Thereupon, they (i.e., those people from the mixed population of Hajar) became dispersed among the Arabs. Some remained with the ʿAbd al-Qays and were then reckoned as part of them, with no one gainsaying this attribution.

Once al-Mukaʿbir had got the Banū Tamīm within al-Mushaqqar, he massacred their menfolk and spared only the boys. On that day was killed Qaʿnab al-Riyāḥī, the knight of the Banū Yarbūʿ; two men of the Shann, who served the kings [of Persia] with alternate spells of duty, killed him.[687] The boys were put in boats and conveyed across to Fārs; some of them were castrated as eunuchs. Hubayrah b. Ḥudayr al-ʿAdawī related: After the conquest of Iṣṭakhr, there came to us a number of these deportees, one of them a eunuch and another a tailor.[688] A man of the Banū Tamīm called Ubayy b. Wahb attacked the chain holding the gate
[987] [of the city], cut through it, and escaped. He then recited:

I remember Hind, although it is not the time for remembrance;
    I remember her, even though several months' journey
    separates me from her.

---

687. This encounter was the *Yawm al-Ṣafqah*, described at length in Abū al Faraj Iṣfahānī, *Aghānī*³, XVII, 318–22, cf. Sir Charles Lyall, *Translations from Ancient Arabian Poetry, Chiefly Pre-Islamic*, 87–88. Qaʿnab b. ʿAttāb al-Riyāḥī had been one of the plunderers of the Persian caravan from Yemen (Abū al-Faraj al-Iṣfahānī, op. cit., XVII, 318). Shann were a clan of ʿAbd al-Qays; see Ibn al-Kalbī-Caskel-Strenziok, *Jamharat al-nasab*, I, Table 168, II, 28, 526.

688. Nöldeke, trans. 262 n. 1, pointed out that the Muslims did not conquer Iṣṭakhr till the 640s (actually in 23/643; see *EI*², s.v. Iṣṭakhr [M. Streck-M. J. Morony]), hence the events mentioned here happened almost certainly later than the time of Khusraw I Anūsharwān, since he died early in 579.

[She is] from Ḥijāz, from the highlands, and her people dwell
where the autumn rains pour down, between Zūr and
Minwar.[689]
Ho there, has it come to my people, despite the distance
separating us, that I defended my sacred interests (*dhimārī*)
on that day of the gateway of al-Mushaqqar?
I struck with my sword the panel of the gateway such a blow,
which would have made the most firmly built gateway
spring open.

On that day, Hawdhah b. ʿAlī interceded with al-Mukaʿbir for a hundred of the captives from the Banū Tamīm; the latter granted them to Hawdhah on Easter Day, and Hawdhah freed them. Concerning this, al-Aʿshā recited:

Question Tamīm about him, how it was in the days when they
were sold, when they came to him as captives, all of them
reduced to submissiveness,
In the midst of al-Mushaqqar. among a host of dust-smeared,
dark-colored ones (i.e., the victorious army), unable to
secure any beneficial aid afer the hurt [they had previously
suffered].
He said to the king, "Free a hundred of them," speaking gently,
in a low voice, not raising it.
So he released a hundred from the band of captives, and all of
them became freed of their bonds.
He put them forward openly, on Easter Day, as an offering,
hoping [for a reward] from God for what he had done as a
benefit and had wrought. [988]
But they (i.e., the freed Tamīmīs) did not consider as an act of
benevolence all that which had just been vouchsafed [for
them], even though their spokesman expressed a need for
due acknowledgment (or: spoke the truth about it, *qāla
qāʾiluhā ḥaqq^an bihā*) and exerted himself in that.[690]

689. Nöldeke vocalized *muṣāb* and translated "on the hills of al-Kharīf," but the vocalization *al-maṣāb*, "place where rains pour down," is followed here, with *al-kharīf* in its usual sense of "autumn." Yāqūt, *Buldān*, V, 216, mentions Manwar as a mountain, but clearly had no idea of its location.

690. al-Aʿshā Maymūn, *Dīwān*, no. 13, vv. 62–63, 67–69, 71; cf. Lyall, *Translations of Ancient Arabian poetry*, 88–89.

He describes the Banū Tamīm here as ungrateful.

Hishām related: When Wahriz was close to death—this being toward the end of Anūsharwān's reign—he called for his bow and an arrow, and said, "Set me up," so they did this. He shot the arrow and said, "See where my arrow falls to earth, and make my grave there." His arrow fell behind the monastery—that is, the church near Nu'm, a place called till today "the grave of Wahriz."[691] When the news of Wahriz's death reached Kisrā, he sent out to Yemen a knight called W.y.n (?), who proved a pertinacious tyrant.[692] Hence Hurmuz, the son of Kisrā, dismissed him and apppointed as governor in his stead al-Marūzān.[693] This last remained in Yemen, and had children born there who grew up to the age of puberty.

At this point Kisrā Anūsharwān died, after a reign of forty-eight years.[694]

---

691. Yāqūt, *Buldān,* II, 539, could only conjecture that this place was in the vicinity of Raḥbat Mālik b. Ṭawq, the latter place, in fact, in Syria (ibid., III, 34–36). This *dayr Nu'm* must, however, have been in Yemen.

692. Marquart surmised that this was the al-Bīnajān of al-Ṭabarī, I, 958, pp. 251–52 above, but the editor Nöldeke thought it more probable that there were two separate persons, *W.y.n* and *W.y.najān* (= al-Bīnajān). See *Addenda et emendanda,* p. DXCIII.

693. Thus corrected in *Addenda et emendanda,* loc. cit., following Marquart, from the text's *al-Marwazān,* in the light of the form of the name in parallel Greek and Armenian sources; previously, Nöldeke in his trans. 264 n. 1, had rendered the name as Marwazān.

694. Khusraw I Anūsharwān's reign was 531–79. His name appears on his coins as ḤWSRWB. See on his coins Paruck, *Sāsānian Coins,* 65–66, 380–84, 470–79, Plates XX–XXI, Tables XX–XXV; Göbl, *Sasanian Numismatics,* 52, Table XI, Plate 12; Sellwood, Whitting, and Williams, *An Introduction to Sasanian Coins,* 21, 140–44; Malek, "A Survey of Research on Sasanian Coins," 237.

The Arabic sources devote considerable space to this important reign, concurrent as it was with many events within Arabia significant for the birth of Islam. See Ibn Qutaybah, *Ma'ārif,* 663–64; al-Ya'qūbī, *Ta'rīkh,* I, 186–67; al-Dīnawarī, op. cit., 67–74; al-Mas'ūdī, *Murūj,* II, 196–211 = §§ 618–31; idem, *Tanbīh,* 101–102, tr. 145–46; Ḥamzah al-Iṣfahānī, *Ta'rīkh,* 51–53; Ibn al-Athīr, *Kāmil,* I, 434–42, 455–57. Of Persian sources, see Ṭabarī-Bal'amī, trans. II, 159–64, 219–32. Of modern studies, see Christensen, *Sassanides,* 363–440; Frye, *The Heritage of Persia,* 228–33; idem, "The Political History of Iran under the Sasanians," 153–62, 178; *EI*², s.vv. Anūsharwān (H. Massé), Kisrā and Sāsānids (M. Morony).

Al-Ṭabarī, in company with other early historical writers like al-Ya'qūbī and Ḥamzah al-Iṣfahānī, does not mention Buzurgmihr/Buzurjmihr, famed sage and minister of Anūsharwān so famed in later Islamic lore and legend (al-Dīnawarī, *al-Akhbār al-ṭiwāl,* 72, has a single, brief reference, but Ibn Qutaybah in his *'Uyūn al-*

## [Hurmuz]

Then there assumed the royal power Hurmuz. He was the son of King Anūsharwān, and his mother was the daughter of Khāqān the Elder.[695]

I received reports going back to Hishām b. Muḥammad, who said: This Hurmuz, son of Kisrā, was well educated and full of good intentions of benevolence toward the weak and destitute, but he attacked the power of the nobles, so that they showed themselves hostile and hated him, exactly as he in turn hated them. When he assumed the crown, he gathered round himself the members of the nobility of his kingdom. They enthusiastically called down blessings on his head and offered up thanks for his father. Hurmuz gave them promises of benevolent rule; he was anxious to behave toward his subjects with justice but implacable [989]
against the great men of the kingdom, because of their oppressing the lowly folk.[696]

---

*akhbār* has frequent mentions and quotations from his *ḥikmah*). Extensive mention of him only appears in writers of the mid-fourth/tenth century onward, such as al-Mas'ūdī, al-Tha'ālibī and especially Firdawsī, but thereafter he figures as the epitome of good counsel and wisdom in the "Mirrors for Princes" and similar *adab* works. This paragon may have arisen out of the Burzmihr who was a secretary of Anūsharwān's but who was, according to the *Shāh-nāmah*, executed by that ruler's successor Hormizd IV. Christensen, "La légende du sage Buzurjmihr," 81–128, although now outdated, traced how the stories round him first appeared in Middle Persian literature and then grew in the Islamic period. De Blois, in his *Burzōy's Voyage to India and the Origin of the Book of Kalīlah wa Dimnah*, 48–50, subjects Christensen's ideas to stringent analysis and concludes that Buzurgmihr remains a very shadowy individual, if he existed at all; nor does he think that there are any grounds for identifying him with Khusraw Anūsharwān's physician Burzōy, sent to India, according to the story, to fetch back a copy of the wonderful book *Kalīlah wa-Dimnah*. See also *EI²*, s.v. Buzurgmihr (H. Massé); *EIr*, s.v. Bozorgmehr-e Boḵtagān (Djalal Khaleghi Motlagh).

695. See al-Ṭabarī, I, 899, p. 160 and n. 404. According to al-Dīnawarī, *al-Akhbār al-ṭiwāl*, 74–75, Hormizd was the only son of Anūsharwān's who was born of a noble mother, all the others being *awlād sūqah*.

696. Hormizd's policy of favoring the masses as a counterweight to the upper classes, who represented a threat to his despotic royal power, is stressed in the Arabic sources. Al-Dīnawarī, *al-Akhbār al-ṭiwāl*, 75–77, puts into his mouth a lengthy accession speech enunciating guidelines for his future policy, including protection of the weaker, vulnerable members of society (*al-ḍu'afā' wa-ahl al-ḍi'ah*) against the oppression of the upper classes (*al-'ilyah*). This was a reversal of his father's cultivation of the support of the nobility and the Zoroastrian clergy, and the hostility of these latter entrenched interests was to contribute to Hor-

His justice reached such a point that he once went to Māh in order to spend the summer there.[697] In the course of his journey thither, he gave orders for it to be proclaimed amongst his troops and all the others in his army camp that they were to avoid the cultivated fields and not to cause harm to any of the landholders (*dahāqīn*) there. They were also to keep their mounts under control so that they caused no damage to the fields. He appointed a man who was to familiarize himself with the sort of thing that was going on in the army camp and to punish anyone who transgressed his command.

His own son Kisrā was in the army camp, and one of his riding beasts wandered off and strayed into one of the tilled fields along the way, started grazing, and created damage there. The animal was caught and brought to the man whom Hurmuz had appointed to punish anyone who caused damage to the tillage, or the owner of any beast that caused such damage, and to compel the offender to pay compensation. However, the man was not able to enforce Hurmuz's orders against Kisrā nor against any of those in Kisrā's retinue, hence he brought to Hurmuz's notice the damage he had observed that beast causing. Hurmuz ordered that he should crop that animals's ears and dock its tail, and that he should exact compensation from Kisrā. The man left Hurmuz's presence in order to put the king's orders into effect regarding Kisrā and his riding beast, but Kisrā secretly induced a group of the great men to ask him to go easy in putting the command into effect. They met him and talked to him about this, but he refused to listen. They asked him to delay putting into practice Hurmuz's order to him concerning the beast, until they had a chance to speak with the king and to persuade him to leave the animal alone. He agreed to this. That group of great men went to Hurmuz and told him that the steed that had done the damage was an ill-natured beast and

---

mizd's downfall, blinding, and death, see al-Ṭabarī, I, 993, p. 303 below. Nevertheless, Hormizd's justice is stressed, a justice greater than that of Anūsharwān, in the opinion of Ṭabarī-Bal'amī, tr. II, 246–47. Also, Christian sources praise him for his tolerance, which included special favor for the Nestorian Catholicos at Seleucia-Ctesiphon, Īshō'yahb I (in office 582–95). See Nöldeke, trans. 268 n. 3; Labourt, *Le Christianisme dans l'empire perse,* 200–203; Christensen, *Sassanides,* 441–43; Frye, "The Political History of Iran under the Sasanians," 162.

697. See for this place, al-Ṭabarī, I, 865, p. 97 and n. 249 above.

that it had wandered off and entered the tilled field; they asked Hurmuz to withdraw his order that the beast's ears should be cropped and its tail docked because this would be a bad augury for Kisrā. Despite this, Hurmuz refused their request; on his orders, the steed's ears were cropped and its tail docked, and Kisrā was [990] made to pay compensation in the same amount as other people were made to pay. Then Hurmuz moved off from his army camp.[698]

One day, at the time when the vines were ripening, Hurmuz rode out to Sābāṭ near al-Madā'in. His route went past orchards and vineyards. One of the men from Hurmuz's cavalry division who was riding with him noted a vineyard and saw in it partly ripened grapes. He picked some clusters and gave them to a squire (*ghulām*) who was accompanying him, telling him, "Take these back to our quarters, cook them with some meat, and make a broth out of it, for this is very wholesome and beneficial at this time." The guardian of that vineyard came up to him, gripped him fast and shouted loudly. The man's anxiety about being punished by Hurmuz for picking those grapes reached such a pitch that he handed over to the guardian of the vineyard a belt ornamented with gold, which he was wearing, in exchange for the half-ripe grapes he had picked from his vines, and thereby indemnified himself against punishment. He considered that the guardian's acceptance of the belt from him, and his letting him go free, was an act of grace the guardian had bestowed on him and a kind act he had accorded him.

It is said that Hurmuz was a successful and victorious commander, who never set his hand to anything that he did not attain. He was, moreover, well educated, skillful, and shrewd, but bad intentioned, a defect he inherited from his maternal relations, the Turks. He removed the nobles [from his court and entourage] and killed 13,600 men from the religious classes and from those of good family and noble birth. His sole aim was to win over the lower classes and to make them favorably disposed towards him. He imprisoned a great number of the great men, and degraded them and stripped them of their offices and ranks. He provide well

698. This story also in al-Dīnawarī, *al-Akhbār al-ṭiwāl*, 77–78.

for the mass of troops (*al-jund*), but deprived the cavalrymen (*al-asāwirah*) of resources. Hence a great number of those in his entourage became evil intentioned toward him, as a consequence of the fact that God wished to change their (i.e., the Persians') rule and transfer their royal power to someone else. Everything has its own particular cause.[699]

[991] The Hērbadhs presented Hurmuz with a petition that embodied their desire to persecute the Christians. The king endorsed the document with the words, "Just as our royal throne cannot stand on its two front legs without the two back ones, our kingdom cannot stand or endure firmly if we cause the Christians and adherents of other faiths, who differ in belief from ourselves, to become hostile to us. So renounce this desire to persecute the Christians and become assiduous in good works, so that the Christians and the adherents of other faiths may see this, praise you for it, and feel themselves drawn toward your religion."[700]

I received reports going back to Hishām b. Muḥammad, who said: The Turks marched out against Hurmuz. Other authorities state that, in the eleventh year of his reign, Shābah, the supreme ruler of the Turks,[701] advanced against him with three hundred

---

699. Cf. al-Dīnawarī, *al-Akhbār al-ṭiwāl*, 78, and Al-Mas'ūdī, *Murūj*, II, 211–12, the latter source stating that Hormizd killed thirteen thousand from the upper classes (*al-khawāṣṣ*) of Persia and destroyed the bases of the Zoroastrian state church. The *asāwirah* or mailed, heavy cavalrymen were recruited from the classes of the nobility and gentry (see n. 258 above), while what is here called the *jund* represented the infantry and other less favored elements of the forces.

700. As mentioned in n. 696 above, Nestorian Christian sources give a favorable picture of Hormizd and his policies.

701. Shābah (if this is the correct form of a dubiously written name) was more probably a ruler of the northern Hephthalites, or a vassal ruler in the upper Oxus regions of the Turkish, rather than the Qaghan of the Western Turks. In the 580s, Tardu (Chinese, Ta-t'ou), son of Ishtemi or Istemi (see n. 394 above), was Qaghan of what the Chinese knew as the Western Frontier Region, with Central Asia *stricto sensu* and the fringes of Transoxania controlled by other members of the Turkish ruling house, Taspar (or Taghpar), son of Bumin (r. 572–81), then Nivar (Chinese, She-tu), who was ousted by Apa, son of Muhan (Chinese, Ta-lo-pien), who in 583 founded the state of the Western Turks, until he lost power in 587. See Sinor, "The Establishment and Dissolution of the Türk Empire," 304–306; Sinor and S. G. Klyashtorny, "The Türk Empire," 333–34. None of these names resembles that of Shābah, and these Turkish potentates were in any case too heavily involved in internal warfare and internecine rivalries within Inner Asia to have begun hostilities with an external power like the Sāsānids.

thousand warriors until he reached Bādhghīs and Harāt;[702] that the king of the Byzantines moved into the outer districts of his empire (*al-ḍawāḥī*) with eighty thousand warriors heading toward him;[703] and that the king of the Khazars moved with a large army toward al-Bāb wa-al-Abwāb (i.e., Darband), wreaking damage and

---

702. Bādhghīs is the region of what is now northwestern Afghanistan lying to the north of Herat, the name being known, in the form Wāitigaēsa, since Avestan times. See Yāqūt, *Buldān*, I, 318; Marquart, *Ērānšahr*, 64–65, 67, 70, 77–78; Le Strange, *Lands*, 412–13; Barthold, *Historical Geography*, 47–49; *EI*², s.v. Bādghīs or Bādhghīs (W. Barthold and F. R. Allchin); *EIr*, s.v Bādgīs. I. General and the early period (C. E. Bosworth).

703. The course of Perso-Byzantine relations after the war of 540–45 between Khusraw Anūsharwān and Justinian (see al-Ṭabarī, I, 958–60, p. 252–55 above) until this point is not noted by al-Ṭabarī but was in fact very eventful. There was a prolonged war in Lazica, the westernmost, coastal region of Georgia, the Colchis of Antiquity, from 549 to 561, in which Persia, endeavoring to extend her influence over Armenia and Georgia, had confronted Byzantium, equally concerned to assert a protectorate over these Christian kingdoms (for Sāsānid policy in Persarmenia, that part of eastern Armenia where the Persians claimed control, see *EIr*, s.v. Armenia and Iran. ii. The Pre-Islamic Period. 6. The Sasanian Period. II: Persarmenia [M.L. Chaumont]), and this formed the second of Anūsharwān's wars with the Greeks. The peace treaty of 561, the negotiations for which are described in detail by the Greek historian Menander Protector, giving the text of the Greek version of the treaty *in extenso*, and whose chief Persian representative in them was Īzadh-Gushnasp (later to be a partisan of Bahrām Chūbīn's, see al-Ṭabarī, I, 997, p. 307 below), provided for a fifty years' peace, on analogy with that of 422 between Theodosius II and Bahrām V Gūr, involving Byzantium's paying an annual tribute in return for Persia's renouncing all rights over Lazica and consequent access to the Black Sea. There was also a commercial clause by means of which both powers aimed at controlling—with the imposition of appropriate customs dues—trade conducted by Arab merchants from the Persian Gulf shores and across the Syrian Desert, and a military clause that seems to have aimed at preventing intertribal, or rather, interdynastic hostilities between the respective Arab allies of the Byzantines and Persians, the Jafnids/Ghassānids and the Lakhmids (see Shahîd, "The Arabs in the Peace Treaty of 561," 191–211).

Justinian's expansionist efforts during his long reign were largely concentrated on the west of his empire, and he had been generally content to maintain the status quo in the east. But his nephew and successor Justin II (r. 567–78), having lost much of Italy to thc Germanic Lombards who invaded the Po valley in 568, looked to the east for compensatory military glory. Hence the fifty years' peace lasted only ten years. In 572 Justin renounced payment of the tribute and intervened in Armenia to support a revolt of local Christians against the persecutions and attempts to impose Zoroastrianism of the Persian Marzbān Chihr-Gushnasp from the prominent Suren family. By supporting the Armenian rebels, Justin hoped to take advantage of Anūsharwān's preoccupations in the east with the Turkish Khāqān Sinjibū (see al-Ṭabarī, I, 895–96, pp. 152–53 above).

The result was a third war which began with a Persian invasion of Syria, capturing Daras/Dārā and threatening Antioch. The war dragged on for twenty years,

destruction.[704] [They further state] that two men from the Arabs, one called 'Abbās the Squinter and the other 'Amr the Blue-Eyed One, encamped with a mighty host of Arabs on the banks of the Euphrates and mounted raids against the inhabitants of the Sawād.[705] His enemies became emboldened against him and

---

despite an armistice of 575–78 negotiated on the Persian side by the commander Māhbōdh (whose son Basak (?) is named in al-Ṭabarī, I, 985, p. 291 above, as the fortifier of al-Mushaqqar in eastern Arabia) and on the Greek side by Tiberius (who became emperor as Tiberius II Constantine, r. 578–82, but who was already Caesar and acting emperor after Justin lapsed into insanity in December 574). The truce enabled the *Magister Militum per Orientem* Maurice (subsequently emperor, r. 582–602) to build up his forces for a campaign in the east in 578, but this was preempted by a Persian invasion, under the general Māhbōdh, of the Armenian Taurus region, checked by a counterattack of Maurice which carried the Byzantine offensive as far as the region of Adiabene in northern Mesopotamia. Attempts at a further peace between Tiberius and Anūsharwān were aborted by the Persian king's sudden death in spring 579, for his successor Hormizd preferred to break off relations and continue the war; a sticking-point was the Byzantines' continued refusal to extradite the Armenian leaders of the 572 revolt in Persarmenia.

With the resumption of hostilities, Maurice prepared for war, and now in 580 aimed at involving the Jafnid/Ghassānid al-Mundhir b. al-Ḥārith (r. 569–82) in warfare along the Syrian Desert fringes (see Nöldeke, *Die Ghassânischen Fürsten*, 27–28; Shahîd, *Byzantium and the Arabs in the Sixth Century*, I/1, 396ff.). After further peace negotiations in 580–81 failed, the Byzantine army under Maurice secured resounding victories in Upper Mesopotamia, including at Constantina/ Tall Mawzan, but was still unable to capture the key fortresses of Niṣībīn and Daras/Dārā. The war then continued through Hormizd's reign, with the Byzantine armies commanded by Maurice's brother-in-law Philippicus, by Priscus and then by Phillippicus again till 589, and with fighting concentrated upon such points as Amida/Āmid, Martyropolis/Mayyāfāriqīn, and Daras/Dārā. In 589 Hormizd ordered Bahrām Chūbīn (on whom see n. 706 below), fresh from his victories in the east against the Hephthalites, to invade Siunik' (the region between Lake Sevan and the middle course of the Araxes/Aras river) but Bahrām suffered a decisive defeat at the hands of the Byzantine general Romanus; it was apparently Hormizd's humiliating treament of the momentarily unsuccessful, but until then highly successful, Bahrām (the Greek historians state that the emperor sent to him women's garments, emblems of weakness and cowardice, while Bahrām responded with a letter addressed to his sovereign merely as "Hormizd, son of Khusraw"), which finally provoked him into rebellion against the king.

See on these events, Bury, *A History of the Later Roman Empire from Arcadius to Irene*, I, 441–68, II, 95–110; idem, *History of the Later Roman Empire from the Death of Theodosius to the Death of Justinian*, I, 113–23; M. J. Higgins, *The Persian War of the Emperor Maurice (582–602). Part I. The Chronology, with a Brief History of the Persian Calendar*, 24–41; Christensen, *Sassanides*, 372–74; Stein, *Histoire du Bas-Empire*, II, 503–21; P. Goubert, *Byzance avant l'Islam. I. Byzance et l'Orient sous les successeurs de Justinien. L'Empéreur Maurice*, 63–127; Frye, "The Political History of Iran under the Sasanians," 155–56, 158–60, 162–63; Whitby, "Procopius and the Development of Roman Defences in Upper Mesopotamia," 729–30.

raided his lands. They so encompassed his lands that these last became known as a sieve with many holes. It is further said that enemies had encompassed the land of Persia from all sides like the bowstring over the two curved ends of the bow. Shābah, king of the Turks, sent a message to Hurmuz and the great men of the Persians, announcing his advance with his troops and saying, "Put in good repair the bridges over the rivers and wadis so that I may cross over them to your land, and construct bridges over all those [992] rivers which do not already have them. Also, do likewise regarding all the rivers and wadis that lie along my route from your land to that of the Byzantines, because I have determined on marching against them from your land."

Hurmuz became very fearful at all these threats coming upon him, and sought counsel regarding them. The decision was reached for him to move against the king of the Turks. So Hurmuz sent against him a man from the people of al-Rayy called Bahrām, son of Bahrām Jushnas, known as Jūbīn, with twelve thousand men whom Bahrām had personally selected—mature and experienced men, not youngsters.[706] It is stated alternatively that Hur-

---

*Ḍawāḥī*, sing. *ḍāḥiyah*, literally, "exposed, outer side," was a term specially used in early Islamic times for the zones of advanced frontier defenses marking the Byzantine-Arab frontier in the Taurus region of southeastern Anatolia.

704. It does seem that the Khazars had become established in the eastern Caucasus region by the later sixth century, see Dunlop, *The History of the Jewish Khazars*, 43–45; but we have no precise historical mention of this invasion.

705. These two contemptuous and pejorative names (blueness = haggardness, lividness, or blue-eyedness, being regarded as a defect, reflected in the linking of the color with the *mujrimīn* or sinners at the Last Judgment in Qur'ān, XX, 102) may well be fictitious ones. Nothing is otherwise known of these two raiders from the desert except that al-Mas'ūdī, *Murūj*, II, 212 = § 633, gives 'Amr the further sobriquet of *al-Afwah*, "the big-mouthed one," and unhelpfully says that the raiders came from the direction of Yemen.

706. Bahrām Chūbīn (literally "wooden," but explicable, according to A. Sh. Shahbazi, see below, from his tall and slender physique, hence with the sense of "lance, javelin shaft") stemmed from the great family of Mihrān (see al-Ṭabarī, I, 885, p. 131 and n. 340 above) in Rayy and was commander on the eastern frontiers of the Sāsānid realm. His military exploits in the east and his subsequent usurpation of royal power made such an impression on popular consciousness that there arose a popular romance in Pahlavi, the no longer extant *Wahrām Čōbēn-nāmag*. This romance, together with a *Book of Rustam and Isfandiyār*, was translated into Arabic by a secretary of "Hishām" (the Umayyad caliph Hishām b. 'Abd al-Malik?), one Jabalah b. Sālim. See Ibn al-Nadīm, *Fihrist*, 305, 364, tr. Bayard Dodge, II, 589, 716; Nöldeke, trans. 474–48, Excursus 6; Christensen, *Romanen om Bahrâm Tschôbîn, et rekonstruktionsforsøg*. In his own time, Bahrām had been hailed by

muz mustered at that time all those in his capital registered on the *dīwān* rolls (*al-dīwāniyyah*),[707] amounting to seventy thousand warriors. Bahrām advanced rapidly with the troops who had joined him until he had passed Harāt and Bādhghīs. Shābah was unaware of Bahrām's presence until the latter fixed his encampment in his vicinity. Messages went backward and forward between them, and clashes of arms, and Bahrām killed Shābah with an arrow shot at him. It is said that, in the realm of the Persians, supreme skill in archery was attributed to three men: '.r.sh.sh.yāṭ.y.n's shot in the war between Manūshihr and Afrāsiyāb (text, "Firāsiyāt");[708]
[993] Sūkhrā's shot in the war against the Turks;[709] and this shot of Bahrām's. He declared Shābah's encampment to be lawful booty, and established himself in that place. B.r.mūdhah,[710] Shābah's

many as something of a messianic figure who was to save the Sāsānid kingdom from chaos and to restore the glories of his Arsacid forebears, although subsequent writings on the downfall of the Sāsānid kingdom, written in Pahlavi and stemming from the early Islamic period, generally take what might be called a Persian legitimist view and portray Bahrām as a base-born usurper whose actions contributed to the decline and confusion of the state in its last decades. See K. Czeglédy, "Bahrām Čōbīn and the Persian Apocalyptic Literature," 32–43, and on him on general, Nöldeke, trans. 270 n. 3; Christensen, *Sassanides*, 443–45; Frye, "The Political History of Iran under the Sasanians," 163–65; *EI*², s.v. Bahrām (Cl. Huart and H. Massé); *EIr*, s.v. Bahrām. vii. Bahrām VI Čōbīn (A. Sh. Shahbazi).

707. An anachronistic use of the Islamic administrative term, that used to denote the register of names of the Arab *muqātilah* or warriors and their pay allotments, the system instituted, so the story goes, by the caliph 'Umar I, although the word itself is assumed to stem ultimately from Old Persian *dipi-*, "document, inscription," but probably with even older antecedents. See *EIr*, s.v. Dīvān. i. The term (F. C. de Blois), and also al-Ṭabarī, I, 877, p. 116 above, where *dīwān* is used for the king Fīrūz's perpatetic exchequer.

708. Thus in Nöldeke's text, but n. *e* offers a variety of readings from the manuscripts, with Marquart, in *Addenda et emendanda*, p. DXCIV, following Darmesteter, offering also *Irishshibāṭīr*. For his translation, 271, Nöldeke chose from among the various readings *Arishsātīn*. The first element of the name is clearly the personal name Arish, the MP form of Avestan Erəxša-, of uncertain meaning. In Iranian legendary history, Arish or Kay Arish, the Avestan Kawi Arshan, was the celebrated archer who shot an arrow a prodigious distance to establish the boundary between Iran and Afrāsiyāb's Turan, as mentioned here. The Arsacids traced their descent back to Kay Arish, regarded in the Pahlavi sources as the grandson of Kay Kawād. See Nöldeke, trans. 271 n. 2; Justi, *Namenbuch*, 29–30, 88–89; Mayrhofer, *Die altiranischen Namen*, 38 no. 114; Yarshater, "Iranian National History." 373, 406, 444, 475. Nöldeke was, however, unable to suggest any plausible explanation of the second element *sātīn* (or however it should be read)

709. See I, 877, p. 116 above, for this incident.

710. Again a doubtful rendering of a name that does not look very Turkish in its

son, who was the equal of his father, marched against Bahrām. Bahrām attacked him, put him to flight, and besieged him in a certain fortress of his. Bahrām pressed B.r.mūdhah so hard that he surrendered to him. Bahrām sent him back captive to Hurmuz and plundered immense treasures that were laid up in the fortress. It is said that he transported to Hurmuz wealth, jewels, vessels, weapons, and other plundered items amounting to two hundred fifty-thousand camels' loads. Hurmuz thanked Bahrām for the booty he had gained and which had reached him.

However, Bahrām was afraid of Hurmuz's violence, as were the troops who were with him, so he threw off allegiance to Hurmuz, advanced toward al-Madā'in, showed vexation at Hurmuz's behavior, and proclaimed that Hurmuz's son Abarwīz was more fitted for the royal power than he. Certain of those in Hurmuz's court circle threw in their lot with the rebels. For this reason Abarwīz, fearing Hurmuz, fled to Azerbaijan; a number of the Marzbāns and Iṣbahbadhs joined him there and gave him their allegiance. The great men and the nobles at al-Madā'in, including Bindūyah (text, "Bindī") and Bisṭām, maternal uncles of Abarwīz, rose up, deposed Hurmuz, blinded him with a red-hot needle but left him alive, shrinking from the crime of actually killing him.[711]

---

present form. Al-Dīnawarī, *al-Akhbār al-ṭiwāl,* 81, has the much more Turkish-looking *Y.l.t.kīn* for it, but Nöldeke was very likely correct in suspecting that this was the invention of a later age when names for soldiers, etc., compounded with the ancient Turkish, originally princely, title of *tégin* were becoming familiar within the Islamic world.

711. Bindūyah (a hypocoristic from Winda-(farnah?) "possessing royal glory," see Justi, *Namenbuch,* 368–69, 370–71) and Bisṭām (see on this name n. 237 above) were members of one of the seven greatest families of Persia, regarded as almost on a level with the families of the Arsacids and Sāsānids, that of Spābadh. Their father Shabūr had been killed by Hormizd in his purge of magnates of the realm whom he regarded with suspicion (see al-Ṭabarī, I, 990, p. 297 above), hence the revenge of the two sons in this rebellion against the king. See Nöldeke, trans. 273 n. 1, 439 Excursus 3; *EIr,* s.v. Besṭām o Bendōy (A. Sh. Shahbazi).

The mode of blinding mentioned here (Ar. *samala,* Pers. *mīl kashīdan*) was often employed in order to avoid physical desecration or disfiguring of the body of a person invested with the divinely buttressed aura of kingship, etc. Procopius, *The Persian War,* I.vi.17, states that the Persians used either to pour boiling olive oil into the victim's wide-open eyes or else to prick the eyeballs with a heated needle. Al-Ṭabarī, I, 998, p. 310 below, and other sources state further that Hormizd was shortly afterward murdered, either directly on Khusraw Abarwēz's orders, as the Byzantine chronicler Theophylactus Simocatta alleges, or with his complicity, as

News of this reached Abarwīz, and he set out from Azerbaijan, with his retinue, for the capital, hastening to get there before Bahrām. Having arrived at al-Madā'in, Abarwīz seized the royal power and prepared to defend himself against Bahrām. The two of them met together on the bank of the Nahrawān river,[712] where disputation and confrontation took place between them. Abarwīz sought to convince Bahrām that he would guarantee his security, exalt him in rank, and raise the status of his governorship; but
[994] Bahrām would not accept that.[713]

Various battles took place between them, until Abarwīz was compelled to flee to Byzantium, seeking help from its king, after a fierce battle and a night attack launched by both sides. It is said that Bahrām had with him a detachment of especially strong troops, including a group of three of the leading Turkish warriors, unequalled among the rest of the Turks for their equestrian skills (*furūsiyyah*) and their strength, who had undertaken to Bahrām that they would kill Abarwīz. On the morning after the night attack, Abarwīz stood firm and summoned his troops to give battle to Bahrām, but they were reluctant to stir. The group of three Turks attacked him, but Abarwīz went out to engage them and killed them one by one with his own hand. He then abandoned the battlefield, aware that his followers had been reluctant to fight and were wavering in their allegiance. He went to his father at Ctesiphon, entered his presence, told him what was apparent to him regarding his troops' attitude, and sought his advice. Hurmuz advised him to make his way to Mawrīq (Maurice), the king of the Byzantines, in order to seek help from him. He placed his womenfolk and children in a place secure from Bahrām and set off with a small number of companions, including Bindūyah, Bisṭām and Kurdī, brother of Bahrām Jūbīn. He reached Antioch, and wrote to

al-Ṭabarī says. See Christensen, *Sassanides,* 444.

712. That is, the canal that ran a two hundred miles' course, parallel to and eastward of the Tigris, from near Takrīt in the north to Mādharāyā in the south. See further on the region of Nahrawān n. 615 above.

713. As Nöldeke, trans. 273 n. 1, and 274 n. 2, observed, the course of all these events, which were to culminate in Khusraw Abarwēz's triumph over Bahrām Chūbīn, is extremely confused in the sources, with Theophylactus having the clearest and fullest narrative here. See Christensen, *Sassanides,* 444–45; *EIr,* s.v. Bahrām. vii. Bahrām VI Čōbīn (A. Sh. Shahbazi).

Mawrīq. The latter received him and gave him in marriage his daughter, called Maryam (Mary), who was very precious to him. The complete extent of Hurmuz, son of Kisrā's reign was, according to certain authorities, eleven years, nine months, and ten days, and according to Hishām b. Muḥammad, twelve years.[714]

## [Kisrā II Abarwīz]

Then there assumed the royal power Kisrā Abarwīz.[715] [995]

[He was] the son of Hurmuz, the son of Kisrā Anūsharwān, and was one of the outstanding kings of the dynasty in regard to bravery, one of them with the most incisive judgment, and one with the most far-sighted perceptions. According to what has been mentioned, his strength in battle, valor, successfulness, victoriousness, accumulation of wealth and treasuries, the assistance to his cause of fate and of the times, reached a pitch that had never been vouchsafed to any king more exalted than he. Hence he was called Abarwīz, meaning in Arabic "The Victorious One."

714. For more detailed comment on these events, including Bahrām's revolt, Khusraw Abarwēz's appeal to the Byzantine emperor Maurice, and his alleged marriage to a Byzantine princess, see the second, fuller narrative of these events by al-Ṭabarī at I, 995ff., pp. 305ff. below.

In the Arabic and Persian sources, the story of the three-sided struggle between Hormizd, Khusraw Abarwēz, and Bahrām Chūbīn is given in detail by al-Dīnawarī, *al-Akhbār al-ṭiwāl,* 79–84 and Ṭabarī-Bal'amī, tr. II, 266ff., and more cursorily by al-Ya'qūbī, *Ta'rīkh,* I, 187–91, and al-Mas'ūdī, *Murūj,* II, 212–15 = §§ 633–35. Of modern studies, see Christensen, *Sassanides,* 444–46; Frye, "The Political History of Iran under the Sasanians," 164–65, 178; *EIr,* s.v. Bahrām VI Čōbīn (A. Sh. Shahbazi).

Hormizd IV's period of power was 579–90, see Frye, op. cit., 178. His name appears on his coins as AUHRMZDY. See on his coins Paruck, *Sāsānian Coins,* 66, 384–85, 479–83, Plate XX, Tables XXVI-XXVII; Göbl, *Sasanian Numismatics,* 52, Table XI, Plate 12; Sellwood, Whitting, and Williams, *An Introduction to Sasanian Coins,* 21, 145–47; Malek, "A Survey of Research on Sasanian Numismatics," 237.

The Arabic sources on his reign in general include Ibn Qutaybah, *Ma'ārif,* 664; al-Ya'qūbī, op. cit., I, 187–91; al-Dīnawarī, op. cit., 74–84; al-Mas'ūdī, *Murūj,* II, 195–211 = §§ 617–31; idem, *Tanbīh,* 102, tr. 146; Ḥamzah al-Iṣfahānī, *Ta'rīkh,* 53; Ibn al-Athīr, *Kāmil,* I, 469–72. Of Persian sources, see Ṭabari-Bal'amī, trans. II, 246–53. Of modern studies, see the ones detailed in the previous paragraph.

715. MP *abarwēz,* NP *parwēz,* "victorious." See Justi, *Namenbuch,* 19; Nöldeke, trans. 275 n. 3. This point is the beginning of the second, fuller narrative of events surrounding the deposition of Hormizd, the revolt of Bahrām Chūbīn and the eventual triumph of Khusraw Abarwēz.

It is mentioned that, when he became apprehensive of what his father Hurmuz intended, on account of the scheming of Bahrām Jūbīn over this, and when it had reached the point that Hurmuz imagined that Abarwīz was planning to seize the royal power for himself, Abarwīz left secretly for Azerbaijan. Subsequently, he proclaimed his cause openly there. When he reached that region, a group of the Iṣbahbadhs and others who were there rallied to him and gave him their allegiance, promising to give him aid, but he made no [positive] steps toward that. It is also said that, when Ādhīn Jushnas,[716] who had been sent to combat Bahrām Jūbīn, was killed, the army accompanying Ādhīn Jushnas scattered and finally made its way to al-Madā'in. Jūbīn pursued them, and Hurmuz's[717] position became very unsure. Ādhīn Jushnas's sister, who had been the youthful companion of Abarwīz, wrote to him, informing him of Hurmuz's weak position as a result of what had happened to Ādhīn Jushnas and telling him that the great men of state had resolved upon deposing Hurmuz. She further told him that, if Jūbīn reached al-Madā'in before he could get there, Jūbīn would occupy it. When the letter reached Abarwīz, he gathered together all the troops he could from Armenia and Azerbaijan, and with them marched on al-Madā'in. The leading figures and nobles rallied to him, full of joy at his arrival. He assumed the royal crown and seated himself on his throne. He said: "It is part of our religion to choose piety [above all other things], and part of our considered opinion to do good works. Our grandfather Kisra, son
[996] of Qubādh, was like a parent for you, and our father Hurmuz was a just judge for you; so ensure that you remain obedient and submissive now."

On the third day, Abarwīz went to his father, prostrated himself before him and said, "May God grant you long life, O king! You

716. This name appears variously in the sources. Nöldeke adopted his reading here, see trans. 276 n. 2, on a basis of the readings of al-Ṭabarī and al-Ya'qūbī alone among the sources. Justi, *Namenbuch*, 5, 354–55, interpreted this putative name as from *ādhīn* "ornament" + *gushnasp* "strong, powerful." But Mr F. C. de Blois has pointed out that Justi's translation is certainly wrong: rather, for *ādhīn* read MP *ēwēn* "manner, custom" (NP *ā'īn*), while *gushnasp* means "stallion" and is also the name of a sacred fire. He suggests that a rendering *Ādur-gushnasp would make better sense here.

717. Correcting the name *Bahrām* of the text to *Hurmuz*, as in *Addenda et emendanda*, p. DXCIV, and Nöldeke, trans. 276.

know that I am innocent of what your false-hearted subjects (literally, "hypocrites," *munāfiqūn*) did to you. I went into hiding and made for Azerbaijan out of fear that you had the intention to kill me." Hurmuz gave credence to this apology, saying, "O my dear son, I have two requests to make of you, so aid me in implementing these. The first one is that you should take vengeance on my behalf upon those who took part in my deposition and blinding,[718] and that you should show no mercy toward them. The second one is that you should appoint every day three persons of firm judgment to keep me company and that you should instruct them to come into my presence." Abarwīz showed himself humble and submissive toward him, and said, "O king, may God grant you long life! The rebel Bahrām is threatening us from very near and has on his side courage and bravery; we do not at present have the power to stretch forth our hand against those who perpetrated what they did against you, but if God gives me the upper hand over the false-hearted one, then I shall act as your representative and the willing agent of your hand."

Bahrām got news of Kisrā's approach and of how the people had made Abarwīz king. He hastened toward al-Madā'in with his troops. Abarwīz sent out spies against him. When Bahrām drew near to him, Abarwīz thought that the best course was to negotiate with him peaceably. So he girded on his weapons, and ordered Bindūyah, Bisṭām, a group of the great men whom he trusted, and a thousand men of his troops to put on their best array and gird on their weapons. Abarwīz set out from his fortress with them against Bahrām, with the people calling down blessings on his head, and surrounded by Bindūyah, Bisṭām, and all the other leading figures until he halted on the bank of the Nahrawān river. When Bahrām perceived the full extent of Abarwīz's panoply, he set out on a piebald mount (*birdhawn . . . ablaq*), which he especially held dear, wearing no mailed coat and accompanied by Īzadh [997]
Jushnas[719] and three men who were kinsmen of the king of the Turks. These last had pledged their lives to Bahrām that they

718. That is, on Bindūyah, Bisṭām, and their allies, see al-Ṭabarī, I, 993, p. 303 above.

719. That is, *īzad* "God" + *gushnasp* (see n. 716 above); see Justi, *Namenbuch*, 145–46, 354–55.

would hand over to him Abarwīz as a prisoner, and he had given them extensive wealth as payment for this.

When Bahrām saw Kisrā's fine figure, his splendid outfit, his crown going with him, accompanied by the unfurled banner of Kāwah (*dirafsh-i Kābiyān*), their supremely mighty flag,[720] and when he saw Bindūyah, Bisṭām, and the rest of the great men, their fine weapons, their splendor, and their mounts, he became downcast at all this, and commented to his companions, "Do you not see that the son of a whore has put on flesh and grown fat, has made the transition from youth to manhood experience, has acquired an ample beard and a full-grown mustache,[721] and his body has become stout." While he was uttering these words, having stationed himself on the bank of the Nahrawān river, Kisrā said to one of those standing with him, "Which of these is Bahrām?" One of Bahrām's brothers called Kurdī, who had never wavered in his allegiance to Abarwīz and had remained one of his followers, said, "May God grant you long life, the man on the piebald steed!" Kisrā began his speech with the following words: "O Bahrām, you are one of the supports of our kingdom and a pillar for our subjects; you have exerted yourself nobly in our service. We have seen fit to choose some day auspicious for you[722] in order to appoint you to

---

720. This banner is said to have been originally the apron of the blacksmith Kāwah who, in the Iranian national epic, led a successful revolt against the tyrant Zohāk, although the legend is, according to Christensen, of comparatively late, Sāsānid origin. By that time, it was equated with the royal standard of the Persian kings, and several Arabic authors (e.g., al-Ṭabarī, I, 2174–75; al-Mas'ūdī, *Murūj*, IV, 224 = § 1556; al-Khwārazmī, *Mafātīḥ al-'ulūm*, 115) purport to describe it. By the time of these authors, however, the banner had long ceased to exist, being captured, according to the historians, at the decisive battle of al-Qādisiyyah between the Persians and Arabs in 15/636 or 16/637. See Nöldeke, trans. 278 n. 1; Christensen, *Les Kayanides*, 43; idem, *Sassanides*, 502–504; *EI*², s.v. Kāwah (Ed.).

721. Following the preferred reading of the Sprenger ms. *shāribihī* (text, n. c), for the text's *shabābihi*.

722. That is, auspicious from the astrological aspect. It is emphasized in later Islamic literature, and, in particular, in the works of the third/ninth-century author al-Jāḥiẓ of Baṣrah and apocryphal works attributed to him, that hemerology, the skill of choosing auspicious days for planned actions, had in considerable measure passed to the Arabs from the Persians, with the official astrologers already significant figures at the Sāsānid court. In the *Kitāb al-tāj* or *Kitāb akhlāq al-mulūk*, attributed (but almost certainly falsely) to al-Jāḥiẓ, it is stated that when Ardashīr I Pābagān divided up Persian society into four classes (an item of information that figures extensively in the sources; see Marlow, *Hierarchy and Egalitar-*

the office of Iṣbahbadh of the whole land of Persia." Bahrām, however, replied, "But I have chosen for *you* a day for crucifying you!" Kisrā was filled with trepidation, even though nothing of it showed in his face. Bahrām said to Abarwīz, "O son of an adulteress, raised in the tents of the Kurds!" and other words like it, and accepted nothing whatever of what Abarwīz had offered him. There was mention of Arish, Bahrām's forefather, and Abarwīz reproached him over Arish's obedience to Abarwīz's own forefather Manūshihr.[723] The two of them separated, each one showing the most violent hostility to the other. [998]

Bahrām had a sister called Kurdiyah, one of the most accomplished of women and most endowed of them with qualities, whom he had married.[724] She reproached Bahrām for his evil speech adressed to Kisrā and his attempt to bring him under his own obedience, but he would have none of it. A martial engagement between Kisrā and Bahrām took place. It is said that, on the morning after the night battle, Kisrā sallied forth for combat in person. The three Turks saw him and made for him, but Abarwīz killed them with his own hand. He urged on his troops to battle, but perceived that they were flagging. He decided to go to some other monarch and seek military help from him. He went first to his father [Hurmuz], seeking his advice; Hurmuz considered that Abarwīz's best course was to make his way to the king of the Byzantines. He placed his womenfolk in a secure place and set out with a small body of men, including Bindūyah, Bisṭām, and Bahrām's brother Kurdī. When they left al-Madā'in, the mass of Abarwīz's supporters (*al-qawm*), however, were afraid that Bahrām would restore Hurmuz to the royal power and write to the king of the Byzantines on his behalf that Abarwīz's delegation be

*ianism in Islamic Thought,* 79–83), physicians, scribes, and astrologers formed the third class. See *Kitāb al-tāj,* tr. 53; Gabrieli, "Etichetta di corte e costumi sasanidi nel Kitāb Aḫlāq al-Mulūk di al-Ǧāḥiẓ," 296–97; *EI*², s.v. Ikhtiyārāt (T. Fahd).

723. On Arish, see n. 708 above, where is mentioned the claims of the Arsacids, Bahrām's alleged forebears, to descent from the Kay Arish of Iranian legendary history.

724. As Nöldeke observed, trans. 279 n. 6, such a marriage would be allowable and even praiseworthy in Zoroastrian law and custom, though repugnant to the Muslim Firdawsī, who suppresses mention of it in the *Shāh-nāmah.* It would also have been unacceptable to the pre-Islamic Arabs; see Robertson Smith, *Kinship and Marriage in Early Arabia,* 164.

sent back so that they might be put to death. They told this to Abarwīz and sought permission from him to kill Hurmuz; but he made no reply. Hence Bindūyah, Bisṭām, and some of their followers went to Hurmuz, strangled him to death, and then returned to Kisrā. They said, "You can now proceed under the best possible auguries."[725]

They urged on their mounts and came to the Euphrates, crossed it, and took the way through the desert under the guidance of a man called Khurshīdhān,[726] arriving at a certain monastery on the edge of the cultivated land. While they encamped in the courtyard there, a cavalry squadron of Bahrām's, commanded by a man called Bahrām, son of Siyāwush, came upon them by surprise. Once they became aware of this, Bindūyah woke Abarwīz from his slumber and told him, "Use some stratagem [for escaping], for the enemy are on top of you." Kisrā replied, "I have no means of
[999] escaping," so Bindūyah told him that he would sacrifice his own life for him, and asked him to hand over his weapons and equipment and to flee with his retainers from the monastery. They did this, and hurried on ahead of the enemy until they were able to conceal themselves in the mountains. When Bahrām, son of Siyāwush, arrived, Bindūyah, girded with Abarwīz's weapons and equipment, showed himself to Bahrām from the top of the monastery, and let Bahrām thereby imagine that he was Abarwīz. He asked Bahrām to grant him a respite until the next morning, when he would peacefully deliver himself into his hands. Hence Bahrām left him alone and only later was his stratagem revealed. Bahrām, son of Siyāwush, took Bindūyah back with him to Jūbīn, who consigned Bindūyah to imprisonment in Bahrām's custody.

It is said that Bahrām [Jūbīn] entered the royal palaces at al-Madā'in and sat down on the royal throne. The prominent leaders and great men of state gathered round him, and Bahrām addressed

---

725. These words, and those of other sources, no doubt express the degree of Khusraw's complicity in his father's killing: satisfaction with the result without having to stain his own hands with blood. Khusraw's conduct here was certainly Machiavellian; Nöldeke, 281 n. 1, adduces the parallel of the Russian emperor Alexander I, who in 1801 certainly had prior knowledge of the planned murder of his father Paul I.

726. That is, Khurshēdh, Avestan *hvarə-xšaēta,* literally "sun." See Justi, *Namenbuch,* 180; Bartholomae, *Altiranisches Wörterbuch,* col. 1848.

them, abusing Abarwīz violently and blaming him. Several sessions of argument and disputation took place between him and the prominent leaders, all of whom were averse to him. Nevertheless, Bahrām seated himself on the royal throne and had himself crowned, and the people gave him obedience out of fear.[727] It is said that Bahrām, son of Siyāwush, agreed with Bindūyah on assassinating Jūbīn, but the latter got to know about it, and had Bahrām, son of Siyāwush, executed. Bindūyah, however, escaped and managed to reach Azerbaijan.

Abarwīz journeyed onward until he reached Antioch, and from there wrote to Mawrīq, the king of the Byzantines, sending to him a delegation of his retainers and asking him for military aid.[728]

---

727. Bahrām Chūbīn entered Ctesiphon in summer 590. There was clearly a reluctance among the great men of state in the capital that the ancient house of the Sāsānids should be set aside by Bahrām. The latter, for his part, claimed to be the restorer of the even more ancient house of the Arsacids, who had been displaced by the upstart Ardashīr (I) b. Sāsān, son of a mere shepherd, and he took advantage of apocalyptic beliefs which, so he asserted, foretold himself as the future savior of the land of Iran from such external foes as the Byzantines and the Hephthalites. In Ctesiphon he assumed the complete royal style, being crowned and issuing coins, although according to Theophylactus and al-Dīnawarī, *al-Akhbār al-ṭiwāl,* 90, he hedged his bets by proclaiming to the nobles that he was only acting as regent for Hormizd's young son Shahriyār until the latter should reach maturity. Despite his efforts, Bahrām was never able to persuade the Persian aristocracy and the Zoroastrian clergy that he held a social position above their own or that he enjoyed the divine favor, and a strong party of them continued to favor the cause of Khusraw Abarwēz as successor to his father. Bahrām had accordingly to turn to other elements for support, including that of the Jews; subsequently, Khusraw's commander Māhbōdh slaughtered many Jews in retaliation. See Neusner, "Jews in Iran," 916.

Bahrām VI Chūbīn reigned in Ctesiphon 590–91. His name appears on his coins as VRḤR'N. See on his coins, Paruck, *Sāsānian Coins,* 66–67, 385–86, 483–84, Plate XX, Table XXVII; Göbl, *Sasanian Numismatics,* 52, Table XI, Plate 12; Sellwood, Whitting, and Williams, *An Introduction to Sasanian Coins,* 21, 148–49; Malek, "A Survey of Research on Sasanian Numismatics," 237.

See on his career and reign Nöldeke, trans. 282 n. 2; Christensen, *Sassanides,* 444–45; Czeglédy, "Bahrām Čōbīn and the Persian Apocalyptic Literature," 25–27; *EIr,* s.v. Bahrām. vii. Bahrām VI Čōbīn (A. Sh. Shahbazi).

728. Both the exact date of Khusraw Abarwēz's appeal to Maurice and the exact route he followed from the Persian capital to the Byzantine lands present certain problems. However, it seems likely that the date was the late spring of 590. Antioch, mentioned here by al-Ṭabarī as the place to which Khusraw fled, was deep in Byzantine territory, and it is much more probable, on the basis of fairly exact itineraries in Theophylactus and the *Anonymus Guidi,* that Khusraw and his entourage traveled from the region of Ctesiphon up the Euphrates valley via Fīrūz-

Mawrīq agreed to this, and things went so far that he gave Abarwīz his daughter Maryam in marriage and had her conveyed to him.[729] Furthermore, he sent to Abarwīz his brother Thiyādhūs (Theodosius)[730] with an army of sixty thousand warriors, headed by a man called Sarjīs (Sergius), who was [in practice] in charge of all the army's affairs, and another man whose strength was equal to a thousand men.[731] He laid down as conditions that Abarwīz should

---

Shāpūr/al-Anbār, Hīt and 'Ānah to Circesium/Qarqīsiyā at the confluence of the Khābūr and Euphrates, the first fortified point within Byzantine territory.

Bahrām had tried to purchase Byzantine neutrality in the struggle by offering to cede Niṣībīn and the lands held by the Persians right up to the Tigris. But Maurice must have felt that it was better for Byzantine interests to have a young and inexperienced Khusraw Abarwēz on the throne than the battle-hardened warrior Bahrām, and he may also have hoped to extract concessions for the Christians within the Persian realm if Khusraw were to prevail. At all events, Maurice disregarded the advice of the Senate in Constantinople, which was suspicious of affordng any help to the ancestral foe, and a Byzantine army to be commanded by the *Magister Militum* Narses was promised as aid for Khusraw. See Bury, *A History of the Later Roman Empire from Arcadius to Irene,* II, 112; Higgins, *The Persian War of the Emperor Maurice (582–602), Part I,* 42–54; Goubert, *Byzance avant l'Islam,* I, 131–45.

729. As Nöldeke pointed out, trans. 283 n. 2, the Persian historical tradition and later romantic literature makes this Byzantine princess the mother of Khusraw Abarwēz's son and successor Kawād II Shērōy, whereas the Greek sources do not mention her. Nöldeke did not at the time when he made his translation of al-Ṭabarī know of the Syriac *Anonymus Guidi* (the earlier, greater part of which may, it has recently been suggested, have been written by Elias of Marw: personal communication from Dr. Sebastian Brock). This chronicle does in fact, mention her as one of Khusraw's two Christian wives (see trans. Nöldeke, 10). Another Syriac chronicler like Dionysius of Tell Maḥrē records the marriage with much circumstantial detail, e.g., that she was accompanied to the Persian capital by bishops and clergy and that Khusraw built for her two places of worship (*hayklē*), one dedicated to St. Sergius and the other to Mary, the Mother of Jesus (see trans. Palmer, *The Seventh Century in the West-Syrian Chronicles,* 117). It seems that there was some confusion between the Byzantine princess Maria and the celebrated Shīrīn, Khusraw's beloved, the subject of so many later Persian romances, and Theophylactus makes *Sirē* likewise of Byzantine origin. However, Shīrīn is said by the *Anonymus Guidi,* loc. cit., to have been of Aramaean origin from the district around what was later al-Baṣrah. As the mother of Khusraw's son Mardān Shāh and the mother or foster mother of another son, Shahriyār, she showed herself hostile to Shērōy after her husband's death. The historicity of Khusraw's supposed marriage with Maria must remain very dubious. See von Gutschmid, "Bemerkungen zu Tabari's Sasanidengeschichte," 744; Labourt, *Le Christianisme dans l'empire perse,* 208–209; Garsoïan, "Byzantium and the Sasanians," 579.

730. Nöldeke, trans. 284 n. 1, corrected "brother" to "son," as in al-Dīnawarī, *al-Akhbār al-ṭiwāl,* 92, and later Persian sources.

731. al-Dīnawarī, *al-Akhbār al-ṭiwāl,* 92, speaks of "ten men from among the

treat him with respect and cease requiring the tribute his forefathers had exacted from the kings of the Byzantines. When the Byzantine troops reached Abarwīz, he was filled with joy and allowed them five days' rest after their arrival. Then he reviewed them and appointed officers (*'urafā'*) over them. The army included in its numbers Thiyādhūs, Sarjīs, and the champion warrior who was the equal of a thousand men. He went with them [1000]
until he reached Azerbaijan and encamped on a plain called al-Danaq (?).[732] Bindūyah and a man from the Iṣbahbadhs of that region called Mūshīl[733] with forty thousand warriors met up with him there, and people from Fārs, Iṣbahān, and Khurāsān rushed[734] to Abarwīz's standard.

Bahrām got news of Abarwīz's taking up his position on the plain of al-Danaq and set out toward him from al-Madā'in. Several violent clashes took place between them in which the Byzantine champion was killed. It is said that Abarwīz engaged Bahrām's forces, quite separately from the main body of the army, with just fourteen of his soldiers, including Bahrām's brother Kurdī, Bindūyah, Bisṭām, Sabūr, son of Afriyān, Abādh, son of Farrukhzādh, and Farrukh Hurmuz,[735] in a fierce hand-to-hand fight. The Zoroastrians (*al-Majūs*) assert that Abarwīz got trapped in a defile and Bahrām pursued him thither, but when Bahrām was sure that he had Abarwīz in his power, something that could not be comprehended (i.e., some supernatural power) took the latter up to the

---

Hazārmardān," *hazārmard* "[having the strength of] a thousand men," being a frequent sobriquet of valiant warriors, as Nöldeke, trans. 284 n. 2, points out.

732. Minorsky, "Roman and Byzantine Campaigns in Atropatene," 88–89, discussed the readings for this unidentified name, which include Firdawsī's *Dūk*, and he thought that MP *d.w.k* might lie behind it. He also noted the frequent confusion in Arabic orthography of final *kāf* and *lām* and the existence of a place name Dūl to the southeast of Lake Urmiya. For the probable location of the final battle between Bahrām and the combined forces of the Byzantine army and Khusraw, see n. 736 below,

733. Reading thus for the text's *Mūsīl*, since Nöldeke, trans. 285 n. 3, identified him as Mushel, the Armenian ruler of Mūsh in eastern Anatolia, from the famous Mamikonian family.

734. Following the reading *wa-inqaḍḍa* in *Addenda et emendanda*, p. DXCIV.

735. Following the reconstruction of these names—all fourteen of them being given in Firdawsī's *Shāh-nāmah*—in *Addenda et emendanda*, p. DXCIV, two of them, Sābūr, son of Afriyān, and Abādh, son of Farrukhzād, being to a considerable extent differently rendered in Nöldeke's original edition and his translation, 286, rendering some of the etymological speculations in his n. 2 invalid.

top of the mountain. It is mentioned that the astrologers agreed that Abarwīz would reign for forty-eight years. Abarwīz went out to engage Bahrām in single combat. He wrested Bahrām's spear from his hand and battered his head with it until the spear broke. Bahrām became downhearted about his cause; he grew fearful, and realized that he had no hope of withstanding Abarwīz. Hence he retreated toward Khurāsān and thence to the Turks.[736]

Abarwīz, meanwhile, journeyed to al-Madā'in after he had distributed twenty million [dirhams] among the Byzantine troops and had sent them back to Mawrīq. It is said that Abarwīz wrote a letter to the Christians giving them permission to establish their churches (*'imārat biya'ihim*) and allowing anyone who wished, with the exception of the Zoroastrians, to adopt their faith.[737] In

---

736. Bahrām's troops in the vicinity of Niṣībīn had at the beginning of 591 gone over to Khusraw's side on hearing of the latter's alliance with the Byzantines, so that Khusraw then controlled Upper Mesopotamia. The combined forces of Narses and Khusraw's general Mābōdh captured Seleucia, Ctesiphon, and Weh Andiyōg Shābūr in summer 591, and Bahrām then faced the combined threat of Narses' army plus a mixed Persian-Armenian-Byzantine force under Bindūyah and the Greek general John Mysticus, moving southward from Armenia into Upper Mesopotamia. In Azerbaijan, on a plain to the east of Lake Urmiya, by a river called by the Byzantine historians Balarath, near the fortified point of Ganzakos (identified by Minorsky with the course of the Müri Chay to the south of modern Marāghah), the armies met. Although Bahrām's army included a contingent of "Turks" plus a troop of war elephants, it was decisively defeated, with the victors seizing Bahrām's royal tent, harem, children, and jewels. He himself managed to escape with a small force of some four thousand men to Nīshāpūr and thence across the Oxus to the "land of the Turks." See Higgins, *The Persian War of the Emperor Maurice (582–602), Part I,* 51–54; Minorsky, "The Roman and Byzantine Campaigns in Atropatene," 87–91; Goubert, *Byzance avant l'Islam,* I, 147–62; *EIr,* s.v. Bahrām. vii. Bahrām (VI) Čōbīn (A. Sh. Shahbazi).

737. As Nöldeke noted, trans. 288 n. 1, Zoroastrian church law—like the subsequent Islamic one—prescribed death as the penalty for apostasy from that faith. The Greek and Syriac sources record that Khusraw Anūsharwān had executed high-born Persian converts to Christianity and had put to death the Monophysite Catholicos because he had baptised members of the imperial family; in the Perso-Byzantine treaty of 562 (see n. 703 above), this penalty for proselytism had been prescribed as the reflex of freedom of worship for the Christians. On Khusraw Abarwēz's policy toward the Christians, see Labourt, *Le Christianisme dans l'empire perse,* 208–35; Asmussen, "Christians in Iran," 946. Labourt highlights the great influence at Khusraw's court of his treasurer, the Nestorian Yazdīn, descendant of the martyr Pethion (see n. 487 above) and the official responsible for collecting the land tax. Yazdīn was a member of a rich and influential Nestorian family from the vicinity of Dastagird in eastern Iraq (see on this place, n. 756 below); a

this connection he adduced the fact that Anūsharwān had made a peace agreement with (*kāna hādana*) Qayṣar regarding the tribute that he exacted from the Byzantine ruler, and had stipulated that [1001] those of his [Zoroastrian] compatriots who were in the Byzantine ruler's lands should be kindly treated and that the monarch should build fire temples for them in his lands. Qayṣar, for his part, had made a similar stipulation in regard to the Christians [in the Persian lands].[738]

Bahrām remained among the Turks, highly honored by the king, until Abarwīz intrigued against him by sending a man called Hurmuz.[739] He sent him to the Turks with valuable jewels and other things, and Hurmuz was able to worm his way into the confidence

---

Yezdīnābādh mentioned in Adiabene may reflect their property interests. This family was for long prominent in the financial administration of the Persian realm, and various of its members were generous benefactors of the Nestorian Church. Nevertheless, the see of Seleucia-Ctesiphon remained vacant from the Catholicos Gregory's death in 609 till the end of Khusraw's reign in 628, and Yazdīn was unable to secure authorisation for his replacement (op. cit., 230–31).

738. The peace treaty of autumn 591, which concluded the Byzantine intervention in Persia, involved honors and presents for the Byzantine commanders and for the Armenian allies of Khusraw, with the Prince Sṃbat Bagratuni being appointed Marzbān of Hyrcania/Gurgān. Khusraw now renounced his claims to some two-thirds of Armenia. Maurice recovered the town of Martyropolis, captured by the Persians in 588, and Daras/Dārā was returned to him, although there was no question of the wide range of territory promised to Maurice by Bahrām being relinquished, and Niṣībīn remained firmly in Persian hands. The financial provisions were important, but the twenty million dirhams mentioned by al-Ṭabarī here were in practice a lesser sum, since they had to be set against the arrears of tribute due from the Byzantines in previous years. In the sphere of protocol, the Persian emperor now for the first time agreed to address the Byzantine monarch as Basileus in official correspondence instead of just Caesar (although it was to be Heraclius in 629, after his crushing victory over the Sāsānids, who was formally to adopt the title Basileus, previously used informally; see I. Shahîd, "The Iranian Factor in Byzantium during the Reign of Heraclius," 295–96). According to Theophylactus, Maurice agreed to leave behind at Ctesiphon a force of one thousand Byzantine troops as Khusraw's personal guard. See Nöldeke, trans. 287 n. 1; Bury, *History of the Later Roman Empire from Arcadius to Irene*, II, 112; Goubert, *Byzance avant l'Islam*, I, 163–70; *EIr*, s.v. Byzantine-Iranian Relations. 1. Before the Islamic Conquest (A. Sh. Shahbazi).

739. This man appears in, e.g., al-Dīnawarī, *al-Akhbār al-ṭiwāl*, 80, 83, and al-Ya'qūbī, *Ta'rīkh*, I, 193–94, with the further component to his name of Jarābzīn (with Jalābzīn also found in the sources, including al-Ṭabarī, I, 1030, p. 360–61 and n. 864 below), the Zalabzan of Byzantine Greek historians. See Nöldeke, trans. 289 n. 1.

of Khātūn, the king's wife, and win her over with those jewels and other things, until she engaged agents who secretly brought about Bahrām's death.[740] It is said that Khāqān grieved over his killing, and sent a message to Kurdiyah, Bahrām's sister and wife, informing her of the fate that had come upon Bahrām through his respon-

740. The story of Bahrām's murder through feminine wiles is narrated in considerable detail by al-Dīnawarī, *al-Akhbār al-ṭiwāl*, 98–100, also in al-Ya'qūbī, *Ta'rīkh*, I, 193–94, at fair length, laconically in al-Mas'ūdī, *Murūj*, II, 222–23 = §§ 642–43, and Ṭabarī-Bal'amī, trans. II, 302–303. Bahrām's troops are said to have feared for their continued safety among the "Turks" after their commander's death and to have returned to the security of the fastnesses of Daylam in the Elburz mountains, where Sāsānid control was negligible, taking part later in the revolt of Bisṭām.

At-Ṭabarī records nothing of the fates of Khusraw Abarwēz's two great-uncles Bindūyah and Bisṭām (on whom see n. 711 above). Al-Dīnawarī, op. cit., 101–105, and al-Ya'qūbī, op. cit., I, 194–95, deal with them at length and in the same romantic guise as the legends around Bahrām Chūbīn's end, concluding with Bisṭām's revolt and eventual death through the craftiness of Kurdiyah, Bahrām's sister. Certain Greek and Armenian sources have more prosaic but much briefer references. Theophylactus states that Khusraw took vengeance on all those who had been involved in the deposition and blinding of his father Hormizd, and had Bindūyah thrown into the Tigris; the Armenian historian Sebeos says that Bisṭām fled to "Parthia" and was later treacherously killed by a "Kushan" ruler of the east. The *Anonymus Guidi*, tr. 8–9, also records their deaths. There was thus in Nöldeke's time little hard historical fact on the revolt, but in his trans. 478–87, Excursus 7, he extracted what he could out of the meager evidence. He concluded that Khusraw probably dealt with Bindūyah fairly quickly, but that Bisṭām, who had been appointed Marzbān of Khurāsān, did not rebel until 591 or early 592, and that he maintained himself virtually independent in northern Persia till the end of 595, since coins of his are extant, dated to what are called years 2–6 of his reign. We now know considerably more, above all through the information given by al-Dīnawarī (known to Nöldeke but still in manuscript and apparently not fully accessible to him) and from fresh numismatic evidence. It seems accordingly that Bisṭām held power ca. 590–96 over a considerable stretch of territory in the north, from Media/Jibāl and the Caspian provinces to Khurāsān as far as the Oxus, with the backing of many local magnates and troops from Bahrām Chūbīn's former army. He minted coins at Rayy, under the name PYLWCY WSTḤM, i.e., Pērōz Vistahm, with dates extending over seven regnal years. See on his coins Paruck, *Sāsānian Coins*, 67, 386, Plate XX; Göbl, *Sasanian Numismatics*, 53, Table XI, Plate 13; Sellwood, Whitting, and Williams, *An Introduction to Sasanian Coins*, 21, 150–51; Malek, "A Survey of Research on Sasanian Numismatics," 237. The coin sequence, and information in Christian sources, indicate that it was not till 596 that Khusraw Abarwēz managed through intrigue to procure Bisṭām's death and thus end his separatist movement; he also slew some sixty members of the families of Bindūyah and Bisṭām. These killings were to form one of the accusations laid at Khusraw's door when he himself was deposed and executed over thirty years later; see al-Ṭabarī, I, pp. 1046–47, 1051–52, 1053–54, pp. 382–84, 387–88, 390–91 below. See *EIr*, s.v. Besṭām o Bendōy (A. Sh. Shahbazi).

sibility and asking if he could marry her to his brother N.ṭrā (?). For this reason (i.e., his responsibility for the killing of Bahrām) he divorced Khātūn. It is said that Kurdiyah gave Khāqān a soft answer but refused N.ṭrā. She gathered round herself the warriors who had been with her brother, and set off with them from the land of the Turks toward the borders of the kingdom of Persia. N.ṭrā the Turk pursued her with twelve thousand warriors, but she killed him with her own hand. She proceeded onward and wrote to her brother Kurdī, who subsequently secured for her from Abarwīz a grant of safe conduct and security (*amān*). When she reached Abarwīz, he married her. He was highly taken with her, and thanked her for having (previously) reproached Bahrām.[741] Abarwīz showed himself grateful and acted in a kindly way toward Mawrīq.[742]

After Kisrā had reigned for fourteen years, the Byzantines deposed Mawrīq and killed him, also exterminating all his heirs, apart from one of his sons who fled to Kisrā, and they raised to the throne as their king a man named Fūqā (Phocas).[743] When Kisrā heard the news of the Byzantines' breaking their allegiance to Mawrīq and their killing him, he became violently aroused, re- [1002]
garded it with revulsion, and was gripped by anger.[744] He gave

741. There does not seem to be any firm historical information that Khusraw did marry Kurdiya, though it would not be unexpected. The story involving N.trā, a name which does not look possible as a Turkish one, must be pure legend.

742. See n. 738 above.

743. Text, Qūfā. On the revolution in Constantinople that led to the dethronement and murder in 602 of Maurice and his sons and his replacement as emperor by the Thracian centurion Phocas, see Bury, *A History of the Later Roman Empire from Arcadius to Irene,* II, 86–94. In fact, Theodosius, Maurice's eldest son and intended heir over the Balkan, Anatolian, and Near Eastern lands of the empire, seems to have escaped death with the rest of his brothers only for a short while after their execution, although rumors were rife that he had escaped to Persia, as reported here by al-Ṭabarī and by certain Byzantine historians, including Theophylactus. It seems to have been enemies of Phocas who subsequently spread abroad these rumors that Theodosius had survived the bloodbath, made his way to Persia, and then ended his days in the wastes of Colchis (i.e., western Caucasia). But Khusraw Abarwēz might well have given shelter to some Byzantine claimant, whether genuine or not, as is implied by the Armenian historian Sebēos, in order to use him in as a pawn in any future Perso-Byzantine conflict, as surmised by Nöldeke, trans. 290 n. 2.

744. The killing of Maurice was, nevertheless, only a pretext for the beginning of hostilities, since there had been tension with Persia already in the latter years of

asylum to Mawrīq's son, who had come to him as a refugee, crowned him, and set him up as king of the Byzantines, then sent him back with a mighty army headed by three of his commanders. The first one was called Rumiyūzān (?).[745] Kisrā sent him to Syria, which he then subdued and penetrated as far as Palestine.[746] He came to the city of Jerusalem (*Bayt al-Maqdis*) and took action against its bishop and all the priests in the city and the rest of the Christians over the Cross [of Jesus], which had been placed in a chest of gold and buried, with a vegetable garden planted on top of it. He pressed them hard until they showed him the spot. He then dug it out with his own hand and sent it to Kisrā in the twenty-fourth year of his reign.[747] The second commander was called Shāhīn and was the Fādhūsbān of the West. He proceeded onward until he captured Egypt and Alexandria and the land of Nubia, and sent back to Kisrā the keys of the city of Alexandria in the twenty-

---

Maurice's reign. See Bury, *A History of the Later Roman Empire from Arcadius to Irene,* II, 198–99; Higgins, *The Persian Wars of Emperor Maurice (582–602),* passim.

745. Identified by Nöldeke, trans. 290 n. 3, with the Romīzān of Michael the Syrian and Barhebraeus and the Rhousmiazan of Theophanes. Nöldeke also thought it possible that Barhebraeus was correct in identifying him with the other Persian commander Shahrbarāz mentioned a few lines further on (see on the meaning of this name, n. 749 below), with Shahrbarāz being another component of Romīzān's name (but in that place, we have Shahrbarāz equated with Farru(k)hān). It was Shahrbarāz who was actually the Persian commander who conquered Jerusalem in 614, hence this would fit with what al-Ṭabarī goes on to say of Rumiyūzān's conquests in Syria and Palestine.

746. After appearing in Syria, the Persian army had occupied Damascus in 613 and had appeared in Palestine in spring 614 after defeating the Byzantine forces in the Ḥawrān between al-Darā'ah and Boṣrā (possibly the battle referred to in *Sūrat al-Rūm,* Qur'ān, XXX, 2–3, see al-Ṭabarī, I, 1005, 1007, pp. 324, 327 and n. 761 below). See R. Schick, *The Christian Communities of Palestine from Byzantine to Islamic Rule. A Historical and Archaeological Study,* 20ff.

747. The capture of Jerusalem probably took place in June 614, when the city suffered a three days' sacking at the hands of the Sāsanīd troops. The "bishop" was the Patriarch Zacharias, installed at Jerusalem by Phocas's general Bonosus in 609 but now carried off into captivity in Persia; he remained titular Patriarch until his death in exile around the time of the Byzantines' final defeat of the Persian, i.e., ca. 627–28, with Modestus acting as his *locum tenens* in the years of the Persian occupation of Palestine and Syria. The True Cross was certainly carried off by the victors, not to be restored until 629, but the Sponge and the Spear were preserved and taken to Constantinople. See Nöldeke, trans. 291 n. 1; Bury, *A History of the Later Roman Empire from Arcadius to Irene,* II, 214; 39, 46; Schick, *The Christian Communities of Palestine from Byzantine to Islamic Rule,* 33–39, 46.

eighth year of his reign.[748] The third commander was called Farruhān (i.e., Farrukhān), who had the rank of Shahrbarāz. He led an expedition to attack Constantinople, until he halted on the bank of the strait (i.e., the Bosphorus) just near the city, and made his encampment there.[749] Kisrā ordered him to devastate the land of the Byzantines, as an expression of his anger at the Byzantines' violence against Mawrīq and as an act of vengeance upon them for him. But none of the Byzantines acknowledged Mawrīq's son as their ruler or offered him any obedience. However, they killed Fūqā, the king whom they had raised to the throne as ruler over them, when his evil doing, his impiety toward God, and his reprehensible behavior became apparent to them. They raised to royal [1003]
power over themselves a man called Hiraql (Heraclius).[750]

---

748. MP *shāhēn,* literally "falcon," see Justi, *Namenbuch,* 274–75. Shāhīn's army probably moved from Palestine against Egypt in autumn 616, so that the capture of Alexandria was probably in 617. See A. J. Butler, *The Arab Conquest of Egypt and the Last Thirty Years of the Roman Dominion,* 70–83.

749. Regarding the form Farruhān for the fairly common Persian name Farrukhān (an ancient patronymic from Farrukh, literally "fortunate, joyful"; see Justi, *Namenbuch,* 94–95, and Gignoux, *Noms propres sassanides,* 82–83 nos. 352, 354), Nöldeke, trans. 292 n. 2, noted that the Pahlavi script does not distinguish between the letters *h* and *kh.* Shahrwarāz/Shahrbarāz is a name and not a rank (*martabah*), with the meaning of "boar (i.e., valiant warrior) of the land," occurring in Middle Persian onomastic, although the simple name Warāz/Barāz is more common, see al-Ṭabarī, I, 895, 960, pp. 152, 255, and nn. 393, 616 above. That Farrukhān could also have the name Shahrbarāz seemed to Nöldeke improbable, but he was not able to resolve the problem. In reality, it was Shāhīn who transferred his scene of operations to Anatolia, penetrating as far as Chalcedon on the shores of the Bosphorus (modern Kadiköy, near Üsküdar or Scutari), probably in 616, and according to certain tales meeting with the Emperor Heraclius for negotiations, an act for which he paid with his life when he returned to Khusraw's court. See Bury, *A History of the Later Roman Empire from Arcadius to Irene,* II, 216–17. Al-Dīnawarī, *al-Akhbār al-ṭiwāl,* 106, states that Shāhīn led an army of twenty-four thousand men to the shores of the "gulf of Constantinople" and encamped there; the confused account of al-Mas'ūdī, *Murūj,* II, 226–27 = § 647, has a romancelike account of Shahrbarāz's exploits from a base at Antioch involving his quarrel with Khusraw and in revenge leading the Byzantine emperor and his army into Persian Mesopotamia.

750. The usurper Phocas's misrule in Constantinople provoked an appeal to the Exarch of the West at Carthage, who had been appointed by Maurice and who had maintained a de facto independence during the eight years of Phocas's reign. The Exarch sent his son Heraclius with a fleet. In autumn 610 Phocas was overthrown and killed, and Heraclius was crowned emperor in his place; Phocas left behind him a reputation in the Byzantine chronicles of tyrannical behavior and ineptitude during a chaotic reign. See Bury, *A History of the Later Roman Empire from Arcadius to Irene,* II, 203–206.

When Hiraql perceived the perilous state the land of the Byzantines was in, with the Persian armies devastating it, their killing of the Byzantine warriors, their carrying off into captivity of the Byzantines' women and children, their plundering of the Byzantines' wealth, and their violation of the inmost parts of their realm, he shed tears before God and made humble petition to Him, imploring Him to rescue him and the people of his kingdom from the Persian armies.[751] He saw in a dream a stout-bodied man, on a lofty throne and accoutred with fine weapons (i.e., the Persian king), set up some distance from his side. Another person came into their presence, threw down that man from his throne, and said to Hiraql, "I have delivered him into your hands." When Hiraql woke up, he told no one about his dream. The next night, Hiraql saw in a dream the man whom he had seen in his previous dream seated on a lofty throne, and the man who had come in upon the two of them now came to him with a long chain in his hand, which he threw round the neck of the man on the throne and held him in his power with it, saying to Hiraql, "Here, I've done it; I have handed Kisrā over to you completely. So march against him now, for victory will be yours, you will be given power over him and you will attain your desire in your campaign." When these dreams came to him successively, he at last recounted them to the great men of the Byzantines and to those of them with

751. The Persian invasion of Anatolia had left the Persian army stationed at Chalcedon on the eastern shore of the Bosphorus, permanently threatening the Byzantine capital. Syria and Palestine were under Persian occupation, and the Christians there suffered massacres and the loss of many religious buildings; the interlude between Heraclius's regaining these provinces and the appearance of the Muslim Arabs in the mid-630s was too brief to enable the Christian communities there to recover their lost position. The Copts and Greeks in Egypt likewise endured massacres and saw the destruction of many churches and monasteries; the Persian forces spread up the Nile valley as far as Syene/Aswan and westward along the Mediterranean coast to the Pentapolis (i.e., the modern Cyrenaica). Phocas's disastrous reign had witnessed the collapse of what remained of the Byzantine *limes* on the Sava and lower Danube, allowing the Avars (who had moved westward from Inner Asia before the expanding power of the first Türk empire there) and Slavs to overrun the Balkans and Greece, with the Avars reaching the suburbs of the capital itself in 617. The situation appeared so desperate that in 618 Heraclius contemplated abandoning Constantinople for Carthage, but was deterred by the Patriarch Sergius. See Bury, *A History of the Later Roman Empire from Arcadius to Irene,* II, 214–18; Butler, *The Arab Conquest of Egypt,* 54–92; Schick, *The Christian Communities of Palestine,* 20–48.

penetrating judgment. They told him that he would be given power over Kisrā, and advised him to lead an expedition against him.

Hiraql prepared for the campaign, and appointed one of his sons as his deputy over the city of Constantinople.[752] He took a different route from that of Shahrbarāz and proceeded onward until he penetrated deeply into Armenia and encamped at Niṣībīn after the space of a year.[753] Shāhīn, the Fādhūsbān of the West,

---

752. On his accession to power, Heraclius had found the empire in desperate straits. He had to quell the revolt in 610–11 at Ancyra of Phocas's brother Comentiolus, which caused a delay to his plans for rebuiliding the Byzantine war machine, and he had to force the untrustworthy general of the army in Cappadocia, Priscus, a brother-in-law of Phocas, to relinquish his command and enter a monastery. Heraclius now endeavored to secure his position in the Balkans by making peace with the Khan of the Avars in 620, agreeing to pay him tribute (even if this relief from Avar attacks was only short-lived). He inaugurated extensive reforms and reorganization in both provincial and central administration. Details are sparse, but it seems that, once the Persians had been pushed out of Anatolia in 623 (see n. 753 below), Heraclius began the extensive settlement there of picked troops, *epilekta,* possibly the genesis of the military theme system which was to develop in the later seventh century as a response to Arab attacks along the Taurus mountains frontier. Naval forces were also built up; the Byzantine fleet was used to transport an army in spring 622 to Lazica so that it could campaign successfully in Armenia, and skillful use of sea power prevented any effective link-up of the Persians with their putative allies in the Balkans, the Avars, Slavs, and Bulghars. The emperor's campaign of revenge was to take on something of the character of a holy war; Byzantine religious feeling had been profoundly shocked by the Persians' carrying off from Jerusalem the True Cross, and the church contributed extensively of its gold and silver for the financing of Heraclius's efforts. Moreover, once Heraclius had achieved his victory, former Byzantine territory recovered, Greek captives returned from Persia and the True Cross restored to Jerusalem, he was to assume formally the title (hitherto used in an informal fashion only) of *basileus,* "emperor," with connotations of divine approval of the royal power; Irfan Shahîd has suggested that, in the assumption of this imperial title, Heraclius was influenced by the example of Christian monarchy in Armena and was also harking back to the Davidic monarchy over Israel. See Bury, *A History of the Later Roman Empire from Arcadius to Irene,* II, 244–45; Shahîd, "The Iranian Factor in Byzantium during the Reign of Heraclius," 295–320.

The son of Heraclius appointed as his deputy in Constantinople was the ten-year-old Constantine, the ephemeral emperor Constantine III in the confused period just after Heraclius's death in February 641. See Bury, 210–26; W. Ensslin, in *The Cambridge Medieval History. IV. The Byzantine Empire. Part II, Government, Church and Civilization,* 36–37; W. E. Kaegi, "New Evidence on the Early Reign of Heraclius," 313–24; Frye, "The Political History of Iran under the Sasanians," 169.

753. Heraclius's initial campaign, the first of his six campaigns against the Persians, was aimed at Shahrbarāz, who was still encamped at Chalcedon. It start-

was at Kisrā's court when Hiraql reached Niṣībīn, because Kisrā [1004] had become angry with him and had dismissed him from that frontier command (*thaghr*). Shāhbarāz, however, was firmly holding the place where he was stationed because of Kisrā's command to him to remain there and not leave it.[754] Kisrā received the news of Hiraql's descent on Niṣībīn with his army, and sent to combat Hiraql one of his commanders called Rāhzādh[755] with twelve thousand warriors, giving him orders to remain at Nīniwā (Nineveh) in the vicinity of the town of al-Mawṣil (Mosul), on the banks of the Tigris, and to prevent the Byzantines from crossing the river. Kisrā had been residing at Daskarat al-Malik[756] when the news about Hiraql reached him.

Rāhzādh put Kisrā's command into effect and encamped in the place he had instructed. Hiraql, however, crossed the Tigris at a different spot and marched toward the district where the Persian army lay. Rāhzādh sent out spies against Hiraql; they came back

---

ed from Cilicia and was largely conducted in Pontus and Cappadocia; in a battle at the opening of 623, at a so far unidentified place, the emperor decisively defeated the Persian commander and thereby relieved the pressure on Constantinople. Further operations were conducted in Cilicia, Armenia, Caucasian Albania, and Azerbaijan during the period 623–26 (for Heraclius's operations in the latter region, see Minorsky, "Roman and Byzantine Campaigns in Atropatene," 91–94), The campaign of 627–28 into Upper Mesopotamia and Persia was actually his sixth one, launched in autumn 627 in the year after Heraclius had repelled a second Avar attack on Constantinople, while Shahrbarāz had again penetrated as far as Chalecedon. See Bury, *A History of the Later Roman Empire,* II, 227–30, 239–41; Frye, "The Political History of Iran under the Sasanians," 169–70.

754. Khusraw's attempt to recall Shahrbarāz from Chalcedon in order to reinforce the Persian defenses in Upper Mesopotamia was foiled, so the story goes, by the Greeks' interception of his letter and the substitution for it of another letter telling Shahrbarāz to remain where he was. See Bury, *A History of the Later Roman Empir from Arcadius to Irene,* II, 242.

755. Text, *Rāhzār.* This man is the Razates (vars. Ryzates, Razastēs) and the Rōzbehān and Rōgwehān of the Syriac ones. See Nöldeke, trans. 294 n. 3; Bury, *A History of the Later Roman Empire from Arcadius to Irene,* II, 241 n. 3.

756. This is the Arabic form of the Persian Dastgird (< MP *dastgird* "landed estate, including all buildings, beasts, persons, etc., within it"; see B. Geiger, "Mittelpersische Wörter und Sachen," 123–28), Syriac Dasqartā, which lay to the northeast of Ctesiphon on the route via Khāniqīn and Ḥulwān to Media/Jibāl, the site being marked today by the ruins of Eski Baghdād. Yāqūt distinguishes it from a Dastjird in Khurāsān by calling this one Dastjird al-Kisrawiyyah, "royal Dastjird." See his *Buldān,* II, 454, and II, 455, for Daskarat al-Malik; Nöldeke, trans. 295 n. 1; Le Strange, *Lands,* 62; Christensen, *Sassanides,* 454–55. The ruins of Khusraw's splendid palace there, sacked by the Byzantines when they entered the town, were admired four centuries later by the Arab traveler Abū Dulaf al-Khazrajī, see his *Second Risālah,* ed. and tr. Minorsky, text § 38, trans. 46, comm. 94.

and told him that Hiraql had ninety thousand warriors. Rāhzādh was now convinced that he and the troops at his disposal were inadequate for withstanding such a number of troops. He wrote several times to Kisrā that Hiraql was pressing heavily on him with forces so numerous and so well equipped that he and his troops could not withstand them. To all that, Kisrā kept on replying that, if he was too weak to withstand those Byzantines, he would not be too weak to get his troops to fight to the last and to lavish their blood in his service. When Rāhzādh had secured the same reply successively for his letter to Kisrā, he got his troops ready for action and attacked the Byzantines. The latter killed Rāhzādh and six thousand of his men. The rest were routed and fled precipitately. The news of the Byzantines' killing of Rāhzādh and the victory gained by Hiraql reached Kisrā. This catastrophe crushed his spirits, and he left Daskarat al-Malik for al-Madā'in and fortified himself within it because he was too weak to stand up to Hiraql in battle.[757] Hiraql advanced until he was near to al- [1005]
Madā'in. But when ever-fresh reports about him kept reaching Kisrā, and he prepared to fight Hiraql, the latter turned back to the Byzantine lands.[758]

Kisrā wrote to the three army commanders who had been defeated, instructing them to send him information about every one of their troops who had shown weakness in that battle or who had not stuck fast to their posts. They were to punish these men according to their degrees of guilt. Through this letter, he provoked them into rebelliousness against him and into seeking ways to preserve themselves safe from him. He also wrote to Shahrbarāz, ordering him to come to him as rapidly as possible and to describe for him what the Byzantines had done in his province.[759]

757. As Nöldeke noted, trans. 296 n. 1, Khusraw's flight from Daskarah/Dastgird was a great blow to his authority, and contributed to the loss of confidence in him which was to lead to his deposition and death. It had been his seat of government almost continuously since 604 because of a prediction that he would die at Ctesiphon. See Christensen, *Sassanides*, 454.

758. Not in fact to Anatolia but northeastward into Azerbaijan and its protective mountains, where he took up quarters in the region of Ganzak for the winter of 627–28. See Bury, *A History of the Later Roman Empire*, II, 241–42; Minorsky, "Roman and Byzantine Campaigns in Atropatene," 91–94.

759. It was this letter that was reportedly intercepted by the Greeks, enabling them to spread disinformation which ensured that Shahrbarāz did not march eastward to shore up the Persian defenses in Iraq; see n. 754 above. The doubts and

It has been said that God's words, "*Alif, lām, mīm*. The Romans have been defeated in the nearer part of the land,[760] but after their defeat they will be victorious within a few years. The affair belongs to God, before and after, and on that day the believers will rejoice in God's succor; He succors whom He pleases, and He is the Mighty, the Compassionate One. The promise of God! God does not fall short in His promise, but most of the people do not know.", were only revealed regarding the affairs of Abarwīz, king of Persia, and Hiraql, king of the Byzantines, and what happened between them, which I have recounted in these stories.[761]

## *Mention of Those Who Say That*

There related to me al-Qāsim b. al-Ḥasan—al-Ḥusayn—Ḥajjāj—Abū Bakr b. ʿAbdallāh—ʿIkrimah,[762] who said: The Byzantines and the Persians fought together in the nearer part of the land. He related: The nearer part of the land [refers to] the Day of

---

suspicions of Khusraw's generals were probably justified, and Shahrbarāz, in particular, must have suspected that the king's ire would be directed at him (cf. the information in the romanticized Arabic report on the authority of ʿIkrimah in al-Ṭabarī, I, 1007–09, pp. 326–30 below). But Khusraw's prestige had fallen so low and his freedom of action in Ctesiphon was so circumscribed that he fell victim to events there at the beginning of 628, while Heraclius was in Azerbaijan. He fell ill, tried to arrange the succession in favor of his son by Shīrīn, Mardānshāh, but was forestalled by his other son Kawād or Shērōy, imprisoned and executed at the end of February. For details of these events, see al-Ṭabarī, I, 1043–45, pp. 379–81 below.

760. *Fī adnā al-arḍ* is usually interpreted as the part of northwestern Arabia adjacent to the Byzantine frontier. See further n. 761 below.

761. *Sūrat al-Rūm*, Qurʾān, XXX, 1–5. The text is usually read with the passive verb *ghulibat al-Rūm* and then the active one *sa-yaghlibūna* and is taken to refer to some battle during the Persian invasion of the Levant 613–14 (see n. 746 above). But a less authoritative, single reading has *ghalabat al-Rūm*, ". . . have been victorious," and *sa-yughlabūna*, "[but] . . . they will be defeated," dubiously taken to refer to the initial Byzantine success against the Arab raid on Muʾtah in 8/630 and the eventual triumph of Muslim arms in Palestine and Syria. See Bell, *A Commentary on the Qurʾān*, II, 69; Paret, *Der Koran. Kommentar und Konkordanz*, 388. Detailed studies on the sūrah and its historical background are E. Beck, "Die Sure ar-Rūm (30)," 335–55; M. Götz, "Zum historischen Hintergrund von Sure 30, 1–5," 111–20.

762. Abū ʿAbdallāh ʿIkrimah (died probably in 105/723–24) was a noted Successor, a *mawlā* or client of Ibn ʿAbbās, and an authority for many of his traditions. See Ibn Saʿd, *Kitāb al-Ṭabaqāt al-kabīr*, V, 212–16; al-Ṭabarī, III, 2483–85; *EI²*, s.v. ʿIkrima (J. Schacht).

Adhriʿāt, where the two armies met, and the Byzantines were defeated.[763] This came to the ears of the Prophet and his companions while they were [still] in Mecca (i.e., before the Hijrah) and caused them distress. The Prophet disliked the Zoroastrian gentiles (*al-ummiyyūn min al-Majūs*) gaining the upper hand over the [1006] Byzantine possessors of written scriptures (*ahl al-kitāb min al-Rūm*). The unbelievers in Mecca, however, rejoiced and hurled abuse; they encountered the Prophet's companions and said, "You are possessors of a written scripture, and the Christians are possessors of a written scripture, while we are unbelievers. Now our brethren, the Persians, have been victorious over your brethren, the possessors of written scriptures, and if you attack us, we shall certainly be victorious over you."[764] At this point, God sent down the revelation "*Alif, lām, mīm.* The Romans have been defeated . . ." to "they are unheeding about the next life."

---

763. Adhriʿat, in Biblical times the capital of Bashan, the Edrei of Num. xxi. 33, is the more recent al-Darāʿah or Deraa just north of the Syrian-Jordanian frontier at the southern edge of the Ḥawrān. See Yāqūt, *Buldān,* I, 130–31; Le Strange, *Palestine,* 383; A,-S. Marmardji, *Textes géographiques arabes sur la Palestine,* 3; *EI²*, s.v. Adhriʿāt (F. Buhl-N. Elisséeff); and n. 746 above. The Cairo text, II, 184, has "the nearest part of the land was, at that time (*yawmaʾidhin,* for the Leiden text's *yawm*) Adhriʿāt," with this reading taken from al-Ṭabarī, *Tafsīr* on Sūrah XXX.

764. Kister has pointed out that the Persians may have tried in the sixth century to exercise some form of indirect control or influence over Ḥijāz, including over Mecca and Medina. The seventh/thirteenth-century, hence comparatively late, author Ibn Saʿīd mentions that, in the time of Qubādh, son of Fayrūz, Qubādh attempted, through the agency of the Kindī chief al-Ḥārith b. ʿAmr (on whom see n. 362 above), to impose the doctrine of Mazdak that he had espoused, and some people in Mecca assented to this summons (*tazandaqa*). Muḥammad b. Ḥabīb actually lists the alleged *zanādiqah* (whoever these may be, however; see below) of Quraysh (*Muḥabbar,* 161). Hence the Meccan pagans might well have retained memories of the connection with Persia, enough to use this as a way of slighting Muḥammad when, at this stage in his mission, he would have had a natural sympathy toward the Christian Byzantines as fellow monotheists. See Kister, "Al-Ḥīra. Some Notes on Its Relations with Arabia," 144–45. On the other hand, earlier Arabic authors, such as Muḥammad b. Ḥabīb, in his *Muḥabbar,* loc. cit., and Ibn Qutaybah, in his *Maʿārif,* 621, state that Quraysh got their *zandaqah* from al-Ḥīrah. De Blois has accordingly suggested that, in early Islamic usage, *zandaqah* nornally means "Manichaeism" and that Manichaeism was conveyed to Mecca by Qurashī traders who derived it from converts to Manichaeism from among the Christian population of al-Ḥīrah, i.e., from elements of the ʿIbād; Ibn Saʿīd's story would have arisen from a confusion and conflation of information in the earlier sources. See de Blois, "The 'Sabians' (Ṣābiʾūn) in Pre-Islamic Arabia," 48–50 and n. 38. See also Nöldeke, trans. 298 n. 1.

Abū Bakr al-Ṣiddīq went forth to the unbelievers (*al-kuffār*) and said, "Have you rejoiced at the victory of your brethren over our brethren? Don't rejoice! May God not give you refreshing solace! By God, the Byzantines will be victorious over the Persians; our Prophet has told us that." Ubayy b. Khalaf al-Jumaḥī came up to him and said, "You lie, O Abū Fuḍayl!"[765] Abū Bakr answered him, "You are a bigger liar, O enemy of God!" He added, "I wager you ten of my young she-camels against ten of yours. If within the next three years the Byzantines are victorious over the Persians, I get the stake; and if the Persians are victorious, you get it." Then Abū Bakr went to the Prophet and told him this. The Prophet said, "I didn't express myself thus: 'a few' (*al-biḍ'*) means a number from three to nine, so raise the stake and extend the period of time with him." Abū Bakr accordingly went out and met Ubayy, and the latter commented, "Perhaps you have come to regret [your wager]?" He replied, "Not at all. Come on, I'll raise the stake with you and extend the period of time: make it a hundred young she-camels over a period up to nine years." Ubayy answered, "I agree."[766]

There related to us al-Qāsim—al-Ḥusayn—Ḥajjāj—Abū Bakr—'Ikrimah, who said: There was in Persia a woman who gave birth only to kings and heroes. Kisrā summoned her and said, "I am [1007] planning to send an army against the Byzantines and to appoint one of your sons as its commander. Advise me, which of them should I nominate?" She replied, "The first one is so-and-so, who is craftier than a fox and more wary than a falcon; then there is Farrukhān, who is more incisive than a spear point; and then there is Shahrbarāz, who is more sagacious (*aḥlam*) than such-and-such.[767] So appoint whichever of them you please." He said, "I appoint the sagacious one," and he appointed Shahrbarāz. He pro-

765. Ubayy was a member of the clan of Jumaḥ, which ranged itself with the Makhzūm-'Abd Shams group within Mecca, largely hostile to Muḥammad; he fought in the army of Quraysh at the battle of Uḥud, and died of wounds received there. See al-Ṭabarī, I, 1407, 1409. "Abū Fuḍayl" was a *kunyah* or patronymic of Abū Bakr's, here used as a familiar form of address. The Cairo text, II, 184, has for this *kunyah* "Abū Faṣīl."

766. The same story in al-Ṭabarī, *Tafsīr*, XX, 13.

767. As suggested in nn. 745, 749 above, the two components of Shahrbarāz Farrukhān's name—if this is indeed one person—have apparently been wrongly separated here and made into two different persons.

ceeded to [the land of] the Byzantines with the Persian army, defeated the Byzantines, slaughtered them, devastated their towns, and cut down their olive trees.

Abū Bakr says:[768] I related this narrative to ʿAṭāʾ al-Khurāsānī,[769] and he asked me, "Have you ever seen the land of Syria?" I said, "No," and he replied, "If you had ever been there you would have seen the towns that were laid waste and the olive trees that were cut down."[770] Later, I actually went to Syria and saw this." ʿAṭāʾ al-Khurāsānī related from Yaḥyā b. Yaʿmar, who said: Qayṣar sent a man called Q.ṭ.mah (?)[771] with a Byzantine army, and Kisrā sent Shahrbarāz. The two met up with each other at Adhriʿāt and Buṣrā, which are the nearest parts of Syria to you (i.e., the Arabs). The Persians encountered the Byzantines and defeated them. The unbelievers of Quraysh in Mecca rejoiced at this; whereas, the Meccans were chagrined. God then sent down the revelation "*Alif, lām, mīm.* The Romans have been defeated . . ." to the end of the section. Then he mentioned further another narrative, like ʿIkrimah's but with additional details. Shahrbarāz kept on relentlessly defeating them and laying waste their towns until he reached the Bosphorus (*al-khalīj*). But then, Kisrā died. News of this reached them, and Shahrbarāz and his followers retreated precipitately. Fortune swung round to give the Byzantines power over the Persians at that point, and they pursued and killed them.

He related: ʿIkrimah said in his narrative: When the Persians were victorious over the Byzantines, Farrukhān was once sitting and drinking, and said to his companions, "I had a dream, and it

---

768. That is, the transmitter Abū Bakr b. ʿAbdallāh b. Muḥammad b. Abī Sabrah, died 162/778–79. See Ibn Ḥajar, *Tahdhīb al-Tahdhīb*, XII, 27–28.

769. That is, the Syrian traditionist and Qurʾān commentator ʿAṭāʾ b. Abī Muslim Maysarah al-Khurāsānī, died 135/752–53. See Ibn Saʿd, *Ṭabaqāt*, VII/2, 102; Ibn Ḥajar, *Tahdhīb al-Tahdhīb*, VII, 212–15; Sezgin, *GAS*, I, 33–34.

770. That is, he saw, after the lapse of more than a century, the effects of devastation, in 613–14, by the invading Persian army. See Nöldeke, trans. 399 n. 4.

771. This name is obscure. Nöldeke, trans. 300 n. 1, adduced as a possibility the Jafnid/Ghassānid al-Nuʿmān b. al-Ḥārith b. Jabalah, to whom Ḥamzah al-Iṣfahānī, *Taʾrīkh*, 103, gives the cognomen (*laqab*) Q.ṭām, but later, in his *Die Ghassânischen Fürsten*, 44, Nöldeke took this as a confusion with the name of the chief of Kindah, Ḥujr b. Umm Qaṭām mentioned in the *Muʿallaqah* of al-Ḥārith b. Ḥillizah, it being in any case difficult to take the name Qaṭām as anything but a female one.

was as if I saw myself on Kisrā's throne."[772] This came to Kisrā's ears, and he wrote to Shahrbarāz, "When this letter of mine reaches you, send to me Farrukhān's head." Shahrbarāz wrote back to him, however, "O king, you will never find anyone like Farrukhān who has inflicted so much damage on the enemy or has
[1008] such a formidable reputation among them; so don't do this!" Kisrā answered him, "Among the men of Persia there is certainly someone who can serve as his replacement, so hasten and send me his head!" Shahrbarāz made further representations to him, which angered Kisrā, and he made no further answer but sent a courier of the postal and intelligence service (*barīd*)[773] to the people of Persia announcing, "I hereby remove Shahrbarāz from power over you and appoint Farrukhān over you in his stead." Then he handed over to the courier a small sheet and instructed him, "When Farrukhān assumes royal authority and his brother gives him obedience, then give him this."[774] When Shahrbarāz read the letter, he said, "I hear and obey!" He got down from his throne. Farrukhān sat down [in his place], and he handed over the paper. Farrukhān then said, "Bring Shahrbarāz before me," and pushed him forward so that his head could be cut off. Shahrbarāz, however, protested, "Don't be in such a hurry, let me write my last testament!" and Farrukhān agreed to this. Shahrbarāz called for a chest and gave him three sheets [of paper from out of it], telling him, "I sent these sheets to Kisrā pleading for you, and now you want to execute me on the pretext of a single letter." At this, Farrukhān gave the royal authority back to his brother.[775]

---

772. The dream predicts Shahrbarāz Farrukhān's later elevation to his forty days' reign in Ctesiphon, see al-Ṭabarī, I, 1062–63, p. 401–403.

773. See on this institution n. 147 above.

774. As emerges a few lines below, the sheet contains an order for Shahrbarāz's execution. The motif of a letter containing a command to kill the unsuspecting bearer is an ancient one, and in Arabic lore is exemplified by the "letter of al-Mutalammis," given to the pre-Islamic poet al-Mutalammis by the Lakhmid ʿAmr b. Hind (see on him n. 414 above) but which he was sharp enough to destroy, whereas his nephew, the poet Ṭarafah, duly delivered his letter and thereby brought about his own death. See *EI*², s.v. al-Mutalammis (Ch. Pellat). Cf. also the parallel use, in different circumstances, of a letter containing orders for an execution, that of Oroetes of Sardis at the behest of King Darius, in Herodotus, III.128.

775. The above story continues the separation of Shahrbarāz-Farrukhān into

Shahrbarāz wrote to Qayṣar, the king of the Byzantines, "I have a request to make to you which couriers cannot carry and no documents can convey. Come and meet me, but with just fifty Byzantine troops, and I will bring just fifty Persian ones." Qayṣar, however, came with five hundred thousand Byzantine troops and began to place spies along the road before him, fearing that Shahrbarāz might be contemplating some act of trickery with him, until his spies returned to him with the information that Shahrbarāz had with him only fifty men. A carpet was spread out for them both, and they met in a brocade tent that had been erected for them. Each of them had a knife by his side. They summoned an interpreter for their negotiations, and Shahrbarāz said, "The ones who laid waste your towns were my brother and my-

---

two different persons, as set forth in nn. 745, 749, 767 above. The second commander involved in the story is presumably in reality the Shāhīn mentioned by al-Ṭabarī at I, 1003, p. 321 above. For the apparently more historical episode of the letter of dismissal and death which Khusraw despatched to Shahrbarāz's second-in-command at the Persian camp in Chalcedon and which was intercepted by the Byzantines and its contents revealed to Shahrbarāz, see Bury, *A History of the Later Roman Empire from Arcadius to Irene,* II, 244. The story became a romantic tale handed down among the Persians, and is listed as such by Ibn al-Nadīm, *Fihrist,* 364 (read *Shahrbarāz* for *Shahrīzād*), tr. II, 716.

The whole story of Shahrbarāz's defection from Khusraw's cause to the side of the Byzantines has recently been discussed, on a basis of the sources available, by Walter E. Kaegi and Paul M. Cobb. They distinguish the Eastern Christian ones from the early Islamic ones. Very similar, though with some variation of details, are the accounts of Theophanes, Michael the Syrian, and Agapius of Manbij; these would seem to go back to the lost Syriac historian Theophilus of Edessa, and in them, Shahrbarāz's defection is attributed to Khusraw's suspicious nature thereby driving his commander into Heraclius's arms. The account in the *Short History* of Nicephorus, however, simply makes Heraclius's triumph against the Persians the result of his excellent strategy and generalship, with no suggestion of internal stresses and suspicions within the Persian camp. At the side of these Christian accounts are the Islamic ones: the one given on the basis of reports from ʿIkrimah given here by al-Ṭabarī, and the much less-noticed one—because concealed within a history that ostensibly deals only with the conquest of Egypt—going back to the traditionist of the Umayyad period al-Zuhrī (see on him n. 789 below) and preserved within the *Futūḥ Miṣr* of Ibn ʿAbd al-Ḥakam (said to have d. 171/787–88). Both Islamic accounts share similarities with the Christian accounts, and could represent a single, original tradition, although al-Zuhrī has the interesting additional feature of a plausible reason for Khusraw's anger with Shahrbarāz, i.e., the latter's procrastination, his failure to launch a decisive assault on Constantinople and thus destroy the Byzantine empire. See Kaegi and Cobb, "Heraclius, Shahrbarāz, and al-Ṭabarī," 121–43.

self, with our stratagems and our valor. But now Kisrā has come to envy us and wants me to kill my brother. When I refused to do this, he ordered my brother to kill me. Hence both of us have thrown off allegiance to him, and are ready to fight at your side against him." Qayṣar said, "You have made the right choice."
[1009] Then one of the two made a sign to his companion, [saying,] "The secret lies between two people; if it goes beyond two people, it will become public knowledge." The other said, "Yes, indeed." So they both fell upon the interpreter and killed him with their knives.[776] God brought about Kisrā's death, and the news of this reached the Messenger of God on the Day of Ḥudaybiyah, causing him and his companions to rejoice.[777]

I received information going back to Hishām b. Muḥammad, who said that in the twentieth year of Kisrā Abarwīz's reign, God sent Muḥammad [as His prophet].[778] The latter remained thirteen years in Mecca, and he emigrated to Medina in the thirty-third year of Kisrā's reign.

---

776. Acording to Nöldeke, trans. 302 n. 1, these negotiations in fact refer to a meeting of Heraclius and Shahrbarāz at the Anatolian town of Arabissos (in Armenia Tertia, what was later Little Armenia, somewhere in the region of the mediaeval town of Elbistan; see Shahîd, *Byzantium and the Arabs in the Sixth Century*, I/1, 610–11) in June 629 after Khusraw Abarwēz had been deposed and killed and after Shahrbarāz had led a rebellion at Ctesiphon against his rival for the direction of state affairs under the youthful new king Kawād II Shērōy, had killed the latter after a reign of only eighteen months, and proclaimed himself ruler, though not of Sāsānid or Arsacid royal stock (see al-Ṭabarī, I, 1061–63, p. 400–403 below, and cf. Christensen, *Sassanides*, 497–98; Frye, "The Political History of Iran under the Sasanians," 170–71; Kaegi and Cobb, "Heraclius, Shahrbarāz, and al-Ṭabarī," loc. cit., noting that an anonymous Syriac chronicle from 724 confirms the Arabic sources regarding the location of the meeting at Arabissos and records the construction of a church by Heraclius and Shahrbarāz, dedicated in the name of Eirēnē, "Peace," at their meeting point). Shahrbarāz's rapid rise to power and ephemeral rule—he was killed by a conspiracy at Ctesiphon led by rival military leaders and great men of state, who subsequently set up as nominal ruler there Khusraw's daughter Būrān (see al-Ṭabarī, I, 1063–64, p. 403–405, below)—was aided by Heraclius's support, who had remained at Ganzak in Azerbaijan during the upheavals within the Persian state (see nn. 758–59).

777. The treaty of Ḥudaybiyah made between Muḥammad and the Meccans was concluded at that place on the edge of the Meccan Ḥaram in Dhū al-Qaʿdah 6/March 628, hence in the month after Khusraw's death. See al-Ṭabarī, *Tafsīr*, XX, 13–14; Buhl, *Das Leben Muhammeds*, 286–90; Watt, *Muhammad at Medina*, 46–52; *EI*², s.v. al-Ḥudaybiya (W. M. Watt).

778. That is, in A.D. 610.

## *Mention of the Account Concerning the Events That Happened When God Wished to Take Away from the People of Persia Rule over Persia, and the Arabs' Overrunning it by Means of God's Favoring Them with His Prophet Muḥammad, Involving the Prophethood, the Caliphate, the Royal Power, and the Dominion, in the Days of Kisrā Abarwīz*[779]

This includes what has been related from Wahb b. Munabbih, which is what was related to us by Ibn Ḥumayd—Salamah—Muḥammad b. Isḥāq, who said: This account of Kisrā is what one of my colleagues related to me from Wahb b. Munabbih: That Kisrā constructed a dam on the "Blind Tigris" (*Dijlah al-ʿAwrāʾ*)[780] and expended on it sums of such magnitude that no one knew their extent. Also, the throne room of his palace (*ṭāq majlisihi*) was built [with such splendor] as had never been seen before. He used to suspend his crown and sit on his throne when he was in public audience. He had 360 men who were prognostica- [1010] tors (*ḥuzāt*),[781] these being learned scholars (*ʿulamāʾ*), including soothsayers, magicians, and astrologers. He related: Among these was a man from the Arabs called al-Sāʾib who used to draw omens from the flight of birds in the manner of the Arabs and who was seldom wrong. Bādhān had sent him to Kisrā from Yemen.[782] Whenever Kisrā was disturbed by some matter, he would order his

---

779. The following is an embellished account of the events leading up to Khusraw's deposition and death, concentrating on the prognostications and portents that pointed to and presaged these events.

780. *al-ʿawrāʾ* (fem.) means "the one-eyed." As applied to the Tigris, it is the estuary, extending nearly one hundred miles, of the combined Euphrates and Tigris before it debouches into the Persian Gulf at Ābādān, i.e., the modern Shaṭṭ al-ʿArab. The appellation "one-eyed" may stem from the fact either of the island of ʿUways being close to the estuary's mouth or of the existence of the sand bar there. See Le Strange, *Lands*, 26, 43; *EI*², s.v. Shaṭṭ al-ʿArab (Amatzia Baram). According to al-Balādhurī, *Futūḥ*, 292, Khusraw had attempted, at the end of his reign, to cope with excessive floods in Lower Iraq by repairing or constructing dams with sluices (*musannayāt*) and diversion channels from the river to feed the canals (*buthūq*) (for these terms, see Bosworth, "Some Remarks on the Terminology of Irrigation Practices and Hydraulic Constructions," 81–82), but without success.

781. The *ḥāzī* was essentially the *kāhin* or soothsayer in his rôle as prognosticator, the term being etymologically connected with the Biblical Hebrew *ḥōzeh* or seer. See Fahd, *La divination arabe*, 112–13.

782. Bādhān was the last Persian governor in Yemen. See al-Ṭabarī, I, 958, p. 252 and n. 609 above.

soothsayers, magicians, and astrologers to be gathered together and would tell them, "Look into this matter and see exactly what it is."

Now when God sent His prophet Muḥammad, Kisrā woke up one morning and found that the arched roof of his royal palace (*ṭāq mulkihi*) had collapsed in the middle without any weight having been put upon it; also, that the [dam on the] "Blind Tigris" had been breached. When he saw all that, he became filled with grief and said, "The arched roof of my royal palace has collapsed in the middle without any weight having been put upon it, and the [dam on the] 'Blind Tigris' has been breached: *Shāh bishikast*," meaning [in Arabic] "the king has been overthrown (literally, 'broken')." Then he summoned his soothsayers, magicians, and astrologers, and summoned al-Sā'ib with them, too. He told them "The arched roof of my royal palace has collapsed in the middle without any weight having been put upon it, and the [dam on the] 'Blind Tigris' has been breached: *Shāh bishikast*. Look into this matter and see exactly what it is."

They left his presence and looked into his affair, but all the quarters of the heavens became covered over for them and the earth became darkened; they exploited to the full the resources of their knowledge, but none of the magicians' magic or the soothsayers' ability to look into the future proved efficacious, nor was the astrologers' knowledge of the stars of any avail. Al-Sā'ib spent the whole of a dark, overcast night on a hillock, where he saw a lightning flash that arose from the direction of Ḥijāz, flew across the heavens, and reached as far as the East. The next morn-
[1011] ing, he looked at what was beneath his feet, and behold, there was a green meadow. He then made a pronouncement in his role as diviner: "If what I was seeing is true, there will arise from Ḥijāz a dominion (*sulṭān*) which will reach the East and from which the earth will grow green and fertile—much more so than from any previous kingdom."[783] When the soothsayers and astrologers spoke together confidentially [about what they had seen] and saw what had happened to themselves, and perceived that only Sā'ib had really seen anything, they said to each other, "You know, by

783. Referring, of course, to the rise of Muḥammad and the birth of the new faith in Mecca.

God, that it can only be something originated from the heavens that has prevented you from utilizing your specialist knowledge; that is because of a prophet who has been already sent [from God], or is just about to be sent, who will take away this present royal power and smash it. But if you announce to Kisrā the impending destruction of his royal power, he will surely kill you, so concoct among yourselves some explanation you can give him that will deflect [his wrath] from you for some length of time." So they went to Kisrā and told him. "We have looked into this matter and have found that your astrological calculators, to whom you entrusted the prognostications for building the roof of your royal palace and likewise for the construction of the dam across the 'Blind Tigris', based their calculations on inauspicious stars. When night and day successively worked on those constructions, the inauspicious stars assumed their most maleficient positions, so that everything based upon those nights and days was destroyed.[784] We can, however, make a calculation for you regarding when you should begin the work of reconstruction, and this will not be destroyed." Kisrā said, "Make the calculation, then." They did this for him and told him, "Now construct it!" So he did that, and was at work on the Tigris for eight months, expending on it an incalculable amount of money. When it was at last completed, Kisrā asked them, "Shall I sit down on top of the dam's wall?" They replied, "Yes." So he called for carpets and coverings and aromatic herbs to be placed on it. He ordered the marzbāns to be gathered together before him, as were also musicians and players (*laʿʿābūn*). Then he went forth and sat down on it. But when once he was installed there, the Tigris dashed the construction away from beneath him, and he was only extricated [from it] at his last gasp. When they had got him out, he gathered together his soothsayers, magicians, and astrologers, executed nearly a [1012]
hundred of them and said, "I let you grow fat and let you come closer to my presence than other people, and I gave you living

784. Belief in the favorable or unfavorable effects of the movements of the heavenly bodies went back to the Ancient Near Eastern civilizations and to the Greeks' division of the planets into beneficent ones, *agathopoioi*, and maleficent ones, *kakopoioi*, and was transmitted to the ancient Arabs. See Fahd, *La divination arabe*, 483ff.; *EI*², s.vv. Nudjūm, aḥkām al- (T. Fahd), Saʿd wa-naḥs (Fahd), al-Saʿdānⁱ (P. Kunitzsch).

allowances, and then you trifle with me!" They responded, "O king, we were at fault, just as those before us were at fault, but we can make a [new] calculation for you, and you can be sure of it, and you can accordingly begin the task of reconstruction on the most reliably auspicious of days!" Kisrā said, "Take care what you say!" They replied, "We will indeed!" Kisrā further said, "Make the calculation, then." They did this for him and told him, "Now construct it!" He expended on it an incalculable amount of money, over a period of eight months from that point.

Then they told him, "We've completed it," and he said, "Shall I, accordingly, go forth and sit down on it?" They replied, "Yes." He was nevertheless reluctant to sit down on it, hence rode one of his steeds and started proceeding over the dam. But while he was traveling along it, the Tigris dashed the construction away, and he only reached safety at his last gasp. He gathered them together again, and said, "By God, I will pass you along [for execution], to the last man of you, and I will tear out your shoulder joints and will throw you beneath the feet of elephants, unless you tell me faithfully the truth about this matter concerning which you have elaborated such a story for me."

They replied, "We won't lie to you any longer, O king. You commanded us, when [the dam on] the Tigris was breached and the arched roof of your royal palace collapsed without any weight having been put on it, to use our specialist knowledge and look into the reason behind it. We did that, but the earth became darkened and all the quarters of the heavens became covered for us. Our specialist knowledge was of no avail (literally, "came back into our hands"), so that none of the magicians' magic nor the soothsayers' ability to look into the future nor the astrologers' knowledge of the stars proved efficacious. We realized that this matter originated in the heavens and that a prophet had already been sent, or was about to be sent, and because of that, something had prevented us from exercising our specialist knowledge. We
[1013] were afraid that if we announced to you the destruction of your royal power, you would kill us. Like everybody else, we did not want to die, so we gave you an evasive answer in order to protect ourselves, as you saw." Kisrā said, "Woe upon you! Why didn't you provide me with the explanation of this matter so that I might have used my own judgment regarding what I should do?" They

replied, "Our fear of you prevented us from doing that." Kisrā, therefore, let them go and gave up concerning himself with [the dam on] the Tigris when this last had got the better of him.

There related to us Ḥumayd—Salamah—Muḥammad b. Isḥāq—al-Faḍl b. ʿĪsā al-Raqāshī—al-Ḥasan al-Baṣrī,[785] [who said] that the Messenger of God's Companions said, "O Messenger of God, how could God prevail over Kisrā by means of you?" The Prophet said, "God sent to him an angel, who put his hand out through the wall of the house where he was, shining with light. When Kisrā saw it, he was alarmed. The angel said, "Why are you so fearful, O Kisrā? God has sent a prophet and sent down upon him a book, so follow him, and you will be secure in this present life of yours and in the next one." Kisrā replied, "I'll think about it."[786]

There related to us Ibn Humayd—Salamah—Muḥammad b. Isḥāq—Abdallāh b. Abī Bakr—al-Zuhrī—Abū Salamah b. ʿAbd al-Raḥmān b. ʿAwf, who said: God sent an angel to Kisrā, when he was in a room of his palace (*aywānihi*) where no one was allowed to come into his presence. Suddenly[787] there was, round about the time of midday at the time he was wont to take a siesta, a figure standing by his head with a staff in his hand. The figure said, "O Kisrā, are you going to submit yourself to God (*a-tuslimu*)? [If not,] I shall break this staff!" He replied, "*Bihil, bihil*" ("Leave, leave!"),[788] so the angelic visitant then left him. Kisrā summoned his guards and chamberlains, and became enraged at them, saying, "Who let this person come into my presence?" They replied, "No one has come into your presence, and we haven't seen this person at all." In the following year, the angel came to him at precisely the same hour as before and spoke the same words to him as

785. That is, the great popular preacher and ascetic of al-Baṣrah in Umayyad times, the Successor Abū Saʿīd [al-] Ḥasan b. Abī al-Ḥasan (died 110/728), subsequently regarded as the proto-Ṣūfī. See *EI*², s.v. Ḥasan al-Basrī (H. Ritter).

786. The following versions of the story of how Khusraw was warned by an angelic visitant are of the same type as the Biblical story of King Belshazzar of Chaldaea, who was warned of the imminent fall of his kingdom by the moving finger writing on the wall of his palace (Daniel, v. 5ff.).

787. Literally, "he was not mindful of it," *lam yarʿihā*, echoing the Qur'ānic phrase *fa-mā raʿawhā*, "they (i.e., the followers of Jesus) did not cherish/look after it," of LVII, 27.

788. Persian *hishtan, hilīdan* "to leave, depart."

before, saying, "Are you going to submit yourself to God? [If not,] I
[1014] shall break this staff!" Kisrā replied three times, "*Bihil, bihil, bihil,*" so the angelic visitant departed from him. Kisrā summoned his chamberlains, guards, and doorkeepers, and became enraged with them, saying to them what he had said to them on the first occasion. They replied, "We didn't see anyone coming into your presence." When the third year came round, the angel came to Kisrā at exactly the same hour as he had come to him previously, and spoke the same words to him as before, saying, "Are you going to submit yourself to God? [If not,] I shall break this staff!" Kisrā replied, "*Bihil, bihil.*" He related: At that, the angel broke his staff and departed. Only a short time afterward, his royal power disintegrated, and his son and the Persian rose in rebellion and finally killed him.

'Abdallāh b. Abī Bakr—al-Zuhrī,[789] [who said,]: I recounted this story to 'Umar b. 'Abd al-'Azīz,[790] from Abū Salamah b. 'Abd al-Raḥmān, and he said: It has been mentioned to me that the angel came into Kisrā's presence with two glass bottles in his hands and then said to him, "Submit yourself [to God]!" and when he did not comply, he smashed one of the bottles against the other and broke them into smithereens. Then he departed. Kisrā's own destruction followed, as is well known.

There related to me Yaḥyā b. Ja'far—'Alī b. 'Āṣim—Khālid al-Ḥadhdhā', who said: I heard 'Abd al-Raḥmān b. Abī Bakrah say:[791] Kisrā, son of Hurmuz, was asleep one night in his palace (*aywān*), the palace of al-Madā'in, and the cavalrymen [of the guard] were

---

789. That is, Muḥammad b. Muslim al-Zuhrī, often referred to as Ibn Shihāb, from the Meccan clan of Zuhrah, one of the founders of the Islamic science of tradition (died 124/742). As a teacher of Ibn Isḥāq, he was a great contributor to the *Sīrah* of the Prophet and was much quoted by al-Ṭabarī for the history of the first three Rightly-Guided caliphs. See Ibn Sa'd, *Ṭabaqāt,* II/2, 136–36; Ibn Ḥajar, *Tahdhīb al-Tahdhīb,* IX, 445–51; *EI*[1], s.v. al-Zuhrī (J. Horovitz).

790. That is, the member of the Umayyad family, governor of Medina and then the caliph 'Umar II (r. 99–101/717–20).

791. 'Abd al-Raḥmān was the eldest son of the Companion Nufay' b. Masrūḥ, called Abū Bakrah, "the man of the pulley," and an Abyssinian *mawlā* of the Prophet. 'Abd al-Raḥmān managed his maternal uncle Ziyād b. Abīhi's property in al-Baṣrah for him, but submitted reluctantly to 'Alī after the Battle of the Camel (al-Ṭabarī, I, 3229, II, 22). See Ibn Sa'd, *Ṭabaqāt,* VII/1, 138; Ibn Qutaybah, *Ma'ārif,* 288–89; *EI*[2], s.v. Abū Bakra (M. T. Houtsma-Ch. Pellat).

posted all around his castle. Suddenly, there appeared a man with a staff who walked up and stood at Kisrā's head and said, "O Kisrā, son of Hurmuz, I am God's messenger to you [with the message] that you should submit yourself [to Him]." He said this three times, while Kisrā lay prostrate, looking at him but returning no answer. Then the angel left him. He related: Kisrā sent for the commander of the guard and said to him, "Did you allow this man to enter my presence?" The commander of the guard replied, "No, I didn't, and no one has come in from our part."

He related: When it was the following year, Kisrā was fearful of that night and sent a message to the commander of the guard, [1015] "Post guards all round my castle and don't let anyone enter my presence." He related: The commander of the guard did that. But when it was that precise hour, behold, there was the angel with the staff standing at his head and saying to him, "O Kisrā, son of Hurmuz, I am God's messenger to you [with the message] that you should submit yourself [to Him]; so do this, and it will be best for you!" He related: Kisrā was looking at him without giving any answer. Then the angel left him. He related: Kisrā sent for the commander of the guard [and upbraided him], "Didn't I order you not to let anyone into my presence?" The commander of the guard replied, "O king, by God, no one has come into your presence from our part; search out whence he came into your presence."

He related: When the next year came round, it was as if he was fearful of that night, and he sent a message to the commander of the guard and the guard itself, "Stand guard all around me during this night, and don't allow any woman or man to enter my presence." They did that. When it was that precise hour, behold, there was the angel again standing by his head and saying, "Kisrā, son of Hurmuz, I am God's messenger to you [with the message that] you should submit yourself [to Him], so do this, and it will be best for you!" This he repeated three times, while Kisrā was looking at him but returning no answer. The angel said, "O Kisrā, you have rebuffed me! By God, God will certainly smash you just as I am smashing this staff of mine!" Then he broke it, and went away. Kisrā sent to his guard and said, "Didn't I order you not to let anyone into my presence this night, neither wife (*ahl*) nor child?" They replied, "No one has come into your presence from our part." He related: Very soon afterward, his son rose in rebellion against him and killed him.[792]

## *[The Encounter at Dhū Qār]*

A further episode [in the story of the fall of the Sāsānid empire] is what happened concerning [the tribal group of] Rabī'ah[793] and the army Kisrā Abarwīz had dispatched for war against them and their subsequent encounter at Dhū Qār.

[1016] It is related from the Prophet that when the Prophet heard the news of Rabī'ah's rout of Kisrā's army, he exclaimed, "This [has been] the first military encounter (*yawm*) in which the Arabs have secured their just due from the Persians (*intaṣafat al-ʿArab min al-ʿAjam*), and it was through me that they were given the victory." The battle of Dhū Qār[794] is also called that of Qurāqir or

---

792. That is, Kawād (II) Shērōy, placed on the throne by the rebels against his father. See al-Ṭabarī, I, 1045–61, pp. 381–99 below.

793. Both Bakr and Taghlib, on opposite sides at Dhū Qār, were accounted parts of the great tribal group of Rabīʿah. See *EI*², s.v. Rabīʿa and Muḍar (H. Kindermann).

794. The battle of Dhū Qār, if this is not too grandiose a word for the encounter, was to assume a position in subsequent Islamic lore greater than its military significance—which was probably just one of several similar clashes along the frontiers with Arabia—would warrant. The saying of the Prophet retailed here, oft-repeated in the sources, sets it up as the first stage in the upsurge of the Arabs against the Persians and their influence in eastern and southern Arabia. It could thus be regarded as a victory for proto-Islam over the Persian infidels, or at least as prefiguring that victory, and in later times a popular romance grew up round it, the *Kitāb Ḥarb Banī Shaybān maʿa Kisrā Anūsharwān.*

The ambiguous rôle in the Dhū Qār events of a Shaybānī leader like Qays b. Masʿūd b. Qays b. Khālid b. Dhī al-Jaddayn (see al-Ṭabarī, I, 1028, p. 356–57 below) tends to confirm the view put forward by F. McG. Donner in his "The Bakr b. Wā'il Tribes and Politics in Northeastern Arabia on the Eve of Islam," 27–33, that the anti-Sāsānid alignment of Shaybān and other Bakrī tribes at Dhū Qār does not represent a decisive turning point in relations between the Sāsānids and the Arab tribes of northeastern Arabia and the frontier region—whatever the views that grew up in Islamic times, outlined in the previous paragraph—but rather, a temporary fluctuation of allegiances, in which one group might move against the Persians and then return to its Persian allegiance later if circumstances so dictated. Donner notes that most of the powerful clans combating the Persians at Dhū Qār seem to have fought on the Sāsānid side against the Muslim Arabs during the 630s and 640s, and concludes that "The theory that the Bakr tribes were, since Dhū Qār, awaiting the opportunity to rise against the Persians is, then, if not positively erroneous, at least dangerously simplistic" (ibid., 33).

The sources (see below) offer no firm date for the *Yawm Dhī Qār,* but the

that of the bend (*al-ḥinw*), the bend of Dhū Qār or the bend of Qurāqir; that of al-Jubābāt; that of Dhū al-'Ujrum; that of al-Ghadhawān; and that of the depression (*al-baṭḥā'*), the depression of Dhū Qār. All of these are places around Dhū Qār.[795]

There was related to me a narrative going back to Abū 'Ubaydah Ma'mar b. al-Muthannā[796]—Abū al-Mukhtār Firās b. Khindif[797] and a number of the scholars (*'ulamā'*) of the Arabs, whom he specified by name: The battle of Dhū Qār was the consequence of al-Nu'mān b. al-Mundhir al-Lakhmī's killing of 'Adī b. Zayd al-'Ibādī. 'Adī was one of Kisrā Abarwīz, son of Hurmuz's, translators (*tarājimah*).[798] The reason for al-Nu'mān (III) b. al-Mundhir (IV)'s killing of 'Adī b. Zayd was what was mentioned to me in an account going back to Hishām b. Muḥammad—Isḥāq b. al-Jaṣṣāṣ,

---

Muslim traditions which place it just after the opening of the Hijrī era (e.g., a few months after the battle of Badr between the pagan Quraysh and the Muslims, hence in the later part of 624, according to Abū al-Faraj al-Iṣfahānī, *Aghānī*[3], XXIV, 76) are clearly too late. The range of years for Dhū Qār is probably between 604 and 611, i.e., before the beginning of Muḥammad's public ministry in Mecca but at a time when he could certainly have heard reports of the victory against the Persians and their allies.

Several Arabic sources treat of the last years of Lakhmid domination in al-Ḥīrah and the desert fringes of eastern Arabia, including al-Ya'qūbī, *Ta'rīkh*, I, 246, II, 47; Muḥammad b. Ḥabīb, *Muḥabbar*, 360–61; al-Mas'ūdī, *Murūj*, II, 227–28, III, 205–209 = §§ 648, 1065–70; idem, *Tanbīh*, 241–43, tr. 318–21; Abū al-Faraj al-Iṣfahānī, *Aghānī*[3], XXIV, 53–71; Yāqūt, *Buldān*, IV, 293–95; Abū al-Baqā', *al-Manāqib al-mazyadiyyah*, I, 373–426. Of modern studies, see Rothstein, *Laḫmiden*, 114–23; Donner, loc. cit.; Bosworth, "Iran and the Arabs before Islam," 607–608; *EI*[2], s.v. Dhū Ḳār (L. Veccia Vaglieri); *EIr*, s.v Dū Qār (Ella Landau-Tasseron).

795. According to Yāqūt, *Buldān*, IV, 293, it lay to the south of what soon afterward became the Arab *miṣr* of al-Kūfah, and cannot have been far from the Euphrates, hence in a region where the nomads' herds could have ready access to water. It seems impossible to pinpoint it more exactly, although there were presumably bituminous springs bubbling to the surface there (*qār, qīr* "pitch, tar").

796. Abū 'Ubaydah (d. 209 or 210/824–25), philologist and grammarian, was a mawlā of Mesopotamian origin who became the most learned authority of his time on the tribal history and lore of the early Arabs. He also achieved a later reputation, which does not in fact seem to be justified, as a zealous supporter of the claims of the Shu'ūbiyyah, those vaunting the cultural supremacy of the 'Ajam, in effect the Persians, over the Arabs. See *EI*[2], s.v. Abū 'Ubayda (H.A.R. Gibb); *EIr*, s.v. Abū 'Obayda Ma'mar (C. E. Bosworth).

797. Following what seems to be the correct emendation, following *Addenda et emendanda*, p. DXCIV, for this personal and tribal name (Khindif b. Muḍar: cf. Ibn al-Kalbī-Caskel-Strenziok, *Jamharat al-nasab*, I, Table 1, II, 2, 347, and also n. 430 above).

798. See on 'Adī, n. 116 above.

who took it from the book of Ḥammād [al-Rāwiyah],[799] and my father also mentioned part of the story to me. He said: Zayd b. Ḥammād b. Zayd b. Ayyūb b. Maḥrūf b. 'Āmir b. 'Uṣayyah b. Imri' al-Qays b. Zayd Manāt b. Tamīm[800] had three sons: the poet 'Adī, who was a handsome man, both poet and orator (*khaṭīb*), who had read the books of the Arabs and the Persians;[801] 'Ammār, who was also called Ubayy; and 'Amr, who was also called Sumayy. They had a uterine brother called 'Adī b. Ḥanẓalah, from the [tribe of] Ṭayyi'. 'Ammār used to stay at Kisrā's court. One of the two of them ardently desired the death of 'Adī b. Zayd; the other was a firm devotee of Christianity. They all belonged to a notable house whose members were close to the Kisrās, eating their food with them and staying at their side, and receiving from them land grants (*qaṭā'i'*).

When al-Mundhir (IV) b. al-Mundhir (III) became king,[802] he entrusted his son al-Nu'mān to 'Adī's care; it was this family who fostered him (and reared him). Now al-Mundhir had another son called al-Aswad, whose mother was Māriyah bt. al-Ḥārith b. Julhum from the [tribe of] Taym al-Ribāb. There fostered[803] and

799. Ḥammād b. Maysarah, called Abū Laylā, al-Rāwiyah ("the great transmitter"), d. 155 or 156/772–73, of Persian mawlā stock, was famed as a collector of ancient Arabic poetry but also suspected of forging some of this. See Sezgin, *GAS*, I, 366–38; *EI*², s.v. Ḥammād al-Rāwiya (J. W. Fück).

800. Nöldeke, trans. 312 n. 5, noted that the appearance of the name Ayyūb in 'Adī's *nasab*, as the poet's great-great-grandfather, indicates the ancientness of Christianity within the family. He further noted that, for Ayyūb to have been born four generations back from 'Adī (who must himself have been born ca. 554, in J. Horovitz's view), he must have been in extreme old age if he is to be identified with the person mentioned (together with the *comes* Angeleios (?), son of Zeid) in the *Martyrium Arethae* as Iōb/Ayyūb, ethnarch of the Christian community in al-Ḥīrah, and as being a member of the entourage of the Lakhmid al-Mundhir III b. al-Nu'mān II. The "house of Ayyūb" was clearly important, through its literacy and its practical skills, in the secretarial and diplomatic service of both the Lakhmids and the Sāsānids. See further Horovitz, "'Adi ibn Zeyd, the Poet of Hira," 32–34 (also translates, 40ff., the detailed account of Abū al-Faraj al-Iṣfahānī in *Aghānī*³, II, 95ff., much fuller than the account given here by al-Ṭabarī); Shahîd, *Byzantium and the Arabs in the Sixth Century*, I/1, 315–18.

801. Nöldeke trans. 313 n. 1, commented that there could hardly have been any books written in Arabic at this time, but only orally transmitted poetry and possibly tales, and that, when the Christian Arabs of a city like al-Ḥīrah did write, they would use Syriac.

802. That is, in ca. 575.

803. This passage in parentheses was supplied by Nöldeke in his text, n. *d*, from the parallel passage in *Aghānī*³, II, 105.

reared him a family from the people of al-Ḥīrah called the Banū Marīnā, who were considered a part of Lakhm and were of noble status (*ashrāf*).[804] As well as these two, al-Mundhir b. al-Mundhir had ten other sons. Because of their handsome appearance, the entire group of his sons were known as al-Ashāhib ("the Shining Ones"), as al-Aʿshā says: [1017]

The sons of al-Mundhir, the Shining Ones, go forth in the
morning in al-Ḥīrah with their swords.[805]

Al-Nuʿmān was red haired (or: had a reddish complexion, *aḥmar*), with a mottled skin, and was short of stature.[806] His mother was called Salmā (or Sulmā) bt. Wāʾil b. ʿAṭiyyah al-Ṣāʾigh ("the goldsmith"), from the people of Fadak; she was a slave girl of al-Ḥārith b. Ḥiṣn b. Ḍamḍam b. ʿAdī b. Janāb's, from [the tribe of] Kalb.[807] Qābūs b. al-Mundhir the Elder, the paternal uncle of al-Nuʿmān and his brothers, had sent ʿAdī b. Zayd and his brothers to Kisrā, son of Hurmuz,[808] these being secretaries and translators of his.

When al-Mundhir b. al-Mundhir died,[809] leaving behind those thirteen sons of his, Iyās b. Qabīṣah al-Ṭāʾī was given charge of his

804. For this family, see Rothstein, *Lahmiden*, 20, 110. It was of such prominence in the life of the city that the poet Imruʾ al-Qays speaks of al-Ḥīrah as *diyār Banī Marīnā*. See *Dīwān*, 200, no. 37 v. 3, and cf. Olinder, *The Kings of Kinda*, 67.

The situation thus evolved in al-Ḥīrah of al-Nuʿmān being supported for the succession there by ʿAdī b. Zayd and al-Aswad by the Banū Marīnā; ʿAdī, however, had a distinct advantage through his honored status at the Sāsānid court. See Rothstein, ibid., 109–10.

805. *Dīwān*, 212, no. 63 v. 14.

806. Nöldeke, trans. 314 n. 1, noted that this description is confirmed, in another context, in *Aghānī*³, XXXI, 2.

807. This maternal origin is confirmed in Ḥamzah al-Iṣfahānī, *Taʾrīkh*, 95, and Abū al-Faraj al-Iṣfahānī, *Aghānī*³, 13, but al-Masʿūdī, *Murūj*, III, 202 = § 1061, says that Salmā was of the Kalb.

As Nöldeke, noted, trans. 314 n. 2, Fadak, a settlement in the Wādī al-Qurā of western Ḥijāz, had a significant Jewish element, famed as workers in precious metals. It is thus possible that Salmā came from this population group; the poet ʿAmr b. Kulthūm al-Taghlibī satirized al-Nuʿmān, that his mother's relatives were smiths and weavers, practicing despised crafts (*Aghānī*³, XI, 58–59, and a satire attributed to al-Nābighah al-Dhubyānī by one of his enemies describes al-Nuʿmān as *wārith al-ṣāʾigh* "heir of the goldsmith" (ibid., XI, 13; cf. Rothstein, *Lahmiden*, 108–109).

808. Following Nöldeke, trans. 314 n. 3, one should read here "Kisrā, son of Qubādh," i.e., Anūsharwān, and not "Kisrā [Abarwīz], son of Hurmuz."

809. That is, in 580.

governmental responsibilities,[810] but only held this office for a few months while Kisrā was searching for a man he could appoint as ruler over the Arabs. At that juncture, Kisrā, son of Hurmuz,[811] summoned ʿAdī b. Zayd and said to him, "Who now remains of al-Mundhir's sons?[812] What sort of persons are they, and is there any good amongst them?" ʿAdī replied, "There are still some of them left from the sons of the recently deceased al-Mundhir b. al-Mundhir; those are real men!" Kisrā said, "Send for them!" So he wrote to the various sons, and they came to Kisrā, who assigned them lodging with ʿAdī b. Zayd. ʿAdī gave preferential treatment in regard to lodging and hospitality to al-Nuʿmān's brothers over al-Nuʿmān himself, and he would let them see that he expected nothing from al-Nuʿmān. He spoke with them individually and privately, and said to each of them, "If the king asks you, 'Can you control the Arabs for me?' then tell him, 'Yes, we can control them all for you, except al-Nuʿmān.'" ʿAdī said to al-Nuʿmān,
[1018] however, "If the king asks you about your brothers, tell him, 'If I can't cope with them, then I can't cope with anybody else!'"[813]

810. That is, Hormizd (see n. 811 below) appointed him as temporary governor of al-Ḥīrah. It was Iyās b. Qabīṣah who was, nearly a quarter of a century later, apppointed (this time by Khusraw II Abarwēz) governor or ruler in al-Ḥīrah after the Lakhmid al-Nuʿmān's deposition in 602. At some point, the Persian king awarded Iyās thirty villages along the Euphrates as a grant for life and made him administrator of the district of ʿAyn al-Tamr (see on this place n. 112 above). See *EI*² Suppl., s.v. Iyās b. Ḳabīṣa al-Ṭāʾī (Ch. Pellat). Nöldeke, 314 n. 5, opined that the Qabīṣah of *Aghānī*¹, II, 22, i.e., Iyās's father, fitted better chronologically for this appointment by Hormizd, but a period of twenty-two years during which Iyās was occupied with other charges along Persia's frontier with the north Arabian desert does not seem an excessive amount out of a man's official career, and in any case, the same passage in *Aghānī*³, II, 106, has "Iyās b. Qabīṣah" for the interim governor in al-Ḥīrah before the choice of al-Nuʿmān was made.

811. Read here "Hurmuz, son of Kisrā."

812. That is, of the progeny of al-Nuʿmān's grandfather al-Mundhir III (r. 504–54).

813. That is, al-Nuʿmān is to stress to Hormizd his ability to cope with rivals and with other unruly elements along the desert fringes of the Persian realm. Nöldeke, trans. 315 n. 3, noted further that in the more detailed account of *Aghānī*³, II, 107–108, ʿAdī gives al-Nuʿmān advice which will project himself to the Persian king as a tough and spartan son of the desert: that he should appear before Hormizd in travel-stained clothes, girt with his sword, and exhibiting a voracious appetite. At the same time, ʿAdī craftily instructs the other brothers to wear their most opulent clothes, to eat in an elegant and restrained manner, and generally to present themselves as refined, ineffective characters, useless for the envisaged task of guarding the frontiers.

There was a man from the Banū Marīnā called ʿAdī b. Aws b. Marīnā, a headstrong fellow who was also a poet and who used to say repeatedly to al-Aswad [b. al-Mundhir b. al-Mundhir], "You know that I expect some favor from you (or perhaps, "am well disposed toward you, am concerned for your welfare," *annī laka rājin*).[814] I beg and implore you not to follow ʿAdī b. Zayd's counsel, for by God, he never has your good interests at heart." But al-Aswad paid no attention to his words.

When Kisrā ordered ʿAdī b. Zayd to bring them into his presence, ʿAdī began to lead them in one by one, so that Kisrā might speak with each of them; he found that he was looking at a group of men whose like he had rarely seen. When he asked them, "Are you able to fulfill this office for me, as your family previously filled it?" They replied, "We can control the Arabs for you, except al-Nuʿmān."

When al-Nuʿmān went into Kisrā's presence, the latter perceived an ugly and ill-favored person. Nevertheless, when Kisrā addressed him and asked, "Can you control the Arabs for me?" he answered, "Yes!" Kisrā asked, "How will you deal with your brethren?" Al-Nuʿmān replied [mockingly], "If I can't cope with them, then I can't cope with anyone!" Kisrā thereupon appointed him ruler, gave him robes of honour and a crown valued at sixty thousand dirhams and set with pearls and gold.[815]

Al-Nuʿmān went forth, having been just appointed thus. [At this point,] ʿAdī b. Aws b. Marīnā said to al-Aswad, "Now you've done it! You have gone against the correct course of action!" Then ʿAdī b. Zayd prepared a feast in a church, and sent a message to Ibn Marīnā, "Come along to me, and bring whomever you like, for I need to say something [to you]." Hence Ibn Marīnā went to him with a group of people. They all feasted and drank at a morning meal in the church. ʿAdī [b. Zayd] said to ʿAdī b. Marīnā, "O ʿAdī, "People like you know how best to recognize good conduct and then to avoid blaming [anyone] for it. I realize that you would have preferred your candidate al-Aswad b. al-Mundhir to have been

814. Nöldeke follows the first of these interpretations in his trans., 316.

815. ʿAdī's scheming has thus secured the authority in al-Ḥīrah for al-Nuʿmān (cf. Rothstein, *Laḫmiden*, 111), but at the price of making powerful enemies in the city.

appointed rather than my candidate al-Nu'mān, but don't blame me for something which you yourself would have done [if you had been able]. I would not like you to hate me for a course of action which you yourself would have followed had you been able. I would further like you to treat me with the same consideration as [1019] I show to you, for my share in the royal power is no more extensive than your own share."

'Adī b. Zayd then arose and went to the church and took an oath that he would not satirize 'Adī b. Marīnā in his poetry, would never intend any wicked act against him, and would never keep back from him anything good.[816] But when 'Adī b. Zayd had finished saying this, 'Adī b. Marīnā stood up and swore a similar oath that he would never cease satirizing 'Adī b. Zayd and never cease intending evil against him as long as he lived. Al-Nu'mān now went forth and took up his residence at al-Ḥīrah.

'Adī b. Aws b. Marīnā recited these verses regarding 'Adī b. Zayd:

Ho there, announce to 'Adī from 'Adī, and do not grieve, even
though your physical power has become worn out.
You are despoiling our places of worship when you have no
need for such gains, merely in order that you may be
praised or your gain may be more complete.[817]
If you are now successful, you will not be successful in a
praiseworthy manner; and if you perish, we shall wish
someone else, and not you, to be not far from us [in
death].[818]

---

816. The Cairo text, II, 196, has here *khabar*, "any piece of information," for *khayr*, "anything good," the latter being the reading, however, in Abū al-Faraj al-Iṣfahānī, *Aghānī*[3], II, 108.

817. Following the emendations in the text, I, 1019 n. *a* and in *Addenda et emendanda*, p. DXCIV for the first hemistich of this verse. The reference here to "despoiling our *hayākil*" seems to refer, as Nöldeke noted, trans. 315 n. 3, to 'Adī's obtaining a loan of eighty thousand dirhams from the bishop of al-Ḥīrah, Jābir b. Sham'ūn, on al-Nu'mān's behalf so that the latter could inflate and strengthen his position in the Persian king's eyes. See *Aghānī*[3], II, 115; Rothstein, *Laḫmiden*, 111 n. 2.

818. Literally, "may someone else, not you, not be far from us [in death]!" *fa-lā yab'ad siwāka*, a motif familiar in ancient Arabian elegiac poetry, in which the spirit of a dead man, a companion, or kinsman, is enjoined *lā tab'ad*, "do not go far away in death!" See Goldziher, *Muhammedanische Studien*, I, 255–56, Eng. tr. C.

You will feel regret like the man of Kusaʿ when your two eyes
see what your hands have wrought.[819]

ʿAdī b. Marīnā likewise said to al-Aswad, "Although you have not been successful, do not be so weak as to forgo seeking vengeance on this man of Maʿadd, who has treated you in this fashion.[820] I have kept on telling you that the crafty wiles of Maʿadd are never at rest, and I enjoined you not to follow his ways; but you acted against my advice." He replied, "What do you want, then?" Ibn Marīnā said, "I want you to hand over to me all the income from your sources of wealth and land," and al-Aswad did that. Ibn Marīnā was [already] very rich and well endowed with estates. No day now ever passed without a present arriving at al-Nuʿmān's portal from Ibn Marīnā, so that the latter became the most honored of men in al-Nuʿmān's eyes, and he did not decide any matter of state without ʿAdī b. Marīnā's instructions. Whenever ʿAdī b. Zayd's name was mentioned in Ibn Marīnā's presence, he would heap praises on him and recount his merits, yet he would add, [1020] "The make-up of a man of Maʿadd is not complete without there being an element of craft and treachery in it."

When the persons in al-Nuʿmān's court circle perceived the high status of Ibn Marīnā in the king's sight, they attached themselves to him and followed him. He began to tell his most trusted followers, "When you see me mentioning ʿAdī b. Zayd with approbation to the king, say, 'Indeed, he is just like you say, but he doesn't leave anybody alone but keeps on saying that the king—he meant al-Nuʿmān—is merely his governor and that he secured al-

R. Barber and S. M. Stern, *Muslim Studies,* I, 231–32; idem, "Beiträge zur arabischen Trauerpoesie," 311–12; *EI*², s.v. Marthiya. 1. (Ch. Pellat), at VI, 603b.

819. The "regret of the man of Kusaʿ" was proverbial for someone who committed an irrevocable action and then repented of it. Kusaʿ is variously described as a clan or subgroup of archers of Qays ʿAylān, Yemen, or Ḥimyar, but no such tribal division is registered by Ibn al-Kalbī in his *Jamharat al-nasab;* clearly, the lexicographers had no real idea of the origin of the saying. See Ibn Manẓūr, *Lisān al-ʿarab,* X, 186–87; al-Zabīdī, *Tāj al-ʿarūs,* V, 494–95.

820. ʿAdī's genealogy, set forth by al-Ṭabarī at I, 1016, p. 340 above, went back to the Zayd Manāt b. Imriʾ al-Qays, one of the two main branches of the great North Arab tribe of Tamīm (see Ibn al-Kalbī-Caskel-Strenziok, *Jamharat al-nasab,* I, Table 59, II, 8, 544; *EI*², s.v. Tamīm b. Murr (M. Lecker) ), whereas most of the Arabs in al-Ḥīrah, from the ruling Lakhmid family downward, stemmed from tribes accounted Yemeni in *nasab.*

Nu'mān's appointment to the office which he now holds.'" They kept on thus repeatedly until they caused the king to be full of hatred toward 'Adī b. Zayd. Also, they wrote a letter in 'Adī's name to one of his stewards (*qahramān*) and then laid a plot against him to seize the letter, which they then brought to al-Nu'mān. The latter read it, and it filled him with rage. He sent a message to 'Adī b. Zayd in these terms: "I beseech you, why haven't you visited me? I have been longing to see you." 'Adī was at this juncture at Kisrā's court; he asked Kisrā for permission to leave, and the latter gave this. But when 'Adī came to al-Nu'mān, he had hardly set eyes on al-Nu'mān before he was thrown into a prison, where no one came to visit him.[821] 'Adī b. Zayd set about composing verses while he was in prison. The first of the verses which he composed there was:

Would that I knew something from the great hero (i.e., the king)! Then would a tenderly persuasive enquiry bring you authentic news [of him]![822]

He further recited many other pieces of poetry.[823]

---

821. In the second of Abū al-Faraj al-Iṣfahānī's accounts of the estrangement between al-Nu'mān and 'Adī, in *Aghānī*[3], II, 115–16, that stemming from al-Mufaḍḍal b. Muḥammad al-Ḍabbī, to the reasons for this estrangement set forth in the first account from Ibn al-Kalbī, essentially that given above by al-Ṭabarī, al-Mufaḍḍal adds another cause, also involving 'Adī's enemy Ibn Marīnā. According to this, 'Adī grew angry with al-Nu'mān because he had prepared for al-Nu'mān and his entourage a splendid feast, but en route for this, al-Nu'mān was intercepted by Ibn Marīnā who invited him on the spot to a feast of his own so that, when al-Nu'mān eventually arrived at 'Adī's feast, he was satiated and oculd not touch any of it. 'Adī was naturally piqued, displayed his anger, reproached al-Nu'mān in verse and broke off relations with him. In retailiation, al-Nu'mān consigned 'Adī to prison.

822. *Dīwān*, 56, no. 7 v. 2, a verse from a long poem, more of which is cited in other sources such as *Aghānī*[3], II, 110.

823. When Nöldeke made his translation, he stated, 319 n. 2, that the verses of 'Adī had to be recovered from scattered citations in later sources. A formal *dīwān* of 'Adī's collected poetry is mentioned in several mediaeval Islamic sources, e.g., Ibn al-Nadīm and Abū al-'Alā' al-Ma'arrī, as being in existence at that time, with various copies circulating in Baghdad. However, the *Dīwān* of 'Adī has now been published by Muḥammad Jabbār al-Mu'aybid on the basis of a unique manuscript, preserved at al-Baṣrah, of the work of Jāhilī poets and called *Kitāb jamharat shu'arā' al-'Arab min al-Jāhiliyyah*; see al-Mu'aybid's Introduction, 20–25.

As Nöldeke commented, loc. cit., the poetry of 'Adī, the product of an urban, Christanised environment, is perceptibly easier to understand than the verses of contemporary Bedouin poets, products of the ruder, harsher desert.

Whenever 'Adī composed some poetry, this came to al-Nu'mān's notice and hearing, and he felt regret for having imprisoned him. He began to send messages to 'Adī, making him various promises and arousing his hopes [of being freed], but shrank from releasing him lest 'Adī should then intend some evil against him. 'Adī thereupon uttered the verse:

I lay awake in a thick, dark cloud in which lightning flashes
continually rose up on the gray mountain peaks.[824]

and also,

That night was long for us and intensely dark.[825] [1021]

And also,

Ho there, the nights and the days are long![826]

When he became wearied of addressing entreaties to al-Nu'mān, he recited poetry in which he reminded him of death and informed him of those kings before him who had perished, saying,

Has farewell been said to him when he was setting out in the
morning or at even?[827]

and many other poems.

He related: Al-Nu'mān once set out for al-Baḥrayn, and [in his absence] a man from Ghassān appeared and wrought whatever violence he willed in al-Ḥīrah. It is said that the person who attacked al-Ḥīrah and then put it to flames was Jafnah b. al-Nu'mān al-Jafnī.[828] 'Adī recited:

---

824. *Dīwān*, 37, no. 3 v. 1.
825. ibid., 59, no. 8 v. 1.
826. ibid., 132, no. 60 v. 1.
827. ibid., 84, no. 16 v. 1.
828. This refers to a major, surprise attack on the Lakhmid capital involving an operation mounted across the Syrian Desert by the Jafnid/Ghassānid prince, who plundered al-Ḥīrah and pitched his *praetorium* or military headquarters there for five days, while the Lakhmid ruler was absent, as 'Adī's scornful verse stresses. The Jafnid/Ghassānid prince would be al-Mundhir b. al-Ḥārith or Arethas (r. 569–82). Nöldeke, *Die Ghassânischen Fürsten*, 27–28, placed the attack in 580–81, commenting that it could not in any case have happened after 591 when the emperor Maurice and Khusraw Abarwēz made peace, since the Byzantine ruler would not have allowed his Syrian vassal to breach the agreement thus; see also

A falcon soared high, and then set both sides of it (i.e., the town
of al-Ḥīrah) in flames, while you were completely occupied
with camels, some of which are sent out to travel by night
while others are left to pasture freely.[829]

When ʿAdī's imprisonment became protracted, he wrote the following verses to his brother Ubayy, who was at Kisrā's court,

Convey the news to Ubayy, however far away he is—is what a
man has come to know any use to him?—
—That your brother, the dear one of your heart, for whom you
were intensely concerned while ever he was safe and sound,
Is shackled with iron fetters in the power of a king, whether
justly or unjustly.
So let me not find you acting like a woman with a child (*dhāt
al-ghulāmi*) if she does not find a suckler of her breast,
seeking for such an one.
So take care to remain in your own land, for if you come to us
you will sleep a dreamless slumber (i.e., will find death)![830]

His brother wrote back to him,

If Fate has betrayed you, then you are no weakling (literally, "weak of outstretched arms"), nor an inactive person, nor a feeble
[1022] one.

---

trans. 320 n. 3. This seems a reasonable argument, and the attack must in any case have happened well before al-Nuʿmān's imprisonment of ʿAdī toward the year 600. Rothstein, *Lakhmiden*, 104 n. 2, 105, 112, however, placed the attack earlier than Nöldeke. More recently, Irfan Shahîd has dated the attack to 575, at the end of the three years' period when al-Mundhir b. al-Ḥārith had withdrawn from Byzantine service and was keen to retaliate on the Lakhmids for their raids on the Syrian frontiers during that period. The Lakhmid ruler at that time would thus be al-Mundhir IV b. al-Mundhir III rather than the energetic al-Nuʿmān III, ruling by ca. 580. The mention of the Jafnid/Ghassānid attacker as being "Jafnah b. al-Nuʿmān al-Jafnī" in the account transmitted by Abū ʿUbaydah is thus both vague and inaccurate.

829. *Dīwān*, 114, no. 25 v. 1.

830. ibid., 164, no. 111 vv. 1–5. The message of the last two verses is that Ubayy should not assume a task, that of avenging his brother ʿAdī, which is no part of his business—at least, not by immediately coming to the Lakhmid court seeking vengeance and instead finding there his own certain death. Nöldeke, trans. 321 n. 1, was uncertain about the rendering of v. 4, but the enlightning emendations in *Addenda et emendanda*, p. DCXIV, and *Glossarium*, p. CCCCLIX, make it clear that the proverbial saying given in Lane, *Lexicon*, 2025a, is being alluded to here.

By God's oath, even if a darkly massed,[831] mighty, crushing force, with gleaming swords,
With a distant roaring sound, advancing across country with an overwhelming host bringing death, with robes of battle intact and enfolding them,[832]
Had I been in the thick of its throng, I would have hastened to you; so know that I would have responded when you asked for succor!
Or if I had been asked for money for you, neither inherited wealth nor wealth which had been earned for some specific purpose would have been held back.
Or [if you had been] in a land and I could have come to you there, neither its distance away nor any fearsome danger would have affrighted me.
Since you are far away from me, the glory of this age and the authority to command are with the enemy.
If, by God, I am bereft of you, an old companion whose loss brings pain, there is no one who can replace you, while ever the autumn rains pour forth.
Indeed, by my life, if I grieve over you, it is as an afflicted, sad one.
Indeed, by my life, if I manage to regain control and find consolation, nevertheless there will be few like you in the lands through which I range.[833]

They assert that, when Ubayy read ʿAdī's letter, he went along to Kisrā and spoke with him [about the affair]. Kisrā thereupon wrote a letter and sent an envoy with it. Al-Nuʿmān's deputy in the exercise of government (*khalīfah*) wrote to al-Nuʿmān that Kisrā had sent a letter to him. At that, ʿAdī's enemies from the [1023]
Banū Buqaylah of Ghassān[834] went along to al-Nuʿmān and said,

---

831. That is, because of the dark color of the massed warriors in their mailed coats.

832. Reading thus, with Abū al-Faraj al-Iṣfahānī, *Aghānī*[1], II, 27, *malfūfu*, as suggested in n. *a;* but *Aghānī*[3], II, 119, chooses the reading of Nöldeke's text, *makfūfu* "with the hems of their robes of battle trimmed short." Both renderings are equally possible in the context.

833. This poem also figures in *Aghānī*[3], II, 119–20. As Nöldeke remarked, 321 n. 3, the poem reads more like an elegy composed after ʿAdī's death than one addressed to him during it.

834. See n. 670 above.

"Kill him immediately!" but he refused. The envoy arrived, having been first accosted by ʿAdī's brother, who gave him money as a bribe and told him to visit ʿAdī first. The envoy went to ʿAdī, the latter being incarcerated in [the fortress of] Ṣinnīn.[835] ʿAdī's brother said, "Go into his presence and see what instructions he gives you." The envoy went into ʿAdī's presence and said, "I have brought the order for your release; what have you got [for me]?" ʿAdī said, "Something you will like very much," and gave him promises, adding, however, "Don't leave me, but give me the letter so that I may convey it to him (i.e., al-Nuʿmān), for by God, if you leave me, then I shall undoubtedly be killed." The envoy replied, "I can't do anything except go to the king and deliver the letter to him personally."

Meanwhile, someone went along to al-Nuʿmān to let him know what was happening. This person came to al-Nuʿmān and told him, "Kisrā's envoy has been to visit ʿAdī, and is going to bring ʿAdī with him. If he does that, he will not spare any of us, neither yourself nor anyone else." Al-Nuʿmān thereupon sent ʿAdī's enemies to him, and they smothered him till he died, and then buried him. The envoy came into al-Nuʿmān's presence with the letter. Al-Nuʿmān hailed him with the words, "Good fortune and welcome!" and sent him four thousand mithqāls[836] (i.e., in silver dirhams) and a slave girl, saying to him, "When you go along to ʿAdī next morning, go in to him and bring him back personally." But when the envoy rode out to there next morning and entered the prison, the guards told him, "He has already been dead for several days; we didn't, however, dare to tell the king out of fear of him, since we knew that he did not desire ʿAdī's death." The envoy returned to al-Nuʿmān and said, "I went into his presence

---

835. This was a fortress of the district of al-Ḥīrah, mentioned in the account of Saʿd b. Abī Waqqāṣ's attack on al-Ḥīrah in 14/635 (al-Ṭabarī, I, 2233). According to Ḥamzah al-Iṣfahānī, *Taʾrīkh*, 90, it was built by the Greek architect Sinnimār, the luckless constructor of al-Khawarnaq (see al-Ṭabarī, I, 851–52, pp. 75–78 above). See Yāqūt, *Buldān*, III, 431; Nöldeke, trans. 322 n. 3 (on the most probable Aramaic etymology of the toponym); Musil, *The Middle Euphrates*, 117–18 (mentioning what he identified as the ruins of Ṣinnīn and its castle); Morony, *Iraq after the Muslim Conquest*, 152.

836. For this measure for precious metals and monetary unit, based on the weight of the Byzantine gold, *solidus*, see Hinz, *Islamische Masse und Gewichte*, 1–8; *EI*², s.v. Makāyil and Mawāzin (E. Ashtor).

[yesterday] and he was still alive!" Al-Nuʿmān told him, "The king sends you to me, and you go to ʿAdī before me? You're lying, and you're only seeking bribe money and stirring up mischief!" He threatened him but then gave him increased largesse and marks of favor, and extracted a promise from him that he would merely tell Kisrā that ʿAdī had died before he could go to him. So the envoy [1024] returned to Kisrā and informed him that ʿAdī had died before he could get access to him. Al-Nuʿmān was filled with remorse at ʿAdī's death, but ʿAdī's enemies behaved menacingly toward him, and he was violently afraid of them.

Al-Nuʿmān went out hunting one day and met one of ʿAdī's sons called Zayd. When he saw him, he recognized his resemblance to ʿAdī and asked him, "Who are you?" The son replied, "I am Zayd b. ʿAdī b. Zayd," Al-Nuʿmān spoke with him and found him to be a finely formed young man, and he rejoiced at this (or, "in him") greatly. He introduced him into his court circle, gave him gifts, made excuses to him over the matter of his father,[837] and fitted him out handsomely with a traveling kit. Then he wrote to Kisrā in these terms: "ʿAdī was, because of his wise counsel and his intelligence, one of those persons who are the supports of kings; but the inevitable fate came upon him, his life span was fulfilled and his sustenance was cut off; no one was more deeply afflicted by his death than myself. Yet a king does not lose one of his men without God sending along a replacement for him, since God has made the king's royal power and exalted status so mighty. Now one of ʿAdī's sons, not inferior to him in qualities, has just reached maturity. Hence I have sent him along to the king; if he sees fit to appoint him in his father's stead, he may do so."

When the young man came to Kisrā, he appointed him to his father's old office and transfered his paternal uncle (i.e., Ubayy) to another post. So it was Zayd who took charge of correspondence dispatched to the land of the Arabs—in particular, [that of] the king. The Arabs gave him a specific, annual payment for filling this office, namely, two chestnut-colored colts, fresh truffles in their season and dried ones, dried and compacted cheese, hides (or, "seasonings," *al-udum*), and other products traded by the Arabs.

---

837. That is, over his being imprisoned and not, of course, over his killing. See Nöldeke, trans. 324 n. 1.

Zayd b. ʿAdī b. Zayd was thus in charge of all this—that is, those functions ʿAdī b. Zayd had exercised. When Zayd had attained such a position in Kisrā's eyes, the latter asked him about al-Nuʿmān; Zayd praised him profusely.

Zayd accordingly remained for several years filling the same [1025] role his father had filled. Kisrā was highly pleased with him, and Zayd used frequently to go into his presence. The Persian kings possessed the description of a [perfect] woman, written down and kept by them, and they used to send that description out to all those lands (i.e., to obtain for themselves such ideal wives and concubines), except that they never had any dealings with the land of the Arabs regarding this and would never seek it. At one point, the king again took steps for seeking out women, and sent out that written description. Then Zayd went into Kisrā's presence and spoke to him about the course of action the king had embarked upon, and said, "I see that the king has sent out letters concerning women who are to be sought out for him [as partners]. I have read the description. I know the house of al-Mundhir very well. Your servant al-Nuʿmān has many daughters and paternal nieces and other members of his family, totaling more than twenty women, who correspond to this description." Kisrā said, "In that case, you should write off concerning them." Zayd replied, "O king, the worst characteristic of the Arabs, and of al-Nuʿmān [in particular], is that they regard themselves as superior in nobility, as they conceive themselves, to the Persians. I am afraid that he will conceal these women. But if I personally go to him with this mission, he will not be able to place them in concealment. So send me, together with a man from your own guard who is a skilled Arabic speaker." Hence Kisrā sent with him a sturdy man. Zayd set off with the latter. He began to treat that man in a noble and friendly fashion until he reached al-Ḥīrah. He went into al-Nuʿmān's presence and extolled the monarch, then went on to say that "He (Kisrā) requires women [as attendants] for his wives and children, and desires to show you honor, hence has sent this mission to you."[838] Al-Nuʿmān asked, "What kind of women are

838. Such a tribute of maidens was regarded by Nöldeke, trans. 325 n. 1, as quite credible, especially as Barhebraeus mentions a "Fast of the Maidens" of the Nestorian Christians commemorating the frustration of Khusraw Abarwēz's at-

these [who are required]?" Zayd answered, "This is the description of them."

The description stemmed from al-Mundhir the Elder's[839] forwarding as a present for Anūsharwān a slave girl whom he had acquired as plunder when he had raided al-Ḥārith the Elder al-Ghassānī, son of Abū Shamir,[840] and whose description he had sent in a letter to Anūsharwān:

"[She is] of medium height, with a clear skin color and fine teeth, white, gleaming like the moon, pronounced eyebrows, dark and wide eyed, with a high, aquiline nose, slender eyelashs over fine eyes, smooth cheeks, with a delectable body, plentiful hair, a good-sized skull so that ear-drops hang far apart, with a high neck, a wide bosom, and well-rounded breasts. [She has] stout shoulder and upper arm bones, fine wrists, delicate hands with long and straight fingers; a pulled-in abdomen, neat waist, slender at the girdle, ample hips, a well-rounded rear and strong thighs, a fine posterior and fleshy buttocks, good-sized knees, filled-out calves so that her ornamental anklets fit snugly, but with delicate ankle bones and feet. [She] walks with slow steps, is somnolent and remains inside in the fierce light of day and has a tender skin where this is exposed. [She is] obedient to her lord and master, not flat-nosed or with a tanned skin, humble and submissive although of noble birth and not brought up in penurious circumstances, modest, sedate, mild in character, and steady minded. [She has] noble maternal relatives[841] and she is satisfied with her paternal lineage, without reference to her clan, and with her clan without reference to her tribe. Experience of life has made her of fine conduct and attainments (*adab*). Her ways of thought are those of [1026]

---

tempt to carry off all the maidens from al-Ḥīrah, and as al-Bīrūnī, *al-Āthār al-bāqiyah*, 314, states that the *ṣawm al-ʿadhārā* marked the relief of the Arabs at being relieved of the tribute of virgins levied by the kings of al-Ḥīrah or else the victory of Dhū Qār, which spared the Arabs from the Persian demand for their maidens.

839. That is, the Lakhmid al-Mundhir III (r. 504–54, interrupted by the Kindī occupation of al-Ḥīrah in the mid-520s).

840. That is, the Jafnid/Ghassānid al-Ḥārith (Arethas) (r. 529–69), son of Abū Shamir Jabalah (d. 528). See Shahîd, *Byzantium and the Arabs in the Sixth Century*, I/1, 69.

841. Following the emendation *al-khāl* of *Addenda et emendanda*, p. DXCIV, for the text's *al-ḥāl*.

noble people, but her actions those of the poor and needy. [She is] skillful with her hands, restrained with her tongue, has a gentle voice; she is an adornment to the house, and puts the enemy to shame. If you wish for [sexual contact with] her, she shows eagerness for it; if you prefer to leave her alone, she is content to abstain. She becomes wide eyed [with sexual longing], her cheeks blush red, her lips tremble, and she hastens toward you before you can fall upon her."[842]

Kisrā accepted this description and ordered it to be set down in permanent form in his chancery registers. [The Persian rulers] kept on handing it down to each other until it finally reached Kisrā, son of Hurmuz.

Zayd read out the description to al-Nuʿmān, but the latter found the topic distasteful, and said to Zayd, with the envoy listening at the same time, "Aren't all the wide-eyed ones (*ʿīn*) of the Sawād
[1027] and Persia enough to fulfill your needs?" The envoy said to Zayd, "What are the 'wide-eyed ones'?"[843] He replied, "Wild cows (*al-baqar*)."[844] Zayd said to al-Nuʿmān, "Kisrā only desires to show you honor; if he had known that this [demand] was distressing for you, he would not have written to you in these terms." Al-Nuʿmān gave them both hospitality for two days and then wrote to Kisrā, "That which the king seeks I do not possess," and he told Zayd, "Make my excuses to the king."

When Zayd went back to Kisrā, he told the envoy who had come with him, "Tell the king everything you heard from al-Nuʿmān, for I shall give him the same account as you and not contradict you at all regarding it." When the two of them went into Kisrā's presence, Zayd said, "This is his letter," and he read it out to him. Kisrā retorted, "Where, then is what you [previously] told me

---

842. This bravura piece of rhetorical prose, with its balanced phrases and rhymes, appears also in Abū al-Faraj al-Iṣfahānī, *Aghānī*³, II, 29–30, with various divergencies of wording. On the theme of descriptions of female beauty in Iranian and Persian literatures, from the Avesta onward, see *EIr* s.v. Erotic Literature (Djalal Khaleghi-Motlagh).

843. *aʿyan*, f. *ʿaynāʾ*, pl. *ʿīn*, "wide-eyed, dark-eyed," is a favorite attribute of the wild cow or oryx, and thence, of women, in early Arabic poetry, appearing in the Qurʾān as a description of the houris of the Paradise intended for the justified believers, e.g., in XXXVII, 47/49, XLIV, 54, LII, 20, LVI, 20.

844. The account in al-Masʿūdī, *Murūj*, III, 205–206 = §§ 1065–66, uses the synonym for wild cow, *mahāt*.

about?" Zayd said, "I told you about their (i.e., the Arabs') tenaciousness in keeping their women from others, and that this arises from their miserable way of life; they prefer starvation and nakedness to satiety and fine clothes, and the fiery and tempestuous winds to the ease and pleasantness of this land of yours, to the point that they call it a prison.[845] Now just ask this envoy who accompanied me about what he (i.e., al-Nuʿmān) said, for I have too great a regard for the king's exalted position to be able to repeat what he said and the answer that he gave the king." Kisrā thereupon asked the envoy, "What did he say?" The envoy replied, "He said, O king, 'Hasn't he got enough from the wild cows of the Sawād without seeking after what we ourselves have?'" Signs of anger became apparent in Kisrā's face and he felt violently moved in his heart, but he merely remarked, "Many a wretch has had worse things than this in mind, yet his intentions have come to naught in the end!" These words became generally circulated and reached the ears of al-Nuʿmān.

Kisrā then remained silent regarding this topic for several months. Al-Nuʿmān, meanwhile, was preparing for whatever might befall and was expecting [the worst], when Kisrā's letter reached him [containing the command]: "Come here, for the king has business with you!" He set off [precipitately] when the king's letter reached him, taking with him his weapons and whatever else he was able [to carry]. He arrived at the two mountains of
Ṭayyi',[846] accompanied by [his wife] Farʿah bt. Saʿd b. Ḥārithah b. [1028]
Lām, who had borne him both a male and a female child, and also [his wife] Zaynab. bt. Aws b. Ḥārithah [b. Lām]. Al-Nuʿmān made for the land of the Ṭayyi', hoping that they would take him in among themselves and protect him, but they refused to do this, saying, "Were it not for the marriage bonds between us, we would

845. Contrasting the harshness and misery of the desert existence of the Bedouins with the ease of life in the *ḥaḍar* or settled lands such as al-Ḥīrah and the Persian lands in Mesopotamia.

846. The "two mountains of Ṭayyi'," Aja' and Salmā, were in what is now the Jabal Shammar of northern Najd, to the south and southeast of modern Ḥā'il, and are often mentioned in old poetry. See al-Bakrī, *Muʿjam mā istaʿjam*, I, 109–10, III, 750; Yāqūt, *Buldān*, I, 94–99, III, 238–39; Musil, *Northern Neǧd, a Topographical Itinerary*, New York 1928, 76–77, 88–89; Thilo, *Die Ortsnamen in der altarabischen Poesie*, 26, 90.

attack you, for we do not want to be drawn into emnity with Kisrā."[847] Al-Nu'mān went onward, but no one would receive him except for the Banū Rawāḥah b. Sa'd from the Banū 'Abs, who said, "We will fight at your side, if you wish," because of an act of favor al-Nu'mān had shown to them over the matter of Marwān al-Qaraẓ. However, he replied, "I don't want to bring about your destruction, for you don't have the strength to prevail over Kisrā."[848] So he traveled onward until he encamped secretly at Dhū Qār amongst the Banū Shaybān. Here he met Hāni' b. Mas'ūd b. 'Āmir b. 'Amr b. Abī Rabī'ah b. Dhuhl b. Shaybān, who was a mighty chief. At that time, the sheikhly rule in Rabī'ah was among the house of Dhū al-Jaddayn, held by Qays b. Mas'ūd b. Qays b. Khālid b. Dhī al-Jaddayn.[849] Kisrā had made a grant to

847. The tribe of Ṭayyi', whose ancient pasture grounds were in northern Najd, as the connection of their name with the two mountains there shows (see n. 846 above), were accounted Yemeni in genealogy. Al-Nu'mān's marriage with two Ṭā'ī wives suggests that the tribe had links with the Lakhmids, but these were not strong enough to offset the need to keep up good relations with the Sāsānids, and it was a man of Ṭayyi', Iyās b. Qabīṣah, whom Khusraw appointed after al-Nu'mān's death as the first, and last, non-Lakhmid governor in al-Ḥīrah and the former Lakhmid lands and who commanded the forces of the Persians and their Arab allies at Dhū Qār (see al-Ṭabarī, I, 1017, p. 341 above). Christianity seems to have acquired some hold among the Ṭayyi' in pre-Islamic times, presumably among those of the tribe who frequented the fringes of Iraq, and Iyās was a Christian. See Ibn al-Kalbī-Caskel-Strenziok, *Jamharat al-nasab,* I, Tables 176, 249–57, II, 57–61, 176; *EI*², s.v. Ṭayyi' (Irfan Shahîd). As Nöldeke noted, trans. 329 n. 2, al-Nu'mān's own adoption of Christianity—the first of his line to do so—was nominal enough for him to remain polygamous and to take at least two wives.

848. The 'Abs were a component of the great North Arab group of Ghaṭafān, part of Qays 'Aylān, with the Banū Rawāḥah coming in the tribal *silsilat al-nasab* five generations after 'Abs himself. Their pasture grounds lay between the Jabal Shammar and northern Ḥijāz, hence just beyond those of Ṭayyi'. The "matter of Marwān al-Qaraẓ" involved al-Nu'mān's securing this man's release from al-Nu'mān's uncle and the previous ruler in al-Ḥīrah 'Amr b. al-Mundhir or b. Hind, and the affair is referred to in the poetry of Zuhayr b. Abī Sulmā (who was born and reared among the Banū 'Abdallāh of Ghaṭafān), as is the magnanimous reception of the fugitive Lakhmid by the Banū Rawāḥah b. Sa'd. See Ibn al-Kalbī-Caskel-Strenziok, *Jamharat al-nasab,* I, Tables 92, 132–33, 136, II, 20–21, 135–36; *EI*², s.v. Ghaṭafān (J. W. Fück); and on al-Nu'mān's flight and attempts to secure *jiwār* or tribal protection, see Rothstein, *Laḫmiden,* 117–18.

849. Dhū al-Jaddayn were one of the leading families of Bakr (see Ibn al-Kalbī-Caskel-Strenziok, *Jamharat al-nasab,* I, Table 144, II, 24), from the Hammām b. Murrah, a dominant branch of the Shaybān. Equally influential with Qays was his son, the poet and warrior Bisṭām. See *EI*², s.v. Bisṭām b. Ḳays (M. J. Kister).

Qays b. Mas'ūd of al-Ubullah,[850] hence al-Nu'mān was fearful of entrusting his family and dependents to him because of that fact; whereas, he knew that Hāni' would protect him as he would his own life.

Al-Nu'mān then (i.e., after leaving his family and dependents with Hāni') proceeded toward Kisrā's court. On the stone bridge of Sābāṭ[851] he met Zayd b. 'Adī, who said to him, "Save yourself, [if you can,] O Little Nu'mān (Nu'aym)!" Al-Nu'mān replied, "You have done this, O Zayd, but by God, if I manage to survive, I shall do with you what I did with your father!" Zayd told him, "Go on, Little Nu'mān, for by God, I have prepared for you at Kisrā's court bonds to hobble your feet which even a high-spirited colt couldn't break!"[852] When the news of his arrival at court reached Kisrā, the latter sent guards to him who put him in fetters, and he consigned him to Khāniqīn.[853] There he remained in gaol until an outbreak

---

850. Al-Ubullah (< Greek Apologos) lay on the right bank of the Euphrates-Tigris estuary, at the mouth of a canal of the same name, the Nahr al-Ubullah. The town existed in Sāsānid times and possibly earlier, and in the later Sāsānid period, at least, came normally within the dominions of the Lakhmids. With the advent of Islam, al-Ubullah was to some extent eclipsed by the *miṣr* of al-Baṣrah, founded further inland, but it continued to be a port of major significance for trade with the Arabian Sea and Indian Ocean shores all through mediaeval Islamic times until the Mongol invasions. See Yāqūt, *Buldān*, I, 76–78; Le Strange, *Lands*, 47–48; Wilson, *The Persian Gulf*, 62–64; Morony, *Iraq after the Muslim Conquest*, 161–62; *EI*², s.v. al-Ubullah (J. H. Kramers). According to Abū al-Faraj al-Iṣfahānī, *Aghānī*³, XXIII, 54, Khusraw made the grant to Qays b. Mas'ūd so that the latter would ward off the tribesmen of Bakr b. Wā'il from the Sawād. See Donner, "The Bakr b. Wā'il Tribes and Politics in Northeastern Arabia on the Eve of Islam," 27–28.

851. See for this, n. 327 above.

852. As Nöldeke noted, trans. 331 n. 2, another brother of Zayd's, 'Amr (not 'Ammār) b. 'Adī b. Zayd, acted as adviser on Arab affairs and translator for Khusraw Abarwēz, and fought at Dhū Qār on the Persian side, where he was killed. See *Aghānī*³, XXIV, 61–62, 73–74. The family of 'Adī b. Zayd continued to be of significance in al-Ḥīrah until well into 'Abbāsid times, when al-Ya'qūbī, *Buldān*, 309, tr. 141, describes them in his own time (late third/ninth century) as among the upper social strata there (*'ilyat ahl al-Ḥīrah*) and still firmly attached to their Christian faith.

853. This town lay to the northeast of Ctesiphon and the later Baghdad on the highway through Jibāl to al-Rayy and Khurāsān; at the present day, it comes just within the borders of Iraq. The early Islamic geographers praise a fine, brick-built bridge there, spanning the Ḥulwān river, an affluent of the Diyālā, and this apparently dated back to the town's pre-Islamic existence. The fact that al-Nu'mān was imprisoned there suggests the presence there of a Sāsānid fortress also. See Yāqūt, *Buldān*, II, 340–41; Le Strange, *Lands*, 62–63; Schwarz, *Iran*, 687–89; Barthold,

of plague occurred and he died in prison. People think that he died at Sābāṭ on account of a verse by al-Aʿshā,

> It happened thus, and he was not able to save his master (i.e., al-Nuʿmān, the master of the noble steed addressed in the preceding verses) from death at Sābāṭ, dying while he was
> [1029] incarcerated.[854]

In fact, he died at Khāniqīn, just a short while before the coming of Islam. Soon afterward, God sent His prophet; al-Nuʿmān's fate was the cause of the battle of Dhū Qār.[855]

There was related to me a narrative going back to Abū ʿUbaydah Maʿmar b. al-Muthannā—Abū al-Mukhtār Firās b. Khindif and a number of the learned scholars of the Arabs whom Abū ʿUbaydah expressly named, as follows:[856] When al-Nuʿmān killed ʿAdī, the latter's brother and son hatched a plot against al-Nuʿmān at Kisrā's court, and falsified a letter sent by al-Nuʿmān to Kisrā exculpating himself with expressions that roused Kisrā's anger. Hence he ordered al-Nuʿmān to be killed. When al-Nuʿmān had become fearful of Kisrā, he had deposited his coat of mail, his valuables, and other arms with Hāniʾ b. Masʿūd b. ʿĀmir al-Khaṣīb b. ʿAmr al-Muzdalif b. Abī Rabīʿah b. Dhuhl b. Shaybān b. Thaʿlabah; this was because al-Nuʿmān had given him two of his daughters in marriage. Abū ʿUbaydah added, however, that "Other

---

*Historical Geography,* 199, 202; *EI²*, s.v. Khāniḳīn (P. Schwarz). In his *Iran im Mittelalter,* 688 n. 1, Schwarz details the information of the Arabic sources on al-Nuʿmān's mode of death: either from plague or through being trampled by elephants.

854. *Dīwān,* 147, no. 33 v.18. Cf. Nöldeke, trans. 331 n.4.

855. This could be considered as true in an indirect way, in that the end of the Lakhmids does seem to have facilitated increased depredations by Bedouin tribes like the Bakr on the now less strongly defended desert fringes of Iraq. Whether Khusraw had any serious reason for thinking that al-Nuʿmān was aiming at a policy more independent of his Persian overlord is impossible now to determine. See Bosworth, "Iran and the Arabs before Islam," 607–608.

Other accounts in the Arabic sources of al-Nuʿmān's fall from favor and his consequent fate are given in al-Yaʿqūbī, *Taʾrīkh,* I, 245–46; al-Masʿūdī, *Murūj,* III, 205–10 = §§ 1065–70; Ḥamzah al-Iṣfahānī, *Taʾrīkh,* 94–95 (al-Dīnawarī, on the other hand, takes very little account of the Lakhmids). See also Nöldeke, trans. 332 n. 1.

856. This is now the continuation of the *riwāyah* from Abū ʿUbaydah begun by al-Ṭabarī at I, 1016, p. 339 above.

authorities state that Hāni' b. Mas'ūd was no longer alive at the time of this happening; the person in question was Hāni' b. Qabīṣah b. Hāni' b. Mas'ūd, and I consider this to be correct."[857]

After Kisrā had had al-Nu'mān killed, he appointed Iyās b. Qabīṣah al-Ṭā'ī as governor over al-Ḥīrah and the other former territories of al-Nu'mān.[858] Abū 'Ubaydah related: When Kisrā had fled from Bahrām [Chūbīn], he passed by Iyās b. Qabīṣah, and the latter gave him a horse and slaughtered a camel for him; in this way, Kisrā showed his gratitude.[859] Kisrā sent a message to Iyās enquiring where al-Nu'mān's deposited possessions were. Iyās replied that al-Nu'mān had found a safe refuge for them among the Bakr b. Wā'il. So Kisrā ordered Iyās to get possession of what al-Nu'mān had left behind and to forward that to him. Iyās sent a message to Hāni', "Send to me the coats of mail and other items [1030] al-Nu'mān entrusted to you" (the lowest estimate of these mailed coats was four hundred, and the highest was eight hundred). But Hāni' refused to hand over what he had engaged to protect.[860]

He related: When Hāni' withheld these, Kisrā was filled with anger and gave out that he would extirpate the Bakr b. Wā'il. At that moment, he had at his court al-Nu'mān b. Zur'ah al-Taghlibī,

---

857. Hāni' b. Qabīṣah b. Mas'ūd al-Shaybānī and Iyās b. Qabīṣah al-Ṭā'ī, or his son Farwah b. Iyās—Iyās being at this point the Persian ruler's viceroy in al-Ḥīrah—are mentioned in al-Balādhurī, *Futūḥ*, 243, as yielding up the city in 12/633 to Khālid b. al-Walīd's forces on the basis of a peace treaty, with the provision that the Ḥīran leaders were now to act as spies for the Arabs against the Persians.

858. Iyās, noted above as involved (unless his son Farwah is meant) in the surrender of al-Ḥīrah to the Arabs, was the son of Khusraw's adviser Qabīṣah, the tribe of Ṭayyi' having links with the Sāsānid ruling house (see n. 847 above). He was thus an appropriate person to appoint as governor in al-Ḥīrah. However, at his side Khusraw placed his commander Nakhīrjān (on this name, see n. 377 above), who was later to play an eminent role in the defense of al-Madā'in against the Arabs (see al-Ṭabarī, I, 2419–22, etc., below), as financial controller and tribute collector. Iyās was to govern in al-Ḥīrah from 600 to 611. See Rothstein, *Laḫmiden*, 110, 116, 120 and n. 1.

859. As Nöldeke, trans. 333 n. 2, commented, this gratitude was rather belated. Al-Mas'ūdī, *Murūj*, II, 216–17, has different details on the fugitive Khusraw's desperate search for a mount, including the detail that al-Nu'mān refused to give the king his own celebrated horse al-Yaḥmūm.

860. This refusal to hand over valuable war material is confirmed by some verses of al-A'shā in Abū al-Faraj al-Iṣfahānī, *Aghānī*[3], XXIV, 79.

who was eager for the destruction of the Bakr b. Wā'il.[861] Al-Nu'mān said to Kisrā, "O best of rulers, shall I show you how Bakr might be attacked unawares?" Kisrā replied, "Yes!" Al-Nu'mān said, "Leave them alone, so that they can go to their summer encampments, for if they do take up these summer quarters they will alight at one of their watering places called Dhū Qār just as a moth falls into a fire, and then you can fall upon them exactly as you wish. I myself can take charge of this and get rid of them for you." Al-Nu'mān's phrase "they will alight just like a moth falling into a fire" was translated for Kisrā, and he accordingly left them alone for the time being.

But then when the Bakr b. Wā'il migrated to their summer quarters, they went along and encamped at the bend of Dhū Qār, one night's journey away from Dhū Qār itself. Kisrā sent al-Nu'mān b. Zur'ah to them with the message that they were to chose one of three courses of action (literally, "aims, targets"). Al-Nu'mān encamped at Hāni''s and told him, "I am the king's envoy to you. I offer you three courses of action. Either you submit yourselves, and the king will make a decision concerning you however he pleases; or you remove yourselves from the land; or be apprised of the imminence of war."[862] They took counsel together, and left the decision to Ḥanẓalah b. Tha'labah b. Sayyār al-'Ijlī, whose advice they regarded as auspicious.[863] Ḥanẓalah told them, "I can't see any other course but fighting, for if you place yourself in his hands, you will be killed and your children enslaved. If you flee, you will die of thirst, and the Tamīm will come upon you and put you to death. So apprise the king of imminent war."

The king sent messages to Iyās, to al-Hārmarz al-Tustarī, whose fortress was at al-Quṭquṭānah, and to Jalābzīn,[864] who held the

---

861. The two tribes of Bakr and Taghlib, although forming the major part of Rabī'ah, were at odds with each other for much of the sixth century. See *EI*², s.v. Bakr b. Wā'il (W. Caskel).

862. Echoing Qur'ān, II, 279, *fa-'dhanū bi-ḥarb*ⁱⁿ *min Allāh wa-rasūlihi.*

863. The 'Ijl b. Lujaym were a component of Bakr; see *EI*², s.v. 'Idjl (W.M. Watt). The *sayyid* Ḥanẓalah b. Tha'labah is described in *Aghānī*³, XXIV, 67, as bald headed, large bellied and with a reddish-brown skin, which Nöldeke, trans. 334 n. 3, regarded as probably an authentic description, since it deviates radically from the usual ideal of the spare desert warrior with long locks of hair.

864. This rendering of the Persian commander's name approaches more closely to the Zalabzan of the Byzantine Greek historians (see n. 739 above) than the

fortress at Bāriq. Kisrā further wrote to [the above-mentioned] Qays b. Mas'ūd b. Qays b. Khālid b. Dhī al-Jaddayn, whom Kisrā [1031] had appointed over the frontier zone (*al-ṭaff*) of Safawān, with instructions to meet up with Iyās, and when they were all assembled, Iyās was to be their leader.[865] The Persians brought along troops and elephants on which were mounted cavalrymen. At this time, the Prophet had already begun his mission and the authority of the Persians had become weak. The Prophet said, "Today the Arabs have received satisfaction from the Persians." Note was taken of that day, and behold, it was the day of the battle.

When the armies of the Persians and their allies drew near, Qays b. Mas'ūd slipped away by night and went to Hāni'. He told him, "Give your troops al-Nu'mān [b. al-Mundhir]'s weapons in order thereby to increase the troops' strength. If they should perish, they will merely share the fate of those who bore them [originally], and you will have acted with all prudence and resolution; and if they are victorious, they will give them back to you."[866] Hāni' did that, and divided out the mailed coats and weapons among the strongest and stoutest of his troops. When the [Persian] army drew near to the Bakr, Hāni' shouted to the latter, "O men of the Bakr tribe! You won't be able to withstand Kisrā's troops and their Arab allies, so gallop back to the desert!" The tribesmen rushed headlong to do that, but Ḥanẓalah b. Tha'labah b. Sayyār sprang up and said to Hāni', "You admittedly want us to flee to safety, but you are thereby increasing the likelihood of your consigning us to destruction!" Thus he persuaded the tribesmen to go back, and he cut through the leather straps of the litters [on the camels] so that the

---

Khunābizīn of the *Naqā'iḍ Jarīr wa-al-Farazdaq*, II, 640, 643, 644; see *Addenda et emendanda*, p. cxcv.

865. The three places mentioned here were points along the zone of frontier posts and fortresses to the west of the middle and lower Euphrates. See Yāqūt, *Buldān*, I, 319–20, III, 225, IV, 374 (al-Quṭquṭānah as the place of al-Nu'mān's imprisonment, but this is less likely than the fortress at Khāniqīn mentioned by al-Ṭabarī at I, 1028, p. 357 above); Morony, *Iraq after the Muslim Conquest*, 151, 153.

866. As noted by Nöldeke, trans. 336 n. 1, Qays b. Mas'ūd was subsequently imprisoned by Khusraw in Sābāṭ on the grounds that he had not prevented Bedouin incursions across the fronier zone of al-Ṭaff, confirmed by poetry allegedly composed by Qays himself in Abū al-Faraj al-Iṣfahānī, *Aghānī*[3], XXIV, 57–59, Abū 'Ubaydah's information here does confirm that Qays may have had a secret understanding with his fellow members of Bakr. However, in al-Ṭabarī, I, 1035, p. 367 below, al-A'shā satirizes Qays for cowardice and flight in battle.

Bakr would not be able to take their womenfolk with them if they were to flee. He therefore acquired the name of "the one who cuts the thongs" (*muqaṭṭiʿ al-wuḍun*), *wuḍun* being the straps securing the saddles and litters, or else "the one who cuts the belly girths" (*muqaṭṭiʿ al-buṭn*), *buṭn* being the straps securing the load-bearing frameworks on draught camels (*al-aqtāb*).[867] Ḥanẓalah also erected a tent for himself in the depression of Dhū Qār and took an oath that he would not flee unless the tent itself fled. Some of them (i.e., the Bakr) went forward, but the greater part of them went back and spent half a month at a watering place getting water for themselves [and their herds].

The Persians came upon them and fought with them at the bend [of Dhū Qār]. The Persians suffered from thirst, hence they fled, without making a stand and being hard pressed, back to al-Jubābāt,[868] with the Bakr and the ʿIjl, the foremost of the Bakr,
[1032] pursuing them. The ʿIjl were in the forefront and fought in an exemplary fashion on that day. The Persian troops came together [at first] in a compact mass, so that people said, "The ʿIjl are finished!" Then [the rest of] the Bakr rallied to the attack and found the ʿIjl standing fast and fighting back. One of their women recited:

If the uncircumcised ones (*al-ghuzal*) gain the victory, they will
ravish us (literally, "place [their penises] inside us");
onwards, may your lives be ransoms for yourselves, O Banū ʿIjl!

She also said, urging on the combattants:

If you put the enemy to flight, we shall embrace [you] and
spread out soft rugs [for you].
But if you flee, we shall avoid [you], showing no tender
affection![869]

---

867. This incident appears also in *Aghānī*³, XXIV, 68–71.

868. Al-Jubābah (thus sing.) is merely noted by Yāqūt, *Buldān*, II, 98, as a place near Dhū Qār, and a watering place of the Abū Bakr b. Kilāb.

869. These three verses of the ʿIjlī woman figure in the account of Dhū Qār in the *Naqāʾiḍ Jarīr wa-al-Farazdaq*, II, 641, while the second and third verses, with a slight variant, are attributed in Ibn Hishām, *Sīrat al-nabī*, ed,. Wüstenfeld, 562 = ed. al-Saqqā et al., III, 72, tr. 374, to Hind bt. ʿUtbah when she urged on Quraysh against the Muslims at the battle of Uḥud, in the year 3/625.

They fought with the Persians at al-Jubābāt for a whole day. Then the Persians suffered thirst and made toward the depression of Dhū Qār. The [tribe of] Iyād, who were auxiliary troops against the Bakr with Iyās b. Qabīṣah,[870] secretly sent a message to the Bakr: "Which is more attractive to you, that we should arise and steal away under cover of night, or stay here and take to flight when you encounter the enemy?" They replied, "Nay, stand fast, and then, when the enemy engage in battle, take to flight with them." He related: Bakr b. Wā'il fell upon the enemy next morning, with their womenfolk (*al-ẓu'un,* literally, "those mounted on camels in litters") standing nearby, inciting the men to fight. Yazīd b. Ḥimār al-Sakūnī, a confederate of the Banū Shaybān, said, "O Banū Shaybān, follow my leadership and let me make an ambush against the enemy." They did that, and made Yazīd b. Ḥimār their leader. Then they concealed themselves in an ambush at a place near Dhū Qār called al-Jubb,[871] and showed themselves stout warriors there. Commanding Iyās b. Qabīṣah's right wing was al-Hāmarz, and over his left wing was al-Jalābzīn; commanding the right wing of Hāni' b. Qabīṣah, the leader of the Bakr, was Yazīd b. Mus'hir al-Shaybānī, and over his left was Ḥanẓalah b. Tha'labah b. Sayyār al-'Ijlī. The people began to urge on their fellows and to compose *rajaz* verses [to encourage them]. Ḥanẓalah b. Tha'labah recited: [1033]

Your hosts have already become a compact mass, so fight
fiercely! What excuse shall I have, since I am strongly
armed and robust?[872]
The bow has a thick string, like the foreleg of a young camel or
stronger.

---

870. The Iyād were a North Arab tribe, whose eponymous forebear was said by the genealogists to be a son of Nizār b. Ma'add and a brother of Rabī'ah and Muḍar. Some Iyād settled at al-Ḥīrah and became Christians; others remained nomadic, and at the end of the sixth century and beginning of the seventh century were among the tribes in the service of the Sāsānids as frontier auxiliaries until their defection from the Persian side as narrated below. See Ibn al-Kalbī-Caskel-Strenziok, *Jamharat al-nasab,* I, Tables 174–75, II, 29–30, 359–60; *EI*², s.v. Iyād (J. W. Fück). For Iyās b. Qabīṣah, see above nn. 810, 858.

871. Literally, "depression, hollow."

872. Following the *mud'*$^{in}$ of the Leiden and Cairo texts and of the *Naqā'iḍ.* Nöldeke's translation, 338, "da ich . . . sterben muss" would require *mūd*$^{in}$ < *awdā,* "he perished."

The celebrated deeds of my people have become clear. Indeed, there is no escape from death.
Here is 'Umayr, whose tribe[873] rushes impetuously forward in battle,[874] with none able to repel it,
Until his reddish-colored horse becomes like a dark-brown one (i.e., with the blood of battle); they have cleared the way, O Banū Shaybān, and stood firm on their own![875]
Myself, my father and my grandfather I give as your ransom!

Ḥanẓalah further recited,

O my people, rejoice in yourselves at fighting! [This is] the most suitable of days for putting the Persians to flight![876]

Yazīd b. al-Mukassir b. Ḥanẓalah b. Tha'labah b. Sayyār recited:

The one of you who flees abandons his wives and the alien under his protection, and flees also from his boon companion.
I am the son of Sayyār, with his toughness and endurance (literally, "hanging on to his bit"); indeed, the sandal thongs have been cut from his own hide.
All men grow in the way of their forefathers, whether nurtured from defective blood or of pure stock.[877]

Firās related: Then they handed over the command, after Hāni',[878] to Ḥanẓalah. He went along to his daughter Māriyah, who was the mother of ten sons, one of these being Jābir b. Abjar,[879] and cut through the leather straps of her litter so that she

---

873. The Cairo text, II, 209, has the reading *taḥtahu* for *ḥayyuhu*, followed in the text of the *Naqā'iḍ Jarīr wa-al-Farazdaq*.

874. Following the emendation in *Addenda et emendanda*, p. DXCV, *taqdumatan*.

875. Following, with the text of the *Naqā'iḍ*, the probable emendations to the second hemistich given in *Addenda et emendanda*, loc. cit., with statements (*khallaw . . . wa-stabaddū*) rather than imperative verbs and commands.

876. These verses of Ḥanẓalah figure in the *Naqā'iḍ*, II, 642.

877. These verses are in the *Naqā'iḍ*, II, 643, with the poet's name as Yazīd al-Mukassir b. Ḥanẓalah, i.e., the son, not the grandson, of the previously cited poet.

878. That is, because, as recorded by al-Ṭabarī at I, 1031, p. 361 above, Hāni' had left the field.

879. Nöldeke noted, trans. 339 n. 3, that the Ḥajjār b. Abjar b. Jābir b. Bujayr al-'Ijlī mentioned in the historical sources was probably Jābir's brother. This Ḥajjār

fell to the ground, and he did the same with the straps of the other women so that they all fell to the ground. The daughter of al-Qarīn, the woman of Shaybān, cried out when the women fell to the ground,

Woe to you, O Banū Shaybān, rank upon rank! If you are put to flight, the uncircumcised ones (*al-qulaq*) will ravish us (literally, "will plunge into us")! [1034]

Seven hundred of the Banū Shaybān cut the arms of the sleeves of their garments from the shoulder pieces so that their arms would be freer for wielding their sword, and then they engaged the enemy fiercely in battle. He related: Al-Hāmarz cried out [in Persian], "Man to man!" (*mard u mard*). Burd b. Ḥārithah al-Yashkurī[880] exclaimed, "What is he saying?" They told him, "He is issuing a summonse to single combat, man to man." He replied, "By your father! He has spoken justly!" Burd advanced against him and slew him. Surayd b. Abī Kāhil recited:[881]

Little Burd (Burayd)[882] is one of us, [who proved himself in battle] when he went out against your hordes, when you did not want to let him draw near to the Marzbān with the bracelets on his arm.[883]

---

was prominent in fighting the Muslims during the *Riddah* wars in al-Baḥrayn during Abū Bakr's caliphate, but apparently became a Muslim under 'Umar, especially as Ibn Sa'd, *Ṭabaqāt,* VI, 161 (but not, e.g., Ibn al-Athīr, *Usd al-ghābah*), devotes a notice to him since, after conversion, he could technically be considered as a Companion of the Prophet; cf. also Donner, "The Bakr b. Wā'il Tribes and Politics in Northeastern Arabia on the Eve of Islam," 31–32. His father Abjar seems, however, to have remained Christian until his death toward the end of 'Alī's reign. See al-Ṭabarī, I, 3460, and Hawting, *The History of al-Ṭabarī, an Annotated Translation,* XVII, *The First Civil War,* 217 and n. 858. Nöldeke further noted the antiquity of the name Abjar/Abgar among the Arabs, going back to the kings of Edessa, among whom some ten of that name are known. See Segal, *Edessa, 'The Blessed City,'* index s.vv. Abgar I, etc.

880. The Banū Yashkur were a tribe of Bakr, with much of the tribe living as sedentaries in al-Yamāmah. See Ibn al-Kalbī-Caskel-Strenziok, *Jamharat al-nasab,* I, Tables 141, 162, II, 26, 592.

881. Surayd b. Abī Kāhil Shabīb al-Yashkurī was a poet of the *mukhaḍram.* See Sezgin, *GAS,* II, 165–66.

882. The parallel verse in the *Naqā'iḍ,* II, 643, has for this name "Yazīd," but the text shortly afterward mentions Burayd as a variant for Yazīd.

883. Abū al-Faraj al-Iṣfahānī, *Aghānī*[3], XXIV, 71, mentions that the Persian cavalrymen of al-Hāmarz rode out against the Bakr wearing arm bracelets (*musaw-*

That is, you did not consider him [as an outstanding warrior].

Ḥanẓalah b. Thaʿlabah b. Sayyār called out, "O my people, don't just stand there facing them, or they will overwhelm you with arrows! The left wing of the Bakr, led by Ḥanẓalah, attacked the [Persian] army's right wing (whose commander, al-Hāmarz, Burd had just killed), and the right wing of the Bakr, led by Yazīd b. Mus'hir, attacked the [Persian] army's left wing (commanded by Jalābzīn). The concealed force under Yazīd b. Ḥimār came up behind them from al-Jubb of Dhū Qār, and launched an attack on the enemy's center, where Iyās b. Qabīṣah was. The Iyād turned round and fled, just as they had undertaken to do, and the Persians also fled.

Salīṭ said: The [Arab] captives whom we took, who were on that day in the Persian forces, related to us thus, saying: When the two sides clashed, Bakr took to flight, so we said, 'They are making for the watering place." But when they crossed the wadi and emerged from the bed of its stream onto the other side, we said, 'This is flight." This happened in the midday heat[884] of a day in the midst
[1035] of summer. A detachment of the ʿIjl approached, tightly packed like a bundle of reeds, with no gaps in between; they did not offer impediment to any fugitives (i.e., from the other branches of the Bakr) and they did not mingle with others of the enemy. Then they urged each other on to the attack, advanced in a mass and hurled themselves frontally at the enemy. There was nothing more to be done; they had made the enemy yield, and these last turned and fled. They slew the Persians and those with them from the depression of Dhū Qār as far as al-Rāḥiḍah.[885] Firās related: I was further informed that they pursued the Persians closely, not looking for plunder or anything else, unti they met up with each other at Adam,[886] a place near Dhū Qār. There were found to be thirty riders from the Banū ʿIjl and sixty from the rest of the Bakr. They killed Jalābzīn, slain by the hand of Ḥanẓalah b. Thaʿlabah. May-

---

*war*) and with pearls in each ear. Variants for the last word of this verse, al-Ṭabarī's *al-musawwarā*, are given in both the *Naqā'iḍ* and the *Aghānī*, and from the latter (where two verses are quoted), the correct rhyme emerges as *-ru* and not *-rā*.

884. *Naqā'iḍ*, II, 644, has *ḥadd*, "intensity, acute part of something," for al-Ṭabarī's *ḥarr*.

885. Unidentified.

886. Yāqūt, *Buldān*, I, 162, knows this only as a place associated with the events of Dhū Qār.

mūn b. Qays (i.e., al-Aʿshā) recited the poem, praising the Banū Shaybān in particular:

I would give as a ransom for the Banū Dhuhl b. Shaybān my she-camel and its rider (i.e., myself) on the day of the encounter, but this would be too little.[887]
They combatted fiercely the vanguard of al-Hāmarz at the bend, the bend of Qurāqir, until he turned and fled.
Qays [b. Masʿūd] escaped from our group, and I commented, "Perhaps, if he were wearing sandals there, he threw them off" (i.e., in order to escape more easily).

This shows that Qays was in fact present at Dhū Qār.

Bukayr, the deaf one (*al-aṣamm*) of the Banū al-Ḥārith b. ʿUbād,[888] eulogised the Banū Shaybān thus:

[O serving girl,] if you pour out wine for those who are wont to enjoy it (or, "deserve it"), then pour it out as an act of honor for the sons of Hammām, [1036]
And for all of the Abū Rabīʾah and the Muḥallim,[889] who attained the foremost place on the most noble of battle days.
They attacked the Free Ones (*Banū al-Aḥrār*)[890] on the day when they encountered them in battle, with Mashrafī swords[891] on the place where the skull rests firmly.
Arabs numbering three thousand and a force of two thousand Persians, from those who wear cloths over their mouths (*banī al-faddām*).[892]

---

887. Following the reading *wa-qallati* of al-Aʿshā, *Dīwān*, 179, no. 40 v. 1; *Naqāʾiḍ*, II, 644; *Aghānī*[3], XXIV, 78; and *Addenda et emendanda*, p. DXCV, I do not see how Nöldeke, trans. 342, got his rendering "[geb' ich . . . ] und meinen Renner" from *wa-fullati*.

888. Al-Ḥārith b. ʿUbād b. Ḍubayʿah were a clan of the important Thaʿlabah branch of Bakr. See Ibn al-Kalbī-Caskel-Strenziok, *Jamharat al-nasab*, I, Table 155, II, 25, 314.

889. Muḥallim b. Dhuhl were a clan of Shaybān. See Ibn al-Kalbī-Caskel-Strenziok, *Jamharat al-nasab*, I, Table 142, II, 421,

890. See for these, n. 604 above.

891. Clearly a superior kind of sword. The lexica give various explanations for the term, including one connecting it with the *mashārif al-Shām*, "the highlands of Syria," possibly the Ḥawrān massif, which would be near the place of origin of the later, famed swords of Damascus. See Lane, *Lexicon*, 1539a.

892. Nöldeke, trans. 343 n. 2, noted the reference here to the *pandām*,

The son of Qays made a charge, and the fame of it for him has traveled as far as the peoples of Iraq and Syria,
[That is,] ʿAmr, and ʿAmr is not decrepit with age or weak minded among them (i.e., his people of Qays), nor inexperienced and a mere youth.[893]

Since al-Aʿshā and al-Aṣamm praised the Banū Shaybān specifically, the Lahāzim[894] grew angry, and Abū Kalbah, one of the Banū Qays,[895] reproached those two poets strongly for this:

May you be mutilated, O two poets of a people of exalted fame! May your noses be cut off with a saw!
I mean the deaf one (*al-aṣamm*) and our weak-sighted one (*aʿshānā*) who, when they both come together, do not find help for [defective] hearing from seeing.
If it had not been for the riders of the Lahāzim, who are not feeble and defenseless, they would not have been able to spend the summer [any longer] at Dhū Qār.
We came upon them from their left side, just as those going to water [their beasts] become intermingled with those returning from the water (i.e troops traveling in opposite directions, with the enemy fleeing and ourselves wheeling
[1037] round and returning to the battle field).[896]

---

*paitidāna*, of the Zoroastrians (cf. Bartholomae, *Altiranisches Wörterbuch*, cols. 830–31), MP *padām*, NP *pandāmah*, worn across the mouth in order to avoid contamination with the breath of sacred objects.

893. These verses also in *Naqāʾiḍ*, II, 644–45; *Aghāni*, XXIV, 77–78.

894 The Lahāzim were a grouping of Bakrī tribes, defined in the Umayyad al-Baṣrah of some eighty years later than this time as the Qays b. Thaʿlabah and their confederates; the ʿAnazah; and the Taymallāt b. Thaʿlabah and their confederates, the ʿIjl. See al-Ṭabarī, II, 448, tr. Hawting, *The History of al-Ṭabarī, an Annotated Translation*, XX, *The Collapse of Sufyānid Authority and the Coming of the Marwānids*, 25–26; cf. Ibn al-Kalbī-Caskel-Strenziok, *Jamharat al-nasab*, II, 27. The term *lahāzim* is said by the lexicographers to be the plural of *lihzimah*, "mastoid bone, hinge of the jawbone with the skull," the idea of hardness being transfered to the solidity of the tribal alliance. See *Glossarium*, p. CDLXXIII; Ullmann, *WbKAS*, II, Letter *lām*, Pt. 2, 1516–19; *EI*[1], s.v. Taimallāt b. Thaʿlaba (G. Levi Della Vida).

895. Attached by Ibn Durayd, *Ishtiqāq*, 355, to the clan of ʿUkābah b. Qays, part of Murrah of Shaybān. See Ibn al-Kalbī-Caskel-Strenziok, *Jamharat al-nasab*, I, Table 141, II, 566.

896. *Naqāʾiḍ*, II, 645, in part quoted, but with additional verses,in *Aghānī*[3], XXIV, 77.

Abū ʿAmr b. al-ʿAlāʾ said: When Abū Kalbah's words reached al-Aʿshā, he commented, "He has spoken truly," and recited verses in extenuation of himself, some of which are:

When a deaf person is linked through a connection with a weak-sighted one, they both wander around distractedly, lost and in distress.
For I am not able to see what he can see, while he is never able to hear my reply.[897]

Al-Aʿshā recited concerning the day of battle,

There came to us from the Free Ones (*Banū al-Aḥrār*) a word that was not conformable.
They wanted to hack down the tree of our nobility, but we were defending ourselves against serious events.[898]

He also recited to Qays b. Masʿūd,

O Qays b. Masʿūd b. Qays b. Khālid, you are a man in whose youthful vigor the whole of Wāʾil[899] places its hopes!
Are you combining in a single year both raiding and journeying abroad? Would that the midwives had drowned Qays [at his birth]![900]

Al-Aʿshā of the Banū Rabīʿah said,[901]

We stood our ground firmly on the morning of Dhū Qār, when [the enemy] tribes were present there in swarms, having come together to give aid.
They had brought on that occasion a dark-colored [army], an intimidatory host, with closely compacted squadrons of riders, a crushing force,

---

897. al-Aʿshā, *Dīwān*, 206, no. 57 vv. 1–2; *Naqāʾiḍ*, II, 645.

898. *Dīwān*, 204, no. 56, vv. 5–6; Naqāʾiḍ, II, 645, with *al-ḥakamā* for *al-khuṭamā* at the end of the second verse.

899. That is, Wāʾil b. Jadīlah b. Asad b. Rabīʿah, from whom sprang the two great tribes of Bakr and Taghlib. See *EI*², s.v. Rabīʿa and Muḍar (H. Kindermann).

900. *Dīwān*, 128, no. 26 vv. 1–2; *Naqāʾiḍ*, II, 645–46.

901. That is, Aʿshā Banī Abī Rabīʿah or Aʿshā Shaybān, ʿAbdallāh b. Khārijah, another of the many poets with this sobriquet, numbered at seventeen by the Arabic literary biographers. This al-Aʿshā was a poet of al-Kūfah and a staunch adherent of the Marwānids, dying ca. 100/718–19. See Nöldeke, trans. 344 n. 6; *EI*², s.v. al-Aʿshā (ed.).

For a hateful day of battle, until the moment when the shades of its blackness fell away from us, revealing us as warriors with unsheathed swords.
They thereupon turned their backs on us totally,[902] and we only had to ward off Nuʿmān b. Zurʿah.[903]
And we drove away the threatening rain-cloud (*ʿāriḍ*) of the free ones as if going to water, just as the sand grouse (*qaṭā*) alight for water at a desert pool with exiguous water.[904]

## *Mention of Those Vassal Rulers Set over the Desert Frontier of the Arabs at al-Ḥīrah as Appointees of the Monarchs of Persia, after ʿAmr b. Hind*

We have already mentioned previously those members of the house of Naṣr b. Rabīʿah who held this power as vassal rulers on [1038] behalf of the monarchs of Persia up to the time of ʿAmr b. Hind's death, and the durations of their respective periods of office as vassal rulers. after ʿAmr b. Hind up to the time when al-Nuʿmān b. al-Mundhir held power.[905]

The person who exercised this office after ʿAmr b. Hind was his [full] brother Qābūs b. al-Mundhir,[906] whose mother was likewise Hind bt. al-Ḥārith b. ʿAmr; he held power for four years, of which eight months fell in the reign of Anūsharwān and three years and four months in the reign of the latter's son Hurmuz.[907] After

---

902. *aktaʿīnā,* also translatable "as if they were completely mutilated," as by Nöldeke, trans. 345.

903. That is, the Taghlibī chief and enemy of the Bakr, who at Khusraw's court advised the course of action that led to the *Yawm Dhī Qār;* see al-Ṭabarī, I, 1030, pp. 359–60 above. According to Abū al-Faraj al-Iṣfahānī, *Aghānī*³, XXIV, 72–73, he escaped from the field of Dhū Qār.

904. *Dīwān,* 281 no. 16 vv. 1–5.

905. See al-Ṭabarī, I, 833–34, 845–46, 850–54, 858ff., 899–900, 946, 981, 1016–30, pp. 44, 67, 74–82, 87ff., 161–63, 237, 286, 339–59 above.

906. The appearance of this purely Persian name, an Arabized form of Kāwūs (< Avestan Kawi-Usan, see Nöldeke, 345 n. 4; Justi, *Namenbuch,* 334–46; Mayrhofer, *Die altiranischen Namen,* nos. 208, 210, 323), among the Lakhmids, is an indication of the strength of Persian cultural influence within the dynasty. See further on this, Bosworth, "Iran and the Arabs before Islam," 609ff.

907. On this count, Qābūs would have reigned from 578 or 579 to 582 or 583, since Khusraw Anūsharwān died in 579, but we know that he was ruling a decade or so before then, since he was defeated by the Jafnid/Ghassānid al-Mundhir b. al-

Qābūs b. al-Mundhir there came to power al-Suhrab,[908] then after him the father of al-Nu'mān, al-Mundhir b. al-Mundhir, who held power for four years;[909] then after him, al-Nu'mān b. al-Mundhir, Abū Qābūs, for twenty-two years, of which seven years and eight months fell in the reign of Hurmuz, son of Anūsharwān, and fourteen years and four months in the reign of Kisrā Abarwīz, son of Hurmuz.[910] Then there held power Iyās b. Qabīṣah al-Ṭā'ī, together with al-Nakhīrajān, for nine years in the reign of Kisrā, son

---

Ḥārith on Ascension Day 570. His four years' reign must have been from 569 or 570 to 573 or 574, i.e., entirely within Anūsharwān's reign, as confirmed by Ḥamzah al-Iṣfahānī, *Ta'rīkh*, 94. See Nöldeke, trans. 345 n. 1; Rothstein, *Laḫmiden*, 72, 102–106. Rothstein, op. cit., 102, pointed out that what we know of Qābūs's military activities does not confirm Ḥamzah's allegation that he was a weak and ineffectual ruler, and he believed that the contemptuous nickname given to Qābūs of Qaynat al-'Urus (read thus for Ḥamzah's *Fitnat al-'Urus*), "slavegirl who looks after the bride's dwelling and wedding outfit," stemmed from some satirical poetry aimed at him.

908. As Nöldeke said, trans. 340 n. 1, this man with so typical a Persian name can hardly have been a Lakhmid (despite what has been said in n. 906 above about Persian cultural influence within the Lakhmid house, the name of Suhrab is totally unattested among them) but must have been a Persian official sent out by Anūsharwān during an interregnum between Qābūs's death and the eventual accession of al-Mundhir IV b. al-Mundhir III. According to Ḥamzah al-Iṣfahānī, *Ta'rīkh*, 94, this official (whose name is corruptly written here as *F.y.sh.h.r.t*) administered al-Ḥīrah for one year only. See Rothstein, *Laḫmiden*, 106–107.

909. Al-Mundhir IV b. al-Mundhir III (also a full brother of 'Amr and Qābūs, since according to Nöldeke, trans. 346 n. 2, a poet cited in the *Ḥamāsah* of Abū Tammām addresses him as ". . . b. Hind") must in fact have reigned rather more than four years, from ca. 574 to 580. Nöldeke mentioned, 346 n. 1, the apparent reluctance of the Christian 'Ibād of al-Ḥīrah to accept the pagan al-Mundhir as ruler, but Rothstein pointed out that all the Lakhmid rulers with the exception of the last one were pagans, and the fact that al-Mundhir was unable immediately to succeed his brother Qābūs must have had other causes. In the process of al-Mundhir's eventual succession to the throne in al-Ḥīrah, 'Adī's father Zayd b. (?) Ḥammād, Anūsharwān's adviser on Arab affairs, may have played a significant rôle. Al-Mundhir had at one point been involved in fighting with the Jafnids/Ghassānids, but we have no exact details of the circumstances of his death. See Rothstein, *Laḫmiden*, 107.

910. Al-Nu'mān III, who is also found with the *kunyah* of Abū al-Mundhir and whose mother was the slavegirl Salmā or Sulmā (see al-Ṭabarī, I, 1017, p. 341 above), reigned 580–602 as the last of the Lakhmid kings in al-Ḥīrah. See Nöldeke, trans. 347 n. 1; Rothstein, *Laḫmiden*, 107–19, 142–43. Al-Nu'mān figures frequently in the lives of the poets who frequented his court in the final florescence of Arabic culture at al-Ḥīrah; he was the first and last of his line to become a Nestorian Christian, however nominally, doubtless under the influence of his upbringing in the family circle of 'Adī b. Zayd. See *EI*², s.v. al-Nu'mān (III) b. al-Mundhir (Irfan Shahîd).

of Hurmuz.[911] According to what Hishām b. Muḥammad has asserted, one year and eight months from the beginning of Iyās b. Qabīṣah's tenure of power, the Prophet was sent [by God] on his mission.[912] His successor Āzādhbih, son of [Ādhur] Māhān (?), son of Mihrbundādh, from Hamadhān, held power for seventeen years, of which fourteen years and eight months fell within the time of Kisrā, son of Hurmuz; eight months in the time of Shīrūyah, son of
[1039] Kisrā; one year and seven months in the time of Ardashīr, son of Shīrūyah; and one month in the time of Būrān-dukht, daughter of Kisrā.[913] Al-Mundhir b. al-Nu'mān b. al-Mundhir then held power. He is the one whom the Arabs called al-Gharūr ("the one who deludes, deceives") and who was killed in al-Baḥrayn at the battle of Juwāthā; he held power for eight months until Khālid b. al-Walīd marched on al-Ḥīrah and was the last survivor of the house of Naṣr b. Rabī'ah. Their power crumbled with the collapse of the royal power in Persia.[914]

911. Iyās's nine years' of governorship was from 602–11, and this was in partnership with the Persian commander Nakhīrjān (on whom, see n. 377 above). Rothstein, *Laḫmiden,* 119–20, suggested that this arrangement could have been the prelude to the incorporation of the Lakhmid territories into the Persian empire as one of its provinces.

912. This is almost certainly too early; the Prophet's *mab'ath* or mission is more probably to be placed in 610 (the call to prophethood, *nubuwwah,* and his nonpublic ministry), and then with ca. 613 as the date for the *risālah* or beginning of his public ministry in Mecca. See Watt, *Muhammad at Mecca,* 59.

913. This means a governorship for Āzādhbih of nineteen years if he held the post till the reign of Būrān or Būrān-dukht (r. 630–31). The reading for his father's name is very uncertain. Marquart suggested [Ādhur] Māhān for a completely undotted consonant skeleton, which would correspond with the name in the Byzantine Greeks historians of Adormaanēs, but this was regarded by the editor Nöldeke as not very probable; the text could be *Bān.y.ān* or numerous other possibilities. See *Addenda et emendanda,* p. DXCV.

914. This later Lakhmid never reigned in al-Ḥīrah but was raised up by the rebels of al-Baḥrayn during the Riddah wars as one of their leaders, doubtless from the prestige of his ancient name and lineage. He is called in the Muslim sources *al-Gharūr,* "the treacherous, deceitful one," but is said to have ruefully called himself, when captured by the Muslims, *al-Maghrūr,* "the deceived one." The accounts of his fate vary: that he was killed at the siege of Juwāthā, the fortress of the 'Abd al-Qays in al-Khaṭṭ (i.e., in al-Baḥrayn); that he was subsequently killed fighting for Musaylimah in al-Yamāmah; and (less probably) that he became a Muslim. See al-Balādhurī, *Futūḥ,* 84; al-Ṭabarī, I, 1737, tr. Ismail K. Poonawala, *The History of al-Ṭabarī, an Annotated Translation,* IX, *The Last Years of the Prophet,* 95, and I, 1959–61, tr. F. M. Donner, ibid., X, *The Conquest of Arabia,* 136–38; Nöldeke, trans. 348 n. 1, with other information on the ultimate fate of the Lakhmid line, including that in al-Mas'ūdī, *Murūj,* III, 209–12 = §§ 1071–72, cf.

According to what Hishām [b. Muḥammad] has asserted, the total of the rulers of the house of Naṣr plus their deputies from the 'Ibād and the Persians, was twenty rulers. He related: The total number of years during which they held power was 522 years and eight months.[915]

## *The Story Returns to the Mention of al-Marūzān, Who Governed Yemen on Behalf of Hurmuz and His Son Abarwīz, and His Successors*[916]

There was related to me a narrative going back to Hishām b. Muḥammad, who said: Hurmuz, son of Kisrā, dismissed W.y.n (?)[917] from Yemen and appointed in his stead al-Marūzān. The latter remained in Yemen long enough to have children born to him there and for these to grow to puberty.[918] But then the people

---

Pellat's index, VI, 268, on the encounter of al-Nu'mān's daughter Ḥurqah/Ḥarīqah/Ḥurayqah with Sa'd b. Abī Waqqāṣ after the Arab victory at al-Qādisiyyah.

Al-Shābushtī, *Kitāb al-diyārāt*, 244–46, mentions the Dayr Hind al-Ṣughrā at al-Ḥīrah, which Hind, the daughter of al-Nu'mān, is said to have built and to have stayed there herself as a nun (*mutarahhibah*) until her death; cf. also the editor Gūrgīs 'Awwād's *dhayl*, 388–90, with information from other sources on the convent and on Hind, and Fiey, *L'Assyrie chrétienne*, III, 215–17. According to the *Anonymus Guidi*, tr. 9, the Catholicos Īshō'yabh II was buried there by Hind when he died. According to the later geographer al-Bakrī, *Mu'jam mā ista'jam*, II, 604–607, Hind and Ḥurqah/Ḥarīqah/Ḥurayqah were the same person (Ḥamzah al-Iṣfahānī, *Ta'rīkh*, 95, makes them two separate persons and mentions a third daughter, *'.n.f.q.y.r* [?]), and al-Bakrī quotes Abū al-Faraj [al-Iṣfahānī] that the tribes of both Hind and her father al-Nu'mān were visible, side by side, in the Dayr Hind al-Awwal (= al-Ṣughrā) during the time of Hārūn al-Rashīd (i.e., ca. A.D. 800). Fiey, op. cit., III, 216 n. 4, suggested that Ḥurqah, etc., was this princess's pagan name before the adoption of Christianity by her father and herself. Concerning Khālid's march on al-Ḥīrah, see Musil, *The Middle Euphrates*, 283–92.

915. Nöldeke, trans. 349 n. 1, basing himself on the figures for each reign in the corrected text of Ḥamzah al-Iṣfahānī's *Ta'rīkh*, found this a remarkably accurate computation.

916. From this point onward, there resumes the story from Ibn al-Kalbī on events in Yemen under Persian rule broken off by al-Ṭabarī at I, 988, p. 294 above, and then on the end of Khusraw Abarwēz's reign and the rule of his successors.

917. See al-Ṭabarī, I, 988, p. 294 above.

918. Such children, born of Persian fathers who were soldiers or officials during the half-century or so of Persian dominance in Yemen, and local Arab mothers, came to form the so-called *Abnā'* or "Sons." The virtual collapse of the Sāsānid empire in 628 left these Abnā' and other surviving representatives of Persian power in Yemen remote and isolated from their homeland with virtually no hope of human replenishments or material help from Persia. Hence when Muḥammad was extending his power into the more distant parts of the Arabian peninsula, the

of one of the mountains of Yemen called al-Maṣāni'[919] rebelled against him and refused to hand over to him the land tax. Al-Maṣāni' is a long mountain, difficult of access, with another mountain adjacent to it with a plain that is not very wide lying between them; moreover, no one can possibly conceive in his mind the idea of climbing up to it. Al-Marūzān proceeded to al-Maṣāni', and when he arrived there he perceived that there was no way up to the mountain except via a single way of access which a
[1040] man could defend single handed.

When al-Marūzān saw that there was no way for him to reach it, he climbed up the mountain which faced the people of al-Maṣāni''s fortress, and looked for the narrowest gap between it and the mountain he himself was on, with nothing but empty space stretching down below him. He realized that the only way of takng the fortress was from that point. So he ordered his troops to form themselves into two ranks and then all to shout out to him with one great shout. He spurred on his horse, it galloped on with all its force and then he hurled it forward and it jumped across the chasm, and lo and behold, he was on the top of the fortress. When the Ḥimyarites saw him and what he had done, they exclaimed, "This man is a *'.y.m!*"—*'.y.m* meaning in Ḥimyarite "devil."[920] Then he herded them together roughly, spoke to them in Persian and ordered them to place each other in shackles. He brought

---

Abnā' were inclined to come to terms with the Prophet, with their leader, the governor Bādhān or Bādham (see n. 609 above) recorded as submitting and becoming a Muslim in 10/631. See *EIr*, s.v. Abnā' (C. E. Bosworth); *EI²* Suppl. s.v. Bādhām, Bādhān (Bosworth).

919. Literally, "the constructions," in this case, fortifications. According to Nöldeke, trans. 350 n. 1, the Paris ms. of this part of al-Ṭabarī's text has a remark identifying al-Maṣāni' with the mountain al-D.l.' and the town of Kawkabān. The plateau and mountain area of al-Maṣāni' and the Jabal Dila' (this last often mentioned by al-Hamdānī, *Ṣifat jazīrat al-'Arab*, 223, 231, 234, etc.) are in fact still known as such and lie to the west-northwest of Ṣan'ā', with the ancient town, now a provincial capital, of Kawkabān located there. See *EI²* s.v. Kawkabān. 4 (A. Grohmann).

920. This mysterious word is not so far attested in South Arabian. Nöldeke, trans. 350 n. 2, cited the lexicographers al-Jawharī and Nashwān al-Ḥimyarī that it meant "a variety of serpent" and adduced Hebr. *'ēmāh*, "something terrifying, frightful." He further suggested that there might be a connection of the word with the 'Emīm, the mythical giants of the land of Moab mentioned in Gen. xiv. 5 and Deut. ii. 10–11; but this is pure speculation, based on what is probably chance resemblance of words.

them all down from their fortress, killing one part of them and enslaving others. He wrote to Kisrā, son of Hurmuz, telling him what he had done. The king marveled at his achievement and wrote back: "Appoint as your deputy whomever you will, and come to me!"

He related: Now al-Marūzān had two sons, one of whom, called Khurrakhusrah, was very fond of Arabic and could recite poetry in it,[921] while the other was a cavalryman who spoke Persian and lived in the fashion of a *dihqān*. Al-Marūzān now appointed his son Khurrakhusrah—Khurrakhusrah being the dearest to him of his sons—as his deputy over Yemen, and traveled onward until, when he was in some region of the Arab lands, he died. He was then placed in a sarcophagus and this was carried along until it was finally brought to Kisrā. The latter ordered that sarcophagus to be placed in his treasury and caused to be inscribed on it "In this sarcophagus lies so-and-so, who did such-and-such," giving the story of what he did at the two mountains.[922] News of Khurrakhusrah's adoption of Arab ways (*ta'arrub*), his relating of Arabic poetry, and his entirely Arab education reached Kisrā, so he dismissed him and appointed as governor Bādhān, who was in fact the last of the Persian governors to be sent out to Yemen.[923] [1041]

Kisrā became puffed up with vainglory because of the vast amount of wealth and all kinds of jewels, utensils, equipment, and horses he had accumulated. He had conquered so many of the lands of his enemies. Events all came together to aid him, and he was granted good fortune in his ventures. However, he was filled with conceit and boastfulness, and was horribly avaricious; he grudged and envied people for their wealth and possessions.[924] He appointed a certain man from the local people (*'ilj*,[925] i.e., one of

---

921. An example of the assimilation of the Abnā' to their local environment if, as is possible, Khurrakhusrah had an Arab mother.

922. The story of al-Marūzān's successful attack on al-Maṣāni' and his eventual death and burial is given in Ibn Qutaybah, *'Uyūn al-akhbār*, I, 178–79, on the basis of the author's readings in the "books of the Persians."

923. The date of Bādhān's appointment is unknown, but as noted in n. 918 above, he remained in Yemen till his conversion to Islam in 10/631.

924. Nöldeke, trans. 351 n. 1, gives a balanced assessment of Abarwēz's character and achievements, concluding that "In sum, Khusraw II is to be considered much more a weak than a bad man."

925. See for this term, n. 210 above.

the Nabataean population of Iraq) called Farrukhzādh, son of Sumayy,[926] from a a village called Khandaq[927] in the *ṭassūj* of Bih-Ardashīr (text, Bahurasīr), to take charge of collecting the arrears of taxation (*al-baqāyā*).[928] This latter person imposed on the people all sorts of evil afflictions, ill-treated them and tyrannized them, confiscating their wealth unlawfully on the plea of extracting the arrears of land tax. He thereby rendered them disaffected, their means of life became straitened, and Kisrā and his rule became hateful to them.

There was related to me a narrative going back to Hishām b. Muḥammad, who said: This Kisrā Abarwīz had accumulated more wealth than any other monarch. His riders reached as far as Constantinople and Ifrīqiyah.[929] He spent the winter in al-Madā'in and the summer in the region between al-Madā'in and Hamadhān.[930] It was said that he had twelve thousand women and slave-girls, 999 elephants, and fifty thousand riding beasts comprising finely bred horses, horses of lesser breed, and mules. He was the most avaricious of mankind regarding jewels, vessels, and the like. Another source, not Hishām, has stated that he had in his palace three thousand women with whom he had sexual relations and thousands of slave girls employed as servants, for

926. Nöldeke, trans. 352 n. 1, implied—as seems reasonable in regard to an Aramaic-speaking "Nabataean" of Iraq—that Sumayy was a Semitic name, adducing the name of the Jewish prophet S.m.y who met Zoroaster at Balkh, according to al-Ṭabarī, I, 681, tr. M. Perlmann. *The History of al-Ṭabarī, an Annotated Translation*, IV, *The Ancient Kingdoms*, 76–77.

927. Literally, "trench, ditch," a place that cannot be identified exactly but which, if it was in the vicinity of Bih-Ardashīr or Seleucia, lay to the west of al-Madā'in (see al-Ṭabarī, I, 819, p. 15 and the references in n. 58 above).

928. On this fiscal and administrative term, see n. 253 above.

929. In early Islamic geographical usage, this region (< Latin Africa, perhaps from the Afri, an indigenous people of the region, or the later Punic-Cartaginian ethnic mixture there, see *EI*², s.v. Ifrīḳiya (M. Talbi), corresponded to modern Tunisia, but is doubtless used in this context in a looser, wider sense of "North Africa" in general. These far-flung raids of Khusraw's are, in any case, pure legend.

930. That is, in that part of the Zagros chain which now forms southern Kurdistan. As Nöldeke noted, trans 353 n. 1, it was ancient practice for rulers, from Achaemenid times onward, to spend the winter on the Mesopotamian plain but to move up to the drier, less torrid Iranian plateau for the summer. It was actually Hamadhān which, some four or five centuries later, the Seljuq sultans preferred as their usual capital, only visiting Baghdad occasionally and normally leaving a *shiḥnah*, a military governor, there.

music making and singing, and such. He also had three thousand male servants at his hand, eighty-five hundred riding beasts on which he could travel, 760 elephants, and twelve thousand mules for conveying his baggage.[931] He gave orders for the building of fire temples and appointed for them twelve thousand hērbadhs for [1042] chanting the Zoroastrian religious formulae (*li-al-zamzamah*).[932]

In the eighteenth year of his reign,[933] Kisrā ordered the sums collected as land tax from his territories and its associated taxes (*tawābi'*) and other sources of income, to be counted up. It was reported back to him that the amount of silver coinage (*al-wariq*)[934] collected from the land tax and other sources of income in that year was 420 million mithqāls [in weight], which, on the basis of seven mithqāls [in weight equaling ten dirhams], is the amount corresponding to six hundred million dirhams (i.e., silver coins). He ordered all this to be transfered to a treasury he had built at the city of Ctesiphon and had called Bahār ḥ.f.r.d (?) Khusraw, together with other sums of money he possessed, comprising coinage of Fayrūz, son of Yazdajird, and Qubādh, son of Fayrūz, amounting to twelve thousand purses (*badrah*), each purse containing four thousand mithqāls in coinage,[935] the whole

931. Substantially the same figures in Ḥamzah al-Iṣfahānī, *Ta'rīkh*, 53, but with an increased figure of six thousand guards (*ḥaras*).

932. *zamzamah*, "humming, mumbling," was the term applied by the Arabs to the liturgical chanting of the Zoroastrian priests and religious scholars or hērbeds. Nöldeke, trans. 353 n. 3, gave the MP and Syriac terms for this chanting, *wāz* and *reṭnā* respectively, and noted such still-surviving memorials of Khusraw Abarwēz's palace building as the Ṭāq/Aywān-i Kisrā (see n. 666 above). More precisely, so Mr F .C. de Blois points out, *wāz*, and perhaps *zamzamah*, refers to the Zoroastrian practice of speaking in a subdued voice while eating.

On the Zoroastrian clergy in general, see Nöldeke, trans. 450–52, Excursus 3, and on the hērbed specifically—hērbed being the oldest religious title attested from the Sāsānid period, as being that of Kerdēr, see n. 122 above—see Chaumont, "Recherches sur le clergé zoroastrien. Le Hērbad," 55–80.

933. This would be the year 607–608.

934. Nöldeke, trans. 354 n. 2, detailed and discussed the information in al-Balādhurī, *Futūḥ*, 464, from Ibn al-Muqaffa' on the collecting of sources of revenue in the Persian empire and adduces the continuity of practice as shown, e.g., in the travel narrative of the Huguenot Sir John Chardin in seventeenth-century Ṣafawid Persia.

935. Conventionally, a *badrah* in early Islamic times contained ten thousand dirhams; but on the equivalence of seven mithqāls in weight equaling ten dirhams, these Sāsānid purses contained 5,720 dirhams. See for the mithqāl, n. 836 above, and for *wariq* = "silver coinage," *EI*[2] s.v. Wariḳ (M.L. Bates)

of this totaling forty-eight million mithqāls, the equivalent according to the proportion seven [to ten] of 68,571,42[8] plus a half and a third of an eighth of a dirham. In addition, there were various kinds of jewels, garments, and the like, whose grand total God alone could enumerate.

Kisrā treated people with contempt and regarded them with
[1043] scorn in a manner no righteous and discerning monarch should adopt. His insolent pride and lack of respect for God reached the point that he gave orders to the man in charge of his personal guard at court, called Zādhān Farrūkh,[936] that he should kill every person held captive in any of his prisons; these persons were counted up, and their number reached thirty-six thousand. However, Zādhān Farrūkh did not take any steps to kill them but gave instructions for a delay in implementing Kisrā's command regarding them, adducing various reasons, which he enumerated to Kisrā. Kisrā incurred for himself the hatred of the subjects of his kingdom for various reasons. First, his contemptuous treatment of them and his belittling of the great men of state. Second, his giving the barbarian (*al-ʿilj*) Farrukhānzādh, son of Sumayy, power over them. Third, his command that all the prisoners should be slain. Fourth, his intention to put to death the troops returning from their defeat at the hands of Hiraql (Heraclius) and the Byzantines. Hence a group of the great men of state went to ʿAqr Bābil,[937] where were Shīrūyah (text, "Shīrī"), son of Abarwīz, and his brothers, and where the king had appointed tutors to educate them. [He had also appointed] cavalry guards (*asāwirah*) to prevent them leaving that place. They now brought out Shīrūyah and

936. A Persian financial official, Zādhān-farrukh, with the nickname of "the one-eyed one," later figures in the Islamic historians' accounts of the *naql al-dīwān* in Iraq, i.e., the change from Persian to Arabic as the administrative language of the finance department, effected by the caliph ʿAbd al-Malik's governor of Iraq and the East, al-Ḥajjāj b. Yūsuf al-Thaqafī. See, e.g., al-Balādhurī, *Futūḥ*, 300–301; al-Jahshiyārī, *Kitāb al-wuzarāʾ wa-al-kuttāb*, 38–39; M. Sprengling, "From Persian to Arabic," 185–90, 194–97. Of course, this Zādhān-farrukh lived some three generations after Khusraw's commander of the guard, and it is unknown whether there was any family connection between the two men. On the name Zādhān-farrukh "the fortunate one," see Justi, *Namenbuch*, 377.

937. The ruins of "the palace" (*ʿaqr*) of Babel lay just to the north of the later Islamic town of al-Ḥillah and slightly to the east of the Sūrā canal. See Le Strange, *Lands*, 72; Morony, *Iraq after the Muslim Conquest*, 150.

entered the town of Bih Ardashīr (text, "Bahurasīr") by night. They released all those in the prisons there, and these freed captives were joined by the fugitive troops whom Kisrā had intended to put to death. They all shouted, "Qubādh (i.e., Shīrūyah) for supreme ruler (*shāhanshāh*)!" The next morning they proceeded to the open space before Kisrā['s palace]. His palace guards took to their heels, and Kisrā himself fled, in great terror, unaccompanied by anyone, to one of the gardens adjacent to his palace called the Bāgh al-Hinduwān. But he was sought out and then apprehended on the day Ādhar of the month Ādhar,[938] and imprisoned in the palace of government (*dār al-mamlakah*). Shīrūyah entered that [1044] palace, and the leading figures gathered round him and proclaimed him king. He sent a message to his father bitterly upbraiding him for his conduct.[939]

There was related to me a narrative going back to Hishām b. Muḥammad, who said: Kisrā Abarwīz had eighteen sons, the eldest of whom was Shahriyār, whom Shīrīn had adopted as a son. The astrologers told Kisrā, "One of your sons will himself have a son, at whose hands this throne will come to ruin and this kingdom be destroyed. The distinguishing sign of this son will be a defect in a certain part of his body." For that reason, Kisrā thereupon kept his sons separated from all women, and they remained for a long time with no access to a woman. At last, Shahriyār complained to Shīrīn about this, sending to her a message in which he complained about his lust for women and asked her to provide him with a woman. If he could have no woman, he would kill himself. She sent a message back to him: "I can't manage to get women into your presence, except a woman of no consequence who wouldn't be suitable for you to touch." He replied, "I don't care who she is, as long as she is a woman!" So she sent to him a

938. Nöldeke, trans. 357 n. 3, noted that in Khusraw's rejoinder to Shērōy's's charges against him, the previous day, Day [ba Ādhar], is named, and that this date would correspond to 25 February 628. He further noted, ibid., 357 n. 2, cf. 381 n. 3, that Armenian historians, among others, mention that it had been prophesied to Khusraw that he would die in India, and this duly occurred in the "house of the Indians."

939. The Christian Greek, Syriac, and Armenian sources on the palace revolution that overthrew Khusraw and brought Shīruyah to power are discussed at length in Nöldeke, trans. 357 n. 4, to which can now be added the *Anonymus Guidi*, tr. 29–30.

maiden whom she was wont to employ for being cupped. According to what is asserted, this maiden was the daughter of one of the Persian nobles, but Shīrīn had become angry with her for some reason or another and had consigned her to the ranks of the cuppers.[940] When Shīrīn introduced the maiden into Shahriyār's presence, he immediately leapt on her, and she became pregnant with Yazdajird. Shīrīn gave orders regarding her, and she was kept carefully confined until she gave birth. The fact of the child's birth was kept secret for five years.

At that point, Shīrīn noticed that Kisrā had acquired a tenderness toward young children, at this time when he was growing old, so she said to him, "O king, would it gladden your heart to see a child of one of your own sons, even though this might entail something untoward?" He replied, "[Yes,] I don't care [what might happen]." She gave commands for Yazdajird to be perfumed and decked out with fine clothes, and she had him brought into Kisrā's presence, saying, "This is Yazdajird, son of Shahriyār!" Kisrā sum-
[1045] moned him, clasped him to his breast, kissed him, yearned toward him, and displayed great affection for him; and from then onward he kept Yazdajird close to him. One day, the boy was playing in his presence when he remembered what had been foretold, so he summoned him, had his clothes taken off, inspected him from the front and the back, and perceived clearly the defect (or, "the defect was clearly apparent," *istabāna al-naqṣ*) in one of his hips. He was now filled with anger and distress, and dragged the boy off in order to dash him to the ground. But Shīrīn clung to him and besought Kisrā by God not to kill him, telling Kisrā, "If this is something that is going to befall this state, then there is no possibility of changing it." He replied. "This boy is the agent of ill-fortune about whom I was informed (i.e., by the astrologers), so get rid of him. I don't want ever to see him again!" Shīrīn therefore gave orders for the boy to be sent to Sijistān; but others say that, on the contrary, he was in the Sawād with his guardians at a village called Khumāniyah.[941]

---

940. On Shīrīn, see n. 729 above. In Islamic times at least, phlebotomy, the function of the cupper, was regarded as particularly menial and degrading, doubtless from the fact that such bodily services were usually performed by slaves. See *EI*[2] Suppl., s.v. Faṣṣād, Ḥadjdjām (M. A. J. Beg).

941. The story of Yazdagird's birth and upbringing is doubtless a popular tale

The Persians rose up against Kisrā and killed him, aided by his son Shīrūyah, son of Maryam, the Byzantine woman (al-Rūmiyyah).[942] The duration of his (i.e., Kisrā's) power was thirty-eight years.[943] After the elapsing of thirty-two years, five months, and fifteen days of his rule, there took place the Prophet's migration from Mecca to Medina.[944]

## *[Qubādh II Shīrūyah]*

After him there succeeded to the royal power Shīrūyah,[945] whose [regnal] name was Qubādh (II).

He was the son of [Kisrā II] Abarwīz, son of Hurmuz (IV), son of Kisrā (I) Anūsharwān. It has been mentioned that the great men of state from the Persians came into Shīrūyah's presence when he had become king and after he had imprisoned his father, and said to him, "It is not fitting that we should have two kings: either you kill Kisrā, and we will be your faithful and obedient servants, or we shall depose you and give our obedience to him just as we [1046]

---

that endeavored to account for the eventual disaster that overtook Yazdagird III, the last of his line to rule in Persia, and the Sāsānid dynasty as a whole.

Khumāniyah must be the Humāniyyah or Humayniyyah on the west bank of the Tigris below al-Madā'in and just below the confluence of that river and the Kūthā canal, a place which later became of some importance in early ʿAbbāsid times. See Nöldeke, "Zur orientalischen Geographie," 94 n. 1; Le Strange, *Lands,* 37.

942. See on the question of Maryam al-Rūmiyyah and the historicity or otherwise of her marriage with Khusraw Abarwēz, al-Ṭabarī, I, 999, p. 312 and n. 729 above.

943. From the beginning of his first reign, Khusraw II Abarwēz ruled for thirty-eight years, 590–628. His name appears on his coins as ḤWSRW. See on his coins Paruck, *Sāsānian Coins,* 67–68, 386–90, 484–91, Plates XX–XXI, Tables XXVIII–XXX; Göbl, *Sasanian Numismatics,* 53–54, Table XII, Plate 13; Sellwood, Whitting, and Williams, *An Introduction to Sasanian Coins,* 21, 152–58; Malek, "A Survey of Research on Sasanian Numismatics," 237–38.

The Arabic sources on his reign include Ibn Qutaybah, *Maʿārif,* 665; al-Yaʿqūbī, *Ta'rīkh,* I, 190–96; al-Dīnawarī, *al-Akhbār al-ṭiwāl,* 84–107; al-Masʿūdī, *Murūj,* II, 214–32 = §§ 634–53; idem, *Tanbīh,* 39, 102, 155–56, tr. 62–63, 146, 213–16; Ḥamzah al-Iṣfahānī, *Ta'rīkh,* 53; Ibn al-Athīr, *Kāmil,* I, 472–81, 492–94. Of Persian sources, see Ṭabarī-Balʿamī, trans. II, 274–301, 304–309, 325–32. Of modern studies, see Christensen, *Sassanides,* 448–96; Frye, *The Heritage of Persia,* 234–35, 239; idem, "The Political History of Iran under the Sasanians," 164–70, 178.

944. This is very accurate, given that the Hijrah took place in Rabīʿ I of the year 1/September 622.

945. Properly Shēroy < *shēr* "lion," with a hypocoristic ending of a type familiar in MP and NP and Arabized as *-awayh(i).* See on this ending Nöldeke, "Persische Studien. I. Persische Koseformen," 388–423. On the name Shērōy/Shīrūyah in general, see Nöldeke, trans. 361 n. 2; Justi, *Namenbuch,* 297.

always did before you secured the royal power." These words struck fear into Shīrūyah's heart and crushed him. He ordered Kisrā to be transported from the palace of government to the house of a man called Mārasfand.[946] Kisrā was set on a common nag, with his head covered, and conveyed to that house escorted by a detachment of troops. On the way, they brought him past a shoemaker who was sitting in a booth that led out on to the road. When the shoemaker saw the detachment of cavalry troops escorting a single rider with a muffled head, he realized that the covered-up figure was Kisrā and he struck at him with a shoemaker's last. One of the troops escorting Kisrā turned on the shoemaker, unsheathed his sword, cut off the shoemaker's head, and then rejoined his comrades.[947]

When Kisrā was installed in Mārasfand's house, Shīrūyah assembled together all the great men of state and the members of leading families who were at court and addressed them: "We have thought fit, in the first place to send an envoy to our father the king setting forth all his evil actions in his government and drawing his attention to various aspects of these." Then he sent for a man from Ardashīr Khurrah, who was called Asfādh Jushnas and who, because of his position as head of the [royal] secretaries,[948] was in charge of governing the kingdom. Shīrūyah said to him, "Off you go to our father the king and tell him in our name that we have not been the cause of the unhappy state into which he has fallen, nor is any member of the subject population responsible, but God has condemned you to His divine retribution in return for your evil conduct. [First,] your crime against your father Hurmuz, your violence toward him, depriving him of the royal power, blinding his eyes, killing him in a most horrible fashion, and all the great burden of guilt you have brought upon yourself by injur-

946. Al-Dīnawarī, *al-Akhbār al-ṭiwāl,* 107, has for this name *II.r.s.f.t.h.*

947. Nöldeke, trans. 362 n. 2, noted that, in Firdawsī, the shoemaker often serves as the outspoken representative of the masses, sometimes with comic touches; even so, he is not allowed here to mock and slight the fallen monarch.

948. Correcting the text's *ra'īs al-katībah* (which would mean something like "head of the cavalry of the military host"; *katībah* = "detachment of cavalry") in the light of the parallel passage in al-Dīnawarī, *al-Akhbār al-ṭiwāl,* 107, who has *ra'īs kuttāb al-rasā'il* "head of the secretaries responsible for official correspondence." Cf. also Nöldeke, trans. 362 n. 3.

ing him. [Second,] your bad treatment of us, your sons, by keeping us from all access to and participation in good things, and from everything which would have brought us ease of life, enjoyment, and happiness. [Third,] your bad treatment of those whom you condemned to perpetual imprisonment, to the point that they [1047] suffered hardship from extreme deprivation, wretched living conditions and food, and separation from their homelands, wives, and children. [Fourth,] your lack of consideration for the women whom you appropriated for yourself; your failure to show them any love or affection and to send them back to live with those men by whom they already had children and progeny; and your keeping them confined in your palace against their wills.[949] [Fifth,] what you have inflicted on your subjects generally in levying the land tax and in treating them with harshness and violence. [Sixth,] your amassing a great amount of wealth, which you exacted from the people with great brutality so that you drove them to consider your rule hateful and thereby brought them into affliction and deprivation. [Seventh,] your stationing the troops for long periods along the frontiers with the Byzantines and on other frontiers, thereby separating them from their families.[950] [Eighth,] your treacherous behavior toward Mawrīq (Maurice), the king of the Byzantines and your ingratitude for his praiseworthy actions on your behalf, in that he sought refuge with you, exerted himself laudably for you, protected you from the malevolence of your enemies, and increased the fame of your name by giving to you in marriage the noblest and most precious in his sight of his daughters. Moreover, you regarded your rightful obligations to him lightly and refused to grant his request of you regarding the return of the wooden [True] Cross, to which neither you nor any of your fellow countrymen had any entitlement or need.[951] You know

949. Nöldeke, trans. 364 n. 2, noted that this complaint about the seizure of married women for the ruler's harem has the ring of authenticity.

950. For this complaint, in early Islamic times technically known as *tajmīr*, see n. 151 above.

951. When Shērōy brought the lengthy war with Heraclius to an end, the return of the True Cross to Jerusalem was one of the provisions of the peace treaty. The Byzantine emperor brought it back to the Holy City personally, but the date of his visit is notoriously difficult to ascertain and has been much discussed. The restoration of the Cross was subsequently celebrated on 14 September 629, but the city

this well [now]. If you have explanations or exculpations to adduce to us and to the subjects, then bring them forward; if you don't have any, then show your contrition swiftly to God and return to Him, until we announce our intentions concerning you."[952]

Asfādh Jushnas committed to his mind this message to Kisrā from Shīrūyah and set off from Shīrūyah's court in order to convey it to him. When he reached the place where Kisrā was imprisoned, he found a man called Jīlinūs (Jālīnūs), the commander of the guard who had been entrusted with keeping ward over Kisrā,
[1048] seated there.[953] He held conversation with Jīlinūs for a while, and then Asfādh Jushnas asked him for permission to go into Kisrā in order to deliver a message from Shīrūyah. Jīlinūs went back and drew the curtain that veiled access to Kisrā, went into his presence, and said to him, "May God grant you long life![954] Asfādh Jushnas is at the gate, has recounted that the king Shīrūyah has sent him to you with a message, and now seeks an audience with you. So decide according to your will what you wish to do." Kisrā

---

was, according to some authorities, recaptured in a March, probably March 630. See Nöldeke, trans. 365 n. 2, 392 n. 1; Bury, *A History of the Later Roman Empire from Arcadius to Irene,* II, 244–45; N. H. Baynes, "The Restoration of the Cross at Jerusalem," 287–99; Schick, *The Christian Communities of Palestine from Byzantine to Islamic Rule,* 50.

952. Nöldeke, trans. 363 n. 1, regarded this denunciation and Khusraw's rejoinder, with their fullest extant texts given here by al-Ṭabarī, as artistic renderings of an exchange of complaints and justifications composed by someone close to the actual events yet writing after the deaths of Khusraw, Shērōy, and the latter's son Ardashīr during the reign of Khusraw's grandson Yazdagird III, when the Sāsānid house was still reigning in Persia. Al-Ya'qūbī, *Ta'rīkh,* I, 196, has only a brief reference to Shērōy's *risālah ghalīẓah,* "harsh letter," but al-Dīnawarī, *al-Akhbār al-ṭiwāl,* 107–10, has quite a lengthy version.

953. Jālīnūs or Jālinūs (whose name looks Greek rather than Persian; possibly he was a Christian and had adopted a Christian name in addition to an unknown, purely Persian one) is described by al-Dīnawarī, *al-Akhbār al-ṭiwāl,* 107, as *ra'īs al-jund al-mustamītah,* "commander of the troops who seek death," the ruler's personal guard (in Middle Persian, the *gyān-abespārān,* "those who sacrifice their lives"). He was later to be a leading general of the Persian troops combating the Arab invaders of Iraq and fell at al-Qādisiyyah. See al-Balādhurī, *Futūḥ,* 258, 260; al-Ṭabarī, I, 2169–72, 2174, etc., tr. Khalid Yahya Blankenship, *The History of al-Ṭabarī, an Annotated Translation,* XI, *The Challenge to the Empires,* 183–86, 188, etc., and I, 2357, tr. Yohanan Friedmann, ibid., XII, *The Battle of al-Qādisiyyah and the Conquest of Syria and Palestine,* 141; Nöldeke, trans. 365 n. 2.

954. As Nöldeke noted, trans. 366 n. 2, the imprisoned Khusraw Abarwēz is treated throughout as a monarch, with the correct etiquette of address observed, so that Jālīnūs adresses him with the formula *anōšag buwād!* "may he be immortal!"

smiled and said in a joking manner, "O Jīlinūs, son of Asfādh (*Jīlinūs Asfādhān*), what you say is contrary to what intelligent persons say. For if it is the case that the message you have mentioned is from the king Shīrūyah, then, in the face of his royal power, it is not for us to grant permission to enter. If we do have authority for granting permission to enter or to exclude, then Shīrūyah is not king. But the relevant aphorism here is what is said, 'God wills a thing, and it is; the king commands a thing, and it is put into execution.'[955] So let Asfādh Jushnas enter and deliver the message he bears."

When Jīlinūs heard this speech, he went out from Kisrā's presence, took Asfādh Jushnas's hand, and said to him, "Arise, and come into Kisrā's presence, in a correct manner." Asfādh Jushnas accordingly stood up, called for one of the attendants accompanying him, and handed him the robe he [ordinarily] wore, pulled out a clean, white cloth from his sleeve and used it to wipe his face.[956] Then he went into Kisrā's presence. When he came face to face with him, he fell down before him in prostration. Kisrā ordered him to get up. Hence he arose and did obeisance before Kisrā. Kisrā was seated on three Khusrawānī rugs woven with gold, which had been laid on a silken carpet, and he was lolling back on three cushions likewise woven with gold. In his hand he had a yellow, well-rounded quince. When he noticed Asfādh Jushnas, he sat up in a cross-legged position and placed the quince on the place [1049]
where he had been sitting. Because it was perfectly round and because of the smoothness of the cushion on the seat, plumped out with its stuffing, it rolled down from the topmost of the three cushions on to the upper one of the three rugs, then from the rug to the carpet, finally rolling off the carpet to the ground, where it rolled some distance, becoming covered with dirt. Asfādh Jushnas

955. Echoing frequent Qur'ānic phraseology, e.g., in XXXVI, 82; XL, 70/68.

956. The text has *shushtaqah* for this cloth. The *Glossarium*, p. CCCXI, has *shustaqah* and adduces the commentary to Abū Dulaf al-Khazrajī's *Qaṣīdah sāsāniyyah* as given in al-Tha'ālibī's *Yatīmat al-dahr;* but the word here should be read as *suftajahu* "his financial draft." See Bosworth, *The Mediaeval Islamic Underworld, The Banū Sāsān in Arabic Society and Literature*, II, *The Arabic Jargon Texts*, Arabic text 7, comm. v. 34, tr. 193. In any case, it seems that the action here is not that of wiping the face clean but of placing the *pandāmah* over the mouth to prevent pollution of a sacred object, in this case, the king's person. See Nöldeke, trans. 367 n. 1, and n. 892 above.

picked it up and rubbed it with his sleeve, moving forward to present it to Kisrā. But the latter gestured to Asfādh Jushnas to keep it away from him, and told him, "Take it away from me!" So Asfādh Jushnas laid it on the ground at the carpet's edge, fell back, stood in his old place, and did obeisance before Kisrā by putting his hand on his breast. Kisrā lowered his head and then uttered the aphorism appropriate to the incident: "When one encounters adversity, there is no means or device (*ḥīlah*) for making things go forward again, and when things do go well, there is no means or device which is able to reverse them. These two things happen in turn, but means and devices are lacking in both cases." Then he said to Asfādh Jushnas, "Thus this quince has rolled down and fallen where it did, and become smeared with dirt. It is for us an announcement, as it were, of the message you have been charged with bringing, what you are going to do with it, and its results. For indeed, the quince, which denotes what is good, fell from the heights to the depths; it did not stay on the coverings of our seat but speedily fell to the ground, ending up far away and covered in dirt.[957] All this happening indicates a bad omen, that the glory of the monarchs has passed into the hands of the common masses, that we have been deprived of royal power, and that it will not remain long in the hands of our successors before it passes to persons who are not of royal stock (*min ahl al-mamlakah*). Now get on with it, and speak about the message you have been charged with delivering and the words with which you have been pro-
[1050] vided!" Asfādh Jushnas then began to retail the message Shīrūyah had charged him to deliver, not leaving out a single word and getting the sequence of its phrases exactly right.

Kisrā made the following answer to that message: Convey back to Shīrūyah, the short-lived one,[958] [the message] from me that it

957. It appears from this that the quince was regarded by the Persians as an emblem of good fortune (perhaps not uninfluenced by the closeness in form of *bih*, "good," and *bihī*, "quince" = the Arabic *safarjalah* used here in al-Ṭabarī's text); cf. *Glossarium*, p. CCXCII. The significance of the quince subsequently became the focus of a minor academic controversy among German orientalists; see the details in Muth, *Die Annalen von aṭ-Ṭabarī im Spiegel der europäischen Bearbeitungen*, 58–59.

958. Prophetic of Shērōy's brief period of power and his early death through epidemic disease or, according to one report, by poisoning, see al-Ṭabarī, I, 1061, p. 399, and n. 984 below.

is not fitting for an intelligent person that he should spread around about anyone [tales of] venial sins and minor misdeeds without having thoroughly convinced himself of their truth and being completely certain in his own mind about them, let alone the gross sins and crimes that you have spread around and published abroad, and that you have imputed to us and laid at our door. Moreover, the person who can best repel with contumely a sinner and condemn the perpetrator of a crime is the one who has kept himself free from all sins and crimes. O man who will be short reigned, O man of little understanding, even if we were guilty of what you have imputed to us, it is unfitting that you should spread it abroad and upbraid us. For if you do not recognize the defects you yourself possess, since you have spread them around concerning us as you have done, you should be fully aware of your own defects. So cut short your blaming us and finding fault with us, since your ill-chosen speech only increases the public awareness of your own ignorance and lack of judgment.

O one devoid of reason, deficient in knowledge! If there is any real basis for your efforts in showing us up publicly as guilty of sins which deserve death for us and you have some real proof for it, then [you should remember that] the judges among your own religious community (i.e., the Zoroastrian one) prevent the son of a man who has merited death from assuming his father's position and keep him from contact with the best people, from sitting with them and from mingling with them, except in a small number of places, much less making him king. Furthermore, we have [1051]
attained—praise be to God and [thanks for] His beneficence!—through our upright behavior and intentions and in our relationship with God, with the adherents of our religious community and faith, and with the whole group of our sons, a position in which we have in no way fallen short nor deserved any proof of guilt or any reproach. We shall explain the situation regarding the sins you have imputed to us and the crimes you have laid at our door, without any attempt on our part to diminish anything in the arguments we have put forward and the proofs we have adduced, if only so that you might acquire fuller knowledge of your own lack of judgment, absence of reason and the evil nature of your actions.

[First,] regarding what you have mentioned in regard to our father Hurmuz, our rejoinder here is that evil and malevolent persons had incited him against us, to the point that he grew suspicious of us and was carried away by hatred and rancor against us. We perceived his revulsion from us and his bad opinion of us, and we accordingly became fearful of remaining in his proximity, so removed ourself from his court out of fear from him and made our way to Azerbaijan. By that time, the royal power had become dissolved and split apart, as is well known. As soon as we received news of what had happened to him, we set out from Azerbaijan for his court. But the false-hearted (*munāfiq*) Bahrām [Chūbīn] assailed us with a great army of rebels, whose conduct merited death, threw off his obedience, and drove us out of the kingdom. We sought asylum in the land of the Byzantines, and came back from there with troops and war materials, and made war on him. As a result, he fled before us and ended up in the land of the Turks, with destruction and perdition, as has been generally known among people.

Finally, when we had achieved firm control of the realm and our authority was made firm and, with the help of God, we had dispeled for our subjects all the afflictions and calamities, on the brink of which they had been, we then said [to ourselves], "One of the best courses of action with which we can inaugurate our ruling policy and begin our royal power is to take vengeance for our
[1052] father, to secure requital for him and to kill all those involved in [shedding] his blood." Then, when we had firmly accomplished all our intentions regarding that and had attained what we were aiming at, we turned our attention to other aspects of the governance of the kingdom. So we put to death everyone who had a share in [shedding] his blood or who had schemed and plotted against him.

[Second,] regarding what you have mentioned concerning our sons, our rebuttal here is that all the sons whom we brought into the world, with the exception of those whom God chose to take back unto Himself, were perfectly sound in the limbs of their bodies. But we appointed for you guards and restrained you from getting mixed up in things that did not concern you, out of a desire to prevent you from doing harm to the land and the subjects. So we established for you ample means for your living expenses, such as for your clothing, for your riding mounts, and for everything you needed, as you well know. In respect to you (i.e., Shīrūyah) in particular, the story is that the astrologers had decreed from your

horoscope (*kitāb mawlidika*) that you would bring evil upon us, or that evil would happen through your agency. Nevertheless, we did not order you to be put to death but put a seal on the document indicating your horoscope and handed it over to our consort Shīrīn's keeping. In confirmation of the fact that we placed full credence in that document with the indication [of the horoscope], it happened that Furumīshā, king of India, wrote to us in the thirty-sixth year of our reign, having sent a delegation of his subjects to us.[959] He wrote about all sorts of things and sent to us and to you, the ensemble of our sons, presents, together with a letter to each one of you. His presents to you—you will recall them!—comprised an elephant, a sword, a white falcon, and a brocade coat woven with gold. When we looked at the presents he had sent you, we found that he had written on his letter to you, in the Indian language, "Keep the contents of this secret." We then gave orders that all the presents or letters he had sent to each of you should be [1053]
passed on to you all, and we [merely] kept back his letter to you because of its superscription. We sent for an Indian scribe and ordered the letter's seal to be broken and its contents to be read out. There was written there, 'Rejoice, be refreshed in spirit and be happy in mind, for you will be crowned on the day Day ba-Ādhar in the month of Ādhar of the thirty-eighth year of Kisrā's reign[960] and be hailed as holder of his royal power and ruler of his lands.' We were convinced that you would only attain to royal power through our own destruction and perdition, yet despite being certain about this, we did not make any reduction in the living allowances, subsidies, presents, and such, previously assigned to you, let alone order you to be put to death. We resealed

959. As correctly conjectured by Nöldeke, trans. 371 n. 1, this name reflects that of a leading king of the early mediaeval northern Deccan, but to be rendered as Pulakesin II (r. ca. 609–42), from the Chālukya dynasty. It would thus have been perfectly possible for Khusraw Abarwēz to have received a delegation from this ruler in the thirty-sixth year of his reign, i.e., 626. See A. L. Basham, *The Wonder That Was India. A Survey of the Culture of the Indian Sub-Continent before the Coming of the Muslims*, 74–75; R. C. Majumdar (ed.), *The History and Culture of the Indian People*, III, *The Classical Age*, 234–41. An alternative interpretation of this name was suggested, however, by von Gutschmid, "Bemerkungen zu Tabari's Sasanidengeschichte," 746: that it represents the common Indian royal title Paramēśa "supreme lord."

960. See al-Ṭabarī, I, 1043, p. 379 and n. 938 above.

Furumīshā's letter with our own seal and entrusted it to our consort Shīrīn, who is still alive and sound in mind and body. If you wish to retrieve from her the indications of your horoscope and Furumīshā's letter to you and read them both in order to bring home to you your contrition and loss, then do it!

[Third,] in regard to what you have mentioned concerning the condition of those condemned to perpetual imprisonment, we say in justification that the ancient kings, from the time of Jayūmart (Kayūmarth) till the reign of Bishtāsb,[961] used to conduct their royal power by means of justice, and then continuously from the time of Bishtāsb till we ourselves assumed power, they conducted it by means of justice combined with religious piety. Now, since you are so devoid of reason, knowledge, and education, ask the authorities (*ḥamalah*) in religion, the basic supports (literally, "tent pegs," *awtād*) of this religious community, about the position of those who rebel against and disobey the kings, who break their oaths, and those who have merited death for their sins, and they will tell you that they do not deserve to be shown mercy or forgiveness. Know that, despite all this, we have only condemned to perpetual imprisonment in our gaols those who, if an equitable
[1054] judgment were to be made, have merited being killed or blinded or having a hand or leg or some other limb cut off. How often have those appointed to guard them, or various of our ministers, mentioned the well-deserved fate of those who merit execution and have said, "Kill them speedily, before they find ways and means of killing *you!*" Yet, because of our wish to spare lives and our dislike of shedding blood, we acted slowly and deliberately with them and left them to God, and we used not to go further in punishing them beyond the imprisonment to which we limited ourselves in inflicting, beyond depriving them of eating meat, drinking wine, and enjoying the fragrance of aromatic herbs. In none of these things that were withheld were we going beyond what is in the precepts of the religious community in regard to keeping those who have merited death from enjoying the pleasures of life and easy circum-

961. That is, from the time of Gayōmard (thus the MP form), the first man, to that of Gushtāsp (Avestan Wištāspa-, MP Wishtāsp), son of Luhrāsp, in whose reign Zoroaster is supposed to have arisen. See Yarshater, "Iranian Common Beliefs and World View," 352–53; idem, "Iranian National History," 376–77, 466–69.

stances. [On the contrary,] we used to allot for them the food, drink, and other necessities for keeping them in good health, and we used not to keep them from access to their womenfolk and from the possibility of contact for siring children and producing progeny while they were imprisoned. Now the news has reached us that you have decided to set free these evil doers and evil wishers who merit execution and to give orders for demolishing their gaol. If you do release them, you will sin against God your Lord, bring down harm upon yourself, and inflict injury on your own faith and the injunctions and legal prescriptions contained in it, which deny mercy and forgiveness for those who deserve execution. In addition to this, [there is the fact] that the enemies of kings never love kingly power, and those who rebel against kings never furnish them obedience. The wise men have given the warning, "Don't hold back from punishing those who have merited punishment, for such hesitation entails an impairment of justice and harmful effects on the governance of the kingdom." Although it may give you a certain feeling of joy when you set free those evil doers, evil wishers, and rebels who deserve execution, you will certainly experience the [baleful] result of that in your conduct of government and the introduction of the severest harm and [1055] calamitousness for the people of your religious community.

[Fifth,][962] regarding your allegations that we have only acquired, gathered together, and laid up in our treasuries wealth, equipment and utensils, grain, and so forth, from the lands of our kingdom by means of the harshest methods of tax gathering, the most pressing demands on our subjects, and the most violent tyranny, rather than from the lands of the enemy by making war on them and forcible seizure by ourselves of their possessions, our reply is as follows. The best answer to any statement uttered with gross ignorance and stupidity is not to give any answer at all, but we have not wished to leave this aside, since not giving an answer is tantamount to affirming the truth [of the original statement]. Our rejoinder to the accusations laid against us is a vigorous rebuttal of

962. As Nöldeke, trans. 374 n. 1, noted, this fifth section of Khusraw's response covers both Shērōy's fifth and sixth accusations without clearly distinguishing the two. Shērōy's seventh and eighth accusations are not addressed by his father, as least in the words that have come down to us.

them, and our clear exculpation is an exposition of what you have sought from us regarding it.

Know, O ignorant one, that, after God, it is only wealth and troops that can uphold the royal authority of monarchs, this being especially the case with the kingdom of Persia, whose lands are surrounded by enemies with gaping mouths ready to gulp down what the kingdom possesses. The only thing that can keep them from it and fend them off from those lands they avidly desire to seize for themselves, is numerous troops and copious quantities of weapons and war material. Now numerous troops and everything necessary for these can only be acquired by having a great deal of wealth and ample quantities of it; and wealth can only be amassed and gathered together, for any contingency which may arise, by strenuous efforts and dedication in levying this land tax. We are not the first ones to have gathered together wealth; on the contrary, we have merely imitated here our forefathers and our predecessors in past times. They collected wealth just as we have, and amassed great quantities of it, so that it might constitute a firm backing for them in strengthening their armies, in upholding their authority, and in [making possible] other things for which wealth must inevitably be amassed. But then the false-hearted one Bahrām, with a gang of people like himself and with desperadoes who merited being put to death, attacked that wealth and those
[1056] jewels in our treasuries. They scattered and dispersed them and went off with a great deal of them, and they left behind in our storehouses of wealth and treasuries only a few of our weapons which they were unable to scatter to the winds or remove or else had no desire for them. When, God be praised, we recovered our kingly power and our authority was firmly reestablished, when the subjects submitted to us and gave obedience, and we removed the calamities which had befallen them, we dispatched to the outlying parts of our land Iṣbabadhs, we appointed below them in those regions Fādhūsbāns, and we nominated over the frontier zones Marzbāns and courageous, energetic, and tough executive officials. All those whom we appointed we provided with a strong backing of numerous troops, and these officials led vigorous campaigns against the hostile kings and the enemies into the lands facing their own territories. From the thirteenth year of our reign

onward,[963] their raids against the enemies, the slaughter they wrought, and the captives they took, [reached to such an extent] that none of those hostile rulers could dare to raise his head even in the heart of his own kingdom except under a protective cover, with fearfulness, or under a grant of protection from us, let alone to mount a raid into any part of our land or to engage in anything unacceptable to us. Hence during all this period of years, there came into our storehouses of wealth and our treasuries what had been seized as plunder from the lands of our enemies, comprising gold, silver, all sorts of jewels, copper, steel, silk, silk brocades (*istabraq*),[964] brocade coats, horses, weapons, captured women and children and male prisoners, whose enormous extent cannot be concealed and whose value is known to everyone.

When at the end of the thirteenth year of our reign we gave instructions for the engraving of new dies for coins (*naqsh sikak ḥadīthah*), so that we might give our orders for beginning the minting of new silver coinage with their aid, there was found at the end of the minting process in our storehouses of wealth, according to what was reported back to us by the persons charged with counting the silver which was left there, apart from the [1057] sums of money which we had instructed should be set aside for paying the salaries of our troops, two hundred thousand purses of silver coinage, containing eight hundred million mithqāls [in weight].[965]

When we perceived that we had made our frontiers secure, had repulsed the enemy from them and from our subjects, had put a muzzle on their mouths, which had been gaping open to swallow up what they had acquired, had extended over them (i.e., the subjects) security, and had preserved the inhabitants of the four outlying quarters of our land from calamities and raids, we gave orders

963. That is, the year 602, when the Byzantine emperor Maurice was overthrown and murdered (see n. 743 above), after which Khusraw could claim to be avenging the death of the usurper Phocas.

964. This is itself a loanword in Arabic (and in Syriac), and an early one, since it is used in the Qur'ān of the silk brocade garments of the saved in Paradise (XVIII, 30/31; XLIV, 53; etc.). See Siddiqi, *Studien über die persischen Fremdwörter*, 8 n. 2, 13; Jeffery, *The Foreign Vocabulary of the Qur'ān*, 58–60.

965. Here, as Nöldeke pointed out, trans. 376 n. 2, not meaning a weight in gold.

for the collection of the arrears of taxation remaining from previous years and for the restoration to their original place of all the gold and silver that had been carried off from our storehouses of wealth and all the jewels and copperware that had come from our treasuries.[966] Hence at the end of the thirtieth year of our reign we gave orders for the engraving of new dies for coins, from which silver coins could be struck, and there was found in our storehouses of wealth, apart from what we had ordered to be set aside for paying the salaries of our troops and apart from the sums of money already counted up for us previously, four hundred thousand purses of silver coinage, containing one billion, six hundred million mithqāls [in weight]. All this in addition to what God added for us to those sums of money from what He presented to us as booty and of His liberality and lavishness upon us, out of the wealth of the rulers of Byzantium which the wind brought us in ships and which we called "plunder of the winds (*fay' al-riyāḥ*)."[967]

From the thirtieth year of our reign to the thirty-eighth, which is the present year, our stores of weath have not ceased growing in extent and richness, our lands in florescence, our subjects in security and tranquility, and our frontiers and peripheral regions in impregnability and strength of defenses. We have now heard that you intend, because of the abysmally low level of your manly virtues, to scatter abroad and destroy all this wealth, acting on the advice of evil doers who merit being put to death.[968] We are now telling you, however, that those treasures and wealth were only

966. These activities, as Nöldeke noted, trans. 377 n. 1, could hardly have been carried out without using violence, with resultant great hardship for the populace, and in the case of the recovery of wealth allegedly filched from the central treasury, the innocent would doubtless suffer equally with the guilty.

967. This may conceivably relate distantly to an actual happening. Ibn Qutaybah, *Ma'ārif*, 665, says that a fleet of the king of Constantinople bearing treasure was cast up on the Mediterranean shores at Alexandria (the *khazā'in al-rīḥ*), and, slightly more circumstantially, al-Mas'ūdī, *Murūj*, II, 227–8 = § 647, says that a fleet of treasure ships of Phocas was thrown up on the Syrian coast at Antioch, where Khusraw's general Shahrbarāz was able to seize the wealth and forward it to his master. Nöldeke, trans. 378 n. 1, cited an authority who suggested that the incident might relate to some treasure that Heraclius despatched to North Africa, before he became involved in the Persian wars, and which was lost at sea.

968. According to Ibn Qutaybah, *Ma'ārif*, 665, Shērōy lightened taxes and did not collect the *kharāj*.

gathered together through exposing one's life to danger and after intense exertion and effort in order to repel by means of them the [1058] enemies who were surrounding the lands of this kingdom and who were pursuing courses aimed at getting full control of what they had acquired. Enemies like these can only be driven off, in all periods and times, and after receiving help from God, by wealth and troops; troops can only be kept strong by wealth; and wealth is only of use when it is available in large and extensive amounts. So don't contemplate dividing out this wealth and don't rush rashly into doing it, for wealth is a protection for your royal power and your land, and a source of strength for you against your enemies.

Asfādh Jushnas then went back to Shīrūyah and related to him what Kisrā had said to him, not leaving out a single word. The great men of state among the Persians came back and told Shīrūyah, "It is not fitting that we should have two kings. Either you give orders for Kisrā to be put to death, and we shall be your servants, furnishing obedience to you, or else we shall depose you and give him obedience [once more]." These words struck fear into Shīrūyah's heart and crushed him. He ordered Kisrā to be executed. Several men who had duties incumbent upon them of vengeance against Kisrā responded to the call to kill him. But every time one of them came to Kisrā, he heaped insults on the man and repelled him strongly. No one would undertake the task of killing Kisrā until finally, a youth named Mihr Hurmuz, son of Mardānshāh, went along to kill him. Mardānshāh was Kisrā's Fādhūsbān over the province of Nīmrūz[969] and one of Kisrā's most obedient and trusty retainers.

Now some two years before his deposition, Kisrā had asked his astrologers and diviners[970] what his end would be, and they had

969. That is, the region of the south, see al-Ṭabarī, I, 894, p. 149, and n. 385 above. The geography ascribed to Moses Khorenac'i defines the *K'usti Nemroy* as extending from Lower Iraq and Hajar, from Iṣfahān, Fārs, and Khūzistān, to Kirmān, Sīstān, Makrān, and Tūrān (both in the later Baluchistan), Zābulistān (in what is now eastern Afghanistan), and Daybul on the coast of Sind. See Marquart, *Ērānšahr*, 25–47.

970. *'āfah*, pl. of *'ā'if*, was the diviner who took auguries from the flight or cries of birds, the practice of *'iyāfah*, ornithomancy. Among the early Arabs, this was essentially that practiced by the Greek and Roman augurs. See Fahd, *La divination arabe*, 371, 432–34.

told him that his fated death (*maniyyatahu*)[971] would come from the direction of Nīmrūz. He accordingly grew suspicious of Mardānshāh and fearful of his proximity, on account of Mardānshāh's great prestige and because there was no one in that region who
[1059] could equal him in strength and power. Kisrā had written to him instructing him to travel quickly to him, until by the time Mardānshāh had reached him, he had turned over in his mind how he might seek a pretext to kill him. But he had not found any fault in Mardānshāh. Kisrā accordingly recoiled from killing him because of his knowledge about Mardānshāh's faithful obedience to him, his good counsel to him and his eagerness to please the king. So he resolved to spare his life but to order his right hand to be cut off, and to compensate him for its loss by a grant of a large sum of money, lavishing wealth on him for this. Hence he sought for a pretext that would enable him to have Mardānshāh's right hand cut off.[972]

Hands and feet and heads used to be cut off in the open space before the royal palace (*raḥbat al-mulk*).[973] On the day when he had ordered Mardānshāh's hand to be cut off, Kisrā sent along a scout and observer (*ʿayn*), who was to come back to him and inform him of what he had heard Mardānshāh and the onlookers who were present saying. When Mardānshāh's right hand was cut off, he took it up with his left hand, kissed it, and placed it in his bosom, and he began to lament over it with his tears streaming down, saying, "Alas for a mild and forbearing [hand], one which used to shoot, and write, and deal blows, and engage in sport, and dispensed largesse!" The man whom Kisrā had sent along as a scout and observer over Mardānshāh went back to Kisrā and told

---

971. *maniyyah*, pls. *manāyā* and perhaps *manūn*, is literally "the determination, decreeing, of a man's fate," hence a synonym for death and a term much used in early Arabic poetry. See Caskel, *Das Schicksal in der altarabischen Poesie*, 22–42; H. Ringgren, *Studies in Arabian Fatalism*, 14–23; Mohamed Abdesselem, *Le thème de la mort dans la poésie arabe des origines à la fin du IIIe/IXe siècle*, 57, cf. 71.

972. The story of the mutilation of the courtier by the ruler because of the prognostication that the courtier's son would bring about Khusraw's death, is given very briefly in al-Yaʿqūbī, *Taʾrīkh*, I, 196, with the tale cut short because of a lacuna in the manuscript used by the editor Houtsma.

973. Nöldeke noted, trans. 380 n. 1, the predilection of Persian kings, from Achaemenid up to Qājār times, for public executions and mutilations.

him what he had seen and heard Mardānshāh doing and saying. At this, Kisrā became full of tenderness and sympathy for him, and regretted his impetuosity regarding Mardānshāh. He sent a message to him via one of the great men of state expressing his regret for what he had done to Mardānshāh and telling him that he would fulfill, so far as was in his power, any request to him which Mardānshāh might make and would facilitate this for him. Mardānshāh sent back a message to Kisrā by that same envoy, invoking blessings on the king and saying, "O king, I have always recognized your beneficence to me, and I thank you for it; I have become fully convinced that what you have inflicted on me was done unwillingly. It was merely a stroke of fate that caused this. But I have one request to make of you: give me oaths that you will fulfill it, so that my mind may be set at rest. Also, send to me, on your solemn undertaking to fulfill the oath, a pious man of God, and then I will reveal and communicate [my request] to you." Kisrā's envoy returned to his master with this message, and Kisrā hastened to put into effect Mardānshāh's request, and swore mighty oaths that he would without fail accede to his request so [1060]
long as this last did not entail anything which would weaken the fabric of his royal power. Kisrā dispatched this message to Mardānshāh via the Chief [Zoroastrian] Priest (literally, "head of the murmurers," *ra'īs al-muzamzimīn*). Mardānshāh sent back a message to Kisrā asking him to order his (Mardānshāh's) execution, in order that the dishonor which [now] attached to him might be thereby effaced.[974] Kisrā gave the requisite order for Mardānshāh's head to be cut off, unwilling, as he asserted, to break his oath.

When Mihr Hurmuz, Mardānshāh's son, came into Kisrā's presence, the latter asked Mihr Hurmuz his name and that of his father and his position in the state. He told him that he was Mihr Hurmuz, son of Mardānshāh, the Fādhūsbān of Nīmrūz. Kisrā said, "You are the son of a a noble, highly sufficient, and competent man whom we requited for his faithfulness and good counsel to us, and for his sufficiency and competence with us, in an undeserving manner; so set to, and get on with what you have been ordered to do!" So Mihr Hurmuz struck, with an axe that he held

974. That is, the dishonor of continuing to live as a mutilated person, hence unable to fill any office in the state or in the Zoroastrian church.

in his hand, several blows at the sinews of Kisrā's neck running down to his shoulder, but these had no effect on Kisrā. The latter was searched, and it was discovered that a jewel in the form of an amulet[975] had been tied on his upper arm (or, "he had tied an amulet on his upper arm"). The amulet protected its wearer from the effects of a sword. The amulet was accordingly taken off Kisrā, and then after that Mihr Hurmuz delivered a single blow which killed him.[976]

The news was brought to Shīrūyah, who tore the front part of the neck of his robe and wept copiously; he gave orders for Kisrā's corpse to be borne to the place of sepulture. This was done. All the great men of state and the people of the classes just below them (*afnā' al-nās*)[977] accompanied his corpse [to the place of burial]. He ordered Mihr Hurmuz executed. Kisrā's tenure of royal power lasted thirty-eight years. He was killed on the day of Māh in the month of Ādhar.[978] Shīrūyah killed seventeen of his brothers, men of good education, bravery, and the manly virtues,[979] on the advice of his minister Fayrūz[980] and at the urging of one of the sons of Yazdīn, who was the official in charge of the [collection of the] land tax (literally, "tithes," *'ushūr*) from the entire lands for
[1061] Kisrā and who was called Shamṭā,[981] that he should put them to death.

975. Apparently the reading here is *kharazah* rather than *ḥirzah*. See *Addenda et emendanda*, p. DXCVI, and *Glossarium*, pp. CCXVII–CCXVIII.

976. Nöldeke, trans. 382 n. 1, discussed the information of other sources, including Christian ones, on the exact mode of Khusraw's execution, but concluded that there was no firm evidence concerning this mode.

977. Arabic *afnā'*, sing. *finw*, is defined in the lexica as "people from mixed groups." Here the meaning clearly relates to people high in the Persian social hierarchy who alone would accompany the catafalque of a king. Nöldeke, trans. 382, has "die Ausgesehnsten der Leute," i.e., the most outstanding, prominent people.

978. Nöldeke, trans. 382 n. 2, gives the equivalent of this date as 29 February 628.

979. The Arabic sources, and also the Christian ones, have various totals for these brothers usually around sixteen to eighteen; Ḥamzah al-Iṣfahānī, *Ta'rīkh*, 54, actually names eighteen of them. See the discussion in Nöldeke, 383 n. 1.

980. Bal'amī's Persian rendering of al-Ṭabarī's *History*, tr. II, 346, makes Shērōy's chief minister Barmak, son of Fīrūz, ancestor of the Barmakī family so prominent in the caliphate during early 'Abbāsid times. Nöldeke, trans. 313 n. 2, thought that this was a later touch inserted by an enemy of the Islamic Barmakīs.

981. The very defective rendering of this name in the text was read thus by the editor Nöldeke, who identified Shamṭā's father Yazdīn from the Christian sources,

Shīrūyah was now afflicted by illness and never enjoyed any of the pleasures of this present world. He died at Daskarat al-Malik. He was an inauspicious figure for the house of Sāsān.[982] When he killed his brothers, he showed violent grief. It is said that, on the day after he had killed them, his two sisters Būrān and Āzar-mīdukht[983] came into his presence and reviled and upbraided him harshly, saying, "Greed for a royal power which is still not yet firmly established has driven you to kill your father and all your brothers, and you have committed acts of dishonor." When he heard those words, he wept bitterly and tore the crown from off his head. All his days he was overwhelmed with cares and afflicted by sickness. It is said that he extirpated every member of his house on whom he could get his hands, and that plague spread during his time until most of the Persians perished.[984] His tenure of royal power lasted eight months.[985]

---

principally the Syriac historians and hagiographers and the conciliar acts of the Nestorian Church, as Khusraw's treasurer Yazdīn (see n. 737 above). One Nestorian author, Thomas of Margā, describes Shamṭā as the real driving force behind the conspiracy to dethrone Khusraw. See Nöldeke, trans. 357 n. 4, 383 n. 3. However, according to the *Anonymus Guidi,* tr. 30–31, Shamṭā soon showed himself overly ambitious for power, was accused of conspiring to seize the throne, arrested, his right hand cut off and consigned to prison by Shērōy.

On the name Yazdīn, see Justi, *Namenbuch,* 147–48. Whether this Yazdīn was the same person as the governor of Armenia for Khusraw Abarwēz, the Yazdēn of the Armenian historian Sebēos (see ibid.), is unclear.

982. And called by the Persians, according to al-Mas'ūdī, *Murūj,* II, 232 = § 653, the equivalent of Arabic *al-ghashūm,* "the tyrannical one." On the other hand, the *Anonymus Guidi,* tr. 30, states that Shērōy's reign was one of peace and security for the Christians of the realm.

983. That is, Shērōy's eventual, ephemeral successors on the Persian throne, see al-Ṭabarī, I, 1063–64, 1064–65, pp. 403–405, 406–407, below.

984. This plague is mentioned in other sources (e.g., Ibn Qutaybah, *Ma'ārif,* 665; al-Mas'ūdī, *Murūj,* II, 232 = § 653; and Ibn al-Athīr, *Kāmil,* I, 497) as having devastated Iraq, with, according to Ibn Qutaybah and Ibn al-Athīr, the king himself dying from the disease. Less probably, the Byzantine historian Theophanes states that Shērōy was poisoned by his hostile stepmother Shīrīn; see Christensen, *Sassanides,* 497 n. 1.

985. Kawād II Shērōy reigned for six or eight months in 628. His name appears on his coins as PYRWCY KW'T. See on his coins Paruck, *Sāsānian Coins,* 68, 390–92, 492, Plate XXII, Table XXX; Göbl, *Sasanian Numismatics,* 54–55, Table XIII, Plate 14; Selwood, Whitting and Williams, *An Introduction to Sasanian Coins,* 21, 159–60; Malek, "A Survey of Research on Sasanian Numismatics," 238.

The other Arabic sources on his reign include Ibn Qutaybah, *Ma'ārif,* 665; al-Ya'qūbī, *Ta'rīkh,* I, 196; al-Dīnawarī, *al-Akhbār al-ṭiwāl,* 110; al-Mas'ūdī, *Murūj,*

## *[Ardashīr III]*

After him there succeeded to the royal power Ardashīr. [He was] the son of [Qubādh II] Shīrūyah, son of [Khusraw II] Abarwīz, son of Hurmuz (IV), son of [Khusraw I] Anūsharwān, and was only a small child. It is said that he was only seven years old, since there was no grown-up person of judgment and experience left of the royal house; hence the great men of the Persian state made him king.[986] A man called Mih Ādhar Jushnas, who held the office of high steward of the table (*ri'āsat aṣḥāb al-mā'idah*),[987] was in charge of his upbringing. He carried on the administration of the kingdom in an excellent fashion, and his firm conduct of it reached a point where no one would have been aware of Ardashīr's youthfulness.

Shahrbarāz was at the frontier with Byzantium with troops whom Kisrā had given him and had named "the fortunate ones" (*al-su'adā'*).[988] Kisrā and Shīrūyah had continuously written to him regarding important matters in which they were involved, and had sought his advice concerning these. But now, since the great men of state of the Persians had not consulted him about
[1062] raising Ardashīr to the throne, he took that as a pretext for making accusations of criminal behavior and demands on them, and went as far as shedding blood, and made it an occasion for endeavoring to seize the royal power and to rise by means of that from the lowly status of serving people to the heights of royal power. Shahrbarāz treated Ardashīr with contempt because of his youth

---

II, 233–34 = § 653; idem, *Tanbīh*, 102, tr. 146; Ḥamzah al-Iṣfahānī, *Ta'rīkh*, 54; Ibn al-Athīr, *Kāmil*, I, 494–97. Of Persian sources, see Ṭabarī-Bal'amī, tr. II, 332–47. Of modern studies, see Christensen, *Sassanides*, 493–97; Frye, "The Political History of Iran under the Sasanians," 170, 178.

986. From this point onward, all the remaining Persian kings and queens, with the exception of the capable, non-Sāsānid Shahrbarāz, who seized power for himself, were set on the throne as puppets of the nobility and great men of state and church.

987. In Persian, *khwān-sālār*, which Nöldeke noted, trans. 386 n. 2, was the term used by Bal'amī in his rendering of al-Ṭabarī's *History*.

988. Shahrbarāz made peace with Heraclius in July 629 at Arabissos in eastern Anatolia (see al-Ṭabarī, I, 1008–1009, pp. 329–30 and n. 776 above), and was thus free to turn his attention to Mesopotamia and take advantage of the unsettled conditions there. Quite possibly he claimed to be the avenger of the murdered Khusraw Abarwēz, since al-Dīnawarī, *al-Akhbār al-ṭiwāl*, 111, says that, when Shahrbarāz entered al-Madā'in, he put to death all those who had conspired to depose and kill Khusraw; cf. also Nöldeke, trans. 387 n. 1.

and acted arrogantly toward the great men of state. He decided to summon together the ruling classes of the people (*al-nās*) for a consultation over the matter of the royal power. He then advanced with his troops.

Meanwhile, Mih Ādhar Jushnas had embarked on fortifying and strengthening the walls and gates of the city of Ctesiphon, and he transfered Ardashīr and the remaining members of the royal house, their womenfolk, the contents of Ardashīr's treasury—that is, money and his treasure chests—and his horses, into the city of Ctesiphon. Shahrbarāz's troops, with whom he now approached, numbered six thousand men from the Persian army on the Byzantine frontiers.[989] He took up a position near the city of Ctesiphon, besieged its inhabitants and fought with them, setting up ballistas against the city, but did not manage to enter it. When he realized that he was not strong enough to take it by force, he sought it by means of craft. He kept on inciting a man named Nīw Khusraw, who was the commander of Ardashīr's guard, and Nāmdār Jushnas, son of Ādhar Jushnas, the Iṣbabadh of Nīmrūz, to treachery, until the two of them opened the gates of the city to Shahbarāz. Thus he entered it, seized a number of the leading men, and killed them, appropriating their wealth for himself and ravishing their womenfolk. At Shahbarāz's behest, a group of men killed Ardashīr, son of Shīrūyah, in the second year of his reign, in the month of Bahman, on the night of the day Abān, in the palace of Khusraw Shāh Qubādh. He had held the royal power for one year and six months.[990]

989. As Nöldeke remarked, trans. 387 n. 2, it was indicative of the chaos and weakness into which the Persian state had fallen that such a modest force was able to take over the capital and secure power for Shahrbarāz himself.

990. Nöldeke noted, trans. 388 n. 4, 432–33, that this date in Bahman, the tenth day of the eleventh month, corresponds to 27 April 630, and that Ardashīr's reign had, on the basis of his coins, two years, the first identical with the seven months making up the last year of his father Kawād II Shērōy and the second one of independent rule beginning on 17 June 629. His reign would thus total one year and slightly under six months. Ardashīr's name appears on his coins as 'RTḤŠTR. See on his coins Paruck, *Sāsānian Coins*, 68–69, 391–92, 491–92, Plate XXII, Table XXXI; Göbl, *Sasanian Numismatics*, 54–55, Table 13, Plate 14; Sellwood, Whitting, and Williams, *An Introduction to Sasanian Coins*, 21, 161–63; Malek, "A Survey of Research on Sasanian Numismatics," 238; *EIr*, s.v. Ardašīr III (A. Sh. Shahbazi).

The other Arabic sources on his reign include Ibn Qutaybah, *Ma'ārif*, 665; al-Ya'qūbī, *Ta'rīkh*, I, 196; al-Dīnawarī, *al-Akhbār al-ṭiwāl*, 110–11 (wrongly named

## [*Shahrbarāz*]

After him, there succeeded to the royal power Shahrbarāz, that is, Farrukhān, for the month of Isfandār(madh); he was not of the
[1063] royal house of the kingdom. He proclaimed himself king, but when he sat down on the royal throne, his belly began to gripe, and this affected him so violently that he had no time to get to a latrine, hence he [swiftly] called for a bowl (*ṭast*), had it set down before the throne, and relieved himself in it.[991]

A man from the people of Iṣṭakhr called Fus Farrūkh, son of Mā(h) Khurshidhān,[992] and two of his brothers were roused to great anger at Shahrbarāz's killing of Ardashīr and his seizure of the royal power. They felt an intense revulsion from that, and came together and swore mutually that they would kill him. All three of them belonged to the king's personal guard. It was [at that time] the custom that, when the king rode out, his personal guard stood in two lines, with their mailed coats, helmets, shields, and swords, and with spears in their hands; then, when the king came up level with one of them, each of them laid his shield on the wooden forepart (*qarabūs*, i.e., pommel) of the king's saddle[993] and placed his forehead on it, as if he were prostrating himself on

---

as Shīrzād); al-Mas'ūdī, *Murūj*, II, 233 = § 653; idem, *Tanbīh*, 102, tr. 146; Ḥamzah al-Iṣfahānī, *Ta'rīkh*, 54; Ibn al-Athīr, *Kāmil*, I, 498. Of Persian sources, see Ṭabari-Bal'amī, trans. II, 347–48. Of modern studies, see Christensen, *Sassanides*, 497–98; Frye, "The Political History of Iran under the Sasanians," 170–71, 178; *EIr*, art. cit.

991. This story is meant to heighten the enormity of Shahrbarāz's temerity and his sacrilege by sitting down on the royal throne when he was not from the royal houses of the Arsacids or the Sāsānids. The ensuing account of the ignominious treatment of his corpse after he had been assassinated likewise highlights this apparent strong sense of legitimacy among the Persian ruling classes. However, as Nöldeke, trans. 388 n. 7, noted, the corollary of this feeling that the direction of the state should never pass into the hands of those outside the ancient ruling dynasties meant that, in an age of epigoni, hopes of an infusion of fresh vigor and military initiative could never be realized, and the Persian realm sank into total collapse, together with the feeble remnants of the Sāsānid royal house.

992. The first component of the name Fus Farrukh must be the MP *pus*, "son," the whole name meaning "fortunate son," see Justi, *Namenbuch*, 256, while Māh-Khwarshēd-ān would presumably be the patronym "son of Māh-Khwarshēd," see ibid., 187.

993. The *qarabūs* was actually made up of two curved pieces of wood, the front one forming the forepart or pommel of the saddle and the rear one forming the troussequin. See Lane, *Lexicon*, 2509b.

the ground. Shahrbarāz rode forth a few days after he had become king. Fus Farrūkh and his two brothers stood close to each other, and when Shahrbarāz drew level with them, Fus Farrūkh struck him with his spear, followed by his two brothers, This took place in the month of Isfandārmadh on the day of Daybadīn.[994] He fell down dead from his horse. They tied a rope round his leg and dragged him to and fro. A man from among the great men of state called Zādhān Farrūkh, son of Shahrdārān, a man called Māhyāy (?), who was the instructor of the cavalrymen (*mu'addib al-asāwirah*), and a large number of the great men of state and members of leading families assisted Fus Farrūkh and his brothers in killing Shahrbarāz. They also aided them in killing the various men who had assassinated Ardashīr, son of Shīrūyah, and they killed various members from the class of the great men of state. They then raised to the throne Būrān, daughter of Kisrā. Shahrbarāz had held the royal power for forty days.[995]

## *[Būrān]*

Then there succeeded to the royal power Būrān, daughter of Kisrā (II) Abarwīz, son of Hurmuz (IV), son of Kisrā (I) Anūshar- [1064]

---

994. The twenty-third day of the twelfth month, i.e., 9 June 630, according to Nöldeke, trans. 389 n. 2.

995. Nöldeke, trans. 390 n. 1, 432–33, pointed out that we actually have a period of forty-two days from Ardashīr III's death on 27 April 630, but that Shahrbarāz's proclamation of himself as ruler days later, hence making a reign of forty days, with Shahrbarāz killed on 9 June. Shahrbarāz did not apparently have time enough as king to mint his own coins. The other Arabic sources on his reign include al-Ya'qūbī, *Ta'rīkh*, I, 196–97; al-Dīnawarī, *al-Akhbār al-ṭiwāl*, 111; al-Mas'ūdī, *Murūj*, II, 233 = § 654; idem, *Tanbīh*, 102, tr. 146; Ibn al-Athīr, *Kāmil*, I, 499. Of Persian sources, see Ṭabarī-Bal'amī, tr. II, 348. Of modern studies, see Christensen, *Sassanides*, 497–98; Frye, "The Political History of Iran under the Sasanians," 170–71, 178.

Some sources add at this point in their list of Sāsānid rulers, between Shahrbarāz and Būrān, Khusraw (III), son of Kawād (II) Shērōy, son of Khusraw (II) Abarwēz (or according to others—and this seems genealogically more likely—son of Khusraw Abarwēz, and not his grandson). See Ibn Qutaybah, *Ma'ārif*, 666; al-Mas'ūdī, *Murūj*, loc. cit.; idem, *Tanbīh*, loc. cit.; al-Khwārazmī, *Mafātīḥ al-'ulūm*, 104, who attributes to him the nickname of Kūtāh/al-Qaṣīr "the short one." These sources state that he had grown up in "the land of the Turks," had heard of the dissensions within Persia and had decided to try his own luck there; but after a "reign" of only three months, apparently in some part of Khurāsān, he was killed by the governor there. See Nöldeke, trans. 433; Christensen, op. cit. 498; Frye, op. cit., 171.

wān.[996] It has been mentioned that she proclaimed on the day when she was hailed as queen, "I will pursue righteousness and ordain justice," and she entrusted Shahrbarāz's office to Fus Farrūkh and invested him with the office of her chief minister. She behaved kindly toward her subjects and spread justice among them. She gave orders for silver coins to be minted, and she repaired masonry bridges (*al-qanāṭir*) and bridges of boats (*al-jusūr*).[997] She remitted for the people the arrears of land tax (*baqāyā*) due, and she wrote to them in general open letters concerning the policies of benevolence toward them that she intended to follow, and she mentioned the topic of the members of the royal house [of the Sāsānids] who had perished. At the same time, she expressed the hope that God would show them, through solicitude for their welfare and firm policies deriving from her elevated position, what would let them realize that lands were not subdued through the strength and energy of men, that military camps were not laid open to plunder through their martial valor, and that victory was not gained through men's stratagems and hatreds extinguished, but all that comes from God, He is exalted and magnified. She further exhorted them to be obedient and urged them to be faithful. Her letters brought together everything that was necessary (i.e., for the subjects' guidance and welfare). She restored the wood of the [True] Cross to the ruler of Byzantium through the

---

996. Also named as Būrān-dukht and, according to Ḥamzah al-Iṣfahānī, *Ta'rīkh,* 54, a sister of Shērōy and the daughter of Khusraw Abarwēz's Byzantine princess wife, Maryam, daughter of Heraclius. Her descent on both sides would thus make her a very acceptable queen. The *Anonymus Guidi,* tr. 32–33, describes Būrān as not only Shērōy's sister but also his wife, this being quite possible in Nöldeke's view, ibid. 32 n. 5. For the name Būrān/Bōrān, see Justi, *Namenbuch,* 70; Gignoux, *Noms propres sassanides en Moyen-Perse épigraphique,* no. 209, cf. no. 208, considered by him as a hypocoristic from * *baurāspa-,* "having bay horses."

Al-Dīnawarī, *al-Akhbār al-ṭiwāl,* 111, mentions as ruling before Būrān the child Juwānshīr, son of Khusraw and Kurdiyah, the sister and wife of Bahrām Chūbīn (see al-Ṭabarī, I, 998, 1001, pp. 309, 316–17 above), whom Abarwēz had married after Bahrām's death; if this piece of information were true, presumably Juwānshīr would have escaped Shērōy's massacre of his brothers, but in any case, must have died after a year. There is no trace of him in Sāsānid coinage.

997. Nöldeke noted, trans. 391 n. 3, that Būrān also built a fire temple at Istīniyā (a village near the later al-Kūfah, according to Yāqūt, *Buldān,* I, 176, *pace* Nöldeke that it was near Baghdad), according to al-Mas'ūdī, Murūj, IV, 86 = § 1412, cf. Morony, *Iraq after the Muslim Conquest,* 283.

intermediacy of the Catholicos called Īshū'hab.[998] Her tenure of royal power lasted one year and four months.[999]

## *[Jushnas Dih]*

Then there succeeded to the royal power after her a man called Jushnas Dih,[1000] from the remote offspring of Abarwīz's paternal uncle. His tenure of royal power was less than a month.

---

998. Restoration of the True Cross had been a prominent point in the peace negotiations begun by Heraclius with Shērōy and dragging on into the times of Shahrbarāz or Būrān, but the Cross was actually restored by Shērōy and was back in Jerusalem in late summer 629 or spring 630; see on the problem of exact dating here, n. 951 above. The Catholicos in question was Īshō'yahb II of Gadāla, formerly bishop of Balad in northern Mesopotamia and in office 628–46; hence he was head of the Nestorian Church when the Arabs arrived in Iraq. See Morony, *Iraq after the Muslim Conquest,* 341, 343–44. Īshō'yahb and several other Nestorian bishops of the Persian empire went on a mission to Heraclius in northern Syria as part of the peace negotiations. See Nöldeke, trans. 392 n. 1; Labourt, *Le Christianisme dans l'empire perse,* 243–45.

999. In Nöldeke's surmise, trans. 433, there was a short interregnum of intrigues and anarchy in the capital Ctesiphon after Shahrbarāz's assassination on 9 June 630. Būrān's coins, extending over three regnal years, began with the regnal year 1, which would have ended on 16 June 630. Her reign must have extended over a year and four or six months, hence into autumn 631. The *Anonymus Guidi,* tr. 33, and the Nestorian *Chronicle of Se'ert* state that she was strangled, according to the latter source, by the general Fīrūz. Būrān's name appears on her coins as BWL'N. See on her coins Paruck, *Sāsānian Coins,* 69, 392–93, Plate XXII; Göbl, *Sasanian Numismatics,* 54–55, Table XIII, Plate 15; Sellwood, Whitting, and Williams, *An Introduction to Sasanian Coins,* 21, 166–68; Malek, "A Survey of Research on Sasanian Numismatics," 238; Jenny Rose, "Three Queens, Two Wives, and a Goddess. The Roles and Images of Women in Sasanian Iran," 43–45.

The other Arabic sources for her reign include Ibn Qutaybah, *Ma'ārif,* 666; al-Ya'qūbī, *Ta'rīkh,* I, 197; al-Dīnawarī, *al-Akhbār al-ṭiwāl,* 111; al-Mas'ūdī, *Murūj,* II, 233 = § 654; idem, *Tanbīh,* 102, tr. 147; Ḥamzah al-Iṣfahānī, *Ta'rīkh,* 54; Ibn al-Athīr, *Kāmil,* I, 499. Of Persian sources, see Ṭabarī-Bal'amī, tr. II, 349–50. Of modern studies, see Christensen, *Sassanides,* 498; Frye, "The Political History of Iran under the Sasanians," 171, 178; *EIr,* s.v. Bōrān (Marie Louise Chaumont).

1000. The form of this ephemeral ruler's name is uncertain, especially in regard to the second element after Jushnas/Gushnasp. variably writen in those sources that mention him, i.e., Ibn Qutaybah, *Ma'ārif,* 666, "one of Kisrā's paternal uncle's progeny"; al-Mas'ūdī, *Murūj,* II, 233–34 = § 654, *Fīrūz J.sh.n.dah,* a descendant of Shābūr, son of Yazdajird [I] the Sinner"; idem, *Tanbīh,* tr. 147, *Fīrūz J.sh.n.t.dah;* Ibn al-Athīr, *Kāmil,* I, 499–500 (al-Dīnawarī's section on the Persian rulers ends essentially with Būrān, and merges into his account of the Arab conquests in Iraq and Persia). The resemblance of the names given by al-Mas'ūdī and Ibn al-Athīr to that of the Fayrūz, son of Mihrān Jushnas who is listed by al-Ṭabarī, I, 1066, p. 408 below, leads one to think that the two persons are really one and the same.

## *[Āzarmīdukht]*

Then there succeeded to the royal power Āzarmīdukht,[1001] daughter of Kisrā (II) Abarwīz, son of Hurmuz (IV), son of Kisrā (I)
[1065] Anūsharwān. It is said that she was one of the most beautiful of the women of the Persians and that she proclaimed, when she assumed the royal power, "Our way of conduct will be that of our father Kisrā, the victorious one,[1002] and if anyone rebels against us, we will shed his blood." It is said that the outstanding great man of Persia was at that time Farrukh Hurmuz, Iṣbahbadh of Khurāsān. He sent a message to her asking her to give herself in marriage to him. She wrote back, "Marriage to a queen is not permissible. I realize full well that your intention in what you are proposing is to satisfy your own [sexual] needs and lust with me; so come to me on such-and-such night." Āzarmīdukht ordered the commander of her guard to lie in wait for him on the night they had agreed to meet together and then kill him. The commander of her guard carried out her orders regarding Farrukh Hurmuz; and at her command, the latter's corpse was dragged out by the feet and thrown down in the open space before the palace of government. Next morning, they found Farrukh Hurmuz slain, and she gave orders for his corpse to be taken away and concealed from sight. It was generally recognized that he could only have been killed for some momentous deed. Rustam, son of Farrukh Hurmuz, the man whom Yazdajird (III) was later to send to combat the Arabs,[1003] was acting as his father's deputy in Khurāsān. When he received the news (i.e., of his father's murder), he came with a mighty

---

1001. This is the Arabic form, virtually identical with that of the Syriac sources, Āzarmīdūkht, of the MP name Āzarmīgdukht. Nöldeke, trans. 393 n. 2, saw its etymology as being most probably "modest (*āzarmīg*) noble maiden"; Justi, *Namenbuch*, 54, gave no opinon. However., Gignoux, in his *Noms propres sassanides en Moyen-Perse épigraphique*, no. 167, cf. no. 166, and in *EIr*, s.v. Āzarmīgduxt, renders it as "daughter of the honored, respected one," i.e., of her father Khusraw Abarwēz; both "honored maiden" and "daughter of the honored one" are possible translations.

1002. Arabic *al-manṣūr* = MP *abarwēz*. According to Ḥamzah al-Iṣfahānī, *Ta'rīkh*, 55, Āzarmīgdukht was *jalīdah qasīmah*, "vigorous and beautiful," and he records that she built a fire temple at a village called al-Q.r.ṭ.mān (?) in the region of Abkhāz (i.e., in western Transcaucasia).

1003. That is, the Persian general vanquished some five years later at al-Qādisiyyah by the Arabs. See *EI*², s.v. Rustam b. Farrukh Hurmuzd (ed.).

army, encamped at al-Madā'in, blinded Āzarmīdukht, and then killed her. According to other authorities, however, she was poisoned. Her tenure of royal power was six months.[1004]

## *[Kisrā III]*

There was then brought forward a man from the stock of Ardashīr (I), son of Bābak, who was living in al-Ahwāz, called Kisrā. [He was] the son of Mihr Jushnas. The great men of state raised him to the throne. He assumed the crown and sat down upon the royal throne, but was killed a few days after his accession.[1005]

## *[Khurrazādh Khusraw]*

It is also said that the one who reigned after Āzarmīdukht was Khurrazādh Khusraw, from the progeny of [Khusraw II] Abarwīz.[1006] It is said that he was found in a fortress near Niṣībīn called al-Ḥijārah (the "Stone Fortress").[1007] When he reached al- [1066]
Madā'in, he remained there a few days only before [the people there] rebelled and rose against him in opposition.

---

1004. Hence Āzarmīgdukht's reign was even shorter than that of her sister Būrān, and would fall at the end of 631 and opening of 632; see Nöldeke, trans. 434. Coins issued by her, one from the mint of Shīrāz, with the effigy of her father Khusraw Abarwēz and with the legend of her own name, have been discovered and identified by M. I. Mochiri. See Selwood, Whitting and Williams, *An Introduction to Sasanian Coins,* 21, 169–70; Malek, "A Survey of Research on Sasanian Numismatics," 238–39.

The other Arabic sources on her reign include Ibn Qutaybah, *Ma'ārif,* 666; al-Ya'qūbī, *Ta'rīkh,* I, 197–98; al-Mas'ūdī, *Murūj,* II, 233 = § 654; *idem, Tanbīh,* 102–103, tr. 147; Ḥamzah al-Iṣfahānī, *Ta'rīkh,* 54–55; Ibn al-Athīr, *Kāmil,* I, 500. Of Persian sources, see Ṭabarī-Bal'amī, tr. II, 350–52. Of modern studies, see Christensen, *Sassanides,* 499; *EIr,* s.v. Āzarmīgduxt (Ph. Gignoux).

1005. The only other Arabic sources clearly mentioning him are al-Ya'qūbī, *Ta'rīkh,* I, 198, and Ibn al-Athīr, *Kāmil,* I, 500.

1006. There seems to be a confusion here of Khurrahzādh and the Farrukhzādh mentioned below as coming after Fīrūz (II). Al-Ya'qūbī, *Ta'rīkh,* I, 198, does not mention Khurrazādh (nor do any other sources) but places Farrukhzādh after Fīrūz.

1007. A town of what is now southeastern Anatolia, in the medieval Islamic province of Diyār Bakr, situated on the upper course of the Tigris about halfway between Āmid/Diyarbekir and Jazīrat Ibn 'Umar, the mediaeval Islamic Ḥiṣn Kayfā. The second part of the name would appear to reflect Syriac *kīp̱ā,* "rock," hence "rock or stone fortress." See Yāqūt, *Buldān,* II, 265; Le Strange, *Lands,* 113; Canard, *H'amdanides,* 84; *EI²,* s.v. Ḥiṣn Kayfā (S. Ory).

## [Fayrūz II]

Those authorities who say that Kisrā (III), son of Mihr Jushnas, succeeded to the royal power after Āzarmīdukht [further relate that,] when Kisrā, son of Mihr Jushnas, was killed, the great men of state in Persia sought for someone from the royal house whom they could raise to the throne. They looked for someone who had in his veins an element of [the blood of] the members of that house, even though it was through maternal relationship. They brought forward a man who was resident in Maysān, called Fayrūz, son of Mihrān Jushnas, who was also called Jushnas Dih.[1008] He was the son of Ṣahārbukht,[1009] daughter of Yazdāndādh (text, "Yazdāndār"), son of Kisrā (I) Anūsharwān. They raised him to the throne against his own will. He was a man with a large head, and when he was crowned he exclaimed, "How tight this crown is!" The great men of state drew a bad omen from his beginning his reign by speaking of tightness and narrowness, hence killed him after he had reigned for [only] a few days. Some people assert that he was killed the moment he uttered those words.[1010]

## [Farrukhzādh Khusraw]

The authorities who say this last go on to say that a man from among the great men of state, called Zādhī,[1011] who had the func-

1008. As noted in n. 1000 above, this Fayrūz may well be identical with the Jushnas Dih mentioned in al-Ṭabarī, I, 1064, p. 405 above; at least, there is some confusion in the sources which seem to mention Fayrūz, i.e., al-Yaʿqūbī, *Taʾrīkh*, I, 198; al-Masʿūdī, *Murūj*, II, 233–34 = § 654 (?); Ibn al-Athīr, *Kāmil*, I, 500.

1009. Written thus here and in Ibn al-Athīr, loc. cit., but reflecting the common rendering in Arabic of Persian *ch* by *ṣ*, cf. Siddiqi, *Studien über die persischen Fremdwörter*, 72, hence probably the name Chahār Bukht, "saved by the four," i.e., the four spirits of water, earth, plants, and beasts, or the four elements, cf. the common Sāsānid name Si Bukht, "saved by the three." See Nöldeke, trans. 396 n. 1; Justi, *Namenbuch*, 151; Gignoux, *Noms propres sassanides*, no. 833. Fayrūz's relationship to the main stem of the Sāsānid royal house was clearly tenuous.

1010. In addition to the exiguous Arabic sources on Fayrūz mentioned in n. 1008 above, see the Persian one of Ṭabarī-Balʿamī, tr. II, 352–53. See also Nöldeke, trans. 396 n. 1. No coins of his seem to be extant.

1011. Thus written in the text, but taken by Nöldeke, trans. 396 and n. 2, as Zādhūyah, which seems likely. Nöldeke also noted that the Marzbān of Sarakhs who made peace with ʿAbdallāh b. ʿĀmir in 31/651–52 when the Arabs arrived in

tion of "Chief of the Servants" (*ra'īs al-khawal*),[1012] proceeded to a place in the western section [of the Persian kingdom], near to Niṣībīn, called Ḥiṣn al-Ḥijārah ("the Stone Fortress"). He brought back a son of Kisrā (II)'s who had escaped to that fortress when Shīrūyah killed all the sons of Kisrā, and who was called Farrukhzādh Khusraw, to the city of Ctesiphon. The people gave him obedience for a short time, but then rebelled and rose in opposition against him. Some sources state that they killed him. His period of royal power was six months.[1013] [1067]

## *[Yazdajird III]*

Some authorities say that the people of Iṣṭakhr got hold of Yazdajird, son of Shahriyār, son of Kisrā (II), at Iṣṭakhr, whither people had fled with him when Shīrūyah killed his brothers.[1014]

---

Khurāsān was called Zādhūyah (al-Balādhurī, *Futūḥ,* 405) and that Zādhūyah is a possible reading for the rather cryptic name Wārī in al-Ṭabarī, I, 893 and n. *a,* p. 147 above.

1012. Presumably an office at the Sāsānid court, something like a major-domo or steward, what would in Islamic times be called a *qahramān,* cf. the use of the word by al-Ṭabarī, I, 1020, p. 346 above.

1013. On the possible confusion of this Farrukhzādh with Khurrahzādh Khusraw, see n. 1006 above. The other Arabic sources on him include Ibn Qutaybah, *Ma'ārif,* 666–67; al-Ya'qūbī, *Ta'rīkh,* I, 198; al-Mas'ūdī, *Murūj,* II, 234 = § 655; idem, *Tanbīh,* 103, tr.147; Ḥamzah al-Iṣfahānī, *Ta'rīkh,* 55; Ibn al-Athīr, *Kāmil,* I, 501. Of Persian sources, see Ṭabarī-Bal'amī, trans. II, 353. He is briefly mentioned by Christensen, *Sassanides,* 499. No coins of his are extant.

Also mentioned as fleetingly holding power between the years 630 and 632, but probably with recognition in certain parts of the realm only, are Hormizd (V), who nevertheless minted some coins as 'WḤRMZDY (see concerning him, n. 1016 below), and Khusraw (IV) (assuming that this person is not the same as Farrukhzādh Khusraw), who minted some coins as ḤWSRWB. See Christensen, *Sassanides,* 499, and for their coins, Paruck, *Sāsānian Coins,* 69–70, 393–94, 493–94, Plates XXII–XXIII, Table XXXI; Göbl, *Sasanian Numismatics,* 54–55. Table XIII, Plate 15; Sellwood, Whitting, and Williams, *An Introduction to Sasanian Coins,* 21, 171–74; Malek, "A Survey of Research on Sasanian Numismatics," 239.

1014. The eight-year-old boy Yazdagird (this age being more probable than the fifteen or sixteen years of certain Christian and later Islamic sources, since Yazdagird's coins show him as beardless until the tenth year of his reign and he is described by al-Ṭabarī, I, 1067, p. 410 below, as being twenty-eight years old when he was killed at Marw in 651) was thus raised to power in Fārs and crowned in the temple of Anāhīd at Iṣṭakhr by a faction opposed to the one in Ctesiphon that had made Farrukhzādh king there. Hostility toward the new king is reflected in the statement of al-Ya'qubī, *Ta'rīkh,* I, 198, that Yazdagird was regarded as ill-omened

When the great men of state among the people of Iṣṭakhr received the news that the people of al-Madā'in had rebelled against Farrukhzādh, they brought Yazdajird to a fire temple called "Ardashīr's fire temple,"[1015] crowned him there and hailed him as king. He was, however, only a young boy. Then they brought him to al-Madā'in and killed Farrukhzādh Khusraw by means of treachery after he had reigned for one year. In this fashion, the way was open for Yazdajird to assume the royal power, except that, compared with the power of his forefathers, his power was like a phantom of the imagination and a vision in a dream (*al-khayāl wa-al-ḥulm*).[1016] The great men of state and the ministers exercised his royal authority because of his youth. The most illustrious and the shrewdest of his ministers was the Chief of the Servants. The power of the Persian kingdom grew weak, and its enemies attacked it boldly from all sides, made incursions into Yazdajird's lands, and devastated parts of them. The Arabs attacked his lands when two years had elapsed of his reign or, it is said alternatively, after four years. His whole life span, until he was killed, was twenty-eight years.[1017]

---

from the start because his mother had been a mere cupper (*ḥajjāmah*) in Khusraw Abarwēz's service, but was brought out from obscurity from sheer necessity; cf. al-Ṭabarī's information, I, 1044, p. 380 above, on Yazdagird's mother). Nöldeke, trans. 397 n. 3, 434, that Yazdagird's accession must have fallen within the Persian year 16 June 632–16 June 633, since the Zoroastrians begin their era in this year of Yazdagird III's accession.

1015. That is, the fire temple at Jūr/Fīrūzābād whose building by Ardashīr I is recorded in al-Ṭabarī, I, 817, p. 11 above.

1016. Nöldeke, trans. 397 n. 5, noted that Yazdagird had considerable trouble in establishing his authority throughout all the Persian lands, with important provinces like Azerbaijan, Mesopotamia, and Khurāsān at first reluctant to acknowledge him. Al-Dīnawarī, *al-Akhbār al-ṭiwāl,* 119, speaks of his struggles when raised to the throne (but anachronistically, it would appear, with Āzarmīgdukht). It seems that Rustam threw his weight behind the new king in the short period before he became embroiled with the invading Arabs. Numismatic evidence (see n. 1013 above) shows the existence of a rival for the throne, Hormizd (V), who challenged Yazdagird's position and whose center of power Armenian sources place in Niṣībīn in Upper Mesopotamia.

1017. Yazdagird III ruled from the end of 632 or the beginning of 633 till his death at Marw in 31/651 (al-Ṭabarī, I, 2872–84, tr. R. S. Humphreys, *The History of al-Ṭabarī, an Annotated Translation,* XV, *The Crisis of the Caliphate. The Reign of 'Uthmān,* 78–90). The Arabs began their probes into Iraq by the end of the second year of his reign, i.e., in 634 or 635, with the major battle for the province coming a year or two later. Yazdagird's name appears on coins as YZDKRTY. See

There are various further historical reports about this ruler Yazdajird and his sons, which I will mention later, if God wills, in their appropriate place, including the conquests by the Muslims of the land of the Persians, and what was the ultimate fate of Yazdajird and his sons.[1018]

---

on his coins, Paruck, *Sāsānian Coins*, 70, 394–96, 494–95, Plate XXIII, Table XXXI; Göbl, *Sasanian Numismatics*, 54–55, Table XIII, Plate 15; Sellwood, Whitting, and Williams, *An Introduction to Sasanian Coins*, 21, 175–78; Malek, "A Survey of Research on Sasanian Numismatics," 240.

The other Arabic sources on Yazdagird's accession and first few years include Ibn Qutaybah, *Ma'ārif*, 666–67; al-Ya'qūbī, *Ta'rīkh*, I, 198; al-Dīnawarī, *al-Akhbār al-ṭiwāl*, 119; al-Mas'ūdī, *Murūj*, II, 234 = § 655; idem, *Tanbīh*, 103, trans. 147; Ḥamzah al-Iṣfahānī, *Ta'rīkh*, 53; Ibn al-Athīr, *Kāmil*, I, 501. Of Persian sources, see Ṭabarī-Bal'amī, trans. II, 353, who merely quotes the fact of Yazdagird's accession and that he reigned for four years, i.e., this source regards his reign as closing with the Arabs' capture of the capital al-Madā'in in March 637 and Yazdagird's subsequent gradual retreat eastward across Persia from Ḥulwān and Iṣfahān to Iṣṭakhr (thus according to such Arabic sources as al-Balādhurī, *Futūḥ*, 315; al-Ṭabarī, I, 2439–40, tr. *The History of al-Ṭabarī, an Annotated Translation. XIII. The Conquest of Iraq, Southwestern Persia and Egypt. The Middle Years of 'Umar's Caliphate*, 20; the *Anonymus Guidi*, tr. 33, has Yazdagird flee via Khūzistān) to Kirmān and then his being killed in Khurāsān. Of modern studies, see Nöldeke, trans. 397 nn. 3–5, 431; Frye, *The Golden Age of Persia. The Arabs in the East*, London 1975, 57–67; 'Abd al-Ḥusain Zarrīnkūb, "The Arab Conquest of Iran and Its Aftermath," 4, 12–25.

1018. One of Yazdagird's sons, Fīrūz (III), spent the rest of his life after his father's death on the far northeastern fringes of the Islamic lands. He seems to have received aid from the Hephthalite or Turkish local ruler of Bactria/Ṭukhāristān, and may, in the surmise of J. Harmatta, have held power in Sistan for a short period ca. 660. He became a Chinese vassal and hoped to make a comeback with Chinese help; but he was driven out of the upper Oxus region by the Arabs, subsequently made his way to the imperial capital Ch'ang-an and died in China. Fīrūz's son, whose name is known only from Chinese sources as Ni-nieh-shih (presumably Narseh) continued to hover round the regions of Sogdia and Ṭukhāristān, stirring up trouble against the Arabs, but China was too distant to give these Sāsānid claimants any effective military support; he had to fall back into China and died there soon after 707. The presence of Sāsānid descendants in the Chinese capital Ch'ang-an seems nevertheless to be attested, according to Chinese sources, into the ninth century. See Marquart, *Ērānšahr*, 68, 133–34; J. Harmatta, "The Middle Persian-Chinese Bilingual Inscription from Hsian and the Chinese-Sāsānian Relations," 373–76; Frye, "The Political History," 176; W. Watson, "Iran and China," 547.

# [The Chronology of the World]

The whole of the period of years that elapsed from Adam's being sent down to earth (i.e., his expulsion from the Garden of Eden) up to the time of the Prophet's Hijrah, according to what the Jews
[1068] among the People of the Book say and according to what they allege is in the all-embracing text of the Torah (*al-Tawrāt al-ṣūrah*) setting forth the lives of the prophets and kings, is 4,642 years and a few months.[1019]

According to what the Christians say and assert in their Torah in the Greek language (i.e., the Septuagint), that extent of time was 5,992 years and a few months.

With regard to the whole of that, according to what the Persian Zoroastrians say, it was 4,182 years, ten months, and nineteen days, with the proviso that included in that span is the period of time between the Hijrah and the killing of Yazdajird—that is, thirty years, two months and fifteen days—and the further proviso that this system of reckoning of theirs and the beginning of their era (*ta'rīkh*) runs from the time of Jayūmart, Jayūmart being Ādam (Adam), the progenitor of all mankind, to whom every human being can be traced back, as I have clearly set forth in this book.

Concerning the learned scholars of Islam, I have mentioned previously what certain of them have said regarding it, and I shall now mention some of those whose fame has not come down to the present day. These persons say that from the time of Ādam to that

---

1019. In n. *a* to his text, Nöldeke cited the origin of this phrase as Syriac *ṣūraṯ kəṯāḇ* "the complete text of the sacred books."

of Nūḥ (Noah) was ten centuries (a century, *qarn*, being a hundred years), between Nūḥ and Ibrāhīm (Abraham), ten centuries (a century being a hundred years again) and between Ibrāhīm and Mūsā, son of ʿImrān (Moses, son of Amram), ten centuries (a century being a hundred years yet again).

## *Mention of Those Who Say That*

There related to us Ibn Bashshār—Abū Dāwūd—Hammām b. Qatādah— ʿIkrimah—Ibn ʿAbbās, who said: Between Ādam and [1069] Nūḥ there were ten centuries, and all of them (i.e., the people of this period) followed a path of divine truth (*sharīʿah min al-ḥaqq*).

There related to us al-Ḥārith b. Muḥammad—Muḥammad b. Saʿd—Muḥammad b. ʿUmar b. Wāqid al-Aslamī,[1020] from several of the learned scholars, who all said: Between Ādam and Nūḥ were ten centuries (a century being a hundred years), between Nūḥ and Ibrāhīm, ten centuries (a century being a hundred years again), and between Ibrāhīm and Mūsā, son of ʿImrān, ten centuries (a century being a hundred years yet again).

It was transmitted from ʿAbd al-Raḥmān b. Mahdī—Abū ʿAwānah—ʿĀṣim al-Aḥwal—Abū ʿUthmān—Salmān, who said: The interval (*al-fatrah*) between Muhammad and ʿĪsā (Jesus), peace be upon them both, was six hundred years.[1021]

It was transmitted from Fuḍayl b. ʿAbd al-Wahhāb—Jaʿfar b. Sulaymān—ʿAwf, who said: Between ʿĪsā and Mūsā was 600 years.

---

1020. That is, the historian al-Wāqidī (130–207/747–823), who derived this *nisbah* from his grandfather's name and that of al-Aslamī from being a mawlā of a member of the Medinan clan of Aslam. Of his many works on the pre-Islamic history of Mecca and Medina and on early Islamic history, only the *Kitāb al-maghāzī* and possibly a *Kitāb al-riddah* survive, but his work was much used by slightly later authors such as Ibn Saʿd. See Sezgin, *GAS*, I, 294–97; *EI*², s.v. al-Wāḳidī (S. Leder).

1021. The literal meaning of *fatrah* is "relaxation, weakening," thence "elapsing, period of time," and the term is especially applied in early Islamic usage to the interval between any two of the numerous prophetic messengers (*rusul*) who preceded the advent of Muḥammad. Al-Jāḥiẓ explained that these intervals were called *fatrah*s because there was a "slackening" of observance, with a reinvigoration of religion when a new *rasūl* came along. It became particularly used, as here, for the lengthy period without any prophets between Jesus and Muḥammad. See *EI*², s.v. Fatra (Ch. Pellat), and n. 1025 below.

There related to me Ya'qūb b. Ibrāhīm—Ibn 'Ulayyah—Sa'īd b. Abī Ṣadaqah—Muḥammad b. Sīrīn, who said: I was informed that Ka'b said that God's words, "O sister of Hārūn (Aaron)" do not refer to Hārūn the brother of Mūsā.[1022] He related: 'Ā'ishah said to him, "You are wrong!" He replied, "O Mother of the Faithful! If the Prophet said it, then he is the most knowledgeable and the best one,[1023] but if not, I find a space of six hundred years between them." He related: She was thereupon silent.

There related to me al-Ḥārith—Muḥammad b. Sa'd—Hishām—his father—Abū Ṣāliḥ—Ibn 'Abbās, who said: Between Mūsā, son of 'Imrān, and 'Īsā, son of Maryam (Mary), was nineteen hundred years, but there was no interval (*fatrah*) between them, because during this period, God sent a thousand prophets from the Banū Isrā'īl (Children of Israel), apart from those whom He sent to other
[1070] nations. Between the birth of 'Īsā and the Prophet was 569 years, in the first part of which He sent three prophets, as in His words, "When We sent to them two persons, and they branded them as liars, We strengthened them with a third person";[1024] the person whom He sent as a strengthener was Sham'ūn (Simon), one of the Apostles. The interval during which God did not send any prophets was 434 years.[1025] When Jesus was raised up (i.e., in his

---

1022. Qur'ān, XIX, 29/28, there being an apparent confusion here of Maryam, the Virgin Mary, with Maryam, the sister of Moses and Aaron. However, J. M. Rodwell in his *The Koran Translated from the Arabic,* 385 n. 2, admitted that Muḥammad seems here to be guilty of an anachronism, but further pointed out that the anachronism might be only apparent, since even if Aaron, the brother of Moses, is meant, Maryam, the Virgin Mary, could be called his sister because she was of Levitical stock. Ka'b (i.e., Ka'b al-Aḥbār, on whom see n. 371 above) is in this tradition implying that the Hārūn/Aaron here is another person. See the extensive discussion in R. Paret, *Der Koran. Kommentar und Konkordanz,* 65.

1023. For the Leiden text's *khayr,* the Cairo text, II, 236, has, following al-Ṭabarī's *Tafsīr,* the reading *akhbar* "giving more faithful reports."

1024. Qur'ān, XXXVI, 13/14. The words occur at the opening of the parable, or rather, story, of the unbelieving town, Antioch being the city commonly identified with this. K. Ahrens referred to a story of St. Peter at Antioch given in Ps.-Clement of Alexandria, see Bell, *A Commentary on the Qur'ān,* II, 138–39. Muslim tradition came to connect the story of the unbelieving town with the legendary character Ḥabīb the Carpenter who urged the town's inhabitants not to reject the three messengers who had been sent to them by God. See *EI²*, s.v. Ḥabīb al-Nadjdjār (G. Vajda).

1025. We thus have an attempt to fill up part at least of the *fatrah* between Jesus

Ascension to Heaven), he was thirty-two years and six months old, and his period of prophethood was thirty months. God raised him [to Heaven] corporeally, and he is still alive at this moment.

There related to me Muḥammad b. Sahl b. ʿAskar—Ismāʿīl b. ʿAbd al-Karīm—ʿAbd al-Ṣamad b. Maʿqil, who heard Wahb [b. Munabbih] say that fifty-six hundred years have elapsed of this present world.

There related to me Ibrāhīm b. Saʿīd al-Jawharī—Yaḥyā b. Ṣāliḥ—al-Ḥasan b. Ayyūb al-Ḥaḍramī—ʿAbd Allāh b. Busr, who said: The Messenger of God said to me: "You will certainly live for a century (*qarn*)!" And he did [in fact] live for a hundred years.

This is what was transmitted from the learned scholars of Islam concerning this, and in what they say there is a very wide variation. This is seen in the fact that al-Wāqidī told the story, on the authority of a group of learned scholars, that they said what I have mentioned as his transmission from them. On the basis of what he said, one must take the whole span of years of this present world up to the birth of our Prophet as being forty-six years, but on the basis of what Ibn ʿAbbās said, as transmitted by Hishām b. Muḥammad—his father—Abū Ṣāliḥ—Ibn ʿAbbās, one must take [1071]
the figure up to the birth of the Prophet as fifty-five hundred years. As for Wahb b. Munabbih, he mentioned what he had to say in one bloc, without breaking it down into details, that is, up to his own time [is a span of] fifty-six hundred years. The entire extent in time of this present world is, according to Wahb, six thousand years, of which there had elapsed up to his own time, in his view, fifty-six hundred years. Wahb b. Munabbih died in the year 114 of the Hijrah [/A.D. 732].[1026] Thus the remainder of the extent of this present world, from the time we are actually in now, is, according

---

and Muḥammad; other Muslim scholars endeavored to find also within it persons who had at least rejected the worship of idols and had followed an ascetic way of life, such as the *ḥanīf*s in pre-Islamic Mecca and the poet-ascetic of al-Ṭāʾif, Umayyah b. Abī al-Ṣalt (on whom see n. 603 above), called collectively the *ahl al-fatrah*. See *EI*², s.v. Fatra (Ch. Pellat).

1026. This is one of the two dates given in the sources for Wahb's death, the other being 110/728–29. See Sezgin, *GAS*, I, 305; *EI*², s.v. Wahb b. Munabbih (R. G. Khoury).

to Wahb's words, 215 years.[1027] This is what Wahb b. Munabbih says, conformable to what Abū Ṣāliḥ transmited from Ibn ʿAbbās.

Some authorities state that from the time of the descent [to earth] of Ādam to the mission of our Prophet is 6,113 years, [this span comprising,] in their view, from Ādam's descent to the earth up to the Flood, 2,256 years; from the Flood to the birth of Ibrāhīm, the Friend of the Merciful One,[1028] 1,079 years; from the birth of Ibrāhīm to Mūsā's exodus with the Banū Isrāʾīl from Egypt, 565 years; from Mūsā's exodus with the Banū Isrāʾīl from Egypt to the building of the Sacred Temple (*al-Bayt al-Maqdis*)—this being four years after the accession to royal power of Sulaymān, son of Dāwūd (Solomon, son of David)—636 years; from the building of the Temple to al-Iskandar's (Alexander the Great's) accession to royal power, 717 years; from al-Iskandar's accession to the birth of
[1072] ʿĪsā, son of Maryam, 369 years; from the birth of ʿĪsā to Muḥammad's mission, 551 years; and from Muḥammad's mission to his Hijrah from Mecca to Medina, thirteen years.

Some authorities have related from Hishām b. Muḥammad al-Kalbī—his father—Abū Ṣāliḥ—Ibn ʿAbbās, who said that from Ādam to Nūḥ was twenty-two hundred years; from Nūḥ to Ibrāhīm, 1,143 years; from Ibrāhīm to Mūsā, 575 years; from Mūsā to Dāwūd, 179 years; from Dāwūd to ʿĪsā, 1,053 years; and from ʿĪsā to Muḥammad, 600 years.

Al-Haytham b. ʿAdī[1029] has related from certain members of the People of the Book, saying that from Ādam to the Flood was 2,256 years; from the Flood to the death of Ibrāhīm, 1,020 years; from Ibrāhīm's death to the Banū Isrāʾīl's entry into Egypt, seventy-five years; from Yaʿqūb's (Jacob's) entry into Egypt to Moses' exodus from it, 430 years; from the building of the Sacred Temple to the accession to royal power of Bukht-Naṣṣar (Nebuchadnezzar) and

---

1027. That is, the period of time between Wahb's death and the date when al-Ṭabarī was writing his *History*, which would bring the latter date up to 319 [/931].

1028. Ibrāhīm/Abraham being called in Muslim lore Khalīl Allāh, the "Friend of God," this being based on Qurʾān, IV, 124/125 "and God took Abraham as a friend," echoing Isa. xli. 8.

1029. That is, the Kūfan *akhbārī* or historian (d. 204, 207 or 209/819–24), a source for al-Yaʿqūbī, al-Ṭabarī, al-Masʿūdī, and other historians. See Sezgin, *GAS*, I, 272; *EI*², s.v. al-Haytham b. ʿAdī (Ch. Pellat).

the destruction of the Sacred Temple,[1030] 446 years; from the accession of Bukht-Naṣṣar to the accession to royal power of al-Iskandar,[1031] 436 years; and from al-Iskandar's accession to the year 206 of the Hijrah [/A.D. 821–822], 1,245 years.

---

1030. The Old Testament Nebuchadnezzar (*nbwkdn'ṣr*, a scribal error in the masoretic text for *nbwkdr'ṣr*), Babylonian Nabû-kudurri-uṣur, "the god Nabu has guarded the estate [succession]," came to power in 605 B.C.; various dates, including 588, 587, and 586 B.C. are given for his sack of Jerusalem and destruction of the Temple there. The extents of time between the events delineated here, going up to Alexander's accession (see below) are, of course, fanciful.

1031. That is, Alexander the Great (365–323 B.C.), whose accession to the throne of Macedon took place in 336 B.C. on his father Philip II's assassination. Al-Ṭabarī's computation of 1,245 years is thus an exaggeration, even if *hijrī* lunar years and not solar ones are used.

# Bibliography of Cited Works

## *Primary Sources: Texts and Translations*


Abū al-Baqā' Hibatallāh al-Ḥillī, *al-Manāqib al-mazyadiyyah fī akhbār al-mulūk al-asadiyyah,* ed. Ṣāliḥ Mūsā Danādika and Muḥammad 'Abd al-Qādir Khuraysāt. 2 parts. Amman, 1404/1984.

Abū Dulaf, Mis'ar b. Muhalhil al-Khazrajī. *Second Risālah,* ed. and English trans. V. Minorsky as *Abū-Dulaf Mis'ar ibn Muhalhil's Travels in Iran (circa A.D. 950).* Cairo, 1955.

Abū Ṣāliḥ al-Armanī. *Ta'rīkh,* ed. and English trans. B. T. A. Evetts as *The Churches and Monasteries of Egypt and Some Neighbouring Countries Attributed to Abû Ṣâliḥ, the Armenian,* Oxford, 1894–95.

'Adī b. Zayd al-'Ibādī. *Dīwān,* ed. Muḥammad Jabbār al-Mu'aybidī, Baghdad, 1385/1965.

Anon. *Ḥudūd al-'ālam,* English trans. and commentary V. Minorsky as *"The Regions of the World." A Persian Geography 372 A.H.–982 A.D.,* 2d ed. C. E. Bosworth, GMS N.S. XI. London, 1970.

Anonymous Syriac Chronicle, known as the *Anonymus Guidi.* German trans. Th. Nöldeke, "Die von Guidi herausgegebene syrische Chronik," *SbWAW,* phil.-hist. Classe, CXXVIII (1893), no. IX, 1–48.

al-A'shā, Maymūn b. Qays. *Dīwān,* ed. R. Geyer as *Gedichte von Abû Baṣîr Maimûn ibn Qais al-A'šâ,* GMS N.S. VI. London, 1928.

al-Azraqī, Abū al-Walīd Muḥammad b. 'Abdallāh. *Kitāb akhbār Makkah,* ed. F. Wüstenfeld as *Geschichte und Beschreibung der Stadt Mekka,* in *Die Chroniken der Stadt Mekka,* I, Leipzig, 1858,

al-Bakrī, Abū' Ubayd 'Abdallāh b. 'Abd al-'Azīz al-Andalusī. *Mu'jam mā ista'jam min asmā' al-bilād wa-al-mawāḍi'*, ed. Muṣṭafā al-Saqqā, 4 parts. Cairo, 1364–71/1945–51.

al-Balādhurī, Abū al-Ḥasan Aḥmad b. Yaḥyā. *Futūḥ al-buldān*, ed. M. J. de Goeje as *Liber expugnationis regionum.* Leiden, 1866.

al-Bīrūnī, Abū al-Rayḥān Muḥammad b. Aḥmad. *al-Āthār al-bāqiyah 'an al-qurūn al-khāliyah*, ed. E. Sachau as *Chronologie orientalischer Völker.* Leipzig, 1878.

al-Dīnawarī, Abū Ḥanīfah Aḥmad b. Dāwūd. *Kitāb al-akhbār al-ṭiwāl*, ed. 'Abd al-Mun'im 'Āmir and Jamāl al-Dīn al-Shayyāl. Cairo, 1960.

Dionysius of Tell Maḥrē. *Chronicle*, English trans. in A. Palmer, S. Brock, and R. Hoyland, *The Seventh Century in the West-Syrian Chronicles.* Liverpool, 1993.

al-Hamdānī, Abū Muḥammad al-Ḥasan b. Aḥmad. *al-Iklīl. al-Juz' al-thāmin*, ed. Nabih Amin Faris. Princeton, 1940. English trans. idem as *The Antiquities of South Arabia, Being a Translation from the Arabic with Linguistic, Geographic, and Historical Notes, of the Eighth Book of Al-Hamdānī's al-Iklīl.* Princeton, 1938.

———. *Ṣifat jazīrat al-'Arab*, ed. Muḥammad 'Alī al-Akwa' al-Ḥiwālī. Riyadh, 1394/1974.

al-Ḥimyarī, Nashwān b. Sa'īd. *Shams al-'ulūm wa-dawā' kalām al-'Arab min al-kulūm*, ed. 'Aẓīmuddīn Aḥmad as *Die auf Südarabien bezüglichen Angaben Našwāns im Šams al-'ulūm*, GMS XXIV. Leiden and London, 1916.

Ibn al-Athīr, 'Izz al-Dīn Abū al-Ḥasan 'Alī b. Muḥammad. *al-Kāmil fī al-ta'rīkh.* 13 vols. Beirut, 1385–87/1965–67.

Ibn al-Athīr, Majd al-Dīn Abū al-Sa'ādāt al-Mubārak b. Muḥammad. *al-Nihāya fī gharīb al-ḥadīth wa-al-athar*, ed. Ṭāhir Aḥmad al-Zāwī and Maḥmūd Muḥammad al-Ṭannāḥī, 5 vols. Cairo, 1383/1963.

Ibn Durayd, Abū Bakr Muḥammad b. al-Ḥasan. *Kitāb al-ishtiqāq*, ed. 'Abd al-Salām Muḥammad Hārūn. Cairo, 1378/1958.

Ibn Ḥajar, Shihāb al-Dīn Abū al-Faḍl Aḥmad b. 'Alī al-'Asqalānī. *Tahdhīb tahdhīb al-kamāl fī ma'rifat al-rijāl*, 12 vols. Hyderabad, 1325–27/1907–1909.

Ibn Hisham, Abū Muḥammad 'Abd al-Malik b. Hishām. *Sīrat al-nabī*, ed. F. Wüstenfeld as *Das Leben Muhammed's nach Muhammed Ibn Ishâk bearbeitet von Abd el-Malik Ibn Hischâm*, 2 vols. Göttingen, 1858–60. Ed. Muṣṭafā al-Saqqā, Ibrāhīm al-Abyārī and 'Abd al-Ḥafīẓ Shalabī, 4 vols. Cairo 1955. English trans. A. Guillaume as *The Life of Muhammad. A Translation of Isḥāq's* [sic] Sīrat Rasūl Allāh. London, 1955.

———. *Kitāb al-tījān fī mulūk Ḥimyar.* Hyderabad, 1347/1928–29.

Ibn al-Kalbī, Abū al-Mundhir Hishām b. Muḥammad. *Jamharat al-nasab*, interpreted and arranged with indices by W. Caskel and G. Strenziok as *Ǧamharat an-nasab. Das genealogische Werk des Hišām ibn Muḥammad al-Kalbī*, 2 vols. Leiden, 1966.

———. *Kitāb al-aṣnām*. Ed. Aḥmad Zakī Pasha. Cairo, 1924. Text and German trans. in Rosa Klinke-Rosenburger, *Das Götzenbuch. Kitâb al-Aṣnâm des Ibn al-Kalbî*. Leipzig, 1941. English trans. Nabih Amin Faris, *The Book of Idols, Being a Translation from the Arabic of the* Kitāb al-Aṣnām *by Hishām Ibn al-Kalbī*. Princeton Oriental Series 14. Princeton, 1952.

Ibn Khurradādhbih, Abū al-Qāsim ʿUbaydallāh b. ʿAbdallāh. *Kitāb al-masālik wa-al-mamālik*, ed. M. J. de Goeje, BGA VI. Leiden 1889.

Ibn Manẓūr, Abū al-Faḍl Muḥammad b. Mukarram. *Lisān al-ʿArab*, 20 vols. Būlāq, 1300–1308/1883–91.

Ibn al-Nadīm, Abū al-Faraj Muḥammad b. Isḥāq al-Warrāq. *Kitāb al-fihrist*, ed. Riḍā Tajaddud. Tehran, 1350/1971. English trans. Bayard Dodge, *The Fihrist of an-Nadīm. A Tenth-Century Survey of Muslim Culture*, Records of Civilization: Sources and Studies LXXXIII. 2 vols. New York and London, 1970.

Ibn Qutaybah, Abū Muḥammad ʿAbdallāh b. Muslim. *Kitāb al-maʿārif*, ed. Tharwat ʿUkāshah. Cairo, 1960.

———. *Kitāb al-shiʿr wa-al-shuʿarāʾ*, ed. M. J. de Goeje as *Liber poësis et poëtarum*. Leiden 1904.

———. *Kitāb ʿuyūn al-akhbār*, 4 vols. Cairo, 1383/1963.

Ibn Rustah, Abū ʿAlī Aḥmad b. ʿUmar, *Kitāb al-aʿlāq al-nafīsah*, ed. M.J. de Goeje, BGA VII. Leiden, 1892. French trans. G. Wiet, *Les atours précieux*. Cairo, 1955.

Ibn Saʿd, Abū ʿAbdallāh Muḥammad b. Saʿd al-Baṣrī. *Kitāb al-ṭabaqāt al-kabīr*, ed. E. Sachau *et alii* as *Ibn Saad. Biographien Muhammeds, seiner Gefährten und der späteren Träger des Islams bis zum Jahre 230 der Flucht*, 9 vols. Leiden, 1905–28.

Ibn Sharyah, ʿAbīd/ʿUbayd b. Sharyah al-Jurhumī. *Akhbār al-Yaman wa-ashʿārihā wa-ansābihāʿ alā al-wafāʾ wa-al-kamāl*, In Ibn Hishām, *Kitāb al-tījān*, 311–488.

Imruʾ al-Qays, Abū al-Ḥārith, etc. Imruʾ al-Qays b. Ḥujr. *Dīwān*, ed. Muḥammad Abū al-Faḍl Ibrāhīm. Cairo 1958.

al-Iṣfahānī, Abū al-Faraj ʿAlī b. al-Ḥusayn. *Kitāb al-aghānī*, 20 vols. Būlāq, 1285/1868–69. 22 vols. Dār al-Kutub, Cairo, 1346–93/1927–73.

al-Iṣfahānī, Ḥamzah b. al-Ḥasan. *Taʾrīkh sinī mulūk al-arḍ wa-al-anbiyāʾ*. Beirut, n.d. [1961].

Ps.-al-Jāḥiẓ, Abū ʿUthmān ʿAmr b. Baḥr. *Kitāb al-tāj*, French tr. Ch. Pellat as *Le livre de la couronne. Kitāb at-Tāǧ (fī aḫlāq al-mulūk). Ouvrage attribué à Ǧāḥiẓ.* Collection UNESCO d'oeuvres représentatives and Commission d'études arabes de l'Association Guillaume Budé. Paris, 1954.

al-Jahshiyārī, Abū 'Abdallāh Muḥammad b. 'Abdūs. *Kitāb al-wuzarā' wa-al-kuttāb,* ed. Muṣṭafā al-Saqqā, Ibrāhīm al-Abyārī and 'Abd al-Ḥafīẓ Shalabī. Cairo, 1401/1980.

Jarīr b. 'Aṭiyyah al-Tamīmī, and al-Farazdaq, Abū Firās Tammām b. Ghālib al-Tamīmī. *Naqā'iḍ Jarīr wa-al-Farazdaq,* ed. A. A. Bevan as *The Naḳā'iḍ of Jarīr and al-Farazdaḳ,* 3 vols. Leiden, 1905–12.

al-Jawālīqī, Abū Manṣūr Mawhūb b. Aḥmad. *Kitāb al-mu'arrab min al-kalām al-'ajamī 'alā ḥurūf al-mu'jam,* ed. Aḥmad Muḥammad Shākir. Cairo 1361/1942.

Ps.-Joshua the Stylite. *Chronicle.* English tr. W. Wright as *The Chronicle of Joshua the Stylite, Composed in Syriac* A.D. *507, with a Translation into English and Notes.* Cambridge, 1882.

al-Khwārazmī, Abū 'Abdallāh Muḥammad b. Aḥmad. *Mafātīḥ al-'ulūm,* ed. G. van Vloten as *Liber Mafâtîh al-olûm explicans vocabula technica scientarum tam arabum tam peregrinum.* Leiden, 1895.

al-Kisā'ī, Muḥammad b. 'Abdallāh. *Qiṣaṣ al-anbiyā',* English trans. W.M. Thackston Jr. as *The Tales of the Prophets of al-Kisa'i,* Library of Classical Arabic Literature II. Boston, 1978.

al-Maqdisī, Abū 'Abdallāh Muḥammad b. Aḥmad. *Aḥsan al-taqāsīm fī ma'rifat al-aqālīm,* ed. M. J. de Goeje, BGA III. Leiden, 1906.

al-Mas'ūdī, Abū al-Ḥasan 'Alī b. al-Ḥusayn. *Murūj al-dhahab wa-ma'ādin al-jawhar.* Ed. and French trans. C. Barbier de Meynard and Pavet de Courteille as *Les prairies d'or,* 9 vols. Paris, 1861–77. Ed. and French trans. Ch. Pellat as *Les prairies d'or,* 7 vols. text and index, 5 vols. trans. Paris and Beirut, 1962–97.

———. *Kitāb al-tanbīh wa-al-ishrāf,* ed. M. J. de Goeje, BGA VIII. Leiden, 1894. French trans. Baron Carra de Vaux, *Le livre de l'avertissement et de la revision.* Paris, 1897.

Muḥammad b. Ḥabīb al-Baghdādī. *Kitāb al-muḥabbar,* ed. Ilse Lichtenstädter, Hyderabad, 1361/1942.

———. *Kitāb al-munammaq,* ed. Khurshīd Aḥmad Fāriq, Hyderabad, 1384/1964.

Pliny the Elder (Plinius Secundus). *Natural History,* text and English trans. H. Rackham, The Loeb Classical Library, 10 vols. London 1938–63.

Procopius of Caesarea. *History of the Wars.* Books I and II, *The Persian Wars,* text and English trans. H. B. Dewing, The Loeb Classical Library. London and New York, 1914.

Qudāmah b. Ja'far, Abū al-Faraj. *Kitāb al-kharāj*, ed. M. J. de Goeje, BGA VI. Leiden 1889.

Qur'ān. English trans. J. M. Rodwell, *The Koran. Translated from the Arabic*, Everyman's Library. London 1909.

al-Samhūdī, Nūr al-Dīn 'Alī b. Aḥmad. *Wafā' al-wafā bi-akhbār dār al-Muṣṭafā*, ed. Muḥammad Muḥyī al-Dīn 'Abd al-Ḥamīd, 4 parts in 2 vols. Cairo, 1374/1955.

al-Shābushtī, Abū al-Ḥasan 'Alī b. Muḥammad. *Kitāb al-diyārāt*, ed. Gūrgīs 'Awwād, 2d rev. ed. Baghdad, 1386/1966.

al-Ṭabarī, Abū Ja'far Muḥammad b. Jarīr. *Jāmi' al-bayān 'an ta'wīl al-Qur'ān* or *Tafsīr*, 30 vols. Cairo 1321–30/1903–12.

———. *Ta'rīkh al-rusul wa-al-mulūk*, ed. M. J. de Goeje et al. as *Annales quos scripsit Abu Djafar . . . at-Tabari*. 13 vols plus 1 vol. *Indices* and 1 vol. *Introductio, glossarium, addenda et emendanda*. Leiden, 1879–1901. Ed. Muḥammad Abū al-Faḍl Ibrāhīm. 10 vols. Cairo, 1960–69. Partial German trans. Th. Nöldeke as *Geschichte der Perser und Araber zur Zeit der Sassaniden*. Leiden, 1878. English trans. *The History of al-Ṭabarī, an Annotated Translation*, 39 vols. Albany 1985–99. I. *General Introduction and From the Creation to the Flood*, trans. F. Rosenthal, 1989. III. *The Children of Israel*, trans. W. M. Brinner, 1991. IV. *The Ancient Kingdoms*, trans. M. Perlmann, 1987. IX. *The Last Years of the Prophet. The Formation of the State*, trans. Ismail K. Poonawala, 1990. X. *The Conquest of Arabia. The Riddah Wars*, trans. F. McG. Donner, 1993. XI. *The Challenge to the Empires*, trans. Khalid Yahya Blankinship, 1993. XII. *The Battle of al-Qādisiyyah and the Conquest of Syria and Palestine*, trans. Y. Friedmann, 1992. XIII. *The Conquest of Iraq, Southwestern Persia and Egypt. The Middle Years of 'Umar's Caliphate*, trans. G. D. A. Juynboll, 1989. XV. *The Crisis of the Early Caliphate*, trans. R. S. Humphreys, 1990. XVII. *The First Civil War. From the Battle of Ṣiffīn to the Death of 'Alī*, trans. G. R. Hawting, 1996. XX. *The Collapse of Sufyānid Authority and the Coming of the Marwānids. The Caliphates of Mu'āwiyah II and Marwān I and the Beginning of the Caliphate of 'Abd al-Malik*, trans. G. R. Hawting, 1989. XXXVII. *The 'Abbāsid Recovery*, trans. P. M. Fields, 1987. Persian trans. Abū 'Alī Muḥammad Bal'amī as *Ta'rīkh-i Ṭabarī*, trans. H. Zotenberg as *Chronique de Abou-Djafar Mo'hammed . . . Tabari, traduite sur la version persane d'Abou-'Ali Mo'hammed Bel'ami*, 4 vols. Paris, 1867–74.

Umayyah b. Abī al-Ṣalt, Abū' Uthmān b. 'Abdallāh al-Thaqafī. *Sharḥ dīwān Umayyah*, ed. Sayf al-Dīn al-Kātib and Aḥmad 'Iṣām al-Kātib. Beirut, 1980.

al-Ya'qūbī, Abū al-'Abbās Aḥmad b. Isḥāq, called Ibn Wāḍiḥ. *Kitāb al-buldān*, ed. M. J. de Goeje, BGA VII. Leiden, 1892. French trans. G. Wiet, *Les pays*. Cairo, 1937.

———. *Ta'rīkh*, ed. M. Th. Houtsma as *Historiae*, 2 vols. Leiden, 1883.

Yāqūt, Abū 'Abdallāh Ya'qūb b. 'Abdallāh al-Ḥamawī al-Rūmī. *Mu'jam al-buldān*, 5 vols. Beirut 1374–76/1955–57.

al-Zabīdī, Muḥammad Murtaḍā. *Tāj al-'arūs min jawāhir al-Qāmūs*, 10 vols. Būlāq 1306–1307/1889–90.

## *Secondary Sources and Reference Works*

Abbott, Nabia. *Two Queens of Baghdad. Mother and Wife of Hārūn al-Rashīd*. Chicago, 1946.

Abdesselem, Mohamed. *Le thème de la mort dans la poésie arabe de la mort des origines à la fin du IIIe/IXe siècle*. Publications de l'Université de Tunis, Faculté des Lettres et des Sciences Humaines, 6th sér.: Philosophie, littérature. vol. X. Tunis, 1972.

Al-Ansary, A. R. *Qaryat al-Fau. A Portrait of Pre-Islamic Civilisation in Saudi Arabia*. Riyadh, 1981.

Altheim, F., and R. Stiehl. *Die Araber in der Alten Welt*. II. *Bis zur Reichstrennung*. V/1. *Weitere Neufunde—Nordafrika bis zur Einwanderung der Wandalen—Dū Nuwās*, 6 vols. in 5. Berlin, 1964–69.

———. *Christentum am Roten Meer*, I. Berlin and New York, 1971.

Al-Wohaibi, Abdullah. *The Northern Hijaz in the Writings of the Arab Geographers 800–1150*. Beirut, 1973.

Andrae, Tor. *Die Person Muhammeds in Lehre und Glauben seiner Gemeinde*. Archives d'Etudes Orientales 16. Stockholm, 1918.

———. *Mohammed, sein Leben und Glaube*. Göttingen, 1932.

Asbaghi, Asya. *Persische Lehnwörter im Arabischen*. Wiesbaden, 1988.

Asmussen, J. P. "Christians in Iran," in *CHI* III/2. Pp. 924–48.

*The Assyrian Dictionary of the Oriental Institute of the University of Chicago*. Vol. VII, *Letters I–J*. Chicago, 1960. Vol. X, *Letter M*. Chicago, 1977.

Bafaqih, M. A. "New Light on the Yazanite Dynasty," in *PSAS* 9 (1979): 5–9.

Barthold, W. *Four Studies on the History of Central Asia. III. A History of the Turkmen People*, English trans. V. and T. Minorsky. Leiden, 1962. Pp. 75–187.

———. *Turkestan Down to the Mongol Invasion*, 3d ed. with an additional chapter . . . and with further Addenda and Corrigenda by C. E. Bosworth, GMS N.S. V. London, 1968.

———. *An Historical Geography of Iran*, English trans. S. Soucek, ed. C. E. Bosworth. Modern Classics in Near Eastern Studies. Princeton, 1984.

Bartholomae, Chr. *Altiranisches Wörterbuch*. Strassburg, 1904.

Basham, A. L. *The Wonder That Was India. A Survey of the Culture of the Indian Sub-Continent Before the Coming of the Muslims*. London, 1954.

Baynes, N. H. "The Restoration of the Cross at Jerusalem," *EHR* 27 (1912): 287–99.

———. "The Emperor Heraclius and the Military Theme System," *EHR* 67 (1952): 380–81.

Beaucamp, Joëlle, and Chr. Robin. "Le Christianisme dans la péninsule arabique d'après épigraphie et l'archéologie," *Travaux et Mémoires* 8 (1981): 45–61.

———. "L' évêché nestorien des Mâšmâhîg dans l'archipel d' al-Baḥrayn (V^e^–IX^e^ siècle)," in D. T. Potts (ed.), *Dilmun*. Berlin, 1983. Pp. 171–96.

Beck, E. "Die Sure ar-Rūm (30)," *Orientalia*, N.S. 13 (1944): 334–55.

Beeston, A. F. L. "Notes on the Mureighan Inscription," *BSOAS* 16 (1954): 389–92.

———. "The Himyarite Problem," *PSAS* 5 (1975): 1–7.

———. "Pre-Islamic Ṣanʿāʾ," in *Ṣanʿāʾ, an Arabian Islamic City*, ed. R. B. Serjeant and R. Lewcock. London, 1983. Pp. 36–38.

———. "Himyarite Monotheism," in *Studies on the History of Arabia. II. Pre-Islamic Arabia*. Proceedings of the Second International Symposium on Studies in the History of Arabia 1399/1979, Riyadh, ed. Abdelqadir M. Abdalla et al. Riyadh, 1404/1984. Pp. 149–54.

———. *Sabaic Grammar*, JSS Monographs 6. Manchester, 1984.

———. "Judaism and Christianity in Pre-Islamic Yemen," in *L'Arabie du Sud, histoire et civilisation*, ed. J. Chelhod et al. Paris, 1984. Pp. 271–78.

———. "The Martyrdom of Azqir," *PSAS* 15 (1985): 5–10.

———. "Hamdānī and the Tabābiʿah," in *Al-Hamdānī, a Great Yemeni Scholar. Studies on the Occasion of His Millennial Anniversary*, ed. Yusuf Mohammad Abdallah. Sanaa, 1407/1986. Pp. 5–15.

———. "The Chain of al-Mandab," in *On Both Sides of the Mandab. Ethiopic, South-Arabic and Islamic Studies Presented to Oscar Löfgren on His Ninetieth Birthday*, ed. Ulla Ehrensvärd and Christopher Toll. Swedish Research Institute in Istanbul Transactions 2. Istanbul, 1989. Pp. 1–6.

———, M. A. Ghul, W. W. Müller, and J. Ryckmans. *Sabaic Dictionary (English-French-Arabic)*, Publication of the University of Sanaa, YAR. Louvain-Beirut, 1982.

Bell, R. *The Origin of Islam in Its Christian Environment*, The Gunning Lectures, Edinburgh University 1925. London, 1926.

———. *A Commentary on the Qur'ān*, ed. C. E. Bosworth and M. E. J. Richardson, JSS Monograph 14, 2 vols. Manchester, 1991.

Benveniste, E. "Le sens du mot persan shâdurvân," in *Mélanges d'orientalisme offerts à Henri Massé*. Tehran, 1342/1963. Pp. 31–37.

Biella, Joan C. *Dictionary of Old South Arabic. Sabaean Dialect*, Harvard Semitic Studies 25. Chico, Calif., 1982.

Birkeland, H. *The Legend of the Opening of Muhammad's Breast*. Oslo, 1955.

Bivar, A. D. H. "The Political History of Iran under the Arsacids," in *CHI* III/1. Pp. 21–99.

———. "The History of Eastern Iran," in *CHI* III/1. Pp. 181–231.

Blachère, R. *Histoire de la littérature arabe des origines à la fin du XV^e^ siècle de J.-C.*, 3 vols. Paris, 1952–64.

de Blois, F. C. "'Freemen' and 'Nobles' in Iranian and Semitic Languages," *JRAS* (1985): 5–15.

———. "Maka and Mazūn," *St Ir* 18 (1989): 157–67.

———. "The Date of the 'Martyrs of Nagrān,'" *AAE* 1 (1990): 110–28.

———. *Burzōy's Voyage to India and the Origin of the Book of Kalīlah wa Dimnah*. Royal Asiatic Society Prize Publication Fund Vol. XXIII. London, 1990.

———. "The 'Sabians' (Ṣābi'ūn) in Pre-Islamic Arabia," *AO* 56 (1995): 39–61.

———. "Ḥijāratun min sijjīl," forthcoming in *AO* .

Bosworth, C. E. "The Armies of the Ṣaffārids," *BSAOS* 31 (1968): 534–54. Repr. in *The Medieval History of Iran, Afghanistan and Central Asia*. London, 1977. No. XVII.

———. "Abū 'Abdallāh al-Khwārazmī on the Technical Terms of the Secretary's Art. A Contribution to the Administrative History of Mediaeval Islam," *JESHO* 12 (1969): 113–64. Repr. in *Medieval Arabic Culture and Administration*. London, 1982. No. XV.

———. "The Kūfichīs or Qufṣ in Persian History," *Iran JBIPS* 14 (1976): 9–17. Repr. in *The Medieval History of Iran, Afghanistan and Central Asia*. No. VIII.

———. The Mediaeval Islamic Underworld. *The Banū Sāsān in Arabic Society and Literature. II. The Arabic Jargon Texts*. Leiden, 1976.

———, "The Terminology of the History of the Arabs in the Jāhiliyya, according to Khwārazmī's 'Keys of the Sciences,'" in *Studies in Juda-*

*ism and Islam. Presented to Shelomo Dov Goitein on the Occasion of His Eightieth Birthday.* English vol. ed. Shelomo Morag, Issachar Ben-Ami, and N. R. Stillman. Jerusalem, 1981. Pp. 27–43. Repr. in *Medieval Arabic Culture and Administration.* No. X.

———, "Iran and the Arabs before Islam," in *CHI* III/1. Pp. 593–612.

———. "Some Remarks on the Terminology of Irrigation Practices and Hydraulic Constructions in the Eastern Arab and Iranian Worlds in the Third–Fifth Centuries A.H., *JIS* 2 (1991): 78–85. Repr. in *The Arabs, Byzantium and Iran. Studies in Early Islamic History and Culture.* Aldershot, 1996. No. III.

———, and Sir Gerard Clauson. "Al-Xwārazmī on the Peoples of Central Asia," *JRAS* (1965): 2–12.

Briend, J. "Sheba. I. Dans la Bible," in *Supplément au dictionnaire de la Bible,* ed. J. Briend, E. Cochenet, H. Cazelles, and A. Feuillet, vol. XII, fasc. 70. Paris, 1996. Cols. 1043–46.

Brock, S. "Christians in the Sasanian Empire: A Case of Divided Loyalties," in *Religion and National Identity,* Studies in Church History XVIII, ed. S. Mews. Oxford, 1982. Pp. 1–19. Repr. in *Syriac Perspectives on Late Antiquity.* London, 1984. No. VI.

Brunner, C. "Geographical and Administrative Divisions. Settlements and Economy," in *CHI* III/2. Pp. 747–77.

Buhl, F. *Das Leben Muhammeds. Deutsch von Hans Heinrich Schaeder.* Leipzig, 1930.

Bury, J.B. *A History of the Later Roman Empire from Arcadius to Irene (395 A.D. to 800 A.D.),* 2 vols. London, 1889.

———. *History of the Later Roman Empire from the Death of Theodosius to the Death of Justinian (A.D. 395 to A.D. 565),* I. London, 1923.

Butler. A. J. *The Arab Conquest of Egypt and the Last Thirty Years of the Roman Dominion,* revised version of the Oxford 1902 edition by P. M. Fraser. Oxford, 1978.

Cameron, Averil. "Agathias on the Sassanians," *DOP* 23–24 (1969–70): 67–183.

———. *Procopius and the Sixth Century.* London, 1985.

Canard, M. *Histoire de la dynastie des H'amdanides de Jazîra et de Syrie,* I. Publications de la Faculté des Lettres d'Alger, IIe sér., tome XXI. Algiers, 1951.

Caskel, W. *Das Schicksal in der altarabischen Poesie. Beiträge zur arabischen Literatur und zur allgemeinen Religionsgeschichte.* Morgenländische Texte und Forschungen, Band 1, Heft 5. Leipzig, 1926.

———. *Aijām al-ʿarab. Studien zur altarabischen Epik,* in *Islamica* 3, Ergänzungsheft. Leipzig, 1930. Pp. 1–99.

Chaumont, M. L. "Recherches sur le clergé zoroastrien. Le Hērbad," *RHR* 158 (1960): 55–80, 161–79.

———. "Les Sassanides et la Christianisme de l'Empire iranien au IIIe siècle de notre ère," *RHR* 165 (1964): 165–202.

Christensen, A. *Romanen om Bahrâm Tschôbîn, et rekonstruktionsforsøg.* Copenhagen, 1907.

———. *Le règne du roi Kawādh I et le communisme mazdakite.* Det Kongelige Danske Videnskabernes Selskabs, historisk-filologiske Meddelelser IX/6. Copenhangen, 1925.

———. "La légende du sage Buzurjmihr," *AO* 3 (1930): 81–128.

———. *Les Kayanides.* Det Kongelige Danske Videnskabernes Selskabs, historisk-filologiske Meddelelser XIX/2. Copenhagen, 1930.

———. "La princesse sur la feuille de myrte et la princesse sur la poie," *AO* 14 (1936): 241–57.

———. *L'Iran sous les Sassanides,* 2d enlarged ed. Copenhagen, 1944.

Clauson, Sir Gerard. *An Etymological Dictionary of Pre-Thirteenth-Century Turkish.* Oxford, 1972.

Conrad, L. "Abraha and Muhammad. Some Observations apropos of Chronology and Literary Topoi," *BSOAS* 50 (1987): 225–40.

Crone, Patricia "Kawād's Heresy and Mazdak's Revolt," *Iran JBIPS* 29 (1991): 21–42.

Czeglédy, K. "Bahrām Čōbīn and the Persian Apocalyptic Literature," *AO Hung.* 8 (1958): 21–43.

Dandamayev, M. A. and Lukonin, V. G. *The Culture and Social Institutions of Ancient Iran.* Cambridge, 1989.

Daryaee, Touraj. "National History or Keyanid History? The Nature of Sasanid Zoroastrian Historiography," *IS* 28 (1995): 129–41.

Dennett, D. C. *Conversion and the Poll Tax in Early Islam.* Harvard Historical Monographs XXII. Cambridge, Mass. 1950.

Doerfer, G. *Türkische und mongolische Elemente im Neupersischen. II–IV. Türkische Elemente.* Akademie der Wissenschaften und der Literatur. Veröffentlichungen der Orientalischen Kommission, Bände XIX–XXI. 3 vols. Wiesbaden, 1965–75.

Donner, F. McG. "The Bakr b. Wā'il Tribes and Politics in Northeastern Arabia on the Eve of Islam," *SI* 51 (1980): 5–38.

———. *The Early Islamic Conquests.* Princeton, 1981.

Dozy, R. P. A. *Supplément aux dictionnaires arabes,* 2 vols. Leiden, 1881.

Dunlop, D. M. *The History of the Jewish Khazars.* Princeton, 1954.

Duri, A. A. *The Rise of Historical Writing among the Arabs,* ed. and English trans. L. I. Conrad. Modern Classics in Near Eastern Studies. Princeton, 1983.

Eilers, W. "Iranisches Lehngut im arabischen Lexikon," *IIJ* 5 (1962): 203–32.

———. "Iran and Mesopotamia," in *CHI* III/1. Pp. 481–504.

Endress, G. "Die arabische Schrift," in *Grundriss der arabischen Philologie. Band I. Sprachwisenschaft*, ed. W. Fischer. Wiesbaden, 1982. Pp. 165–83.

Ensslin, W. "The Government and Administration of the Byzantine Empire," in *The Cambridge Medieval History. IV. The Byzantine Empire*, 2 vols. Part II. *Government, Church and Civilization*, ed. J. M. Hussey. Cambridge, 1966–67. Pp. 1–54.

Fahd, T. *La divination arabe. Etudes religieuses, sociologiques et folkloriques sur le milieu natif de l'Islam.* Leiden, 1966.

———. *Le panthéon de l'Arabie centrale à la veille de l'hégire.* Institut Français d'Archéologie de Beyrouth. Bibliothèque Archéologique et Historique LXXXVIII. Paris, 1968.

Fiey, J. M. *Assyrie chrétienne. Contribution à l'étude de l'histoire et de la géographie ecclésiastique et monastique du nord de l'Iraq.* Recherches publiées sous la direction de l'Institut de Lettres Orientales de Beyrouth XXII, XXII, XLII, 3 vols. Beirut, 1965–68.

———. "Topographie chréienne de Mahozé," *L'Orient syrien* 12 (1967): 397–420. Repr. in *Communautés syriaques en Iran et Irak des origines à 1552*. London, 1979. No. IX.

Frye, R. N. *The Heritage of Persia.* London, 1962.

———. "History and Sasanian Inscriptions," in *Accademia Nazionale dei Lincei. Problemi attuali di scienza e cultura. Atti del convegno internazionale sul themo La Persia nel medioevo (Roma, 31 marzo–5 aprile 1970).* Rome, 1971. Pp. 215–24.

———. *The Golden Age of Persia. The Arabs in the East.* London, 1975.

———. "The Political History of Iran under the Sasanians," in *CHI* III/1. Pp. 116–80.

Fück, J. W. *Die arabischen Studien in Europa bis in den Anfang des 20. Jahrhunderts.* Leipzig, 1955.

Gabrieli, F. "Etichetta di corte c costumi sasanidi nel Kitāb Aḫlāq al-Mulūk di al-Ǧāḥiẓ," *RSO* 11 (1928): 292–305.

———. "La «zandaqa» au I^er^ siècle abbaside," in *L'elaboration de l'Islam. Colloque de Strasbourg 12–13–14 juin 1959.* Paris, 1961. Pp. 23–38.

Gaja, Iwona. "Ḥuǧr b. 'Amr roi de Kinda et l'établissement de la domination ḥimyarite en Arabie centrale," *PSAS* 26 (1996): 65–73.

Garsoïan, Nina. "Byzantium and the Sasanians." in *CHI* III/1. Pp. 568–92.

Gaube, H. *Die südpersische Provinz Arraǧān/Kūh-Gīlūyeh von der arabischen Eroberung bis zur Safawidenzeit. Analyse und Auswertung literarischer und archäologischer Quellen zur historischen Topographie.* Österreichische Akademie der Wissenschaften, phil.-hist. Klasse, Denkschriften, 107. Band. Veröffentlichungen der Kommission für Geschichte Mittelasiens, Band II. Vienna, 1973.

Gaudefroy-Demombynes, M. *Le pélerinage à la Mekke. Etude d'histoire religieuse,* Paris, 1923, repr. Philadelphia, 1977.

———. "Le voile de la Ka'ba," *SI* 2 (1954): 5–21.

Geiger, B. "Zum Postwesen der Perser," *WZKM* 29 (1915): 309–14.

———. "Mittelpersische Wörter und Sache," *WZKM* 42 (1935): 114–28; 44 (1937): 51–64.

Ghirshman, R., and T. Ghirshman. *Les Chionites-Hephtalites.* Mémoires de l'Institut Française d'Archéologie Orientale du Caire LXXX = Mémoires de la Délégation Archéologique Française en Afghanistan XIII. Cairo, 1948.

Gibb, H. A. R. "Arab-Byzantine Relations under the Umayyad Caliphs," in *Studies on the Civilization of Islam,* ed. S. J. Shaw and W. R. Polk. Boston, 1962. Pp. 47–61. Originally in *DOP* 12 (1958): 219–33.

Gignoux, P. "Middle Persian Inscriptions," in *CHI* III/2. Pp. 1205–15.

———. *Iranisches Personennamen. Band II. Mitteliranisches Personennamen,* ed. M. Mayrhofer and R. Schmitt. *Faszikel 2. Noms propres sassanides en moyen-Perse épigraphique.* Vienna, 1986.

Gnoli, G. *The Idea of Iran. An Essay on Its Origin.* Serie Orientale Roma LXII. Rome, 1989.

Göbl, R. *Sasanidische Numismatik.* Brunswick, 1968. Eng. trans. P. Severin, *Sasanian Numismatics.* Manuals of Middle Asian Numismatics I. Brunswick, 1971.

Golden, P. B. *Khazar Studies. An Historico-Philological Inquiry into the Origins of the Khazars.* Bibliotheca Orientalis Hungarica XXV/1–2, 2. vols. Budapest, 1980.

Goldziher, I. *Muhammedanische Studien,* 2 vols. Halle, 1888–89. English trans. C. R. Barber and S. M. Stern, *Muslim Studies,* 2 vols. London, 1967–71.

———. *Abhandlungen zur arabischen Philologie,* 2 vols. Leiden, 1896–97.

———. "Beiträge zur arabischen Trauerpoesie," *WZKM* 16 (1902): 307–39. Repr. in *Gesammelte Schriften,* ed. J. de Somogyi, 6 vols. Hildesheim, 1967–73. Vol. IV, 361–93.

———. "Neuplatonische und gnosische Elemente im Ḥadīt," *ZA* 22 (1908): 317–44. Repr. in *Gesammelte Schriften,* V, 107–34.

Götz, M. "Zum historischen Hintergrund von Sure 30, 1–5," in *Festschrift Werner Caskel zum siebzigsten Geburtstag 5. März 1966,* ed. H. Gräf. Leiden, 1968. Pp. 111–20.

Goubert, P. *Byzance avant l'Islam. I. Byzance et l'Orient sous les successeurs de Justinian. L'Empéreur Maurice.* Paris, 1953.

Greatrex, G. "The Two Fifth-Century Wars between Rome and Persia," *Florilegium* 12 (1993), 1–14.

———. *Rome and Persia at War, 502–532.* ARCA Classical and Medieval Texts, Papers and Monographs 37. Leeds, 1998.

Grignaschi, M. "Quelques spécimens de la littérature sassanide conservée dans les bibliothèques d'Istanbul," *JA* 254 (1966): 1–142.

———. "La *Nihāyatu l-'arab fī aḫbāri-l-Furs wa-l-'Arab* (Première partie)," *BEO* 22 (1969): 15–67.

———. "La riforma tributaria di Ḫosrō I e il feudalesimo sassanide," in *Accademia Nazionale dei Lincei. Problemi attuali di scienza e cultura. Atti del convegno internazionale sul themo La Persia nel medioevo (Roma, 31 marzo–5 aprile 1970).* Rome, 1971. Pp. 87–138.

———. "La *Nihāyatu 'l-'arab fī aḫbāri l-Furs wa-l-'Arab* et les *Siyaru mulūki l-'Ağam* du Ps. Ibn al-Muqaffa'," *BEO* 26 (1973–74): 83–102.

Grousset, R. *L'empire des steppes. Attila. Gengis-Khan. Tamerlan,* 4th ed. Paris, 1952. English tr. Naomi Walford, *The Empire of the Steppes. A History of Central Asia.* New Brunswick, N.J., 1970.

von Grunebaum, G. E. "Abū Du'ād al-Iyādī. Collection of Fragments," *WZKM* 51 (1948–52): 83–105, 249–82. Repr. in *Themes in Medieval Arabic Literature.* London, 1981. No. XI.

von Gutschmid, A. "Bemerkungen zu Tabari's Sasanidengeschichte, übersetzt von Th. Noldeke," *ZDMG* 34 (1880): 721–48.

al-Ḥadīthī, Bahjat 'Abd al-Ghafūr. *Umayyah b. Abī al-Ṣalt, ḥayātuhu wa-shi'ruhu.* Baghdad, 1975.

Halévy, J. "Rapport sur une mission archéologique dans le Yémen," *JA,* sér. VI, vol. 19 (1872): 5–128.

Hannestad, K. "Les relations de Byzance avec la Transcaucase et l'Asie centrale aux 5e et 6e siècles," *Byzantion* 25–27 (1955–57): 421–25.

Harding, G. Lankester. *An Index and Concordance of Pre-Islamic Arabic Names and Inscriptions.* Toronto, 1971.

Harmatta, J. "The Middle Persian-Chinese Bilingual Inscription from Hsian and the Chinese-Sāsānian Relations," in *Accademia Nazionale dei Lincei. Problemi attuali di scienza e cultura. Atti del congegno internazionale sul themo La Persia nel medioevo (Roma, 31 marzo—5 aprile 1970).* Rome, 1971. Pp. 363–76.

Haussig, H. W. "Die Quellen über die zentralasiatische Herkunft der europäische Awaren," *CAJ* 2 (1956): 21–43.

Hawting, G. R. *The First Dynasty of Islam. The Umayyad Caliphate AD 661–750.* London and Sidney, 1986.

Henning, W. B. "Neue Materialen zur Geschichte des Manichäismus," *ZDMG* 90 (1936): 1–18.

———. "The Great Inscription of Šāpūr I," *BSOAS* 10 (1939–42): 832–49. Repr. in Henning, *Collected Papers.* Acta Iranica, deuxième série, Hommages et opera minora V–VI. Tehran and Liège, 1977, I, 601–27.

Herrmann, Georgina. *The Iranian Revival.* The Making of the Past. Oxford, 1977.

Herzfeld, E. *Paikuli. Monument and Inscriptions of the Early History of the Sasanian Empire,* 2 vols. Berlin, 1924.

Higgins, M. J. *The Persian War of the Emperor Maurice (582–602). Part I. The Chronology, with a Brief History of the Persian Calendar.* Catholic University of America. Byzantine Studies I. Washington, D.C., 1939.

Hintze, Almut. *Der Zamyād-Yašt. Edition, Übersetzung, Kommentar.* Beiträge zur Iranistik 15. Wiesbaden, 1994.

Hinz, W. *Islamische Masse und Gewichte umgerechnet ins metrische System,* HdO, Ergänzungsband 1, Heft 1. Leiden, 1955.

———. "Mani and Kardēr," in *Accademia Nazionale dei Lincei. Problemi attuali di scienza e cultura. Atti del congegno internazionale sul themo La Persia nel medioevo (Roma, 31 marzo–5 aprile 1970).* Rome, 1971. Pp. 485–99.

Horowitz, J. "'Adi ibn Zeyd, the Poet of Hira," *IC* 4 (1930): 31–69.

Howard-Johnston, J. "The Two Great Powers in Late Antiquity: A Comparison," in *The Byzantine and Early Islamic Near East. III. States, Resources and Armies,* ed. Averil Cameron. Papers of the Third Workshop on Late Antiquity and Early Islam = Studies in Late Antiquity and Early Islam 1. Princeton, 1995. Pp. 157–226.

Humbach, H., and Skjaervø, P.O. *The Sassanian Inscription of Paikuli.* Part I. *Supplement to Herzfeld's Paikuli* (Humbach). Part III. 1. *Text* (Humbach). Part III. 2. *Commentary* (Skjaervø). Wiesbaden and Tehran, 1978–83.

Hunter, Erica C. D. "Syriac Inscriptions from al Hira," *OC* 80 (1996): 66–81.

Hyatt, H. M. *The Church of Abyssinia.* London, 1928.

Jeffery, A. *The Foreign Vocabulary of the Qur'ān.* The Gaekwad's Oriental Series LXXXIX. Baroda, 1938.

Justi, F. *Iranisches Namenbuch.* Marburg, 1895.

Juwaideh, Wadie. *The Introductory Chapters of Yāqūt's Mu'jam al-Buldān, Translated and Annotated.* Leiden, 1959.

Kaegi, W. E. "New Evidence on the Early Reign of Heraclius," *BZ* 66 (1973): 308–30.

———, and P. M. Cobb. "Heraclius, Shahrbarāz, and al-Ṭabarī," in H. Kennedy (ed.), *Al-Ṭabarī. A Medieval Muslim Historian and His Work*. Princeton, 1999. Pp. 121–43.

Kamil, Murad. "An Ethiopian Inscription Found at Mareb," *JSS* 9 (1964): 56–57.

Kettenhofen, E. *Die römisch-persischen Kriege des 3. Jahrhunderts n. Chr. nach der Inscrift Šāpuhrs I. an der Ka'be-ye Zartošt (ŠKZ)*. Beihefte zum TAVO. Reihe B. (Geisteswissenschaften) Nr. 55. Wiesbaden, 1982.

Kister, M. J. "The Campaign of Ḥulubān. A New Light on the Expedition of Abraha," *Le Muséon* 78 (1965): 425–36. Repr. in *Studies in Jāhiliyya and Early Islam*. London, 1980. No. IV.

———. "Al-Ḥīra. Some Notes on Its Relations with Arabia," *Arabica* 15 (1968): 143–69. Repr. in *Studies in Jāhiliyya and Early Islam*. No. III.

———. "Some Reports Concerning Mecca. From Jāhiliyya to Islam," *JESHO* 15 (1972): 61–93. Repr. in *Studies in Jāhiliyya and Early Islam*. No. II.

———. "' . . . And He Was Born Circumcised. . . . ' Some Notes on Circumcision in Ḥadīth," *Oriens* 34 (1994): 10–30.

———, and M. Plessner. "Notes on Caskel's Ǧamharat an-nasab," *Oriens* 25–26 (1976): 48–68. Repr. in Kister, *Society and Religion from Jāhiliyya to Islam*. Aldershot, 1990. No. III.

Krenkow, F. "The Two Oldest Books on Arabic Folklore," *IC* 2 (1928): 55–89, 204–36.

Labourt, J. *Le Christianisme dans l'empire perse sous la dynastie sassanide, 224–632*, Bibliothèque de l'enseignement de l'histoire ecclésiastique IX. Paris, 1904.

Lammens, H. "L'âge de Mahomet et la chronologie de la Sîra," *JA*, sér. X, vol. 17 (1911): 209–50.

———. *Le berceau de l'Islam. L'Arabie occidentale à la veille de l'Hégire. I. Le climat—les Bédouins*. Rome, 1914.

———. "L'avènement des Marwānides et le califat de Marwān Ier," *MUSJ* 12 (1927): 44–147.

———. "Le culte des bétyles et les processions religieuses chez les arabes préislamiques," in *L'Arabie occidentale avant l'Hégire*. Beirut, 1928. Pp. 101–79. Originally in *BIFAO* 17 (1919–20): 39–101.

Landberg, le Comte de, and K. V. Zetterstéen. *Glossaire daṯînois*, 3 vols. Leiden, 1920–42.

Lane, E. W. *An Arabic-English Lexicon, Derived from the Best and Most Copious Oriental Sources . . .*, 8 parts. London, 1863–93.

Lang, D. M. "Iran, Armenia and Georgia," in *CHI* III/1. Pp. 505–36.

Latham, J. D., and W. F. Paterson. *Saracen Archery. An English Version and Exposition of a Mameluke Work on Archery (ca. A.D. 1368).* London, 1970.

Lecker, M. *The Banū Sulaym. A Contribution to the Study of Early Islam,* Max Schloessinger Memorial Series. Monograph IV. Jerusalem, 1989.

———. "Abū Mālik ʿAbdallāh b. Sām of Kinda, a Jewish Convert to Islam," *Isl.* 71 (1994): 280–282.

———. "Kinda on the Eve of Islam and During the Ridda," *JRAS* 3d ser., vol. 4 (1994): 333–56.

———. "The Conversion of Ḥimyar to Judaism and the Jewish Banū Hadl of Medina," *WO* 26 (1995): 129–36.

———. "The Death of the Prophet Muhammad's Father: Did Wāqidī Invent Some of the Evidence?" *ZDMG* 145 (1995): 9–27.

———. "Judaism among Kinda and the *Ridda* of Kinda." *JAOS* 115 (1995): 635–50.

Le Strange, G. *Palestine under the Moslems. A Description of Syria and the Holy Land from A.D. 650 to 1500.* London, 1890.

———. *The Lands of the Eastern Caliphate. Mesopotamia, Persia, and Central Asia from the Moslem Conquest to the Time of Timur,* Cambridge Geographical Series. Cambridge, 1905.

Lings, M. *Muhammad, His Life Based on the Earliest Sources.* London, 1983.

Litvinsky, B.A. "The Hephthalite Empire," in *History of Civilizations of Central Asia. III. The Crossroads of Civilization A.D. 250 to 750,* ed. B. A. Litvinsky. UNESCO Paris, 1996. Pp. 135–62.

Löfgren, O. "ʿAlqama b. D̠ī Ǧadan und seine Dichtung nach der Iklīl-Auswahl in der Bibliotheca Ambrosiana," in *Al-Hudud. Festschrift für Maria Höfner zum 80. Geburtstag,* ed. R. G. Stiegner. Graz, 1981. Pp. 199–209.

Løkkegaard, F. *Islamic Taxation in the Classic Period, with Special Reference to Circumstances in Iraq.* Copenhagen, 1950.

Loth, O. "Die Vulkanregionen von Arabien nach Yāḳūt," *ZDMG* 22 (1868): 365–82.

Lukonin, V. G. "Political, Social and Administrative Institutions: Taxes and Trade," in *CHI* III/2. Pp. 681–746.

Lyall, Sir Charles J. *Translations of Ancient Arabian Poetry, Chiefly Pre-Islamic.* London, 1885.

MacKenzie, D. N. *A Concise Pahlavi Dictionary.* London, 1971.

Majumdar, R. C., ed. *The History and Culture of the Indian People. III. The Classical Age.* Bombay, 1954.

Malek, Hodge Mehdi. "A Survey of Research on Sasanian Numismatics," *NC* 153 (1993): 227–69.

Markwart, J. *A Catalogue of the Provincial Capitals of Ērānshahr (Pahlavi Text, Version and Commentary)*, ed. G. Messina. Analecta Orientalia 3. Rome, 1931.

Marlow, Louise. *Hierarchy and Egalitarianism in Islamic Thought.* Cambridge Studies in Islamic Civilization. Cambridge, 1997.

Marmardji, A.-S. *Textes géographiques arabes sur la Palestine. Recuellis, mis en ordre alphabétique et traduits en français.* Paris, 1951.

Marquart, J. "Beiträge zur Geschichte und Sage von Erān," *ZDMG* 49 (1895): 628–72.

———. *Ērānšahr nach der Geographie des Ps. Moses Xorenacʿi.* AKGW Göttingen, phil.-hist. Kl., N.F. III/2. Berlin, 1901.

———. *Osteuropäische und ostasiatische Streifzüge. Ethnologische und historisch-topographische Studien zur Geschichte des 9. und 10. Jahrhunderts (ca. 840–940).* Leipzig, 1903.

———, and J. J. M. de Groot. "Das Reich Zābul und der Gott Žūn vom 6.-9. Jahrhundert," in *Festschrift Eduard Sachau zum siebigsten Geburtstage gewidmet von Freunden und Schulern*, ed. G. Weil. Berlin, 1915. Pp. 248–92.

Mayrhofer, M. *Iranische Personennamenbuch. Band I. Die altiranischen Namen. Faszikel 1. Die awestischen Namen.* Österreichische Akademie der Wissenschaften, philos.-hist. Klasse, Sonderpublikation der Iranischen Kommission. Vienna, 1977.

Minorsky, V. "Roman and Byzantine Campaigns in Atropatene," *BSOAS* 11 (1943–46): 243–65. Repr. in *Bīst maqāla-yi Minorsky/Iranica. Twenty Articles.* Publications of the University of Tehran 775. Tehran, 1964. No. 6.

———. *A History of Sharvān and Darband in the 10th-11th Centuries.* Cambridge, 1958.

Moravcsik, Gy. *Byzantinoturcica. I. Die byzantinischen Quellen der Geschichte der Türkvölker. II, Sprachreste der Türkvölker in den byzantinischen Quellen*, 2 vols. Berlin, 1958.

Morony, M. J. *Iraq after the Muslim Conquest.* Princeton Studies on the Near East. Princeton, 1984.

Morrison, G. "The Sassanian Genealogy in Masʿūdī," in *Al-Masʿudi Millenary Commemoration Volume*, ed. S. Maqbul Ahmad and A. Rahman. Aligarh, 1960. Pp. 42–44.

Müller, W. W. "Eine hebraeisch-sabaeische Bilinguis aus Bait al-Ašwal," in *Neue Ephemeris für semitischer Epigraphie. II.* Wiesbaden, 1974. Pp. 117–23.

———. "Ancient Castles Mentioned in the Eighth Volume of al-Hamdānī's Iklīl and Evidence of Them in Pre-Islamic Inscription [sic]," in *Al-Hamdānī, a Great Yemeni Scholar. Studies on the Occasion of His Millennial Anniversary,* ed. Yusuf Mohammad Abdallah. Sanaa, 1407/1986. Pp. 139–57.

———. "L'écriture *zabūr* du Yémen pré-islamique dans la tradition arabe," in *Textes du Yémen antique inscrits sur bois (with an English summary),* ed. J. Ryckmans, W. W. Müller, and Yusuf M. Abdallah. Publications de l'Institut orientaliste de Louvain 43. Louvain-la-Neuve, 1994. Pp. 35–39.

Musil, A. *The Middle Euphrates. A Topographical Itinerary.* New York, 1927.

———. *Northern Neǧd. A Topographical Itinerary.* New York, 1928.

Muth, F.-C. *Die Annalen von aṭ-Ṭabarī im Spiegel der europäischen Bearbeitungen.* Heidelberger Orientalistische Studien 6. Frankfurt-am-Main, 1983.

Nagel, T. *Alexander der Grosser in der frühislamiscchen Volksliteratur.* Beiträge zur Sprach- und Kulturgeschichte des Orients 28. Walldorf-Hessen, 1978.

Naval Intelligence Division. Admiralty Handbooks. *Persia.* London, 1945.

Neusner, J. "Jews in Iran," in *CHI* III/2. Pp. 909–23.

Newby, G. H. "Abraha and Sennacherib. A Talmudic Parallel to the Tafsīr on Sūrat al-Fīl," *JAOS* 94 (1974): 431–37.

Nöldeke, Th. "Zum orientalischen Geographie," *ZDMG* 28 (1874): 93–102.

———. "Ueber den syrischen Roman von Kaiser Julian," *ZDMG* 28 (1974): 263–92.

———. *Die Ghassânischen Fürsten aus dem Hause Gafna's.* AKAW Berlin, philos.-hist. Abhandlungen, Berlin, 1887.

———. *Persische Studien. I. Persische Koseformen,* SbWAW, phil.-hist. Cl. CXVI. Vienna, 1888. Pp. 388–423.

———. *Geschichte des Qorāns.* Vol. I, 2d ed. Leipzig, 1909. Vol. II, 2d ed. F. Schwally. Leipzig, 1919. Vol. III, *Die Geschichte des Korantexts* by G. Bergstrasser and O. Pretzl, 2d ed. Leipzig, 1938.

———. *Das iranische Nationalepos,* 2d ed. Berlin and Leipzig, 1920.

Olinder, G. *The Kings of Kinda of the Family of Ākil al-Murār.* Lunds Universitets Årsskrift, N.F. Avd. 1, Bd 23, Nr. 6. Lund-Leipzig, 1927.

———. "Āl al-Ǧaun of the Family of Ākil al-Murār," *MO* 25 (1931): 208–29.

Paret, R. *Der Koran. Kommentar und Konkordanz.* Stuttgart etc., 1980.

Paruck, Furdoonjee D. I. *Sāsānian Coins.* Bombay, 1924.

Piacentini, Valeria F. "*Madīna/shahr, qarya/dih, nāḥiya/rustāq*. The City as Political-Administrative Institution: the Continuity of a Sasanian Model," *JSAI* 17 (1994): 85–107.
Pirenne, Jacqueline. "Who Was the Suleyman Visited by al-Hamdani's Bilqis, Queen of Himyar?" In *Al-Hamdānī, a Great Yemeni Scholar. Studies on the Occasion of His Millennial Anniversary*, ed. Yusuf Mohammad Abdallah. Sanaa, 1407/1986. Pp. 27–45.
Potts. D. T. "Gundešapur and the *Gondeisos*," *IA* 24 (1989): 323–35.
———. *The Arabian Gulf in Antiquity*, 2 vols. Oxford, 1990.
Pulleyblank, E. G. "The Consonantal System of Old Chinese. Part II," *AM*, N.S. 9 (1963): 206–65.
Qudratullah Fatimi, S. "The Twin Ports of Daybul. A Study in the Early Maritime History of Sind," in *Sind through the Centuries. Proceedings of an International Seminar Held in Karachi in Spring 1975*, ed. Hamida Khuhro. Karachi, 1981. Pp. 97–105.
Ringgren, H. *Studies in Arabian Fatalism*. Uppsala Universitets Årsskrift 1955 no. 2. Uppsala and Wiesbaden, 1955.
Robin, Chr. "Résultats épigraphiques et archéologiques de deux brefs séjours en République Arabe du Yémen," *Semitica* 26 (1976): 167–93.
———, ed. *L'Arabie antique de Karib'īl à Mahomet. Nouvelles données sur l'histoire des Arabes grâce aux inscriptions* . Aix-en-Provence 1992 = *RMMM* no. 61 (1991–93).
———. "La Tihāma yéménite avant l'Islam: notes d'histoire et de géographie historique," *AAE* 6 (1995): 22–35.
———. "Le royaume ḥujride, dit «royaume de Kinda», entre Ḥimyar et Byzance," *CRAIBL* (1996): 665–714.
———, "Sheba. II. Dans les inscriptions d'Arabie du Sud," in *Supplément au dictionnaire de la Bible*, ed. J. Briend, E. Cochenet, H. Cazelles and A. Feuillet, vol. XII, fasc. 70. Paris, 1996. Cols. 1047–1254.
Rose, Jenny. "Three Queens, Two Wives, and a Goddess. The Roles and Images of Women in Sasanian Iran," in *Women in the Medieval Islamic World. Power, Patronage and Piety*, ed. G. R. G. Hambly. The New Middle Ages 6. New York, 1998. Pp. 29–54.
Rothstein, G. *Die Dynastie der Laḫmiden in al-Ḥîra. Ein Versuch zur arabisch-persischen Geschichte zur Zeit der Sasaniden*. Berlin, 1899.
Rothstein, J. G. *De chronographo arabo anonymo, qui codice Berolinensi Sprengriano tricesimo continetur*. Diss. Bonn, 1877.
Rubin, Z. "Diplomacy and War in the Relations between Byzantium and the Sassanids in the Fifth Century A.D.," in *The Defence of the Roman and Byzantine East*, ed. P.W. Freeman and D. L. Kennedy. Proceedings of a Colloquium held at the University of Sheffield in April 1986. BAR International Series 297, i–ii = British Institute of

Archaeology at Ankara Monograph 8. Oxford, 1986. Part ii, pp. 677–95.

———. "Byzantium and Southern Arabia. The Policy of Anastasius," in *The Eastern Frontier of the Roman Empire*, ed. D. H. French and C. S. Lightfoot. Proceedings of a Colloquium Held at Ankara in September 1988. BAR International Series 553 = British Institute of Archaeology at Ankara Monograph 11. Oxford, 1989. Part ii, pp. 383–420.

———. "The Reforms of Khusrō Anūshirwān," in *The Byzantine and Early Islamic Near East. III. States, Resources and Armies*, ed. Averil Cameron. Papers of the Third Workshop on Late Antiquity and Early Islam = Studies in Late Antiquity and Early Islam 1. Princeton, 1995. Pp. 227–96.

Ryckmans, G. *Les noms propres sud-sémitiques.* Bibliothèque du Muséon 2, 2 vols. Louvain, 1934–35.

———. "Le Qayl en Arabie méridionale préislamique," in *Hebrew and Semitic Studies Presented to G.R. Driver in Celebration of His Seventieth Birthday*, ed. D. W. Thomas and W. D. McHardy. Oxford, 1963. Pp. 144–55.

Ryckmans, J. *L'Institution monarchique en Arabie méridionale avant l'Islam. Ma'în et Saba.* Bibliothèque du Muséon 28. Louvain, 1951.

———. "Le Christianisme en Arabie du Sud préislamique," in *Accademia Nazionale dei Lincei. Atti del Convegno internazionale sul thema L'Oriente christiano nella storia della civilità.* Rome, 1964, Pp. 413–53.

Schick, R. *The Christian Communities of Palestine from Byzantine to Islamic Rule. A Historical and Archaeological Study.* Studies in Late Antiquity and Early Islam 2. Princeton, 1995.

Schimmel, Annemarie. *And Muhammad Is His Messenger. The Veneration of the Prophet in Islamic Piety.* Durham, N.C., 1985.

Schwarz, P. *Iran im Mittelalter*, 9 parts. Leipzig, Zwickau, Stuttgart and Berlin, 1896–1935.

Segal, J. B. *Edessa, 'The Blessed City.'* Oxford, 1970.

Sellheim, R. "Ṭāq-i Bustān und Kaiser Julian (361–363)," *Oriens* 34 (1994): 354–66.

Sellwood, D. "Numismatics. (b) Minor States in Southern Iran," *CHI* III/1. Pp. 299–321.

———, P. Whitting, and R. Williams. *An Introduction to Sasanian Coins.* London, 1985.

Serjeant, R. B. "Ṣan'ā', the 'Protected,' Hijrah," in *Ṣan'ā', an Arabian Islamic City*, ed. R. B. Serjeant and R. Lewcock. London, 1983. Pp. 39–43.

———, and R. Lewcock. "The Church (al-Qalīs) of Ṣanʿāʾ and Ghumdān Castle," in ibid. Pp. 44–48.

Shahbazi, A. Shahpur. "On the Xwadāy-nāmag," in *Acta Iranica*, troisième série, Textes et Mémoires, XVI, *Iranica Varia: Papers in Honor of Professor Ehsan Yarshater*. Leiden, 1990. Pp. 208–29.

Shahîd, Irfān (as I. Kawar). "The Arabs in the Peace Treaty of A.D. 561," *Arabica* 3 (1956): 181–213. Repr. in Shahîd. *Byzantium and the Semitic Orient Before the Rise of Islam*. London, 1988. No. VII.

———. "Byzantium and Kinda," *BZ* 53 (1960): 57–73. Repr. in Shahîd. *Byzantium and the Semitic Orient Before the Rise of Islam*. No. IV.

Shahîd, Irfan. "Procopius and Kinda," BZ 53 (1960): 74–78. Repr. in Shahîd. *Byzantium and the Semitic Orient Before the Rise of Islam*. No. V.

———. *The Martyrs of Najrân. New Documents*. Société des Bollandistes, Subsidia. Hagiographica 49. Brussels, 1971.

———. "The Iranian Factor in Byzantium during the Reign of Heraclius," *DOP* 26 (1971): 295–320.

———. "Theodor Nöldeke's "Geschichte der Perser und Araber zur Zeit der Sasaniden": an Evaluation," *IJMES* 8 (1977): 117–22.

———. "Byzantium and South Arabia," *DOP* 33 (1979): 23–94. Repr. in *Byzantium and the Semitic Orient before the Rise of Islam*. No. IX.

———. "Two Qur'ānic Sūras: al-Fīl and Qurayš," in *Studia Arabica et Islamica. Festschrift for Iḥsān ʿAbbās*, ed. Wadād al-Qāḍī. Beirut, 1981. Pp. 429–36.

———. *Byzantium and the Arabs in the Fourth Century*. Washington D.C., 1984.

———. *Byzantium and the Arabs in the Fifth Century*. Washington D.C. 1989.

———. *Byzantium and the Arabs in the Sixth Century. I. Part 1. Political and Military History. Part 2. Ecclesiastical History*. Washington D.C., 1995.

Shaked, S. "Some Iranian Themes in Islamic Literature," *St Ir* 21 (1991): 143–58. Repr. in Shaked, *From Zoroastrian Iran to Islam*. Aldershot, 1995. No. XII.

Shboul, Ahmad M. H. *Al-Masʿūdī and His World. A Muslim Humanist and His Interest in Non-Muslims*. London, 1979.

Siddiqi, A. *Studien über die persischen Fremdwörter im klassischen Arabisch*. Göttingen, 1919.

Sinor, D. "The Establishment and Dissolution of the Türk Empire," in *The Cambridge History of Early Inner Asia*, ed. D. Sinor. Cambridge, 1990. Pp. 285–316.

———, and S. G. Klyashtorny. "The Türk Empire," in *History of Civilizations of Central Asia. III. The Crossroads of Civilization* A.D. *250 to 750*, ed. B. A. Litvinsky. UNESCO Paris, 1996. Pp. 327–47.

Smith, S. "Events in Arabia in the 6th Century A.D.," *BSOAS* 16 (1954): 425–68.

Smith, W. Robertson. *Kinship and Marriage in Early Arabia.* Cambridge, 1885.

———. *Lectures on the Religion of the Semites. First Series. The Fundamental Institutions.* Burnett Lectures 1888–89. London, 1894.

von Soden, W. *Akkadisches Handwörterbuch*, 3 vols. Wiesbaden, 1959–81.

Sourdel, D. *Le vizirat ʿabbāside de 749 à 936 (132 à 324 de l'Hégire)*, 2 vols. Damascus, 1959–60.

Sprengling, M. "From Persian to Arabic," *AJSLL* 56 (1939): 175–224, 325–36.

Stein, E. *Histoire du Bas-Empire. I. De l'état romain à l'état byzantin (284–476).* Paris, 1959. *II. De la disparition de l'Empire d'Occident à la mort de Justinian (476–565).* Paris, 1949.

Taqizadeh, S. H., with W. B. Henning. "The Dates of Mani's Life." Translated from the Persian [of S. H. Taqizadeh], introduced and concluded by W. B. Henning, *AM*, N.S. 6 (1957): 106–21. Repr. in Henning, *Collected Papers*, II, 505–20.

Thilo, U. *Die Ortsnamen in der altarabischen Poesie. En Beitrag zur vor- und frühislamischen Dichtung und zur historischen Topographie Nordarabiens.* Schriften der Max Freiherr von Oppenheim-Stiftung, Heft 3. Wiesbaden, 1958.

Thompson, R. C. *A Dictionary of Assyrian Botany.* London, 1949.

Torrey. *The Jewish Foundation of Islam.* The Hilda Stich Stroock Lectures at the Jewish Institute of Religion. New York, 1933. Repr. with an introduction by F. Rosenthal. New York, 1967.

Trimingham, J. S. *Christianity among the Arabs in Pre-Islamic Times.* Arab Background Series. London and Beirut, 1979.

Ullmann, M. *Wörterbuch der klassischen arabischen Sprache. II. Letter* lām, Part 2. Wiesbaden, 1991.

Vajda, G. "Les zindîqs en pays d'Islam au début de la période abbaside," *RSO* 17 (1938): 173–229.

van Vloten, G. "Dämonen, Geister und Zauber bei den altern Arabern. Mitteilungen aus Djâhitz' Kitâb al-haiwân," *WZKM* 7 (1893): 169–87, 233–47; 8 (1894): 59–73, 290–92.

Watson, W. "Iran and China," in *CHI* III/1. Pp. 537–58.

Watt, W. Montgomery. *Muhammad at Mecca.* Oxford, 1953.

———. *Muhammad at Medina.* Oxford, 1956.

Wellhausen, J. *Reste arabischen Heidentums gesammelt und erläutert,* 2d ed. Berlin, 1897.
Whitby, M. "Procopius and the Development of Roman Defences in Upper Mesopotamia," in *The Defence of the Roman and Byzantine East,* ed. P. W. Freeman and D. L. Kennedy. Proceedings of a Colloquium held at the University of Sheffield in April 1986. BAR International Series 297, i–ii = British Institute of Archaeology at Ankara Monograph 8. Oxford, 1986. Part ii, pp. 717–35.
———. "Procopius' Description of Dara (*Buildings* II.1–3)," in ibid., 737–83.
Widengren, G. "Xosrau Anōšurvān, les Hephtalites et les peuples turcs. Etude préliminaire des sources," *OS* 1 (1952): 69–94.
———. "Recherches sur le feudalisme iranien," *OS* 5 (1956): 79–182.
———. "Manichaeism and Its Background," in *CHI* III/2. Pp. 965–90.
Wiesehöfer, J. *Die antike Persien, von 550 v. Chr. bis 650 n. Chr.*, Munich and Zürich, 1994. English trans. Azizeh Azodi, *Ancient Persia, from 550 B.C. to 650 A.D.* London and New York, 1996.
———. *Die 'dunklen Jahrhunderte' der Persis. Untersuchungen zu Geschichte und Kultur von Fārs in frühhellenistischer Zeit (330–140 v. Chr.).* Munich, 1994.
Wilson, Sir Arnold T. *The Persian Gulf. An Historical Sketch from the Earliest Times to the Beginning of the Twentieth Century.* London, 1928.
Wright, W. *A Grammar of the Arabic Language,.* 3d ed. revised W., Robertson Smith and M. J. de Goeje, 2 vols. Cambridge, 1896–98.
Yarshater, E. "Were the Sasanians Heirs to the Achaemenids?" In *Accademia Nazionale dei Lincei. Problemi attuali di scienza e cultura. Atti del convegno internazionale sul themo La Persia nel medioevo (Roma, 31 marzo–5 aprile 1970).* Rome, 1971. Pp. 517–31.
———. "Iranian Common Beliefs and World-View," in *CHI* III/1. Pp. 343–58.
———. "Iranian National History," in ibid. Pp. 359–480.
———. "Mazdakism," in *CHI* III/2. Pp. 991–1024.
Zaehner, R. C. *The Dawn and Twilight of Zoroastrianism.* London, 1961.
Zarrīnkūb, ʿAbd al-Ḥusain. "The Arab Conquest of Iran and Its Aftermath," in *CHI* IV. Pp.1–56.
Zeimal, E. V. "The Kidarite Kingdom in Central Asia," in *History of Civilizations of Central Asia. III. The Crossroads of Civilization A.D. 250 to 750,* ed. B. A. Litvinsky. UNESCO Paris, 1996. Pp. 119–33.

# Index

*The index contains proper names of persons, places, and tribal and other groups, as well as topographical data, occurring in the text (and sometimes in the footnotes also), together with technical terms; where the latter are explained in the footnotes, they are also noted.*

*The definite article* al-, *the abbreviation* b. *(for* ibn *"son") and* bt. *(for* bint *"daughter") and everything in parentheses have been disregarded for purposes of alphabetization.*

B

G



H

I

L

N

T

Z